THE ILLUSTRATED BOOK

of

WORLD RANKINGS

THE ILLUSTRATED BOOK

of

WORLD RANKINGS

Fifth Edition

Edited by

George Thomas Kurian

2001 Library Reference Edition published by Sharpe Reference
Sharpe Reference is an imprint of *M.E. Sharpe* INC.

M.E. Sharpe INC.
80 Business Park Drive
Armonk, NY 10504

Library of Congress Cataloging-in-Publication Data

The illustrated book of world rankings / edited by George Thomas Kurian—5th ed.
p. cm.
Includes bibliographical references and index.
ISBN 0-7656-8026-2 (alk. paper)
  1. Statistics. 2. Social indicators. 3. Economic indicators. 4. Quality of life—
  Statistics. I. Kurian, George Thomas.

HA155 .K87 2001   00-046373
310—dc21   CIP

Printed and bound in the United States of America

The paper used in this publication meets the minimum requirements of
American National Standard for Information Sciences
Permanence of Paper for Printed Library Materials,
ANSI Z 39.48-1984

BM (c) 10 9 8 7 6 5 4 3 2 1

Table of Contents

Preface

THE ILLUSTRATED BOOK OF WORLD RANKINGS is designed as an international scorecard that compares and ranks over 190 nations of the world according to their performance in almost 300 key areas.

The output and refinement of international statistics have reached a level where it is now possible, timely, and logical to convert this raw data into indicators of comparative performance. Such rankings are widely used in business and industry—the *Fortune 500* list is perhaps the most familiar American example. Nation-states function within an environment as competitive as corporations, and an evaluation of their track records is vastly more significant.

THE ILLUSTRATED BOOK OF WORLD RANKINGS includes over 50,000 variables that measure national achievement by using no less than 300 specific performance yardsticks, making it one of the most comprehensive databases ever attempted in the field of international affairs. Interpreted sensibly, the data in these rankings will help not only to explain and evaluate national behavior, but sometimes even to predict it.

Numbers may be used to terrify, as well as to comfort; to inform, as well as to amuse; to encourage, as well as to edify; to accuse, as well as to honor; and the numbers in this book do all of these. Perhaps one of the most important contributions of these rankings is to test popular perceptions of national performance and environments. Most of us hold on to perceived notions of alien cultures, notions that are often stereotyped and embedded in prejudice. We may believe that Icelanders are the best read, Americans the most productive, Germans the most efficient, Indians the poorest, and so on. While the rankings bear out these perceptions in some cases, they disprove them even more often. Some of these rankings can also tell us what makes nations tick; why some of them are rich, while others are powerless and dependent; why some are cauldrons of change, while others are mired in inertia. An effort has been made in each ranking to briefly analyze and interpret the data, but the analyses hew closely to the framework of facts. There has been no attempt to predict trends or force conclusions, although the temptation to do so has frequently been very great.

THE ILLUSTRATED BOOK OF WORLD RANKINGS is not simply concerned with bestowing superlatives (although it indirectly measures excellence), but with establishing the proper rung on which each nation stands. All nations for which comparable data are available are represented in the lists of rankings, even those that are not currently independent. Only in the rhetoric of the United Nations General Assembly are all nations equal, but in the real world of nations inequality is the rule, and this work underscores just how unequal the nations are in each area of performance.

The selection of data to be included is based on five concepts: availability, comparability, usability, reliability, and rankability. Much of the available data are derived from the publications of the four principal agencies engaged in the collection of international statistics: the United Nations, the World Bank, the International Monetary Fund, and the U.S. Agency for International Development. Despite the efforts of these agencies, there are several subjects on which there are no data for any country and others for which available data are fragmentary. In the *UN Statistical Yearbook* there is only one complete table—"Population"—which provides data for each country. Even in this table the figures for many countries represent estimates and conjectures based on sample surveys.

From this pool of available data, my first task was to select comparable data, that is, series that have information on at least twenty countries. The problems of comparability are discussed in detail below.

The third element is usability. Do the figures really tell us something? Does the ranking add to our knowledge or give us some new insight? Does it provide a backdrop to some emerging trend or a clue to some problem or solution?

The fourth element is reliability. Have the statistics been collected by an international organization without any revealed bias? If they were collected by national organizations, have they been checked for reliability and verified through independent sources?

The fifth element is rankability. Not all valid data are rankable: the spread between the highest and the lowest units may be too small in some cases to be statistically significant. For example, the age of suffrage varies only by a few years among countries. As emphasized earlier, we are treating inequalities, and where there are no discernible inequalities, ranking becomes pointless.

One significant feature of this work is that the geographical coverage is as complete as the sources permit. Another is the broad-spectrum characteristic of the indicators themselves. With so many rankings, every important segment of national activity has been included. Some crucial subjects, such as defense spending, have been examined from different angles: per capita, as percentage of Gross National Product (GNP), and so on. The comprehensiveness of the lists of rankings is essential since what may be considered of minor importance in large industrialized countries may be critical for small countries. The production of phosphates, for example, is more important for Nauru than even GNP or population. Indeed, with the growing web of interdependence, some apparently trivial indicators can affect the economies of superpowers.

One source of unending despair in international statistics is the comparability of data. Strictly speaking, data used in rankings should be based on identical definitions, relate to the same calendar year or other base period, use the same techniques of collection, and be presented in the same form. Few, if any, of these conditions are ideally met in the rankings in this book. First of all, definitions vary from country to country even for terms that one might imagine could be defined only in one way, such as birth, death, marriage, and households. Also, the year or base period varies even more widely. Agricultural or housing censuses are held once every twenty or thirty years, and sometimes censuses are begun but never completed because of lack of funds or because of a change of government in the intervening period. There are also discontinuities in the publication of collected data resulting from political instability or civil war. Finally, the methodology and techniques of data collection vary from country to country.

Only a few countries have the necessary personnel skilled in data-gathering and data-analysis procedures. Poor countries, faced with the constant demand for statistics beyond the resources that their trained personnel can collect, may find ingenious ways of reporting fabricated data. Given these circumstances, I have invariably taken *the best available data for the latest available year* for each country. In practice this means that data for varying years have been used together, and some of the information may go back to the 1960s. If some readers feel this method offends scientific requirements, they should remember that these rankings can only reflect the state of the art in international statistics; the rankings are no better and no worse than the sources from which they are derived.

A further caveat must be entered here about the quality and reliability of data from developing countries. In general there is a direct relationship between the quality and availability of data and the level of economic development. This is attributable not only to the lack of resources and expertise in developing countries, but also to deliberate distortions of facts. Many developing countries manipulate data to suit their self-image. Because the appearance of economic might or of rapid development or of a literate and healthy population are important national assets, data in these areas may be modified to back up the official claims. (In one recent case with an ironic twist, Singapore—which has had phenomenal economic growth in recent years—has been accused of doctoring, or at the very least misinterpreting, various economic indicators to show that it is poorer than it really is in order to continue to qualify for the special concessions granted developing countries by international financial agencies.) In addition, there is a prohibition against collection and publication of data in some developing countries. There are many more countries that consider dissemination of data about their failing economies undesirable for political reasons. Data on developing countries are therefore subject to more serious qualifications and should be used with greater caution.

It must be pointed out here that in most cases only the aggregate or total figures have been derived from the sources cited and that per capita figures or share of total figures are based on my own calculations. In general, an effort has been made to present the rankings in their most meaningful form, particularly by minimizing the impact of sheer physical size on national performance. Because the book is aimed at a general rather than specialized audience, I have also tried to avoid, perhaps not always success-fully, the scholarly trappings and buzzwords that may turn off the lay reader. Technical notes are limited to the bare minimum. Scholars who need more information on the vintage and quality of the data and the methodology used for collecting data in each case are advised to consult the source or sources cited at the end of each ranking.

I wish to acknowledge that this book, like many others before it, could not have been written without the support and encouragement of my wife, Annie Kurian.

Every effort has been made to make the work as comprehensive, up-to-date, and accurate as possible. However, errors and inadequacies (for which the author assumes full responsibility) are inevitable in a work of such a large scope, and the author welcomes criticisms, corrections, and suggestions for inclusion in further editions.

GEORGE THOMAS KURIAN

Notes on Format and Entry Order

Each ranking or group of related rankings is preceded by an introduction highlighting the salient features and peculiarities of the topic covered. When countries have the same figures and are "tied," they are ranked alphabetically.

Unless otherwise noted, all data in this edition refer to the year 1998. There is usually a time lag of a year or two between collection of data by the major international organizations and their publication in book or electronic format. Rankings derived from published statistics suffer additional delays. However, careful students and observers who are interested in monitoring or analyzing trends will find that the rankings remain valid over a period of time. Because the rankings hew as closely as possible to the original sources, the deficiencies of these sources are sometimes reflected in the order of the ranking. Even standard sources, such as the *UN Statistical Yearbook*, do not provide data for nonreporting countries. Users sometimes wonder why countries like the United States do not appear in certain rankings. They have to remember that the international statistical reporting systems are far from perfect and that there is a long way to go before all countries are represented in every ranking.

Prologue

The Use of Statistics

A reader confronted with the over 50,000 pieces of data in this book might well ask the questions: What do they tell us? How do they add to our knowledge of the world?

Supreme Court Justice Louis Brandeis once remarked that nothing so clearly proved the finiteness of human intelligence as its inability to truly comprehend the number one billion. For example, *if every minute* had been counted since the day Christ was born, the number would have reached one billion in 1902. There are large numbers that one can grasp only in the gross, without understanding their true significance. Yet this book is full of millions and billions and some figures that are in the trillions.

The learning process starts, as Paul Lazarsfeld said, only when one attaches a number to an idea. Numbers must therefore be looked upon as stages and as tools in the learning process, not as ends in themselves. Pythagoras contended that number is the sole inner reality of each thing. According to the *New Catholic Encyclopedia*: "Number is a way of knowing the quantity, intensity, order and structure of material reality. With the aid of statistics and probability, number affords scientists the opportunity of predicting and controlling countable or measurable things or events with varying degrees of success." A number thus relates to the discreteness, the individuality, and what German philosophers, especially Immanuel Kant, described as *das Ding an sich* of each material object. A total subsumes all numbers within its sets but does not destroy or cancel any of them, for without each of them the total would be materially different.

Thus, numbers have a philosophical basis, but they have a strong practical application as well. It has been estimated that a person of average intelligence can have a personal, caring, and meaningful relationship with not more than fif-teen or twenty people; he or she could sustain and manage face-to-face, first-name-basis relationships with not more than sixty to seventy people; and he or she could be familiar with, keep track of, or remember the names of not more than 500 to 600 people. With all others he or she can have only what is best described as a *statistical relationship.* Therefore, in a world of six billion people, it is important that we evolve statistical systems that will enable us to establish such a relationship with the masses of people living outside our own little "puddle." These people are the amorphous "they" who constitute the rest of the world for each one of us.

Statistics is a science of indicators by which to judge the total human environment, or, as the American Statistical Association defines it, "to illustrate the conditions and prospects of society." Quantification is thus an important preliminary step leading to "qualitification," to coin a word. It is a diagnostic tool enabling us not only to present large sets of data and describe activities, events, and phenomena to those without direct, first-hand knowledge, but also to assess growth, determine excellence, detect flaws, and recognize dangers.

Viewed thus, numbers are important in themselves and in the trends and directions to which they point. Many of the policies and decisions that affect the lives of millions are taken on the basis of what Plato called the idols of the cave: opinions, prejudices, semantic distinctions, conventional wisdom, and so on. Facts are the best cure for opinions, and statistical systems provide the best antidote for biased and ill-informed judgments. Such statistics need not always be based on actual enumeration; they can be the assessments and guesstimates of knowledgeable people. And the statistics do not have to be exact figures, which may rarely be available and even where available may soon become out of date.

Thus, when it is noted that the earth's population is six billion, the figure could be off the mark by several millions or by just a few hundreds. Nobody knows for sure and nobody ever will. (In any case, it changed while you were reading this sentence.) But what is important is the general order of magnitude. For the same reason, rounded figures are used in most rankings of this book because they serve our purposes as well as exact figures.

The vast array of numbers in this book has three purposes: to present the totality of the human situation at the dawn of the twenty-first century; to describe this totality in terms of the component national groups, that is, to determine how the earth's total resource pie is cut into unequal shares and how each national share is multiplied or depleted; and to interpret the data in the wider context of national growth or decline and, where possible, to suggest solutions or alternative avenues of development.

Throughout this book nations and territories are treated as homogeneous units, whereas, in actuality, they are not. Nations are mosaics of differing racial, linguistic, religious, and social segments, as well as occupational and age groups, each of them subdivided into still smaller units. Sometimes these groups share a common heritage, common economic interests or political experiences, and sometimes they do not. Even nations that rank high on the Ethnic Homogeneity Index, such as South Korea or Japan, are homogeneous only in a cultural and ethnic sense and exhibit deep social fissures and divisions. Just as global aggregates mask variations within the component national groups, so do national aggregates presented in this book mask smaller variations within domestic groups. A statement such as "Only 10 percent of the Afghans are literate" might be true of a whole nation but could be inaccurate in reference to particular groups within a country. Similarly, there are immensely rich persons in statistically poor countries and extremely well-fed persons in statistically starving countries. While we invariably have to break up larger units into smaller ones to gain new insights into national behavior and performance, there are

limits on such efforts because there are very little data available on groups or units smaller than nation-states or cities. Nations and cities are therefore the lowest levels at which we can attempt to construct a system of rankings such as this one.

Statistics can be presented several meaningful ways—gross total, percentage, growth rate, per capita rate, ratio, and so on—and in at least four primary modes: rhetorical, gross, comparative, and interpretative. The rhetorical is the non-numerical or symbolic expression of a fact or belief, such as when God tells Abraham his children will one day be more numerous than the sands of the seashore. The gross presentation simply establishes the broad order of magnitude, such as the statement: "There are sixteen million Jews in the world today." The comparative presents the data in the context of the whole, as well as in relation to others, such as the statement: "Arabs outnumber Jews by twenty to one." The interpretative tries to derive factual conclusions from the data, such as the statement: "The fact that the Jewish population is dispersed over eighty countries is a cause of their strength rather than a weakness, although the reverse is true of other peoples whose strengths lie in their concentration."

The statistics presented in this volume have three areas of use:

• *To understand the past.* Each datum in this book is the sum of historical experiences, resources, successes, and failures, and it cannot be understood without some reference to the past. The present is the legacy of the past, and it will always remain a riddle to those who do not understand the past. For example, Senegal's prosperity today can be understood only in light of the French colonial policies of the nineteenth century. Furthermore, the international borders of almost all nations are the results of a series of historical accidents, and these borders, in turn, determine the size of a country, the level of population, the extent of natural resources, and so on.

• *To analyze the present.* The rankings calibrate and audit national performance, compare such performances with other nation-states and territories, highlight successes and failures, and assess national development strategies and ideologies.

• *To plan for the future.* Each datum is not merely a statement of fact, but also a call to some sort of action, remedy, or correction or at least concern. The statement, for example, that "75 percent of Chadians live in absolute poverty" is a direct pointer to a tragic situation and should be looked upon as a cry of agony rather than a simple fact. Further, these numbers indicate where each country is heading, how fast, and what efforts will be needed to get there.

For most people, statistics are dry bones. Yet, their very dry nature makes them valuable in a study of nations where our judgments must be grounded in fact. At the same time, it must be remembered that each "dry bone" in this book refers to human beings with flesh and blood or some situation relating to human beings. In the final analysis, therefore, this book is about people. But it requires intelligence, imagination, and, even more than these, compassion to see beyond numbers and to grasp the vast and imponderable human predicament with which these numbers deal.

Introduction

In her 1946 book, *Mystery on the Desert*, Maria Reiche describes a series of strange lines made by the Nazea Indians in the plains of Peru, some of them covering many square miles. For years, people assumed that these lines were the remnants of ancient irrigation ditches. Then in 1939 Paul Kosok of Long Island University discovered that their true meaning could only be seen from high in the air. When viewed from an airplane, these seemingly random lines form enormous drawings of birds, insects, and animals.

Similarly, the enormous mass of numbers presented in this book may not make much sense until they are viewed from a certain perspective. Rankings are not an idle exercise for stirring curiosity. They are diagnostic tools for analyzing through the prism of numbers the patterns of growth or decline among nations as well as in the global village. They are also forecasting tools that enable us to extrapolate numbers into the future, as far as the eye can see. By viewing the whole procession, as it were, from the top, one can determine the direction in which the nations of the world are going, detect subtle tremors and tectonic faults, and distinguish between the significant and the random.

In the third edition of *The Book of World Rankings* in 1989, an attempt was made to use the rankings as a kind of instrument panel for gauging the state of the world. It was an optimistic report. In fact, the 1990s became the golden decade of the twentieth century in which enormous strides were made in technology, with the Internet being a prime example. The collapse of the Soviet Union and the end of the Cold War brought large peace dividends leading to unprecedented prosperity for many developed nations. The 1989 report concluded that "the spaceship earth was functioning smoothly," and all systems were go. It is tempting—if somewhat risky—to treat a new study of the rankings as an instrument panel that can be used to determine the state of the world at the beginning of the twenty-first century. Unfortunately, the conclusions are somewhat grimmer than they were in 1990. There are at least six storm clouds on the horizon, and, if the numbers in this book are any guide, the outlook is choppy.

1. Global Economy. At no time in modern history has the gulf between the rich and poor nations—and indeed between the rich and poor in every country—been as great as it is today. The old military "Iron Curtain" that basically divided Europe into a western bloc of First World nations and an eastern bloc of Second World nations has been replaced by an economic Iron Curtain largely dividing the globe by north and south. The northern nations tend to be rich, powerful, and technologically advanced, while the southern nations tend to be poor, powerless, and technologically undeveloped. The first group consists primarily of twelve "super nations," led by the United States, followed by Japan, Germany, United Kingdom, France, Italy, Canada, Spain, Netherlands, Switzerland, Australia, and Sweden. There are also some fifteen other nations, all of them European, within the orbit of the First World. The second group consists of the remaining 165 nations of the world ranging from Brazil to Nauru. These nations are generally referred to as the Third World.

The First World nations are the engines that drive modern civilization. These twenty-seven countries now account for a staggering 80 percent of the Gross Global Product (GGP), estimated at $30 to $38 trillion per year. The income of the top twenty nations is thirty-seven times the income of the bottom twenty, and the percentage has doubled in the last twenty years. In 1999, all African countries south of the Sahara Desert had a combined Gross Domestic Product (GDP) of $500 billion—just 2 percent of the global total. As the numbers in this book attest, the rich indeed are getting richer and the poor poorer. The heavy concentration of wealth and power in the hands of a few nations is producing a new kind of hegemonic imperialism that is far more insidious than and far more destructive to the identity and independence of smaller nations than conventional nineteenth-century imperialism. In fact, under the guise of globalization, Western nations are pushing to eradicate the last vestiges of national identities of developing countries. Already, the U.S. dollar has become the international standard for currency exchange, English has become the international lingua franca, and the global economy is being wired so that it can be controlled from New York, Zurich, or London.

2. Demographics. The twenty-first century will witness one of the most important demographic transitions in modern history. The birthrate in all developed nations of the Western world is—or soon will likely be—below the replacement level. This is called the "birth dearth." It means that the populations in these countries in 2100 could be below what they were in 2000. Beginning around 2010 and persisting until the twenty-second century, there may well be massive labor shortages in these countries. These shortages could force them to import labor at both the lower and higher end of the scale, from menial workers on the lower end to information industry workers, scientists, and engineers on the higher end. Furthermore, the birthrate in developing countries, particularly in India and parts of Africa, will probably continue to be very high, with a doubling of the population every twenty to forty years. Because of this contrast in birthrates, people living in the Third World will form nearly 80 percent of the global population in 2100. The heavy concentration of wealth and power in the developed world will be countered by the heavy concentration of population in developing countries. As a result, a greater proportion of the world's population may well be poorer, more illiterate, and more poorly fed, clothed, and housed in 2100 than in 2000.

3. Diverse Nations. The massive import of labor from the Third World by Western nations will have several unintended consequences, not the least of which will be the change in their ethnic makeup and national character. Nationhood is not merely a geographic concept: it flows from a sense of shared history and heritage, common aspirations and hopes, common traditions, common language, and common values. Every nation has, in Winston Churchill's phrase, a theme or characteristic mode of life. The large-scale influx of aliens into a society can alter that theme. If the number of aliens in a society rises greatly, it can generate linguistic, religious, cultural, and economic conflicts and reshape a national consensus on key issues. This is a situation that European countries in particular may confront later in this century. For example, the Swiss, Austrians, and Germans may become minorities in their respective countries within the next 100 years. The effects of this transition cannot yet be known, but historical precedents and recent conflicts indicate a strong potential for violence.

4. Military Power. The rankings illustrate the vastly changed military situation that followed the end of the Cold War. With the rise of the United States as the world's sole superpower, it appears improbable that another world war will break out any time soon. There is no comparable nation or group of nations on earth that has the resources to wage such a war for an extended period of time. But assuring peace is a different proposition. For one, there is no guarantee that U.S. military or political leadership will always be wise or effective. There also remains the possibility of brushfire wars in small nations that can take a heavy toll and embroil other nations in their conflicts. Unlike conventional wars, which often lead to decisive conclusions, these brushfire wars can fester for years without any resolution. Places like the Middle East and the Balkans will likely remain hot spots for decades.

5. Corruption. Until the end of the Cold War, the political classification of nations was based on whether they were free or unfree, with unfree generally meaning communist. At the end of the 1990s, the organization Freedom House issued a report, which stated that about 80 percent of the world was finally free of the worst kind of dictators. For many countries of the Third World, however, the transition to freedom created new problems. As the Corruption rankings show, there are more governments today that are not only corrupt, but also inept and inefficient. The generation of political leaders that produced Sukarno in Indonesia and Mobutu in Zaire (now the Democratic Republic of Congo) has left a legacy of oppression, greed, and conflict that has profoundly impoverished their nations. Although there are more democratic countries today than ever before, democracy remains weak or nonexistent throughout much of the globe. In many countries, especially in the Muslim world, democratic institutions are not only moribund, but a sham. In many former Soviet bloc countries, democracy has been for a decade difficult to maintain and in some places appears close to collapse. In Africa, democracy has faced even greater obstacles, making the future very uncertain.

6. Energy. The real doomsday indicator of the twenty-first century will be energy. Between 2025 and 2040, the world may run out of oil. Nothing seems likely to replace oil as a cheap and efficient source of energy, and no technology is in place that can serve as a universal resource, particularly for transportation. Even if new alternatives are found, it could take decades to construct the necessary infrastructure and to make them available for large-scale use. For poor nations, the end of the oil era could bring even greater economic difficulties.

For those who believe that the world is on an ever-ascendant curve of peace, progress, and prosperity, these rankings will be a sober reality check. While the future remains unpredictable, it is likely that problems may well get worse in many parts of the world in the twenty-first century.

THE ILLUSTRATED BOOK

of

WORLD RANKINGS

Chapter 1

Geography and Climate

Geographers have identified at least ten "macroregions" in the world based on a number of political and geophysical factors, including size. A few are tidy divisions that have some tectonic basis, such as North America and South America, but others are obviously political in nature, such as Russia, Commonwealth of Independent States (CIS), Eastern Europe, Mongolia, and Africa south of the Sahara Desert. The United Nations has adopted a different division into eight macroregions on the basis of demographic features, while in other classifications, there are twenty-two subregions within the larger macrodivisions.

Rank	Region/Continent	Land Mass (million sq. km.)	Rank	Region/Continent	Land Mass (million sq. km.)	Rank	Region/Continent	Land Mass (million sq. km.)
1	Russia, CIS, Eastern Europe and Mongolia	24.8	4	South America	17.6	8	South Asia	6.1
2	North America	24.0	5	Africa South of the Sahara	17.0	9	Europe	3.9
3	Middle East and North Africa	18.1	6	East Asia	10.8	10	South East Asia	3.9
			7	Oceania	7.7			

Source: World Data

Among the principal responsibilities of a sovereign nation is the defense of its borders. Some national borders correspond to natural physical boundaries, but most were determined by historical accidents or were settled through warfare and guaranteed by peace treaties. In the case of many African nations, they are arbitrary lines drawn across maps by colonial rulers and mapmakers and were never properly demarcated. The length of the borders, the number of neighbors, the political and ethnic compatibility of these neighbors, and the pressures of claims from subgroups within nations and territorial ambitions are among the more crucial determinants of foreign policy. Borders are also important because, as in the case of the United States-Mexican border, they require heavy surveillance and checkpoints against illegal immigrants and contraband goods. Throughout the nineteenth and twentieth centuries, national borders were quite fluid and kept changing following wars and the collapse of colonial administrations. National borders tend to be more stable today.

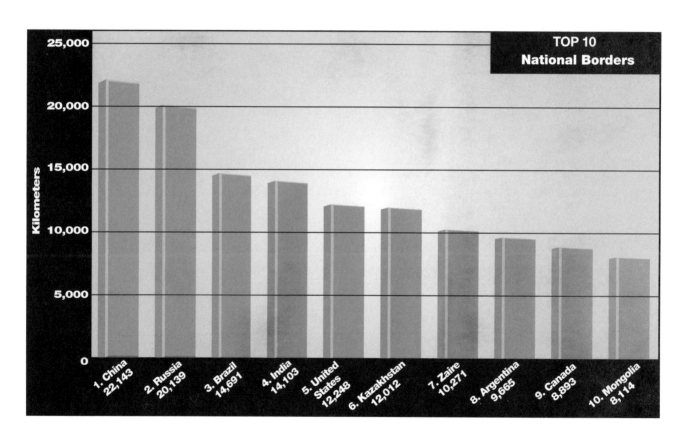

TOP 10 National Borders

1. China 22,143
2. Russia 20,139
3. Brazil 14,691
4. India 14,103
5. United States 12,248
6. Kazakhstan 12,012
7. Zaire 10,271
8. Argentina 9,665
9. Canada 8,893
10. Mongolia 8,114

Rank	Country/Entity	Borders (km)	Rank	Country/Entity	Borders (km)	Rank	Country/Entity	Borders (km)
11	Sudan	7,697	20	Chad	5,968	29	Angola	5,198
12	Colombia	7,408	21	Myanmar (Burma)	5,876	30	Laos	5,083
13	Mali	7,243	22	Niger	5,697	31	Mauritania	5,074
14	Peru	6,940	23	Zambia	5,664	32	Venezuela	4,993
15	Pakistan	6,774	24	Afghanistan	5,529	33	South Africa	4,973
16	Bolivia	6,743	25	Congo, Dem. Rep. of	5,504	34	Thailand	4,863
17	Algeria	6,343	26	Iran	5,440	35	Cameroon	4,591
18	Uzbekistan	6,221	27	Ethiopia	5,311	36	Mozambique	4,571
19	Chile	6,171	28	Central African Republic	5,203	37	Ukraine	4,558

Rank	Country/Entity	Borders (km)	Rank	Country/Entity	Borders (km)	Rank	Country/Entity	Borders (km)
38	Mexico	4,538	76	Somalia	2,366	114	Latvia	1,078
39	Saudi Arabia	4,415	77	Syria	2,253	115	Bhutan	1,075
40	Libya	4,383	78	Yugoslavia	2,234	116	Netherlands	1,027
41	Bangladesh	4,246	79	Sweden	2,205	117	Israel	1,006
42	Nigeria	4,047	80	Ghana	2,093	118	Slovenia	999
43	Botswana	4,013	81	Azerbaijan	2,013	119	Burundi	974
44	Namibia	3,935	82	Ecuador	2,010	120	Sierra Leone	958
45	Paraguay	3,920	83	Morocco	2,002	121	Lesotho	909
46	Kyrgyzstan	3,878	84	Benin	1,989	122	Rwanda	893
47	Vietnam	3,818	85	Hungary	1,952	123	United Arab Emirates	867
48	Turkmenistan	3,736	86	Spain	1,903	124	Macedonia	748
49	Tajikistan	3,651	87	Italy	1,899	125	Gambia	740
50	Iraq	3,631	88	Czech Republic	1,880	126	Guinea-Bissau	724
51	Germany	3,621	89	Switzerland	1,852	127	Albania	720
52	Kenya	3,446	90	Croatia	1,843	128	Costa Rica	639
53	Tanzania	3,402	91	Bulgaria	1,808	129	Estonia	557
54	Guinea	3,399	92	Yemen	1,746	130	Panama	555
55	Burkina Faso	3,192	93	Suriname	1,707	131	El Salvador	545
56	Poland	3,114	94	Guatemala	1,687	132	Equatorial Guinea	539
57	Côte d'Ivoire	3,110	95	North Korea	1,673	133	Swaziland	535
58	Belarus	3,098	96	Togo	1,647	134	Belize	516
59	Zimbabwe	3,066	97	Eritrea	1,630	135	Djibouti	508
60	Nepal	2,926	98	Jordan	1,619	136	Kuwait	464
61	France	2,892	99	Liberia	1,585	137	Lebanon	454
62	Malawi	2,881	100	Uruguay	1,564	138	Brunei	381
63	Uganda	2,698	101	Honduras	1,520	139	Ireland	360
64	Egypt	2,689	102	Georgia	1,461	140	United Kingdom	360
65	Malaysia	2,669	103	Tunisia	1,424	141	Luxembourg	359
66	Senegal	2,640	104	Moldova	1,389	142	Dominican Republic	275
67	Finland	2,628	105	Belgium	1,385	143	Haiti	275
68	Turkey	2,627	106	Oman	1,374	144	South Korea	238
69	Indonesia	2,602	107	Bosnia and Herzegovina	1,369	145	Andorra	125
70	Cambodia	2,572	108	Slovakia	1,355	146	Liechtenstein	78
71	Gabon	2,551	109	Lithuania	1,273	147	Denmark	68
72	Norway	2,515	110	Armenia	1,254	148	Qatar	60
73	Romania	2,508	111	Nicaragua	1,231	149	San Marino	39
74	Austria	2,496	112	Portugal	1,214	150	Cuba	29
75	Guyana	2,462	113	Greece	1,210	151	Monaco	4.4

Source: World Data

1.2 National Coastlines

A coastline is a national resource that also has strategic advantages. Historically, no sizable landlocked nation has become powerful or prosperous, with the exceptions of Austria and Switzerland. A coastline ensures participation in world commerce, provides access to coastal fishing grounds, and extends territorial sovereignty over offshore mineral deposits. It also may promote the development of a strong navy, the development of ports and harbors, and the creation of coastal towns and cities. Attractive beaches often bring in additional revenues.

Rank	Country/Entity	Coastlines (km)	Rank	Country/Entity	Coastlines (km)	Rank	Country/Entity	Coastlines (km)
1	Canada	243,791	6	Australia	25,760	11	Greece	13,676
2	Indonesia	54,716	7	Norway	21,925	12	United Kingdom	12,429
3	Russia	37,653	8	United States	19,924	13	Mexico	9,330
4	Philippines	36,289	9	New Zealand	15,134	14	Brazil	7,491
5	Japan	29,751	10	China	14,500	15	Turkey	7,200

Rank	Country/Entity	Coastlines (km)	Rank	Country/Entity	Coastlines (km)	Rank	Country/Entity	Coastlines (km)
16	India	7,000	62	Tanzania	1,424	108	Suriname	386
17	Chile	6,435	63	Estonia	1,393	109	Albania	362
18	Croatia	5,790	64	Sri Lanka	1,340	110	Trinidad and Tobago	362
19	Solomon Islands	5,313	65	United Arab Emirates	1,318	111	Bulgaria	354
20	Papua New Guinea	5,152	66	Costa Rica	1,290	112	Guinea-Bissau	350
21	Italy	4,996	67	Dominican Republic	1,288	113	Comoros	340
22	Argentina	4,989	68	Eritrea	1,151	114	Guinea	320
23	Iceland	4,988	69	Tunisia	1,148	115	Djibouti	314
24	Spain	4,964	70	Kiribati	1,143	116	Georgia	310
25	Madagascar	4,828	71	Fiji	1,129	117	El Salvador	307
26	Malaysia	4,675	72	Finland	1,126	118	Guatemala	306
27	Cuba	3,738	73	Pakistan	1,046	119	Equatorial Guinea	296
28	Bahamas	3,542	74	Jamaica	1,022	120	Israel	273
29	Vietnam	3,444	75	Algeria	998	121	Lebanon	225
30	France	3,427	76	Cape Verde	965	122	Romania	225
31	Denmark	3,379	77	Nicaragua	910	123	São Tomé and Príncipe	209
32	Colombia	3,280	78	Gabon	885	124	Yugoslavia	199
33	Thailand	3,219	79	Nigeria	853	125	Singapore	193
34	Sweden	3,218	80	Sudan	853	126	Syria	193
35	Somalia	3,025	81	Honduras	820	127	Mauritius	177
36	Kazakhstan	2,909	82	Azerbaijan	800	128	Congo, Dem. Rep. of	169
37	South Africa	2,881	83	Mauritania	754	129	Bahrain	161
38	Venezuela	2,800	84	Uruguay	680	130	Brunei	161
39	Ukraine	2,782	85	Cyprus	648	131	Saint Lucia	158
40	Saudi Arabia	2,640	86	Maldives	644	132	Antigua and Barbuda	153
41	Vanuatu	2,528	87	Bangladesh	580	133	Dominica	148
42	North Korea	2,495	88	Liberia	579	134	Malta	140
43	Panama	2,490	89	Qatar	563	135	Saint Kitts and Nevis	135
44	Mozambique	2,470	90	Ghana	539	136	Benin	121
45	Egypt	2,450	91	Kenya	536	137	Grenada	121
46	Iran	2,440	92	Latvia	531	138	Lithuania	108
47	Peru	2,414	93	Senegal	531	139	Bermuda	103
48	South Korea	2,413	94	Côte d'Ivoire	515	140	Barbados	97
49	Germany	2,389	95	Puerto Rico	501	141	Saint Vincent and the Grenadines	84
50	Ecuador	2,237	96	Kuwait	499			
51	Oman	2,092	97	Poland	491	142	Gambia	80
52	Myanmar (Burma)	1,930	98	Seychelles	491	143	Belgium	64
53	Yemen	1,906	99	Netherlands	451	144	Iraq	58
54	Morocco	1,835	100	Cambodia	443	145	Togo	56
55	Portugal	1,793	101	Uzbekistan	420	146	Dem. Rep. of Congo	37
56	Haiti	1,771	102	Tonga	419	147	Slovakia	32
57	Libya	1,770	103	Samoa	403	148	Nauru	30
58	Turkmenistan	1,768	104	Cameroon	402	149	Jordan	26
59	Angola	1,600	105	Sierra Leone	402	150	Tuvalu	24
60	Namibia	1,489	106	Guyana	400	151	Bosnia and Herzegovina	20
61	Ireland	1,448	107	Belize	386	152	Monaco	4.1

Source: World Data

1.3 Total Land Area

Total land area of the planet is estimated at 133.5 million square kilometers (51.57 million square miles) representing 29.2 percent of the planet. This land is divided among 192 independent nation states or 266 territorial units including dependencies. Of these, the top seventeen nations occupy nearly two-thirds of the land area. But total land area by itself may not be as significant as the arable or inhabitable area of countries. Thus, Russia, the largest by far of all countries, has only 26 percent arable land; while Canada, the second largest, has 6 percent; and China, 11 percent. This factor scales these giants down in size considerably so that they roughly match the United States, which has 45 percent of territory in arable land or cultivated pasture. Two other large countries, Argentina and India, also have almost half of their land cultivated or arable. Nevertheless, land area is an important element in geopolitics. It measures a country's physical size and often—but not always—correlates to its population.

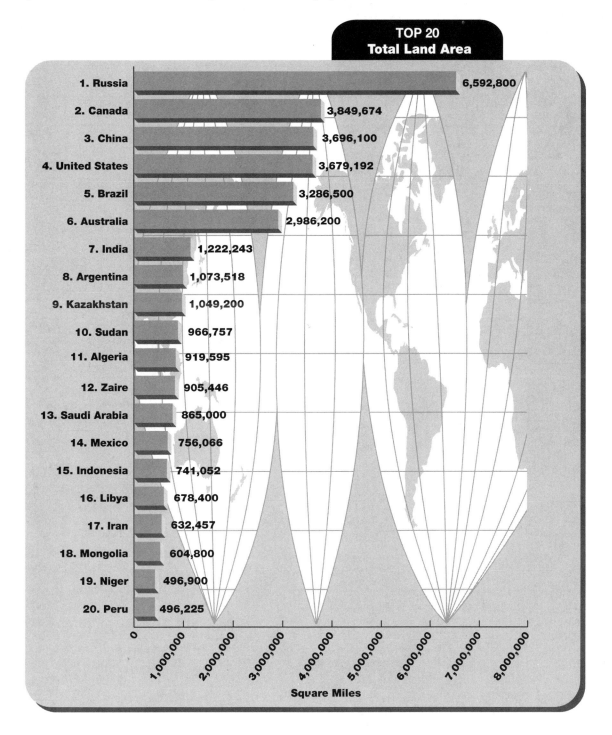

**TOP 20
Total Land Area**

Rank	Country	Square Miles
1.	Russia	6,592,800
2.	Canada	3,849,674
3.	China	3,696,100
4.	United States	3,679,192
5.	Brazil	3,286,500
6.	Australia	2,986,200
7.	India	1,222,243
8.	Argentina	1,073,518
9.	Kazakhstan	1,049,200
10.	Sudan	966,757
11.	Algeria	919,595
12.	Zaire	905,446
13.	Saudi Arabia	865,000
14.	Mexico	756,066
15.	Indonesia	741,052
16.	Libya	678,400
17.	Iran	632,457
18.	Mongolia	604,800
19.	Niger	496,900
20.	Peru	496,225

Square Miles

Rank	Country/Entity	Land Area (sq. mi.)	Rank	Country/Entity	Land Area (sq. mi.)	Rank	Country/Entity	Land Area (sq. mi.)
21	Chad	495,755	78	Uganda	93,070	135	Moldova	13
22	Mali	482,077	79	Ghana	92,098	136	Belgium	11,787
23	Angola	481,354	80	Romania	91,699	137	Lesotho	11,720
24	South Africa	472,281	81	Laos	91,429	138	Armenia	11,500
25	Colombia	440,831	82	Guyana	83,044	139	Albania	11,100
26	Ethiopia	437,794	83	Belarus	80,153	140	Solomon Islands	10,954
27	Bolivia	424,164	84	Kyrgyzstan	78,600	141	Equatorial Guinea	10,831
28	Mauritania	398	85	Senegal	75,951	142	Burundi	10,740
29	Egypt	385,229	86	Syria	71,498	143	Haiti	10,695
30	Tanzania	364,017	87	Cambodia	70,238	144	Rwanda	10,169
31	Nigeria	356,669	88	Uruguay	68,037	145	Macedonia	9,928
32	Venezuela	352,144	89	Tunisia	63,378	146	Djibouti	8,950
33	Pakistan	339,697	90	Suriname	63,251	147	Belize	8,867
34	Namibia	318,580	91	Bangladesh	57,295	148	El Salvador	8,124
35	Mozambique	313,661	92	Nepal	56,827	149	Israel	7,992
36	Turkey	300,948	93	Tajikistan	55,300	150	Slovenia	7,821
37	Chile	292,135	94	Greece	50,949	151	Fiji	7,056
38	Zambia	290,586	95	Nicaragua	50,838	152	Kuwait	6,880
39	Myanmar (Burma)	261,228	96	North Korea	47,399	153	Swaziland	6,704
40	Afghanistan	251,825	97	Malawi	45,747	154	Bahamas	5,382
41	Somalia	246	98	Eritrea	45,300	155	Vanuatu	4,707
42	Central African Republic	240,324	99	Benin	43,500	156	Qatar	4,412
			100	Honduras	43,277	157	Jamaica	4,244
43	Madagascar	226,658	101	Bulgaria	42,855	158	Gambia	4,127
44	Kenya	224,961	102	Cuba	42,804	159	Lebanon	3,950
45	Botswana	224,607	103	Guatemala	42,042	160	Cyprus	3,572
46	France	210,026	104	Iceland	39,699	161	Puerto Rico	3,515
47	Yemen	205,356	105	Yugoslavia	39,449	162	Brunei	2,226
48	Ukraine	203,100	106	South Korea	38,330	163	Trinidad and Tobago	1,980
49	Thailand	198,115	107	Liberia	38,250	164	Cape Verde	1,557
50	Spain	194,898	108	Hungary	35,920	165	Samoa	1,093
51	Turkmenistan	188,500	109	Portugal	35,574	166	Luxembourg	999
52	Cameroon	183,569	110	Jordan	34,342	167	Mauritius	788
53	Papua New Guinea	178,704	111	Azerbaijan	33,400	168	Comoros	719
54	Morocco	177,117	112	Austria	32,378	169	São Tomé and Príncipe	386
55	Sweden	173,732	113	Czech Republic	30,450	170	Kiribati	313
56	Uzbekistan	172,700	114	United Arab Emirates	30	171	Dominica	290
57	Iraq	167,975	115	Panama	29,157	172	Tonga	290
58	Paraguay	157,048	116	Sierra Leone	27,699	173	Bahrain	268
59	Zimbabwe	150,872	117	Ireland	27,137	174	Singapore	247
60	Japan	145,850	118	Georgia	26,900	175	Saint Lucia	238
61	Germany	137,823	119	Sri Lanka	25,332	176	Andorra	181
62	Congo, Rep. of	132,047	120	Lithuania	25,213	177	Seychelles	176
63	Finland	130,559	121	Latvia	24,946	178	Antigua and Barbuda	171
64	Malaysia	127,584	122	Togo	21,925	179	Barbados	166
65	Vietnam	127,246	123	Croatia	21,829	180	Saint Vincent and the Grenadines	150
66	Norway	125,050	124	Bosnia and Herzegovina	19,741	181	Grenada	133
67	Côte d'Ivoire	123,847	125	Costa Rica	19,730	182	Malta	122
68	Poland	120,728	126	Slovakia	18,933	183	Maldives	115
69	Oman	118,150	127	Dominican Republic	18,704	185	Saint Kitts and Nevis	104
70	Italy	116,334	128	Bhutan	18,150	186	Liechtenstein	62
71	Philippines	115,680	129	Estonia	17,462	187	San Marino	24
72	Burkina Faso	105,946	130	Denmark	16,639	188	Bermuda	21
73	Ecuador	105,037	131	Netherlands	16,033	189	Tuvalu	9.4
74	New Zealand	104,454	132	Switzerland	15,940	190	Nauru	8.2
75	Gabon	103,347	133	Taiwan	13,969	191	Monaco	.75
76	Guinea	94,926	134	Guinea-Bissau	13,948			
77	United Kingdom	94,251						

Source: World Data

This ranking rates countries by the elevation of their highest point, often the highest national peak. It may be noted that the first seven countries share the high Himalayan and Central Asian mountain ranges and the next five share the Andes.

Rank	Country/Entity	Elevation Meters	Feet	Rank	Country/Entity	Elevation Meters	Feet	Rank	Country/Entity	Elevation Meters	Feet
1	China	8,848	29,028	51	Vietnam	3,143	10,312	100	South Korea	1,950	6,398
2	Nepal	8,848	29,028	52	Saudi Arabia	3,133	10,279	101	Sierra Leone	1,947	6,390
3	Pakistan	8,611	28,250	53	Lebanon	3,083	10,115	102	Swaziland	1,862	6,109
4	India	7,817	25,645	54	Malawi	3,048	10,000	103	Guinea	1,828	6,000
5	Bhutan	7,541	24,740	55	Brazil	3,014	9,888	104	Niger	1,798	5,900
6	Russia	7,495	24,590	56	Algeria	3,003	9,852	105	Jordan	1,754	5,755
7	Afghanistan	7,485	24,557	57	Germany	2,963	9,721	106	Côte d'Ivoire	1,752	5,748
8	Argentina	7,485	24,557	58	Philippines	2,954	9,690	107	Burundi	1,706	5,600
9	Chile	6,880	22,572	59	Andorra	2,946	9,665	108	Gabon	1,574	5,165
10	Peru	6,768	22,205	60	Bulgaria	2,925	9,596	109	Tunisia	1,544	5,065
11	Bolivia	6,400	21,000	61	Greece	2,917	9,570	110	United Arab Emirates	1,527	5,010
12	Ecuador	6,267	20,561	62	Madagascar	2,880	9,450	111	Congo, Rep. of	1,500	4,921
13	United States	6,194	20,320	63	Honduras	2,870	9,400	112	Liberia	1,380	4,528
14	Myanmar (Burma)	6,096	20,000	64	Yugoslavia	2,863	9,393	113	United Kingdom	1,343	4,406
15	Canada	5,950	19,520	65	Guyana	2,835	9,304	114	Finland	1,324	4,344
16	Tanzania	5,894	19,340	66	Cape Verde	2,829	9,281	115	Fiji	1,323	4,341
17	Colombia	5,775	18,947	67	Laos	2,816	9,242	116	Suriname	1,286	4,218
18	Iran	5,771	18,934	68	Syria	2,814	9,232	117	Central African Republic	1,280	4,200
19	Mexico	5,700	18,701	69	Albania	2,750	9,023				
20	Kenya	5,199	17,058	70	North Korea	2,744	9,003	118	Bangladesh	1,229	4,034
21	Turkey	5,185	17,011	71	Haiti	2,677	8,783	119	Botswana	1,219	4,000
22	Congo, Dem. Rep. of	5,109	16,762	72	Czech Republic	2,654	8,707	120	Israel	1,208	3,963
23	Indonesia	5,030	16,503	73	Egypt	2,642	8,668	121	Equatorial Guinea	1,200	3,937
24	Venezuela	5,002	16,411	74	Angola	2,620	8,595	122	Ireland	1,041	3,414
25	Uganda	4,876	16,000	75	Liechtenstein	2,599	8,527	123	Tonga	1,030	3,380
26	France	4,807	15,771	76	Zimbabwe	2,595	8,517	124	Hungary	1,015	3,330
27	Italy	4,731	15,521	77	Thailand	2,595	8,514	125	Togo	986	3,235
28	Switzerland	4,634	15,203	78	Romania	2,543	8,343	126	Trinidad and Tobago	940	3,085
29	Ethiopia	4,618	15,153	79	Sri Lanka	2,524	8,281	127	Belize	914	3,000
30	Rwanda	4,532	14,870	80	Yemen	2,513	8,245	128	Seychelles	912	2,993
31	Papua New Guinea	4,509	14,793	81	Poland	2,499	8,199	129	Ghana	884	2,900
32	Mongolia	4,362	14,311	82	Norway	2,470	8,104	130	Grenada	840	2,757
33	Guatemala	4,220	13,845	83	Cameroon	2,438	8,000	131	Mauritius	826	2,711
34	Morocco	4,165	13,665	84	Nicaragua	2,438	8,000	132	Cambodia	762	2,500
35	Malaysia	4,101	13,455	85	Mozambique	2,436	7,992	133	Burkina Faso	717	2,352
36	Taiwan	3,997	13,113	86	El Salvador	2,417	7,933	134	Mali	701	2,300
37	Costa Rica	3,819	12,530	87	Somalia	2,406	7,894	135	Belgium	694	2,277
38	Austria	3,797	12,457	88	Comoros	2,361	7,746	136	Benin	610	2,001
39	Japan	3,776	12,388	89	Jamaica	2,256	7,402	137	Paraguay	609	1,998
40	New Zealand	3,764	12,349	90	Australia	2,228	7,310	138	Uruguay	609	1,998
41	Yemen	3,760	12,336	91	Sudan	2,133	7,000	139	Luxembourg	559	1,835
42	Greenland	3,700	12,139	92	Zambia	2,133	7,000	140	Senegal	487	1,600
43	Iraq	3,609	11,840	93	Iceland	2,119	6,952	141	Mauritania	457	1,500
44	Lesotho	3,482	11,425	94	Sweden	2,111	6,926	142	Netherlands	322	1,051
45	Spain	3,478	11,411	95	Nigeria	2,042	6,699	143	Guinea-Bissau	300	1,000
46	Panama	3,477	11,410	96	São Tomé and Príncipe	2,024	6,640	144	Denmark	173	568
47	South Africa	3,377	11,081					145	Bahrain	135	443
48	Dominican Republic	3,175	10,417	97	Cuba	1,994	6,552	146	Bahamas	63	206
49	Libya	3,150	10,335	98	Portugal	1,993	6,539	147	Maldives	24	80
50	Chad	3,145	10,318	99	Cyprus	1,952	6,406				

Source: George Thomas Kurian, *Geo-Data: World Geographical Encyclopedia*

The annual world precipitation is estimated at 430,000 cubic kilometers (103,000 cubic miles) of which 320,000 cubic kilometers (77,000 cubic miles) fall on the oceans and 110,000 cubic kilometers (26,000 cubic miles) fall on land. By continents, Asia receives the most precipitation (32,690 cubic kilometers, or 7,840 cubic miles), followed by South America (29,335 cubic kilometers, or 7,000 cubic miles), Africa (20,780 cubic kilometers, or 4,985 cubic miles), North America (13,910 cubic kilometers, or 3,340 cubic miles), Europe (7,165 cubic kilometers, or 1,720 cubic miles), and Oceania (6,405 cubic kilometers, or 1,540 cubic miles). As with other natural resources, there is wide disparity in the distribution of rainfall. Parts of the Sahara receive rain only once in several years while Cherrapunji in northeast India receives an average of 2.95 centimeters (1.16 inches) every day of the year.

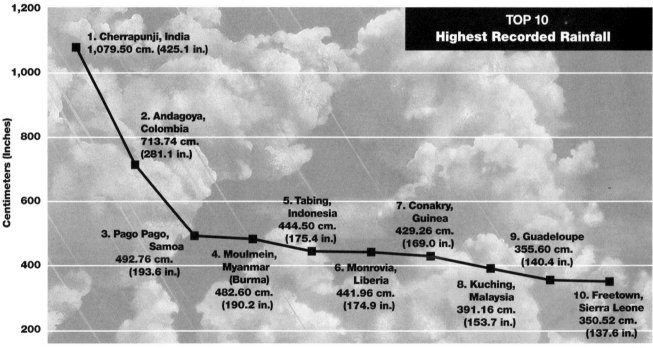

TOP 10 Highest Recorded Rainfall

Centimeters (Inches)

1. Cherrapunji, India 1,079.50 cm. (425.1 in.)
2. Andagoya, Colombia 713.74 cm. (281.1 in.)
3. Pago Pago, Samoa 492.76 cm. (193.6 in.)
4. Moulmein, Myanmar (Burma) 482.60 cm. (190.2 in.)
5. Tabing, Indonesia 444.50 cm. (175.4 in.)
6. Monrovia, Liberia 441.96 cm. (174.9 in.)
7. Conakry, Guinea 429.26 cm. (169.0 in.)
8. Kuching, Malaysia 391.16 cm. (153.7 in.)
9. Guadeloupe 355.60 cm. (140.4 in.)
10. Freetown, Sierra Leone 350.52 cm. (137.6 in.)

Rank	Country/Entity	Rainfall Centimeters	Inches	Rank	Country/Entity	Rainfall Centimeters	Inches	Rank	Country/Entity	Rainfall Centimeters	Inches
11	Madang, Papua New Guinea	347.98	137.2	22	Prince Rupert, Canada	241.30	95.3	32	Martinique	203.20	80.4
12	Yakutat, United States	335.28	132.0	23	Singapore	241.30	95.0	33	Bergen, Norway	200.66	78.8
13	Brunei	332.74	131.0	24	Seychelles	233.68	92.5	34	Cococ (Keeling) Islands	198.12	78.2
14	Cayenne, French Guiana	320.40	126.1	25	Colombo, Sri Lanka	233.68	92.3	35	Ho Chi Minh City, Vietnam	198.12	78.1
15	Tulagi, Solomon Islands	312.42	123.4	26	Paramaribo, Suriname	231.14	91.0	36	Abidjan, Côte d'Ivoire	195.58	77.1
16	Los Evangelistas, Chile	302.26	119.4	27	Réunion	228.60	90.5	37	Nagasaki, Japan	190.50	75.5
17	Suva, Fiji	297.18	117.1	28	Georgetown, Guyana	226.60	88.7	38	Santa Isabel, Equatorial Guinea	190.50	74.9
18	Iquitos, Peru	274.32	107.7	29	Bolama, Guinea-Bissau	218.44	85.9	39	Belize	187.96	74.4
19	Vaupes, Brazil	266.70	105.4	30	Hong Kong	215.90	85.1	40	Dacca, Bangladesh	187.96	73.9
20	Libreville, Gabon	248.92	98.8	31	Manila, Philippines	208.28	82.0	41	Taipei, Taiwan	185.42	72.7
21	Tela, Honduras	243.84	96.1					42	Lagos, Nigeria	182.88	72.3

Rank	Country/Entity	Rainfall Centimeters	Inches	Rank	Country/Entity	Rainfall Centimeters	Inches	Rank	Country/Entity	Rainfall Centimeters	Inches
43	San Jose, Costa Rica	180.34	70.8	76	Barbados	127.00	50.3	114	Saint Helena	81.28	32.1
44	Santa Elena, Venezuela	180.34	70.7	77	Seoul, South Korea	124.46	49.2	115	Kingston, Jamaica	78.74	31.5
45	San Salvador, El Salvador	177.80	70.0	78	Auckland, New Zealand	124.46	49.1	116	Istanbul, Turkey	78.74	31.5
46	Thursday Island, Australia	170.18	67.5	79	Gamble, Ethiopia	124.46	48.8	117	Bone, Algeria	78.74	31.0
47	Vientiane, Laos	170.18	67.5	80	Artigas, Uruguay	124.46	48.6	118	Lome, Togo	78.74	31.0
48	Kisangani, Dem. Rep. of Congo	170.18	67.1	81	Havana, Cuba	121.92	48.2	119	Göteberg, Sweden	76.20	30.5
49	Vera Cruz, Mexico	167.64	65.7	82	Mombasa, Kenya	119.38	47.3	120	Kaolack, Senegal	76.20	30.3
50	San Juan, Puerto Rico	162.56	64.2	83	Genoa, Italy	119.38	46.6	121	Monaco	76.20	30.1
51	Saint Clair, Trinidad and Tobago	162.56	64.2	84	Djibouti	116.84	46.0	122	Gibraltar	76.20	30.1
52	Canton, China	162.56	63.6	85	Corrientes, Argentina	116.84	46.4	123	Luxembourg	73.66	29.2
53	Yaounde, Cameroon	154.94	61.2	86	Nassau, Bahamas	116.84	46.4	124	Krakow, Poland	73.66	28.6
54	Bangui, Central African Empire	154.94	60.8	87	Babo Dioulasso, Burkina Faso	116.84	46.4	125	Rhodes, Greece	71.12	28.5
55	Kampala, Uganda	154.94	60.7	88	Bamako, Mali	111.76	44.1	126	Helsinki, Finland	71.12	27.6
56	Sofala, Mozambique	152.40	59.9	89	Quito, Ecuador	111.76	43.9	127	Falkland Islands	68.58	26.8
57	Oursso, Rep. of Congo	149.86	58.6	90	Noumea, New Caledonia	109.22	43.5	128	Aarhus, Denmark	68.58	26.6
58	Bangkok, Thailand	147.32	57.8	91	Wau, Sudan	109.22	43.3	129	Haifa, Israel	66.40	26.2
59	Hamilton, Bermuda	147.32	57.6	92	Durres, Albania	109.22	42.9	130	Amsterdam, Netherlands	66.40	25.6
60	Nova Lisboa, Angola	144.78	57.0	93	Dar es Salaam, Tanzania	106.68	41.9	131	Sofia, Bulgaria	63.50	25.0
61	Faeroe Islands	142.24	56.2	94	Cardiff, United Kingdom	106.68	41.9	132	Prerov, Czech Republic	63.50	24.8
62	Katmandu, Nepal	142.24	56.2	95	Cork, Ireland	104.14	41.3	133	Budapest, Hungary	60.96	24.2
63	Santo Domingo, Dominican Republic	142.24	55.8	96	Zurich, Switzerland	104.14	40.9	134	Cluj, Rumania	60.96	24.0
64	Kumasi, Ghana	139.70	55.2	97	Durban, South Africa	101.60	39.7	135	Barcelona, Spain	58.42	23.5
65	Phnom Penh, Cambodia	139.70	54.8	98	Concepción, Bolivia	99.60	38.6	136	Niamey, Niger	55.88	21.6
66	Braganca, Portugal	137.16	53.8	99	Balovale, Zambia	96.52	38.3	137	Valetta, Malta	50.80	20.3
67	Antananarive, Madagascar	134.62	53.4	100	São Tomé, São Tomé and Príncipe	96.52	38.0	138	Maun, Botswana	45.72	18.2
68	Port-au-Prince, Haiti	134.62	53.3	101	Cherbourg, France	93.98	37.3	139	Mogadiscio, Somalia	43.18	16.9
69	Zomba, Malawi	134.62	52.9	102	Am Timan, Chad	93.98	37.2	140	Tunis, Tunisia	40.64	16.5
70	Cotonou, Benin	132.80	52.4	103	Rawalpindi, Pakistan	91.44	36.5	141	Kermanshah, Iran	40.64	16.4
71	Asuncion, Paraguay	132.80	51.8	104	Pyongyang, North Korea	91.44	36.4	142	Aleppo, Syria	38.10	15.5
72	Guatemala City, Guatemala	129.54	51.8	105	Petropavlovsk, Russia	91.44	35.9	143	Mosul, Iraq	38.10	15.2
73	Bathurst, Gambia	129.54	51.0	106	Tangier, Morocco	88.90	35.3	144	Tripoli, Libya	38.10	15.1
74	La Guerite, Saint Christopher Nevis	129.54	50.9	107	Beirut, Lebanon	88.90	35.1	145	Nicosia, Cyprus	38.10	14.6
75	Mauritius	129.54	50.6	108	Split, Yugoslavia	88.90	35.1	146	Windhoek, Namibia	35.56	14.3
				109	Les Escaldes, Andorra	88.90	34.3	147	Kabul, Afghanistan	33.20	12.6
				110	Munich, Germany	86.36	34.1	148	Nema, Mauritania	29.52	11.6
				111	Reykjavik, Iceland	86.36	33.9	149	Amman, Jordan	27.46	10.9
				112	Innsbruck, Austria	86.36	33.8	150	Porto da Praia, Cape Verde	26.30	10.2
				113	Salisbury, Zimbabwe	83.82	32.6	151	Ulan Bator, Mongolia	19.50	7.7
								152	Alexandria, Egypt	17.78	7.0
								153	Kuwait	12.85	5.1
								154	Sharjah, United Arab Emirates	10.47	4.2
								155	Muscat, Oman	10.00	3.9
								156	Dhahran, Saudi Arabia	8.89	3.5
								157	Kamaran, Yemen	8.25	3.4

Source: World Data

Outside of Antarctica, there are few places that totally exclude human activity because of cold weather. Human settlements do not thrive in places where temperatures are consistently below zero because of the extra burdens imposed on the human body as well as the extra costs involved in heating, clothing, snow removal, and so on. There are thirty countries where the coldest recorded temperature is below 0° F. Of these, the four coldest are within or close to the Arctic Circle. The following ranking is limited to cities and does not include remote or mountainous regions where colder temperatures may have been reached.

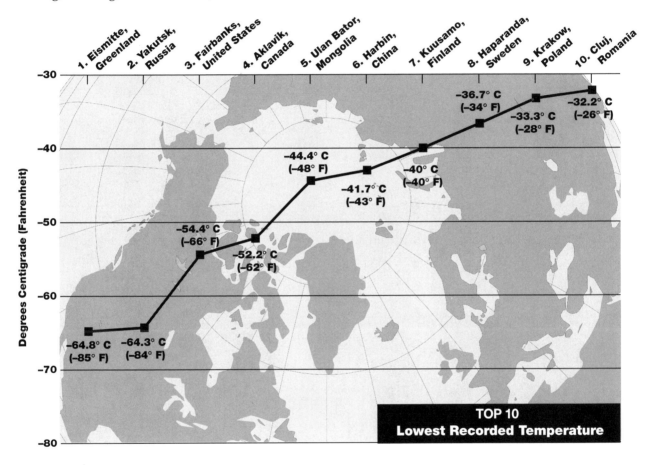

TOP 10
Lowest Recorded Temperature

Rank	Country/Entity	Temperature °C	°F	Rank	Country/Entity	Temperature °C	°F	Rank	Country/Entity	Temperature °C	°F
11	Prerov, Czech Republic	-30.6	-26	20	Belgrade, Yugoslavia	-25.6	-14	30	Srinagar, India	-20.0	-4
12	Debrecen, Hungary	-30.0	-22	21	Lyon, France	-25.0	-13	31	Les Escaldes, Andorra	-17.8	0
13	Trondheim, Norway	-30.0	-22	22	Kermanshah, Iran	-25.0	-13	32	Burgos, Spain	-17.8	0
14	Erzurum, Turkey	-30.0	-22	23	Aarhus, Denmark	-24.4	-12	33	Perth, United Kingdom	17.8	0
15	Kushiro, Japan	-28.3	-19	24	Seoul, South Korea	-24.4	-12	34	Amsterdam, Netherlands	-16.1	3
16	Pyongyang, North Korea	-28.3	-19	25	Zurich, Switzerland	-24.4	-12	35	Thorshavn, Faroe Islands	-13.3	8
17	Nurnberg, Germany	-27.8	-18	26	Luxembourg	-23.3	-10	36	Dublin, Ireland	-13.3	8
18	Sofia, Bulgaria	-27.2	-17	27	Akureyi, Iceland	-22.2	-8	37	Aleppo, Syria	-12.8	9
19	Innsbruck, Austria	-26.7	-16	28	Kabul, Afghanistan	-22.2	-6				
				29	Ushuaia, Argentina	-21.1	-6				

Rank	Country/Entity	°C	°F
38	Braganca, Portugal	-12.2	10
39	Punta Arenas, Chile	-11.7	11
40	Stanley, Falkland Islands	-11.1	12
41	Mosul, Iraq	-11.1	12
42	Chihuahua, Mexico	-11.1	12
43	Canberra, Australia	-10.0	14
44	Venice, Italy	-10.0	14
45	Tsabong, Botswana	-9.4	15
46	Thessaloniki, Greece	-9.4	15
47	Cusco, Peru	-8.9	16
48	Fort Flatters, Algeria	-7.2	19
49	Riyadh, Saudi Arabia	-7.2	19
50	Cangamba, Angola	-6.7	20
51	Bela Vista, Brazil	-6.7	20
52	Kimberley, South Africa	-6.7	20
53	Durres, Albania	-6.1	21
54	Amman, Jordan	-6.1	21
55	Christchurch, New Zealand	-6.1	21
56	Nicosia, Cyprus	-5.0	23
57	Sabhah, Libya	-4.4	24
58	Artigas, Uruguay	-4.4	24
59	Sucre, Bolivia	-3.9	25
60	Quito, Ecuador	-3.9	25
61	Windhoek, Namibia	-3.9	25
62	Rawalpindi, Pakistan	-3.9	25
63	Jerusalem, Israel	-3.3	26
64	Monaco	-2.8	27
65	Marrakech, Morocco	-2.8	27
66	Katmandu, Nepal	-2.8	27
67	Gabes, Tunisia	-2.8	27
68	Bulawayo, Zimbabwe	-2.2	28
69	Wadi Halfa, Sudan	-2.2	28
70	Bilma, Niger	-1.7	29
71	Asunción, Paraguay	-1.7	29
72	Bogota, Colombia	-1.1	30
73	Beirut, Lebanon	-1.1	30
74	Asmara, Ethiopia	-0.6	31
75	Hong Kong	0.0	32
76	Chicoa, Mozambique	0.0	32
77	Taipei, Taiwan	0.0	32
78	Vientiane, Laos	0.0	32
79	Kuwait	0.6	33
80	Cairo, Egypt	1.1	34
81	Antananrive, Madagascar	1.1	34
82	Valetta, Malta	1.1	34
83	Gibraltar	1.7	35
84	Faya, Chad	2.8	37
85	Araouane, Mali	2.8	37
86	Sharjah, United Arab Emirates	2.8	37
87	Balovale, Zambia	3.3	38
88	Kouroussa, Guinea	3.9	39
89	Atar, Mauritania	3.9	39
90	Hamilton, Bermuda	4.4	40
91	Réunion	4.4	40
92	Nassau, Bahamas	5.0	41
93	Guatemala City, Guatemala	5.0	41
94	Nairobi, Kenya	5.0	41
95	Zomba, Malawi	5.0	41
96	Hanoi, Vietnam	5.0	41
97	Iringa, Tanzania	5.6	42
98	Havana, Cuba	6.1	43
99	Dacca, Bangladesh	6.1	43
100	Maiduguri, Nigeria	6.1	43
101	Mandalay, Myanmar (Burma)	6.7	44
102	San Salvador, El Salvador	7.2	45
103	Bathurst, Gambia	7.2	45
104	Ngaoundere, Cameroon	7.8	46
105	Bobo Dioulasso, Burkina	7.8	46
106	Kaolack, Senegal	8.9	48
107	Merida, Venezuela	8.9	48
108	Belize	9.4	49
109	San José, Costa Rica	9.4	49
110	Mauritius	10.0	50
111	Saint Helena	10.0	50
112	Bangkok, Thailand	10.0	50
113	Lira, Uganda	10.0	50
114	Kalemi, Dem. Rep. of Congo	10.0	50
115	Kumasi, Ghana	10.6	51
116	Muscat, Oman	10.6	51
117	Noumea, New Caledonia	11.1	52
118	Saint Clair, Trinidad and Tobago	11.1	52
119	Brazzaville, Rep. of Congo	12.2	54
120	Camp Jacob, Guadeloupe	12.2	54
121	Phnom Penh, Cambodia	12.8	55
122	Suva, Fiji	12.8	55
123	Porto de Praia, Cape Verde	13.3	56
124	Kingston, Jamaica	13.3	56
125	Martinique	13.3	56
126	São Tomé, São Tomé and Príncipe	13.3	56
127	Bangui, Central African Republic	13.9	57
128	Bouake, Côte d'Ivoire	13.9	57
129	Aden, Yemen	13.9	57
130	Port-au-Prince, Haiti	14.4	58
131	Tela, Honduras	14.4	58
132	Penfui, Indonesia	14.4	58
133	Manila, Philippines	14.4	58
134	Berbera, Somalia	14.4	58
135	Lome, Togo	14.4	58
136	Santo Domingo, Dominican Republic	15.0	59
137	Bolama, Guinea-Bissau	15.0	59
138	Colombo, Sri Lanka	15.0	59
139	Mayoumba, Gabon	15.6	60
140	San Juan, Puerto Rico	15.6	60
141	Barbados	16.1	61
142	Santa Isabel, Equatorial Guinea	16.1	61
143	Saint Kitts and Nevis	16.1	61
144	Monrovia, Liberia	16.7	62
145	Madang, Papua New Guinea	16.7	62
146	Freetown, Sierra Leone	16.7	62
147	Paramaribo, Suriname	16.7	62
148	Lethem, Guyana	17.2	63
149	Djibouti	17.2	63
150	Kuala Lumpur, Malaysia	17.8	64
151	Benin	18.3	65
152	Cayenne, French Guyana	18.3	65
153	Kamaran, Yemen	18.9	66
154	Singapore	18.9	66
155	Pago Pago, Samoa	19.4	67
156	Seychelles	19.4	67
157	Cocos (Keeling) Islands	20.0	68
158	Tulagi, Solomon Islands	20.0	68
159	Brunei	21.1	70

Source: World Data

The limits of human physiological tolerance of heat has not been established precisely, but human beings have been reported to survive temperatures of more than 135° F, although not for more than a few days. Such high temperatures are reached every year in the forbidding Rub al-Khali in Saudi Arabia, in the kavirs of the Central Plateau in Iran, and in the Sahara in northern Africa. Desert winds, like the harmattan in the Sahara, tend to intensify the heat and shrivel all living things. African and Asian countries and Australia lead the list. Phoenix in the United States is the hottest in the Americas, and Spain occupies that rank in Europe.

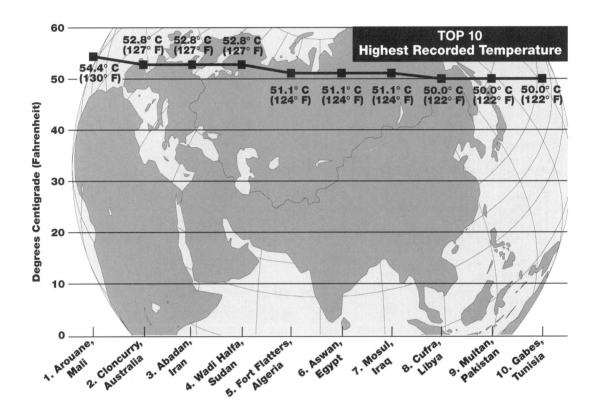

Rank	Country/Entity	Temperature °C	°F	Rank	Country/Entity	Temperature °C	°F	Rank	Country/Entity	Temperature °C	°F
11	Faya, Chad	49.4	121	21	Guaymas, Mexico	47.2	117	32	Palermo, Italy	45.0	113
12	Nema, Mauritania	48.9	120	22	Chicao, Mozambique	47.2	117	33	Urumchi, China	44.4	112
13	Marrakech, Morocco	48.8	120	23	Berbera, Somalia	47.2	117	34	Haifa, Israel	44.4	112
14	Dhahran, Saudi Arabia	48.9	120	24	Seville, Spain	47.2	117	35	Maiduguri, Nigeria	44.4	112
15	Lucknow, India	48.3	119	25	Aleppo, Syria	47.2	117	36	Kandahar, Afghanistan	43.9	111
16	Kuwait	48.3	119	26	Santiago del Estero, Argentina	46.7	116	37	Mandalay, Myanmar (Burma)	43.9	111
17	Sharjah, United Arab Emirates	47.8	118	27	Nicosia, Cyprus	46.7	116	38	Gambela, Ethiopia	43.9	111
18	Phoenix, United States	47.8	118	28	Bilma, Niger	46.7	116	39	Toulouse, France	43.9	111
19	Ouagadougou, Burkina, Faso	47.8	118	29	Muscat, Oman	46.7	116	40	Aden, Yemen	43.9	111
20	Djibouti	47.2	117	30	Iraklion, Crete, Greece	45.6	114	41	Regina, Canada	43.3	110
				31	Kaolack, Senegal	45.6	114	42	Asunción, Paraguay	43.3	110
								43	Maun, Botswana	43.3	110

Rank	Country/Entity	°C	°F
44	Cangamba, Angola	42.8	109
45	Ndele, Central African Republic	42.8	109
46	Kouroussa, Guinea	42.8	109
47	Amman, Jordan	42.8	109
48	Adana, Turkey	42.8	109
49	Montevideo, Uruguay	42.8	109
50	Dacca, Bangladesh	42.2	108
51	Uruguaiana, Brazil	42.2	108
52	Vientiane, Laos	42.2	108
53	Tulear, Madagascar	42.2	108
54	Keetmanshoop, Namibia	42.2	108
55	Kazalinsk, Russia	42.2	108
56	Hanoi, Vietnam	42.2	108
57	Balovale, Zambia	42.2	108
58	Varna, Bulgaria	41.7	107
59	Beirut, Lebanon	41.7	107
60	Lagos, Portugal	41.7	107
61	Durban, South Africa	41.7	107
62	Belgrade, Yugoslavia	41.7	107
63	Oursso, Rep. of Congo	41.1	106
64	Bathurst, Gambia	41.1	106
65	Bolama, Guinea-Bissau	41.1	106
66	Phnom Penh, Cambodia	40.6	105
67	San Salvador, El Salvador	40.6	105
68	Veletta, Malta	40.6	105
69	Bucharest, Rumania	40.6	105
70	Kamaran, Yemen	40.6	105
71	Havana, Cuba	40.0	104
72	Bouake, Côte d'Ivoire	40.0	104
73	Bangkok, Thailand	40.0	104
74	Budapest, Hungary	39.4	103
75	Ngaoundere, Cameroon	38.9	102
76	Santa Isabel, Equatorial Guinea	38.9	102
77	Osaka, Japan	38.9	102
78	Maracaibo, Venezuela	38.9	102
79	Concepción, Bolivia	38.2	101
80	Taipei, Taiwan	38.3	101
81	Port-au-Prince, Haiti	38.3	101
82	Penfui, Indonesia	38.3	101
83	Manila, Philippines	38.3	101
84	Geneva, Switzerland	38.3	101
85	Saint Clair, Trinidad and Tobago	38.3	101
86	Prerov, Czech Republic	37.8	100
87	Frankfurt, Germany	37.8	100
88	Accra, Ghana	37.8	100
89	Pyongyang, North Korea	37.8	100
90	Rabaul, Papua New Guinea	37.8	100
91	Iquitos, Peru	37.8	100
92	Kigoma, Tanzania	37.8	100
93	Lira, Uganda	37.8	100
94	Hamilton, Bermuda	37.2	99
95	Brunei	37.2	99
96	Santiago, Chile	37.2	99
97	Libreville, Gabon	37.2	99
98	Seoul, South Korea	37.2	99
99	Luxembourg	37.2	99
100	Karonga, Malawi	37.2	99
101	Kuala Lumpur, Malaysia	37.2	99
102	Katmandu, Nepal	37.2	99
103	Noumea, New Caledonia	37.2	99
104	Bulawayo, Zimbabwe	37.2	99
105	Colombo, Sri Lanka	37.2	99
106	Paramaribo, Suriname	37.2	99
107	London, United Kingdom	37.2	99
108	Vienna, Austria	36.7	98
109	Cartagena, Colombia	36.7	98
110	Santo Domingo, Dominican Republic	36.7	98
111	Guayquil, Ecuador	36.7	98
112	Suva, Fiji	36.7	98
113	Warsaw, Poland	36.7	98
114	Pago Pago, Samoa	36.7	98
115	Freetown, Sierra Leone	36.7	98
116	Belize	38.1	97
117	Cayenne, French Guiana	36.1	97
118	Gibraltar	36.1	97
119	Lethem, Guyana	36.1	97
120	Hong Kong	36.1	97
121	Kingston, Jamaica	36.1	97
122	Monrovia, Liberia	36.1	97
123	Ulan Bator, Mongolia	36.1	97
124	Singapore	36.1	97
125	Stockholm, Sweden	36.1	97
126	Kinshasa, Zaire	36.1	97
127	Tela, Honduras	35.6	96
128	Mombasa, Kenya	35.6	96
129	Fort-de-France, Martinique	35.6	96
130	Christchurch, New Zealand	35.6	96
131	Tulagi, Solomon Islands	35.6	96
132	Durres, Albania	35.0	95
133	Bridgetown, Barbados	35.0	95
134	Cotonou, Benin	35.0	95
135	Mauritius	35.0	95
136	Amsterdam, Netherlands	35.0	95
137	Trondheim, Norway	35.0	95
138	Nassau, Bahamas	34.4	94
139	Cape Verde	34.4	94
140	Cocos (Keeling) Islands	34.4	94
141	San Juan, Puerto Rico	34.4	94
142	Lome, Togo	34.4	94
143	Monaco	33.9	93
144	San Jose, Costa Rica	33.3	92
145	Camp Jacob, Guadeloupe	33.3	92
146	Seychelles	33.3	92
147	Les Escaldes, Andorra	32.8	91
148	Copenhagen, Denmark	32.8	91
149	Saint Kitts and Nevis	32.8	91
150	São Tomé, and Príncipe	32.8	91
151	Kuusamo, Finland	32.2	90
152	Guatemala City, Guatemala	32.2	90
153	Ivigtut, Greenland	30.0	86
154	Dublin, Ireland	30.0	86
155	Réunion	28.9	84
156	Akureyri, Iceland	28.3	83
157	Saint Helena	27.8	82
158	Stanley, Falkland Islands	24.4	76
159	Thorshavn, Faroe Islands	21.1	70

Source: World Weather Guide

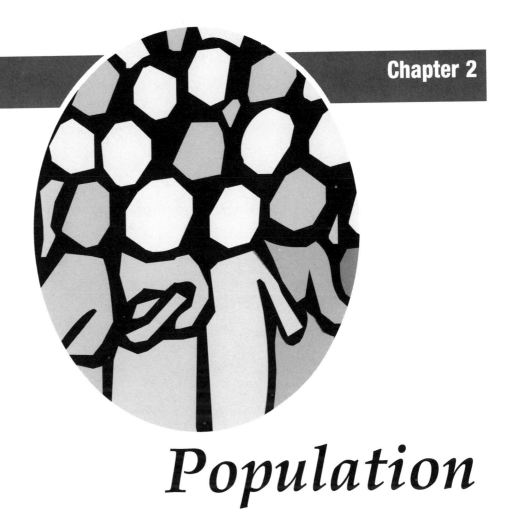

Chapter 2

Population

Global population passed the 6 billion mark in 1999 and is expected to reach 7.1 billion by 2020. Since the earth's carrying capacity—the optimum population in relation to the planet's resources—has been determined by leading demographers to be about 5 billion, we are even at this stage overcrowded, and are beginning to strain at the limits of sustainability. But what makes the numbers even more ominous is the heavy demographic imbalance among nations and regions. Many nations that have the least capacity to sustain large populations are the most populous, while most Western nations, which largely control the global economy, are facing what has been described as a "birth dearth"—a declining population that is far below the replacement level. Some forty-two of the world's poorer nations—including China and India—account for nine-tenths of the world population. Population figures are among the most accurate in this book, helped by the fact that most modern nations conduct periodic censuses. The margin of error in national censuses has been estimated to be no more than 4 to 5 percent. However, there are many countries—especially Saudi Arabia and Afghanistan, to name just two—where censuses are not conducted, either because of religious reasons or because of opposition to the enumeration of women and children.

Rank	Country/Entity	Population	Rank	Country/Entity	Population	Rank	Country/Entity	Population
1	China	1,251,238,000	38	Afghanistan	25,825,000	75	Hungary	10,065,000
2	India	1,000,849,000	39	Peru	25,232,000	76	Senegal	10,052,000
3	United States	273,131,000	40	Uzbekistan	24,449,000	77	Malawi	10,000,000
4	Indonesia	206,143,000	41	Venezuela	23,707,000	78	Portugal	9,988,000
5	Brazil	163,947,000	42	Uganda	22,805,000	79	Niger	9,962,000
6	Pakistan	152,231,000	43	Malaysia	22,710,000	80	Zambia	9,664,000
7	Russia	146,394,000	44	Nepal	22,449,000	81	Tunisia	9,514,000
8	Bangladesh	127,118,000	45	Iraq	22,427,000	82	Sweden	8,859,000
9	Japan	126,680,000	46	Romania	22,405,000	83	Bulgaria	8,206,000
10	Nigeria	113,829,000	47	Taiwan	22,024,000	84	Rwanda	8,155,000
11	Mexico	97,367,000	48	Saudi Arabia	21,505,000	85	Bolivia	8,137,000
12	Germany	82,100,000	49	North Korea	21,386,000	86	Dominican Republic	8,130,000
13	Vietnam	77,311,000	50	Mozambique	19,124,000	87	Austria	8,080,000
14	Philippines	74,723,000	51	Australia	18,943,000	88	Azerbaijan	7,993,000
15	Egypt	64,560,000	52	Sri Lanka	18,940,000	89	Chad	7,557,000
16	Turkey	64,431,000	53	Ghana	18,888,000	90	Guinea	7,539,000
17	Iran	62,127,000	54	Yemen	16,942,000	91	Switzerland	7,165,000
18	Thailand	61,806,000	55	Côte d'Ivoire	15,818,000	92	Somalia	7,141,000
19	Ethiopia	59,680,000	56	Netherlands	15,777,000	93	Hong Kong	6,885,000
20	United Kingdom	59,313,000	57	Syria	15,727,000	94	Haiti	6,884,000
21	France	59,087,000	58	Cameroon	15,456,000	95	Benin	6,306,000
22	Italy	57,723,000	59	Kazakhstan	15,348,000	96	Honduras	6,281,000
23	Congo, Dem. Rep. of	50,481,000	60	Chile	15,018,000	97	Tajikistan	6,213,000
24	Ukraine	49,890,000	61	Madagascar	14,873,000	98	Israel	5,939,000
25	Myanmar (Burma)	48,081,000	62	Ecuador	12,411,000	99	El Salvador	5,839,000
26	South Korea	46,858,000	63	Burkina Faso	11,576,000	100	Burundi	5,736,000
27	South Africa	43,426,000	64	Angola	11,178,000	101	Georgia	5,449,000
28	Spain	40,017,000	65	Zimbabwe	11,163,000	102	Laos	5,407,000
29	Poland	38,654,000	66	Cuba	11,159,000	103	Slovakia	5,398,000
30	Colombia	38,297,000	67	Guatemala	11,090,000	104	Paraguay	5,359,000
31	Argentina	36,578,000	68	Cambodia	10,981,000	105	Denmark	5,316,000
32	Sudan	34,476,000	69	Yugoslavia	10,731,000	106	Finland	5,167,000
33	Tanzania	31,271,000	70	Greece	10,561,000	107	Togo	5,081,000
34	Canada	30,626,000	71	Mali	10,429,000	108	Nicaragua	4,923,000
35	Algeria	29,910,000	72	Czech Republic	10,290,000	109	Jordan	4,839,000
36	Kenya	28,809,000	73	Belgium	10,224,000	110	Kyrgyzstan	4,761,000
37	Morocco	28,307,000	74	Belarus	10,164,000	111	Turkmenistan	4,721,000

Rank	Country/Entity	Population	Rank	Country/Entity	Population	Rank	Country/Entity	Population
112	Sierra Leone	4,717,000	148	Gambia	1,336,000	184	Samoa	177,000
113	Papua New Guinea	4,705,000	149	Trinidad and Tobago	1,289,000	185	French Guiana	159,000
114	Croatia	4,677,000	150	Guinea-Bissau	1,235,000	186	Saint Lucia	155,000
115	Libya	4,493,000	151	Gabon	1,226,000	187	Guam	152,000
116	Norway	4,452,000	152	Mauritius	1,171,000	188	Mayotte	149,000
117	Moldova	4,301,000	153	Gaza Strip	1,128,000	189	São Tomé and Príncipe	140,000
118	Eritrea	3,985,000	154	Swaziland	985,000	190	Virgin Islands (U.S.)	120,000
119	Puerto Rico	3,888,000	155	Cyprus	856,000	191	Saint Vincent and the	113,000
120	New Zealand	3,841,000	156	Fiji	813,000		Grenadines	
121	Bosnia and Herzegovina	3,838,000	157	Guyana	787,000	192	Micronesia	109,000
122	Armenia	3,804,000	158	Réunion	714,000	193	Grenada	101,000
123	Ireland	3,736,000	159	Djibouti	669,000	194	Tonga	98,200
124	Lithuania	3,699,000	160	Bhutan	658,000	195	Aruba	95,200
125	Costa Rica	3,594,000	161	Bahrain	646,000	196	Jersey	85,900
126	Lebanon	3,563,000	162	Qatar	589,000	197	Kiribati	85,500
127	Central African Republic	3,445,000	163	Comoros	563,000	198	Seychelles	80,100
128	Albania	3,365,000	164	Equatorial Guinea	466,000	199	Dominica	77,000
129	Uruguay	3,247,000	165	Solomon Islands	442,000	200	Isle of Man	71,200
130	Singapore	3,225,000	166	Macau	434,000	201	Northern Mariana Islands	69,400
131	Liberia	2,924,000	167	Luxembourg	432,000	202	Antigua and Barbuda	69,100
132	United Arab Emirates	2,826,000	168	Guadeloupe	424,000	203	Andorra	66,100
133	Panama	2,809,000	169	Suriname	415,000	204	Guernsey	65,400
134	Congo, Rep. of	2,717,000	170	Cape Verde	406,000	205	Marshall Islands	65,400
135	Jamaica	2,592,000	171	Martinique	382,000	206	American Samoa	63,800
136	Mauritania	2,582,000	172	Malta	380,000	207	Bermuda	62,500
137	Oman	2,447,000	173	Brunei	323,000	208	Greenland	56,100
138	Mongolia	2,440,000	174	Bahamas	297,000	209	Faroe Islands	44,500
139	Latvia	2,428,000	175	Western Sahara	284,000	210	Saint Kitts and Nevis	42,800
140	Lesotho	2,129,000	176	Maldives	278,000	211	Monaco	32,100
141	Macedonia	2,023,000	177	Iceland	276,000	212	Liechtenstein	31,700
142	Slovenia	1,977,000	178	Barbados	266,000	213	Gibraltar	27,200
143	West Bank	1,946,000	179	Belize	250,000	214	San Marino	26,500
144	Kuwait	1,924,000	180	French Polynesia	230,000	215	Palau	18,500
145	Namibia	1,648,000	181	Netherlands Antilles	217,000	216	Nauru	10,600
146	Botswana	1,464,000	182	New Caledonia	208,000	217	Tuvalu	10,600
147	Estonia	1,439,000	183	Vanuatu	187,000			

Source: Demographic Yearbook

The demographic profile of the world is going to change dramatically in the twenty-first century. It will be the most significant shift in population distribution of the past 1,000 years. A key factor in this shift is decline in human fertility and the resulting decline in birthrates in advanced countries. With the exception of the United States, all technologically advanced countries (including Japan in Asia) will likely have a smaller population in 2100 than they had in 2000. This will also trigger changes in migratory patterns. Since before the time of Columbus, the West has colonized the world and almost all emigration was outward to the colonies and imperial possessions. This trend is being reversed as the former colonizing countries are becoming magnets for immigration. Certain smaller European countries, such as Luxembourg, Liechtenstein, Austria, and Switzerland, may lose much of their historical cultural character. The first stages of this massive demographic shift have already begun. By 2020 the global population will reach 8 billion, but western Europe will account for only about 300 million people, or 3.75 percent.

Rank	Country/Entity	Population	Rank	Country/Entity	Population	Rank	Country/Entity	Population
1	China	1,403,169,000	40	Canada	36,454,000	79	Cuba	11,744,000
2	India	1,340,865,000	41	Nepal	35,259,000	80	Rwanda	11,304,000
3	United States	323,691,000	42	Yemen	34,682,000	81	Greece	11,148,000
4	Indonesia	261,802,000	43	Kenya	33,936,000	82	Yugoslavia	11,117,000
5	Pakistan	244,211,000	44	Peru	33,757,000	83	Dominican Republic	11,085,000
6	Brazil	194,793,000	45	Malaysia	33,645,000	84	Portugal	10,348,000
7	Nigeria	183,962,000	46	Uzbekistan	33,002,000	85	Czech Republic	10,309,000
8	Bangladesh	170,879,000	47	Venezuela	32,911,000	86	Togo	10,146,000
9	Russia	141,311,000	48	Mozambique	30,392,000	87	Belarus	10,132,000
10	Mexico	124,976,000	49	Ghana	26,516,000	88	Belgium	9,819,000
11	Japan	123,961,000	50	Taiwan	26,444,000	89	Haiti	9,600,000
12	Philippines	105,503,000	51	Cameroon	26,059,000	90	Hungary	9,515,000
13	Vietnam	99,153,000	52	Madagascar	25,988,000	91	Burundi	9,432,000
14	Congo, Dem. Rep. of	92,852,000	53	Côte d'Ivoire	25,268,000	92	Azerbaijan	9,169,000
15	Ethiopia	89,943,000	54	North Korea	24,937,000	93	Sweden	9,125,000
16	Egypt	88,701,000	55	Syria	24,563,000	94	Tajikistan	9,059,000
17	Turkey	84,116,000	56	Sri Lanka	23,095,000	95	Laos	8,923,000
18	Iran	83,241,000	57	Australia	22,672,000	96	Honduras	8,662,000
19	Germany	77,984,000	58	Romania	21,839,000	97	Hong Kong	8,568,000
20	Thailand	70,788,000	59	Mali	19,677,000	98	Paraguay	8,470,000
21	Myanmar (Burma)	64,280,000	60	Senegal	19,497,000	99	Austria	8,076,000
22	United Kingdom	62,111,000	61	Burkina Faso	19,239,000	100	Jordan	8,005,000
23	France	58,908,000	62	Angola	19,207,000	101	El Salvador	7,852,000
24	Sudan	58,621,000	63	Chile	18,774,000	102	Nicaragua	7,826,000
25	Italy	53,263,000	64	Guatemala	18,123,000	103	Israel	7,728,000
26	South Korea	52,409,000	65	Niger	17,983,000	104	Libya	7,718,000
27	Colombia	50,246,000	66	Netherlands	17,089,000	105	Switzerland	7,547,000
28	South Africa	48,983,000	67	Ecuador	16,904,000	106	Bulgaria	7,517,000
29	Tanzania	46,693,000	68	Kazakhstan	16,536,000	107	Eritrea	7,471,000
30	Ukraine	46,046,000	69	Cambodia	15,880,000	108	Sierra Leone	7,375,000
31	Argentina	45,347,000	70	Zambia	14,695,000	109	Papua New Guinea	7,044,000
32	Saudi Arabia	43,255,000	71	Somalia	13,312,000	110	Turkmenistan	6,220,000
33	Afghanistan	43,050,000	72	Chad	12,831,000	111	Kyrgyzstan	6,068,000
34	Algeria	43,045,000	73	Tunisia	12,216,000	112	Liberia	5,737,000
35	Uganda	42,772,000	74	Bolivia	12,193,000	113	Slovakia	5,579,000
36	Poland	40,427,000	75	Zimbabwe	12,162,000	114	Denmark	5,527,000
37	Iraq	39,713,000	76	Malawi	12,052,000	115	Georgia	5,178,000
38	Morocco	39,008,000	77	Benin	11,920,000	116	Central African Republic	5,133,000
39	Spain	38,737,000	78	Guinea	11,836,000	117	Finland	5,110,000

Rank	Country/Entity	Population	Rank	Country/Entity	Population	Rank	Country/Entity	Population
118	Costa Rica	4,935,000	152	Swaziland	1,434,000	186	French Guiana	238,000
119	Norway	4,824,000	153	Trinidad and Tobago	1,431,000	187	São Tomé and Príncipe	212,000
120	Singapore	4,821,000	154	Estonia	1,299,000	188	Guam	211,000
121	Mauritania	4,765,000	155	Cyprus	1,067,000	189	Saint Lucia	196,000
122	Oman	4,680,000	156	Djibouti	1,045,000	190	Grenada	147,000
123	Lebanon	4,613,000	157	Fiji	1,037,000	191	Virgin Islands (U.S.)	143,000
124	Moldova	4,594,000	158	Bhutan	1,031,000	192	Saint Vincent and the	136,000
125	New Zealand	4,551,000	159	Comoros	1,022,000		Grenadines	
126	Croatia	4,469,000	160	Bahrain	895,000	193	Marshall Islands	132,000
127	Albania	4,155,000	161	Réunion	882,000	194	Micronesia	131,000
128	Puerto Rico	4,104,000	162	Guyana	804,000	195	Northern Mariana Islands	124,000
129	Ireland	4,039,000	163	Equatorial Guinea	783,000	196	Aruba	105,000
130	United Arab Emirates	3,959,000	164	Qatar	764,000	197	Tonga	104,000
131	Congo, Rep. of	3,945,000	165	Solomon Islands	749,000	198	Kiribati	98,000
132	Bosnia and Herzegovina	3,918,000	166	Macau	601,000	199	American Samoa	96,000
133	Armenia	3,838,000	167	Cape Verde	512,000	200	Dominica	93,000
134	Uruguay	3,748,000	168	Guadeloupe	512,000	201	Jersey	91,000
135	Panama	3,620,000	169	Suriname	503,000	202	Seychelles	91,000
136	Lithuania	3,584,000	170	Luxembourg	497,000	203	Guernsey	79,000
137	Mongolia	3,328,000	171	Brunei	490,000	204	Andorra	78,000
138	West Bank	3,304,000	172	Maldives	465,000	205	Antigua and Barbuda	71,000
139	Kuwait	3,216,000	173	Western Sahara	442,000	206	Bermuda	71,000
140	Jamaica	3,153,000	174	Martinique	432,000	207	Isle of Man	71,000
141	Gaza Strip	2,699,000	175	Malta	395,000	208	Greenland	58,000
142	Lesotho	2,625,000	176	Belize	383,000	209	Saint Kitts and Nevis	57,000
143	Gambia	2,399,000	177	Bahamas	377,000	210	Faroe Islands	45,000
144	Macedonia	2,167,000	178	Iceland	322,000	211	Liechtenstein	38,000
145	Namibia	2,154,000	179	Mayotte	321,000	212	San Marino	37,000
146	Latvia	2,099,000	180	Netherlands Antilles	321,000	213	Monaco	34,000
147	Slovenia	2,019,000	181	French Polynesia	309,000	214	Gibraltar	27,000
148	Guinea-Bissau	1,925,000	182	Vanuatu	305,000	215	Palau	24,000
149	Gabon	1,675,000	183	New Caledonia	277,000	216	Tuvalu	15,000
150	Botswana	1,601,000	184	Barbados	274,000	217	Nauru	12,000
151	Mauritius	1,469,000	185	Samoa	254,000			

Source: World Population Prospects

2.3 Population Density

Population density is the most common indicator of the relation of people to available land. The global density of population is 6.7 people per square kilometer (17.3 per square mile), which may seem low, except that overall density figures obscure unequal distribution of population within countries. Generally, a certain level of density is required for civilizations to flourish, which is why cities and large urban agglomerations have proven more prosperous than rural communities. But there is a critical threshold which, when passed, leads to overcrowding, crime, traffic jams, and unsanitary health conditions. The densest nations are generally the smallest—many of them are islands—where there is little room to grow. The major exception is Bangladesh where 120 million people live in a space roughly the size of the state of Wisconsin.

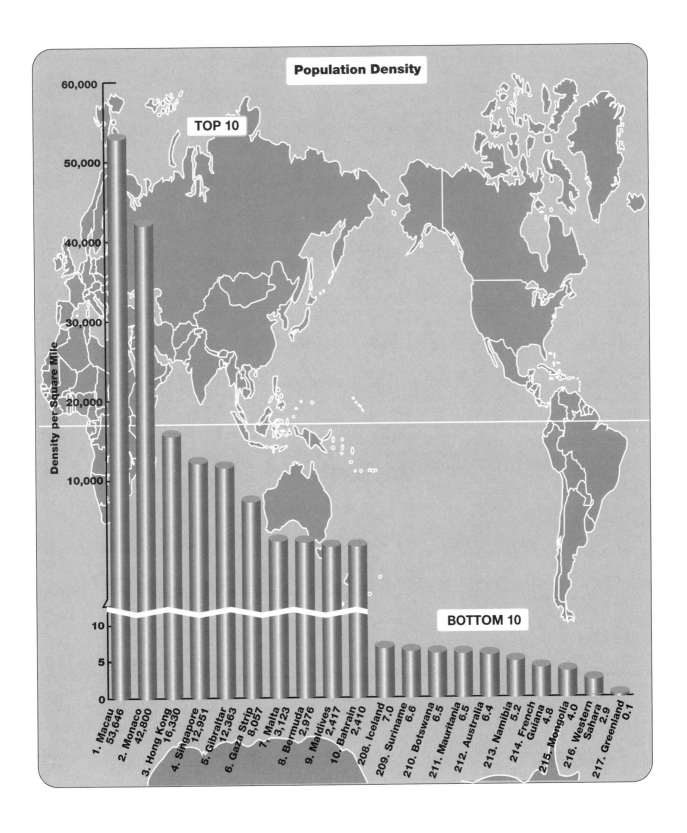

Population Density

TOP 10

BOTTOM 10

Density per Square Mile

60,000

50,000

40,000

30,000

20,000

10,000

10

5

0

1. Macau 53,646
2. Monaco 42,800
3. Hong Kong 16,330
4. Singapore 12,951
5. Gibraltar 12,363
6. Gaza Strip 8,057
7. Malta 3,123
8. Bermuda 2,976
9. Maldives 2,417
10. Bahrain 2,410
208. Iceland 7.0
209. Suriname 6.6
210. Botswana 6.5
211. Mauritania 6.5
212. Australia 6.4
213. Namibia 5.2
214. French Guiana 4.8
215. Mongolia 4.0
216. Western Sahara 2.9
217. Greenland 0.1

Rank	Country/Entity	Density (per sq. mi.)	Rank	Country/Entity	Density (per sq. mi.)	Rank	Country/Entity	Density (per sq. mi.)
11	Bangladesh	2,231.0	71	Czech Republic	337.9	132	Iraq	133.5
12	Guernsey	2,180.0	72	Armenia	331.2	133	Qatar	133.4
13	Jersey	1,908.9	73	Moldova	330.8	134	Senegal	132.3
14	Barbados	1,602.4	74	Gambia	323.7	135	Mexico	128.8
15	Taiwan	1,576.6	75	Isle of Man	322.2	136	Kenya	128.1
16	Mauritius	1,486.0	76	Poland	320.2	137	Côte d'Ivoire	127.0
17	Nauru	1,292.7	77	Denmark	319.5	138	Belarus	126.8
18	Aruba	1,269.3	78	Nigeria	319.1	139	Ecuador	118.2
19	South Korea	1,222.6	79	Thailand	312.0	140	Fiji	115.2
20	San Marino	1,121.5	80	Albania	303.2	141	Tajikistan	112.4
21	Puerto Rico	1,106.1	81	Slovakia	285.1	142	Burkina Faso	109.3
22	Tuvalu	1,070.7	82	France	281.3	143	Afghanistan	102.6
23	Mayotte	1,027.6	83	Portugal	280.8	144	Palau	98.4
24	Netherlands	984.0	84	Hungary	280.2	145	Iran	97.9
25	Marshall Islands	934.3	85	Kuwait	279.7	146	Latvia	97.3
26	Lebanon	887.2	86	Indonesia	275.6	147	Nicaragua	96.7
27	Virgin Islands (U.S.)	882.2	87	Kiribati	273.2	148	Panama	96.3
28	Martinique	876.1	88	Yugoslavia	272.0	149	South Africa	92.3
29	Japan	868.4	89	Dominica	265.5	150	Guinea-Bissau	88.5
30	Belgium	867.4	90	Guatemala	263.8	151	United Arab Emirates	87.5
31	West Bank	857.3	91	Cape Verde	260.8	152	Colombia	86.9
32	American Samoa	828.6	92	Cuba	260.7	153	Tanzania	85.7
33	India	818.9	93	Slovenia	252.6	154	Eritrea	85.2
34	Rwanda	801.9	94	Austria	249.6	155	Cameroon	84.2
35	Comoros	783.0	95	Uganda	245.0	156	Estonia	82.4
36	Grenada	759.4	96	Romania	244.3	157	Faroe Islands	82.4
37	Israel	756.9	97	Cyprus	239.6	158	Guinea	79.4
38	Saint Vincent and the Grenadines	751.8	98	Azerbaijan	239.3	159	Yemen	79.1
			99	Togo	231.7	160	Liberia	77.5
39	Sri Lanka	747.7	100	Syria	220.0	161	United States	75.6
40	Réunion	737.6	101	Malawi	218.6	162	Djibouti	74.7
41	Guam	727.3	102	Turkey	214.1	163	Zimbabwe	74.0
42	El Salvador	718.7	103	Croatia	214.0	164	Venezuela	67.3
43	Netherlands Antilles	704.5	104	Ukraine	214.0	165	Madagascar	65.6
44	Saint Lucia	651.3	105	Greece	207.3	166	Kyrgyzstan	61.7
45	Trinidad and Tobago	651.0	106	Ghana	205.1	167	Mozambique	61.0
46	Philippines	644.9	107	Spain	204.8	168	Laos	59.1
47	Haiti	643.7	108	Macedonia	203.8	169	Congo, Dem. Rep. of	55.8
48	United Kingdom	629.3	109	Georgia	203.1	170	Bahamas	55.2
49	Guadeloupe	617.2	110	Bosnia and Herzegovina	194.9	171	Chile	51.4
50	Jamaica	610.7	111	Bulgaria	191.5	172	Sweden	51.0
51	Vietnam	604.9	112	Myanmar (Burma)	184.1	173	Peru	50.8
52	Germany	595.6	113	Costa Rica	182.2	174	Brazil	49.7
53	Burundi	534.1	114	Lesotho	181.7	175	Uruguay	47.7
54	Liechtenstein	512.9	115	Malaysia	178.4	176	Equatorial Guinea	43.0
55	Italy	496.2	116	Sierra Leone	170.3	177	Solomon Islands	40.4
56	Pakistan	495.3	117	Egypt	167.6	178	Vanuatu	39.7
57	Seychelles	455.1	118	Samoa	161.9	179	Finland	39.6
58	North Korea	451.2	119	Morocco	159.8	180	New Zealand	36.8
59	Switzerland	449.5	120	Cambodia	156.3	181	Bhutan	36.3
60	Dominican Republic	432.6	121	Tunisia	150.1	182	Sudan	35.7
61	Luxembourg	432.4	122	French Polynesia	149.0	183	Norway	35.6
62	Saint Kitts and Nevis	411.5	123	Swaziland	146.9	184	Argentina	34.1
63	Antigua and Barbuda	405.3	124	Lithuania	146.7	185	Paraguay	34.1
64	Micronesia	402.5	125	Brunei	145.1	186	Zambia	33.3
65	Nepal	395.9	126	Benin	145.0	187	Algeria	32.5
66	Northern Mariana Islands	377.2	127	Honduras	144.6	188	New Caledonia	29.0
67	Andorra	365.2	128	Uzbekistan	141.6	189	Somalia	29.0
68	São Tomé and Príncipe	362.7	129	Jordan	140.3	190	Belize	28.2
69	Tonga	339.2	130	Ireland	137.7	191	Papua New Guinea	26.3
70	China	338.5	131	Ethiopia	136.3	192	Turkmenistan	25.0

Rank	Country/Entity	Density (per sq. mi.)	Rank	Country/Entity	Density (per sq. mi.)	Rank	Country/Entity	Density (per sq. mi.)
193	Saudi Arabia	24.8	198	Oman	20.5	203	Central African Republic	14.3
194	Angola	23.2	199	Niger	20.4	204	Gabon	11.9
195	Russia	22.2	200	Bolivia	19.2	205	Guyana	9.5
196	Mali	21.6	201	Chad	15.2	206	Canada	8.0
197	Congo, Rep. of	20.6	202	Kazakhstan	14.6	207	Libya	7.4

Source: Population Division, US Census Bureau

2.4 Percentage of Children in the Population

One of the clearest indicators of a surging population is the percentage of children under the age of fifteen. In all countries with a high population growth rate, children represent 40 to 52 percent of the population. In this ranking more than 100 countries in the world have a young population, and none of these countries are developed. On the other hand all nations in the bottom of the ranking are in Europe or North America. The less developed nations are having a long-running baby boom whose ripple effects will be felt well beyond the twenty-first century.

Rank	Country/Entity	Percentage of Population Aged 14 and Under	Rank	Country/Entity	Percentage of Population Aged 14 and Under	Rank	Country/Entity	Percentage of Population Aged 14 and Under
1	Marshall Islands	51.0	39	Iraq	45.2	77	Guyana	40.8
2	Gaza Strip	50.3	40	Madagascar	45.1	78	Uzbekistan	40.8
3	Togo	49.8	41	Nicaragua	45.1	79	Lesotho	40.7
4	Niger	48.7	42	Zimbabwe	45.1	80	Bhutan	40.6
5	Benin	48.3	43	Cape Verde	45.0	81	Tonga	40.6
6	Burkina Faso	48.3	44	Ghana	45.0	82	Samoa	40.5
7	Chad	48.1	45	Congo, Rep. of	44.7	83	Turkmenistan	40.5
8	Nigeria	47.9	46	West Bank	44.6	84	Kuwait	40.4
9	Kenya	47.8	47	Afghanistan	44.5	85	Kiribati	40.3
10	Comoros	47.6	48	Pakistan	44.5	86	Paraguay	40.1
11	Yemen	47.6	49	Iran	44.3	87	Philippines	39.6
12	Senegal	47.5	50	Guinea	44.1	88	Djibouti	39.4
13	Congo, Dem. Rep. of	47.3	51	Mauritania	44.1	89	Suriname	39.3
14	Solomon Islands	47.3	52	Guatemala	44.0	90	Haiti	39.2
15	Swaziland	47.3	53	Algeria	43.9	91	Vietnam	39.0
16	Syria	47.3	54	Belize	43.9	92	Ecuador	38.8
17	Uganda	47.3	55	Guinea-Bissau	43.9	93	El Salvador	38.7
18	Zambia	47.3	56	Sierra Leone	43.9	94	Myanmar (Burma)	38.6
19	Tanzania	47.2	57	Gambia	43.8	95	Mexico	38.3
20	Cambodia	47.0	58	Central African Republic	43.2	96	Venezuela	38.3
21	Mayotte	47.0	59	Liberia	43.2	97	Fiji	38.2
22	Maldives	46.9	60	Sudan	43.0	98	American Samoa	38.1
23	São Tomé and Príncipe	46.9	61	Tajikistan	42.9	99	Costa Rica	37.9
24	Côte d'Ivoire	46.8	62	Botswana	42.8	100	Kyrgyzstan	37.5
25	Honduras	46.8	63	Lebanon	42.6	101	Saint Vincent and the Grenadines	37.2
26	Ethiopia	46.6	64	Grenada	42.5	102	Morocco	37.0
27	Burundi	46.4	65	Nepal	42.3	103	Peru	37.0
28	Cameroon	46.4	66	Jordan	42.2	104	Egypt	36.9
29	Micronesia	46.4	67	Saudi Arabia	42.1	105	Saint Kitts and Nevis	36.9
30	Mozambique	46.4	68	Mongolia	41.9	106	Saint Lucia	36.8
31	Eritrea	46.1	69	Papua New Guinea	41.9	107	Malaysia	36.7
32	Malawi	46.1	70	Nauru	41.8	108	Indonesia	36.6
33	Mali	46.1	71	Angola	41.7	109	Dominican Republic	36.5
34	Rwanda	45.6	72	Equatorial Guinea	41.7	110	French Polynesia	36.0
35	Somalia	45.6	73	Namibia	41.7	111	India	36.0
36	Vanuatu	45.5	74	Bangladesh	41.5	112	Sri Lanka	35.3
37	Laos	45.4	75	Bolivia	41.2	113	Turkey	35.0
38	Libya	45.4	76	Oman	41.0			

Rank	Country/Entity	Percentage of Population Aged 14 and Under	Rank	Country/Entity	Percentage of Population Aged 14 and Under	Rank	Country/Entity	Percentage of Population Aged 14 and Under
114	United Arab Emirates	34.9	149	Greenland	27.7	184	United States	21.5
115	Panama	34.8	150	Puerto Rico	27.2	185	Latvia	21.4
116	Tunisia	34.8	151	Taiwan	27.1	186	Hungary	21.3
117	Brazil	34.7	152	Ireland	26.7	187	Czech Republic	21.0
118	South Africa	34.6	153	Netherlands Antilles	26.0	188	Canada	20.9
119	Tuvalu	34.6	154	Cyprus	25.4	189	Bulgaria	20.5
120	Brunei	34.5	155	Poland	25.4	190	Slovenia	20.0
121	Jamaica	34.4	156	Slovakia	25.0	191	Portugal	19.9
122	Gabon	33.8	157	Guadeloupe	24.9	192	Gibraltar	19.6
123	Seychelles	33.6	158	Georgia	24.8	193	Bermuda	19.5
124	Trinidad and Tobago	33.5	159	Macedonia	24.8	194	Croatia	19.4
125	French Guiana	33.4	160	Aruba	24.4	195	Hong Kong	19.4
126	Dominica	33.3	161	Faroe Islands	24.4	196	Finland	19.3
127	Colombia	33.1	162	San Marino	24.4	197	Greece	19.3
128	Albania	33.0	163	Uruguay	24.4	198	France	19.1
129	Azerbaijan	32.8	164	Barbados	24.1	199	Spain	19.1
130	Israel	32.6	165	Macau	24.1	200	United Kingdom	19.1
131	New Caledonia	32.6	166	Iceland	24.0	201	Norway	18.8
132	Bahamas	32.2	167	Northern Mariana Islands	23.8	202	Sweden	18.8
133	Kazakhstan	31.9	168	Bosnia and Herzegovina	23.5	203	Netherlands	18.4
134	Bahrain	31.7	169	New Zealand	23.2	204	Belgium	18.2
135	Argentina	30.6	170	Singapore	23.2	205	Denmark	17.5
136	Antigua and Barbuda	30.4	171	Martinique	23.1	206	Austria	17.4
137	Armenia	30.3	172	Russia	23.1	207	Isle of Man	17.3
138	Palau	30.3	173	Belarus	23.0	208	Luxembourg	17.3
139	Guam	30.0	174	South Korea	23.0	209	Guernsey	17.0
140	Mauritius	29.7	175	Liechtenstein	23.0	210	Switzerland	16.8
141	North Korea	29.5	176	Yugoslavia	22.8	211	Andorra	16.3
142	Réunion	29.5	177	Lithuania	22.6	212	Japan	15.9
143	Chile	29.4	178	Romania	22.4	213	Italy	15.7
144	Virgin Islands (U.S.)	28.9	179	Cuba	22.3	214	Jersey	15.5
145	Thailand	28.8	180	Estonia	22.2	215	Germany	14.6
146	Moldova	27.9	181	Australia	22.1	216	Monaco	12.3
147	Qatar	27.8	182	Malta	21.9			
148	China	27.7	183	Ukraine	21.5			

Source: UN Statistical Yearbook

2.5 Population Aged 65 and Over

This ranking is the reverse of the numbers presented in the ranking on the percentage of children, but the numbers are the result not merely of a low birthrate. People in developed countries live longer than those in developing countries. Every additional year in the life-expectancy table has a bearing on the proportion of seniors in the population. But, ultimately, over two or three generations, the aggregate will tend to decline although the percentage will continue to grow because of the fewer number of babies being born. But until then, the percentage of seniors in most developed societies will rise as high as 25 percent.

Rank	Country/Entity	Percentage of Population Aged 65 and Over	Rank	Country/Entity	Percentage of Population Aged 65 and Over	Rank	Country/Entity	Percentage of Population Aged 65 and Over
1	Monaco	28.7	7	Germany	20.8	14	France	19.9
2	Sweden	22.0	8	Belgium	20.7	15	Luxembourg	19.9
3	Italy	21.1	9	Bulgaria	20.5	16	Denmark	19.7
4	Norway	21.1	10	Switzerland	20.2	17	Spain	19.4
5	United Kingdom	21.1	11	Austria	20.1	18	Hungary	19.0
6	Japan	20.9	12	Greece	20.0	19	Portugal	19.0

Rank	Country/Entity	Percentage of Population Aged 65 and Over	Rank	Country/Entity	Percentage of Population Aged 65 and Over	Rank	Country/Entity	Percentage of Population Aged 65 and Over
20	Finland	18.6	78	Gabon	8.1	137	Venezuela	5.7
21	Ukraine	18.4	79	Haiti	8.1	138	Costa Rica	5.6
22	Czech Republic	17.8	80	Azerbaijan	7.9	139	Guyana	5.6
23	Netherlands	17.8	81	Albania	7.8	140	Iran	5.6
24	Croatia	17.4	82	Lebanon	7.7	141	Micronesia	5.6
25	Latvia	17.3	83	Grenada	7.6	142	Nepal	5.6
26	Uruguay	17.2	84	Panama	7.5	143	Chad	5.5
27	Estonia	16.8	85	Greenland	7.4	144	Bangladesh	5.4
28	Romania	16.8	86	Brazil	7.3	145	Bhutan	5.4
29	United States	16.8	87	El Salvador	7.3	146	Somalia	5.4
30	Belarus	16.0	88	Suriname	7.3	147	Botswana	5.3
31	Canada	16.0	89	Thailand	7.3	148	Congo, Dem. Rep. of	5.3
32	Yugoslavia	15.7	90	Mauritius	7.2	149	Madagascar	5.3
33	Lithuania	15.7	91	Turkey	7.2	150	Paraguay	5.3
34	Australia	15.5	92	Vietnam	7.2	151	Philippines	5.3
35	New Zealand	15.4	93	Peru	7.0	152	Sudan	5.3
36	Russia	15.4	94	Lesotho	6.9	153	Togo	5.3
37	Barbados	15.3	95	Morocco	6.9	154	Honduras	5.2
38	Ireland	15.2	96	Namibia	6.9	155	Laos	5.2
39	Iceland	15.1	97	Pakistan	6.9	156	Mozambique	5.2
40	San Marino	15.1	98	Bahamas	6.8	157	Sierra Leone	5.2
41	Cyprus	14.9	99	Nauru	6.8	158	Iraq	5.1
42	Malta	14.9	100	Nigeria	6.8	159	Nicaragua	5.1
43	Slovakia	14.9	101	São Tomé and Príncipe	6.7	160	Niger	5.1
44	Poland	14.6	102	Sri Lanka	6.6	161	Zimbabwe	5.1
45	Slovenia	14.5	103	Bolivia	6.5	162	Senegal	5.0
46	Georgia	14.4	104	Colombia	6.5	163	Uganda	5.0
47	Andorra	13.7	105	South Africa	6.5	164	Gambia	4.9
48	Bermuda	13.3	106	Uzbekistan	6.5	165	Kenya	4.9
49	Puerto Rico	13.2	107	Ecuador	6.4	166	Solomon Islands	4.9
50	Macedonia	13.0	108	Tonga	6.4	167	Angola	4.8
51	Argentina	12.9	109	Equatorial Guinea	6.3	168	Maldives	4.8
52	Moldova	12.6	110	Indonesia	6.3	169	Rwanda	4.8
53	Israel	12.5	111	Myanmar (Burma)	6.3	170	Guinea-Bissau	4.7
54	Liechtenstein	12.3	112	Ethiopia	6.2	171	Swaziland	4.7
55	Cuba	12.3	113	North Korea	6.2	172	Congo, Rep.of	4.6
56	Dominica	11.8	114	Liberia	6.2	173	Fiji	4.6
57	Bosnia and Herzegovina	11.6	115	Mexico	6.2	174	Comoros	4.5
58	Antigua and Barbuda	11.1	116	Tajikistan	6.2	175	Guinea	4.5
59	Saint Kitts and Nevis	10.7	117	Burkina Faso	6.1	176	Jordan	4.5
60	Seychelles	10.6	118	India	6.1	177	Libya	4.3
61	Aruba	10.2	119	Mali	6.1	178	Vanuatu	4.3
62	Taiwan	9.7	120	Mauritania	6.1	179	Yemen	4.3
63	Chile	9.7	121	Turkmenistan	6.1	180	Afghanistan	4.2
64	Armenia	9.6	122	Belize	6.0	181	Zambia	4.2
65	Jamaica	9.4	123	Dominican Republic	6.0	182	Brunei	4.1
66	South Korea	9.3	124	Eritrea	6.0	183	Benin	4.0
67	Kazakhstan	9.2	125	Malawi	6.0	184	Tanzania	4.0
68	Tuvalu	9.2	126	Samoa	6.0	185	Oman	3.8
69	Singapore	9.1	127	Central African Republic	5.9	186	Bahrain	3.7
70	Saint Vincent and the Grenadines	8.9	128	Ghana	5.9	187	Saudi Arabia	3.6
			129	Algeria	5.8	188	Côte d'Ivoire	3.4
71	Saint Lucia	8.7	130	Egypt	5.8	189	Djibouti	3.4
72	Trinidad and Tobago	8.7	131	Guatemala	5.8	190	Papua New Guinea	3.2
73	China	8.6	132	Malaysia	5.8	191	Kuwait	2.8
74	Palau	8.6	133	Mongolia	5.8	192	United Arab Emirates	2.1
75	Cape Verde	8.4	134	Burundi	5.7	193	Qatar	2.0
76	Kyrgyzstan	8.3	135	Cameroon	5.7			
77	Tunisia	8.3	136	Kiribati	5.7			

Source: UN Statistical Yearbook

Birthrates measure gross additions to the population and, when used in combination with death rates, provide estimates of total population growth. Statistics on birthrates are subject to error because in many countries they are based on civil registers only and ignore births in private homes or with the aid of untrained midwives. Some mothers may hide their pregnancies and deliveries.

Many countries do not include infants who are born alive but die within the first twenty-four hours of life. It may be noted that almost all of the top fifty countries are in either Africa or the Middle East, where culture and religion combine to encourage women to have as many babies as possible. As countries become more prosperous or educated, the birthrates tend to fall.

Rank	Country/Entity	Birthrate per 1,000 Population	Rank	Country/Entity	Birthrate per 1,000 Population	Rank	Country/Entity	Birthrate per 1,000 Population
1	Niger	54.5	47	Ghana	38.2	93	Samoa	26.7
2	Uganda	51.1	48	American Samoa	37.8	94	Venezuela	26.7
3	Somalia	50.0	49	Gabon	37.6	95	Marshall Islands	26.1
4	Sierra Leone	49.1	50	Côte d'Ivoire	37.2	96	Kyrgyzstan	26.0
5	Ethiopia	48.2	51	Botswana	37.1	97	Colombia	25.9
6	Guinea	48.2	52	Nepal	36.6	98	India	25.9
7	Angola	47.7	53	Pakistan	36.4	99	Malaysia	25.6
8	Yemen	47.7	54	Solomon Islands	36.2	100	Vietnam	25.6
9	Liberia	47.5	55	Namibia	35.9	101	Morocco	25.3
10	Mali	47.4	56	Honduras	35.8	102	Saint Lucia	25.2
11	Burkina Faso	47.0	57	Guatemala	35.4	103	Lebanon	24.9
12	Mauritania	46.9	58	Lesotho	35.4	104	Peru	24.9
13	Gaza Strip	46.7	59	Micronesia	35.0	105	Kuwait	24.3
14	Benin	46.0	60	São Tomé and Príncipe	34.9	106	Virgin Islands (U.S.)	24.3
15	West Bank	46.0	61	Saudi Arabia	34.3	107	Guam	24.0
16	Comoros	45.8	62	Iraq	34.1	108	Tunisia	23.9
17	Senegal	45.5	63	Nicaragua	33.8	109	Costa Rica	23.8
18	Nigeria	45.4	64	Iran	33.7	110	Dominican Republic	23.5
19	Congo, Dem. Rep. of	44.9	65	Sudan	33.7	111	Brunei	23.3
20	Laos	44.3	66	Haiti	33.5	112	Saint Vincent and the Grenadines	23.3
21	Mayotte	43.7	67	Bolivia	33.2			
22	Oman	43.7	68	Turkmenistan	33.0	113	Jamaica	23.2
23	Afghanistan	43.0	69	Uzbekistan	33.0	114	Monaco	22.9
24	Cambodia	43.0	70	Vanuatu	33.0	115	Fiji	22.7
25	Swaziland	42.9	71	Jordan	32.9	116	New Caledonia	22.7
26	Rwanda	42.8	72	Belize	32.8	117	Bahamas	22.5
27	Burundi	42.7	73	Kenya	32.4	118	North Korea	22.5
28	Congo, Rep. of	42.5	74	Papua New Guinea	32.4	119	Panama	22.5
29	Mozambique	42.5	75	Cape Verde	31.9	120	Indonesia	22.4
30	Zambia	42.4	76	Zimbabwe	31.6	121	Turkey	22.3
31	Maldives	41.8	77	Western Sahara	31.4	122	Mongolia	22.0
32	Chad	41.6	78	Paraguay	31.3	123	Palau	22.0
33	Malawi	41.6	79	Kiribati	31.0	124	Grenada	21.3
34	Bhutan	41.3	80	Mexico	30.4	125	Suriname	21.3
35	Togo	41.2	81	French Guiana	29.2	126	Israel	21.2
36	Madagascar	41.1	82	Northern Mariana Islands	29.0	127	Bahrain	21.0
37	Tanzania	41.0	83	Philippines	28.7	128	French Polynesia	21.0
38	Equatorial Guinea	40.8	84	Algeria	28.5	129	Antigua and Barbuda	20.9
39	Guinea-Bissau	40.3	85	Tajikistan	28.2	130	Brazil	20.8
40	Libya	40.0	86	Egypt	27.8	131	Greenland	20.7
41	Syria	40.0	87	El Salvador	27.7	132	Seychelles	20.0
42	Gambia	39.9	88	Myanmar (Burma)	27.4	133	Argentina	19.9
43	Eritrea	39.8	89	South Africa	27.4	134	Qatar	19.9
44	Cameroon	39.3	90	Tonga	27.0	135	Chile	19.7
45	Central African Republic	39.2	91	Tuvalu	27.0	136	Réunion	19.6
46	Djibouti	38.6	92	Bangladesh	26.8	137	Saint Kitts and Nevis	19.4

Rank	Country/Entity	Birthrate per 1,000 Population	Rank	Country/Entity	Birthrate per 1,000 Population	Rank	Country/Entity	Birthrate per 1,000 Population
138	Azerbaijan	19.2	165	Macedonia	14.9	192	Isle of Man	11.4
139	Guyana	19.0	166	Taiwan	14.7	193	Guernsey	11.2
140	Nauru	18.8	167	United States	14.7	194	Slovakia	11.2
141	United Arab Emirates	18.7	168	Australia	14.1	195	San Marino	11.1
142	Guadeloupe	18.5	169	Macau	14.1	196	Andorra	11.0
143	Dominica	18.4	170	Ireland	13.9	197	Austria	10.8
144	Mauritius	18.3	171	Norway	13.9	198	Sweden	10.8
145	Netherlands Antilles	18.3	172	Luxembourg	13.7	199	Lithuania	10.6
146	Sri Lanka	17.9	173	Cuba	13.5	200	Croatia	10.5
147	Thailand	17.8	174	Armenia	13.3	201	Hungary	10.4
148	Uruguay	17.8	175	Barbados	13.3	202	Romania	10.4
149	Aruba	17.4	176	Ukraine	13.0	203	Hong Kong	10.0
150	Puerto Rico	17.2	177	Yugoslavia	13.0	204	Georgia	9.9
151	Martinique	16.8	178	Denmark	12.9	205	Greece	9.7
152	Kazakhstan	16.7	179	France	12.6	206	Japan	9.5
153	Albania	16.6	180	Canada	12.5	207	Belarus	9.3
154	Gibraltar	16.5	181	Jersey	12.5	208	Germany	9.3
155	New Zealand	16.3	182	United Kingdom	12.5	209	Russia	9.3
156	Trinidad and Tobago	16.3	183	Moldova	12.3	210	Slovenia	9.3
157	China	16.2	184	Netherlands	12.3	211	Italy	9.2
158	Iceland	16.0	185	Malta	12.2	212	Spain	9.2
159	Singapore	16.0	186	Poland	12.0	213	Estonia	9.0
160	Ecuador	15.8	187	Finland	11.8	214	Czech Republic	8.8
161	Cyprus	15.4	188	Liechtenstein	11.7	215	Bulgaria	8.6
162	Faroe Islands	15.4	189	Switzerland	11.7	216	Latvia	7.9
163	Bermuda	15.1	190	Portugal	11.5	217	Bosnia and Herzegovina	6.5
164	South Korea	15.1	191	Belgium	11.4			

Source: UN Statistical Yearbook

2.7 Rate of Natural Increase

The rate of natural increase is the difference between birthrates and death rates. In many Western societies, the rate is negative, because more people are dying than are being born. The rate of natural increase is the effective indicator of population growth and is thus connected with the related concept of the replacement level of population.

Rank	Country/Entity	Rate of Natural Increase per 1,000 Population	Rank	Country/Entity	Rate of Natural Increase per 1,000 Population	Rank	Country/Entity	Rate of Natural Increase per 1,000 Population
1	Gaza Strip	41.4	20	Madagascar	31.2	39	Cameroon	27.4
2	West Bank	39.0	21	Laos	30.6	40	Belize	27.1
3	Oman	38.9	22	Botswana	30.5	41	Iran	27.1
4	Mayotte	37.7	23	Mali	30.3	42	Burkina Faso	27.0
5	Yemen	37.3	24	Saudi Arabia	30.1	43	Micronesia	27.0
6	Comoros	35.5	25	Uganda	30.1	44	Uzbekistan	27.0
7	Maldives	34.2	26	Nigeria	30.0	45	Vanuatu	26.8
8	Syria	34.0	27	Jordan	29.9	46	Togo	26.3
9	Senegal	33.7	28	Niger	29.9	47	São Tomé and Príncipe	26.2
10	American Samoa	33.6	29	Guinea	29.8	48	Northern Mariana Islands	26.0
11	Libya	33.1	30	Honduras	29.4	49	Turkmenistan	26.0
12	Somalia	33.1	31	Angola	29.0	50	Paraguay	25.9
13	Benin	33.0	32	Pakistan	28.5	51	Mexico	25.6
14	Swaziland	32.3	33	Cambodia	28.0	52	Nepal	25.4
15	Liberia	32.2	34	Congo, Rep. of	27.9	53	Eritrea	25.1
16	Solomon Islands	32.1	35	Guatemala	27.9	54	French Guiana	25.1
17	Ethiopia	32.0	36	Ghana	27.8	55	Afghanistan	25.0
18	Mauritania	31.7	37	Nicaragua	27.8	56	Mozambique	25.0
19	Congo, Dem. Rep. of	31.4	38	Bhutan	27.4	57	Burundi	24.9

Rank	Country/Entity	Rate of Natural Increase per 1,000 Population	Rank	Country/Entity	Rate of Natural Increase per 1,000 Population	Rank	Country/Entity	Rate of Natural Increase per 1,000 Population
58	Cape Verde	24.8	112	New Caledonia	17.2	165	Macedonia	7.3
59	Lesotho	24.8	113	Malawi	17.1	166	Australia	7.2
60	Equatorial Guinea	24.6	114	Turkey	16.8	167	Kazakhstan	6.5
61	Zambia	24.4	115	Bahamas	16.6	168	Faroe Islands	6.4
62	Chad	24.3	116	Saint Vincent and the Grenadines	16.6	169	Cuba	6.3
63	Iraq	24.3				170	United States	5.9
64	Namibia	24.1	117	French Polynesia	16.5	171	Armenia	5.8
65	Sierra Leone	24.0	118	Qatar	16.5	172	Canada	5.3
66	Tanzania	24.0	119	India	16.3	173	Ireland	5.2
67	Djibouti	23.6	120	South Africa	16.3	174	Hong Kong	5.1
68	Côte d'Ivoire	23.4	121	United Arab Emirates	15.8	175	Liechtenstein	5.0
69	Gabon	23.3	122	Israel	15.2	176	Malta	4.7
70	Rwanda	23.1	123	Suriname	14.7	177	Slovenia	4.5
71	Philippines	22.9	124	Bangladesh	14.6	178	Monaco	4.4
72	Western Sahara	22.8	125	Indonesia	14.5	179	Luxembourg	4.3
73	Algeria	22.6	126	Mongolia	14.4	180	San Marino	4.3
74	Gambia	22.5	127	Nauru	14.3	181	Barbados	4.2
75	Papua New Guinea	22.4	128	Antigua and Barbuda	14.2	182	Georgia	3.5
76	Central African Republic	22.2	129	Chile	14.2	183	Netherlands	3.5
77	Kuwait	22.1	130	Réunion	14.2	184	Norway	3.5
78	Marshall Islands	22.1	131	Palau	14.0	185	France	3.4
79	Sudan	22.0	132	Grenada	13.4	186	Switzerland	2.8
80	Venezuela	22.0	133	Dominica	13.1	187	Jersey	2.6
81	Kenya	21.6	134	Seychelles	13.0	188	Ukraine	2.5
82	Tajikistan	21.2	135	Greenland	12.7	189	Yugoslavia	2.5
83	Tonga	21.2	136	Azerbaijan	12.6	190	Finland	2.2
84	El Salvador	21.1	137	Zimbabwe	12.6	191	Japan	2.1
85	Malaysia	20.8	138	Netherlands Antilles	12.5	192	Poland	1.9
86	Samoa	20.7	139	Argentina	12.0	193	Slovakia	1.6
87	Lebanon	20.6	140	Guadeloupe	12.0	194	United Kingdom	1.6
88	Bolivia	20.4	141	Sri Lanka	12.0	195	Denmark	1.3
89	Brunei	20.3	142	Albania	11.9	196	Belgium	1.0
90	Colombia	20.0	143	Brazil	11.6	197	Austria	0.9
91	Guam	20.0	144	Mauritius	11.6	198	Guernsey	0.8
92	Kiribati	20.0	145	Ecuador	11.4	199	Moldova	0.5
93	Guinea-Bissau	19.7	146	Aruba	11.2	200	Spain	0.5
94	Costa Rica	19.6	147	Macau	10.9	201	Portugal	0.3
95	Saint Lucia	19.3	148	Singapore	10.9	202	Sweden	0.2
96	Egypt	19.2	149	Thailand	10.4	203	Greece	0.1
97	Virgin Islands (U.S.)	18.8	150	Saint Kitts and Nevis	10.0	204	Croatia	-0.1
98	Morocco	18.6	151	Martinique	9.7	205	Italy	-0.3
99	Vietnam	18.6	152	Guyana	9.5	206	Lithuania	-1.0
100	Peru	18.5	153	Trinidad and Tobago	9.4	207	Germany	-1.4
101	Jamaica	18.2	154	Puerto Rico	9.3	208	Romania	-1.6
102	Fiji	18.1	155	China	9.1	209	Isle of Man	-1.8
103	Haiti	18.0	156	Iceland	8.8	210	Czech Republic	-2.1
104	Tunisia	18.0	157	South Korea	8.7	211	Belarus	-3.7
105	Tuvalu	18.0	158	Taiwan	8.6	212	Hungary	-3.7
106	Dominican Republic	17.8	159	New Zealand	8.4	213	Estonia	-3.9
107	Kyrgyzstan	17.8	160	Gibraltar	8.2	214	Bulgaria	-5.4
108	Myanmar (Burma)	17.5	161	Uruguay	7.8	215	Russia	-5.7
109	Bahrain	17.4	162	Bermuda	7.7	216	Latvia	-5.9
110	Panama	17.3	163	Cyprus	7.7	217	Bosnia and Herzegovina	-9.0
111	North Korea	17.2	164	Andorra	7.6			

Source: UN Statistical Yearbook

Death has a medical as well as legal definition, and they differ widely. The most common definition is the permanent dis-appearance of all evidence of life at any time after live birth has taken place. Death statistics are also subject to error because not all deaths are reported, and there are thousands of missing persons whose ultimate fate is a mystery. Death rates are higher in developing countries because of lower life expectancy, famine, and higher incidence of fatal illnesses. Countries in Africa with large numbers of people infected with AIDS have some of the highest death rates in the world.

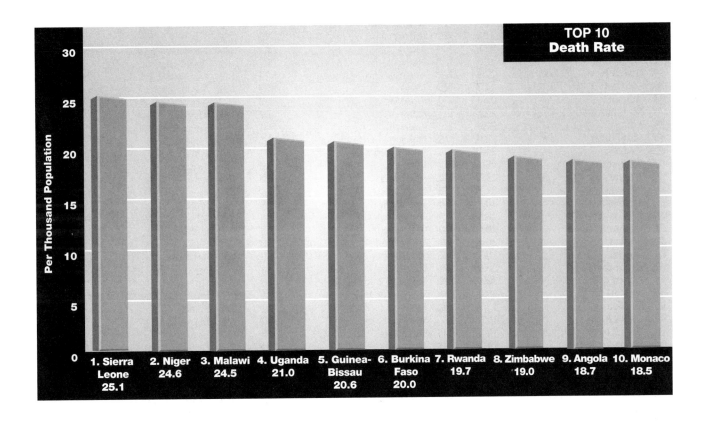

TOP 10
Death Rate

Rank	Country/Entity	Death Rate per 1,000 Population	Rank	Country/Entity	Death Rate per 1,000 Population	Rank	Country/Entity	Death Rate per 1,000 Population
11	Guinea	18.4	24	Bosnia and Herzegovina	15.5	37	Bulgaria	14.0
12	Afghanistan	18.0	25	Haiti	15.5	38	Bhutan	13.9
13	Zambia	18.0	26	Nigeria	15.4	39	Côte d'Ivoire	13.8
14	Burundi	17.8	27	Liberia	15.3	40	Latvia	13.8
15	Mozambique	17.5	28	Mauritania	15.2	41	Laos	13.7
16	Gambia	17.4	29	Cambodia	15.0	42	Congo, Dem. Rep. of	13.5
17	Chad	17.3	30	Djibouti	15.0	43	Isle of Man	13.2
18	Mali	17.1	31	Russia	15.0	44	Belarus	13.0
19	Central African Republic	17.0	32	Togo	14.9	45	Benin	13.0
20	Tanzania	17.0	33	Eritrea	14.7	46	Estonia	12.9
21	Somalia	16.9	34	Congo, Rep. of	14.6	47	Bangladesh	12.2
22	Equatorial Guinea	16.2	35	Gabon	14.3	48	Romania	12.0
23	Ethiopia	16.2	36	Hungary	14.1	49	Cameroon	11.9

Rank	Country/Entity	Death Rate per 1,000 Population	Rank	Country/Entity	Death Rate per 1,000 Population	Rank	Country/Entity	Death Rate per 1,000 Population
50	Moldova	11.8	107	Kyrgyzstan	8.2	163	Nicaragua	6.0
51	Namibia	11.8	108	Greenland	8.0	164	Samoa	6.0
52	Senegal	11.8	109	Micronesia	8.0	165	Syria	6.0
53	Sudan	11.7	110	Palau	8.0	166	Uzbekistan	6.0
54	Denmark	11.6	111	Argentina	7.9	167	Algeria	5.9
55	Lithuania	11.6	112	Grenada	7.9	168	Bahamas	5.9
56	Nepal	11.2	113	Indonesia	7.9	169	Colombia	5.9
57	South Africa	11.1	114	New Zealand	7.9	170	Sri Lanka	5.9
58	Kiribati	11.0	115	Pakistan	7.9	171	Saint Lucia	5.9
59	Czech Republic	10.9	116	Puerto Rico	7.9	172	Tunisia	5.9
60	United Kingdom	10.9	117	Cyprus	7.7	173	Philippines	5.8
61	Kenya	10.8	118	Macedonia	7.6	174	Tonga	5.8
62	Portugal	10.8	119	Maldives	7.6	175	Belize	5.7
63	Germany	10.7	120	Mongolia	7.6	176	Dominican Republic	5.7
64	Croatia	10.6	121	Armenia	7.5	177	Chile	5.5
65	Lesotho	10.6	122	Guatemala	7.5	178	New Caledonia	5.5
66	Swaziland	10.6	123	Malta	7.5	179	Turkey	5.5
67	Sweden	10.6	124	Bermuda	7.4	180	Virgin Islands (U.S.)	5.5
68	Ukraine	10.5	125	Japan	7.4	181	Paraguay	5.4
69	Yugoslavia	10.5	126	Thailand	7.4	182	Réunion	5.4
70	Belgium	10.4	127	Canada	7.2	183	Dominica	5.3
71	Ghana	10.4	128	Cuba	7.2	184	Gaza Strip	5.3
72	Guernsey	10.4	129	Iceland	7.2	185	North Korea	5.3
73	Yemen	10.4	130	Cape Verde	7.1	186	Panama	5.2
74	Comoros	10.3	131	China	7.1	187	Singapore	5.1
75	Kazakhstan	10.2	132	Martinique	7.1	188	Jamaica	5.0
76	Norway	10.1	133	Seychelles	7.0	189	Hong Kong	4.9
77	Poland	10.1	134	Tajikistan	7.0	190	Malaysia	4.8
78	Papua New Guinea	10.0	135	Turkmenistan	7.0	191	Mexico	4.8
79	Uruguay	10.0	136	Vietnam	7.0	192	Oman	4.8
80	Austria	9.9	137	West Bank	7.0	193	Slovenia	4.8
81	Jersey	9.9	138	Australia	6.9	194	Albania	4.7
82	Madagascar	9.9	139	Libya	6.9	195	Venezuela	4.7
83	Myanmar (Burma)	9.9	140	Trinidad and Tobago	6.9	196	Fiji	4.6
84	Iraq	9.8	141	San Marino	6.8	197	French Polynesia	4.5
85	Finland	9.6	142	Antigua and Barbuda	6.7	198	Nauru	4.5
86	Greece	9.6	143	Liechtenstein	6.7	199	Ecuador	4.4
87	India	9.6	144	Mauritius	6.7	200	Lebanon	4.3
88	Guyana	9.5	145	Morocco	6.7	201	American Samoa	4.2
89	Italy	9.5	146	Netherlands Antilles	6.7	202	Costa Rica	4.2
90	Slovakia	9.5	147	Saint Vincent and the Grenadines	6.7	203	Saudi Arabia	4.2
91	Luxembourg	9.4				204	French Guiana	4.1
92	Saint Kitts and Nevis	9.4	148	Azerbaijan	6.6	205	Solomon Islands	4.1
93	Brazil	9.2	149	Botswana	6.6	206	Guam	4.0
94	France	9.2	150	El Salvador	6.6	207	Marshall Islands	4.0
95	Barbados	9.1	151	Iran	6.6	208	Bahrain	3.6
96	Bolivia	9.1	152	Suriname	6.6	209	Andorra	3.4
97	Faroe Islands	9.0	153	Guadeloupe	6.5	210	Qatar	3.4
98	Tuvalu	9.0	154	Georgia	6.4	211	Macau	3.2
99	Switzerland	8.9	155	Honduras	6.4	212	Brunei	3.0
100	Netherlands	8.8	156	South Korea	6.4	213	Jordan	3.0
101	United States	8.8	157	Peru	6.4	214	Northern Mariana Islands	3.0
102	Ireland	8.7	158	Aruba	6.2	215	United Arab Emirates	2.9
103	Spain	8.7	159	Vanuatu	6.2	216	Kuwait	2.2
104	Egypt	8.6	160	Taiwan	6.1	217	São Tomé and Príncipe	0.7
105	Western Sahara	8.6	161	Israel	6.0			
106	Gibraltar	8.3	162	Mayotte	6.0			

Source: UN Statistical Yearbook

The annual growth rate is the bottom line of all demographic inquiries. It is the clearest indicator of population trends and forms the basis of all extrapolations of the current numbers into the future. Annual growth rates tend to be stable over the short haul, but are sensitive to various factors, such as immigration, fertility, social development, and, interestingly, the state of women's education.

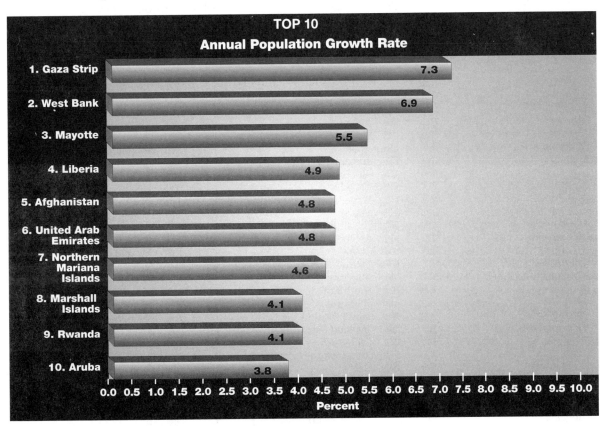

Rank	Country/Entity	Percent, 1994–1999	Rank	Country/Entity	Percent, 1994–1999	Rank	Country/Entity	Percent, 1994–1999
11	Belize	3.7	29	Mali	3.2	47	Pakistan	2.8
12	Eritrea	3.7	30	Comoros	3.1	48	Uganda	2.8
13	Solomon Islands	3.7	31	Congo, Dem. Rep. of	3.1	49	Djibouti	2.7
14	French Guiana	3.6	32	Nicaragua	3.1	50	Guatemala	2.7
15	Gambia	3.6	33	Nigeria	3.1	51	Hong Kong	2.7
16	Saudi Arabia	3.6	34	American Samoa	3.0	52	Paraguay	2.7
17	Togo	3.6	35	Bahrain	3.0	53	Sierra Leone	2.7
18	Jordan	3.5	36	Bhutan	3.0	54	Brunei	2.6
19	Kuwait	3.5	37	Maldives	3.0	55	Equatorial Guinea	2.6
20	Oman	3.5	38	Niger	3.0	56	Mauritania	2.6
21	Western Sahara	3.5	39	Somalia	3.0	57	Nepal	2.6
22	Benin	3.4	40	Sudan	3.0	58	Syria	2.6
23	Mozambique	3.4	41	Côte d'Ivoire	2.9	59	Vanuatu	2.6
24	Senegal	3.4	42	Cameroon	2.9	60	Malaysia	2.5
25	Angola	3.3	43	Madagascar	2.9	61	Bolivia	2.4
26	Honduras	3.3	44	Burkina Faso	2.8	62	Cambodia	2.4
27	Iraq	3.3	45	Chad	2.8	63	Ethiopia	2.4
28	Yemen	3.3	46	Laos	2.8	64	Guinea-Bissau	2.4

Rank	Country/Entity	Percent, 1994–1999	Rank	Country/Entity	Percent, 1994–1999	Rank	Country/Entity	Percent, 1994–1999
65	Israel	2.4	117	Tunisia	1.5	169	Saint Vincent and the Grenadines	0.6
66	Congo, Rep. of	2.3	118	Turkey	1.5	170	Cuba	0.5
67	Ghana	2.3	119	Tuvalu	1.5	171	Netherlands	0.5
68	Papua New Guinea	2.3	120	Vietnam	1.5	172	Norway	0.5
69	Philippines	2.3	121	Brazil	1.4	173	Switzerland	0.5
70	Algeria	2.2	122	Chile	1.4	174	Trinidad and Tobago	0.5
71	Tanzania	2.2	123	French Polynesia	1.4	175	Andorra	0.4
72	Egypt	2.1	124	Iran	1.4	176	Denmark	0.4
73	Lesotho	2.1	125	Luxembourg	1.4	177	France	0.4
74	Palau	2.1	126	Turkmenistan	1.4	178	Yugoslavia	0.4
75	Venezuela	2.1	127	Argentina	1.3	179	Armenia	0.3
76	Central African Republic	2.0	128	Fiji	1.3	180	Finland	0.3
77	Ecuador	2.0	129	Guernsey	1.3	181	Greece	0.3
78	São Tomé and Príncipe	2.0	130	Kyrgyzstan	1.3	182	Jersey	0.3
79	Zambia	2.0	131	New Zealand	1.3	183	Spain	0.3
80	Costa Rica	1.9	132	Samoa	1.3	184	Suriname	0.3
81	Kiribati	1.9	133	Virgin Islands (U.S.)	1.3	185	Tonga	0.3
82	Morocco	1.9	134	Australia	1.2	186	United Kingdom	0.3
83	Netherlands Antilles	1.9	135	Botswana	1.2	187	Belgium	0.2
84	Réunion	1.9	136	Guam	1.2	188	Germany	0.2
85	Singapore	1.9	137	Sri Lanka	1.2	189	Greenland	0.2
86	India	1.8	138	Albania	1.1	190	Italy	0.2
87	Macau	1.8	139	Canada	1.1	191	Japan	0.2
88	New Caledonia	1.8	140	Jamaica	1.1	192	Portugal	0.2
89	Peru	1.8	141	Nauru	1.1	193	Slovakia	0.2
90	Qatar	1.8	142	Puerto Rico	1.1	194	Slovenia	0.2
91	Uzbekistan	1.8	143	Azerbaijan	1.0	195	Sweden	0.2
92	Bahamas	1.7	144	China	1.0	196	Austria	0.1
93	Colombia	1.7	145	Cyprus	1.0	197	Barbados	0.1
94	Dominican Republic	1.7	146	Guadeloupe	1.0	198	Burundi	0.1
95	Kenya	1.7	147	South Korea	1.0	199	Georgia	0.1
96	Libya	1.7	148	Mauritius	1.0	200	Isle of Man	0.1
97	Mexico	1.7	149	Saint Kitts and Nevis	1.0	201	Poland	0.1
98	Myanmar (Burma)	1.7	150	Thailand	1.0	202	Faroe Islands	0.0
99	Namibia	1.7	151	Zimbabwe	1.0	203	North Korea	0.0
100	Panama	1.7	152	Dominica	0.9	204	Czech Republic	-0.1
101	Bangladesh	1.6	153	Malawi	0.9	205	Lithuania	-0.1
102	Cape Verde	1.6	154	Micronesia	0.9	206	Croatia	-0.2
103	El Salvador	1.6	155	Taiwan	0.9	207	Moldova	-0.2
104	Indonesia	1.6	156	United States	0.9	208	Belarus	-0.3
105	Lebanon	1.6	157	Bosnia and Herzegovina	0.8	209	Gibraltar	-0.3
106	San Marino	1.6	158	Grenada	0.8	210	Romania	-0.3
107	South Africa	1.6	159	Ireland	0.8	211	Russia	-0.3
108	Saint Lucia	1.6	160	Liechtenstein	0.8	212	Hungary	-0.4
109	Tajikistan	1.6	161	Macedonia	0.8	213	Bulgaria	-0.6
110	Antigua and Barbuda	1.5	162	Uruguay	0.8	214	Estonia	-0.8
111	Gabon	1.5	163	Iceland	0.7	215	Ukraine	-0.8
112	Guinea	1.5	164	Malta	0.7	216	Latvia	-1.0
113	Haiti	1.5	165	Martinique	0.7	217	Kazakhstan	-1.8
114	Mongolia	1.5	166	Bermuda	0.6			
115	Seychelles	1.5	167	Guyana	0.6			
116	Swaziland	1.5	168	Monaco	0.6			

Source: Demographic Yearbook

Chapter 3

Vital Statistics and Family

3.1 Life Expectancy at Birth: Male

Expectation of life is defined as the average number of years a person has a chance to live under normal conditions of health on the basis of actuarial tables. It is one of the indicators that has steadily risen for the past 500 years. In the ancient and medieval worlds, the average life expectancy rarely exceeded forty, and life was, in the words of philosopher Thomas Hobbes (1588–1679), "nasty, short and brutish." Today life expectancy of up to eighty years is common in most industrial countries, and even in Africa it is rarely below fifty. Medical advances are the single most important factor in the continuing rise in life expectancy.

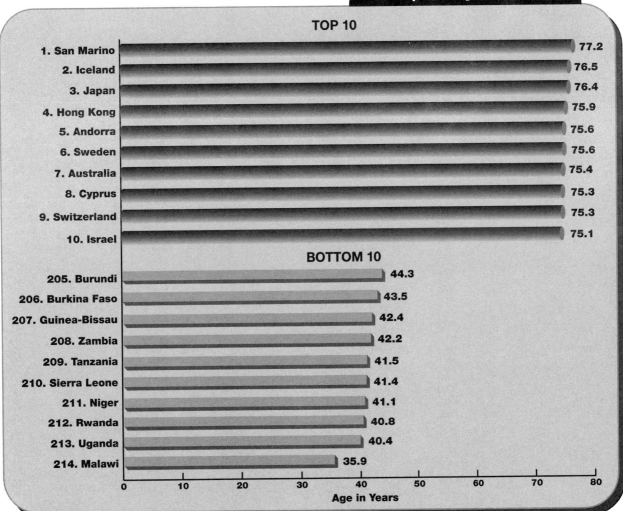

Life Expectancy at Birth: Male

TOP 10

Rank	Country	Age
1. San Marino		77.2
2. Iceland		76.5
3. Japan		76.4
4. Hong Kong		75.9
5. Andorra		75.6
6. Sweden		75.6
7. Australia		75.4
8. Cyprus		75.3
9. Switzerland		75.3
10. Israel		75.1

BOTTOM 10

Rank	Country	Age
205. Burundi		44.3
206. Burkina Faso		43.5
207. Guinea-Bissau		42.4
208. Zambia		42.2
209. Tanzania		41.5
210. Sierra Leone		41.4
211. Niger		41.1
212. Rwanda		40.8
213. Uganda		40.4
214. Malawi		35.9

Age in Years

Rank	Country/Entity	Age	Rank	Country/Entity	Age	Rank	Country/Entity	Age
11	Malta	74.9	18	Jamaica	74.4	25	France	73.7
12	Norway	74.9	19	Kuwait	74.4	26	Martinique	73.7
13	Spain	74.9	20	Singapore	74.4	27	Austria	73.5
14	Canada	74.7	21	United Kingdom	74.4	28	Gibraltar	73.4
15	Greece	74.6	22	Italy	74.1	29	New Zealand	73.4
16	Netherlands	74.6	23	Cuba	73.9	30	Belgium	73.0
17	Dominica	74.5	24	United Arab Emirates	73.9	31	Bermuda	73.0

Rank	Country/Entity	Age	Rank	Country/Entity	Age	Rank	Country/Entity	Age
32	Brunei	73.0	89	Bahamas	68.0	147	Marshall Islands	61.9
33	Guam	73.0	90	Tonga	68.0	148	São Tomé and Príncipe	61.8
34	Faroe Islands	72.8	91	Moldova	67.9	149	Turkmenistan	61.4
35	Finland	72.8	92	Trinidad and Tobago	67.9	150	Greenland	60.7
36	Denmark	72.6	93	Oman	67.7	151	Mongolia	60.0
37	Luxembourg	72.6	94	Ecuador	67.5	152	Bolivia	59.8
38	Germany	72.5	95	Paraguay	67.5	153	Western Sahara	59.8
39	Lebanon	72.5	96	Poland	67.5	154	Botswana	59.5
40	Ireland	72.3	97	Algeria	67.2	155	India	59.1
41	Bosnia and Herzegovina	72.1	98	Armenia	67.2	156	Northern Mariana Islands	59.0
42	Guadeloupe	72.1	99	Suriname	67.2	157	Bangladesh	58.0
43	Micronesia	72.0	100	Bulgaria	67.1	158	Lesotho	58.0
44	Monaco	72.0	101	Samoa	67.0	159	Myanmar (Burma)	58.0
45	United States	72.0	102	Saint Lucia	67.0	160	Russia	58.0
46	Costa Rica	71.9	103	Thailand	67.0	161	Zimbabwe	58.0
47	Chile	71.8	104	Dominican Republic	66.9	162	Yemen	57.4
48	Netherlands Antilles	71.8	105	Virgin Islands (U.S.)	66.7	163	Iraq	57.3
49	Taiwan	71.8	106	Belize	66.6	164	Guyana	57.2
50	Réunion	71.7	107	Azerbaijan	66.5	165	Madagascar	57.0
51	Barbados	71.6	108	Liechtenstein	66.5	166	Nepal	57.0
52	Antigua and Barbuda	71.5	109	Mauritius	66.5	167	Papua New Guinea	57.0
53	Portugal	71.3	110	Mexico	66.5	168	Brazil	56.7
54	Aruba	71.1	111	Gaza Strip	66.2	169	Comoros	56.4
55	Bahrain	71.1	112	Iran	66.1	170	Ghana	56.2
56	Panama	71.0	113	Belarus	66.0	171	South Africa	55.7
57	Sri Lanka	71.0	114	Philippines	66.0	172	Namibia	54.7
58	Saint Vincent and the Grenadines	71.0	115	Seychelles	66.0	173	Cameroon	54.5
			116	Vietnam	66.0	174	Kenya	54.2
59	Uruguay	70.9	117	Peru	65.9	175	Mayotte	54.0
60	Slovenia	70.3	118	Tajikistan	65.7	176	Gabon	53.8
61	Macedonia	70.1	119	West Bank	65.7	177	Senegal	53.7
62	Venezuela	70.1	120	Cape Verde	65.5	178	Sudan	53.6
63	Czech Republic	70.0	121	El Salvador	65.5	179	Nigeria	53.5
64	Fiji	70.0	122	Colombia	65.4	180	Swaziland	53.2
65	Malaysia	70.0	123	Egypt	65.4	181	Cambodia	52.0
66	Saudi Arabia	69.9	124	Lithuania	65.3	182	Congo, Dem. Rep. of	51.3
67	Argentina	69.6	125	Ukraine	65.3	183	Bhutan	51.0
68	Puerto Rico	69.6	126	Uzbekistan	65.1	184	Laos	51.0
69	Turkey	69.5	127	Estonia	65.0	185	Benin	50.7
70	Romania	69.3	128	Maldives	65.0	186	Côte d'Ivoire	50.0
71	Palau	69.1	129	Vanuatu	65.0	187	Liberia	50.0
72	Yugoslavia	69.1	130	Honduras	64.8	188	Eritrea	49.1
73	American Samoa	69.0	131	Hungary	64.8	189	Togo	48.8
74	North Korea	69.0	132	Morocco	64.8	190	Djibouti	48.7
75	South Korea	69.0	133	Jordan	64.4	191	Congo, Rep. of	48.6
76	New Caledonia	69.0	134	Latvia	64.2	192	Equatorial Guinea	48.4
77	Solomon Islands	69.0	135	Nauru	64.0	193	Ethiopia	48.4
78	Georgia	68.9	136	Tuvalu	64.0	194	Somalia	47.4
79	Qatar	68.8	137	Kyrgyzstan	63.9	195	Haiti	47.3
80	Slovakia	68.8	138	Libya	63.9	196	Afghanistan	46.4
81	Croatia	68.6	139	French Guiana	63.4	197	Mali	46.4
82	French Polynesia	68.4	140	Nicaragua	63.4	198	Chad	46.3
83	Syria	68.4	141	Kazakhstan	63.2	199	Mauritania	46.1
84	Tunisia	68.4	142	Indonesia	63.0	200	Guinea	46.0
85	China	68.2	143	Pakistan	63.0	201	Mozambique	45.5
86	Grenada	68.2	144	Saint Kitts and Nevis	63.0	202	Gambia	45.4
87	Macau	68.1	145	Kiribati	62.0	203	Angola	44.9
88	Albania	68.0	146	Guatemala	61.9	204	Central African Republic	44.7

Source: Population and Vital Statistics Report

In every society, women generally live longer than men. As a result, there are more widows than widowers in most countries. There is no commonly accepted medical explanation for this universal phenomenon.

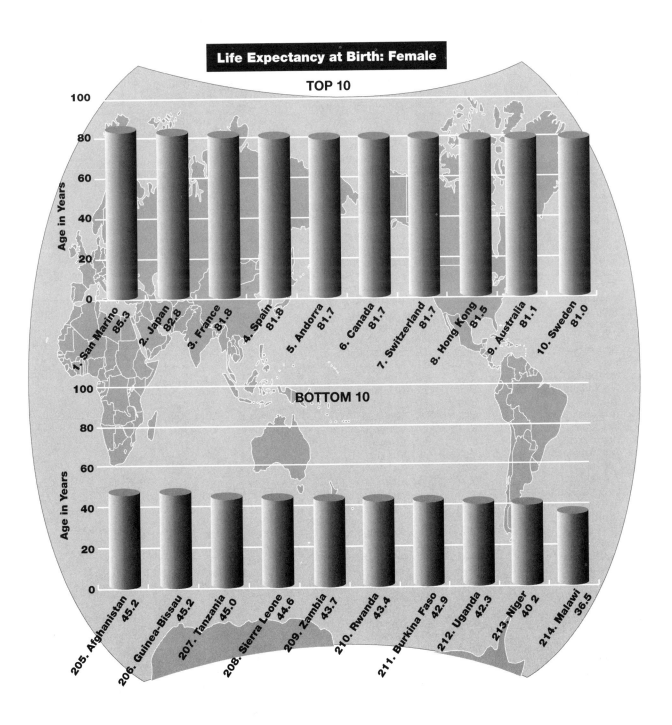

Life Expectancy at Birth: Female

TOP 10

Age in Years

1. San Marino 85.3
2. Japan 82.8
3. France 81.8
4. Spain 81.8
5. Andorra 81.7
6. Canada 81.7
7. Switzerland 81.7
8. Hong Kong 81.5
9. Australia 81.1
10. Sweden 81.0

BOTTOM 10

Age in Years

205. Afghanistan 45.2
206. Guinea-Bissau 45.2
207. Tanzania 45.0
208. Sierra Leone 44.6
209. Zambia 43.7
210. Rwanda 43.4
211. Burkina Faso 42.9
212. Uganda 42.3
213. Niger 40.2
214. Malawi 36.5

Rank	Country/Entity	Age	Rank	Country/Entity	Age	Rank	Country/Entity	Age
11	Iceland	80.6	72	Bahrain	75.3	132	Honduras	69.2
12	Norway	80.6	73	Estonia	75.0	133	Nauru	69.0
13	Italy	80.5	74	Fiji	75.0	134	Saint Kitts and Nevis	69.0
14	Dominica	80.4	75	North Korea	75.0	135	Vanuatu	69.0
15	Gibraltar	80.4	76	Sri Lanka	75.0	136	Vietnam	69.0
16	Netherlands	80.4	77	Bulgaria	74.9	137	Iran	68.7
17	Martinique	80.3	78	Ukraine	74.7	138	Turkmenistan	68.6
18	Finland	80.2	79	Latvia	74.6	139	Morocco	68.5
19	Austria	80.1	80	Azerbaijan	74.5	140	Greenland	68.4
20	Monaco	80.0	81	Macedonia	74.4	141	Nicaragua	68.1
21	Belgium	79.8	82	Turkey	74.4	142	Cape Verde	67.5
22	Cyprus	79.8	83	Yugoslavia	74.3	143	Libya	67.5
23	Greece	79.8	84	Hungary	74.2	144	West Bank	67.5
24	United Kingdom	79.7	85	Qatar	74.2	145	Guatemala	67.1
25	Faroe Islands	79.6	86	Albania	74.0	146	Kiribati	67.0
26	Liechtenstein	79.5	87	American Samoa	74.0	147	Brazil	66.8
27	Malta	79.5	88	Armenia	74.0	148	Indonesia	66.0
28	Luxembourg	79.1	89	Malaysia	74.0	149	Botswana	65.6
29	New Zealand	79.1	90	Mauritius	74.0	150	São Tomé and Príncipe	65.6
30	Bermuda	79.0	91	Solomon Islands	74.0	151	Marshall Islands	65.0
31	Germany	79.0	92	Saint Vincent and the Grenadines	74.0	152	Pakistan	65.0
32	Guam	79.0				153	Northern Mariana Islands	64.0
33	Kuwait	79.0	93	Colombia	73.4	154	Mongolia	63.5
34	Singapore	78.9	94	Saudi Arabia	73.4	155	Bolivia	63.2
35	United States	78.9	95	Grenada	73.2	156	Western Sahara	63.1
36	Guadeloupe	78.8	96	Mexico	73.1	157	Lesotho	63.0
37	Portugal	78.6	97	Palau	73.0	158	Maldives	63.0
38	Israel	78.5	98	Seychelles	73.0	159	Guyana	62.8
39	Puerto Rico	78.5	99	French Polynesia	72.8	160	Myanmar (Burma)	62.0
40	Brunei	78.0	100	Trinidad and Tobago	72.8	161	Zimbabwe	62.0
41	Réunion	78.0	101	Kazakhstan	72.7	162	Swaziland	61.4
42	Ireland	77.9	102	Ecuador	72.6	163	Comoros	61.0
43	Lebanon	77.9	103	Kyrgyzstan	72.6	164	Iraq	60.4
44	Chile	77.8	104	El Salvador	72.4	165	India	60.3
45	Denmark	77.8	105	Suriname	72.4	166	South Africa	60.2
46	Slovenia	77.8	106	Micronesia	72.0	167	Madagascar	60.0
47	Bosnia and Herzegovina	77.7	107	Paraguay	72.0	168	Ghana	59.9
48	Netherlands Antilles	77.7	108	Russia	72.0	169	Senegal	59.3
49	Taiwan	77.7	109	Saint Lucia	72.0	170	Papua New Guinea	59.0
50	Cuba	77.6	110	Thailand	72.0	171	Yemen	58.4
51	Costa Rica	77.5	111	Tonga	72.0	172	Bangladesh	58.0
52	Uruguay	77.5	112	Macau	71.8	173	Mayotte	58.0
53	Bahamas	77.2	113	Oman	71.8	174	Cameroon	57.2
54	Barbados	77.2	114	Uzbekistan	71.8	175	Gabon	57.2
55	Aruba	77.1	115	China	71.7	176	Nepal	57.0
56	Czech Republic	76.9	116	Moldova	71.5	177	Namibia	56.6
57	Argentina	76.8	117	Tajikistan	71.5	178	Sudan	56.4
58	Slovakia	76.7	118	Dominican Republic	71.3	179	Nigeria	55.9
59	Georgia	76.5	119	Syria	71.3	180	Cambodia	55.0
60	Panama	76.5	120	Samoa	71.0	181	Benin	54.7
61	United Arab Emirates	76.5	121	Peru	70.9	182	Kenya	54.6
62	Lithuania	76.1	122	Tunisia	70.7	183	Congo, Dem. Rep. of	54.5
63	Poland	76.1	123	Virgin Islands (U.S.)	70.7	184	Laos	54.0
64	Croatia	76.0	124	Belize	70.6	185	Congo, Rep. of	53.4
65	South Korea	76.0	125	Philippines	70.0	186	Bhutan	53.0
66	New Caledonia	76.0	126	Tuvalu	70.0	187	Liberia	53.0
67	Venezuela	76.0	127	Jordan	69.9	188	Côte d'Ivoire	52.2
68	Antigua and Barbuda	75.8	128	French Guiana	69.7	189	Eritrea	52.1
69	Jamaica	75.8	129	Algeria	69.5	190	Mauritania	52.1
70	Belarus	75.7	130	Egypt	69.5	191	Djibouti	52.0
71	Romania	75.4	131	Gaza Strip	69.3	192	Equatorial Guinea	51.6

Rank	Country/Entity	Age	Rank	Country/Entity	Age	Rank	Country/Entity	Age
193	Ethiopia	51.6	197	Mali	49.7	201	Central African Republic	48.3
194	Togo	51.5	198	Chad	49.3	202	Angola	48.1
195	Haiti	51.3	199	Gambia	48.7	203	Burundi	47.3
196	Somalia	50.6	200	Mozambique	48.4	204	Guinea	47.0

Source: World Data

3.3 Fertility Rate

Fertility rate is the average number of children that would be borne by a woman, typically aged fifteen to forty-nine, in a calendar year, expressed per 1,000 women. It assumes that all childbearing women live to the end of their childbearing age and bear children at an average rate. Generally, decline in birthrates is associated with declines in fertility, but there may be other social factors that influence birthrates. Calculating fertility rates requires analysis of the changing age structure of the female population over time, and changing infant and maternal mortality rates.

Rank	Country/Entity	Fertility Rate	Rank	Country/Entity	Fertility Rate	Rank	Country/Entity	Fertility Rate
1	Albania	20.4	36	Libya	5.9	71	Mongolia	4.5
2	Ecuador	11.4	37	Malawi	5.9	72	Tajikistan	4.5
3	Gaza Strip	8.0	38	Saudi Arabia	5.9	73	Bolivia	4.4
4	Yemen	7.6	39	Cambodia	5.8	74	São Tomé and Príncipe	4.4
5	Niger	7.4	40	Madagascar	5.7	75	Vanuatu	4.4
6	Uganda	7.1	41	West Bank	5.7	76	Kenya	4.3
7	Ethiopia	7.0	42	Tanzania	5.6	77	Belize	4.2
8	Marshall Islands	7.0	43	Chad	5.5	78	Paraguay	4.2
9	Somalia	7.0	44	Equatorial Guinea	5.5	79	Qatar	4.1
10	Oman	6.9	45	Zambia	5.5	80	Turkmenistan	4.1
11	Burkina Faso	6.8	46	American Samoa	5.4	81	Nicaragua	4.0
12	Maldives	6.8	47	Djibouti	5.4	82	Uzbekistan	4.0
13	Mauritania	6.8	48	Gabon	5.4	83	Western Sahara	4.0
14	Mayotte	6.8	49	Guinea-Bissau	5.4	84	French Polynesia	3.9
15	Angola	6.7	50	Cameroon	5.3	85	Zimbabwe	3.9
16	Comoros	6.7	51	Eritrea	5.3	86	Grenada	3.8
17	Benin	6.6	52	Ghana	5.3	87	Samoa	3.8
18	Guinea	6.6	53	Tuvalu	5.3	88	French Guiana	3.7
19	Mali	6.6	54	Central African Republic	5.2	89	Kuwait	3.7
20	Burundi	6.5	55	Gambia	5.2	90	Mexico	3.7
21	Sierra Leone	6.5	56	Côte d'Ivoire	5.1	91	Philippines	3.7
22	Nigeria	6.4	57	Micronesia	5.1	92	Algeria	3.6
23	Liberia	6.3	58	Pakistan	5.1	93	Cape Verde	3.6
24	Senegal	6.3	59	Nepal	5.0	94	Egypt	3.5
25	Congo, Dem. Rep. of	6.2	60	Solomon Islands	5.0	95	United Arab Emirates	3.5
26	Laos	6.2	61	Honduras	4.9	96	Tonga	3.4
27	Afghanistan	6.1	62	Iraq	4.9	97	Kiribati	3.3
28	Mozambique	6.1	63	Lesotho	4.9	98	Malaysia	3.3
29	Syria	6.1	64	Namibia	4.9	99	Myanmar (Burma)	3.3
30	Togo	6.1	65	Guatemala	4.8	100	South Africa	3.3
31	Rwanda	6.0	66	Haiti	4.8	101	Bangladesh	3.2
32	Swaziland	6.0	67	Iran	4.7	102	El Salvador	3.2
33	Bhutan	5.9	68	Papua New Guinea	4.7	103	India	3.2
34	Congo, Rep. of	5.9	69	Sudan	4.6	104	Palau	3.2
35	Jordan	5.9	70	Botswana	4.5	105	Vietnam	3.2

Rank	Country/Entity	Fertility Rate	Rank	Country/Entity	Fertility Rate	Rank	Country/Entity	Fertility Rate
106	Guam	3.1	144	Macedonia	2.2	181	Belarus	1.7
107	Kyrgyzstan	3.1	145	Netherlands Antilles	2.2	182	Canada	1.7
108	Morocco	3.1	146	Romania	2.2	183	Finland	1.7
109	Venezuela	3.1	147	Cyprus	2.1	184	France	1.7
110	Bahrain	3.0	148	Guadeloupe	2.1	185	South Korea	1.7
111	Jamaica	3.0	149	Iceland	2.1	186	Luxembourg	1.7
112	Peru	3.0	150	Mauritius	2.1	187	Singapore	1.7
113	Brunei	2.9	151	Moldova	2.1	188	Sweden	1.7
114	Colombia	2.9	152	Poland	2.1	189	Ukraine	1.7
115	Greenland	2.9	153	Sri Lanka	2.1	190	United Kingdom	1.7
116	Israel	2.9	154	Saint Vincent and the Grenadines	2.1	191	Belgium	1.6
117	Lebanon	2.9				192	Guernsey	1.6
118	New Caledonia	2.9	155	Bahamas	2.0	193	Hungary	1.6
119	Tunisia	2.9	156	Lithuania	2.0	194	Macau	1.6
120	Costa Rica	2.8	157	Martinique	2.0	195	Austria	1.5
121	Fiji	2.8	158	New Zealand	2.0	196	Croatia	1.5
122	Gibraltar	2.8	159	Puerto Rico	2.0	197	Liechtenstein	1.5
123	Dominican Republic	2.7	160	Seychelles	2.0	198	Netherlands	1.5
124	Faroe Islands	2.7	161	Thailand	2.0	199	San Marino	1.5
125	Suriname	2.7	162	Trinidad and Tobago	2.0	200	Slovakia	1.5
126	Argentina	2.6	163	United States	2.0	201	Switzerland	1.5
127	Indonesia	2.6	164	Dominica	1.9	202	Czech Republic	1.4
128	Panama	2.6	165	Norway	1.9	203	Greece	1.4
129	Saint Kitts and Nevis	2.6	166	Yugoslavia	1.9	204	Japan	1.4
130	Turkey	2.6	167	Aruba	1.8	205	Latvia	1.4
131	Virgin Islands (U.S.)	2.6	168	Australia	1.8	206	Portugal	1.4
132	Kazakhstan	2.5	169	Barbados	1.8	207	Russia	1.4
133	Nauru	2.5	170	Bermuda	1.8	208	Estonia	1.3
134	Saint Lucia	2.5	171	China	1.8	209	Germany	1.3
135	Northern Mariana Islands	2.4	172	Cuba	1.8	210	Jersey	1.3
136	Uruguay	2.4	173	Denmark	1.8	211	Slovenia	1.3
137	Azerbaijan	2.3	174	Ireland	1.8	212	Spain	1.3
138	Brazil	2.3	175	Isle of Man	1.8	213	Bulgaria	1.2
139	Chile	2.3	176	Malta	1.8	214	Italy	1.2
140	North Korea	2.3	177	Taiwan	1.8	215	Monaco	1.2
141	Réunion	2.3	178	Andorra	1.7	216	Hong Kong	1.1
142	Georgia	2.2	179	Antigua and Barbuda	1.7	217	Bosnia and Herzegovina	1.0
143	Guyana	2.2	180	Armenia	1.7			

Source: Demographic Yearbook

3.4 Household Size

The definition of a family has become controversial in recent decades. It involves religious, juridical, and social concerns that have eluded clear and precise formulation. Generally, a family is used in the sense of nuclear or extended family consisting of a man and woman living together in a formal or informal relationship with children, parents, siblings, or other close relatives. The blood relationship between one or more of these persons constitutes the nexus of the relationship. A household, on the other hand, may be just an aggregation of individuals with or without a common head and with no legal or religiously ordained bonds between them. In developing societies, families tend to be fairly large because of both the large number of children and the persistence of the tradition of extended families. Differing definitions limit the international comparability of the data.

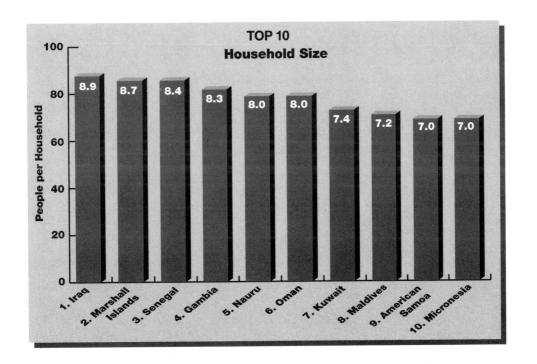

Rank	Country/Entity	People per Household	Rank	Country/Entity	People per Household	Rank	Country/Entity	People per Household
11	Algeria	6.9	23	Kenya	6.2	35	Honduras	5.7
12	United Arab Emirates	6.8	24	Syria	6.2	36	Swaziland	5.7
13	Kiribati	6.6	25	Jordan	6.1	37	Bangladesh	5.6
14	Saudi Arabia	6.6	26	Tajikistan	6.1	38	Cambodia	5.6
15	Sierra Leone	6.6	27	Congo, Dem. Rep. of	6.0	39	Comoros	5.6
16	Bahrain	6.5	28	Laos	6.0	40	Djibouti	5.6
17	Niger	6.4	29	Benin	5.9	41	India	5.6
18	Qatar	6.4	30	Brunei	5.8	42	Mali	5.6
19	Tuvalu	6.4	31	Morocco	5.8	43	Myanmar (Burma)	5.6
20	Pakistan	6.3	32	Nicaragua	5.8	44	Nepal	5.6
21	Afghanistan	6.2	33	Solomon Islands	5.8	45	Togo	5.6
22	Burkina Faso	6.2	34	Botswana	5.7	46	Turkmenistan	5.6

Rank	Country/Entity	People per Household	Rank	Country/Entity	People per Household	Rank	Country/Entity	People per Household
47	Yemen	5.6	96	Ethiopia	4.5	144	Guadeloupe	3.4
48	Uzbekistan	5.5	97	Indonesia	4.5	145	Moldova	3.4
49	Bhutan	5.4	98	Turkey	4.5	146	Greece	3.3
50	Côte d'Ivoire	5.4	99	Haiti	4.4	147	Ireland	3.3
51	Lebanon	5.3	100	Panama	4.4	148	Malta	3.3
52	Sudan	5.3	101	Zambia	4.4	149	Martinique	3.3
53	Venezuela	5.3	102	Malawi	4.3	150	Uruguay	3.3
54	Cameroon	5.2	103	Jamaica	4.2	151	Antigua and Barbuda	3.2
55	Guatemala	5.2	104	Kyrgyzstan	4.2	152	Argentina	3.2
56	Namibia	5.2	105	Singapore	4.2	153	Belarus	3.2
57	Tanzania	5.2	106	China	4.1	154	Gibraltar	3.2
58	Guyana	5.1	107	Costa Rica	4.1	155	Hong Kong	3.2
59	Iran	5.1	108	Ecuador	4.1	156	Lithuania	3.2
60	Mexico	5.1	109	Georgia	4.1	157	Russia	3.2
61	Peru	5.1	110	Guinea-Bissau	4.1	158	Ukraine	3.2
62	Tunisia	5.1	111	New Caledonia	4.1	159	Croatia	3.1
63	Vanuatu	5.1	112	Trinidad and Tobago	4.1	160	Estonia	3.1
64	Liberia	5.0	113	Gabon	4.0	161	Latvia	3.1
65	Mauritania	5.0	114	Guam	4.0	162	Portugal	3.1
66	Belize	4.9	115	Kazakhstan	4.0	163	Romania	3.1
67	Egypt	4.9	116	São Tomé and Príncipe	4.0	164	Slovenia	3.1
68	Ghana	4.9	117	Slovakia	4.0	165	Virgin Islands (U.S.)	3.1
69	Malaysia	4.9	118	Saint Lucia	4.0	166	Bulgaria	3.0
70	Mayotte	4.9	119	Bahamas	3.9	167	Liechtenstein	3.0
71	Somalia	4.9	120	Chad	3.9	168	Czech Republic	2.9
72	Angola	4.8	121	Dominican Republic	3.9	169	Iceland	2.9
73	Azerbaijan	4.8	122	Saint Vincent and the Grenadines	3.9	170	New Zealand	2.9
74	El Salvador	4.8				171	Japan	2.8
75	North Korea	4.8	123	Suriname	3.9	172	Canada	2.7
76	Lesotho	4.8	124	Bolivia	3.8	173	Australia	2.6
77	Seychelles	4.8	125	Chile	3.8	174	Bermuda	2.6
78	Uganda	4.8	126	Macedonia	3.8	175	France	2.6
79	Vietnam	4.8	127	Thailand	3.8	176	Guernsey	2.6
80	Zimbabwe	4.8	128	Grenada	3.7	177	Jersey	2.6
81	Armenia	4.7	129	Israel	3.7	178	Luxembourg	2.6
82	Central African Republic	4.7	130	South Korea	3.7	179	San Marino	2.6
83	Congo, Rep. of	4.7	131	Netherlands Antilles	3.7	180	United States	2.6
84	French Polynesia	4.7	132	Saint Kitts and Nevis	3.7	181	Austria	2.5
85	Guinea	4.7	133	Aruba	3.6	182	Netherlands	2.4
86	Madagascar	4.7	134	Bosnia and Herzegovina	3.6	183	United Kingdom	2.4
87	Nigeria	4.7	135	Dominica	3.6	184	Norway	2.3
88	Paraguay	4.7	136	Puerto Rico	3.6	185	Denmark	2.2
89	Rwanda	4.7	137	Taiwan	3.6	186	Finland	2.2
90	Burundi	4.6	138	Yugoslavia	3.6	187	Germany	2.2
91	Northern Mariana Islands	4.6	139	Barbados	3.5	188	Monaco	2.2
92	Papua New Guinea	4.6	140	Cyprus	3.5	189	Switzerland	2.2
93	South Africa	4.6	141	Macau	3.5	190	Sweden	2.1
94	Sri Lanka	4.6	142	Réunion	3.5			
95	Equatorial Guinea	4.5	143	French Guiana	3.4			

Source: Demographic Yearbook

3.5 Legitimate Births

It has been said that there are no illegitimate children, only illegitimate parents. Nevertheless, some societies seem more likely to have a larger proportion of its births outside of wedlock. The highest percentage of illegitimate births are among blacks, whether in the developed or developing world. In the United States, close to 75 percent of all births are to unmarried black women. This also applies to many Caribbean countries, where blacks are in the majority, as well as to most of sub-Saharan Africa.

Rank	Country/Entity	Percentage of Legitimate Births	Rank	Country/Entity	Percentage of Legitimate Births	Rank	Country/Entity	Percentage of Legitimate Births
1	Egypt	100.0	41	Germany	86.6	81	Aruba	63.2
2	Kuwait	100.0	42	Slovakia	86.0	82	Chile	61.9
3	Tunisia	99.8	43	Portugal	85.5	83	Puerto Rico	59.6
4	Brunei	99.6	44	Russia	85.4	84	Peru	57.8
5	Cyprus	99.6	45	Liechtenstein	85.3	85	Faroe Islands	57.5
6	South Korea	99.5	46	Netherlands	84.5	86	Cape Verde	55.2
7	Macau	99.3	47	Czech Republic	84.4	87	Northern Mariana Islands	53.9
8	Japan	99.0	48	Canada	83.8	88	Denmark	53.5
9	Israel	98.5	49	Kyrgyzstan	83.2	89	Costa Rica	53.4
10	Azerbaijan	97.5	50	Fiji	82.7	90	Norway	52.4
11	Taiwan	97.2	51	Georgia	82.3	91	Netherlands Antilles	51.6
12	Gibraltar	97.1	52	Tuvalu	82.2	92	New Caledonia	48.1
13	Greece	97.1	53	Hungary	81.5	93	Sweden	47.0
14	Djibouti	96.8	54	Bolivia	80.9	94	Venezuela	47.0
15	Monaco	96.8	55	Tonga	80.6	95	Bahamas	44.7
16	Turkmenistan	96.5	56	Ireland	77.8	96	Réunion	44.1
17	Sri Lanka	96.3	57	Isle of Man	76.1	97	Samoa	43.5
18	Malta	95.8	58	South Africa	75.9	98	Belize	41.6
19	Uzbekistan	95.8	59	Austria	75.2	99	Guam	41.3
20	Zimbabwe	95.8	60	Colombia	75.2	100	Guadeloupe	39.3
21	San Marino	95.2	61	Australia	75.0	101	Iceland	39.1
22	Poland	95.0	62	Bulgaria	74.3	102	Virgin Islands (U.S.)	38.4
23	Rwanda	94.9	63	Uruguay	73.8	103	French Polynesia	37.2
24	Hong Kong	94.5	64	Latvia	73.6	104	Guatemala	34.8
25	Philippines	93.9	65	Guernsey	73.2	105	Martinique	34.1
26	Lithuania	93.3	66	Mozambique	73.1	106	Dominican Republic	32.8
27	Switzerland	93.2	67	Mauritius	72.8	107	El Salvador	30.6
28	Tajikistan	93.0	68	Mexico	72.5	108	Botswana	28.8
29	Macedonia	91.5	69	American Samoa	72.0	109	Greenland	28.0
30	Belarus	91.0	70	United States	70.5	110	Seychelles	27.2
31	Italy	90.2	71	Slovenia	70.2	111	Barbados	26.9
32	Moldova	89.6	72	Paraguay	68.7	112	Panama	25.5
33	Spain	89.5	73	United Kingdom	68.0	113	Antigua and Barbuda	23.4
34	Mayotte	89.2	74	Ecuador	67.9	114	French Guiana	20.3
35	Ukraine	89.2	75	Argentina	67.5	115	Saint Kitts and Nevis	19.2
36	Belgium	88.7	76	Finland	66.9	116	Jamaica	14.9
37	Jersey	88.1	77	Estonia	66.1	117	Saint Lucia	14.2
38	Armenia	87.7	78	Bermuda	63.9	118	Guinea-Bissau	11.3
39	Kazakhstan	87.6	79	France	63.9	119	São Tomé and Príncipe	9.8
40	Luxembourg	87.3	80	New Zealand	63.3			

Source: World Data

3.6 Induced Abortions

During the past fifty years the number of countries where abortion is legal and socially acceptable has grown from thirty to more than fifty. This development is closely related to the rise of the feminist movement, which has successfully linked abortion rights to women's rights as a whole. The terms "reproductive rights" and "choice" have been used to emphasize the fact that abortion represents above all a woman's freedom from the age-old fear of unwanted pregnancies. It is also a weapon in the armory of family planning and planned parenthood advocates. But abortion remains illegal in the vast majority of countries, and the battle over this issue is fought on many grounds, even in technologically advanced countries. In most countries abortion is defined as the interruption of pregnancy before twenty-eight weeks of gestation, causing the death of the infant. Late-term abortions are unusual and have not gained public acceptance. Abortion is permitted on request even by a minor in forty-one countries, for social and economic reasons in fifty-five countries, for fetal impairment in seventy-eight countries, for rape or incest in eighty-one countries, to preserve the mental or physical health of the mother in ninety-five countries, and to save the mother's life in one hundred and seventy-three countries. However, the data suffer from serious inadequacies resulting from poor reporting. In many countries (including those where it is legal) abortion is often done surreptitiously.

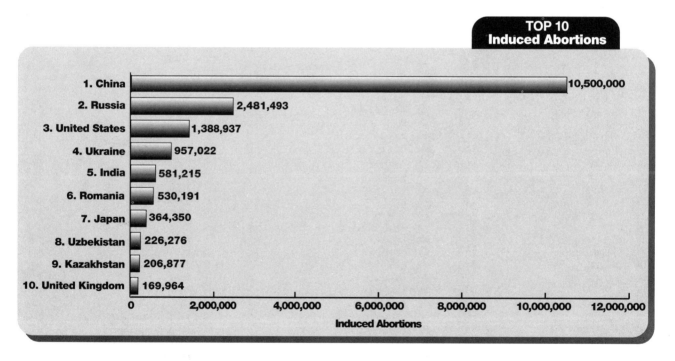

TOP 10 Induced Abortions

Rank	Country	Induced Abortions
1. China		10,500,000
2. Russia		2,481,493
3. United States		1,388,937
4. Ukraine		957,022
5. India		581,215
6. Romania		530,191
7. Japan		364,350
8. Uzbekistan		226,276
9. Kazakhstan		206,877
10. United Kingdom		169,964

Rank	Country/Entity	Number of Induced Abortions	Rank	Country/Entity	Number of Induced Abortions	Rank	Country/Entity	Number of Induced Abortions
11	France	162,902	19	Georgia	68,883	27	Sweden	32,293
12	Italy	124,334	20	Czech Republic	61,590	28	Kyrgyzstan	31,389
13	Cuba	124,059	21	Moldova	52,003	29	Estonia	28,403
14	Bulgaria	107,416	22	Azerbaijan	42,134	30	Armenia	27,958
15	Germany	103,586	23	Lithuania	42,023	31	Latvia	26,795
16	Canada	99,971	24	Tajikistan	40,078	32	Tunisia	23,300
17	Belarus	85,685	25	Turkmenistan	39,068	33	Netherlands	20,811
18	Hungary	74,491	26	Slovakia	34,883	34	Macedonia	18,754

Rank	Country/Entity	Number of Induced Abortions	Rank	Country/Entity	Number of Induced Abortions	Rank	Country/Entity	Number of Induced Abortions
35	Hong Kong	17,600	45	Philippines	2,315	55	French Guiana	388
36	Denmark	17,598	46	Martinique	1,753	56	Seychelles	387
37	Israel	17,164	47	Swaziland	1,145	57	Jersey	313
38	Singapore	15,690	48	Belize	990	58	Vanuatu	113
39	Norway	14,909	49	Greenland	962	59	Bermuda	92
40	Greece	11,977	50	Poland	874	60	Chile	67
41	New Zealand	11,460	51	Iceland	775	61	Faroe Islands	26
42	Slovenia	11,324	52	Barbados	723	62	Botswana	17
43	Finland	10,013	53	Dominican Republic	562	63	Trinidad and Tobago	9
44	Réunion	4,302	54	Guadeloupe	561			

Source: World Data

3.7 Contraceptive Use

The main contraceptive methods are intrauterine devices, oral contraceptives, sterilization, and abortion. The French "morning-after pill" is another popular method in Europe, but it is not in large-scale use in the United States. Because of the sensitive nature of the topic, the data are subject to serious limitations and may represent only estimates or educated guesses.

Rank	Country/Entity	Percentage of Married Women of Childbearing Age Using Contraceptives	Rank	Country/Entity	Percentage of Married Women of Childbearing Age Using Contraceptives	Rank	Country/Entity	Percentage of Married Women of Childbearing Age Using Contraceptives
1	Hong Kong	86	32	New Zealand	69	62	Mexico	53
2	China	83	33	Portugal	66	63	Trinidad and Tobago	53
3	United Kingdom	82	34	Sri Lanka	66	64	Algeria	52
4	Finland	80	35	Iran	65	65	Belarus	50
5	Belgium	79	36	Vietnam	65	66	Dominica	50
6	South Korea	79	37	Dominican Republic	64	67	Morocco	50
7	Denmark	78	38	Panama	64	68	South Africa	50
8	Italy	78	39	Peru	64	69	Bangladesh	49
9	Netherlands	78	40	Turkey	63	70	Nicaragua	49
10	Sweden	78	41	Bahamas	62	71	Venezuela	49
11	Brazil	77	42	Jamaica	62	72	Malaysia	48
12	France	77	43	North Korea	62	73	Zimbabwe	48
13	Australia	76	44	Mongolia	61	74	Belize	47
14	Bulgaria	76	45	Tunisia	60	75	Egypt	47
15	Norway	76	46	Japan	59	76	Honduras	47
16	Costa Rica	75	47	Kazakhstan	59	77	Latvia	47
17	Germany	75	48	Lithuania	59	78	Saint Lucia	47
18	Mauritius	75	49	Spain	59	79	Bolivia	45
19	Poland	75	50	Saint Vincent and the Grenadines	58	80	Fiji	41
20	Singapore	74				81	India	41
21	Slovakia	74	51	Ecuador	57	82	Saint Kitts and Nevis	41
22	Thailand	74	52	Romania	57	83	Libya	40
23	Canada	73	53	Paraguay	56	84	Philippines	40
24	Hungary	73	54	Uzbekistan	56	85	Syria	36
25	Colombia	72	55	Barbados	55	86	Jordan	35
26	Austria	71	56	Indonesia	55	87	Kuwait	35
27	Switzerland	71	57	Grenada	54	88	Botswana	33
28	United States	71	58	Antigua and Barbuda	53	89	Kenya	33
29	Cuba	70	59	Bahrain	53	90	Qatar	32
30	Estonia	70	60	El Salvador	53	91	Guatemala	31
31	Czech Republic	69	61	Lebanon	53	92	Guyana	31

Rank	Country/Entity	Percentage of Married Women of Childbearing Age Using Contraceptives	Rank	Country/Entity	Percentage of Married Women of Childbearing Age Using Contraceptives	Rank	Country/Entity	Percentage of Married Women of Childbearing Age Using Contraceptives
93	Namibia	29	105	Madagascar	17	117	Oman	9
94	Nepal	29	106	Myanmar (Burma)	17	118	Burkina Faso	8
95	Zambia	25	107	Benin	16	119	Congo, Dem. Rep. of	8
96	Lesotho	23	108	Cameroon	16	120	Sudan	8
97	Malawi	22	109	Central African Republic	15	121	Mali	7
98	Comoros	21	110	Uganda	15	122	Yemen	7
99	Ghana	20	111	Iraq	14	123	Nigeria	6
100	Swaziland	20	112	Senegal	13	124	Eritrea	5
101	Laos	19	113	Gambia	12	125	Ethiopia	4
102	Haiti	18	114	Togo	12	126	Niger	4
103	Pakistan	18	115	Côte d'Ivoire	11	127	Mauritania	3
104	Tanzania	18	116	Burundi	9	128	Guinea	2

Source: World Bank

3.8 Age-Dependency Ratio

Age-dependency ratio is an indicator of the number of persons below fifteen and above sixty-five that are supported by the working-age population. In a young population with a strong cohort of children or an old population with a large percentage of seniors the problem is very acute.

Rank	Country/Entity	Dependents as Percentage of Working-Age Population, 1998	Rank	Country/Entity	Dependents as Percentage of Working-Age Population, 1998	Rank	Country/Entity	Dependents as Percentage of Working-Age Population, 1998
1	Chad	1.2	30	Nigeria	0.9	59	El Salvador	0.7
2	Yemen	1.1	31	Oman	0.9	60	Iran	0.7
3	Angola	1.0	32	Rwanda	0.9	61	Kyrgyzstan	0.7
4	Benin	1.0	33	Senegal	0.9	62	Libya	0.7
5	Burkina Faso	1.0	34	Sierra Leone	0.9	63	Mongolia	0.7
6	Congo, Dem. Rep. of	1.0	35	Tanzania	0.9	64	Papua New Guinea	0.7
7	Congo, Rep. of	1.0	36	Zambia	0.9	65	Philippines	0.7
8	Ethiopia	1.0	37	Bangladesh	0.8	66	Sudan	0.7
9	Malawi	1.0	38	Bolivia	0.8	67	Turkmenistan	0.7
10	Mali	1.0	39	Botswana	0.8	68	Vietnam	0.7
11	Niger	1.0	40	Cambodia	0.8	69	Albania	0.6
12	Togo	1.0	41	Gabon	0.8	70	Argentina	0.6
13	Uganda	1.0	42	Gambia	0.8	71	Azerbaijan	0.6
14	West Bank and Gaza	1.0	43	Haiti	0.8	72	Chile	0.6
15	Burundi	0.9	44	Honduras	0.8	73	Colombia	0.6
16	Côte d'Ivoire	0.9	45	Iraq	0.8	74	Costa Rica	0.6
17	Cameroon	0.9	46	Jordan	0.8	75	Dominican Republic	0.6
18	Central African Republic	0.9	47	Lesotho	0.8	76	Ecuador	0.6
19	Eritrea	0.9	48	Namibia	0.8	77	India	0.6
20	Ghana	0.9	49	Nepal	0.8	78	Indonesia	0.6
21	Guatemala	0.9	50	Pakistan	0.8	79	Israel	0.6
22	Guinea	0.9	51	Paraguay	0.8	80	Jamaica	0.6
23	Guinea-Bissau	0.9	52	Saudi Arabia	0.8	81	Kuwait	0.6
24	Kenya	0.9	53	Syria	0.8	82	Lebanon	0.6
25	Laos	0.9	54	Tajikistan	0.8	83	Malaysia	0.6
26	Madagascar	0.9	55	Uzbekistan	0.8	84	Mexico	0.6
27	Mauritania	0.9	56	Zimbabwe	0.8	85	Morocco	0.6
28	Mozambique	0.9	57	Algeria	0.7	86	Panama	0.6
29	Nicaragua	0.9	58	Egypt	0.7	87	Peru	0.6

Rank	Country/Entity	Dependents as Percentage of Working-Age Population, 1998	Rank	Country/Entity	Dependents as Percentage of Working-Age Population, 1998	Rank	Country/Entity	Dependents as Percentage of Working-Age Population, 1998
88	South Africa	0.6	109	Greece	0.5	130	Slovakia	0.5
89	Sweden	0.6	110	Hungary	0.5	131	Spain	0.5
90	Tunisia	0.6	111	Ireland	0.5	132	Sri Lanka	0.5
91	Uruguay	0.6	112	Italy	0.5	133	Switzerland	0.5
92	Venezuela	0.6	113	Japan	0.5	134	Thailand	0.5
93	Armenia	0.5	114	Kazakhstan	0.5	135	Trinidad and Tobago	0.5
94	Australia	0.5	115	North Korea	0.5	136	Turkey	0.5
95	Austria	0.5	116	Latvia	0.5	137	Ukraine	0.5
96	Belarus	0.5	117	Lithuania	0.5	138	United Kingdom	0.5
97	Belgium	0.5	118	Macedonia	0.5	139	United States	0.5
98	Brazil	0.5	119	Mauritius	0.5	140	Yugoslavia	0.5
99	Bulgaria	0.5	120	Moldova	0.5	141	Bosnia and Herzegovina	0.4
100	Canada	0.5	121	Myanmar (Burma)	0.5	142	Cuba	0.4
101	China	0.5	122	Netherlands	0.5	143	Czech Republic	0.4
102	Croatia	0.5	123	New Zealand	0.5	144	Hong Kong	0.4
103	Denmark	0.5	124	Norway	0.5	145	South Korea	0.4
104	Estonia	0.5	125	Poland	0.5	146	Singapore	0.4
105	Finland	0.5	126	Portugal	0.5	147	Slovenia	0.4
106	France	0.5	127	Puerto Rico	0.5	148	United Arab Emirates	0.4
107	Georgia	0.5	128	Romania	0.5			
108	Germany	0.5	129	Russia	0.5			

Source: UN Statistical Yearbook

3.9 Marriage Rate

Marriage rate is a term that traditionally expresses in statistical terms the percentage of males and females who are legally wedded to one another in a religious or civil ceremony. However, the very institution of marriage has come into question in the latter half of the twentieth century, making it difficult to assign a clear and specific meaning to the term. Most of the statistics refer to conventional society, and the existence of subcultures within a society complicates data collection and analysis. Although common-law marriages have always existed, they were assumed to exist outside the bounds of legitimate relationships and thus not worthy of statistical attention. However, within recent decades the number of people living together without the imprimatur of a formal ceremony has become so large that marriage rates have become far from accurate.

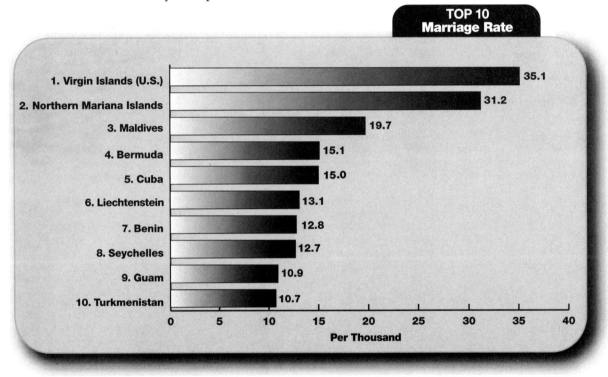

TOP 10 Marriage Rate

Rank		Per Thousand
1. Virgin Islands (U.S.)		35.1
2. Northern Mariana Islands		31.2
3. Maldives		19.7
4. Bermuda		15.1
5. Cuba		15.0
6. Liechtenstein		13.1
7. Benin		12.8
8. Seychelles		12.7
9. Guam		10.9
10. Turkmenistan		10.7

Rank	Country/Entity	Marriage Rate per 1,000	Rank	Country/Entity	Marriage Rate per 1,000	Rank	Country/Entity	Marriage Rate per 1,000
11	Bangladesh	10.2	23	Syria	8.6	35	American Samoa	7.8
12	Cyprus	9.6	24	Barbados	8.5	36	China	7.8
13	Fiji	9.6	25	Egypt	8.3	37	Iraq	7.8
14	Tajikistan	9.6	26	Tonga	8.2	38	Kuwait	7.8
15	Mauritius	9.5	27	Ukraine	8.2	39	Mongolia	7.8
16	North Korea	9.3	28	Greenland	8.1	40	Taiwan	7.8
17	Bahamas	9.2	29	Jordan	8.0	41	Uzbekistan	7.8
18	Sri Lanka	9.2	30	Aruba	7.9	42	Turkey	7.7
19	Moldova	9.1	31	Belarus	7.9	43	Albania	7.6
20	Puerto Rico	9.0	32	Iran	7.9	44	Indonesia	7.6
21	United States	8.8	33	Singapore	7.9	45	Macedonia	7.6
22	Kazakhstan	8.6	34	Thailand	7.9	46	Monaco	7.5

Rank	Country/Entity	Marriage Rate per 1,000	Rank	Country/Entity	Marriage Rate per 1,000	Rank	Country/Entity	Marriage Rate per 1,000
47	San Marino	7.4	82	Yugoslavia	5.7	117	Suriname	4.7
48	Russia	7.3	83	Panama	5.6	118	Armenia	4.6
49	Mexico	7.2	84	Trinidad and Tobago	5.6	119	Finland	4.6
50	Brunei	7.1	85	Canada	5.5	120	Iceland	4.6
51	Costa Rica	7.1	86	United Kingdom	5.5	121	Estonia	4.5
52	Bosnia and Herzegovina	7.0	87	Austria	5.4	122	Ireland	4.4
53	Philippines	6.9	88	Poland	5.4	123	Latvia	4.4
54	South Korea	6.8	89	Venezuela	5.4	124	Mali	4.4
55	Romania	6.8	90	Bahrain	5.3	125	Bulgaria	4.3
56	Denmark	6.7	91	French Guiana	5.3	126	Faroe Islands	4.3
57	Chile	6.5	92	Hungary	5.3	127	Grenada	4.3
58	Isle of Man	6.5	93	Netherlands	5.3	128	Swaziland	4.3
59	Azerbaijan	6.4	94	Czech Republic	5.2	129	El Salvador	4.2
60	Israel	6.4	95	Germany	5.2	130	Martinique	4.2
61	Japan	6.4	96	Gibraltar	5.2	131	Slovenia	4.2
62	Portugal	6.4	97	Kiribati	5.2	132	Saint Vincent and the Grenadines	4.2
63	Belize	6.3	98	Netherlands Antilles	5.2			
64	Luxembourg	6.3	99	Belgium	5.1	133	Peru	4.1
65	Ecuador	6.2	100	Macau	5.1	134	Cape Verde	3.8
66	Malta	6.2	101	Slovakia	5.1	135	Dominican Republic	3.6
67	New Zealand	6.2	102	Brazil	5.0	136	Paraguay	3.6
68	Uruguay	6.2	103	Croatia	5.0	137	South Africa	3.6
69	Jamaica	6.1	104	New Caledonia	5.0	138	Sweden	3.4
70	Nauru	6.1	105	Antigua and Barbuda	4.9	139	Dominica	3.3
71	Argentina	6.0	106	Georgia	4.9	140	Nicaragua	3.3
72	Australia	6.0	107	Honduras	4.9	141	Saint Lucia	3.2
73	Lithuania	6.0	108	Réunion	4.9	142	Qatar	2.8
74	Tunisia	6.0	109	Bolivia	4.8	143	United Arab Emirates	2.7
75	French Polynesia	5.9	110	France	4.8	144	Rwanda	2.6
76	Greece	5.9	111	Norway	4.8	145	Colombia	2.3
77	Hong Kong	5.9	112	Spain	4.8	146	Togo	2.3
78	Guernsey	5.8	113	Guadeloupe	4.7	147	Andorra	2.0
79	Kyrgyzstan	5.8	114	Guatemala	4.7	148	Botswana	1.5
80	Switzerland	5.8	115	Italy	4.7			
81	Algeria	5.7	116	Samoa	4.7			

Source: World Data

3.10 Divorce Rate

There is less dispute about what is a divorce than about what is a marriage. Divorce is universally defined as the final legal dissolution of a marriage conferring on the parties the right to remarry in accordance with the laws in each country. Divorce is strictly a legal privilege that is not extended to people in consensual unions. Divorce is permitted in almost all religions except Catholicism, and there are some Catholic countries in which divorce is barred. The data are obtained from legal records.

Rank	Country/Entity	Number of Divorces per 1,000 Population	Rank	Country/Entity	Number of Divorces per 1,000 Population	Rank	Country/Entity	Number of Divorces per 1,000 Population
1	Cuba	6.0	29	Belgium	2.1	57	Croatia	1.0
2	China	4.6	30	France	2.0	58	Poland	1.0
3	Russia	4.6	31	Guadeloupe	2.0	59	Venezuela	1.0
4	United States	4.6	32	Germany	1.9	60	Cyprus	0.8
5	Belarus	4.3	33	Iceland	1.9	61	Martinique	0.8
6	Ukraine	4.0	34	Kuwait	1.8	62	Slovenia	0.8
7	Estonia	3.7	35	Luxembourg	1.8	63	Syria	0.8
8	Puerto Rico	3.7	36	Bahamas	1.7	64	Albania	0.7
9	Moldova	3.4	37	Slovakia	1.7	65	Ecuador	0.7
10	Latvia	3.2	38	Azerbaijan	1.6	66	Serbia	0.7
11	Uruguay	3.2	39	Egypt	1.6	67	Greece	0.7
12	Czech Republic	3.0	40	Israel	1.6	68	Mauritius	0.7
13	United Kingdom	3.0	41	Romania	1.5	69	Spain	0.7
14	Lithuania	2.8	42	Uzbekistan	1.5	70	Bermuda	0.6
15	Australia	2.7	43	Barbados	1.4	71	Brazil	0.6
16	Canada	2.7	44	Japan	1.4	72	Chile	0.5
17	Finland	2.7	45	Singapore	1.4	73	El Salvador	0.5
18	Kazakhstan	2.7	46	Turkmenistan	1.4	74	Iran	0.5
19	New Zealand	2.7	47	Dominican Republic	1.3	75	Jamaica	0.5
20	Norway	2.7	48	Reunion	1.3	76	Libya	0.5
21	Netherlands Antilles	2.6	49	Bahrain	1.2	77	Turkey	0.5
22	Denmark	2.5	50	Jordan	1.2	78	Italy	0.4
23	Sweden	2.5	51	Kyrgyzstan	1.2	79	Mexico	0.4
24	Suriname	2.5	52	Portugal	1.2	80	Macedonia	0.3
25	Austria	2.3	53	South Korea	1.2	81	Guatemala	0.2
26	Hungary	2.3	54	Brunei	1.1	82	Nicaragua	0.2
27	Netherlands	2.2	55	Costa Rica	1.1			
28	Switzerland	2.2	56	United Arab Emirates	1.1			

Source: World Data

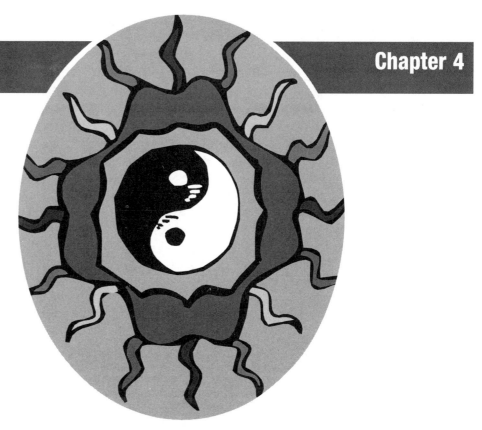

Chapter 4

Race and Religion

According to the *World Christian Encyclopedia* edited by David Barrett, George Thomas Kurian, and Todd Johnson, there are more than 27,000 religions, cults, and sects in the world. Of these, only six may be called world religions, that is, they have a sizable number of adherents in more than two countries: Christianity, Islam, Hinduism, Buddhism, Confucianism, and Judaism. Almost no country includes religious affiliations in its national censuses. The data are therefore collected from the religious groups themselves and are more likely than not to suffer from inflated numbers. Because religion is idiosyncratic it is difficult to measure the depth or intensity of one's faith, and religious censuses may not reflect the state of religious beliefs. But the data do give a broad picture of the religious landscape in an age when some observers expected that religion would die out.

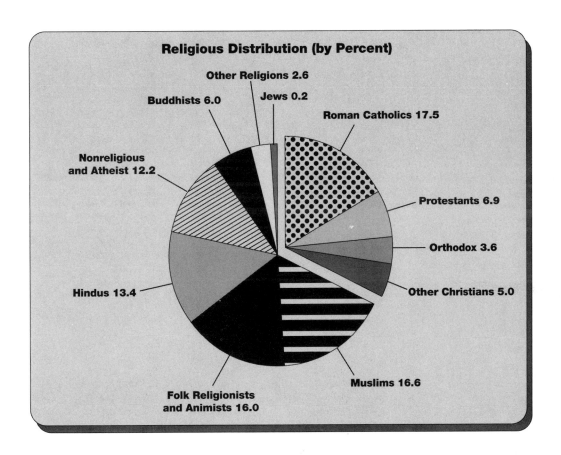

Religious Distribution (by Percent)

Other Religions 2.6
Buddhists 6.0
Jews 0.2
Roman Catholics 17.5
Nonreligious and Atheist 12.2
Protestants 6.9
Orthodox 3.6
Other Christians 5.0
Hindus 13.4
Muslims 16.6
Folk Religionists and Animists 16.0

Religious Distribution

Christians	33.0	Folk Religionists and Animists	16.0
Roman Catholics	17.5	Hindus	13.4
Protestants	6.9	Nonreligious and Atheists	12.2
Orthodox	3.6	Buddhists	6.0
Other	5.0	Other	2.6
Muslims	16.6	Jews	0.2

Source: Encyclopedia Britannica

Ethnic homogeneity is generally considered a source of national strength. Consider Japan and China, which, for the most part, have unique mono-cultures. But ethnic homogeneity is often achieved at great cost and through brutal persecution of minorities. The bloodstained history of Turkey is one example. Turks, who moved into Asia Minor and Anatolia only about six centuries ago, have managed to kill or forcibly convert the original inhabitants of the land, suppress the Kurds, massacre the Armenians, and wipe out the Greeks. Ironically, developed societies in the West are moving toward ethnic pluralism (either voluntarily or involuntarily because of labor shortages), while traditional societies in Asia and Africa are moving toward ethnic homogeneity. When mixed with religious and linguistic chauvinism, the quest for ethnic homogeneity may prove to be a bloody one.

Rank	Country/Entity	Ethnic Homogeneity by Percentage	Rank	Country/Entity	Ethnic Homogeneity by Percentage	Rank	Country/Entity	Ethnic Homogeneity by Percentage
1	North Korea	100	44	Costa Rica	90	87	India	72
2	South Korea	100	45	Denmark	90	88	Uzbekistan	71
3	Algeria	99	46	Egypt	90	89	Zimbabwe	71
4	Austria	99	47	France	90	90	Cape Verde	70
5	Iceland	99	48	Honduras	90	91	Georgia	70
6	Japan	99	49	Hungary	90	92	Madagascar	70
7	Lesotho	99	50	Ireland	90	93	Panama	70
8	Morocco	99	51	Italy	90	94	Nicaragua	69
9	Norway	99	52	Malta	90	95	Mauritius	68
10	Portugal	99	53	Mongolia	90	96	Macedonia	67
11	Yemen	99	54	Rwanda	90	97	Venezuela	67
12	Bangladesh	98	55	Saudi Arabia	90	98	Moldova	65
13	Greece	98	56	Syria	90	99	Switzerland	65
14	Jordan	98	57	Romania	89	100	Tajikistan	65
15	Poland	98	58	Andorra	88	101	Brunei	64
16	Taiwan	98	59	New Zealand	88	102	Yugoslavia	63
17	Tunisia	98	60	Comoros	86	103	Estonia	62
18	Turkey	98	61	Slovakia	86	104	Djibouti	60
19	Armenia	97	62	Vietnam	86	105	Mexico	60
20	Libya	97	63	Bulgaria	85	106	Uganda	60
21	Swaziland	97	64	Nepal	85	107	Malaysia	59
22	Netherlands	96	65	Somalia	85	108	Colombia	58
23	Botswana	95	66	Sweden	85	109	Guatemala	56
24	Chile	95	67	Australia	84	110	Niger	56
25	Czech Republic	95	68	Burundi	84	111	Brazil	55
26	Germany	95	69	Israel	83	112	Ecuador	55
27	Haiti	95	70	United States	83	113	Kyrgyzstan	52
28	Lebanon	95	71	Russia	82	114	Sudan	52
29	Liberia	95	72	United Kingdom	82	115	Cuba	51
30	Paraguay	95	73	Lithuania	80	116	Guyana	51
31	Puerto Rico	95	74	Luxembourg	80	117	Iran	51
32	Spain	95	75	Belarus	78	118	Latvia	51
33	Argentina	94	76	Croatia	78	119	Afghanistan	50
34	El Salvador	94	77	Cyprus	78	120	Bhutan	50
35	Finland	93	78	Jamaica	76	121	Eritrea	50
36	Solomon Islands	93	79	Singapore	76	122	Laos	50
37	China	92	80	Iraq	75	123	Mali	50
38	Philippines	91	81	South Africa	75	124	Namibia	50
39	Slovenia	91	82	Thailand	75	125	Fiji	49
40	Albania	90	83	Sri Lanka	74	126	Belgium	48
41	Azerbaijan	90	84	Dominican Republic	73	127	Congo, Rep. of	48
42	Bahrain	90	85	Turkmenistan	73	128	Indonesia	45
43	Cambodia	90	86	Ukraine	73	129	Malawi	45

Rank	Country/Entity	Ethnic Homogeneity by Percentage	Rank	Country/Entity	Ethnic Homogeneity by Percentage	Rank	Country/Entity	Ethnic Homogeneity by Percentage
130	Kuwait	45	143	Angola	37	156	Côte d'Ivoire	23
131	Peru	45	144	Suriname	37	157	Kenya	21
132	Ghana	44	145	Senegal	36	158	Nigeria	20
133	Trinidad and Tobago	43	146	Gabon	35	159	United Arab Emirates	19
134	Gambia	42	147	Guinea	35	160	Equatorial Guinea	15
135	Kazakhstan	41	148	Central African Republic	34	161	Mozambique	15
136	Belize	40	149	Cameroon	31	162	Burkina	10
137	Bosnia and Herzegovina	40	150	Bolivia	30	163	Papua New Guinea	10
138	Canada	40	151	Guinea-Bissau	30	164	Togo	10
139	Ethiopia	40	152	Sierra Leone	30	165	Congo, Dem. Rep of	5
140	Mauritania	40	153	Benin	25	166	Tanzania	5
141	Oman	40	154	Pakistan	25	167	Zambia	5
142	Qatar	40	155	Chad	24			

Source: World Factbook

4.3 Christians

Christianity is perhaps the only true world religion because it has adherents and churches in virtually every country in the world. The Christian presence is truly universal, with only six countries in the world without native Christians: Saudi Arabia, Yemen, Maldives, Afghanistan, Comoros, and Mauritania. Christians form the majority of the population in 123 of 191 countries. Although historically Christianity is perceived as a Western religion, its present strength lies in the developing world, especially in Africa and Latin America, where many Christian churches are experiencing a revival. Nearly 29 percent of the world Christian population lives in Europe, 16 percent in North America, 27 percent in South America, 16 percent in Africa, and 10 percent in Asia.

Rank	Country/Entity	Percentage of Total Population	Rank	Country/Entity	Percentage of Total Population	Rank	Country/Entity	Percentage of Total Population
1	Holy See	100.0	25	São Tomé and Príncipe	95.8	49	Tonga	92.9
2	Malta	98.3	26	Palau	95.7	50	Finland	92.8
3	Faeroe Islands	98.1	27	Solomon Islands	95.7	51	Bermuda	92.7
4	Cook Islands	97.8	28	Croatia	95.2	52	Portugal	92.4
5	Guatemala	97.7	29	Dominican Republic	95.2	53	Bahamas	92.3
6	Paraguay	97.7	30	Cape Verde	95.1	54	Namibia	92.3
7	Ecuador	97.6	31	Papua New Guinea	95.1	55	San Marino	92.2
8	El Salvador	97.7	32	Dominica	94.8	56	Slovenia	92.1
9	Poland	97.4	33	Saint Kitts	94.8	57	Burundi	92.1
10	Iceland	97.2	34	Venezuela	94.8	58	Denmark	91.6
11	Ireland	97.2	35	Greece	94.7	59	Anguilla	91.5
12	Peru	97.2	36	Kiribati	94.4	60	Brazil	91.4
13	Barbados	97.0	37	Norway	94.3	61	Congo, Rep. of	91.1
14	Grenada	97.0	38	Cyprus	94.2	62	Lesotho	91.1
15	Honduras	97.0	39	Angola	94.1	63	Belize	90.8
16	Puerto Rico	97.0	40	Bolivia	94.1	64	Gabon	90.6
17	Seychelles	96.9	41	Antigua	93.9	65	Austria	89.8
18	Colombia	96.7	42	Luxembourg	93.9	66	Philippines	89.7
19	Costa Rica	96.6	43	Spain	93.6	67	Tuvalu	89.3
20	Samoa	96.6	44	Andorra	93.4	68	Chile	89.2
21	Mexico	96.3	45	Monaco	93.2	69	Saint Vincent and the Grenadines	89.1
22	Aruba	96.2	46	Liechtenstein	93.0			
23	Saint Lucia	96.1	47	Vanuatu	93.0	70	Uganda	88.7
24	Haiti	95.8	48	Argentina	92.9	71	Equatorial Guinea	88.4

Rank	Country/Entity	Percentage of Total Population	Rank	Country/Entity	Percentage of Total Population	Rank	Country/Entity	Percentage of Total Population
72	Switzerland	88.4	114	Ethiopia	57.7	156	Syria	7.8
73	Belgium	88.3	115	Russia	57.4	157	Brunei	7.7
74	Panama	88.2	116	Fiji	56.8	158	China	7.1
75	Romania	88.0	117	Ghana	55.4	159	Taiwan	6.3
76	Lithuania	87.6	118	Cameroon	54.2	160	India	6.2
77	Hungary	87.3	119	Lebanon	53.0	161	Israel	5.8
78	Swaziland	86.9	120	Guyana	51.0	162	Senegal	5.5
79	Slovakia	85.6	121	Eritrea	50.5	163	Oman	4.9
80	United States	84.7	122	Suriname	50.4	164	Azerbaijan	4.6
81	French Guiana	84.6	123	Tanzania	50.4	165	Djibouti	4.5
82	Jamaica	84.1	124	Madagascar	49.5	166	Jordan	4.1
83	Armenia	84.0	125	Nigeria	45.9	167	Guinea	4.0
84	New Zealand	83.5	126	Congo, Dem. Rep. of	45.5	168	Gambia	3.9
85	South Africa	83.1	127	Cuba	44.5	169	Saudi Arabia	3.7
86	Ukraine	83.0	128	Togo	42.6	170	Japan	3.6
87	Rwanda	82.7	129	South Korea	40.8	171	Iraq	3.2
88	United Kingdom	82.6	130	Liberia	39.3	172	Libya	3.1
89	Zambia	82.4	131	Mozambique	38.4	173	Pakistan	2.5
90	Italy	82.1	132	Albania	35.4	174	Nepal	2.4
91	Bulgaria	81.0	133	Bosnia	35.0	175	Turkmenistan	2.3
92	Netherlands	80.4	134	Mauritius	32.6	176	Thailand	2.2
93	Canada	79.5	135	Côte d'Ivoire	31.8	177	Laos	2.1
94	Australia	79.3	136	Benin	28.0	178	North Korea	2.1
95	Kenya	79.3	137	Chad	22.8	179	Tajikistan	2.1
96	Malawi	76.8	138	Burkina	16.7	180	Mali	2.0
97	Germany	75.8	139	Kazakhstan	16.7	181	Uzbekistan	1.7
98	Nauru	75.0	140	Sudan	16.7	182	Somalia	1.4
99	France	70.7	141	Egypt	15.1	183	Mongolia	1.3
100	Belarus	70.3	142	Guinea-Bissau	13.2	184	Comoros	1.2
101	Moldova	68.8	143	Indonesia	13.1	185	Cambodia	1.1
102	Sweden	67.9	144	Kuwait	12.7	186	Bangladesh	0.7
103	Serbia	67.9	145	Singapore	12.3	187	Bhutan	0.5
104	Central African Republic	67.8	146	Sierra Leone	11.5	188	Turkey	0.5
105	Zimbabwe	67.5	147	United Arab Emirates	11.1	189	Algeria	0.3
106	Latvia	67.9	148	Bahrain	10.5	190	Iran	0.3
107	Uruguay	65.3	149	Kyrgyzstan	10.4	191	Afghanistan	0.0
108	Trinidad and Tobago	64.6	150	Qatar	10.4	192	Maldives	0.0
109	Macedonia	63.7	151	Sri Lanka	9.4	193	Mauritania	0.0
110	Estonia	63.5	152	Palestine	8.6	194	Morocco	0.0
111	Czech Republic	63.0	153	Malaysia	8.3	195	Niger	0.0
112	Georgia	62.2	154	Myanmar (Burma)	8.3	196	Tunisia	0.0
113	Botswana	59.9	155	Vietnam	8.3	197	Yemen	0.0

Source: World Christian Encyclopedia

4.4 Catholics

Although Christians are ranked elsewhere, the Catholic Church deserves special consideration. It is the largest single religious body in the world, and it is also the most organized. Historically, Catholics are baptized just after birth and confirmed after childhood. Once their names are entered in the parish register, they remain listed as Catholics until death. This practice varies from that of Protestants, many of whom list only active communicants as members. Virtually all of Latin America is Catholic. The Catholic Church is also an efficient collector of statistics, and its *Annuario* is an outstanding publication.

Rank	Country/Entity	Percentage of Total Population	Rank	Country/Entity	Percentage of Total Population	Rank	Country/Entity	Percentage of Total Population
1	Italy	99.5	31	Austria	85.0	61	French Polynesia	30.0
2	Spain	99.0	32	Cuba	85.0	62	Kenya	28.0
3	Guam	98.0	33	Panama	85.0	63	Tokelau	28.0
4	Malta	98.0	34	Puerto Rico	85.0	64	United States	28.0
5	Saint Pierre and Miquelon	98.0	35	Philippines	83.0	65	Mauritius	26.0
6	Luxembourg	97.0	36	Aruba	82.0	66	Central African Republic	25.0
7	Portugal	97.0	37	Haiti	80.0	67	Suriname	22.8
8	Slovenia	96.0	38	Dominica	77.0	68	Papua New Guinea	22.0
9	Venezuela	96.0	39	Croatia	76.5	69	American Samoa	20.0
10	Bolivia	95.0	40	Belgium	75.0	70	Malawi	20.0
11	Colombia	95.0	41	El Salvador	75.0	71	Bahamas	19.0
12	Costa Rica	95.0	42	Gibraltar	74.0	72	Solomon Islands	19.0
13	Dominican Republic	95.0	43	Hungary	67.5	73	United Kingdom	16.0
14	Ecuador	95.0	44	Uruguay	66.0	74	Bosnia	15.0
15	Guadeloupe	95.0	45	Rwanda	65.0	75	New Zealand	15.0
16	Martinique	95.0	46	Belize	62.0	76	Vanuatu	15.0
17	Monaco	95.0	47	Burundi	62.0	77	Norfolk Island	11.7
18	Nicaragua	95.0	48	Slovakia	60.3	78	Albania	10.0
19	Poland	95.0	49	New Caledonia	60.0	79	Christmas Island	8.2
20	Reunion	94.0	50	Kiribati	52.6	80	Romania	6.0
21	Ireland	93.0	51	Congo, Rep. of	50.0	81	Jamaica	5.0
22	Argentina	90.0	52	Switzerland	47.6	82	Barbados	4.0
23	Brazil	90.0	53	Canada	46.0	83	Macedonia	4.0
24	France	90.0	54	Czech Republic	39.2	84	Serbia	4.0
25	Paraguay	90.0	55	Angola	38.0	85	Norway	3.8
26	Saint Lucia	90.0	56	Germany	37.0	86	Anguilla	3.0
27	Seychelles	90.0	57	Netherlands	36.0	87	Indonesia	3.0
28	Chile	89.0	58	Virgin Islands	34.0	88	Sweden	1.5
29	Mexico	80.0	59	Uganda	33.0	89	Burma	1.0
30	Liechtenstein	87.3	60	Trinidad and Tobago	32.2	90	Bulgaria	0.5

Source: World Christian Encyclopedia

Islam is the second largest religion in the world, both in the number of adherents (about one billion) and in the number of countries (forty-one) where it is professed by the majority of the population. Islam is an expansionary religion whose symbol is the sword. Along with its strict legal code known as the *Sharia*, Islam is distinguished by a number of factors, particularly its approval of polygamy (Muhammad himself had thirteen wives in addition to numerous concubines), its easy divorce laws, and its straightforward theology.

Rank	Country/Entity	Percentage of Total Population	Rank	Country/Entity	Percentage of Total Population	Rank	Country/Entity	Percentage of Total Population
1	Maldives	99.2	41	Indonesia	54.7	81	Uganda	5.2
2	Mauritania	99.1	42	Burkina Faso	48.6	82	Mongolia	4.8
3	Yemen	98.9	43	Malaysia	47.7	83	Gabon	4.6
4	Tunisia	98.9	44	Sierra Leone	45.9	84	Panama	4.4
5	Morocco	98.3	45	Eritrea	44.7	85	Germany	4.4
6	Somalia	98.3	46	Nigeria	43.9	86	Equatorial Guinea	4.1
7	Afghanistan	98.1	47	Kazakhstan	42.7	87	Nepal	3.9
8	Comoros	98.0	48	Lebanon	42.4	88	Netherlands	3.8
9	Turkey	97.2	49	Guinea-Bissau	39.9	89	Belgium	3.6
10	Algeria	96.7	50	Albania	38.8	90	Greece	3.3
11	Libya	96.1	51	Tanzania	31.8	91	Cape Verde	2.8
12	Pakistan	96.1	52	Ethiopia	30.4	92	Liechtenstein	2.7
13	Iraq	96.0	53	Côte d'Ivoire	30.1	93	Switzerland	2.7
14	Iran	95.6	54	Macedonia	28.3	94	Myanmar (Burma)	2.4
15	Djibouti	94.1	55	Cameroon	21.2	95	South Africa	2.4
16	Saudi Arabia	93.7	56	Benin	20.0	96	Cambodia	2.3
17	Jordan	93.5	57	Ghana	19.7	97	Croatia	2.3
18	Niger	90.7	58	Georgia	19.3	98	Sweden	2.3
19	Syria	89.3	59	Togo	18.9	99	Austria	2.2
20	Senegal	87.6	60	Singapore	18.4	100	Israel	2.0
21	Oman	87.4	61	Mauritius	16.9	101	Madagascar	2.0
22	Gambia	86.9	62	Serbia (incl. Kosovo)	16.2	102	United Kingdom	2.0
23	Bangladesh	85.8	63	Liberia	16.0	103	Ukraine	1.7
24	Egypt	84.4	64	Central African Republic	15.6	104	Saint Vincent	1.5
25	Azerbaijan	83.7	65	Malawi	14.8	105	China	1.5
26	Tajikistan	83.6	66	Suriname	13.9	106	United States	1.5
27	Kuwait	83.0	67	India	12.1	107	Burundi	1.4
28	Qatar	82.7	68	Bulgaria	11.9	108	Argentina	1.3
29	Bahrain	82.4	69	Mozambique	10.5	109	Congo, Rep. of	1.3
30	Mali	81.9	70	Sir Lanka	9.0	110	Denmark	1.3
31	Turkmenistan	87.2	71	Guyana	8.1	111	Romania	1.3
32	Uzbekistan	76.2	72	Rwanda	7.9	112	Australia	1.2
33	United Arab Emirates	75.6	73	Russia	7.6	113	Italy	1.2
34	Palestine	73.5	74	Kenya	7.3	114	Congo, Dem. Rep. of	1.1
35	Sudan	70.3	75	France	7.1	115	Zambia	1.1
36	Guinea	67.3	76	Fiji	6.9	116	Canada	1.0
37	Brunei	64.4	77	Trinidad and Tobago	6.8	117	Luxembourg	1.0
38	Kyrgyzstan	60.8	78	Thailand	6.8	118	Norway	1.0
39	Bosnia	60.0	79	Philippines	6.2			
40	Chad	59.1	80	Moldova	5.5			

Source: World Christian Encyclopedia

4.6 Jews

Jews are among the most widely dispersed communities in the world, and the word "diaspora" has been applied most properly to their dispersion, which began shortly after the destruction of the Temple by Emperor Titus in 70 A.D. In succeeding waves, known as galut in Hebrew, they first reached northern Africa and Spain, then Russia and northern Europe, and finally the Americas, where the first Sephardic Jews are believed to have arrived soon after the Spaniards. Isolated groups of Jews are also believed to have migrated to Cochin in India and even as far as China, where their presence was recorded by medieval travelers.

Their present concentration in North America and Israel, which was established in 1948, is a much later phenomenon and is the product of what might be called remigration as a result of persecution. Jews are among the few communities that succeeded—for hundreds and even thousands of years—in maintaining their sense of nationhood without a home nation. The impact of Jewish presence in a country cannot be measured adequately by numbers alone because their many contributions have had a vastly disproportionate imprint in almost every country in which they have resided.

Rank	Country/Entity	Percentage of Total Population	Rank	Country/Entity	Percentage of Total Population	Rank	Country/Entity	Percentage of Total Population
1	Israel	82	6	Uruguay	2	11	Bulgaria	0.8
2	West Bank	12	7	Moldova	1.5	12	Turkey	0.2
3	Luxembourg	3	8	Algeria	1	13	Morocco	0.2
4	Argentina	2	9	France	1			
5	United States	2	10	Tunisia	1			

Source: World Christian Encyclopedia

4.7 Hindus

Until the end of the nineteenth century, Hindus were restricted almost entirely to the Indian subcontinent. Upper-class Hindus were barred by Vedic injunctions from crossing the sea, let alone emigrating to other countries. The British who ruled India until 1947 had other ideas. They viewed Indians as hard workers who caused little political trouble. As a result, they began transporting Indians to many of their possessions, including Fiji, Guyana, Mauritius, Trinidad, and Tobago. So many

came and raised families that in all of these places Indians became the majority group. Most of these immigrants were lower-class Hindus. After World War II, a second wave of immigration brought Hindus to the shores of Great Britain, the United States, and Canada. Most of them were educated professionals. The percentage of people of Western origin practicing any form of Hinduism is minuscule.

Rank	Country/Entity	Percentage of Total Population	Rank	Country/Entity	Percentage of Total Population	Rank	Country/Entity	Percentage of Total Population
1	Nepal	90	6	Suriname	27.4	11	Guadeloupe	5
2	India	83	7	Bhutan	25	12	Martinique	5
3	Mauritius	52	8	Trinidad and Tobago	24.3	13	Indonesia	2
4	Fiji	42	9	Bangladesh	16	14	Thailand	0.5
5	Guyana	33	10	Sri Lanka	15			

Source: World Christian Encyclopedia

Chapter 5

Politics and International Relations

5.1 Age of Nations

If the 191 nations of the world were divided into younger nations and older nations, surprisingly three-fourths would fall into the former category, because they were founded in the twentieth century. Only sixteen, including the United States, were founded before 1800. Most of the younger nations have had an existence as part of colonial empires, but they became nations in the modern sense only within the last 100 years. In the rankings below, the age of nations is determined by unbroken independence and systemic continuity. Thus, Egypt, Israel, and India, although historic civilizations, became nations only recently. Some European nations can trace their history back over a millennium, while most of Latin America became independent in the nineteenth century.

Rank	Country/Entity	Date Formed	Rank	Country/Entity	Date Formed	Rank	Country/Entity	Date Formed
1	China	1253 B.C.	47	Norway	June 7, 1905	93	Guinea	Oct. 2, 1958
2	Ethiopia	1000 B.C.	48	Iran	Oct. 7, 1906	94	Cameroon	Jan. 1, 1960
3	Japan	660 B.C.	49	New Zealand	Sept. 26, 1907	95	Zimbabwe	Apr. 18, 1960
4	Denmark	800	50	Bulgaria	Oct. 5, 1908	96	Togo	Apr. 27, 1960
5	Sweden	836	51	Bhutan	Mar. 24, 1910	97	Madagascar	June 26, 1960
6	France	Aug. 843	52	South Africa	May 31, 1910	98	Zaire	June 30, 1960
7	San Marino	855	53	Albania	Nov. 28, 1912	99	Somalia	July 1, 1960
8	Uganda	Oct. 9, 1062	54	Argentina	July 9, 1916	100	Benin	Aug. 1, 1960
9	United Kingdom	Oct. 14, 1066	55	Finland	Dec. 6, 1917	101	Niger	Aug. 3, 1960
10	Portugal	1140	56	Austria	Oct. 13, 1918	102	Burkina	Aug. 5, 1960
11	Andorra	Dec 6. 1288	57	Poland	Nov. 10, 1918	103	Côte d'Ivoire	Aug. 7, 1960
12	Thailand	1350	58	Hungary	Nov. 16, 1918	104	Chad	Aug. 11, 1960
13	Spain	1492	59	Yemen	Dec. 1918	105	Central African	Aug. 13, 1960
14	Switzerland	Sept. 22, 1499	60	Yugoslavia	Dec. 1, 1918		Republic	
15	Nepal	Nov. 13, 1769	61	Afghanistan	Aug. 19, 1919	106	Congo, Rep. of	Aug. 15, 1960
16	United States	July 4, 1776	62	Ireland	Dec. 6, 1921	107	Cyprus	Aug. 16, 1960
17	Haiti	Jan. 1, 1804	63	Egypt	Feb. 28, 1922	108	Gabon	Aug. 17, 1960
18	Liechtenstein	July 12, 1806	64	Turkey	Oct. 29, 1923	109	Senegal	Aug. 20, 1960
19	Colombia	July 20, 1810	65	Mongolia	Mar. 13, 1931	110	Malta	Sept. 21, 1960
20	Mexico	Sept. 16, 1810	66	Saudi Arabia	Sept. 23, 1932	111	Mali	Sept. 22, 1960
21	Chile	Sept. 16, 1810	67	Iraq	Oct. 3, 1932	112	Nigeria	Oct. 1, 1960
22	Paraguay	May 14, 1811	68	Lebanon	Nov. 26, 1941	113	Mauritania	Nov. 28, 1960
23	Venezuela	July 5, 1811	69	Iceland	June 17, 1944	114	Sierra Leone	April 27, 1961
24	Netherlands	Mar. 30, 1814	70	Indonesia	Aug. 17, 1945	115	Kuwait	June 19, 1961
25	Peru	July 28, 1821	71	Vietnam	Sept. 2, 1945	116	Tanzania	Dec. 9, 1961
26	Costa Rica	Sept. 15, 1821	72	Taiwan	Oct. 25, 1945	117	Samoa	Jan. 1962
27	Guatemala	Sept. 15, 1821	73	Syria	April 17, 1946	118	Burundi	July 1, 1962
28	Ecuador	May 24, 1822	74	Jordan	May 25, 1946	119	Rwanda	July 1, 19162
29	Brazil	Sept. 7, 1822	75	Philippines	July 4, 1946	120	Algeria	July 5, 1962
30	Bolivia	Aug. 6, 1825	76	Pakistan	Aug. 14, 1947	121	Jamaica	Aug. 6, 1962
31	Uruguay	Aug. 25, 1828	77	India	Aug. 15, 1947	122	Trinidad and	Aug. 31, 1962
32	Greece	Feb. 3, 1830	78	Myanmar (Burma)	Jan. 4, 1948		Tobago	
33	Belgium	Oct. 4, 1830	79	Sri Lanka	Feb. 4, 1948	123	Kenya	Dec. 12, 1963
34	Nicaragua	April 30, 1838	80	Israel	May 14, 1948	124	Malawi	July 6, 1964
35	Honduras	Nov. 5, 1838	81	South Korea	Aug. 15, 1948	125	Zambia	Oct. 24, 1964
36	El Salvador	Jan. 30, 1841	82	North Korea	Sept. 9, 1948	126	Gambia	Feb. 18, 1965
37	Dominican Republic	Feb. 27, 1844	83	Oman	Dec. 20, 1951	127	Maldives	July 26, 1965
38	Liberia	July 26, 1847	84	Libya	Dec. 24, 1951	128	Singapore	Aug. 9, 1965
39	Monaco	Feb. 2, 1861	85	Laos	Oct. 23, 1953	129	Guyana	May 26, 1966
40	Italy	Mar. 17, 1861	86	Cambodia	Nov. 9, 1953	130	Botswana	Sept. 30, 1966
41	Luxembourg	May 10, 1867	87	Germany	May 5, 1955	131	Lesotho	Oct. 4, 1966
42	Canada	July 1, 1867	88	Sudan	Jan. 1956	132	Barbados	Nov. 30, 1966
43	Romania	May 21, 1877	89	Morocco	Mar. 2, 1956	133	Nauru	Jan. 31, 1968
44	Australia	Jan. 1, 1901	90	Tunisia	Mar. 20, 1956	134	Mauritius	Mar. 12, 1968
45	Cuba	May 20, 1902	91	Ghana	Mar. 6, 1957	135	Swaziland	Sept. 6, 1968
46	Panama	Nov. 3, 1903	92	Malaysia	Aug. 31, 1957	136	Equatorial Guinea	Oct. 12, 1968

Rank	Country/Entity	Date Formed	Rank	Country/Entity	Date Formed	Rank	Country/Entity	Date Formed
137	Tonga	June 4, 1970	154	Djibouti	June 27, 1977	170	Estonia	Aug. 20, 1991
138	Fiji	Oct. 10, 1970	155	Solomon Islands	July 7, 1978	171	Latvia	Aug. 21, 1991
139	Bangladesh	Mar. 26, 1971	156	Tuvalu	Oct. 1, 1978	172	Ukraine	Aug. 24, 1991
140	Bahrain	Aug. 15, 1971	157	Dominica	Nov. 3, 1978	173	Belarus	Aug. 25, 1991
141	Qatar	Sept. 3, 1971	158	Saint Lucia	Feb. 2, 1979	174	Moldova	Aug. 27, 1991
142	United Arab Emirates	Dec. 2, 1971	159	Kiribati	July 12, 1979	175	Azerbaijan	Aug. 30, 1991
143	Bahamas	July 10, 1973	160	Saint Vincent and the Grenadines	Oct. 27, 1979	176	Kyrgyzstan	Aug. 31, 1991
144	Grenada	Feb. 7, 1974				177	Uzbekistan	Aug. 31, 1991
145	Guinea-Bissau	Sept. 10, 1974	161	Vanuatu	July 30, 1980	178	Lithuania	Sept. 6, 1991
146	Mozambique	June 25, 1975	162	Belize	Sept. 21, 1981	179	Tajikistan	Sept. 9, 1991
147	Cape Verde	July 5, 1975	163	Antigua and Barbuda	Nov. 21, 1981	180	Armenia	Sept. 23, 1991
148	Comoros	July 6, 1975				181	Turkmenistan	Oct 27, 1991
149	São Tomé and Príncipe	July 12, 1975	164	Saint Kitts and Nevis	Sept. 19, 1983	182	Russia	Dec. 8, 1991
150	Papua New Guinea	Sept. 16, 1975	165	Brunei	Jan. 1, 1984	183	Kazakhstan	Dec. 16, 1991
151	Angola	Nov. 11, 1975	166	Namibia	Mar. 21, 1990	184	Bosnia	Mar. 3, 1992
152	Suriname	Nov. 25, 1975	167	Georgia	April 1, 1991	185	Macedonia	April 1992
153	Seychelles	June 29, 1976	168	Croatia	June 15, 1991	186	Czech Republic	Jan. 1, 1993
			169	Slovenia	June 25, 1991	187	Slovakia	Jan. 1, 1993
						188	Eritrea	May 24, 1994

Source: Encyclopadia Britannica

5.2 Most Powerful Nations

Decisions affecting foreign policy and international conflicts or negotiations are usually made by national leaders on the basis of their perceptions of their own power or that of others, summed up in the term *realpolitik*. Although perceptions of power are often blurred or diffuse, they contain concrete elements and ingredients that can be identified and even measured broadly. One of the most successful attempts to do so is by Ray Cline in *World Power Assessment*, in which he presents an overall conceptual methodology that incorporates military, economic, geopolitical, and psychological factors. He has also devised a calibrated scale of perceived power on which the rank of each nation can be determined. There are five basic elements in his scale: (1) Critical Mass (population plus territory); (2) Economic Capability; (3) Military Capability; (4) Strategic Purpose; and (5) National Will. The last is a mix of many intangible factors, such as ethnic cohesiveness (generally only ethnically homo-geneous nations become great powers, although the United States is apparently an exception), political stability, and a national sense of destiny. The rating adds the first three elements to form a subtotal. This subtotal is then multiplied by the combined value of the last two elements, which is labeled "Purpose and Will," to form the total.

Rank	Country/Entity	Critical Mass	Economic Capability	Military Capability	Subtotal	Purpose and Will	Total
1	United States	100	146	188	434	0.7	304
2	Russia	90	30	121	241	1.0	241
3	Brazil	80	50	3	98	1.4	137
4	Germany	30	34	13	77	1.5	116
5	Japan	44	28	5	77	1.4	108
6	Australia	50	22	1	73	1.2	88
7	China	75	23	41	139	0.6	83
8	France	28	33	21	82	0.9	74
9	United Kingdom	29	21	18	68	1.0	68
10	Canada	56	30	1	87	0.7	61
11	Indonesia	56	4	1	61	0.9	55
12	Taiwan	14	3	12	29	1.7	49
13	South Korea	20	5	8	33	1.4	46

Rank	Country/Entity	Critical Mass	Economic Capability	Military Capability	Subtotal	Purpose and Will	Total
14	Egypt	25	—	13	38	1.2	46
15	South Africa	23	9	4	36	1.1	40
16	Vietnam	28	—	11	39	1.0	39
17	Saudi Arabia	12	18	—	30	1.3	39
18	Israel	—	1	22	22	1.7	39
19	Spain	25	9	5	39	1.0	39
20	India	52	11	8	71	0.5	36
21	Italy	29	14	5	48	0.7	34
22	Argentina	31	7	2	40	0.8	32
23	Chile	15	4	—	19	1.3	25
24	Philippines	27	3	—	30	0.8	24
25	Netherlands	—	17	2	19	1.2	23
26	Pakistan	25	2	1	28	0.8	22
27	Nigeria	26	2	—	28	0.8	22
28	Mexico	27	5	—	32	0.7	22
29	Norway	15	5	1	21	1.0	21
30	North Korea	5	—	10	15	1.4	21
31	Thailand	17	2	1	20	1.0	20
32	Turkey	26	3	7	36	0.5	18
33	Iran	18	12	2	32	0.5	16
34	Syria	5	—	10	15	1.0	15
35	Iraq	5	5	7	17	0.8	14

Source: Cline, *World Power Assessment*

5.3 Corruption Index

Corruption is a clandestine industry that nets about $3.5 billion a year, much of it stocked away in Swiss vaults or other safe money havens. This industry extends to every branch of government in nondemocratic governments that have no system of public accountability. In parts of Asia and Africa, corruption is so prevalent that an ordinary citizen bribes on the average thirty-two public officials in the course of a year. Corruption has spread even to the International Olympic Committee and other honored institutions. In many countries, bribes are an accepted form of business. In almost all African countries and most Asian countries, illegal commissions are openly demanded before any project is approved or any sale is completed. In some countries, rates are published for each transaction and each level of public servant. The list extends from the lowest customs clerk to heads of state. Mobutu Sese Seko of Zaire amassed over $15 billion and President Suharto of Indonesia over $25 billion by openly stealing from their state treasuries. Based on reports of bribes paid by multinationals to government officials, the Berlin-based group Transparency International has devised a Corruption Index, with zero being the most corrupt and ten the least corrupt.

Rank	Country/Entity	Corruption Index	Rank	Country/Entity	Corruption Index	Rank	Country/Entity	Corruption Index
1	New Zealand	9.8	9	Iceland	9.1	17	France	8.4
2	United Kingdom	9.7	10	Netherlands	9.0	18	Japan	8.3
3	Liechtenstein	9.6	11	Austria	8.9	19	Hungary	8.2
4	Switzerland	9.5	12	Czech Republic	8.9	20	Monaco	8.2
5	Luxembourg	9.4	13	United States	8.8	21	Cyprus	8.1
6	Sweden	9.3	14	Finland	8.7	22	Germany	8.0
7	Canada	9.2	15	Ireland	8.6	23	Singapore	7.9
8	Denmark	9.1	16	Spain	8.5	24	Uruguay	7.8

Rank	Country/Entity	Corruption Index	Rank	Country/Entity	Corruption Index	Rank	Country/Entity	Corruption Index
25	Malta	7.7	73	Guyana	4.3	121	Laos	2.6
26	Bulgaria	7.6	74	Puerto Rico	4.3	122	Lebanon	2.5
27	Cuba	7.5	75	Uzbekistan	4.3	123	Mozambique	2.5
28	Costa Rica	7.4	76	Belarus	4.2	124	Cameroon	2.4
29	Estonia	7.3	77	Chile	4.2	125	Libya	2.4
30	Greece	7.2	78	Ethiopia	4.2	126	Swaziland	2.4
31	Slovenia	7.1	79	Georgia	4.2	127	Cape Verde	2.3
32	Croatia	7.0	80	Guatemala	4.2	128	Angola	2.2
33	Poland	6.9	81	Venezuela	4.2	129	Brunei	2.1
34	Portugal	6.8	82	Mexico	4.1	130	Comoros	2.1
35	Armenia	6.7	83	Tunisia	4.1	131	Senegal	2.1
36	Latvia	6.6	84	Ukraine	4.1	132	Benin	1.9
37	South Korea	6.6	85	Algeria	4.1	133	Grenada	1.9
38	Slovakia	6.5	86	Bahrain	4.0	134	Lesotho	1.9
39	Vietnam	6.4	87	Colombia	4.0	135	Malawi	1.9
40	Bhutan	6.3	88	Honduras	4.0	136	Burkina	1.8
41	Mongolia	6.2	89	India	3.9	137	Congo, Rep. of	1.8
42	Italy	6.1	90	Moldova	3.9	138	Namibia	1.8
43	Romania	6.0	91	Nepal	3.9	139	Turkey	1.8
44	Yugoslavia	5.9	92	Solomon Islands	3.9	140	Zambia	1.8
45	Qatar	5.8	93	Yemen	3.9	141	Central Africa Republic	1.7
46	Argentina	5.7	94	Ecuador	3.8	142	Ghana	1.6
47	Bolivia	5.6	95	Botswana	3.7	143	Togo	1.6
48	Iran	5.5	96	Lithuania	3.7	144	Tanzania	1.5
49	North Korea	5.4	97	São Tomé and Príncipe	3.7	145	Chad	1.4
50	Oman	5.3	98	Tajikistan	3.7	146	Gabon	1.4
51	Philippines	5.2	99	Azerbaijan	3.6	147	Indonesia	1.4
52	Russia	5.1	100	Burma	3.6	148	Kenya	1.4
53	Ivory	5.0	101	Samoa	3.6	149	Tonga	1.4
54	Kuwait	4.9	102	Burundi	3.5	150	Jordan	1.3
55	Papua New Guinea	4.9	103	Panama	3.5	151	Congo, Dem. Rep. of	1.3
56	Tuvalu	4.9	104	Sri Lanka	3.5	152	Haiti	1.2
57	Jamaica	4.8	105	Maldives	3.4	153	Mauritania	1.2
58	Kyrgyzstan	4.8	106	Malaysia	3.3	154	Pakistan	1.1
59	Nicaragua	4.8	107	Morocco	3.2	155	Rwanda	1.1
60	Albania	4.7	108	South Africa	3.2	156	Saudi Arabia	1.1
61	Fiji	4.7	109	United Arab Emirates	3.2	157	Sierra Leone	1.1
62	Mauritius	4.7	110	Côte d'Ivoire	3.1	158	Uganda	1.1
63	Peru	4.7	111	Syria	3.1	159	Zimbabwe	1.0
64	Taiwan	4.7	112	Egypt	3.0	160	Equatorial Guinea	1.0
65	Trinidad and Tobago	4.7	113	Mali	2.9	161	Somalia	0.9
66	Brazil	4.6	114	Seychelles	2.9	162	Sudan	0.8
67	El Salvador	4.6	115	Madagascar	2.8	163	Gambia	0.8
68	Paraguay	4.5	116	Thailand	2.8	164	Guinea	0.7
69	Turkmenistan	4.5	117	Bangladesh	2.7	165	Niger	0.6
70	Cambodia	4.4	118	Djibouti	2.7	166	Guinea-Bissau	0.6
71	Suriname	4.4	119	Kazakhstan	2.7	167	Liberia	0.5
72	Dominican Republic	4.3	120	Eritrea	2.6	168	Nigeria	0.4

Source: Transparency International

Foreign Aid and Assistance

Development assistance is money in the form of grants or concessional loans to poorer nations of the world by rich nations who belong to the Development Assistance Committee of the Organization for Economic Cooperation and Development, and international bodies, such as the United Nations and World Bank. Development assistance was originally conceived as a philanthropic act, but during the course of the Cold War, it became a means of rewarding faithful allies and keeping the less powerful nations subservient to great power interests. After the Cold War was over, many nations, including the United States, became less willing to share their wealth with poorer nations. As a result, the grant element in development assistance has been decreasing for years. The only exception to this trend is in Scandinavia, where Sweden and Norway have set a remarkable example by writing off all loans to developing nations.

5.4 Official Development Assistance per Capita

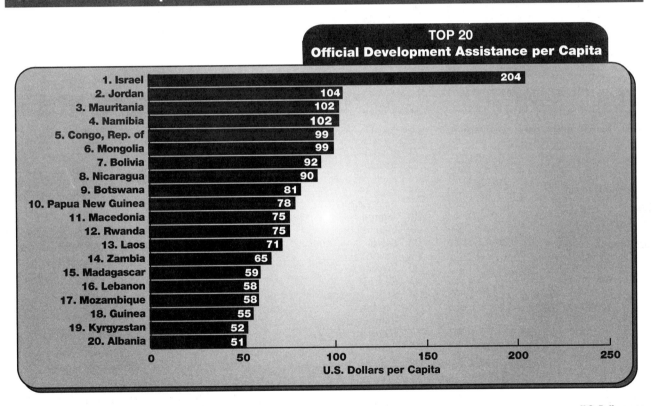

TOP 20 Official Development Assistance per Capita

Rank	Country	U.S. Dollars per Capita
1.	Israel	204
2.	Jordan	104
3.	Mauritania	102
4.	Namibia	102
5.	Congo, Rep. of	99
6.	Mongolia	99
7.	Bolivia	92
8.	Nicaragua	90
9.	Botswana	81
10.	Papua New Guinea	78
11.	Macedonia	75
12.	Rwanda	75
13.	Laos	71
14.	Zambia	65
15.	Madagascar	59
16.	Lebanon	58
17.	Mozambique	58
18.	Guinea	55
19.	Kyrgyzstan	52
20.	Albania	51

U.S. Dollars per Capita

Rank	Country/Entity	U.S. Dollars per Capita, 1997	Rank	Country/Entity	U.S. Dollars per Capita, 1997	Rank	Country/Entity	U.S. Dollars per Capita, 1997
21	El Salvador	51	30	Haiti	44	39	Malawi	34
22	Honduras	51	31	Mali	44	40	Eritrea	33
23	Senegal	49	32	Uganda	41	41	Latvia	33
24	Slovenia	49	33	Benin	39	42	Egypt	32
25	Panama	47	34	Angola	37	43	Côte d'Ivoire	31
26	Georgia	46	35	Cambodia	36	44	Chad	31
27	Lesotho	46	36	Cameroon	36	45	Tanzania	31
28	Armenia	45	37	Burkina Faso	35	46	Guatemala	29
29	Estonia	44	38	Niger	35	47	Togo	29

Rank	Country/Entity	U.S. Dollars per Capita, 1997	Rank	Country/Entity	U.S. Dollars per Capita, 1997	Rank	Country/Entity	U.S. Dollars per Capita, 1997
48	Zimbabwe	29	70	Moldova	15	92	Congo, Dem. Rep. of	4
49	Ghana	28	71	Slovakia	13	93	Indonesia	4
50	Jamaica	28	72	Syria	13	94	Ukraine	4
51	Central African Republic	27	73	Vietnam	13	95	Brazil	3
52	Lithuania	27	74	South Africa	12	96	Iran	3
53	Sierra Leone	27	75	Ethiopia	11	97	China	2
54	Bulgaria	25	76	Croatia	10	98	India	2
55	Paraguay	24	77	Czech Republic	10	99	Nigeria	2
56	Azerbaijan	23	78	Thailand	10	100	Turkmenistan	2
57	Yemen	23	79	Chile	9	101	Hong Kong	1
58	Tunisia	21	80	Dominican Republic	9	102	Kuwait	1
59	Peru	20	81	Philippines	9	103	Mexico	1
60	Burundi	19	82	Romania	9	104	Myanmar (Burma)	1
61	Nepal	19	83	Algeria	8	105	Saudi Arabia	1
62	Sri Lanka	19	84	Bangladesh	8	106	Venezuela	1
63	Morocco	17	85	Kazakhstan	8	107	Singapore	0
64	Poland	17	86	Colombia	7	108	Turkey	0
65	Tajikistan	17	87	Argentina	6	109	Costa Rica	-1
66	Uruguay	17	88	Uzbekistan	6	110	South Korea	-3
67	Hungary	16	89	Pakistan	5	111	Malaysia	-11
68	Kenya	16	90	Russia	5			
69	Ecuador	15	91	Belarus	4			

Source: OECD

5.5 Gross Official Development Assistance

Rank	Country/Entity	U.S. Dollars (millions)	Rank	Country/Entity	U.S. Dollars (millions)	Rank	Country/Entity	U.S. Dollars (millions)
1	China	2,359	31	Cameroon	424	61	Mongolia	203
2	Egypt	1,915	32	Jordan	408	62	Malaysia	202
3	India	1,595	33	Haiti	407	63	El Salvado	180
4	Indonesia	1,258	34	Napal	404	64	Namibia	180
5	Bangladesh	1,251	35	Burkina Faso	397	65	Ecuador	176
6	Vietnam	1,163	36	Algeria	389	66	Mauritania	171
7	Israel	1,066	37	Ukraine	380	67	Chad	167
8	Pakistan	1,050	38	Papua New Guinea	361	68	Colombia	166
9	Mozambique	1,039	39	Guinea	359	69	Iran	164
10	Russia	1,017	40	Romania	356	70	Georgia	162
11	Tanzania	998	41	Rwanda	350	71	Eritrea	158
12	Poland	902	42	Mali	349	72	Syria	156
13	Bosnia and Herzegovina	876	43	Zambia	349	73	Slovakia	155
14	Côte d'Ivoire	798	44	Cambodia	337	74	Tunisia	148
15	Ghana	701	45	Angola	335	75	Uzbekistan	144
16	Thailand	690	46	Brazil	329	76	Armeia	138
17	Ethiopia	648	47	Honduras	318	77	Togo	128
18	Bolivia	628	48	Yemen	310	78	Lithuania	128
19	Philippines	607	49	Niger	291	79	Cong, Dem. Rep. of	126
20	Nicaragua	562	50	Laos	281	80	Central African Republic	120
21	Morocco	528	51	Albania	242	81	Dominican Republic	120
22	South Africa	512	52	Lebanon	236	82	Iraq	115
23	Senegal	502	53	Guatemala	233	83	South Korea	109
24	Peru	501	54	Bulgaria	232	84	Botswana	106
25	Madagascar	494	55	Kyrgyzstan	216	85	Sierra Leone	106
26	Sri Lanka	490	56	Benin	210	86	Yugoslavia	106
27	Kenya	474	57	Hungary	209	87	Chile	105
28	Uganda	471	58	Sudan	209	88	Tajikistan	105
29	Czech Republic	447	59	Kazakhstan	207	89	Latvia	97
30	Malawi	434	60	Nigeria	204	90	Cuinea-Bissau	96

Rank	Country/Entity	U.S. Dollars (millions)	Rank	Country/Entity	U.S. Dollars (millions)	Rank	Country/Entity	U.S. Dollars (millions)
91	Macedonia	92	102	Gabon	45	113	Uruguay	24
92	Estonia	90	103	Mauritius	40	114	Panama	22
93	Azerbaijan	89	104	Slovenia	40	115	Jamaica	18
94	Cuba	80	105	Croatia	39	116	Turkmenistan	17
95	Argentina	77	106	Gambia	38	117	Mexico	15
96	Burundi	77	107	Venezuela	37	118	Trinidad and Tobago	14
97	Paraguay	76	108	Moldova	33	119	Turkey	14
98	Lesotho	66	109	Belarus	28	120	Libya	7
99	Congo, Rep. of	65	110	Costa Rica	27	121	Kuwait	6
100	Myanmar (Burma)	59	111	Oman	27	122	United Arab Emirates	4
101	Zimbabwe	47	112	Saudi Arabia	25	123	Singapore	2

Source: World Development Report

5.6 Refugees

Refugees were until recently a humanitarian concern and not a problem in international law. Since the 1950s, there has been a massive flow of national populations across borders and, in some cases, across oceans, both legally and illegally. Legitimate refugees generally flee religious persecution, genocide, or civil strife. The grant of asylum to refugees is now generally acknowledged as a human right by the United Nations and by a handful of nations.

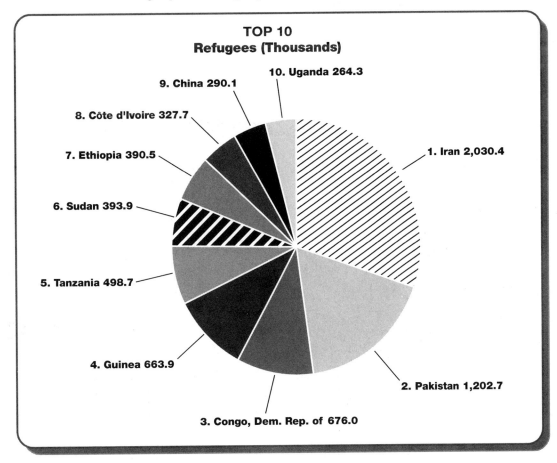

TOP 10
Refugees (Thousands)

9. China 290.1
10. Uganda 264.3
8. Côte d'Ivoire 327.7
7. Ethiopia 390.5
1. Iran 2,030.4
6. Sudan 393.9
5. Tanzania 498.7
4. Guinea 663.9
2. Pakistan 1,202.7
3. Congo, Dem. Rep. of 676.0

Rank	Country/Entity	Refugees by Country of Asylum (thousands)	Rank	Country/Entity	Refugees by Country of Asylum (thousands)	Rank	Country/Entity	Refugees by Country of Asylum (thousands)
11	India	233.4	39	Saudi Arabia	9.9	67	Dominican Republic	0.6
12	Kenya	223.6	40	Angola	9.4	68	Nicaragua	0.6
13	Algeria	190.3	41	Belize	8.5	69	Swaziland	0.6
14	Zambia	131.1	42	Nigeria	8.5	70	Zimbabwe	0.6
15	Nepal	126.8	43	Turkey	8.2	71	United Arab Emirates	0.5
16	Iraq	113.0	44	Libya	7.7	72	Chile	0.3
17	Thailand	108.0	45	Gambia	6.9	73	Botswana	0.2
18	Senegal	65.0	46	Hong Kong	6.9	74	Colombia	0.2
19	Yemen	53.5	47	Benin	6.0	75	Ecuador	0.2
20	Cameroon	46.4	48	Egypt	6.0	76	El Salvador	0.2
21	Central African Republic	36.6	49	Kuwait	3.8	77	Malaysia	0.2
22	Ghana	35.6	50	Burkina Faso	2.8	78	Mozambique	0.2
23	Mexico	34.6	51	Lebanon	2.4	79	Tunisia	0.2
24	Vietnam	34.4	52	Philippines	2.3	80	Chad	0.1
25	Bangladesh	30.7	53	Brazil	2.2	81	Honduras	0.1
26	Syria	27.8	54	Namibia	2.2	82	Indonesia	0.1
27	Niger	25.8	55	Eritrea	2.1	83	Morocco	0.1
28	Djibouti	25.1	56	Solomon Islands	2.0	84	Paraguay	0.1
29	Costa Rica	23.2	57	Cuba	1.7	85	Uruguay	0.1
30	South Africa	22.6	58	Guatemala	1.6	86	Bahamas	0.0
31	Congo, Rep. of	20.5	59	Venezuela	1.6	87	Cambodia	0.0
32	Mali	18.2	60	Malawi	1.3	88	Cyprus	0.0
33	Mauritania	15.9	61	Burundi	1.0	89	Fiji	0.0
34	Guinea-Bissau	15.4	62	Jordan	0.9	90	Jamaica	0.0
35	Sierra Leone	13.5	63	Panama	0.9	91	South Korea	0.0
36	Togo	12.6	64	Gabon	0.8	92	Singapore	0.0
37	Argentina	10.4	65	Bolivia	0.7	93	Sri Lanka	0.0
38	Papua New Guinea	10.2	66	Peru	0.7			

Source: UN High Commission for Refugees

5.7 Voter Turnout

Poor voter turnout is the Achilles heel of representative democracy. It is an exhibition of political apathy by a portion of the electorate that, to paraphrase Abraham Lincoln, results in government of, by, and for a minority of politically active people. For example, in the United States, voter turn out in presidential elections is less than 60 percent and in nonpresidential elections 40 percent, despite massive get-the-vote-out campaigns. Generally, poorer and less educated people do not vote, and there are vested interests who would prefer to keep it that way. To reverse this universal trend, some European countries have made voting compulsory subject to penalties, but even this measure has not led to higher voter turn out at the polling booth.

Rank	Country/Entity	Percentage of Voter Turnout at Last Elections for Lower or Single House	Rank	Country/Entity	Percentage of Voter Turnout at Last Elections for Lower or Single House	Rank	Country/Entity	Percentage of Voter Turnout at Last Elections for Lower or Single House
1	Turkmenistan	100	9	Iraq	94	17	Luxembourg	88
2	Vietnam	100	10	Uzbekistan	94	18	Mongolia	88
3	Laos	99	11	Cyprus	93	19	Mozambique	88
4	Cuba	98	12	Angola	91	20	New Zealand	88
5	Guyana	98	13	Belgium	91	21	Cambodia	87
6	Malta	97	14	Uruguay	91	22	Iceland	87
7	Australia	96	15	El Salvador	89	23	Seychelles	87
8	Tunisia	95	16	Indonesia	89	24	South Africa	87

Rank	Country/Entity	Percentage of Voter Turnout at Last Elections for Lower or Single House	Rank	Country/Entity	Percentage of Voter Turnout at Last Elections for Lower or Single House	Rank	Country/Entity	Percentage of Voter Turnout at Last Elections for Lower or Single House
25	Sweden	87	66	Panama	74	106	Nepal	62
26	Austria	86	67	Slovenia	74	107	Thailand	62
27	Azerbaijan	86	68	Albania	73	108	Kyrgyzstan	61
28	Chile	86	69	Honduras	73	109	Syria	61
29	Samoa	86	70	Latvia	72	110	Yemen	61
30	Ethiopia	85	71	Lesotho	72	111	Barbados	60
31	Turkey	85	72	Malaysia	72	112	Jamaica	60
32	Denmark	84	73	United Kingdom	72	113	Madagascar	60
33	Tajikistan	84	74	Côte d'Ivoire	71	114	Venezuela	60
34	Brazil	82	75	Costa Rica	71	115	Bulgaria	59
35	Italy	82	76	Croatia	71	116	Japan	59
36	Papua New Guinea	81	77	France	71	117	Macedonia	58
37	Kuwait	80	78	Bolivia	70	118	Mexico	58
38	Malawi	80	79	Estonia	70	119	Morocco	58
39	Mauritius	80	80	Canada	69	120	Djibouti	57
40	Germany	79	81	Gambia	69	121	Ukraine	57
41	Israel	79	82	Bahamas	68	122	Zimbabwe	57
42	Moldova	79	83	Ecuador	68	123	Armenia	56
43	Argentina	78	84	Finland	68	124	Central African Republic	56
44	Netherlands	78	85	Georgia	68	125	Hungary	55
45	Norway	78	86	Saint Kitts and Nevis	68	126	Lithuania	53
46	Botswana	77	87	Philippines	67	127	São Tomé and Príncipe	52
47	Cape Verde	77	88	Portugal	67	128	Chad	49
48	Iran	77	89	Suriname	67	129	United States	49
49	Nicaragua	77	90	Algeria	66	130	Egypt	48
50	Spain	77	91	Ireland	66	131	Poland	48
51	Benin	76	92	Paraguay	66	132	Jordan	47
52	Cameroon	76	93	Saint Lucia	66	133	Burkina Faso	45
53	Czech Republic	76	94	Saint Vincent and the Grenadines	66	134	Guinea-Bissau	45
54	Greece	76				135	Lebanon	44
55	Kazakhstan	76	95	Ghana	65	136	Dominican Republic	42
56	Romania	76	96	Kenya	65	137	Switzerland	42
57	Sri Lanka	76	97	Russia	65	138	Senegal	41
58	Belize	75	98	Togo	65	139	Singapore	41
59	Dominica	75	99	South Korea	64	140	Zambia	40
60	Fiji	75	100	Solomon Islands	64	141	Niger	39
61	Maldives	75	101	Peru	63	142	Colombia	36
62	Namibia	75	102	Trinidad and Tobago	63	143	Pakistan	35
63	Slovakia	75	103	Antigua and Barbuda	62	144	Haiti	31
64	Vanuatu	75	104	Grenada	62	145	Mali	22
65	Bangladesh	74	105	Guinea	62	146	Comoros	20

Source: Interparliamentary Union

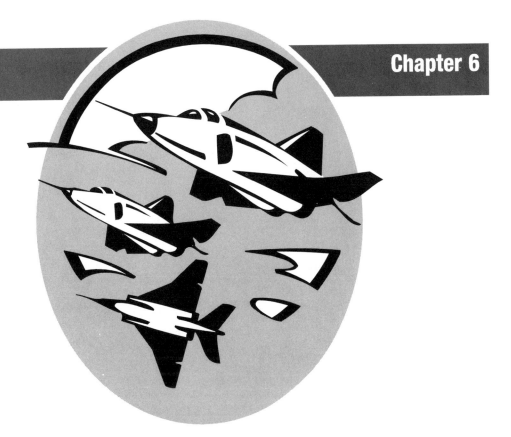

Military Power

6.1 Military Personnel

Military personnel is the strength of a nation's standing army. Some nations have conscriptions in peacetime as well as wartime, whereas other nations have voluntary armies in which men and women who wish to pursue a military career enlist. Serving in the military was previously considered a privilege for a citizen, and one of the most honorable things a person could do for one's country. There are more than a dozen nations that have no standing armies at all, either because they have good neighbors or because they fear an army-led coup. Military power generally consists of an army, navy, and air force.

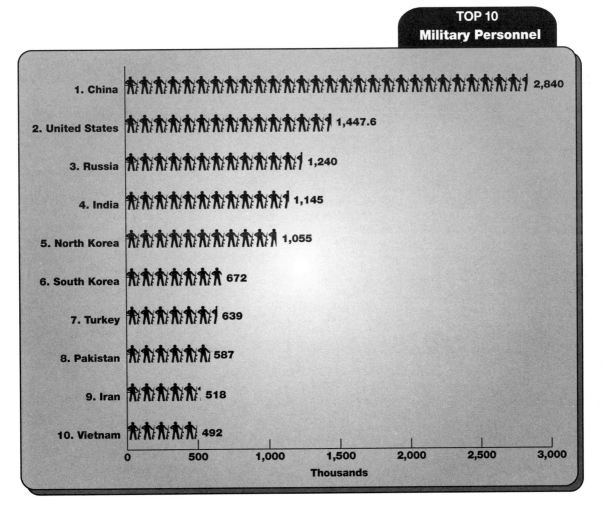

TOP 10 Military Personnel

- 1. China — 2,840
- 2. United States — 1,447.6
- 3. Russia — 1,240
- 4. India — 1,145
- 5. North Korea — 1,055
- 6. South Korea — 672
- 7. Turkey — 639
- 8. Pakistan — 587
- 9. Iran — 518
- 10. Vietnam — 492

Thousands

Rank	Country/Entity	Military Personnel, 1997 (thousands)	Rank	Country/Entity	Military Personnel, 1997 (thousands)	Rank	Country/Entity	Military Personnel, 1997 (thousands)
11	Egypt	450.0	18	Italy	325.2	25	Romania	227.0
12	Myanmar (Burma)	429.0	19	Syria	320.0	26	United Kingdom	213.8
13	Iraq	387.5	20	Brazil	314.7	27	Spain	197.5
14	Ukraine	387.4	21	Indonesia	284.0	28	Morocco	196.3
15	France	380.8	22	Thailand	266.0	29	Israel	175.0
16	Taiwan	376.0	23	Poland	241.8	30	Mexico	175.0
17	Germany	347.1	24	Japan	235.6	31	Greece	162.3

Rank	Country/Entity	Military Personnel, 1997 (thousands)	Rank	Country/Entity	Military Personnel, 1997 (thousands)	Rank	Country/Entity	Military Personnel, 1997 (thousands)
32	Colombia	146.3	72	Czech Republic	44.0	112	Djibouti	9.6
33	Cambodia	140.5	73	Oman	43.5	113	New Zealand	9.6
34	Jordan	130.0	74	Guatemala	40.7	114	Slovenia	9.6
35	Peru	125.0	75	Bosnia and Herzegovina	40.0	115	Mongolia	9.0
36	Algeria	124.0	76	Zimbabwe	39.0	116	Côte d'Ivoire	8.4
37	Bangladesh	121.0	77	Slovakia	35.8	117	Botswana	7.5
38	Sri Lanka	115.3	78	Kazakhstan	35.1	118	Mali	7.4
39	Yugoslavia	114.2	79	Tunisia	35.0	119	Guinea-Bissau	7.3
40	Malaysia	111.5	80	United Arab Emirates	35.0	120	Ghana	7.0
41	Angola	110.5	81	Tanzania	34.6	121	Tajikistan	7.0
42	Philippines	110.5	82	Norway	33.6	122	Togo	7.0
43	Saudi Arabia	105.5	83	Bolivia	33.5	123	Namibia	5.7
44	Chile	94.3	84	Denmark	32.9	124	Lithuania	5.3
45	Belarus	80.0	85	Finland	31.0	125	Niger	5.3
46	Sudan	79.7	86	Laos	29.0	126	Brunei	5.0
47	South Africa	79.4	87	El Salvador	28.4	127	Central African Republic	5.0
48	Venezuela	79.0	88	Uruguay	25.6	128	Malawi	5.0
49	Nigeria	77.0	89	Chad	25.4	129	Benin	4.8
50	Bulgaria	75.8	90	Dominican Republic	24.5	130	Gabon	4.7
51	Argentina	73.0	91	Kenya	24.2	131	Latvia	4.5
52	Singapore	70.0	92	Zambia	21.6	132	Papua New Guinea	4.3
53	Azerbaijan	66.7	93	Madagascar	21.0	133	Bhutan	4.0
54	Yemen	66.3	94	Paraguay	20.2	134	Fiji	3.6
55	Libya	65.0	95	Honduras	18.8	135	Estonia	3.5
56	Canada	61.6	96	Burundi	18.5	136	Jamaica	3.3
57	Portugal	59.3	97	Nicaragua	17.0	137	Switzerland	3.3
58	Armenia	58.6	98	Mauritania	15.7	138	Trinidad and Tobago	2.1
59	Croatia	58.0	99	Macedonia	15.4	139	Lesotho	2.0
60	Australia	57.4	100	Kuwait	15.3	140	Malta	2.0
61	Ecuador	57.1	101	Senegal	13.4	141	Guyana	1.6
62	Lebanon	55.1	102	Cameroon	13.1	142	Suriname	1.4
63	Rwanda	55.0	103	Ireland	12.7	143	Equatorial Guinea	1.3
64	Sweden	53.4	104	Kyrgyzstan	12.2	144	Belize	1.1
65	Cuba	53.0	105	Qatar	11.8	145	Cape Verde	1.1
66	Netherlands	52.8	106	Bahrain	11.0	146	Bahamas	0.9
67	Hungary	49.1	107	Moldova	11.0	147	Gambia	0.8
68	Uzbekistan	49.0	108	Burkina Faso	10.0	148	Luxembourg	0.8
69	Nepal	46.0	109	Congo, Rep. of	10.0	149	Barbados	0.6
70	Austria	45.5	110	Cyprus	10.0	150	Antigua and Barbuda	0.2
71	Belgium	44.5	111	Guinea	9.7	151	Seychelles	0.2

Source: Military Balance

6.2 Military Personnel per Capita

The number of enlisted personnel in the three services or branches—the army, navy, and air force—varies according to the defense needs of the country. Israel, for example, is an embattled nation and thus keeps a large army in constant readiness. Numbers alone, however, do not assure military superiority, although large countries such as China have the advantage in this respect, as was proved during the Korean War. In the absence of any immediate threat, most countries tend to downsize their military personnel and to rely on superiority in weaponry.

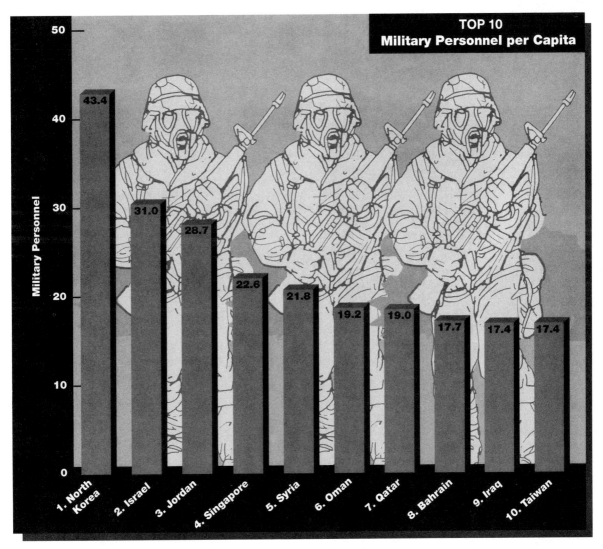

TOP 10 Military Personnel per Capita

Military Personnel

- 1. North Korea — 43.4
- 2. Israel — 31.0
- 3. Jordan — 28.7
- 4. Singapore — 22.6
- 5. Syria — 21.8
- 6. Oman — 19.2
- 7. Qatar — 19.0
- 8. Bahrain — 17.7
- 9. Iraq — 17.4
- 10. Taiwan — 17.4

Rank	Country/Entity	Military Personnel per Thousand, 1997	Rank	Country/Entity	Military Personnel per Thousand, 1997	Rank	Country/Entity	Military Personnel per Thousand, 1997
11	Brunei	16.2	16	Lebanon	14.3	21	Croatia	12.1
12	Armenia	15.5	17	United Arab Emirates	13.6	22	Libya	11.5
13	Djibouti	15.4	18	Cambodia	13.5	23	Yugoslavia	10.7
14	Greece	15.4	19	Cyprus	13.0	24	Angola	10.4
15	South Korea	14.7	20	Bosnia and Herzegovina	12.8	25	Romania	10.1

Rank	Country/Entity	Military Personnel per Thousand, 1997	Rank	Country/Entity	Military Personnel per Thousand, 1997	Rank	Country/Entity	Military Personnel per Thousand, 1997
26	Turkey	10.0	68	Belize	4.6	110	China	2.3
27	Myanmar (Burma)	9.2	69	Fiji	4.6	111	Zambia	2.3
28	Bulgaria	9.1	70	Belgium	4.4	112	Argentina	2.1
29	Azerbaijan	8.8	71	Thailand	4.4	113	Guyana	2.1
30	Russia	8.4	72	Bolivia	4.3	114	Kazakhstan	2.1
31	Iran	8.3	73	Czech Republic	4.3	115	Nepal	2.1
32	Uruguay	8.0	74	Pakistan	4.3	116	Uzbekistan	2.1
33	Macedonia	7.8	75	Algeria	4.2	117	Brazil	2.0
34	Belarus	7.7	76	Germany	4.2	118	Canada	2.0
35	Norway	7.6	77	Colombia	4.0	119	Japan	1.9
36	Ukraine	7.6	78	Paraguay	4.0	120	Luxembourg	1.9
37	Egypt	7.2	79	Yemen	4.0	121	Mexico	1.9
38	Morocco	7.2	80	Congo, Rep. of	3.9	122	South Africa	1.9
39	Rwanda	7.1	81	Gabon	3.9	123	Latvia	1.8
40	Kuwait	7.0	82	Nicaragua	3.9	124	Trinidad and Tobago	1.6
41	Slovakia	6.6	83	Mongolia	3.8	125	Central African Republic	1.5
42	Chile	6.5	84	Tunisia	3.8	126	Madagascar	1.5
43	France	6.5	85	Guatemala	3.6	127	Philippines	1.5
44	Mauritania	6.5	86	United Kingdom	3.6	128	Indonesia	1.4
45	Vietnam	6.5	87	Chad	3.5	129	Lithuania	1.4
46	Sri Lanka	6.3	88	Ireland	3.5	130	Senegal	1.4
47	Denmark	6.2	89	Venezuela	3.5	131	Guinea	1.3
48	Guinea-Bissau	6.2	90	Netherlands	3.4	132	Jamaica	1.3
49	Poland	6.2	91	Zimbabwe	3.4	133	India	1.2
50	Finland	6.0	92	Namibia	3.3	134	Tajikistan	1.2
51	Portugal	6.0	93	Suriname	3.3	135	Tanzania	1.2
52	Sweden	6.0	94	Honduras	3.2	136	Togo	1.2
53	Italy	5.7	95	Australia	3.1	137	Bangladesh	1.0
54	Laos	5.7	96	Bhutan	3.1	138	Lesotho	1.0
55	Austria	5.6	97	Burundi	3.1	139	Papua New Guinea	1.0
56	Saudi Arabia	5.5	98	Dominican Republic	3.1	140	Burkina Faso	0.9
57	United States	5.4	99	Bahamas	3.0	141	Cameroon	0.9
58	Malaysia	5.3	100	Equatorial Guinea	3.0	142	Benin	0.8
59	Malta	5.2	101	Cape Verde	2.8	143	Kenya	0.8
60	Peru	5.1	102	Kyrgyzstan	2.7	144	Mali	0.7
61	Botswana	5.0	103	New Zealand	2.6	145	Nigeria	0.7
62	El Salvador	5.0	104	Seychelles	2.6	146	Côte d'Ivoire	0.6
63	Spain	5.0	105	Moldova	2.5	147	Gambia	0.6
64	Slovenia	4.9	106	Estonia	2.4	148	Niger	0.6
65	Ecuador	4.8	107	Sudan	2.4	149	Malawi	0.5
66	Hungary	4.8	108	Antigua and Barbuda	2.3	150	Switzerland	0.5
67	Cuba	4.7	109	Barbados	2.3	151	Ghana	0.4

Source: Military Balance

6.3 Military Expenditures

In terms of the Gross Global Product, military expenditures constitute not merely a small burden, but have actually decreased from 7.06 percent in 1960 to 3.8 percent in 2000. Ironically, the decrease comes mainly from the large military powers following the winding down of the Cold War. In developing countries, however, defense expenditures have continued to grow during the same period, from 1.78 percent of the Gross National Product (GNP) to 4.8 percent. Western nations have contributed to this buildup by selling arms and sophisticated weapons to poorer nations who then cut their education and health budgets to maintain their military.

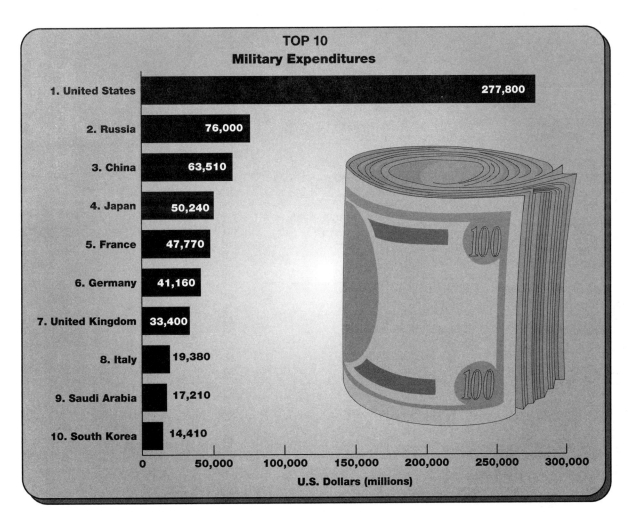

TOP 10
Military Expenditures

Rank	Country	U.S. Dollars (millions)
1. United States		277,800
2. Russia		76,000
3. China		63,510
4. Japan		50,240
5. France		47,770
6. Germany		41,160
7. United Kingdom		33,400
8. Italy		19,380
9. Saudi Arabia		17,210
10. South Korea		14,410

U.S. Dollars (millions)

Rank	Country/Entity	Military Expenditures in U.S. Dollars (millions), 1995	Rank	Country/Entity	Military Expenditures in U.S. Dollars (millions), 1995	Rank	Country/Entity	Military Expenditures in U.S. Dollars (millions), 1995
11	Taiwan	13,140	15	Israel	8,734	19	India	7,831
12	Brazil	10,900	16	Spain	8,652	20	Turkey	6,606
13	Canada	9,077	17	Australia	8,401	21	Sweden	6,042
14	Iraq	9,007	18	Netherlands	8,012	22	North Korea	6,000

Rank	Country/Entity	Military Expenditures in U.S. Dollars (millions), 1995	Rank	Country/Entity	Military Expenditures in U.S. Dollars (millions), 1995	Rank	Country/Entity	Military Expenditures in U.S. Dollars (millions), 1995
23	Greece	5,056	70	Bangladesh	502	117	Mozambique	69
24	Switzerland	5,034	71	Cyprus	495	118	Tanzania	69
25	Poland	4,887	72	Jordan	481	119	Burkina Faso	68
26	Argentina	4,684	73	Kazakhstan	426	120	Macedonia	63
27	Belgium	4,449	74	Lebanon	410	121	Haiti	59
28	Iran	4,191	75	Uruguay	410	122	Kyrgyzstan	57
29	Thailand	4,014	76	Afghanistan	408	123	Guinea	51
30	Singapore	3,970	77	Cuba	350	124	Honduras	51
31	Pakistan	3,740	78	Tunisia	345	125	Costa Rica	50
32	Yugoslavia	3,608	79	Slovenia	344	126	Congo, Rep. of	48
33	Ukraine	3,588	80	Qatar	330	127	Burundi	46
34	Syria	3,563	81	Nigeria	324	128	Liberia	45
35	Norway	3,508	82	Azerbaijan	304	129	Mali	43
36	Kuwait	3,488	83	Bahrain	273	130	Nepal	42
37	Indonesia	3,398	84	Brunei	269	131	Sierra Leone	41
38	Denmark	3,118	85	Angola	225	132	Suriname	39
39	South Africa	2,895	86	Botswana	225	133	Chad	34
40	Portugal	2,690	87	Moldova	222	134	Nicaragua	34
41	Egypt	2,653	88	Zimbabwe	220	135	Mauritania	33
42	Romania	2,520	89	Tajikistan	209	136	Fiji	32
43	Malaysia	2,444	90	Turkmenistan	196	137	Malta	32
44	Finland	2,381	91	Georgia	194	138	Central African Republic	30
45	Czech Republic	2,368	92	Guatemala	191	139	Jamaica	28
46	Mexico	2,321	93	Kenya	173	140	Lesotho	28
47	Chile	2,243	94	Albania	157	141	Madagascar	28
48	Austria	2,106	95	Luxembourg	142	142	Togo	28
49	Yemen	2,082	96	Bolivia	132	143	Swaziland	27
50	Uzbekistan	2,062	97	Uganda	126	144	Benin	24
51	Colombia	2,000	98	Dominican Republic	122	145	Djibouti	22
52	Libya	1,999	99	Paraguay	121	146	Malawi	21
53	United Arab Emirates	1,880	100	Estonia	118	147	Niger	21
54	Myanmar (Burma)	1,833	101	Ethiopia	118	148	Mongolia	20
55	Oman	1,735	102	Rwanda	118	149	Congo, Dem. Rep. of	17
56	Morocco	1,375	103	Papua New Guinea	107	150	Gambia	15
57	Algeria	1,238	104	Gabon	104	151	Mauritius	14
58	Philippines	1,151	105	Cameroon	102	152	Barbados	13
59	Bulgaria	1,073	106	Zambia	102	153	Bahamas	9
60	Peru	989	107	El Salvador	101	154	Belize	9
61	Hungary	961	108	Côte d'Ivoire	98	155	Seychelles	8
62	Sudan	882	109	Cambodia	90	156	Somalia	8
63	Venezuela	854	110	Ghana	87	157	Guinea-Bissau	7
64	New Zealand	740	111	Trinidad and Tobago	82	158	Guyana	7
65	Ireland	689	112	Armenia	79	159	Cape Verde	4
66	Ecuador	611	113	Lithuania	78	160	Equatorial Guinea	2
67	Sri Lanka	585	114	Senegal	76	161	São Tomé and Príncipe	1
68	Slovakia	577	115	Latvia	74			
69	Vietnam	544	116	Laos	72			

Source: World Military Expenditures and Arms Transfers

6.4 Military Expenditures per Capita

Military expenditures are not strictly comparable across national borders. A U.S. soldier costs more to train and equip than a whole battalion of troops in Russia, Asia, or Africa. Much of the defense budgets in Western nations are accounted for by heavy equipment and weaponry—tanks, missiles, submarines, aircraft, and so on. Military hardware has a short life cycle and tends to get obsolete within five to ten years. Large scale training exercises are very expensive unless the costs are shared by several nations. Military expenditures also tend to be subject to high cost overruns because of corruption and inefficiency.

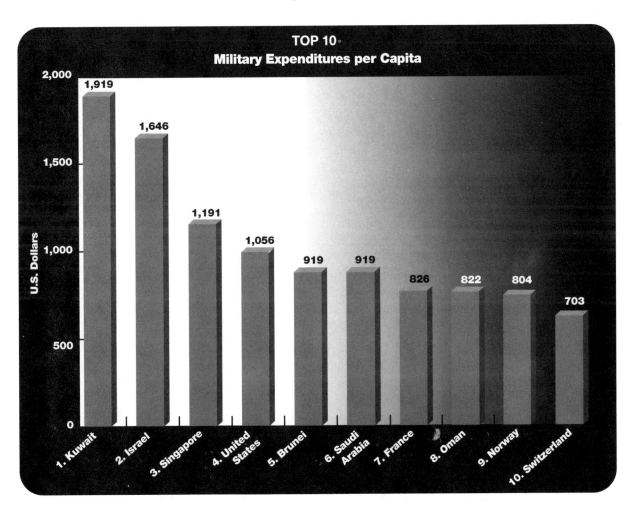

Rank	Country/Entity	Military Expenditures in U.S. Dollars per Capita, 1995	Rank	Country/Entity	Military Expenditures in U.S. Dollars per Capita, 1995	Rank	Country/Entity	Military Expenditures in U.S. Dollars per Capita, 1995
11	Sweden	683	17	United Kingdom	572	23	Bahrain	473
12	Cyprus	672	18	Iraq	528	24	Finland	467
13	United Arab Emirates	643	19	Netherlands	518	25	Australia	465
14	Taiwan	618	20	Russia	513	26	Belgium	439
15	Qatar	617	21	Germany	496	27	Japan	401
16	Denmark	596	22	Greece	482	28	Libya	381

Military Power **83**

Rank	Country/Entity	Military Expenditures in U.S. Dollars per Capita, 1995	Rank	Country/Entity	Military Expenditures in U.S. Dollars per Capita, 1995	Rank	Country/Entity	Military Expenditures in U.S. Dollars per Capita, 1995
29	Luxembourg	348	74	Barbados	50	119	Gambia	13
30	Italy	338	75	Moldova	50	120	Kyrgyzstan	13
31	South Korea	320	76	Turkmenistan	48	121	Mauritius	12
32	Canada	319	77	Morocco	47	122	Jamaica	11
33	Portugal	273	78	Algeria	43	123	Zambia	11
34	Austria	264	79	Egypt	43	124	Central African Republic	10
35	North Korea	255	80	Fiji	42	125	Guyana	10
36	Syria	236	81	Belize	41	126	Cambodia	9
37	Czech Republic	229	82	Myanmar (Burma)	41	127	Cape Verde	9
38	Spain	221	83	Peru	41	128	Haiti	9
39	New Zealand	211	84	Azerbaijan	40	129	Honduras	9
40	Ireland	193	85	Bahamas	40	130	Senegal	9
41	Slovenia	176	86	Venezuela	40	131	Sierra Leone	9
42	Chile	158	87	Tunisia	39	132	Burundi	8
43	Yugoslavia	158	88	Georgia	37	133	Cameroon	8
44	Botswana	155	89	Tajikistan	36	134	India	8
45	Yemen	147	90	Cuba	32	135	Mongolia	8
46	Argentina	137	91	Sri Lanka	32	136	Nicaragua	8
47	Poland	127	92	Sudan	32	137	Burkina Faso	7
48	Uruguay	127	93	Macedonia	30	138	Côte d'Ivoire	7
49	Bulgaria	125	94	Pakistan	30	139	Guinea	7
50	Malaysia	125	95	Latvia	29	140	São Tomé and Príncipe	7
51	Seychelles	124	96	Swaziland	28	141	Togo	7
52	Jordan	117	97	Kazakhstan	25	142	Vietnam	7
53	Romania	115	98	Mexico	25	143	Equatorial Guinea	6
54	Lebanon	111	99	Papua New Guinea	25	144	Guinea-Bissau	6
55	Slovakia	108	100	Afghanistan	24	145	Kenya	6
56	Turkey	108	101	Armenia	23	146	Uganda	6
57	Hungary	95	102	Paraguay	23	147	Chad	5
58	Gabon	90	103	Angola	22	148	Ghana	5
59	Suriname	90	104	Liberia	21	149	Mali	5
60	Uzbekistan	90	105	Lithuania	21	150	Bangladesh	4
61	Malta	87	106	Rwanda	20	151	Benin	4
62	Estonia	80	107	Zimbabwe	20	152	Mozambique	4
63	South Africa	71	108	Bolivia	19	153	Nigeria	3
64	Ukraine	70	109	Congo, Rep. of	19	154	Ethiopia	2
65	Thailand	69	110	El Salvador	18	155	Madagascar	2
66	Brazil	68	111	Guatemala	17	156	Malawi	2
67	Iran	65	112	Indonesia	17	157	Nepal	2
68	Trinidad and Tobago	64	113	Dominican Republic	16	158	Niger	2
69	Albania	56	114	Philippines	16	159	Tanzania	2
70	Colombia	55	115	Costa Rica	15	160	Somalia	1
71	Ecuador	54	116	Laos	15	161	Congo, Dem. Rep. of	0
72	China	53	117	Lesotho	15			
73	Djibouti	52	118	Mauritania	15			

Source: World Military Expenditures and Arms Transfers

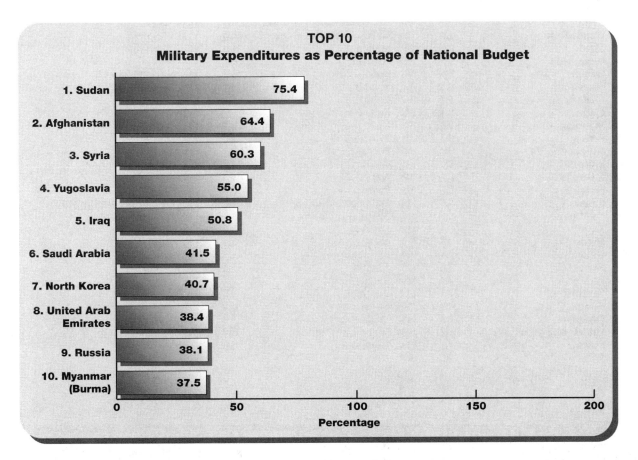

6.5 Military Expenditures as Percentage of National Budget

The impact of military expenditures is most clearly felt on national budgets. Military needs get priority from budget makers, partly because of perceived threats from other nations, but also because of the substantial influence wielded by the defense establishment in national affairs.

TOP 10
Military Expenditures as Percentage of National Budget

Rank	Country/Entity	Military Expenditures as Percentage of National Budget, 1995	Rank	Country/Entity	Military Expenditures as Percentage of National Budget, 1995	Rank	Country/Entity	Military Expenditures as Percentage of National Budget, 1995
11	Taiwan	34.9	26	Equatorial Guinea	21.0	41	Yemen	14.5
12	Oman	33.9	27	Brunei	20.1	42	Guatemala	14.2
13	Somalia	30.0	28	China	18.5	43	Djibouti	13.9
14	Sierra Leone	28.9	29	Ecuador	18.3	44	Morocco	13.8
15	Libya	28.0	30	Turkey	17.6	45	Egypt	13.7
16	Argentina	27.0	31	Chile	17.5	46	Senegal	13.7
17	Pakistan	25.3	32	United States	17.4	47	Iran	13.6
18	Kuwait	25.2	33	Cyprus	17.1	48	South Korea	13.6
19	Burundi	24.8	34	Cambodia	16.7	49	Liberia	13.3
20	Singapore	24.0	35	Mozambique	16.6	50	Uganda	13.3
21	Rwanda	23.3	36	Colombia	16.2	51	Botswana	12.7
22	Jordan	21.7	37	Gambia	16.2	52	India	12.7
23	Haiti	21.6	38	Sri Lanka	15.7	53	Zambia	12.6
24	Laos	21.3	39	Thailand	15.2	54	Malaysia	12.4
25	Israel	21.1	40	Bahrain	14.8	55	Burkina Faso	12.0

Rank	Country/Entity	Military Expenditures as Percentage of National Budget, 1995	Rank	Country/Entity	Military Expenditures as Percentage of National Budget, 1995	Rank	Country/Entity	Military Expenditures as Percentage of National Budget, 1995
56	Albania	11.3	89	Guinea	7.0	122	Netherlands	4.4
57	Romania	11.2	90	Mongolia	7.0	123	Latvia	4.3
58	Congo, Rep. of	11.1	91	Swaziland	7.0	124	Côte d'Ivoire	4.2
59	Vietnam	10.9	92	Algeria	6.9	125	Japan	4.2
60	Greece	10.8	93	Dominican Republic	6.8	126	Denmark	4.1
61	Zimbabwe	10.5	94	Slovakia	6.8	127	Trinidad and Tobago	4.0
62	Cameroon	10.2	95	South Africa	6.7	128	Brazil	3.9
63	Togo	10.2	96	Central African Republic	6.6	129	Italy	3.9
64	Bangladesh	9.9	97	Czech Republic	6.6	130	Malawi	3.9
65	Chad	9.7	98	France	6.6	131	Azerbaijan	3.8
66	Lebanon	9.7	99	Norway	6.5	132	Congo, Dem. Rep. of	3.7
67	Gabon	9.6	100	Bulgaria	6.3	133	Turkmenistan	3.7
68	Bolivia	9.5	101	Tunisia	6.3	134	Belgium	3.5
69	Mali	9.4	102	Venezuela	6.3	135	Slovenia	3.5
70	Qatar	9.4	103	Kenya	6.2	136	Ireland	3.4
71	Mauritania	9.3	104	Fiji	6.0	137	New Zealand	3.3
72	Peru	9.3	105	Switzerland	6.0	138	Guyana	3.0
73	Ethiopia	9.2	106	Portugal	5.9	139	Estonia	2.9
74	Indonesia	8.9	107	Ghana	5.8	140	Costa Rica	2.7
75	Australia	8.8	108	Nepal	5.8	141	Bahamas	2.5
76	Honduras	8.7	109	Sweden	5.8	142	Lesotho	2.5
77	Benin	8.6	110	Papua New Guinea	5.6	143	São Tomé and Príncipe	2.5
78	Philippines	8.5	111	Spain	5.6	144	Georgia	2.4
79	Tanzania	8.4	112	Poland	5.4	145	Barbados	2.3
80	Niger	7.9	113	Nicaragua	5.3	146	Austria	2.2
81	Ukraine	7.8	114	Suriname	5.3	147	Lithuania	2.1
82	Guinea-Bissau	7.6	115	Finland	5.1	148	Malta	2.0
83	El Salvador	7.4	116	Mexico	5.1	149	Luxembourg	1.9
84	Seychelles	7.4	117	Belize	5.0	150	Mauritius	1.6
85	Paraguay	7.3	118	Germany	5.0	151	Jamaica	1.4
86	Uruguay	7.3	119	Madagascar	5.0	152	Cape Verde	1.3
87	United Kingdom	7.2	120	Nigeria	5.0	153	Kyrgyzstan	1.1
88	Canada	7.1	121	Hungary	4.6			

Source: World Military Expenditures and Arms Transfers

6.6 Military Expenditures as Percentage of Combined Education and Health Expenditures

Military expenditures have been regarded since the 1960s as socially unproductive compared to expenditures on education, health, and social welfare, which are considered socially beneficial and ameliorative. A comparison between these types of expenditures reveals a government's sense of priorities. More progressive nations tend to invest more in education and health and to hold the line on military expenditures.

Rank	Country/Entity	Military Expenditures as Percentage of Combined Education and Health Expenditures	Rank	Country/Entity	Military Expenditures as Percentage of Combined Education and Health Expenditures	Rank	Country/Entity	Military Expenditures as Percentage of Combined Education and Health Expenditures
1	Syria	373	7	Qatar	192	13	Brunei	125
2	Oman	293	8	Ethiopia	190	14	Cuba	125
3	Iraq	271	9	Saudi Arabia	151	15	Pakistan	125
4	Myanmar (Burma)	222	10	Jordan	138	16	Mozambique	121
5	Angola	208	11	Russia	132	17	China	114
6	Yemen	197	12	Singapore	129	18	Sri Lanka	107

Rank	Country/Entity	Military Expenditures as Percentage of Combined Education and Health Expenditures	Rank	Country/Entity	Military Expenditures as Percentage of Combined Education and Health Expenditures	Rank	Country/Entity	Military Expenditures as Percentage of Combined Education and Health Expenditures
19	Israel	106	56	South Africa	41	93	Dominican Republic	22
20	Nicaragua	97	57	Mauritania	40	94	Netherlands	22
21	Honduras	92	58	United Kingdom	40	95	Norway	22
22	Kuwait	88	59	Peru	39	96	Guyana	21
23	Turkey	87	60	Togo	39	97	Italy	21
24	Tanzania	77	61	Iran	38	98	Belgium	20
25	Chad	74	62	Malaysia	38	99	Denmark	18
26	Morocco	72	63	Uruguay	38	100	Hungary	18
27	Congo, Dem. Rep. of	71	64	Congo, Rep. of	37	101	Spain	18
28	Greece	71	65	Fiji	37	102	Uganda	18
29	Libya	71	66	Guinea	37	103	Cyprus	17
30	Thailand	71	67	Madagascar	37	104	Czech Republic	17
31	Chile	68	68	Nepal	35	105	New Zealand	16
32	El Salvador	66	69	Panama	34	106	Sweden	16
33	Zimbabwe	66	70	Central African Republic	33	107	Canada	15
34	India	65	71	Nigeria	33	108	Finland	15
35	Zambia	63	72	Senegal	33	109	Côte d'Ivoire	14
36	South Korea	60	73	Venezuela	33	110	Switzerland	14
37	Bolivia	57	74	Portugal	32	111	Ghana	12
38	Colombia	57	75	Guatemala	31	112	Ireland	12
39	Mali	53	76	Tunisia	31	113	Japan	12
40	Egypt	52	77	Burkina Faso	30	114	Algeria	11
41	Albania	51	78	Haiti	30	115	Gambia	11
42	Argentina	51	79	Poland	30	116	Niger	11
43	Gabon	51	80	Bulgaria	29	117	Swaziland	11
44	Indonesia	49	81	France	29	118	Hong Kong	10
45	Cameroon	48	82	Germany	29	119	Luxembourg	10
46	Lesotho	48	83	Suriname	27	120	Malta	10
47	United States	46	84	Ecuador	26	121	Austria	9
48	Sudan	44	85	Romania	25	122	Trinidad and Tobago	9
49	United Arab Emirates	44	86	Australia	24	123	Jamaica	8
50	Burundi	42	87	Kenya	24	124	Barbados	5
51	Paraguay	42	88	Malawi	24	125	Costa Rica	5
52	Bahrain	41	89	Brazil	23	126	Mexico	5
53	Bangladesh	41	90	Namibia	23	127	Mauritius	4
54	Papua New Guinea	41	91	Sierra Leone	23			
55	Philippines	41	92	Botswana	22			

Source: Human Development Report

Richer nations spend less on their defense establishment than poorer nations in terms of their Gross National Product (GNP). This anomaly has become even more acute since the end of the Cold War. Richer nations have downsized effectively while poorer nations continue to seek the security that comes from expensive military hardware. "Rogue" nations often lead the ranking, particularly in trouble spots such as East Asia and the Middle East.

Rank	Country/Entity	Military Expenditures as Percentage of GDP	Rank	Country/Entity	Military Expenditures as Percentage of GDP	Rank	Country/Entity	Military Expenditures as Percentage of GDP
1	North Korea	27.2	49	Turkey	3.9	97	Australia	2.2
2	Oman	15.6	50	Zimbabwe	3.9	98	Italy	2.2
3	Kuwait	12.9	51	Uzbekistan	3.8	99	Kenya	2.2
4	Saudi Arabia	12.8	52	Mozambique	3.7	100	Bolivia	2.1
5	Israel	12.1	53	Yemen	3.7	101	Brazil	2.1
6	Tajikistan	11.0	54	United States	3.6	102	Indonesia	2.1
7	Qatar	10.2	55	Chile	3.5	103	Netherlands	2.1
8	Iraq	8.3	56	Haiti	3.5	104	Ethiopia	2.0
9	Myanmar (Burma)	7.6	57	Latvia	3.5	105	Finland	2.0
10	Eritrea	7.5	58	Nigeria	3.5	106	Gabon	2.0
11	Croatia	6.8	59	Suriname	3.5	107	Philippines	2.0
12	Albania	6.7	60	Ecuador	3.4	108	Tunisia	2.0
13	Botswana	6.7	61	Georgia	3.4	109	Congo, Rep. of	1.9
14	Brunei	6.5	62	Bulgaria	3.3	110	Guinea	1.9
15	Russia	6.5	63	South Korea	3.3	111	Peru	1.9
16	Sri Lanka	6.5	64	France	3.1	112	Mali	1.8
17	Angola	6.4	65	Seychelles	3.1	113	Slovenia	1.8
18	Armenia	6.2	66	Namibia	3.0	114	South Africa	1.8
19	Sierra Leone	5.9	67	Ukraine	3.0	115	Zambia	1.8
20	Azerbaijan	5.8	68	United Kingdom	3.0	116	Bangladesh	1.7
21	Cambodia	5.7	69	Guinea-Bissau	2.9	117	Cape Verde	1.7
22	China	5.7	70	Mauritania	2.9	118	Denmark	1.7
23	Pakistan	5.7	71	Sweden	2.9	119	Germany	1.7
24	Jordan	5.6	72	Congo, Dem. Rep. of	2.8	120	Hungary	1.7
25	Bahrain	5.5	73	India	2.8	121	Mongolia	1.7
26	Singapore	5.5	74	Poland	2.8	122	Senegal	1.7
27	Cuba	5.4	75	Portugal	2.8	123	Belgium	1.6
28	Cyprus	5.2	76	Turkmenistan	2.8	124	Switzerland	1.6
29	Djibouti	5.2	77	Chad	2.7	125	Argentina	1.5
30	United Arab Emirates	5.2	78	Colombia	2.6	126	Canada	1.5
31	Libya	5.1	79	Fiji	2.6	127	El Salvador	1.5
32	Iran	5.0	80	Kazakhstan	2.6	128	Nicaragua	1.5
33	Lesotho	5.0	81	Kyrgyzstan	2.6	129	Papua New Guinea	1.5
34	Greece	4.8	82	Slovakia	2.6	130	Spain	1.5
35	Syria	4.8	83	Belize	2.5	131	Benin	1.4
36	Egypt	4.5	84	Tanzania	2.5	132	Ghana	1.4
37	Lebanon	4.4	85	Thailand	2.5	133	Guatemala	1.4
38	Lithuania	4.3	86	Togo	2.5	134	Panama	1.4
39	Morocco	4.3	87	Burkina Faso	2.4	135	Honduras	1.3
40	Sudan	4.3	88	Cameroon	2.4	136	New Zealand	1.3
41	Belarus	4.2	89	Central African Republic	2.4	137	Paraguay	1.3
42	Malaysia	4.2	90	Czech Republic	2.4	138	Malawi	1.2
43	Moldova	4.2	91	Estonia	2.4	139	Venezuela	1.2
44	Burundi	4.1	92	Norway	2.4	140	Dominican Republic	1.1
45	Laos	4.1	93	Uganda	2.4	141	Ireland	1.1
46	Algeria	4.0	94	Mauritius	2.3	142	Malta	1.1
47	Vietnam	4.0	95	Romania	2.3	143	Trinidad and Tobago	1.1
48	Gambia	3.9	96	Uruguay	2.3	144	Equatorial Guinea	1.0

Rank	Country/Entity	Military Expenditures as Percentage of GDP	Rank	Country/Entity	Military Expenditures as Percentage of GDP	Rank	Country/Entity	Military Expenditures as Percentage of GDP
145	Guyana	1.0	150	Niger	0.9	155	Luxembourg	0.7
146	Japan	1.0	151	Antigua and Barbuda	0.8	156	Bahamas	0.6
147	Austria	0.9	152	Madagascar	0.8	157	Costa Rica	0.6
148	Côte d'Ivoire	0.9	153	Mexico	0.8	158	Jamaica	0.6
149	Nepal	0.9	154	Barbados	0.7			

Source: World Military Expenditures and Arms Transfers

6.8 Exports of Conventional Weapons

The world arms trade is a multibillion dollar industry with a global reach and powerful international lobbies. Much of the industry is directly patronized by the United States, France, Russia, and other countries, which promote these sales to improve their balance of trade. The "merchants of death," as these arms lobbies are called, specialize in inflaming hostilities and sabotaging peace moves.

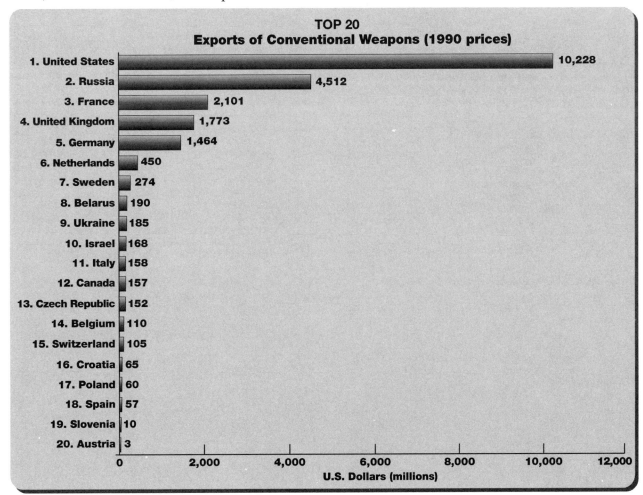

TOP 20
Exports of Conventional Weapons (1990 prices)

- 1. United States — 10,228
- 2. Russia — 4,512
- 3. France — 2,101
- 4. United Kingdom — 1,773
- 5. Germany — 1,464
- 6. Netherlands — 450
- 7. Sweden — 274
- 8. Belarus — 190
- 9. Ukraine — 185
- 10. Israel — 168
- 11. Italy — 158
- 12. Canada — 157
- 13. Czech Republic — 152
- 14. Belgium — 110
- 15. Switzerland — 105
- 16. Croatia — 65
- 17. Poland — 60
- 18. Spain — 57
- 19. Slovenia — 10
- 20. Austria — 3

U.S. Dollars (millions)

Source: World Military Expenditures and Arms Transfers

In a military sense, the world is divided into patron states and client states. Client states in the arms industry are those with a hunger for armaments and military hardware. Arms supply is extremely lucrative and also affords an opportunity for flagrant corruption on a large scale. Middle Eastern Arab nations are among the world's leaders in imports of sophisticated military hardware, but because they lack trained personnel to use them, often allow them to remain idle for years.

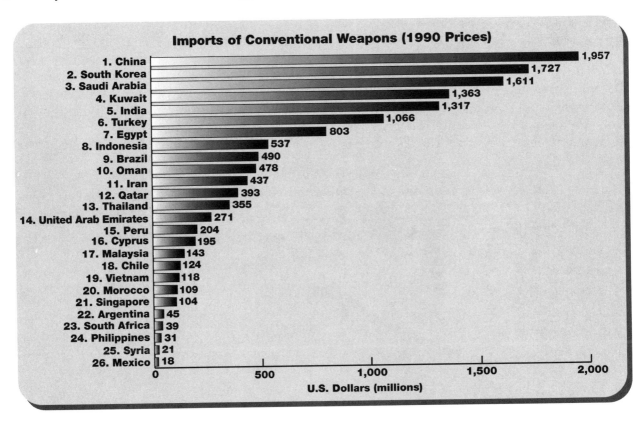

Imports of Conventional Weapons (1990 Prices)

Rank	Country	U.S. Dollars (millions)
1.	China	1,957
2.	South Korea	1,727
3.	Saudi Arabia	1,611
4.	Kuwait	1,363
5.	India	1,317
6.	Turkey	1,066
7.	Egypt	803
8.	Indonesia	537
9.	Brazil	490
10.	Oman	478
11.	Iran	437
12.	Qatar	393
13.	Thailand	355
14.	United Arab Emirates	271
15.	Peru	204
16.	Cyprus	195
17.	Malaysia	143
18.	Chile	124
19.	Vietnam	118
20.	Morocco	109
21.	Singapore	104
22.	Argentina	45
23.	South Africa	39
24.	Philippines	31
25.	Syria	21
26.	Mexico	18

Source: World Military Expenditures and Arms Transfers

In his classic book *Study of War,* Quincy Wright distinguished four types of wars: balance of power wars, civil wars, defensive wars, and imperial wars or wars of conquest. To these may be added world wars, which combine two or more of these elements. In the following table, countries are ranked on the basis of war and war-related deaths from 1945 to 2000.

Rank	Country/Entity	War-Related Deaths, 1945–2000	Rank	Country/Entity	War-Related Deaths, 1945–2000	Rank	Country/Entity	War-Related Deaths, 1945–2000
1	Vietnam	2,994,000	18	Somalia	550,000	35	Egypt	79,000
2	China	2,610,000	19	Angola	355,000	36	El Salvador	75,000
3	Nigeria	2,011,000	20	Colombia	323,000	37	Turkey	70,000
4	Rwanda	2,000,000	21	Lebanon	246,000	38	Sri Lanka	42,000
5	Afghanistan	1,505,000	22	Iraq	227,000	39	Cameroon	32,000
6	North Korea	1,305,000	23	Liberia	225,000	40	Laos	30,000
7	South Korea	1,250,000	24	Sierra Leone	220,000	41	Yemen	30,000
8	Cambodia	1,221,000	25	Congo, Dem. Rep. of	220,000	42	Chile	28,000
9	Sudan	1,106,000	26	Burundi	218,000	43	Peru	26,000
10	Mozambique	1,080,000	27	Kuwait	200,000	44	Taiwan	26,000
11	Bangladesh	1,000,000	28	Greece	160,000	45	Israel	24,000
12	India	856,000	29	Yugoslavia	145,000	46	Argentina	20,000
13	Indonesia	691,000	30	Guatemala	141,000	47	Hungary	20,000
14	Ethiopia	614,000	31	Algeria	104,000	48	Myanmar (Burma)	20,000
15	Uganda	613,000	32	United States	95,000	49	Syria	20,000
16	Russia (Chechnya)	600,000	33	Philippines	84,000	50	Guinea-Bissau	15,000
17	Iran	588,000	34	Nicaragua	80,000	51	Pakistan	8,000

Source: Melvin Small and David Singer: *Resort to Arms*

Chapter 7

Economy

The two most commonly used measures of national output are Gross Domestic Product (GDP) and Gross National Product (GNP). Each of these measures represents an aggregate value of goods and services produced in a country. The GDP, the more basic of the two, is a measure of the total value of goods produced entirely within a country. The GNP, the more comprehensive measure, is composed of both the GDP and the net income from current transactions with other countries. When income received from other countries is greater than payments to them, a country's GNP is greater than its GDP. In theory, if all national accounts could be equilibrated, the global summation of GDP would equal GNP. GNP and GDP are normally presented in nominal terms, that is, in current value and according to existing exchange rates. Because of the distortions inherent in exchange rates and because inflation rates vary among nations, both GNP and GDP may be presented in constant values by deflating currencies to a certain base year, or they may also be presented in purchasing power parities, that is, scaled according to the cost of living indexes. The total Gross Global Product (GGP) in 1999 was $38 trillion. Of this, nearly $20 trillion, or 53 percent, was generated by the seven trillion-dollar economies: the United States, Japan, Germany, France, the United Kingdom, Italy, and China. With 4 percent of the global population, the United States generates 21 percent of the GGP.

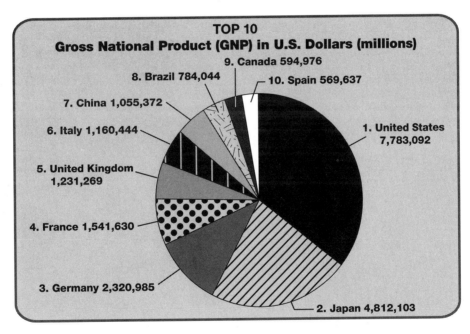

TOP 10
Gross National Product (GNP) in U.S. Dollars (millions)

9. Canada 594,976
8. Brazil 784,044
10. Spain 569,637
7. China 1,055,372
6. Italy 1,160,444
5. United Kingdom 1,231,269
4. France 1,541,630
3. Germany 2,320,985
2. Japan 4,812,103
1. United States 7,783,092

Rank	Country/Entity	GNP in U.S. Dollars (millions)	Rank	Country/Entity	GNP in U.S. Dollars (millions)	Rank	Country/Entity	GNP in U.S. Dollars (millions)
11	South Korea	485,209	23	Indonesia	221,533	35	Iran	108,614
12	Netherlands	403,057	24	Turkey	199,307	36	Singapore	101,834
13	Russia	394,861	25	Denmark	184,347	37	Malaysia	98,195
14	Australia	382,705	26	Thailand	165,759	38	Israel	94,402
15	India	357,391	27	Hong Kong	163,834	39	Philippines	88,372
16	Mexico	348,627	28	Norway	158,973	40	Colombia	87,125
17	Argentina	319,293	29	Saudi Arabia	143,430	41	Venezuela	79,317
18	Switzerland	305,238	30	Poland	138,909	42	Egypt	72,164
19	Taiwan	285,030	31	South Africa	130,151	43	Chile	70,510
20	Belgium	272,382	32	Finland	127,398	44	Ireland	65,137
21	Sweden	231,905	33	Greece	122,430	45	Pakistan	64,638
22	Austria	225,373	34	Portugal	109,472	46	Peru	63,672

Rank	Country/Entity	GNP in U.S. Dollars (millions)	Rank	Country/Entity	GNP in U.S. Dollars (millions)	Rank	Country/Entity	GNP in U.S. Dollars (millions)
47	New Zealand	59,539	105	Afghanistan	5,666	163	Togo	1,485
48	Myanmar (Burma)	55,700	106	Trinidad and Tobago	5,553	164	Swaziland	1,458
49	Czech Republic	53,952	107	Congo, Dem. Rep. of	5,201	165	Lesotho	1,368
50	Ukraine	52,625	108	Botswana	5,070	166	Gaza Strip	1,256
51	United Arab Emirates	49,307	109	Estonia	4,899	167	Virgin Islands (U.S.)	1,246
52	Hungary	45,760	110	Nepal	4,863	168	Greenland	1,218
53	Bangladesh	44,090	111	Senegal	4,777	169	Isle of Man	1,210
54	Algeria	43,927	112	Gabon	4,752	170	Aruba	1,181
55	Kuwait	35,152	113	Georgia	4,656	171	Liberia	1,174
56	Morocco	34,380	114	Bahrain	4,514	172	Andorra	1,155
57	Nigeria	33,393	115	Bosnia and Herzegovina	4,455	173	Central African Republic	1,104
58	Romania	31,787	116	Mauritius	4,444	174	Mauritania	1,093
59	Libya	29,476	117	Honduras	4,426	175	Mongolia	998
60	Puerto Rico	25,380	118	Yemen	4,405	176	Burundi	924
61	Uzbekistan	24,236	119	Papua New Guinea	4,185	177	Faroe Islands	890
62	Vietnam	24,008	120	Jamaica	3,956	178	San Marino	883
63	Belarus	22,082	121	Martinique	3,942	179	Eritrea	852
64	North Korea	21,800	122	Azerbaijan	3,886	180	Monaco	793
65	Kazakhstan	21,317	123	Guinea	3,830	181	Sierra Leone	762
66	Yugoslavia	20,039	124	Guadeloupe	3,706	182	Liechtenstein	714
67	Uruguay	20,035	125	Madagascar	3,575	183	Somalia	706
68	Slovakia	19,801	126	Zambia	3,536	184	Guyana	677
69	Slovenia	19,550	127	Malta	3,498	185	Belize	614
70	Tunisia	19,433	128	Namibia	3,428	186	Saint Lucia	558
71	Croatia	19,343	129	French Polynesia	3,418	187	Northern Mariana Islands	550
72	Luxembourg	18,837	130	Bahamas	3,288	188	Suriname	544
73	Ecuador	18,785	131	Cambodia	3,162	189	Seychelles	537
74	Cuba	16,900	132	New Caledonia	3,017	190	Djibouti	500
75	Syria	16,643	133	Angola	3,012	191	Gibraltar	500
76	Guatemala	16,582	134	Guam	2,993	192	Antigua and Barbuda	489
77	Sri Lanka	14,781	135	Turkmenistan	2,987	193	Equatorial Guinea	444
78	Dominican Republic	14,148	136	West Bank	2,917	194	Cape Verde	436
79	Lebanon	13,900	137	Haiti	2,864	195	Gambia	407
80	Oman	13,808	138	Réunion	2,864	196	Solomon Islands	350
81	Iraq	11,500	139	Mali	2,656	197	Bhutan	315
82	Cyprus	10,839	140	Burkina Faso	2,579	198	Maldives	301
83	El Salvador	10,704	141	Albania	2,540	199	Grenada	300
84	Paraguay	10,183	142	Mozambique	2,405	200	Saint Vincent and the Grenadines	272
85	Côte d'Ivoire	10,152	143	Netherlands Antilles	2,400			
86	Bulgaria	9,750	144	Benin	2,227	201	Guinea-Bissau	264
87	Kenya	9,654	145	Kyrgyzstan	2,211	202	Saint Kitts and Nevis	256
88	Costa Rica	9,275	146	Jersey	2,198	203	American Samoa	253
89	Cameroon	8,610	147	Macedonia	2,187	204	Vanuatu	238
90	Panama	8,373	148	Malawi	2,129	205	Dominica	225
91	Lithuania	8,360	149	Bermuda	2,128	206	Micronesia	213
92	Zimbabwe	8,208	150	Armenia	2,112	207	Comoros	209
93	Sudan	7,917	151	Tajikistan	2,010	208	Samoa	199
94	Bolivia	7,564	152	Fiji	2,007	209	Tonga	177
95	Iceland	7,513	153	Moldova	1,974	210	Palau	160
96	Qatar	7,429	154	Niger	1,962	211	Marshall Islands	97
97	Macau	7,350	155	Laos	1,924	212	Nauru	81
98	Brunei	7,151	156	Nicaragua	1,907	213	Kiribati	76
99	Ghana	6,982	157	Congo, Rep. of	1,827	214	Western Sahara	60
100	Jordan	6,755	158	Barbados	1,741	215	Mayotte	54
101	Tanzania	6,632	159	Rwanda	1,680	216	São Tomé and Príncipe	40
102	Ethiopia	6,507	160	Chad	1,629	217	Tuvalu	7
103	Uganda	6,068	161	French Guiana	1,543			
104	Latvia	5,995	162	Guernsey	1,531			

Source: UN Statistical Yearbook

7.2 GNP per Capita

The problem with the Gross National Product (GNP) is that it does not reflect income disparities within a country and is frequently unreliable when employed as a measure of national well-being. It has been humorously suggested that what is wrong with the GNP is that it is gross. As a derived average, per capita GNP suffers from equally serious flaws. It fails to reflect the distributional inequalities of income, and it is easily affected by population estimates. Thus, when it is said that Kuwait has a per capita income of $22,000, it does not reveal that the average Kuwaiti receives only about $2,000 and that the emir has an income of $12 billion. Nevertheless, per capita income is one of the most closely watched indicators in the world.

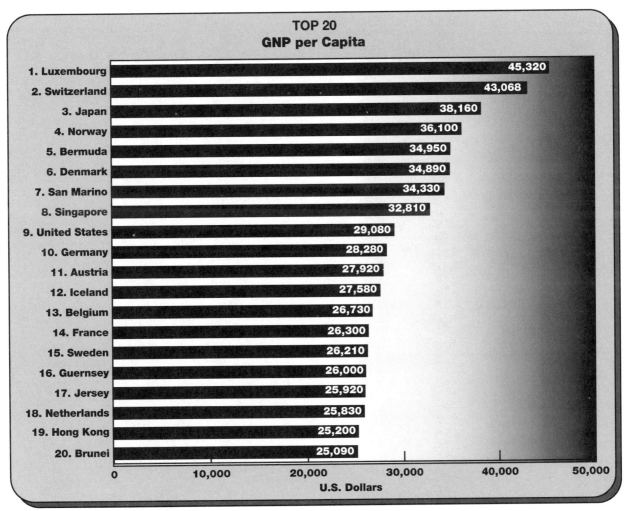

TOP 20 GNP per Capita

Rank	Country	GNP per Capita
1.	Luxembourg	45,320
2.	Switzerland	43,068
3.	Japan	38,160
4.	Norway	36,100
5.	Bermuda	34,950
6.	Denmark	34,890
7.	San Marino	34,330
8.	Singapore	32,810
9.	United States	29,080
10.	Germany	28,280
11.	Austria	27,920
12.	Iceland	27,580
13.	Belgium	26,730
14.	France	26,300
15.	Sweden	26,210
16.	Guernsey	26,000
17.	Jersey	25,920
18.	Netherlands	25,830
19.	Hong Kong	25,200
20.	Brunei	25,090

U.S. Dollars

Rank	Country/Entity	GNP per Capita in U.S. Dollars	Rank	Country/Entity	GNP per Capita in U.S. Dollars	Rank	Country/Entity	GNP per Capita in U.S. Dollars
21	Monaco	25,000	27	Australia	20,650	33	Andorra	18,000
22	Finland	24,790	28	Faroe Islands	20,220	34	Ireland	17,790
23	Liechtenstein	23,000	29	Italy	20,170	35	Macau	17,550
24	Kuwait	22,110	30	Canada	19,640	36	Gibraltar	17,500
25	Greenland	21,870	31	Guam	19,600	37	Isle of Man	16,810
26	United Kingdom	20,870	32	United Arab Emirates	18,290	38	Aruba	16,640

Rank	Country/Entity	GNP per Capita in U.S. Dollars	Rank	Country/Entity	GNP per Capita in U.S. Dollars	Rank	Country/Entity	GNP per Capita in U.S. Dollars
39	Israel	16,180	99	Belize	2,670	158	Côte d'Ivoire	710
40	New Zealand	15,830	100	Peru	2,610	159	Lesotho	680
41	New Caledonia	15,330	101	Fiji	2,460	160	Congo, Rep. of	670
42	Cyprus	14,930	102	Latvia	2,430	161	Tuvalu	650
43	French Polynesia	14,910	103	Saint Vincent and	2,420	162	Turkmenistan	640
44	Spain	14,490		the Grenadines		163	Cameroon	620
45	Taiwan	13,230	104	Lithuania	2,260	164	Iraq	600
46	Bahamas	11,830	105	Colombia	2,180	165	Mayotte	600
47	Virgin Islands (U.S.)	11,740	106	Belarus	2,150	166	Armenia	560
48	Greece	11,640	107	Namibia	2,110	167	Guinea	550
49	Qatar	11,570	108	Tunisia	2,110	168	Senegal	540
50	Netherlands Antilles	11,500	109	Paraguay	2,000	169	Azerbaijan	510
51	Portugal	11,010	110	Micronesia	1,920	170	Pakistan	500
52	French Guiana	10,580	111	Yugoslavia	1,900	171	Liberia	490
53	South Korea	10,550	112	El Salvador	1,810	172	Kyrgyzstan	480
54	Martinique	10,000	113	Tonga	1,810	173	Moldova	460
55	Slovenia	9,840	114	Iran	1,780	174	Mauritania	440
56	Malta	9,330	115	Dominican Republic	1,750	175	Bhutan	430
57	Guadeloupe	9,200	116	Marshall Islands	1,610	176	Nicaragua	410
58	Argentina	8,950	117	West Bank	1,600	177	Comoros	400
59	Palau	8,800	118	Guatemala	1,580	178	Laos	400
60	Northern Mariana Islands	8,730	119	Ecuador	1,570	179	Ghana	390
61	Bahrain	7,820	120	Jamaica	1,550	180	Mongolia	390
62	Antigua and Barbuda	7,380	121	Cuba	1,540	181	Benin	380
63	Nauru	7,210	122	Jordan	1,520	182	Haiti	380
64	Saudi Arabia	7,150	123	Swaziland	1,520	183	India	370
65	Puerto Rico	7,010	124	Algeria	1,500	184	Zambia	370
66	Seychelles	6,910	125	Romania	1,410	185	Bangladesh	360
67	Barbados	6,590	126	Kazakhstan	1,350	186	Gambia	340
68	Saint Kitts and Nevis	6,260	127	Vanuatu	1,340	187	Kenya	340
69	Uruguay	6,130	128	Suriname	1,320	188	Togo	340
70	Oman	6,050	129	Gaza Strip	1,260	189	Tajikistan	330
71	Libya	5,540	130	Morocco	1,260	190	Uganda	330
72	Czech Republic	5,240	131	Egypt	1,200	191	Central African Republic	320
73	Chile	4,820	132	Philippines	1,200	192	Vietnam	310
74	Brazil	4,790	133	Myanmar (Burma)	1,190	193	Cambodia	300
75	Malaysia	4,530	134	Maldives	1,180	194	Western Sahara	300
76	Hungary	4,510	135	Bulgaria	1,170	195	São Tomé and Príncipe	290
77	American Samoa	4,300	136	Samoa	1,140	196	Sudan	290
78	Réunion	4,300	137	Syria	1,120	197	Nigeria	280
79	Trinidad and Tobago	4,250	138	Indonesia	1,110	198	Yemen	270
80	Gabon	4,120	139	Macedonia	1,100	199	Angola	260
81	Croatia	4,060	140	Bosnia and Herzegovina	1,090	200	Mali	260
82	Mauritius	3,870	141	Cape Verde	1,090	201	Afghanistan	250
83	Mexico	3,700	142	Equatorial Guinea	1,060	202	Burkina Faso	250
84	Slovakia	3,680	143	Ukraine	1,040	203	Madagascar	250
85	Poland	3,590	144	Uzbekistan	1,020	204	Chad	230
86	Saint Lucia	3,510	145	Bolivia	970	205	Eritrea	230
87	Venezuela	3,480	146	Papua New Guinea	930	206	Guinea-Bissau	230
88	Estonia	3,360	147	Kiribati	910	207	Nepal	220
89	Lebanon	3,350	148	North Korea	900	208	Malawi	210
90	Botswana	3,310	149	Solomon Islands	870	209	Rwanda	210
91	South Africa	3,210	150	China	860	210	Tanzania	210
92	Grenada	3,140	151	Georgia	860	211	Niger	200
93	Turkey	3,130	152	Guyana	800	212	Sierra Leone	160
94	Panama	3,080	153	Sri Lanka	800	213	Burundi	140
95	Dominica	3,040	154	Djibouti	780	214	Mozambique	140
96	Thailand	2,740	155	Albania	760	215	Congo, Dem. Rep. of	110
97	Costa Rica	2,680	156	Honduras	740	216	Ethiopia	110
98	Russia	2,680	157	Zimbabwe	720	217	Somalia	110

Source: UN Statistical Yearbook

GNP is an indicator of economic performance, not resources. Generally, GNP tends to go up rather than down because of increases in population, improved and new technologies, expansion in financial markets, and so on. But the rate of GNP growth is what concerns economists. Generally, higher rate of annual GNP growth is achieved at certain stages of a nation's economic growth, and such growth is as often achieved by small and poor nations as by the large and rich ones. Thus, at one time, Botswana had one of the highest GNP growth rates in the world, exceeding 11 percent per year. But it is now conceded that an extremely high GNP growth rate is inflationary by nature and tends to be counterproductive in the long haul.

Rank	Country/Entity	Average GNP Annual Growth, 1990–1997	Rank	Country/Entity	Average GNP Annual Growth, 1990–1997	Rank	Country/Entity	Average GNP Annual Growth, 1990–1997
1	Guyana	12.9	45	Denmark	2.5	88	Italy	1.0
2	Equatorial Guinea	12.1	46	Lesotho	2.5	89	Solomon Islands	1.0
3	China	10.0	47	Papua New Guinea	2.5	90	Côte d'Ivoire	0.9
4	Singapore	6.7	48	Australia	2.4	91	Ecuador	0.9
5	Chile	6.4	49	Costa Rica	2.3	92	Finland	0.9
6	Vietnam	6.1	50	Turkey	2.3	93	Tanzania	0.9
7	South Korea	6.0	51	Albania	2.2	94	Burkina Faso	0.8
8	Indonesia	5.9	52	Ethiopia	2.2	95	Canada	0.8
9	Thailand	5.9	53	Nepal	2.2	96	Jamaica	0.8
10	Malaysia	5.8	54	Bhutan	2.0	97	Malawi	0.8
11	Ireland	5.6	55	Bolivia	2.0	98	Dominica	0.7
12	Taiwan	5.3	56	Pakistan	2.0	99	Germany	0.7
13	Lebanon	4.9	57	Portugal	2.0	100	Nigeria	0.7
14	Peru	4.6	58	Tunisia	2.0	101	Samoa	0.7
15	Uganda	4.4	59	Brazil	1.9	102	Trinidad and Tobago	0.5
16	India	4.3	60	Iran	1.9	103	Fiji	0.4
17	Maldives	4.3	61	Netherlands	1.9	104	Belize	0.3
18	Argentina	4.2	62	United Kingdom	1.9	105	Mali	0.3
19	Poland	4.2	63	Antigua and Barbuda	1.8	106	Slovakia	0.3
20	Slovenia	4.2	64	Saint Vincent and the Grenadines	1.8	107	Hungary	0.2
21	Sri Lanka	4.0				108	Mexico	0.2
22	Saint Kitts and Nevis	4.0	65	Benin	1.7	109	Morocco	0.2
23	Laos	3.9	66	Seychelles	1.7	110	Sweden	0.2
24	Norway	3.8	67	United States	1.7	111	Paraguay	0.0
25	Mauritius	3.7	68	Nicaragua	1.6	112	Senegal	0.0
26	Sudan	3.7	69	Philippines	1.6	113	Gabon	-0.1
27	Dominican Republic	3.5	70	Guatemala	1.5	114	Romania	-0.1
28	El Salvador	3.5	71	Mauritania	1.5	115	South Africa	-0.2
29	Uruguay	3.5	72	Ghana	1.4	116	Venezuela	-0.2
30	Bangladesh	3.3	73	Japan	1.4	117	Czech Republic	-0.3
31	Hong Kong	3.3	74	Tonga	1.4	118	Kenya	-0.3
32	Syria	3.3	75	Belgium	1.3	119	Suriname	-0.5
33	Malta	3.0	76	Botswana	1.3	120	Switzerland	-0.5
34	Panama	3.0	77	Grenada	1.3	121	Gambia	-0.6
35	Eritrea	2.9	78	Spain	1.3	122	Kiribati	-0.6
36	Egypt	2.8	79	New Zealand	1.2	123	Swaziland	-0.6
37	Jordan	2.8	80	Austria	1.1	124	Zimbabwe	-0.7
38	Saint Lucia	2.8	81	Namibia	1.1	125	Zambia	-0.9
39	Cambodia	2.7	82	Cape Verde	1.0	126	Central African Republic	-1.0
40	Croatia	2.7	83	Chad	1.0	127	Togo	-1.2
41	Guinea	2.7	84	France	1.0	128	Mongolia	-1.4
42	Colombia	2.6	85	Greece	1.0	129	Yemen	-1.5
43	Israel	2.6	86	Guinea-Bissau	1.0	130	Algeria	-1.6
44	Mozambique	2.6	87	Honduras	1.0	131	Madagascar	-1.6

Rank	Country/Entity	Average GNP Annual Growth, 1990–1997	Rank	Country/Entity	Average GNP Annual Growth, 1990–1997	Rank	Country/Entity	Average GNP Annual Growth, 1990–1997
132	São Tomé and Príncipe	-1.7	143	Haiti	-4.4	154	Kyrgyzstan	-9.7
133	Micronesia	-1.8	144	Belarus	-5.6	155	Angola	-10.0
134	Niger	-1.9	145	Uzbekistan	-5.6	156	Armenia	-10.7
135	Bulgaria	-2.0	146	Rwanda	-5.7	157	Moldova	-10.8
136	Macedonia	-2.1	147	Sierra Leone	-5.7	158	Ukraine	-12.6
137	Saudi Arabia	-2.5	148	Burundi	-5.9	159	Turkmenistan	-14.6
138	Estonia	-2.8	149	Lithuania	-7.1	160	Georgia	-14.9
139	Congo, Rep. of	-2.9	150	Latvia	-7.3	161	Azerbaijan	-16.0
140	Comoros	-3.1	151	Kazakhstan	-7.4	162	Tajikistan	-16.1
141	Cameroon	-3.3	152	Russia	-7.9			
142	Vanuatu	-3.5	153	Congo, Dem. Rep. of	-9.6			

Source: UN Statistical Yearbook

7.4 GNP Annual Growth Rate per Capita

Countries that experience high to moderate GNP growth rate may not have a commensurate growth rate in per capita income. This is explained by the fact that without proper intervention by the government, money generally tends to move up and stay there without ever trickling down to the bottom stratum of society. Contrary to conventional wisdom, prosperity is seldom a tide that lifts all boats; it lifts some boats more than others. Even countries that report high per capita income may have serious distributional inequities that are masked by the figures. Thus, it would be wrong to assume on the basis of this ranking that all people in countries with a low per capita income are poor or that all people in countries with a high per capita income are rich.

Rank	Country/Entity	GNP Annual Growth Rate per Capita, 1990–1997	Rank	Country/Entity	GNP Annual Growth Rate per Capita, 1990–1997	Rank	Country/Entity	GNP Annual Growth Rate per Capita, 1990–1997
1	Guyana	12.0	27	Albania	2.0	52	United States	0.7
2	Equatorial Guinea	9.6	28	Portugal	1.9	53	Austria	0.5
3	China	8.9	29	Saint Lucia	1.9	54	Brazil	0.5
4	Ireland	5.0	30	Bangladesh	1.7	55	Costa Rica	0.5
5	South Korea	5.0	31	Maldives	1.7	56	Finland	0.5
6	Chile	4.8	32	Sudan	1.7	57	France	0.5
7	Singapore	4.7	33	Dominican Republic	1.6	58	Greece	0.5
8	Thailand	4.7	34	United Kingdom	1.5	59	Hungary	0.5
9	Saint Kitts and Nevis	4.4	35	El Salvador	1.4	60	Turkey	0.5
10	Taiwan	4.4	36	Hong Kong	1.4	61	Dominica	0.4
11	Slovenia	4.3	37	Antigua and Barbuda	1.3	62	Syria	0.4
12	Indonesia	4.2	38	Laos	1.3	63	Eritrea	0.3
13	Poland	4.0	39	Netherlands	1.3	64	Iran	0.3
14	Vietnam	4.0	40	Uganda	1.3	65	Lesotho	0.3
15	Malaysia	3.3	41	Australia	1.2	66	Mozambique	0.3
16	Norway	3.3	42	Panama	1.2	67	Romania	0.3
17	Lebanon	3.0	43	Japan	1.1	68	Tunisia	0.3
18	Argentina	2.9	44	Spain	1.1	69	Germany	0.2
19	Peru	2.9	45	Saint Vincent and the Grenadines	1.1	70	Papua New Guinea	0.2
20	Uruguay	2.8	46	Tonga	1.1	71	Seychelles	0.2
21	Croatia	2.7	47	Belgium	1.0	72	Guinea	0.1
22	Sri Lanka	2.7	48	Grenada	1.0	73	Cambodia	0.0
23	India	2.5	49	Egypt	0.8	74	Ethiopia	0.0
24	Mauritius	2.5	50	Italy	0.8	75	Slovakia	0.0
25	Malta	2.2	51	Colombia	0.7	76	Jamaica	-0.1
26	Denmark	2.1				77	Czech Republic	-0.2

Rank	Country/Entity	GNP Annual Growth Rate per Capita, 1990–1997	Rank	Country/Entity	GNP Annual Growth Rate per Capita, 1990–1997	Rank	Country/Entity	GNP Annual Growth Rate per Capita, 1990–1997
78	Nepal	-0.3	107	Honduras	-1.9	136	Niger	-5.3
79	Sweden	-0.3	108	Malawi	-1.9	137	Belarus	-5.6
80	Trinidad and Tobago	-0.3	109	Côte d'Ivoire	-2.0	138	Comoros	-5.7
81	Bolivia	-0.4	110	Jordan	-2.0	139	Congo, Rep. of	-5.7
82	Canada	-0.4	111	Chad	-2.1	140	Yemen	-5.8
83	New Zealand	-0.4	112	Tanzania	-2.1	141	Saudi Arabia	-5.9
84	Pakistan	-0.5	113	Nigeria	-2.2	142	Cameroon	-6.1
85	Samoa	-0.5	114	Solomon Islands	-2.2	143	Vanuatu	-6.1
86	Israel	-0.6	115	South Africa	-2.2	144	Latvia	-6.2
87	Philippines	-0.7	116	Venezuela	-2.4	145	Haiti	-6.5
88	Suriname	-0.8	117	Belize	-2.5	146	Kazakhstan	-6.9
89	Bhutan	-0.9	118	Mali	-2.5	147	Lithuania	-7.0
90	Fiji	-1.1	119	Kiribati	-2.6	148	Rwanda	-7.5
91	Guatemala	-1.1	120	Senegal	-2.6	149	Uzbekistan	-7.6
92	Benin	-1.2	121	Gabon	-2.7	150	Russia	-7.8
93	Guinea-Bissau	-1.2	122	Paraguay	-2.7	151	Sierra Leone	-8.2
94	Botswana	-1.3	123	Macedonia	-2.8	152	Burundi	-8.3
95	Bulgaria	-1.3	124	Zimbabwe	-3.0	153	Kyrgyzstan	-10.5
96	Cape Verde	-1.3	125	Central African Republic	-3.1	154	Moldova	-10.6
97	Ecuador	-1.3	126	Kenya	-3.1	155	Armenia	-11.6
98	Ghana	-1.3	127	Mongolia	-3.4	156	Ukraine	-12.3
99	Mauritania	-1.3	128	Swaziland	-3.7	157	Congo, Dem. Rep. of	-12.8
100	Nicaragua	-1.3	129	Zambia	-3.7	158	Angola	-13.3
101	Switzerland	-1.3	130	Algeria	-3.9	159	Georgia	-14.8
102	Namibia	-1.5	131	Micronesia	-3.9	160	Azerbaijan	-16.9
103	Burkina Faso	-1.6	132	Gambia	-4.2	161	Tajikistan	-17.9
104	Mexico	-1.6	133	Togo	-4.2	162	Turkmenistan	-18.0
105	Morocco	-1.6	134	Madagascar	-4.4			
106	Estonia	-1.7	135	São Tomé and Príncipe	-4.4			

Source: UN Statistical Yearbook

Income Disparities

There are startling disparities in income between the poorest 20 percent of households and the richest 10 percent of households in every country in the world. Such disparities exist even in socialist countries where governments are committed to their elimination. Contrary to public perceptions, increasing democratization or socialization does not by itself produce greater economic egalitarianism. They only facilitate better mobility between economic classes and promote more economic opportunities. Actually, during the 1990s, income disparities between the rich and the poor increased throughout the world and the trend is likely to continue in the twenty-first century.

7.5 Income Disparity: Poorest Households

Rank	Country/Entity	Percentage of National Income Received by Lowest 20 Percent of Households	Rank	Country/Entity	Percentage of National Income Received by Lowest 20 Percent of Households	Rank	Country/Entity	Percentage of National Income Received by Lowest 20 Percent of Households
1	Slovakia	11.9	7	Libya	10.1	13	Slovenia	9.5
2	Turkey	11.9	8	Luxembourg	10.0	14	Ukraine	9.5
3	Belarus	11.1	9	Rwanda	9.7	15	Bangladesh	9.4
4	Japan	10.9	10	Laos	9.6	16	Poland	9.3
5	Czech Republic	10.5	11	Latvia	9.6	17	Suriname	9.3
6	Malawi	10.4	12	Hungary	9.5	18	Romania	9.2

Rank	Country/Entity	Percentage of National Income Received by Lowest 20 Percent of Households	Rank	Country/Entity	Percentage of National Income Received by Lowest 20 Percent of Households	Rank	Country/Entity	Percentage of National Income Received by Lowest 20 Percent of Households
19	Sri Lanka	8.9	57	Isle of Man	6.4	95	Guyana	4.0
20	Egypt	8.7	58	Paraguay	6.0	96	Mauritius	4.0
21	Indonesia	8.7	59	Switzerland	6.0	97	Nigeria	4.0
22	Ethiopia	8.6	60	Syria	6.0	98	Sudan	4.0
23	India	8.5	61	Uruguay	6.0	99	Zimbabwe	4.0
24	Israel	8.4	62	Jordan	5.9	100	Zambia	3.9
25	Pakistan	8.4	63	Tunisia	5.9	101	Australia	3.8
26	Bulgaria	8.3	64	Jamaica	5.8	102	Honduras	3.8
27	Spain	8.3	65	Madagascar	5.8	103	Iran	3.8
28	Netherlands	8.2	66	Canada	5.7	104	Botswana	3.7
29	Lithuania	8.1	67	Bolivia	5.6	105	Fiji	3.7
30	Benin	8.0	68	France	5.6	106	Finland	3.7
31	Chad	8.0	69	Sierra Leone	5.6	107	Russia	3.7
32	Myanmar (Burma)	8.0	70	Thailand	5.6	108	Bahamas	3.6
33	Togo	8.0	71	China	5.5	109	Colombia	3.6
34	Belgium	7.9	72	El Salvador	5.5	110	Mauritania	3.6
35	Cyprus	7.9	73	Ecuador	5.4	111	Venezuela	3.6
36	Ghana	7.9	74	Hong Kong	5.4	112	Chile	3.5
37	Vietnam	7.8	75	Sweden	5.3	113	Denmark	3.5
38	Nepal	7.6	76	Yugoslavia	5.3	114	Senegal	3.5
39	Kazakhstan	7.5	77	Portugal	5.2	115	Kenya	3.4
40	Niger	7.5	78	New Zealand	5.1	116	Gabon	3.3
41	South Korea	7.4	79	Singapore	5.1	117	South Africa	3.3
42	Bermuda	7.2	80	Lebanon	5.0	118	Puerto Rico	3.2
43	Taiwan	7.1	81	Liberia	5.0	119	Réunion	3.1
44	Barbados	7.0	82	Peru	4.9	120	Guinea	3.0
45	Congo, Rep. of	7.0	83	Iceland	4.7	121	Kyrgyzstan	3.0
46	Germany	7.0	84	Ireland	4.6	122	Lesotho	2.8
47	Algeria	6.9	85	Malaysia	4.6	123	Swaziland	2.8
48	Moldova	6.9	86	United Kingdom	4.6	124	Norway	2.6
49	Tanzania	6.9	87	Argentina	4.4	125	Trinidad and Tobago	2.6
50	Côte d'Ivoire	6.8	88	Dominican Republic	4.2	126	Brazil	2.1
51	Italy	6.8	89	Nicaragua	4.2	127	Guatemala	2.1
52	Uganda	6.8	90	United States	4.2	128	Guinea-Bissau	2.1
53	Turkmenistan	6.7	91	Mexico	4.1	129	Iraq	2.1
54	Estonia	6.6	92	Seychelles	4.1	130	Panama	2.0
55	Morocco	6.6	93	Austria	4.0			
56	Philippines	6.5	94	Costa Rica	4.0			

Source: World Bank

7.6 Income Disparity: Richest Households

Rank	Country/Entity	Percentage of National Income Received by Highest 10 Percent of Households	Rank	Country/Entity	Percentage of National Income Received by Highest 10 Percent of Households	Rank	Country/Entity	Percentage of National Income Received by Highest 10 Percent of Households
1	Liberia	73.0	14	Paraguay	46.0	27	Guyana	40.0
2	Kyrgyzstan	57.0	15	Lebanon	45.0	28	Myanmar (Burma)	40.0
3	Swaziland	54.5	16	Barbados	44.0	29	Nicaragua	39.8
4	Gabon	54.4	17	Congo, Rep. of	43.5	30	Dominican Republic	39.6
5	Réunion	51.4	18	Lesotho	43.4	31	Colombia	39.5
6	Brazil	51.3	19	Botswana	42.9	32	Mexico	39.2
7	Kenya	47.7	20	Senegal	42.8	33	Benin	39.0
8	South Africa	47.3	21	Venezuela	42.7	34	Turkey	39.0
9	United States	46.9	22	Guinea-Bissau	42.4	35	Russia	38.7
10	Zimbabwe	46.9	23	Panama	42.2	36	Malaysia	37.9
11	Mauritius	46.7	24	Honduras	41.9	37	Fiji	37.8
12	Guatemala	46.6	25	Iran	41.7	38	Sierra Leone	37.8
13	Chile	46.1	26	Malawi	40.1	39	Ecuador	37.6

Rank	Country/Entity	Percentage of National Income Received by Highest 10 Percent of Households	Rank	Country/Entity	Percentage of National Income Received by Highest 10 Percent of Households	Rank	Country/Entity	Percentage of National Income Received by Highest 10 Percent of Households
40	Thailand	37.1	69	Mauritania	30.4	98	Moldova	25.8
41	Seychelles	35.6	70	Tanzania	30.2	99	Denmark	25.6
42	Argentina	35.2	71	Chad	30.0	100	Indonesia	25.6
43	Madagascar	34.9	72	Nepal	29.8	101	Taiwan	25.5
44	Jordan	34.7	73	El Salvador	29.5	102	Italy	25.3
45	Puerto Rico	34.7	74	Niger	29.3	103	Pakistan	25.2
46	Sudan	34.6	75	Uruguay	29.3	104	Sri Lanka	25.2
47	Peru	34.3	76	Vietnam	29.0	105	Kazakhstan	24.9
48	Costa Rica	34.1	77	Austria	28.7	106	Bermuda	24.7
49	Luxembourg	34.0	78	New Zealand	28.7	107	Bulgaria	24.7
50	Trinidad and Tobago	33.6	79	Côte d'Ivoire	28.5	108	Germany	24.4
51	Singapore	33.5	80	India	28.4	109	Rwanda	24.2
52	Portugal	33.4	81	Australia	28.0	110	Canada	24.1
53	Uganda	33.4	82	Lithuania	28.0	111	Slovenia	23.8
54	Bahamas	32.1	83	United Kingdom	27.8	112	Bangladesh	23.7
55	Philippines	32.1	84	South Korea	27.6	113	Czech Republic	23.5
56	Jamaica	31.9	85	Ethiopia	27.5	114	Israel	23.1
57	Bolivia	31.7	86	Yugoslavia	27.4	115	Hungary	22.6
58	Guinea	31.7	87	Ghana	27.3	116	Latvia	22.1
59	Japan	31.6	88	Iceland	27.3	117	Poland	22.1
60	Algeria	31.5	89	Switzerland	27.0	118	Netherlands	21.9
61	Estonia	31.3	90	Finland	26.9	119	Spain	21.8
62	Hong Kong	31.3	91	Turkmenistan	26.9	120	Belgium	21.5
63	Nigeria	31.3	92	Egypt	26.7	121	Ukraine	20.8
64	Zambia	31.3	93	Isle of Man	26.6	122	Romania	20.2
65	China	30.9	94	Norway	26.6	123	Belarus	19.4
66	Tunisia	30.7	95	Ireland	26.5	124	Sweden	18.6
67	Morocco	30.5	96	Laos	26.4	125	Slovakia	18.2
68	Togo	30.5	97	France	26.1			

Source: World Bank

Because there is no universal definition of poverty line, international statistical collection agencies have adopted the rate of $1 per day, or $365 per year, as a minimum that could be applied to even the poorest countries. It is described as absolute poverty. On this basis, nearly one billion people—one-sixth of the planet's population—live in poverty so stark and dehumanizing that it is inconceivable to most people living in industrialized countries. This is also the segment of the world's population that has the highest birthrate, so more and more children are condemned to such misery.

Rank	Country/Entity	Percentage of Population Below Poverty Line of (U.S.) $1 a Day	Rank	Country/Entity	Percentage of Population Below Poverty Line of (U.S.) $1 a Day	Rank	Country/Entity	Percentage of Population Below Poverty Line of (U.S.) $1 a Day
1	Azerbaijan	68.1	22	Nepal	42.0	43	Argentina	25.5
2	Sierra Leone	68.0	23	India	40.9	44	Zimbabwe	25.5
3	Zambia	68.0	24	Philippines	40.6	45	Hungary	25.3
4	Haiti	65.0	25	Sri Lanka	40.6	46	Dominican Republic	24.5
5	Chad	64.0	26	Cameroon	40.0	47	Poland	23.8
6	Niger	63.0	27	Kyrgyzstan	40.0	48	Belarus	22.5
7	Mauritania	57.0	28	Cambodia	39.0	49	Paraguay	21.8
8	Uganda	55.0	29	Mongolia	36.3	50	Chile	21.6
9	Malawi	54.0	30	Burundi	36.2	51	Romania	21.5
10	Peru	53.5	31	Ecuador	35.0	52	Tunisia	19.9
11	Rwanda	51.2	32	Kazakhstan	34.6	53	Yemen	19.1
12	Tanzania	51.1	33	Jamaica	34.2	54	Thailand	18.0
13	Vietnam	50.9	34	Pakistan	34.0	55	Brazil	17.4
14	Nicaragua	50.3	35	Senegal	33.4	56	Indonesia	17.4
15	Honduras	50.0	36	Benin	33.0	57	Colombia	16.9
16	Lesotho	49.2	37	Togo	32.3	58	Malaysia	15.5
17	El Salvador	48.3	38	Ukraine	31.7	59	Jordan	15.0
18	Laos	46.1	39	Ghana	31.4	60	Algeria	12.2
19	Nigeria	43.0	40	Venezuela	31.3	61	Mexico	10.1
20	Bangladesh	42.7	41	Russia	30.9	62	Estonia	8.9
21	Kenya	42.0	42	Morocco	26.0	63	China	8.4

Source: Human Development Report

7.8 Inflation Rate

Inflation is the one fact of economics with which not merely economists but also lay people, especially those in charge of households, are all too familiar. Even normal and healthy economic systems experience a slow but constant inflation in prices given the push of population growth and pull of finite and depleting resources. Inflation can create significant economic imbalances when incomes do not rise commensurately. The process is accelerated in times of internal and external stress. Economists distinguish between various types of inflation, such as creeping inflation, galloping inflation, and stagflation, but these distinctions are only academic. Uncontrolled inflation poses a threat not merely to economic systems, but also to the political stability of countries.

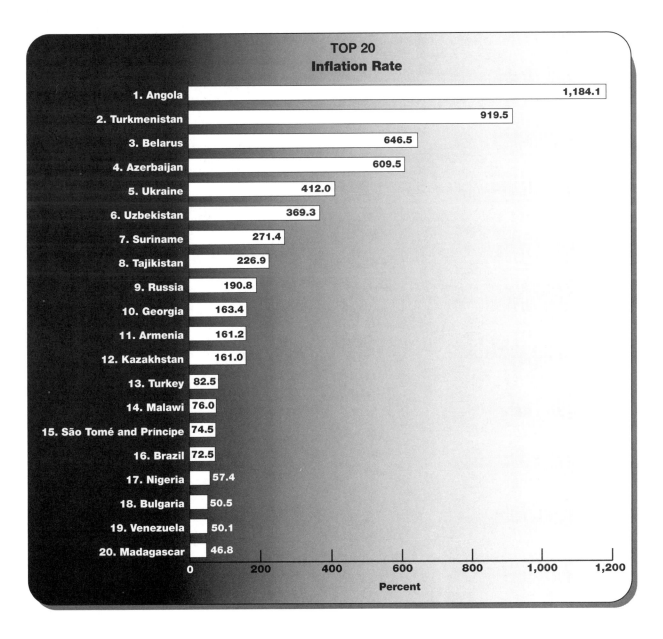

TOP 20
Inflation Rate

Rank	Country	Percent
1.	Angola	1,184.1
2.	Turkmenistan	919.5
3.	Belarus	646.5
4.	Azerbaijan	609.5
5.	Ukraine	412.0
6.	Uzbekistan	369.3
7.	Suriname	271.4
8.	Tajikistan	226.9
9.	Russia	190.8
10.	Georgia	163.4
11.	Armenia	161.2
12.	Kazakhstan	161.0
13.	Turkey	82.5
14.	Malawi	76.0
15.	São Tomé and Príncipe	74.5
16.	Brazil	72.5
17.	Nigeria	57.4
18.	Bulgaria	50.5
19.	Venezuela	50.1
20.	Madagascar	46.8

Percent

Rank	Country/Entity	Inflation Rate, 1995	Rank	Country/Entity	Inflation Rate, 1995	Rank	Country/Entity	Inflation Rate, 1995
21	Zambia	46.2	63	South Africa	10.2	105	Tunisia	4.8
22	Guinea-Bissau	45.9	64	Guatemala	10.0	106	Italy	4.7
23	Mozambique	44.2	65	Syria	10.0	107	Namibia	4.7
24	Uruguay	41.7	66	El Salvador	9.8	108	Spain	4.7
25	Ghana	39.9	67	Peru	9.8	109	Hong Kong	4.6
26	Iran	39.7	68	Solomon Islands	9.8	110	Argentina	4.5
27	Kyrgyzstan	38.5	69	Israel	9.6	111	Mauritania	4.4
28	Lithuania	37.2	70	Botswana	9.2	112	Mauritius	4.2
29	Mexico	35.8	71	Czech Republic	9.1	113	Trinidad and Tobago	4.2
30	Romania	35.5	72	Greece	9.0	114	Gabon	3.9
31	Estonia	34.5	73	Slovakia	9.0	115	Sweden	3.9
32	Tanzania	34.0	74	Cambodia	8.9	116	Portugal	3.8
33	Sierra Leone	32.2	75	Togo	8.9	117	Saint Lucia	3.8
34	Mongolia	29.9	76	Bangladesh	8.8	118	Oman	3.7
35	Algeria	28.3	77	Indonesia	8.7	119	Brunei	3.6
36	Poland	27.4	78	Uganda	8.6	120	Grenada	3.6
37	Honduras	25.2	79	Sri Lanka	8.5	121	Finland	3.1
38	Hungary	24.1	80	Bhutan	8.3	122	Saint Kitts and Nevis	3.0
39	Latvia	23.9	81	Egypt	8.3	123	Canada	2.9
40	Costa Rica	23.8	82	Burkina Faso	8.0	124	Iceland	2.9
41	Haiti	23.7	83	India	8.0	125	Bahamas	2.8
42	Zimbabwe	23.4	84	Kenya	8.0	126	United Kingdom	2.8
43	Ecuador	23.3	85	Lesotho	7.9	127	Belize	2.7
44	Jamaica	22.4	86	Guyana	7.7	128	Panama	2.7
45	Colombia	21.1	87	Philippines	7.4	129	Singapore	2.6
46	Laos	19.8	88	Swaziland	7.1	130	United States	2.5
47	Vietnam	19.5	89	Comoros	7.0	131	Norway	2.4
48	Papua New Guinea	16.7	90	Dominican Republic	7.0	132	Saint Vincent and	2.4
49	Cameroon	16.0	91	Maldives	6.7		the Grenadines	
50	Pakistan	14.3	92	Nepal	6.7	133	Senegal	2.3
51	Côte d'Ivoire	14.1	93	Chad	6.6	134	Austria	2.2
52	Ethiopia	13.7	94	Morocco	6.5	135	Belgium	2.1
53	China	12.8	95	Thailand	6.5	136	Luxembourg	2.1
54	Mali	12.5	96	Fiji	6.3	137	Netherlands	2.1
55	Chile	12.3	97	Equatorial Guinea	5.8	138	France	1.7
56	Burundi	12.2	98	Guinea	5.3	139	Denmark	1.5
57	Central African Republic	11.7	99	South Korea	5.3	140	Bahrain	1.4
58	Bolivia	11.5	100	Kuwait	5.2	141	Ireland	1.2
59	Nicaragua	11.2	101	Niger	5.2	142	Barbados	0.3
60	Congo	11.0	102	Malaysia	5.1	143	Switzerland	0.3
61	Albania	10.3	103	Saudi Arabia	5.0	144	Japan	-.6
62	Paraguay	10.2	104	Gambia	4.8	145	New Zealand	-1.7

Source: World Bank

Value Added in Key Areas as Percentage of Gross Domestic Product (GDP)

Every gainful human activity confers or creates economic value, but at different rates. The investment of a certain amount of capital, energy, or labor results in the end product being more valuable than the original parts. Translated into shares of the Gross Domestic Product (GDP)—or the proportion of GDP contributed by a particular sector—value added becomes a means of determining the role that each sector plays in an economy. Thus, agriculture, being the most labor intensive of all economic activities and also the most subject to the vagaries of nature, is the least efficient of all sectors and contributes least to the overall economy in most advanced countries. Those countries where agriculture is the most prominent sector are also the poorest. On the same scale, services fare better than manufacturing and in the so-called post-industrialized economies, tend to perform better and contribute more to the GDP. Value added is an index of sectoral efficiency and performance.

7.9 Value Added in Manufacturing as Percentage of Gross Domestic Product (GDP)

Rank	Country/Entity	Value Added in Manufacturing as Percentage of GDP, 1998	Rank	Country/Entity	Value Added in Manufacturing as Percentage of GDP, 1998	Rank	Country/Entity	Value Added in Manufacturing as Percentage of GDP, 1998
1	Belarus	37	37	Georgia	18	73	Burundi	11
2	China	37	38	Honduras	18	74	Cameroon	11
3	Malaysia	34	39	Kyrgyzstan	18	75	Madagascar	11
4	Slovenia	29	40	Spain	18	76	Norway	11
5	Thailand	29	41	Tunisia	18	77	Yemen	11
6	Moldova	28	42	Turkey	18	78	Kenya	10
7	Egypt	26	43	United States	18	79	Mozambique	10
8	Indonesia	26	44	Uruguay	18	80	Nepal	10
9	South Korea	26	45	Chile	17	81	Saudi Arabia	10
10	Lithuania	26	46	Dominican Republic	17	82	Algeria	9
11	Argentina	25	47	Estonia	17	83	Azerbaijan	9
12	Armenia	25	48	Lebanon	17	84	Central African Republic	9
13	Finland	25	49	Lesotho	17	85	Mauritania	9
14	Hungary	25	50	Morocco	17	86	Panama	9
15	Romania	25	51	Pakistan	17	87	Papua New Guinea	9
16	Germany	24	52	Poland	17	88	Togo	9
17	Singapore	24	53	Sri Lanka	17	89	Uganda	9
18	South Africa	24	54	Venezuela	17	90	Benin	8
19	Brazil	23	55	Zimbabwe	17	91	Congo, Rep. of	8
20	Ecuador	22	56	Costa Rica	16	92	Ghana	8
21	El Salvador	22	57	Eritrea	16	93	Hong Kong	7
22	Peru	22	58	Jamaica	16	94	Myanmar (Burma)	7
23	Philippines	22	59	Laos	16	95	Tanzania	7
24	Burkina Faso	21	60	Nicaragua	16	96	Cambodia	6
25	Latvia	21	61	Rwanda	16	97	Mali	6
26	United Kingdom	21	62	Malawi	15	98	Niger	6
27	Austria	20	63	Paraguay	15	99	Sierra Leone	6
28	Italy	20	64	Senegal	15	100	Ukraine	6
29	Mexico	20	65	Australia	14	101	Angola	5
30	Côte d'Ivoire	19	66	Namibia	14	102	Botswana	5
31	Colombia	19	67	Guatemala	13	103	Nigeria	5
32	France	19	68	Jordan	13	104	Bolivia	4
33	India	19	69	Uzbekistan	13	105	Guinea	4
34	Bangladesh	18	70	Chad	12	106	Macedonia	0
35	Belgium	18	71	Kazakhstan	12			
36	Bulgaria	18	72	Zambia	12			

Source: World Development Report

Rank	Country/Entity	Value Added in Agriculture as Percentage of GDP, 1998	Rank	Country/Entity	Value Added in Agriculture as Percentage of GDP, 1998	Rank	Country/Entity	Value Added in Agriculture as Percentage of GDP, 1998
1	Albania	63	39	Paraguay	25	77	Kazakhstan	10
2	Myanmar (Burma)	59	40	Mauritania	24	78	Namibia	10
3	Congo, Dem. Rep. of	58	41	Bangladesh	23	79	Eritrea	9
4	Central African Republic	55	42	Bulgaria	23	80	Russia	9
5	Laos	52	43	Honduras	23	81	Brazil	8
6	Cambodia	51	44	Guinea	22	82	Chile	8
7	Burundi	49	45	Sri Lanka	22	83	Uruguay	8
8	Kyrgyzstan	46	46	Guatemala	21	84	Argentina	7
9	Tanzania	46	47	Azerbaijan	19	85	Jamaica	7
10	Mali	45	48	China	18	86	Latvia	7
11	Sierra Leone	44	49	Yemen	18	87	Panama	7
12	Uganda	43	50	Zimbabwe	18	88	Peru	7
13	Cameroon	42	51	Egypt	17	89	Hungary	6
14	Togo	42	52	Philippines	17	90	South Korea	6
15	Armenia	41	53	Senegal	17	91	Saudi Arabia	6
16	Niger	41	54	Bolivia	16	92	Estonia	5
17	Nepal	40	55	Indonesia	16	93	Mexico	5
18	Benin	39	56	Morocco	16	94	Slovakia	5
19	Chad	39	57	Zambia	16	95	Slovenia	5
20	Malawi	39	58	Romania	15	96	Botswana	4
21	Ghana	37	59	Turkey	15	97	Finland	4
22	Mozambique	34	60	Angola	14	98	Poland	4
23	Nicaragua	34	61	Belarus	14	99	South Africa	4
24	Rwanda	34	62	Costa Rica	14	100	Venezuela	4
25	Mongolia	33	63	Lithuania	14	101	Australia	3
26	Burkina Faso	32	64	Tunisia	14	102	Italy	3
27	Georgia	32	65	Colombia	13	103	Jordan	3
28	Nigeria	32	66	El Salvador	13	104	Spain	3
29	Haiti	31	67	Algeria	12	105	France	2
30	Madagascar	31	68	Congo, Rep. of	12	106	Norway	2
31	Moldova	31	69	Dominican Republic	12	107	United Kingdom	2
32	Kenya	29	70	Ecuador	12	108	United States	2
33	Papua New Guinea	28	71	Lebanon	12	109	Austria	1
34	Uzbekistan	28	72	Macedonia	12	110	Belgium	1
35	Vietnam	26	73	Malaysia	12	111	Germany	1
36	Côte d'Ivoire	25	74	Ukraine	12	112	Hong Kong	0
37	India	25	75	Lesotho	11	113	Singapore	0
38	Pakistan	25	76	Thailand	11			

Source: World Development Report

7.11 Value Added in Services as Percentage of GDP

Rank	Country/Entity	Value Added in Services as Percentage of GDP, 1998	Rank	Country/Entity	Value Added in Services as Percentage of GDP, 1998	Rank	Country/Entity	Value Added in Services as Percentage of GDP, 1998
1	Hong Kong	85	39	Madagascar	56	77	Vietnam	43
2	Panama	76	40	Namibia	56	78	Belarus	42
3	Belgium	72	41	Kenya	55	79	Guinea	42
4	France	72	42	Peru	55	80	Niger	42
5	Jordan	72	43	Zambia	55	81	Uzbekistan	42
6	Australia	71	44	Ecuador	54	82	Algeria	41
7	United States	71	45	Morocco	54	83	Indonesia	41
8	Poland	70	46	Paraguay	53	84	Malawi	41
9	Austria	68	47	Bolivia	52	85	Burkina Faso	40
10	Mexico	68	48	Côte d'Ivoire	52	86	Malaysia	40
11	Estonia	67	49	Philippines	52	87	Mongolia	40
12	United Kingdom	67	50	Sri Lanka	52	88	Tanzania	40
13	Italy	66	51	Venezuela	52	89	Congo, Rep. of	39
14	Norway	66	52	Botswana	51	90	Uganda	39
15	Singapore	65	53	South Korea	51	91	Ghana	38
16	Costa Rica	64	54	Bulgaria	50	92	Nepal	38
17	Uruguay	64	55	Egypt	50	93	Togo	37
18	Kazakhstan	63	56	Pakistan	50	94	Azerbaijan	36
19	Finland	62	57	Bangladesh	49	95	Cameroon	36
20	Latvia	62	58	Colombia	49	96	Papua New Guinea	36
21	Slovakia	62	59	Russia	49	97	Cambodia	34
22	Eritrea	61	60	Saudi Arabia	49	98	Mali	34
23	Lebanon	61	61	Thailand	49	99	Moldova	34
24	Macedonia	61	62	Haiti	48	100	Yemen	34
25	Guatemala	60	63	Mozambique	48	101	China	33
26	Hungary	60	64	Romania	48	102	Angola	32
27	El Salvador	59	65	Ukraine	48	103	Burundi	32
28	Senegal	59	66	Benin	47	104	Sierra Leone	32
29	Jamaica	58	67	Honduras	47	105	Myanmar (Burma)	31
30	Tunisia	58	68	Lesotho	47	106	Kyrgyzstan	30
31	Zimbabwe	58	69	Chad	46	107	Central African Republic	27
32	Chile	57	70	Lithuania	46	108	Laos	27
33	Slovenia	57	71	Georgia	45	109	Nigeria	27
34	South Africa	57	72	India	45	110	Congo, Dem. Rep. of	25
35	Turkey	57	73	Mauritania	45	111	Armenia	23
36	Argentina	56	74	Germany	44	112	Albania	19
37	Brazil	56	75	Nicaragua	44			
38	Dominican Republic	56	76	Rwanda	43			

Source: World Development Report

Chapter 8

Business and Investment

8.1 Companies

Joint-stock investment companies, known as public companies (or limited companies in the United Kingdom and elsewhere), have become the world's most popular form of business corporation since the nineteenth century. It has also allowed mass participation in the economy by a large body of investors who have neither the time nor the money to go into business themselves. Over the years, government regulations have successfully reduced the risk to investors and have also controlled, though not eliminated, opportunities for corruption and greed by management. The number of publicly listed companies on a nation's stock exchanges is an index of vigor of a free market economy. Its absence, on the other hand, is an indication of a controlled or socialist economy, such as the one that prevailed in the former Soviet Union.

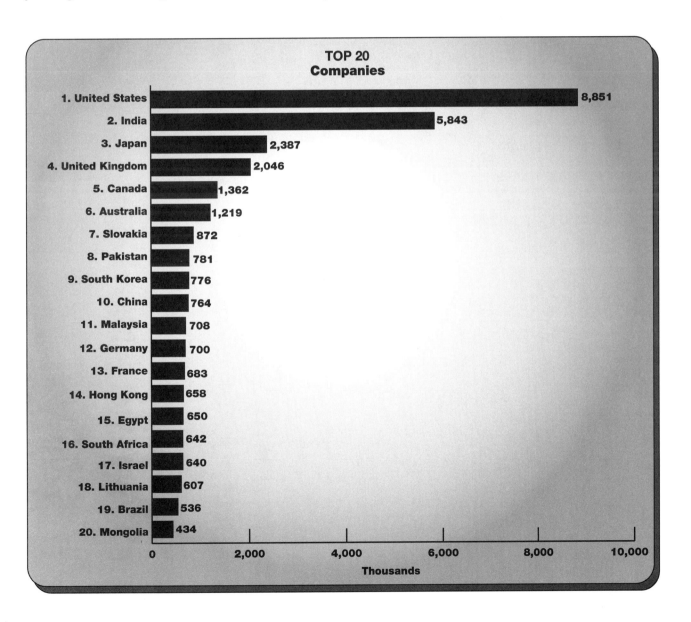

TOP 20
Companies

1. United States — 8,851
2. India — 5,843
3. Japan — 2,387
4. United Kingdom — 2,046
5. Canada — 1,362
6. Australia — 1,219
7. Slovakia — 872
8. Pakistan — 781
9. South Korea — 776
10. China — 764
11. Malaysia — 708
12. Germany — 700
13. France — 683
14. Hong Kong — 658
15. Egypt — 650
16. South Africa — 642
17. Israel — 640
18. Lithuania — 607
19. Brazil — 536
20. Mongolia — 434

Thousands

Rank	Country/Entity	Number of Publicly Listed Domestic Companies, 1997	Rank	Country/Entity	Number of Publicly Listed Domestic Companies, 1997	Rank	Country/Entity	Number of Publicly Listed Domestic Companies, 1997
21	Thailand	431	44	Nigeria	182	67	Hungary	49
22	Spain	384	45	Portugal	148	68	Jamaica	49
23	Singapore	303	46	Poland	143	69	Morocco	49
24	Chile	295	47	Jordan	139	70	Ecuador	41
25	Indonesia	282	48	Belgium	138	71	Côte d'Ivoire	35
26	Czech Republic	276	49	Argentina	136	72	Tunisia	34
27	Iran	263	50	Finland	124	73	Kyrgyzstan	27
28	Turkey	257	51	Honduras	119	74	Slovenia	26
29	Peru	248	52	Costa Rica	114	75	Estonia	22
30	Sweden	245	53	Austria	101	76	Ghana	21
31	Sri Lanka	239	54	Nepal	98	77	Panama	21
32	Denmark	237	55	Venezuela	91	78	Uruguay	16
33	Italy	235	56	Ireland	83	79	Bulgaria	15
34	Greece	230	57	Croatia	77	80	Namibia	13
35	Philippines	221	58	Romania	76	81	Botswana	12
36	Switzerland	216	59	Kuwait	74	82	Bolivia	11
37	Russia	208	60	Saudi Arabia	70	83	Lebanon	9
38	Bangladesh	202	61	Zimbabwe	64	84	Guatemala	7
39	Netherlands	201	62	Paraguay	60	85	Dominican Republic	6
40	Mexico	198	63	Armenia	59	86	Zambia	6
41	Norway	196	64	El Salvador	59	87	Uzbekistan	4
42	New Zealand	190	65	Kenya	58			
43	Colombia	189	66	Latvia	50			

Source: Economist Intelligence

Net Foreign Direct Investment

Foreign direct investment is one of the principal agents of globalization. Net foreign direct investment happens at three levels: (1) by multinationals through their subsidiaries in countries belonging to the Organization for Economic Cooperation and Development (OECD) without any political strings; (2) by multinationals in developing countries with some political risk through the intermediation of international organizations or consortia; and (3) by donor OECD countries in developing countries as part of sometimes overlapping political or economic programs. Total net foreign direct investment tripled to an estimated $619 billion in 1998 from $198 billion in 1980. By linking national economies together through strategic investments, net foreign direct investment has brought a large degree of stability to the global economic system and also helped to exploit the potential of many countries without the capital structure to do so.

8.2 Net Foreign Direct Investment

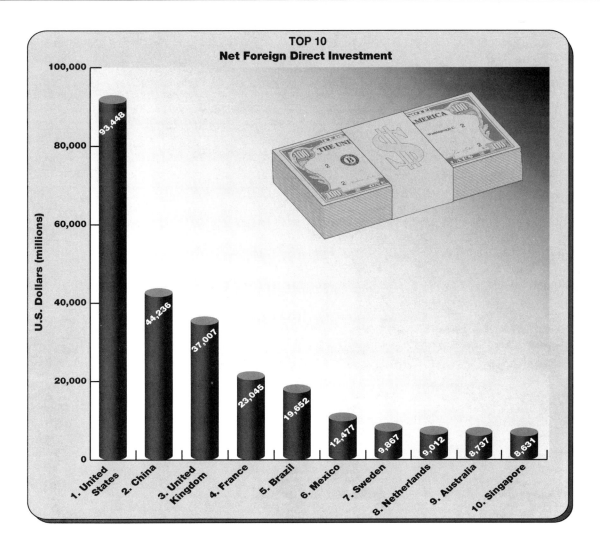

TOP 10
Net Foreign Direct Investment

U.S. Dollars (millions)

- 1. United States — 93,448
- 2. China — 44,236
- 3. United Kingdom — 37,007
- 4. France — 23,045
- 5. Brazil — 19,652
- 6. Mexico — 12,477
- 7. Sweden — 9,867
- 8. Netherlands — 9,012
- 9. Australia — 8,737
- 10. Singapore — 8,631

Rank	Country/Entity	Foreign Investment in Millions of U.S. Dollars, 1997	Rank	Country/Entity	Foreign Investment in Millions of U.S. Dollars, 1997	Rank	Country/Entity	Foreign Investment in Millions of U.S. Dollars, 1997
11	Canada	7,132	51	Ukraine	623	91	Armenia	51
12	Argentina	6,645	52	Bolivia	601	92	Georgia	50
13	Russia	6,241	53	Ecuador	577	93	Iran	50
14	Colombia	5,982	54	Latvia	521	94	Kyrgyzstan	50
15	Spain	5,556	55	Bulgaria	498	95	Albania	48
16	Switzerland	5,506	56	Sri Lanka	430	96	Cameroon	45
17	Chile	5,417	57	Dominican Republic	405	97	Mozambique	35
18	Malaysia	5,106	58	Croatia	388	98	Senegal	30
19	Venezuela	5,087	59	Lithuania	355	99	Lesotho	29
20	Poland	4,908	60	Angola	350	100	Nepal	23
21	Indonesia	4,677	61	Côte d'Ivoire	327	101	Jordan	22
22	Thailand	3,745	62	Slovenia	321	102	Kenya	20
23	Italy	3,700	63	Tunisia	316	103	Kuwait	20
24	Norway	3,545	64	Uzbekistan	285	104	Tajikistan	20
25	India	3,351	65	Estonia	266	105	Chad	15
26	Japan	3,200	66	Paraguay	250	106	Macedonia	15
27	South Korea	2,844	67	Cambodia	203	107	Mali	15
28	Denmark	2,792	68	Belarus	200	108	Madagascar	14
29	Ireland	2,727	69	Papua New Guinea	200	109	El Salvador	11
30	Israel	2,706	70	Uganda	180	110	Congo, Rep. of	9
31	New Zealand	2,650	71	Nicaragua	173	111	Algeria	7
32	Austria	2,354	72	Slovakia	165	112	Mongolia	7
33	Finland	2,128	73	Uruguay	160	113	Central African Republic	6
34	Hungary	2,079	74	Tanzania	158	114	Ethiopia	5
35	Peru	2,030	75	Lebanon	150	115	Sierra Leone	4
36	Vietnam	1,800	76	Jamaica	137	116	Benin	3
37	South Africa	1,725	77	Namibia	137	117	Haiti	3
38	Portugal	1,713	78	Bangladesh	135	118	Mauritania	3
39	Nigeria	1,539	79	Ghana	130	119	Malawi	2
40	Kazakhstan	1,321	80	Honduras	122	120	Niger	2
41	Czech Republic	1,286	81	Botswana	100	121	Burundi	1
42	Philippines	1,222	82	Guatemala	90	122	Congo, Dem. Rep. of	1
43	Romania	1,215	83	Laos	90	123	Guinea	1
44	Morocco	1,200	84	Turkmenistan	85	124	Rwanda	1
45	Panama	1,030	85	Myanmar (Burma)	80	125	Burkina Faso	0
46	Greece	984	86	Syria	80	126	Eritrea	0
47	Egypt	891	87	Zambia	70	127	Togo	0
48	Turkey	805	88	Zimbabwe	70	128	Yemen	-138
49	Pakistan	713	89	Moldova	60	129	Germany	-344
50	Azerbaijan	650	90	Costa Rica	57	130	Saudi Arabia	-1,129

Source: World Development Report

8.3 Net Foreign Direct Investment as Percentage of Gross Domestic Product (GDP)

Rank	Country/Entity	Investment as Percentage of GDP, 1993–1995	Rank	Country/Entity	Investment as Percentage of GDP, 1993–1995	Rank	Country/Entity	Investment as Percentage of GDP, 1993–1995
1	Vanuatu	16.0	9	Grenada	9.0	18	Swaziland	5.5
2	Saint Vincent and the Grenadines	12.6	10	Malaysia	7.2	19	Jamaica	5.3
			11	Vietnam	7.0	20	China	5.2
3	Saint Lucia	12.0	12	Trinidad and Tobago	6.3	21	Laos	5.1
4	Hungary	10.8	13	Singapore	6.0	22	Solomon Islands	4.9
5	Seychelles	10.6	14	Czech Republic	5.7	23	Nicaragua	4.4
6	Papua New Guinea	9.9	15	Antigua and Barbuda	5.6	24	Costa Rica	4.3
7	Angola	9.6	16	Cambodia	5.5	25	Tanzania	4.3
8	Saint Kitts and Nevis	9.6	17	Dominica	5.5	26	Suriname	4.2

Rank	Country/Entity	Investment as Percentage of GDP, 1993–1995	Rank	Country/Entity	Investment as Percentage of GDP, 1993–1995	Rank	Country/Entity	Investment as Percentage of GDP, 1993–1995
27	Belize	3.8	66	Romania	1.2	105	Armenia	0.3
28	Ghana	3.7	67	Venezuela	1.2	106	Benin	0.3
29	Maldives	3.6	68	Bulgaria	1.1	107	Central African Republic	0.3
30	Fiji	3.5	69	Sweden	1.1	108	Estonia	0.3
31	Colombia	3.4	70	Guinea	1.0	109	Kuwait	0.3
32	Peru	3.3	71	Lithuania	1.0	110	Lebanon	0.3
33	Azerbaijan	3.2	72	Norway	1.0	111	Madagascar	0.3
34	Latvia	3.2	73	Slovakia	1.0	112	Mauritania	0.3
35	Albania	3.1	74	Comoros	0.9	113	Ukraine	0.3
36	Panama	3.1	75	Morocco	0.9	114	Burundi	0.2
37	Poland	3.1	76	Slovenia	0.9	115	Côte d'Ivoire	0.2
38	Mexico	2.9	77	Djibouti	0.8	116	Denmark	0.2
39	Ecuador	2.8	78	Spain	0.8	117	Georgia	0.2
40	Mozambique	2.8	79	Tajikistan	0.8	118	Ireland	0.2
41	Bolivia	2.6	80	Barbados	0.7	119	Nepal	0.2
42	Chile	2.6	81	Brazil	0.7	120	Belarus	0.1
43	Gambia	2.6	82	Equatorial Guinea	0.7	121	Congo, Rep. of	0.1
44	Paraguay	2.6	83	Pakistan	0.7	122	Ethiopia	0.1
45	Malta	2.4	84	Uruguay	0.7	123	Haiti	0.1
46	Dominican Republic	2.3	85	Zimbabwe	0.7	124	Iceland	0.1
47	Indonesia	2.3	86	Cape Verde	0.6	125	Jordan	0.1
48	Uganda	2.2	87	Chad	0.6	126	Malawi	0.1
49	Philippines	1.9	88	Russia	0.6	127	Niger	0.1
50	Moldova	1.7	89	Argentina	0.5	128	Sierra Leone	0.1
51	Nigeria	1.7	90	Australia	0.5	129	Canada	-0.2
52	Zambia	1.7	91	Guatemala	0.5	130	South Korea	-0.2
53	Botswana	1.6	92	Guyana	0.5	131	Austria	-0.3
54	Lesotho	1.6	93	Kyrgyzstan	0.5	132	Italy	-0.3
55	Namibia	1.5	94	Sri Lanka	0.5	133	Japan	-0.3
56	Tunisia	1.5	95	Turkey	0.5	134	Israel	-0.5
57	Cameroon	1.4	96	Uzbekistan	0.5	135	Bahrain	-0.6
58	Honduras	1.4	97	Yemen	0.5	136	United States	-0.6
59	Oman	1.4	98	Croatia	0.4	137	Germany	-0.8
60	Egypt	1.3	99	El Salvador	0.4	138	United Kingdom	-1.1
61	Kazakhstan	1.3	100	Guinea-Bissau	0.4	139	Finland	-1.3
62	Portugal	1.3	101	India	0.4	140	Gabon	-1.4
63	Thailand	1.3	102	Kenya	0.4	141	Netherlands	-1.4
64	Greece	1.2	103	Mauritius	0.4	142	Saudi Arabia	-1.5
65	Mongolia	1.2	104	Syria	0.4	143	Switzerland	-2.3

Source: World Development Report

Risk Assessment

Risk assessment is an economic concept that has gained wide currency among developmental and investment specialists. It is also an industry engaged in scanning the performance of nations on a number of scales and providing an evaluation of a nation's potential in the immediate future, and the political risk attendant on a financial investment or loan. It helps answer the questions: Will a nation repay its loans on time, and does it have the capacity to meet its financial obligations?

What are its domestic and international trade policies designed to achieve in the short term? What is its track record in dealing with international financial organizations? The International Credit Rating Group (ICRG) is a body that advises donor nations, banks, and investors on the viability of national economies and the potential pitfalls of extending loans. *Institutional Investor,* a distinguished magazine in the field, devised the rating system.

8.4 Composite International Credit Rating Group (ICRG) Assessment

Rank	Country/Entity	ICRG Assessment, 1999	Rank	Country/Entity	ICRG Assessment, 1999	Rank	Country/Entity	ICRG Assessment, 1999
1	Norway	88.3	40	Lithuania	73.5	79	Venezuela	62.8
2	Netherlands	87.8	41	Estonia	73.0	80	Yemen	62.8
3	Ireland	87.5	42	Philippines	73.0	81	Malawi	61.8
4	Singapore	87.5	43	Uruguay	73.0	82	Brazil	61.5
5	Switzerland	87.3	44	Tunisia	72.8	83	Ecuador	61.5
6	Finland	86.5	45	Morocco	72.3	84	Armenia	61.0
7	Denmark	86.0	46	Panama	72.3	85	Togo	60.8
8	Austria	84.8	47	Dominican Republic	72.0	86	Albania	60.5
9	Sweden	83.5	48	Syria	71.5	87	Guinea	60.5
10	Japan	83.3	49	Jamaica	71.3	88	Vietnam	60.3
11	Canada	82.8	50	Latvia	71.0	89	Belarus	59.8
12	Germany	82.8	51	Croatia	70.8	90	Zambia	59.8
13	United States	82.8	52	Malaysia	70.8	91	Ukraine	59.0
14	Botswana	82.0	53	Egypt	69.0	92	Honduras	58.8
15	Portugal	82.0	54	Kazakhstan	69.0	93	Tanzania	58.8
16	France	81.8	55	Saudi Arabia	69.0	94	Mozambique	58.5
17	United Kingdom	81.3	56	South Africa	68.8	95	Ethiopia	57.8
18	Italy	80.8	57	Guatemala	68.3	96	Romania	57.8
19	Belgium	80.5	58	Bolivia	67.5	97	Colombia	57.3
20	Poland	80.5	59	Côte d'Ivoire	67.3	98	Nigeria	56.3
21	Australia	80.0	60	Papua New Guinea	67.0	99	Azerbaijan	56.0
22	Slovenia	79.5	61	Thailand	67.0	100	Turkey	56.0
23	Spain	79.5	62	Mali	66.5	101	Lebanon	55.3
24	Hungary	77.8	63	Iran	66.3	102	Haiti	55.0
25	Namibia	77.8	64	Mexico	66.3	103	Myanmar (Burma)	55.0
26	Slovakia	77.8	65	Mongolia	66.3	104	Niger	54.8
27	New Zealand	77.5	66	Peru	66.3	105	Moldova	54.5
28	El Salvador	76.8	67	Bangladesh	66.0	106	Pakistan	53.5
29	Czech Republic	76.5	68	Madagascar	66.0	107	Algeria	52.8
30	Argentina	76.3	69	Burkina Faso	65.5	108	Zimbabwe	52.0
31	Costa Rica	76.3	70	Israel	64.8	109	Congo, Rep. of	50.0
32	Greece	76.3	71	Kenya	63.8	110	Russia	49.8
33	Hong Kong	76.3	72	Sri Lanka	63.8	111	Indonesia	48.5
34	Bulgaria	75.5	73	Cameroon	63.5	112	Nicaragua	47.8
35	China	75.5	74	India	63.3	113	Angola	46.5
36	South Korea	74.5	75	Paraguay	63.0	114	Congo, Dem. Rep. of	39.5
37	Chile	74.0	76	Senegal	63.0	115	Sierra Leone	29.5
38	Jordan	73.8	77	Uganda	63.0			
39	Kuwait	73.5	78	Ghana	62.8			

Source: International Credit Rating Group

8.5 Institutional Investor Credit Rating

Rank	Country/Entity	Credit Rating, 1999	Rank	Country/Entity	Credit Rating, 1999	Rank	Country/Entity	Credit Rating, 1999
1	Switzerland	92.7	12	Canada	83.0	23	Hong Kong	61.8
2	Germany	92.5	13	Finland	82.2	24	Slovenia	58.4
3	United States	92.2	14	Ireland	81.8	25	China	57.2
4	Netherlands	91.7	15	Singapore	81.3	26	Poland	56.7
5	France	90.8	16	Spain	80.3	27	Kuwait	56.5
6	United Kingdom	90.2	17	Sweden	79.7	28	Greece	56.1
7	Austria	88.7	18	Italy	79.1	29	Hungary	55.9
8	Norway	86.8	19	Portugal	76.1	30	Saudi Arabia	54.4
9	Japan	86.5	20	Australia	74.3	31	Israel	54.3
10	Denmark	84.7	21	New Zealand	73.1	32	Botswana	53.5
11	Belgium	83.5	22	Chile	61.8	33	South Korea	52.7

Rank	Country/Entity	Credit Rating, 1999	Rank	Country/Entity	Credit Rating, 1999	Rank	Country/Entity	Credit Rating, 1999
34	Malaysia	51.0	59	Paraguay	31.3	84	Uganda	20.3
35	Tunisia	50.3	60	El Salvador	31.2	85	Russia	20.0
36	Thailand	46.9	61	Romania	31.2	86	Honduras	19.8
37	Uruguay	46.5	62	Papua New Guinea	30.4	87	Burkina Faso	18.8
38	Mexico	46.0	63	Ghana	29.5	88	Myanmar (Burma)	18.7
39	South Africa	45.8	64	Bulgaria	28.6	89	Tanzania	18.3
40	Colombia	44.5	65	Dominican Republic	28.1	90	Cameroon	18.1
41	India	44.5	66	Bolivia	28.0	91	Mozambique	17.9
42	Egypt	44.4	67	Jamaica	28.0	92	Ukraine	17.2
43	Philippines	43.3	68	Indonesia	27.9	93	Nigeria	16.8
44	Morocco	43.2	69	Kazakhstan	27.9	94	Togo	16.6
45	Estonia	42.8	70	Vietnam	27.8	95	Benin	16.3
46	Argentina	42.7	71	Iran	27.7	96	Ethiopia	16.2
47	Slovakia	41.3	72	Guatemala	27.2	97	Zambia	16.1
48	Panama	39.9	73	Zimbabwe	26.5	98	Guinea	15.4
49	Croatia	39.0	74	Ecuador	25.5	99	Mali	15.4
50	Costa Rica	38.4	75	Algeria	25.2	100	Belarus	11.9
51	Latvia	38.0	76	Bangladesh	25.0	101	Nicaragua	11.6
52	Brazil	37.4	77	Nepal	24.4	102	Angola	11.5
53	Jordan	37.3	78	Côte d'Ivoire	24.3	103	Haiti	11.2
54	Turkey	36.9	79	Kenya	24.1	104	Congo, Dem. Rep. of	11.1
55	Peru	35.0	80	Syria	23.0	105	Georgia	10.9
56	Venezuela	34.4	81	Senegal	21.7	106	Albania	10.7
57	Sri Lanka	33.3	82	Malawi	20.4	107	Congo, Rep. of	9.7
58	Lebanon	31.9	83	Pakistan	20.4	108	Sierra Leone	6.3

Source: Institutional Investor

8.6 Gross Domestic Investment

Two major indicators of development are the rate of national saving and the rate of domestic investment. It is also one of three major components of Gross Domestic Product expenditures, the others being government expenditure and private consumption. The amount of investment capital generated internally determines the ability of a nation to sustain development in the various economic sectors. Most modern economies also supplement domestic investment with foreign investment. This is especially true of developing countries, which do not have sufficient capital and are therefore dependent on attracting foreign investors and providing them with the right incentives.

Rank	Country/Entity	Millions of Dollars (U.S.)	Rank	Country/Entity	Millions of Dollars (U.S.)	Rank	Country/Entity	Millions of Dollars (U.S.)
1	Lesotho	84	14	Saint Kitts and Nevis	39	26	Hong Kong	32
2	Mozambique	70	15	Honduras	38	27	Indonesia	32
3	Congo, Rep. of	51	16	Grenada	36	28	Mauritius	32
4	Kazakhstan	49	17	South Korea	36	29	Singapore	32
5	Turkmenistan	46	18	Jordan	35	30	Jamaica	31
6	Bhutan	45	19	Moldova	35	31	Malta	30
7	Cape Verde	42	20	Ukraine	35	32	Syria	30
8	Macedonia	42	21	Macau	33	33	Vanuatu	30
9	Thailand	42	22	Saint Vincent and	33	34	Belarus	29
10	China	41		the Grenadines		35	Estonia	29
11	Gaza Strip	41	23	Algeria	32	36	Japan	29
12	São Tomé and Príncipe	41	24	Georgia	32	37	Seychelles	29
13	Malaysia	39	25	Guyana	32	38	Panama	28

Rank	Country/Entity	Millions of Dollars (U.S.)	Rank	Country/Entity	Millions of Dollars (U.S.)	Rank	Country/Entity	Millions of Dollars (U.S.)
39	Tanzania	28	87	Hungary	21	135	Mauritania	16
40	Aruba	27	88	Morocco	21	136	Poland	16
41	Chile	27	89	New Zealand	21	137	Denmark	15
42	Costa Rica	27	90	Slovenia	21	138	Ethiopia	15
43	Gabon	27	91	Suriname	21	139	Fiji	15
44	Réunion	27	92	Turkey	21	140	Finland	15
45	Sri Lanka	27	93	Argentina	20	141	Iceland	15
46	United Arab Emirates	27	94	Benin	20	142	Senegal	15
47	Austria	26	95	Czech Republic	20	143	United Kingdom	15
48	Bahrain	26	96	Egypt	20	144	Uruguay	15
49	Botswana	26	97	El Salvador	20	145	Uzbekistan	15
50	Russia	26	98	Kenya	20	146	Angola	14
51	Equatorial Guinea	25	99	Kyrgyzstan	20	147	Bangladesh	14
52	Mali	25	100	Netherlands	20	148	Guinea	14
53	Nicaragua	25	101	Saudi Arabia	20	149	Ireland	14
54	Portugal	25	102	Somalia	20	150	Sweden	14
55	San Marino	25	103	Spain	20	151	Togo	14
56	Antigua and Barbuda	24	104	Yemen	20	152	Zambia	14
57	Cyprus	24	105	Cambodia	19	153	Barbados	13
58	Dominica	24	106	Canada	19	154	Bulgaria	13
59	Iran	24	107	Comoros	19	155	Burundi	13
60	Israel	24	108	Ecuador	19	156	Central African Republic	13
61	Namibia	24	109	Iraq	19	157	Laos	13
62	Saint Lucia	24	110	Luxembourg	19	158	Malawi	13
63	Taiwan	24	111	Maldives	19	159	Trinidad and Tobago	13
64	Belize	23	112	Mongolia	19	160	Uganda	13
65	Dominican Republic	23	113	Pakistan	19	161	Venezuela	13
66	Germany	23	114	Papua New Guinea	19	162	Bermuda	12
67	India	23	115	Qatar	19	163	Côte d'Ivoire	12
68	Mexico	23	116	Vietnam	19	164	Djibouti	12
69	Norway	23	117	Belgium	18	165	Myanmar (Burma)	12
70	Paraguay	23	118	France	18	166	Madagascar	11
71	Philippines	23	119	Lithuania	18	167	Romania	11
72	Slovakia	23	120	South Africa	18	168	Albania	10
73	Tunisia	23	121	Swaziland	18	169	Lebanon	10
74	Australia	22	122	Zimbabwe	18	170	Liberia	10
75	Burkina Faso	22	123	Italy	17	171	Niger	10
76	Colombia	22	124	Oman	17	172	Armenia	9
77	Guinea-Bissau	22	125	Puerto Rico	17	173	Latvia	9
78	Libya	22	126	Sudan	17	174	Nigeria	9
79	Nepal	22	127	United States	17	175	Sierra Leone	8
80	Peru	22	128	Bolivia	16	176	Faroe Islands	4
81	Switzerland	22	129	Cameroon	16	177	Congo, Dem. Rep. of	3
82	Azerbaijan	21	130	Chad	16	178	Croatia	3
83	Bahamas	21	131	Gambia	16	179	Mayotte	3
84	Brazil	21	132	Ghana	16	180	Rwanda	3
85	French Polynesia	21	133	Guatemala	16	181	Haiti	2
86	Greece	21	134	Kuwait	16			

Source: World Bank

8.7 Largest Market Capitalization

Market capitalization is an investment term that means the total value of all stocks and bonds traded on all the stock exchanges in a country. In the case of highly developed countries, market capitalization is an index of the vigor of a free market economy, and the rate of increase in market capitalization is an index of the pace of economic growth. It may be noted that the market capitalization of the major economic superpowers is comparable to the Gross Domestic Product of these countries.

Rank	Country/Entity	Market Capitalization, Millions of Dollars (U.S.)	Rank	Country/Entity	Market Capitalization, Millions of Dollars (U.S.)	Rank	Country/Entity	Market Capitalization, Millions of Dollars (U.S.)
1	United States	8,484,433	18	Singapore	150,215	35	Austria	33,953
2	Japan	3,088,850	19	South Korea	138,817	36	Luxembourg	32,692
3	United Kingdom	1,740,246	20	India	122,605	37	Turkey	30,020
4	Germany	670,997	21	Belgium	119,831	38	Portugal	24,660
5	France	591,123	22	China	113,755	39	Greece	24,178
6	Canada	486,268	23	Mexico	106,540	40	Czech Republic	18,077
7	Hong Kong	449,381	24	Thailand	99,828	41	Colombia	17,137
8	Switzerland	402,104	25	Indonesia	91,106	42	Egypt	14,173
9	Netherlands	378,721	26	Philippines	80,649	43	Peru	12,291
10	Australia	311,988	27	Denmark	71,648	44	Pakistan	10,639
11	Malaysia	307,179	28	Chile	65,940	45	Venezuela	10,055
12	Taiwan	273,608	29	Finland	63,078	46	Morocco	8,705
13	Italy	258,160	30	Norway	57,423	47	Poland	8,390
14	Sweden	247,217	31	Argentina	44,679	48	Jordan	4,551
15	Spain	242,779	32	New Zealand	38,288	49	Bangladesh	4,551
16	South Africa	241,571	33	Russia	37,230			
17	Brazil	216,990	34	Israel	35,934			

Source: Economist Intelligence

Largest Businesses and Banks

The largest business corporations and banks in the world are giant multinationals, which have both a substantial domestic base in one country and branches and affiliates in all the major trading and industrial nations of the world. Because of the constant mergers and acquisitions in the business world, new rankings are created periodically. The rank is based on sales, but a number of other rankings exist—by assets, profits, employees, capitalization, and so on—and in each case the rank order can vary considerably. It may be noted that seventeen out of the world's largest businesses are Japanese and eleven are American.

8.8 Largest Businesses

Rank	Business	Country/Entity	Sales in Billions of Dollars (U.S.)	Rank	Business	Country/Entity	Sales in Billions of Dollars (U.S.)
1	General Motors	United States	168.4	8	Maribeni	Japan	124.0
2	Ford Motor	United States	147.0	9	Exxon	United States	119.4
3	Mitsui	Japan	144.9	10	Sumitomo	Japan	119.3
4	Mitsubishi	Japan	140.2	11	Toyoto Motor	Japan	108.7
5	Itocchu	Japan	135.5	12	Wal-Mart Stores	United States	106.1
6	Daimler/Chrysler	Germany	133.0	13	General Electric	United States	79.2
7	Royal Dutch/Shell	United Kingdom/ Netherlands	128.2	14	Nissho Iwai	Japan	78.9
				15	Nippon Telephone	Japan	78.3

Rank	Business	Country/Entity	Sales in Billions of Dollars (U.S.)
16	IBM	United States	75.9
17	Hitachi	Japan	75.7
18	AT&T	United States	74.5
19	Nippon Life Insurance	Japan	72.6
20	Mobil	United States	72.3
21	British Petroleum	United States	69.9
22	Matsushita Electrical	Japan	68.1
23	Volkswagen	Germany	66.5
24	Daewoo	South Korea	65.2
25	Siemens	Germany	63.7
26	Nissan Motor	Japan	59.1
27	Allianz	Germany	56.6
28	U.S. Postal Service	United States	56.4
29	Philip Morris	United States	54.5
30	Unilever	United Kingdome/ Netherlands	52.1
31	Fiat	Italy	50.5
32	Sony	Japan	50.3
33	Dai-Ichi	Japan	49.1
34	IRI	Italy	49.1
35	Nestles	Switzerland	48.9
36	Toshiba	Japan	48.4
37	Honda Motor	Japan	47.0
38	Elf Aquitaine	France	46.8
39	Tomen	Japan	46.5

Source: Forbes

8.9 Largest Banks

Rank	Bank	Country/Entity	Capital in Millions of Dollars (U.S.)
1	HSBC Holdings	United Kingdom	25,716
2	Bank of Tokyo-Mitsubishi	Japan	24,323
3	Credit Agricole	France	22,235
4	Chase Manhattan	United States	21,095
5	Citicorp	United States	20,109
6	Deutsche Bank	Germany	18,517
7	Bank of America	United States	17,181
8	ABN-Amro Bank	Netherlands	16,098
9	Sumitomo Bank	Japan	15,724
10	Union Bank of Switzerland	Switzerland	15,743
11	Fuji Bank	Japan	15,724
12	Dai Ichi Kangyo	Japan	15,162
13	Sanwa Bank	Japan	15,161
14	Sakura Bank	Japan	14,772
15	Bank of China	China	13,737
16	Nations Bank	United States	12,662
17	Barclays Bank	United Kingdom	12,635
18	Industrial Bank of Japan	Japan	12,384
19	Gourpe Caisse d'Espargne	France	12,368
20	National Westminster Bank	United Kingdom	11,914
21	Banque Nationale de Paris	France	11,612
22	Credit Suisse Group	Switzerland	11,611
23	J.P. Morgan & Co	United States	11,469
24	Rabobank Nederland	Netherlands	11,423
25	Industrial and Commercial Bank	China	11,172
26	Companie Financiere de Paribas	France	10,765
27	Societe General	France	10,735
28	Swiss Bank Corp	Switzerland	10,264
29	Dresdner Bank	Germany	9,325
30	First Chicago NBD Corp	United States	9,318
31	Lloyds TSB Group	United Kingdom	8,937
32	Long-Term Credit Bank	Japan	8,489
33	Tokai Bank	Japan	8,487
34	Westdeutsche Landesbank Girozcentrale	Germany	8,320
35	Commerzbank	Germany	8,157
36	Bank One Corp	United States	8,107
37	Credit Mutuel	France	8,065
38	National Australia Bank	Australia	8,042
39	Asahi Bank	Japan	7,871
40	First Union Corp	United States	7,790

Source: American Banker

8.10 Business Environment Index

This ranking measures what is generally known as the business climate, a term which describes the sum total of all the factors that favor the free market. The eight major categories on which the scale is based are market potential, tax policies, labor market policies, infrastructure, access to capital, official corruption, level of available skills, and political environment.

Rank	Country/Entity	Business Environment Index	Rank	Country/Entity	Business Environment Index	Rank	Country/Entity	Business Environment Index
1	Netherlands	8.78	17	Austria	7.89	33	Greece	6.64
2	United Kingdom	8.74	18	Spain	7.89	34	Mexico	6.58
3	United States	8.64	19	Chile	7.82	35	Brazil	6.38
4	Canada	8.61	20	Portugal	7.75	36	Peru	6.38
5	Singapore	8.56	21	Japan	7.68	37	South Africa	6.23
6	Denmark	8.43	22	Taiwan	7.61	38	Indonesia	6.20
7	Switzerland	8.42	23	Italy	7.53	39	Colombia	6.04
8	New Zealand	8.29	24	South Korea	7.26	40	Turkey	5.97
9	Ireland	8.28	25	Argentina	7.18	41	Egypt	5.92
10	Sweden	8.24	26	Hungary	7.14	42	Saudi Arabia	5.90
11	Germany	8.23	27	Malaysia	7.11	43	Slovakia	5.90
12	France	8.21	28	Israel	6.98	44	Sri Lanka	5.90
13	Australia	8.20	29	Philippines	6.88	45	India	5.77
14	Finland	8.17	30	Poland	6.84	46	Romania	5.77
15	Belgium	8.13	31	Thailand	6.79			
16	Norway	8.12	32	Czech Republic	6.74			

Source: Economist Intelligence

8.11 Global Competitiveness

This ranking assesses the ability of an economy to achieve sustained high growth over a period of time. It assumes that such growth is directly related to the degree of competition in an economy, especially its freedom from overt government intervention and from monopolistic tendencies historically embedded in capitalist societies. Some economies are more open and transparent than others and foster international trade and globalization. Any level of chauvinism and protectionism would decrease the level of global competitiveness. The role of government is as important as the existence of a large cadre of internationally trained managers, the level of technological capability, and the country's participation in international trade and investment flows.

Rank	Country/Entity	Global Competitiveness Index	Rank	Country/Entity	Global Competitiveness Index	Rank	Country/Entity	Global Competitiveness Index
1	Singapore	5	11	Denmark	38	21	Portugal	71
2	United States	15	12	Canada	39	22	France	73
3	Luxembourg	24	13	Malaysia	47	23	Iceland	75
4	Ireland	24	14	China	49	24	Belgium	76
5	Netherlands	27	15	Australia	51	25	Austria	79
6	United Kingdom	27	16	Germany	58	26	Hungary	80
7	Finland	31	17	Taiwan	62	27	Japan	89
8	Switzerland	32	18	Chile	65	28	Israel	91
9	Norway	33	19	Sweden	66	29	Italy	94
10	New Zealand	33	20	Spain	68	30	Brazil	97

Rank	Country/Entity	Global Competitiveness Index	Rank	Country/Entity	Global Competitiveness Index	Rank	Country/Entity	Global Competitiveness Index
31	Mexico	99	35	Czech Republic	106	39	South Africa	117
32	Indonesia	100	36	India	111	40	Thailand	120
33	Turkey	101	37	South Korea	113	41	Venezuela	123
34	Argentina	104	38	Greece	114			

Source: Economist Intelligence

8.12 Economic Freedom Index

Freedom is generally associated with the individual, but there are corporate freedoms that a democratic society requires to thrive. Among these are business freedom (also called economic freedom), religious freedom, academic freedom, and so on. The Index of Economic Freedom, reproduced below, is prepared by the Heritage Foundation, and it ranks countries on the basis of ten criteria that measure government role in restricting or enlarging the sphere of freedom in relation to the economy. These criteria are trade policy, taxation, monetary policy, the banking system, foreign investment regulations, property rights, government consumption, rule making by government, size of the black market, and wage and price controls. The ranking is on a scale of one to five, with one being the most free.

Rank	Country/Entity	Economic Freedom Index	Rank	Country/Entity	Economic Freedom Index	Rank	Country/Entity	Economic Freedom Index
1	Singapore	1.30	29	Panama	2.40	57	Turkey	2.80
2	Bahrain	1.70	30	Thailand	2.40	58	Uganda	2.80
3	New Zealand	1.75	31	El Salvador	2.45	59	Indonesia	2.85
4	Switzerland	1.90	32	Sri Lanka	2.45	60	Latvia	2.85
5	United States	1.90	33	Sweden	2.45	61	Malta	2.85
6	Luxembourg	1.95	34	France	2.50	62	Paraguay	2.85
7	Taiwan	1.95	35	Italy	2.50	63	Greece	2.90
8	United Kingdom	1.95	36	Spain	2.50	64	Hungary	2.90
9	Bahamas	2.00	37	Trinidad and Tobago	2.55	65	South Africa	2.90
10	Ireland	2.00	38	Argentina	2.60	66	Benin	2.95
11	Australia	2.05	39	Barbados	2.60	67	Ecuador	2.95
12	Japan	2.05	40	Cyprus	2.60	68	Gabon	2.95
13	Belgium	2.10	41	Jamaica	2.60	69	Morocco	2.95
14	Canada	2.10	42	Portugal	2.60	70	Poland	2.95
15	United Arab Emirates	2.10	43	Bolivia	2.65	71	Colombia	3.00
16	Austria	2.15	44	Oman	2.65	72	Ghana	3.00
17	Chile	2.15	45	Philippines	2.65	73	Lithuania	3.00
18	Estonia	2.15	46	Swaziland	2.70	74	Kenya	3.05
19	Czech Republic	2.20	47	Uruguay	2.70	75	Slovakia	3.05
20	Netherlands	2.20	48	Botswana	2.75	76	Zambia	3.05
21	Denmark	2.25	49	Jordan	2.75	77	Mali	3.10
22	Finland	2.25	50	Namibia	2.75	78	Mongolia	3.10
23	Germany	2.30	51	Tunisia	2.75	79	Slovenia	3.10
24	Iceland	2.30	52	Costa Rica	2.80	80	Honduras	3.15
25	South Korea	2.30	53	Guatemala	2.80	81	Papua New Guinea	3.15
26	Norway	2.35	54	Israel	2.80	82	Fiji	3.20
27	Kuwait	2.40	55	Peru	2.80	83	Pakistan	3.20
28	Malaysia	2.40	56	Saudi Arabia	2.80			

Source: Heritage Foundation

Chapter 9

Finance

External Public Debt

Only about twenty nations in the world live within their budgets or have a surplus, the United States being the latest entrant into this exclusive club. All the others carry an enormous burden of public debt created over the years through borrowing, often recklessly, from international financial groups or development banks. Total external public debt in 2000 was estimated at over $2.1 trillion and growing. Even though most of this debt is at low interest, it creates an intolerable burden for low- and middle-income countries where, in some cases, the debt repayment is more than the national income, and interest payments require further indebtedness. As a result, countries or regions go through intermittent financial crises, the last memorable one being the Asian financial crisis in 1997.

9.1 External Public Debt

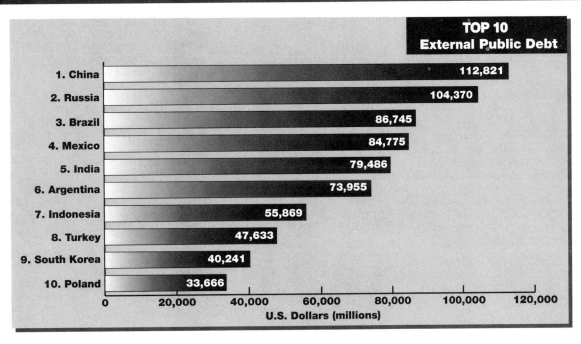

TOP 10 External Public Debt

Rank	Country	U.S. Dollars (millions)
1.	China	112,821
2.	Russia	104,370
3.	Brazil	86,745
4.	Mexico	84,775
5.	India	79,486
6.	Argentina	73,955
7.	Indonesia	55,869
8.	Turkey	47,633
9.	South Korea	40,241
10.	Poland	33,666

Rank	Country/Entity	External Public Debt in U.S. Dollars (millions)	Rank	Country/Entity	External Public Debt in U.S. Dollars (millions)	Rank	Country/Entity	External Public Debt in U.S. Dollars (millions)
11	Algeria	28,741	27	Czech Republic	12,275	43	Tanzania	6,054
12	Egypt	26,804	28	South Africa	11,246	44	Mozambique	5,430
13	Venezuela	26,680	29	Côte d'Ivoire	10,427	45	Zambia	5,233
14	Philippines	25,950	30	Ethiopia	9,427	46	Kenya	5,108
15	Pakistan	23,565	31	Tunisia	9,427	47	Panama	5,074
16	Nigeria	22,631	32	Sudan	8,998	48	Nicaragua	4,819
17	Thailand	22,009	33	Angola	8,885	49	Ghana	4,691
18	Peru	20,177	34	Congo, Dem. Rep. of	8,617	50	Slovakia	4,658
19	Vietnam	18,839	35	Iran	8,256	51	Myanmar (Burma)	4,640
20	Morocco	18,640	36	Yugoslavia	8,165	52	Uruguay	4,528
21	Malaysia	16,808	37	Romania	8,122	53	Chile	4,364
22	Syria	16,254	38	Bulgaria	7,721	54	Congo, Rep. of	4,284
23	Colombia	15,273	39	Cameroon	7,688	55	Croatia	4,217
24	Hungary	14,941	40	Jordan	7,020	56	Bolivia	4,144
25	Bangladesh	14,578	41	Ukraine	6,978	57	Honduras	3,910
26	Ecuador	12,376	42	Sri Lanka	6,641	58	Madagascar	3,871

Rank	Country/Entity	External Public Debt in U.S. Dollars (millions)	Rank	Country/Entity	External Public Debt in U.S. Dollars (millions)	Rank	Country/Entity	External Public Debt in U.S. Dollars (millions)
59	Gabon	3,671	86	Papua New Guinea	1,311	113	Latvia	322
60	Dominican Republic	3,460	87	Macedonia	1,251	114	Djibouti	253
61	Yemen	3,418	88	Turkmenistan	1,242	115	Azerbaijan	233
62	Uganda	3,202	89	Togo	1,207	116	São Tomé and Príncipe	227
63	Zimbabwe	3,124	90	Mauritius	1,187	117	Cape Verde	219
64	Senegal	3,110	91	Georgia	1,168	118	Estonia	214
65	Guinea	3,008	92	Burkina Faso	1,139	119	Swaziland	210
66	Jamaica	2,921	93	Liberia	1,061	120	Equatorial Guinea	209
67	Costa Rica	2,840	94	Lithuania	1,049	121	Belize	199
68	Guatemala	2,834	95	Burundi	1,022	122	Comoros	181
69	Kazakhstan	2,822	96	Rwanda	994	123	Maldives	153
70	Mali	2,687	97	Chad	939	124	Samoa	144
71	Oman	2,567	98	Haiti	897	125	Seychelles	131
72	El Salvador	2,427	99	Sierra Leone	893	126	Malta	125
73	Lebanon	2,356	100	Guinea-Bissau	838	127	Fiji	124
74	Nepal	2,340	101	Central African Republic	804	128	Saint Lucia	119
75	Laos	2,247	102	Moldova	785	129	Grenada	92
76	Malawi	2,073	103	Kyrgyzstan	730	130	Solomon Islands	92
77	Mauritania	2,037	104	Tajikistan	669	131	Bhutan	87
78	Cambodia	2,031	105	Belarus	652	132	Dominica	86
79	Uzbekistan	2,028	106	Mongolia	643	133	Saint Vincent and the Grenadines	86
80	Somalia	1,853	107	Lesotho	624			
81	Trinidad and Tobago	1,529	108	Albania	603	134	Eritrea	76
82	Paraguay	1,488	109	Botswana	522	135	Tonga	60
83	Benin	1,393	110	Armenia	512	136	Saint Kitts and Nevis	60
84	Guyana	1,345	111	Gambia	407	137	Vanuatu	39
85	Niger	1,331	112	Barbados	350			

Source: World Bank

9.2 External Public Debt as Percentage of Gross National Product (GNP)

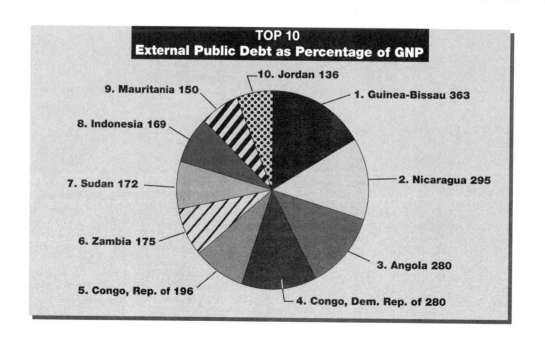

TOP 10
External Public Debt as Percentage of GNP

10. Jordan 136
9. Mauritania 150
8. Indonesia 169
7. Sudan 172
6. Zambia 175
5. Congo, Rep. of 196
4. Congo, Dem. Rep. of 280
3. Angola 280
2. Nicaragua 295
1. Guinea-Bissau 363

Rank	Country/Entity	External Public Debt as Percentage of GNP	Rank	Country/Entity	External Public Debt in U.S. Dollars (millions)	Rank	Country/Entity	External Public Debt in U.S. Dollars (millions)
11	Ethiopia	135	44	Russia	62	77	Uganda	35
12	Sierra Leone	131	45	Jamaica	60	78	Rwanda	34
13	Syria	128	46	Mauritius	60	79	Burkina	34
14	Côte d'Ivoire	124	47	Bolivia	59	80	Colombia	32
15	Cameroon	100	48	Moldova	58	81	Croatia	31
16	Laos	92	49	Senegal	58	82	Nepal	31
17	Gabon	91	50	Tunisia	56	83	Armenia	30
18	Madagascar	89	51	Central African Republic	55	84	Brazil	29
19	Macedonia	87	52	Niger	55	85	Egypt	29
20	Turkmenistan	83	53	Peru	55	86	Ukraine	29
21	Mali	82	54	Ghana	54	87	Dominican Republic	28
22	Bulgaria	79	55	Morocco	54	88	Poland	28
23	Yemen	79	56	Argentina	52	89	El Salvador	27
24	Ecuador	78	57	Kyrgyzstan	50	90	Romania	26
25	Panama	78	58	Mongolia	49	91	Georgia	25
26	Malawi	77	59	Turkey	49	92	Kazakhstan	25
27	Nigeria	76	60	Chile	48	93	Paraguay	25
28	Thailand	76	61	Benin	46	94	Bangladesh	23
29	Vietnam	76	62	Lesotho	46	95	Guatemala	23
30	Mozambique	74	63	Czech Republic	45	96	Albania	20
31	Burundi	72	64	Slovakia	45	97	India	20
32	Guinea	72	65	Pakistan	43	98	South Africa	19
33	Tanzania	70	66	Kenya	45	99	Lithuania	17
34	Malaysia	69	67	South Korea	43	100	Haiti	16
35	Papua New Guinea	69	68	Lebanon	41	101	Uzbekistan	15
36	Zimbabwe	69	69	Mexico	41	102	China	14
37	Togo	68	70	Sri Lanka	41	103	Azerbaijan	14
38	Algeria	66	71	Tajikistan	40	104	Estonia	13
39	Gambia	66	72	Venezuela	40	105	Iran	12
40	Philippines	66	73	Chad	38	106	Eritrea	12
41	Hungary	63	74	Costa Rica	37	107	Latvia	11
42	Honduras	62	75	Uruguay	37	108	Botswana	10
43	Cambodia	62	76	Trinidad and Tobago	36	109	Belarus	5

Source: World Bank, *World Development Indicators*

Nations are subject to constant scrutiny and monitoring by lender organizations regarding their creditworthiness. One element of such scrutiny is the debt-service ratio, which determines the extent of burden that repayment places on a nation's economic base. The debt-service ratio varies according to various factors, such as international reserves, export revenues, and the size of the national budget, out of which the repayment has to be made. Countries caught in a vicious circle of more borrowing, coupled with reduced solvency, may find themselves subject to the IMF's tough fiscal discipline. The ratio of external debt to international reserves, however, is less susceptible to interpretation in isolation. A low ratio, for example, may mean either that the country has little need to borrow, or that it has substantial debt but also the means to repay it. A high ratio, on the other hand, may not be alarming if a country also has high export earnings.

Rank	Country/Entity	Debt-Service Ratio	Rank	Country/Entity	Debt-Service Ratio	Rank	Country/Entity	Debt-Service Ratio
1	São Tomé and Príncipe	44.1	44	Romania	12.7	87	Togo	5.9
2	Argentina	40.1	45	Gabon	12.3	88	Lesotho	5.8
3	Turkmenistan	31.9	46	Uzbekistan	12.1	89	South Africa	5.8
4	Iran	31.0	47	Lebanon	11.8	90	Georgia	5.6
5	Nicaragua	30.3	48	Bulgaria	11.6	91	Russia	5.5
6	Ecuador	28.1	49	Mongolia	11.4	92	Ukraine	5.4
7	Venezuela	27.1	50	Burkina Faso	10.7	93	Oman	5.3
8	Morocco	26.2	51	Czech Republic	10.5	94	Albania	5.2
9	Pakistan	26.2	52	Papua New Guinea	10.5	95	Congo, Rep. of	5.2
10	Brazil	25.2	53	Costa Rica	10.4	96	Armenia	5.0
11	Madagascar	24.6	54	Rwanda	10.3	97	Bhutan	5.0
12	Algeria	24.4	55	Senegal	10.1	98	Dominican Republic	4.9
13	Cape Verde	22.3	56	Jordan	9.6	99	Sri Lanka	4.9
14	Mauritania	22.1	57	Tanzania	9.5	100	Lithuania	4.6
15	Peru	22.0	58	Ethiopia	9.4	101	Paraguay	4.4
16	Bolivia	21.7	59	Slovakia	9.2	102	Kazakhstan	4.3
17	Mexico	21.5	60	Malawi	9.1	103	Kyrgyzstan	4.3
18	Burundi	21.0	61	Mali	9.0	104	Tajikistan	4.2
19	Sierra Leone	19.4	62	Bangladesh	8.7	105	Poland	4.0
20	Guinea	18.7	63	Niger	8.4	106	Seychelles	3.9
21	Zambia	18.4	64	Gambia	8.3	107	Saint Kitts and Nevis	3.9
22	India	18.2	65	Moldova	8.1	108	Samoa	3.6
23	Cameroon	16.8	66	Myanmar (Burma)	7.9	109	South Korea	3.2
24	Ghana	16.8	67	Chad	7.8	110	Comoros	3.0
25	Colombia	16.1	68	China	7.8	111	Laos	3.0
26	Honduras	16.1	69	Guatemala	7.8	112	Latvia	2.9
27	Hungary	16.1	70	Belize	7.7	113	Malaysia	2.9
28	Côte d'Ivoire	16.0	71	Benin	7.6	114	Djibouti	2.8
29	Kenya	15.5	72	Nigeria	7.5	115	Thailand	2.6
30	Panama	15.5	73	Egypt	7.3	116	Yemen	2.3
31	Trinidad and Tobago	15.3	74	Dominica	7.0	117	Central African Republic	1.9
32	Zimbabwe	15.3	75	Syria	7.0	118	Swaziland	1.9
33	Angola	15.0	76	Tonga	7.0	119	Fiji	1.8
34	Uganda	14.8	77	Macedonia	6.9	120	Belarus	1.4
35	Guinea-Bissau	14.5	78	Vietnam	6.9	121	Cambodia	1.0
36	Mozambique	14.2	79	Croatia	6.7	122	Vanuatu	0.9
37	Tunisia	14.2	80	Mauritius	6.7	123	Equatorial Guinea	0.5
38	Guyana	14.0	81	Philippines	6.7	124	Estonia	0.5
39	Turkey	14.0	82	Maldives	6.6	125	Malta	0.5
40	Jamaica	13.9	83	Nepal	6.2	126	Solomon Islands	0.5
41	Indonesia	13.5	84	Azerbaijan	6.0	127	Eritrea	0.1
42	Haiti	13.3	85	Chile	5.9			
43	Uruguay	12.8	86	El Salvador	5.9			

Source: World Bank

9.4 International Reserves

International reserves are to the financial health of a nation what a pulse is to the health of an individual. International reserves comprise the sum of the following items: (1) a country's reserve position in the International Monetary Fund (IMF); (2) a quota subscribed in the country's own currency, constituting a level up to which transactions may be affected within the IMF system; (3) a country's holdings of gold and foreign exchange; (4) and holdings of special drawing rights (SDRs), an unconditional credit allocation, within a quota system set up by the IMF, of currency needed by a country to maintain stability of foreign exchange transactions or markets. At appropriate accounting intervals these four elements are combined into a single unit of account, the SDR, and summed up. The portion of the total reserves comprised by foreign exchange is very significant as an indicator of the country's international liquidity (ability to pay its debts immediately in hard or convertible currencies). The ratio of external debt to total reserves, however, is less susceptible to interpretation in isolation. A low ratio, for example, may mean either that the country has little need to borrow, or that it has substantial debt, but also the means to repay it. A high ratio, on the other hand, is no reason for alarm if a country also has high export earnings.

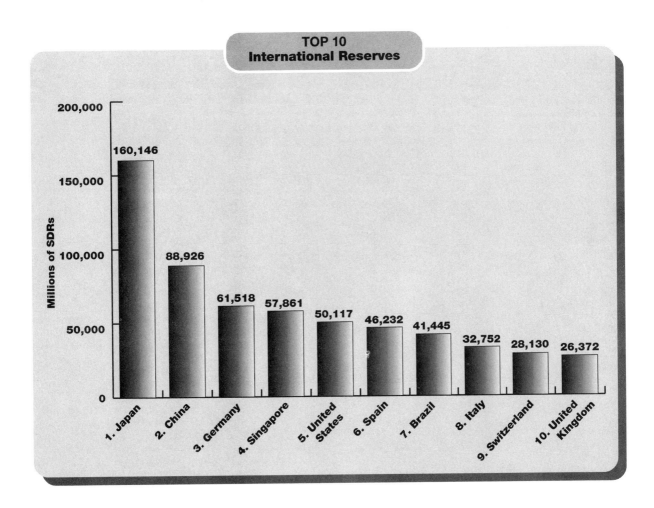

Rank	Country/Entity	International Reserves, 1997 (millions of SDRs)	Rank	Country/Entity	International Reserves, 1997 (millions of SDRs)	Rank	Country/Entity	International Reserves, 1997 (millions of SDRs)
11	South Korea	24,555	55	Ecuador	1,662	99	Moldova	204
12	France	23,732	56	Ukraine	1,364	101	Benin	184
13	Thailand	22,679	57	Panama	1,337	102	Madagascar	182
14	Norway	20,538	58	Sri Lanka	1,277	103	Central African Republic	165
15	Netherlands	20,460	59	Bangladesh	1,226	104	Rwanda	145
16	India	18,963	60	Oman	1,211	105	Netherlands Antilles	138
17	Malaysia	18,946	61	Jordan	1,198	106	Myanmar (Burma)	136
18	Mexico	17,135	62	Tunisia	1,121	107	Aruba	135
19	Canada	15,315	63	Kazakhstan	1,113	108	Chad	123
20	Austria	15,221	64	Malta	1,076	109	Bhutan	119
21	Indonesia	14,759	65	Bahrain	1,045	110	Mauritania	118
22	Argentina	14,335	66	Uruguay	918	111	Malawi	107
23	Poland	13,996	67	Pakistan	913	112	Gabon	105
24	Egypt	13,260	68	Cyprus	911	113	Burundi	103
25	Israel	12,868	69	Costa Rica	825	114	Haiti	90
26	Belgium	12,610	70	Yemen	786	115	Congo, Rep. of	83
27	Chile	11,928	71	Bolivia	781	116	Togo	80
28	Russia	11,895	72	Guatemala	769	117	Sudan	75
29	Turkey	11,697	73	El Salvador	744	118	Gambia	74
30	Portugal	11,692	74	Kenya	668	119	Suriname	74
31	Denmark	11,301	75	Ghana	640	120	Mongolia	73
32	Greece	11,205	76	Côte d'Ivoire	634	121	Maldives	69
33	Australia	10,511	77	Mauritius	606	122	Niger	66
34	Sweden	10,431	78	Paraguay	595	123	Luxembourg	59
35	Venezuela	9,921	79	Jamaica	590	124	Djibouti	52
36	Czech Republic	8,659	80	Estonia	447	125	Congo, Dem. Rep. of	45
37	Philippines	7,600	81	Ethiopia	421	126	Samoa	45
38	Peru	7,578	82	Lesotho	420	127	Belize	43
39	Finland	7,470	83	Uganda	414	128	Saint Lucia	43
40	Colombia	7,173	84	Papua New Guinea	407	129	Antigua and Barbuda	32
41	Saudi Arabia	6,826	85	Trinidad and Tobago	386	130	Saint Kitts and Nevis	28
42	United Arab Emirates	6,455	86	Honduras	366	131	Cameroon	27
43	Hungary	6,173	87	Zimbabwe	343	132	Grenada	27
44	Lebanon	5,645	88	Tanzania	331	133	Vanuatu	27
45	Nigeria	5,564	89	Iceland	299	134	Sierra Leone	24
46	Ireland	5,472	90	Mali	297	135	Tonga	22
47	Algeria	4,835	91	Dominican Republic	263	136	Solomon Islands	21
48	Botswana	3,961	92	Fiji	257	137	Seychelles	19
49	New Zealand	3,308	93	Senegal	256	138	Saint Vincent and the Grenadines	19
50	Morocco	2,993	94	Barbados	249	139	Dominica	18
51	South Africa	2,828	95	Burkina Faso	238	140	Guinea-Bissau	12
52	Kuwait	2,460	96	Guyana	232			
53	Slovakia	2,181	97	Bahamas	220			
54	Romania	1,747	98	Swaziland	209			

Source: IMF

9.5 Balance of Payments

Balance of payments is the summary of all external transactions of a current nature between one country and the rest of the world. The account shows a country's net overseas receipts and obligations, including not only the trade of goods and merchandise (the balance of trade), but also invisible items such as services, interest, and dividends, investments, tourism, and workers' remittances. Any international transaction automatically creates a deficit in the balance of payments of one country and a surplus in that of another.

Rank	Country/Entity	Balance of Payments in U.S. Dollars (millions), 1997	Rank	Country/Entity	Balance of Payments in U.S. Dollars (millions), 1997	Rank	Country/Entity	Balance of Payments in U.S. Dollars (millions), 1997
1	Japan	94,350	49	Fiji	4.2	96	Papua New Guinea	-192.2
2	France	39,470	50	Burundi	4.0	97	Aruba	-195.8
3	Italy	32,403	51	Mauritania	0.0	98	Malta	-207.0
4	China	29,718	52	São Tomé and Príncipe	-1.6	99	Cambodia	-209.9
5	Netherlands	27,684	53	Kiribati	-2.3	100	Chad	-228.2
6	Switzerland	23,714	54	Guinea-Bissau	-15.2	101	Zambia	-239.0
7	Singapore	15,032	55	Maldives	-15.9	102	Congo, Rep. of	-251.9
8	Belgium	13,939	56	Comoros	-18.9	103	Costa Rica	-254.0
9	United Kingdom	10,300	57	Djibouti	-18.9	104	Mozambique	-260.3
10	Norway	8,017	58	Tonga	-19.3	105	Lesotho	-264.3
11	Kuwait	7,935	59	Vanuatu	-19.3	106	Moldova	-267.7
12	Taiwan	7,688	60	Ethiopia	-23.0	107	Equatorial Guinea	-268.1
13	Sweden	7,407	61	Gambia	-23.6	108	Albania	-272.2
14	United Arab Emirates	6,701	62	Antigua and Barbuda	-24.7	109	Macedonia	-275.5
15	Finland	6,664	63	Solomon Islands	-27.7	110	Uruguay	-287.4
16	Russia	4,050	64	Cape Verde	-29.7	111	Bahrain	-303.7
17	Venezuela	3,909	65	Belize	-31.9	112	Laos	-305.5
18	Algeria	3,500	66	Marshall Islands	-35.8	113	Armenia	-306.5
19	Brunei	2,875	67	Dominica	-38.7	114	Bangladesh	-327.3
20	Spain	2,486	68	Saint Kitts and Nevis	-40.1	115	Latvia	-345.0
21	Luxembourg	2,342	69	Central African Republic	-43.5	116	Jamaica	-382.2
22	Iran	2,213	70	Bhutan	-46.5	117	Cyprus	-382.7
23	Ireland	1,984	71	Haiti	-47.7	118	Uganda	-387.8
24	Denmark	921	72	Swaziland	-49.1	119	Sri Lanka	-394.7
25	Botswana	722	73	Oman	-57.0	120	Myanmar (Burma)	-412.0
26	Nigeria	552	74	Togo	-58.3	121	Congo, Dem. Rep. of	-415.0
27	Syria	483	75	Seychelles	-63.2	122	Nepal	-418.1
28	Bulgaria	427	76	Senegal	-70.4	123	Kenya	-454.1
29	Honduras	272	77	Tajikistan	-74.0	124	Bahamas	-472.1
30	Saudi Arabia	257	78	Grenada	-74.9	125	Paraguay	-482.9
31	Gabon	237	79	Guinea	-91.1	126	Georgia	-534.7
32	Faroe Islands	146	80	Malawi	-92.7	127	Ghana	-540.9
33	Bermuda	125	81	Rwanda	-92.7	128	Bolivia	-550.8
34	El Salvador	95.9	82	Saint Vincent and the Grenadines	-92.9	129	Estonia	-561.9
35	Netherlands Antilles	93.3				130	Trinidad and Tobago	-579.0
36	Mauritius	91.1	83	Benin	-96.6	131	Uzbekistan	-584.0
37	Namibia	90.4	84	Saint Lucia	-99.3	132	Tunisia	-595.0
38	Suriname	72.9	85	Cameroon	-101.1	133	Turkmenistan	-596.0
39	Micronesia	63.8	86	Guyana	-106.0	134	Nicaragua	-619.0
40	Yemen	51.6	87	Burkina Faso	-122.2	135	Guatemala	-633.5
41	Slovenia	36.5	88	Sierra Leone	-126.5	136	Tanzania	-707.4
42	Côte d'Ivoire	34.6	89	Iceland	-133.0	137	Egypt	-711.0
43	Jordan	29.3	90	Kyrgyzstan	-138.5	138	Ecuador	-743.0
44	Mongolia	28.2	91	Madagascar	-149.0	139	Belarus	-787.6
45	San Marino	10.7	92	Niger	-151.7	140	Kazakhstan	-794.2
46	Samoa	9.1	93	Dominican Republic	-163.0	141	Zimbabwe	-827.0
47	Barbados	7.1	94	Morocco	-169.0	142	Sudan	-828.1
48	Eritrea	4.9	95	Mali	-178.0	143	Angola	-866.0

Rank	Country/Entity	Balance of Payments in U.S. Dollars (millions), 1997	Rank	Country/Entity	Balance of Payments in U.S. Dollars (millions), 1997	Rank	Country/Entity	Balance of Payments in U.S. Dollars (millions), 1997
144	Azerbaijan	-915.8	156	Turkey	-2,679	168	Austria	-4,996
145	Lithuania	-981.3	157	India	-2,965	169	Portugal	-5,527
146	Hungary	-982.0	158	Thailand	-3,024	170	Poland	-5,744
147	Panama	-1,240.3	159	Czech Republic	-3,271	171	Colombia	-5,888
148	Ukraine	-1,355.0	160	Israel	-3,398	172	Mexico	-7,454
149	Germany	-1,520.0	161	Peru	-3,407	173	South Korea	-8,167
150	Vietnam	-1,664.0	162	Chile	-4,057	174	Canada	-10,304
151	Pakistan	-1,755.0	163	Philippines	-4,351	175	Argentina	-12,035
152	South Africa	-1,931.0	164	New Zealand	-4,750	176	Australia	-12,731
153	Slovakia	-1,961.0	165	Malaysia	-4,792	177	Brazil	-33,840
154	Romania	-2,137.0	166	Greece	-4,860	178	United States	-155,380
155	Croatia	-2,342.7	167	Indonesia	-4,889			

Source: IMF

9.6 Central Government Expenditures as Percentage of Gross Domestic Product (GDP)

The extent and scope of government expenditures or consumption is an integral part of Gross Domestic Product and ranks only next to personal consumption as influencing the growth rate of GDP. Government expenditures are designed to redistribute the national wealth, advance social policy goals, and buttress the weaker sectors of the economy. Government expenditures also reflect the division between proactive governments that espouse state intervention in the economy or command economies of the socialist model. On the other hand, government expenditures are a smaller portion of the GDP in free market or laissez-faire economies.

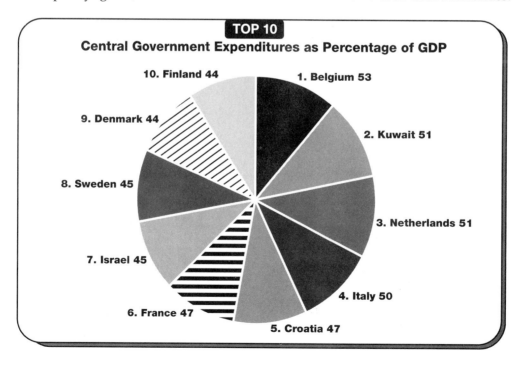

TOP 10

Central Government Expenditures as Percentage of GDP

10. Finland 44
9. Denmark 44
8. Sweden 45
7. Israel 45
6. France 47
5. Croatia 47
4. Italy 50
3. Netherlands 51
2. Kuwait 51
1. Belgium 53

Rank	Country/Entity	Central Government Expenditures as Percentage of GDP	Rank	Country/Entity	Central Government Expenditures as Percentage of GDP	Rank	Country/Entity	Central Government Expenditures as Percentage of GDP
11	United Kingdom	44	34	Jordan	31	57	Gambia	20
12	Bulgaria	43	35	Latvia	30	58	Sierra Leone	20
13	Egypt	43	36	Nicaragua	30	59	Madagascar	19
14	Greece	43	37	Australia	29	60	Peru	19
15	Ireland	43	38	Papua New Guinea	29	61	Venezuela	19
16	Oman	43	39	Sri Lanka	29	62	South Korea	18
17	Poland	43	40	Costa Rica	28	63	Philippines	18
18	Czech Republic	42	41	Panama	28	64	Dominican Republic	17
19	Namibia	41	42	Kenya	27	65	Zambia	17
20	Austria	40	43	Lithuania	27	66	Cameroon	16
21	Brazil	39	44	Russia	27	67	Ecuador	16
22	Norway	39	45	Syria	27	68	India	16
23	Spain	39	46	Turkey	27	69	Indonesia	16
24	Yemen	39	47	Lebanon	26	70	El Salvador	15
25	Botswana	38	48	Switzerland	26	71	Singapore	15
26	Portugal	38	49	Bolivia	24	72	Colombia	14
27	New Zealand	36	50	Malaysia	23	73	Mexico	14
28	Albania	34	51	Mauritius	23	74	Paraguay	13
29	Germany	34	52	Pakistan	23	75	United Arab Emirates	12
30	Lesotho	33	53	United States	23	76	Thailand	11
31	South Africa	33	54	Ghana	21	77	Guatemala	9
32	Romania	32	55	Mongolia	21			
33	Uruguay	32	56	Chile	20			

Source: *World Development Report*

9.7 Highest Corporate Marginal Tax Rate

Tax codes are arcane, cumbersome, and taxpayer unfriendly. They reflect not merely the fiscal needs of government, but also the prevailing social and political philosophy. There are systems that levy almost punitive tax rates on the wealthy as a means of redistributing wealth. "Soak the rich" is not only a populist slogan, but also a means of reducing the existing disparities between the lower and upper classes. In certain countries, as in Scandinavia, for example, it is also a means of paying for the welfare state, and it has become an acceptable fiscal tool in almost every country in the world.

Rank	Country/Entity	Highest Corporate Tax Rate, 1998 (percentage)	Rank	Country/Entity	Highest Corporate Tax Rate, 1998 (percentage)	Rank	Country/Entity	Highest Corporate Tax Rate, 1998 (percentage)
1	Saudi Arabia	45	30	Spain	35	59	Ukraine	30
2	Switzerland	45	31	Sri Lanka	35	60	Uruguay	30
3	Egypt	40	32	United States	35	61	Lithuania	29
4	India	40	33	Zambia	35	62	Finland	28
5	Slovakia	40	34	Austria	34	63	South Korea	28
6	Belgium	39	35	Denmark	34	64	Malaysia	28
7	Cameroon	39	36	Mexico	34	65	Nigeria	28
8	Canada	38	37	Philippines	34	66	Norway	28
9	Japan	38	38	Argentina	33	67	Sweden	28
10	Malawi	38	39	France	33	68	Estonia	26
11	Romania	38	40	Jamaica	33	69	Singapore	26
12	Zimbabwe	38	41	New Zealand	33	70	Bolivia	25
13	Italy	37	42	Azerbaijan	32	71	Dominican Republic	25
14	Portugal	37	43	Ireland	32	72	Ecuador	25
15	Australia	36	44	United Kingdom	31	73	El Salvador	25
16	Israel	36	45	Bulgaria	30	74	Latvia	25
17	Poland	36	46	China	30	75	Turkey	25
18	Côte d'Ivoire	35	47	Costa Rica	30	76	Vietnam	25
19	Colombia	35	48	Germany	30	77	Hungary	18
20	Czech Republic	35	49	Guatemala	30	78	Hong Kong	17
21	Ghana	35	50	Indonesia	30	79	Botswana	15
22	Greece	35	51	Kazakhstan	30	80	Brazil	15
23	Kenya	35	52	Kyrgyzstan	30	81	Chile	15
24	Morocco	35	53	Nicaragua	30	82	Honduras	15
25	Namibia	35	54	Paraguay	30	83	Panama	15
26	Netherlands	35	55	Peru	30	84	Papua New Guinea	15
27	Russia	35	56	Tanzania	30	85	Iran	12
28	Senegal	35	57	Thailand	30	86	Kuwait	6
29	South Africa	35	58	Uganda	30			

Source: World Development Report

Kautilya, the great Indian political philosopher who lived some 2,300 years ago, said that taxes should be collected as bees collect honey, without any harm to the flower. In the twenty-first century, the principle remains the same although the mandatory nature of taxes does not render the process entirely painless. In all countries, tax revenues form the lion's share of most government revenues, but the percentage varies widely. In certain Arab oil-producing countries, much of the government income is derived from state enterprises. In fact, there are five countries in the world—all Arab—without income taxes of any kind. In addition to personal and corporate income taxes, there are numerous other taxes that make up tax revenues, such as sales taxes, excise duties, customs, levies, and tolls.

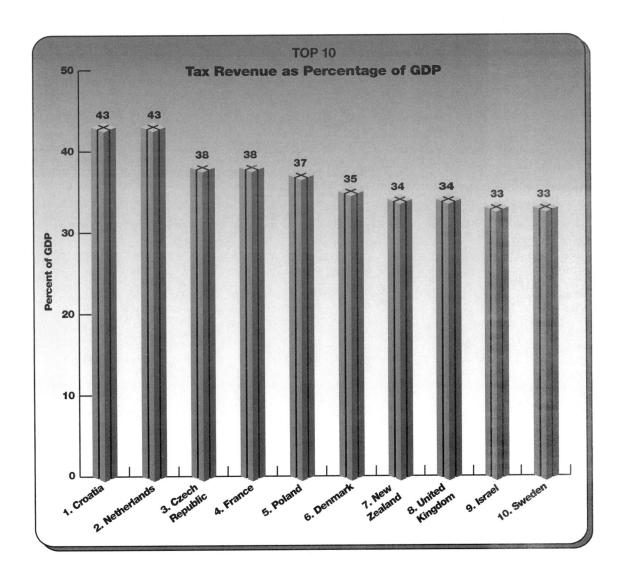

Rank	Country/Entity	Tax Revenue as Percentage of GDP	Rank	Country/Entity	Tax Revenue as Percentage of GDP	Rank	Country/Entity	Tax Revenue as Percentage of GDP
11	Germany	30	22	Fiji	21	34	Peru	14
12	Bulgaria	29	23	Malaysia	21	35	Turkey	14
13	Uruguay	28	24	Mongolia	20	36	Zambia	13
14	Saint Vincent and the Grenadines	25	25	United States	19	37	Bolivia	12
			26	Albania	18	38	El Salvador	12
15	Lithuania	24	27	Chile	18	39	India	10
16	Nicaragua	24	28	South Korea	18	40	Bahrain	9
17	Grenada	23	29	Mauritius	18	41	Nepal	9
18	Latvia	23	30	Sri Lanka	18	42	Madagascar	8
19	Australia	22	31	Thailand	17	43	Oman	8
20	Costa Rica	22	32	Russia	16	44	Bhutan	6
21	Belize	21	33	Pakistan	15	45	Kuwait	1

Source: World Development Report

9.9 Gross Domestic Savings as Percentage of GDP

Gross domestic savings are the key to building capital at both the personal and the national levels. The level of savings is considered a key not only to the level of capital accumulation, but also to the quality of the population's work ethic. Savings require deferment of immediate satisfactions for the sake of future financial security.

Gross domestic savings are higher in two different situations: in certain cultures, family values associated with a strong work ethic provide incentives for savings. In others, the absence of a consumer culture may encourage savings because there are fewer opportunities for spending.

Rank	Country/Entity	Gross Domestic Savings as Percentage of GDP, 1995	Rank	Country/Entity	Gross Domestic Savings as Percentage of GDP, 1995	Rank	Country/Entity	Gross Domestic Savings as Percentage of GDP, 1995
1	Gabon	48	28	Botswana	23	55	Poland	19
2	Angola	43	29	Congo, Rep. of	23	56	Sweden	19
3	China	42	30	Germany	23	57	Argentina	18
4	Papua New Guinea	39	31	Australia	22	58	Estonia	18
5	Malaysia	37	32	India	22	59	Kuwait	18
6	Indonesia	36	33	Italy	22	60	Portugal	18
7	South Korea	36	34	Mauritius	22	61	South Africa	18
8	Thailand	36	35	Panama	22	62	Tajikistan	18
9	Iran	34	36	Spain	22	63	Colombia	16
10	Hong Kong	33	37	Brazil	21	64	Dominican Republic	16
11	Japan	31	38	Cameroon	21	65	Latvia	16
12	Slovakia	30	39	Canada	21	66	Lithuania	16
13	Algeria	29	40	Denmark	21	67	Pakistan	16
14	Chile	29	41	Ecuador	21	68	Vietnam	16
15	Netherlands	29	42	Hungary	21	69	Philippines	15
16	Norway	29	43	Romania	21	70	United Kingdom	15
17	Ireland	27	44	Slovenia	21	71	United States	15
18	Switzerland	27	45	Venezuela	21	72	Honduras	14
19	Austria	26	46	Belarus	20	73	Sri Lanka	14
20	New Zealand	26	47	Côte d'Ivoire	20	74	Israel	13
21	Russia	26	48	Czech Republic	20	75	Kenya	13
22	Bulgaria	25	49	France	20	76	Morocco	13
23	Grenada	25	50	Tunisia	20	77	Uruguay	13
24	Trinidad and Tobago	25	51	Turkey	20	78	Fiji	12
25	Belgium	24	52	Iceland	19	79	Nepal	12
26	Costa Rica	24	53	Kazakhstan	19	80	Guinea	11
27	Finland	24	54	Mexico	19	81	Mauritania	11

Rank	Country/Entity	Gross Domestic Savings as Percentage of GDP, 1995	Rank	Country/Entity	Gross Domestic Savings as Percentage of GDP, 1995	Rank	Country/Entity	Gross Domestic Savings as Percentage of GDP, 1995
82	Peru	11	93	Uganda	7	104	Djibouti	-5
83	Ghana	10	94	Central African Republic	6	105	Guinea-Bissau	-5
84	Jamaica	10	95	Egypt	6	106	Burundi	-7
85	Kyrgyzstan	10	96	El Salvador	6	107	Tanzania	-7
86	Mali	10	97	Azerbaijan	4	108	Albania	-8
87	Senegal	10	98	Macedonia	4	109	Comoros	-8
88	Swaziland	9	99	Malawi	4	110	Georgia	-9
89	Togo	9	100	Madagascar	3	111	Lesotho	-9
90	Bangladesh	8	101	Zambia	3	112	Sierra Leone	-9
91	Ethiopia	7	102	Croatia	1	113	Eritrea	-27
92	Greece	7	103	Moldova	-1	114	Armenia	-29

Source: World Development Report

Chapter 10

Trade

Exports and Imports

"Export or perish" is the watch-phrase of most nations in the world. The economic strength of nations is directly proportional to export-driven trade. Exports may be of primary commodities as in the case of developing nations, manufactured commodities in the case of industrialized or industrializing nations, and services and invisibles as in the case of post-industrial nations. However, higher export values may be achieved at the expense of domestic consumption and consequent lower standard of living. Two international organizations keep a tab on global exports and imports: the World Trade Organization (WTO)

and the International Monetary Fund (IMF). The WTO assures that trade is conducted according to the many agreements that govern the trade relations of nations, and the IMF monitors the international reserves that are affected by the extent and volume of trade. Ideally, the total global exports and total global imports should match, but in all the years that records have been kept, they have not done so. In fact, one of the great mysteries of international trade is that a substantial part of trade goes unreported and unaccounted for. Part of the reason may be poor accounting procedures, and part of it may be simple old-fashioned smuggling.

10.1 Exports

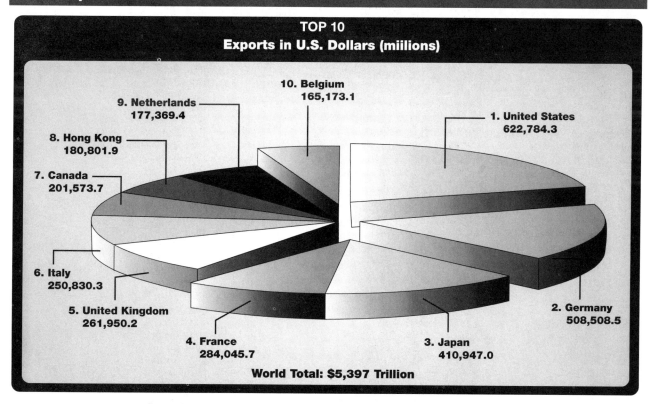

TOP 10
Exports in U.S. Dollars (miilions)

- 10. Belgium 165,173.1
- 9. Netherlands 177,369.4
- 8. Hong Kong 180,801.9
- 7. Canada 201,573.7
- 6. Italy 250,830.3
- 5. United Kingdom 261,950.2
- 4. France 284,045.7
- 3. Japan 410,947.0
- 2. Germany 508,508.5
- 1. United States 622,784.3

World Total: $5,397 Trillion

Rank	Country/Entity	Exports in U.S. Dollars (millions)	Rank	Country/Entity	Exports in U.S. Dollars (millions)	Rank	Country/Entity	Exports in U.S. Dollars (millions)
11	China	148,779.6	18	Russia	79,910.0	25	Ireland	48,153.2
12	South Korea	129,714.6	19	Mexico	79,488.6	26	Denmark	47,221.8
13	Singapore	125,153.1	20	Malaysia	74,120.1	27	Brazil	46,505.4
14	Taiwan	115,724.0	21	Australia	60,534.0	28	Indonesia	45,418.0
15	Spain	100,955.5	22	Austria	57,141.5	29	Saudi Arabia	42,584.0
16	Sweden	82,880.5	23	Thailand	56,743.2	30	Finland	40,556.5
17	Switzerland	80,454.9	24	Norway	48,955.0	31	South Africa	27,339.9

Rank	Country/Entity	Exports in U.S. Dollars (millions)	Rank	Country/Entity	Exports in U.S. Dollars (millions)	Rank	Country/Entity	Exports in U.S. Dollars (millions)
32	India	26,330.0	93	Zimbabwe	1,895.5	154	Afghanistan	235.1
33	United Arab Emirates	24,756.0	94	Turkmenistan	1,880.7	155	French Polynesia	226.2
34	Portugal	23,185.6	95	Botswana	1,848.8	156	Cambodia	219.1
35	Poland	22,863.3	96	Liechtenstein	1,817.7	157	Jersey	209.2
36	Turkey	21,598.7	97	Iceland	1,802.5	158	Réunion	208.7
37	Puerto Rico	21,051.2	98	Jordan	1,782.0	159	Ethiopia	201.7
38	Argentina	20,962.6	99	Cameroon	1,757.9	160	Uganda	171.4
39	Iran	19,868.0	100	Malta	1,748.3	161	Bosnia and Herzegovina	171.0
40	Israel	19,046.0	101	Netherlands Antilles	1,558.9	162	Mozambique	164.0
41	Venezuela	18,914.2	102	Mauritius	1,555.8	163	Togo	162.2
42	Philippines	17,447.2	103	Kenya	1,391.9	164	Guadeloupe	162.0
43	Czech Republic	17,099.1	104	Cyprus	1,391.0	165	Belize	161.7
44	Chile	15,901.1	105	Jamaica	1,386.9	166	French Guiana	158.2
45	New Zealand	13,745.4	106	Namibia	1,321.4	167	Georgia	154.4
46	Kuwait	12,944.4	107	Latvia	1,303.8	168	Solomon Islands	142.2
47	Hungary	12,867.0	108	Ghana	1,234.4	169	Albania	141.3
48	Nigeria	11,886.5	109	Panama	1,202.5	170	Rwanda	131.9
49	Ukraine	11,566.5	110	Bolivia	1,181.4	171	Saint Lucia	119.7
50	Libya	11,211.7	111	North Korea	1,095.0	172	Central African Republic	119.5
51	Greece	10,954.6	112	Macedonia	1,086.3	173	Gibraltar	116.2
52	Colombia	10,327.8	113	Zambia	1,049.2	174	Sierra Leone	115.8
53	Algeria	8,555.5	114	Gabon	1,040.9	175	Lesotho	109.1
54	Slovenia	8,315.8	115	Congo, Rep. of	948.5	176	Burkina Faso	105.4
55	Pakistan	8,157.9	116	Yemen	933.9	177	Eritrea	86.0
56	Romania	8,084.5	117	Myanmar (Burma)	920.7	178	Micronesia	78.2
57	Luxembourg	7,743.0	118	Paraguay	819.6	179	Haiti	74.3
58	Slovakia	6,690.2	119	El Salvador	812.7	180	Burundi	68.7
59	Iraq	6,659.0	120	Swaziland	751.8	181	Bhutan	67.1
60	Oman	5,917.4	121	Tajikistan	748.6	182	Equatorial Guinea	61.7
61	Peru	5,575.1	122	Moldova	745.5	183	Dominica	54.2
62	Tunisia	5,517.4	123	Honduras	656.0	184	Seychelles	51.8
63	Bulgaria	5,184.4	124	Guinea	625.9	185	Saint Vincent and the Grenadines	50.4
64	Kazakhstan	4,974.4	125	Senegal	605.1			
65	Morocco	4,728.1	126	Lebanon	572.7	186	Gaza Strip	49.4
66	Belarus	4,706.8	127	Azerbaijan	547.4	187	Andorra	48.9
67	Yugoslavia	4,704.1	128	Fiji	544.5	188	Somalia	44.0
68	Croatia	4,511.7	129	Sudan	523.9	189	Benin	43.0
69	Ecuador	4,361.5	130	Nicaragua	509.2	190	Antigua and Barbuda	39.8
70	Bahrain	4,092.1	131	Congo, Dem. Rep. of	506.0	191	Guam	39.2
71	Syria	3,969.9	132	American Samoa	488.2	192	Aruba	37.5
72	Cuba	3,860.0	133	Mongolia	473.3	193	Bermuda	35.3
73	Egypt	3,444.1	134	Malawi	472.4	194	Maldives	34.4
74	Lithuania	3,354.9	135	Mauritania	471.0	195	Guinea-Bissau	33.2
75	Qatar	3,212.9	136	Tanzania	416.1	196	Nauru	28.9
76	Angola	3,178.9	137	Kyrgyzstan	408.9	197	Saint Kitts and Nevis	27.7
77	Uzbekistan	3,109.0	138	Guyana	404.0	198	Marshall Islands	23.1
78	Côte d'Ivoire	3,105.0	139	Liberia	389.0	199	West Bank	22.6
79	Virgin Islands (U.S.)	3,026.3	140	Greenland	363.6	200	Gambia	21.5
80	Vietnam	2,985.2	141	Madagascar	359.9	201	Grenada	20.1
81	Papua New Guinea	2,624.6	142	Suriname	357.1	202	Vanuatu	17.6
82	Bahamas	2,592.6	143	New Caledonia	354.8	203	Samoa	17.5
83	Sri Lanka	2,391.4	144	Mali	330.3	204	Djibouti	17.3
84	Costa Rica	2,217.5	145	Faroe Islands	321.3	205	Tonga	14.0
85	Bangladesh	2,137.6	146	Niger	311.9	206	Comoros	11.4
86	Uruguay	2,116.5	147	Laos	300.4	207	Mayotte	8.2
87	Brunei	2,093.9	148	Nepal	286.3	208	São Tomé and Príncipe	6.5
88	Estonia	2,074.1	149	Armenia	270.9	209	Kiribati	5.2
89	Macau	2,017.3	150	Northern Mariana Islands	263.0	210	Cape Verde	5.0
90	Dominican Republic	2,007.8	151	Chad	261.0	211	Tuvalu	0.7
91	Trinidad and Tobago	1,960.4	152	Martinique	241.9	212	Palau	0.5
92	Guatemala	1,935.5	153	Barbados	237.5			

Source: International Trade Statistics

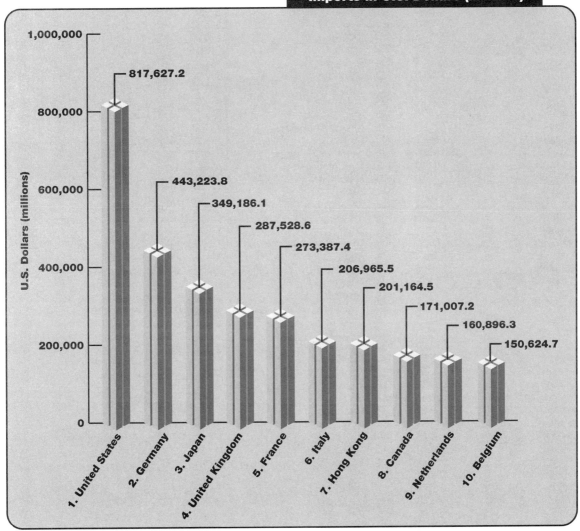

TOP 10
Imports in U.S. Dollars (millions)

U.S. Dollars (millions)

- 817,627.2 — 1. United States
- 443,223.8 — 2. Germany
- 349,186.1 — 3. Japan
- 287,528.6 — 4. United Kingdom
- 273,387.4 — 5. France
- 206,965.5 — 6. Italy
- 201,164.5 — 7. Hong Kong
- 171,007.2 — 8. Canada
- 160,896.3 — 9. Netherlands
- 150,624.7 — 10. Belgium

Rank	Country/Entity	Imports in U.S. Dollars (millions)	Rank	Country/Entity	Imports in U.S. Dollars (millions)	Rank	Country/Entity	Imports in U.S. Dollars (millions)
11	South Korea	150,334.3	23	Brazil	53,736.7	35	India	28,654.8
12	China	132,083.5	24	Russia	46,680.0	36	Philippines	28,487.4
13	Singapore	131,480.2	25	Denmark	41,626.4	37	South Africa	27,737.0
14	Spain	121,255.4	26	Indonesia	40,628.7	38	Greece	25,926.8
15	Taiwan	102,554.4	27	Ireland	35,767.7	39	Saudi Arabia	23,343.5
16	Switzerland	79,365.3	28	Turkey	35,707.5	40	Czech Republic	20,915.0
17	Malaysia	77,292.3	29	Norway	34,309.2	41	Argentina	20,121.7
18	Mexico	73,993.0	30	Portugal	34,121.9	42	United Arab Emirates	17,410.0
19	Thailand	71,387.4	31	Finland	30,904.9	43	Hungary	15,466.3
20	Austria	65,662.5	32	Iran	30,712.1	44	Puerto Rico	15,387.3
21	Australia	65,427.0	33	Israel	29,579.0	45	Chile	14,903.1
22	Sweden	63,986.8	34	Poland	28,929.9	46	New Zealand	13,957.7

Rank	Country/Entity	Imports in U.S. Dollars (millions)	Rank	Country/Entity	Imports in U.S. Dollars (millions)	Rank	Country/Entity	Imports in U.S. Dollars (millions)
47	Colombia	13,863.1	103	Macau	2,018.6	159	Kyrgyzstan	522.3
48	Egypt	11,739.0	104	Martinique	1,969.8	160	Aruba	486.9
49	Pakistan	11,703.6	105	Qatar	1,927.4	161	Guyana	483.8
50	Romania	11,435.3	106	Guadeloupe	1,901.3	162	Gibraltar	436.0
51	Ukraine	11,335.5	107	Bosnia and Herzegovina	1,879.0	163	American Samoa	427.5
52	Venezuela	10,791.3	108	Netherlands Antilles	1,868.3	164	Eritrea	423.6
53	Luxembourg	9,861.5	109	Brunei	1,820.5	165	Greenland	421.1
54	Algeria	9,830.6	110	Latvia	1,817.5	166	Congo, Dem. Rep. of	420.0
55	Slovenia	9,491.7	111	Iceland	1,751.4	167	Mongolia	415.3
56	Peru	9,224.0	112	Honduras	1,727.5	168	Congo, Rep. of	408.4
57	Nigeria	8,839.3	113	Kenya	1,695.9	169	Benin	408.0
58	Morocco	8,551.5	114	Botswana	1,636.6	170	Cambodia	403.9
59	Kuwait	7,789.8	115	Macedonia	1,484.1	171	Northern Mariana Islands	392.2
60	Croatia	7,787.8	116	Myanmar (Burma)	1,419.3	172	Georgia	379.0
61	Tunisia	7,698.2	117	Bolivia	1,396.3	173	Niger	355.3
62	Slovakia	6,611.0	118	Namibia	1,374.3	174	Gaza Strip	339.3
63	Lebanon	5,990.0	119	Turkmenistan	1,364.0	175	Saint Lucia	300.3
64	Liberia	5,760.0	120	Papua New Guinea	1,298.6	176	Rwanda	291.1
65	Belarus	5,563.6	121	Zambia	1,237.7	177	Central African Republic	265.5
66	Yugoslavia	5,548.6	122	Cameroon	1,204.3	178	Belize	258.3
67	Libya	5,357.5	123	Sudan	1,161.5	179	Antigua and Barbuda	245.9
68	Bulgaria	5,125.0	124	Senegal	1,139.2	180	Chad	243.0
69	Iraq	4,833.9	125	Trinidad and Tobago	1,136.2	181	Faroe Islands	238.2
70	Syria	4,708.8	126	Andorra	1,055.5	182	Somalia	228.0
71	Lithuania	4,558.8	127	Tanzania	1,021.5	183	Haiti	226.0
72	Oman	4,248.6	128	Nicaragua	1,009.2	184	Togo	222.0
73	Ecuador	4,195.2	129	Lesotho	977.0	185	Djibouti	214.4
74	Cyprus	3,982.5	130	Swaziland	962.6	186	Cape Verde	210.1
75	Vietnam	3,924.0	131	Afghanistan	936.4	187	Seychelles	206.5
76	Panama	3,799.0	132	Liechtenstein	906.4	188	Burundi	204.5
77	Kazakhstan	3,781.0	133	French Polynesia	880.7	189	Maldives	191.4
78	Jordan	3,722.7	134	Nepal	855.9	190	Solomon Islands	170.6
79	Bahrain	3,624.8	135	New Caledonia	842.2	191	Sierra Leone	149.9
80	Guatemala	3,292.5	136	Moldova	840.7	192	Mayotte	144.3
81	Virgin Islands (U.S.)	3,200.3	137	Fiji	830.5	193	Gambia	141.3
82	Estonia	3,197.2	138	Tajikistan	799.2	194	Samoa	130.9
83	Paraguay	3,135.9	139	French Guiana	783.3	195	Saint Vincent and the Grenadines	129.9
84	Costa Rica	3,029.7	140	Ethiopia	771.6			
85	Bahamas	2,919.9	141	Barbados	766.0	196	Micronesia	129.1
86	Jamaica	2,916.4	142	Guinea	687.0	197	Bhutan	128.0
87	Uzbekistan	2,892.7	143	Gabon	680.8	198	Grenada	117.2
88	Uruguay	2,865.7	144	Armenia	673.9	199	Saint Kitts and Nevis	110.7
89	Sri Lanka	2,833.2	145	Azerbaijan	667.6	200	Dominica	109.6
90	Malta	2,803.0	146	Malawi	647.4	201	West Bank	102.5
91	Zimbabwe	2,726.2	147	Suriname	639.8	202	Marshall Islands	75.1
92	Réunion	2,711.1	148	Guam	610.7	203	Vanuatu	73.5
93	Bangladesh	2,708.8	149	Mali	601.8	204	Tonga	69.1
94	Dominican Republic	2,626.4	150	Albania	601.0	205	Guinea-Bissau	63.5
95	Côte d'Ivoire	2,447.0	151	Mauritania	600.0	206	Equatorial Guinea	61.6
96	El Salvador	2,261.8	152	Bermuda	588.9	207	Comoros	52.8
97	North Korea	2,238.0	153	Laos	564.1	208	São Tomé and Príncipe	30.4
98	Cuba	2,185.0	154	Madagascar	549.5	209	Kiribati	26.4
99	Ghana	2,145.4	155	Mozambique	544.0	210	Palau	25.1
100	Yemen	2,087.4	156	Jersey	537.1	211	Nauru	17.8
101	Angola	2,041.9	157	Burkina Faso	536.0	212	Tuvalu	17.6
102	Mauritius	2,022.8	158	Uganda	524.4			

Source: International Trade Statistics

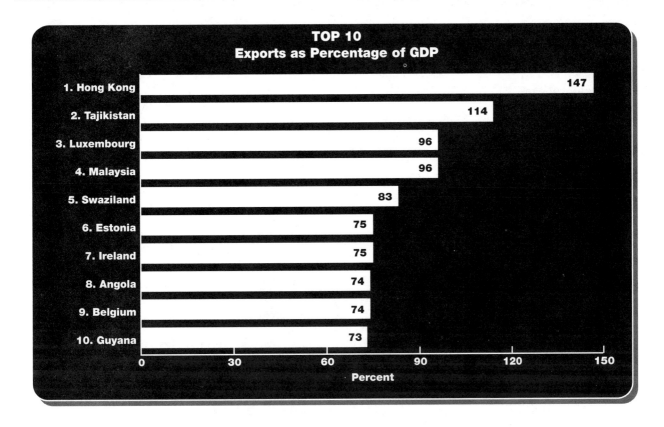

TOP 10
Exports as Percentage of GDP

Rank	Country	Percent
1. Hong Kong		147
2. Tajikistan		114
3. Luxembourg		96
4. Malaysia		96
5. Swaziland		83
6. Estonia		75
7. Ireland		75
8. Angola		74
9. Belgium		74
10. Guyana		73

Rank	Country/Entity	Exports as Percentage of GDP	Rank	Country/Entity	Exports as Percentage of GDP	Rank	Country/Entity	Exports as Percentage of GDP
11	Jamaica	69	35	Croatia	40	59	Eritrea	30
12	Slovakia	63	36	Panama	39	60	Tanzania	30
13	Congo, Rep. of	62	37	Trinidad and Tobago	39	61	Chile	29
14	Gabon	61	38	Austria	38	62	Ecuador	29
15	Papua New Guinea	61	39	Finland	38	63	Israel	29
16	Lithuania	58	40	Norway	38	64	Malawi	29
17	Mauritius	58	41	Canada	37	65	Poland	28
18	Slovenia	56	42	Macedonia	37	66	Portugal	28
19	Kuwait	55	43	Honduras	36	67	Romania	28
20	Gambia	53	44	Iceland	36	68	United Kingdom	28
21	Netherlands	53	45	Philippines	36	69	Algeria	27
22	Czech Republic	52	46	Sri Lanka	36	70	Azerbaijan	27
23	Fiji	51	47	Switzerland	36	71	Morocco	27
24	Mauritania	50	48	Vietnam	36	72	Venezuela	27
25	Botswana	49	49	Denmark	35	73	Cameroon	26
26	Bulgaria	49	50	Hungary	35	74	Dominican Republic	26
27	Tunisia	45	51	Kazakhstan	35	75	Italy	26
28	Belarus	43	52	Moldova	35	76	Kyrgyzstan	26
29	Latvia	43	53	Kenya	33	77	Ghana	25
30	Djibouti	42	54	South Korea	33	78	Indonesia	25
31	Thailand	42	55	New Zealand	32	79	Mexico	25
32	Côte d'Ivoire	41	56	Senegal	32	80	Armenia	24
33	Costa Rica	41	57	Togo	31	81	Nepal	24
34	Sweden	41	58	Zambia	31	82	Spain	24

Rank	Country/Entity	Exports as Percentage of GDP	Rank	Country/Entity	Exports as Percentage of GDP	Rank	Country/Entity	Exports as Percentage of GDP
83	France	23	95	Lesotho	21	107	Bangladesh	14
84	Germany	23	96	Australia	20	108	Guinea-Bissau	13
85	Madagascar	23	97	Grenada	20	109	Sierra Leone	13
86	Greece	22	98	Turkey	20	110	Burundi	12
87	Mali	22	99	Comoros	19	111	India	12
88	Russia	22	100	Uruguay	19	112	Peru	12
89	South Africa	22	101	Central African Republic	18	113	Uganda	12
90	China	21	102	Georgia	17	114	United States	11
91	Egypt	21	103	Pakistan	16	115	Argentina	9
92	El Salvador	21	104	Colombia	15	116	Japan	9
93	Guinea	21	105	Ethiopia	15	117	Brazil	7
94	Iran	21	106	Albania	14			

Source: World Development Report

10.4 Imports as Percentage of GDP

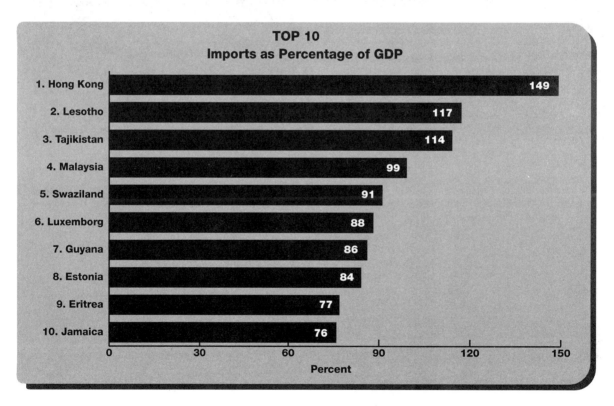

TOP 10
Imports as Percentage of GDP

Rank	Country	Percent
1. Hong Kong		149
2. Lesotho		117
3. Tajikistan		114
4. Malaysia		99
5. Swaziland		91
6. Luxemborg		88
7. Guyana		86
8. Estonia		84
9. Eritrea		77
10. Jamaica		76

Rank	Country/Entity	Imports as Percentage of GDP	Rank	Country/Entity	Imports as Percentage of GDP	Rank	Country/Entity	Imports as Percentage of GDP
11	Gambia	72	18	Lithuania	61	25	Croatia	53
12	Belgium	69	19	Slovakia	61	26	Fiji	53
13	Tanzania	68	20	Djibouti	59	27	Botswana	52
14	Congo	66	21	Angola	58	28	Kuwait	49
15	Armenia	62	22	Slovenia	57	29	Macedonia	49
16	Mauritius	62	23	Czech Republic	56	30	Tunisia	49
17	Ireland	61	24	Mauritania	54	31	Latvia	48

Rank	Country/Entity	Imports as Percentage of GDP	Rank	Country/Entity	Imports as Percentage of GDP	Rank	Country/Entity	Imports as Percentage of GDP
32	Thailand	48	61	Morocco	35	90	Poland	26
33	Belarus	47	62	Nepal	35	91	Ethiopia	25
34	Sri Lanka	47	63	Côte d'Ivoire	34	92	Guinea	25
35	Vietnam	47	64	El Salvador	34	93	Turkey	25
36	Netherlands	46	65	Ghana	34	94	Italy	23
37	Bulgaria	45	66	Greece	34	95	Spain	23
38	Honduras	45	67	South Korea	34	96	Bangladesh	22
39	Papua New Guinea	45	68	Iceland	33	97	Germany	22
40	Comoros	44	69	Egypt	32	98	Mexico	22
41	Philippines	44	70	Kyrgyzstan	32	99	Russia	22
42	Moldova	43	71	Norway	32	100	South Africa	22
43	Costa Rica	42	72	Romania	32	101	Venezuela	22
44	Israel	40	73	Switzerland	32	102	Uganda	21
45	Malawi	40	74	Burundi	31	103	Australia	20
46	Panama	40	75	Madagascar	31	104	Cameroon	20
47	Zambia	40	76	Algeria	30	105	Colombia	20
48	Austria	39	77	Finland	30	106	France	20
49	Azerbaijan	39	78	New Zealand	30	107	Uruguay	20
50	Gabon	39	79	Denmark	29	108	China	19
51	Kenya	39	80	Dominican Republic	29	109	Pakistan	19
52	Albania	38	81	Georgia	29	110	Peru	18
53	Mali	38	82	Trinidad and Tobago	29	111	Iran	16
54	Portugal	38	83	United Kingdom	29	112	India	15
55	Hungary	37	84	Central African Republic	27	113	United States	13
56	Kazakhstan	37	85	Chile	27	114	Argentina	8
57	Senegal	37	86	Ecuador	27	115	Brazil	8
58	Sweden	36	87	Grenada	27	116	Japan	8
59	Canada	35	88	Indonesia	27			
60	Guinea-Bissau	35	89	Sierra Leone	27			

Source: World Development Report

10.5 Trade as Percentage of GDP

Rank	Country/Entity	Trade as Percentage of GDP	Rank	Country/Entity	Trade as Percentage of GDP	Rank	Country/Entity	Trade as Percentage of GDP
1	Hong Kong	297	22	Jordan	121	43	Barbados	96
2	Tajikistan	228	23	Mauritius	120	44	Tanzania	96
3	Antigua and Barbuda	218	24	Equatorial Guinea	113	45	Bulgaria	94
4	Malta	198	25	Slovenia	113	46	Croatia	93
5	Malaysia	194	26	Namibia	110	47	Tunisia	93
6	Bahrain	191	27	Belize	109	48	Latvia	91
7	Swaziland	186	28	Dominica	109	49	Thailand	90
8	Luxembourg	184	29	Czech Republic	108	50	Oman	89
9	Estonia	160	30	Lithuania	108	51	Yemen	88
10	Guyana	159	31	São Tomé and Príncipe	108	52	Macedonia	86
11	Jamaica	145	32	Papua New Guinea	106	53	Armenia	85
12	Belgium	143	33	Fiji	104	54	Bhutan	85
13	Saint Lucia	141	34	Gambia	104	55	Sri Lanka	83
14	United Arab Emirates	139	35	Kuwait	104	56	Vietnam	83
15	Lesotho	138	36	Mauritania	104	57	Paraguay	82
16	Ireland	136	37	Mozambique	102	58	Costa Rica	81
17	Angola	132	38	Botswana	101	59	Nigeria	81
18	Seychelles	129	39	Djibouti	101	60	Honduras	80
19	Congo, Rep. of	128	40	Gabon	101	61	Philippines	80
20	Uzbekistan	125	41	Cyprus	99	62	Panama	79
21	Slovakia	124	42	Netherlands	99	63	Moldova	78

Rank	Country/Entity	Trade as Percentage of GDP	Rank	Country/Entity	Trade as Percentage of GDP	Rank	Country/Entity	Trade as Percentage of GDP
64	Austria	77	93	New Zealand	62	122	Georgia	46
65	Sweden	77	94	Nepal	60	123	Germany	46
66	Côte d'Ivoire	76	95	Romania	60	124	Guinea	46
67	Nicaragua	76	96	Ghana	59	125	Burkina Faso	45
68	Cape Verde	75	97	Kyrgyzstan	58	126	Turkey	45
69	Zimbabwe	74	98	Algeria	57	127	Russia	44
70	Kenya	72	99	Greece	57	128	South Africa	44
71	Canada	71	100	United Kingdom	57	129	Burundi	43
72	Norway	71	101	Ecuador	56	130	France	43
73	Zambia	71	102	Chile	55	131	Uruguay	41
74	Iceland	70	103	Dominican Republic	55	132	Australia	40
75	Lebanon	70	104	El Salvador	55	133	China	40
76	Saudi Arabia	70	105	Egypt	54	134	Sierra Leone	40
77	Israel	69	106	Madagascar	54	135	Ethiopia	39
78	Kazakhstan	69	107	Indonesia	53	136	Mali	38
79	Malawi	69	108	Laos	53	137	Bangladesh	37
80	Senegal	69	109	Poland	53	138	Cambodia	36
81	Finland	68	110	Albania	52	139	Pakistan	36
82	Switzerland	68	111	Italy	50	140	Colombia	35
83	Trinidad and Tobago	68	112	Venezuela	49	141	Uganda	33
84	Hungary	67	113	Bolivia	48	142	Niger	30
85	South Korea	67	114	Guinea-Bissau	48	143	Peru	30
86	Azerbaijan	66	115	Mexico	48	144	India	27
87	Portugal	66	116	Grenada	47	145	United States	24
88	Togo	65	117	Guatemala	47	146	Haiti	17
89	Benin	64	118	Spain	47	147	Japan	17
90	Comoros	64	119	Cameroon	46	148	Argentina	16
91	Denmark	64	120	Central African Republic	46	149	Brazil	16
92	Morocco	62	121	Chad	46	150	Suriname	11

Source: International Trade Statistics

10.6 Terms of Trade

Terms of trade indicates change in the level of export prices expressed as a percentage of import price. It is calculated by dividing export prices by 100. A country's ranking on this scale shows the profitability of its international trade if it were conducted under barter arrangements. The unit values of the index are derived from the *Handbook of International Trade and Development Statistics*.

Rank	Country/Entity	Terms of Trade, 1995 (1987=100)	Rank	Country/Entity	Terms of Trade, 1995 (1987=100)	Rank	Country/Entity	Terms of Trade, 1995 (1987=100)
1	Botswana	152	15	South Africa	111	29	Chad	103
2	India	150	16	Benin	110	30	Mali	103
3	Jordan	128	17	Israel	109	31	Mauritius	103
4	Japan	127	18	Poland	109	32	Netherlands	103
5	Mozambique	124	19	Turkey	109	33	South Korea	102
6	Dominican Republic	123	20	New Zealand	108	34	Sweden	102
7	Argentina	120	21	Italy	107	35	United Kingdom	102
8	Pakistan	114	22	Senegal	107	36	United States	102
9	Philippines	114	23	Bulgaria	106	37	Australia	101
10	Spain	114	24	France	106	38	Belgium	101
11	Uruguay	112	25	Mauritania	106	39	Brazil	101
12	Gambia	111	26	China	105	40	Niger	101
13	Greece	111	27	Jamaica	105	41	Canada	100
14	Romania	111	28	Burkina Faso	103	42	Denmark	100

Rank	Country/Entity	Terms of Trade, 1995 (1987=100)	Rank	Country/Entity	Terms of Trade, 1995 (1987=100)	Rank	Country/Entity	Terms of Trade, 1995 (1987=100)
43	Paraguay	100	66	Tunisia	91	89	Zimbabwe	84
44	Thailand	100	67	Gabon	90	90	Algeria	83
45	Kenya	98	68	Ireland	90	91	Peru	83
46	Hungary	97	69	Morocco	90	92	Tanzania	83
47	Germany	96	70	Papua New Guinea	90	93	Madagascar	82
48	Egypt	95	71	Togo	90	94	Venezuela	82
49	Finland	95	72	El Salvador	89	95	Côte d'Ivoire	81
50	Lebanon	95	73	Sierra Leone	89	96	Colombia	80
51	Nicaragua	95	74	Singapore	89	97	Cameroon	79
52	Norway	95	75	Kuwait	88	98	Indonesia	79
53	Bangladesh	94	76	Sri Lanka	88	99	Syria	78
54	Chile	94	77	Austria	87	100	Honduras	77
55	Congo	93	78	Hong Kong	87	101	Oman	77
56	Guatemala	93	79	Malawi	87	102	Ethiopia	74
57	United Arab Emirates	93	80	Angola	86	103	Ecuador	71
58	Costa Rica	92	81	Czech Republic	86	104	Bolivia	67
59	Guinea-Bissau	92	82	Nigeria	86	105	Ghana	64
60	Malaysia	92	83	Panama	86	106	Switzerland	60
61	Mexico	92	84	Slovakia	86	107	Uganda	58
62	Portugal	92	85	Trinidad and Tobago	86	108	Burundi	52
63	Saudi Arabia	92	86	Nepal	85	109	Haiti	52
64	Central African Republic	91	87	Zambia	85			
65	Guinea	91	88	Yemen	84			

Source: International Trade Statistics

10.7 Export-Import Ratio

The relation between exports and imports is dependent on a number of factors. Imports are unpopular with economic policymakers because they represent the failure of import-substitution measures and demonstrate the country's dependence on foreign producers. Economic self-sufficiency is the national ideal in many countries where protectionism is high. Since economic self-sufficiency is an impossible ideal, many nations with low export potential try to achieve a better import-export ratio by imposing import controls and high tariffs. They also classify imports into various classes ranging from essential to prohibited and permit imports only through state agencies or through a rigorous system of licenses. The efficiency of such controls and licensing varies from country to country. Foiling these official efforts is the universal activity of smuggling, which is not reflected in these rankings.

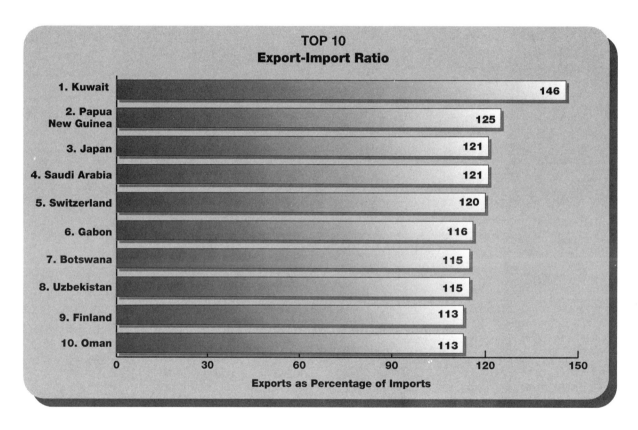

TOP 10 Export-Import Ratio

Rank. Country	Exports as Percentage of Imports
1. Kuwait	146
2. Papua New Guinea	125
3. Japan	121
4. Saudi Arabia	121
5. Switzerland	120
6. Gabon	116
7. Botswana	115
8. Uzbekistan	115
9. Finland	113
10. Oman	113

Exports as Percentage of Imports

Rank	Country/Entity	Exports as Percentage of Imports	Rank	Country/Entity	Exports as Percentage of Imports	Rank	Country/Entity	Exports as Percentage of Imports
11	Norway	112	20	France	105	29	Panama	100
12	Trinidad and Tobago	112	21	Slovakia	105	30	Chile	99
13	Russia	111	22	Bulgaria	103	31	Ireland	99
14	Singapore	111	23	Denmark	103	32	Slovenia	99
15	Venezuela	111	24	Germany	103	33	Austria	97
16	Italy	110	25	Côte d'Ivoire	101	34	Spain	97
17	Netherlands	110	26	United Kingdom	101	35	Canada	96
18	Sweden	108	27	China	100	36	Latvia	96
19	Belgium	106	28	Hong Kong	100	37	South Korea	95

Rank	Country/Entity	Exports as Percentage of Imports	Rank	Country/Entity	Exports as Percentage of Imports	Rank	Country/Entity	Exports as Percentage of Imports
38	Mauritius	95	69	Hungary	83	100	Guinea	66
39	Mexico	95	70	New Zealand	83	101	Pakistan	66
40	Czech Republic	94	71	Portugal	83	102	Egypt	65
41	Costa Rica	93	72	Lithuania	82	103	Lesotho	65
42	Mongolia	93	73	Jamaica	81	104	Madagascar	65
43	Syria	93	74	Australia	80	105	Bangladesh	64
44	Cameroon	92	75	Sri Lanka	80	106	Benin	64
45	Philippines	92	76	Honduras	79	107	Greece	61
46	Argentina	91	77	Senegal	79	108	Peru	61
47	Malaysia	91	78	Togo	79	109	Macedonia	60
48	Namibia	91	79	Angola	78	110	El Salvador	59
49	Ukraine	91	80	Kenya	77	111	Ethiopia	59
50	Estonia	90	81	Colombia	76	112	Niger	59
51	Kazakhstan	90	82	Croatia	76	113	Tanzania	56
52	Poland	90	83	Gambia	75	114	Burkina Faso	55
53	South Africa	90	84	India	75	115	Mali	55
54	Uruguay	90	85	Vietnam	75	116	Chad	51
55	United States	90	86	Central African Republic	73	117	Burundi	47
56	Zambia	89	87	Guatemala	73	118	Nicaragua	46
57	Algeria	88	88	Bolivia	72	119	Malawi	45
58	Indonesia	87	89	Brazil	72	120	Uganda	45
59	Moldova	87	90	Israel	72	121	Albania	43
60	Belarus	86	91	Morocco	71	122	Armenia	41
61	Turkey	85	92	Ghana	70	123	Sierra Leone	37
62	Dominican Republic	84	93	Nepal	70	124	Mozambique	36
63	Mauritania	84	94	Yemen	70	125	Haiti	27
64	Romania	84	95	Congo, Rep. of	69	126	Guinea-Bissau	25
65	Thailand	84	96	Jordan	69	127	Lebanon	22
66	Tunisia	84	97	Kyrgyzstan	69	128	Nigeria	20
67	Zimbabwe	84	98	Cambodia	68			
68	Ecuador	83	99	Laos	67			

Source: World Development Report

Chapter 11

Agriculture

Farms

Agriculture is the only true universal economic activity. There are nations without any industries and without any mines, but none without farms. Agricultural data collection is fairly extensive because governments consider it one of their prime and traditional responsibilities. Agriculture is characterized by many dichotomies: between traditional slash-and-burn and modern farming; between rain-fed and irrigated; between subsistence and commercial; between owner-operated and commercial; between owner-operated and rented; between large and small; and between labor-intensive and mechanized. In almost all countries, agriculture is the least efficient and least productive sector of the economy despite large state subsidies. It is also the sector that receives the smallest share of investment capital and credit. Farmers also tend to be universally conservative, sticking to their traditional crops and resisting large-scale introduction of new crops and land-use techniques.

11.1 Number of Farms

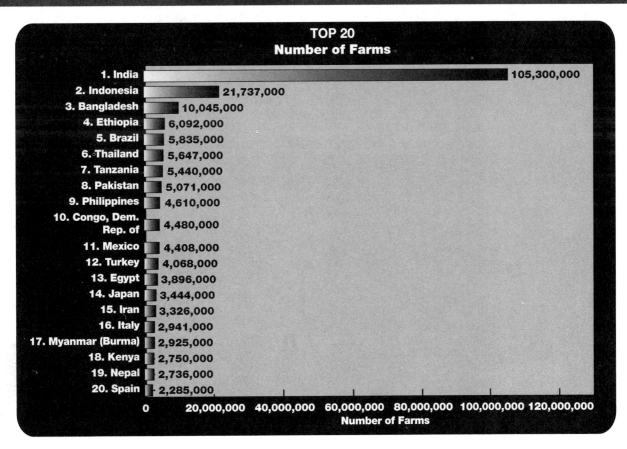

TOP 20
Number of Farms

Rank	Country/Entity	Number of Farms
1. India		105,300,000
2. Indonesia		21,737,000
3. Bangladesh		10,045,000
4. Ethiopia		6,092,000
5. Brazil		5,835,000
6. Thailand		5,647,000
7. Tanzania		5,440,000
8. Pakistan		5,071,000
9. Philippines		4,610,000
10. Congo, Dem. Rep. of		4,480,000
11. Mexico		4,408,000
12. Turkey		4,068,000
13. Egypt		3,896,000
14. Japan		3,444,000
15. Iran		3,326,000
16. Italy		2,941,000
17. Myanmar (Burma)		2,925,000
18. Kenya		2,750,000
19. Nepal		2,736,000
20. Spain		2,285,000

Number of Farms

Rank	Country/Entity	Number of Farms	Rank	Country/Entity	Number of Farms	Rank	Country/Entity	Number of Farms
21	United States	2,073,000	26	Uganda	1,704,000	31	South Korea	1,500,000
22	Poland	2,030,000	27	China	1,650,000	32	Madagascar	1,453,000
23	Morocco	1,900,000	28	Mozambique	1,605,000	33	Yugoslavia	1,176,000
24	Burkina Faso	1,860,000	29	Peru	1,574,000	34	Malawi	1,136,000
25	Sri Lanka	1,817,000	30	Colombia	1,548,000	35	Rwanda	1,112,000

Rank	Country/Entity	Number of Farms	Rank	Country/Entity	Number of Farms	Rank	Country/Entity	Number of Farms
36	Angola	1,067,000	89	Bhutan	160,000	142	Belize	11,000
37	Zimbabwe	1,000,000	90	Slovenia	157,000	143	Hong Kong	11,000
38	Cameroon	926,000	91	Ireland	153,000	144	Samoa	11,000
39	Malaysia	920,000	92	Australia	150,000	145	Estonia	10,400
40	Algeria	899,000	93	Congo, Rep. of	143,000	146	New Caledonia	10,300
41	Greece	862,000	94	Lebanon	143,000	147	Martinique	10,200
42	Cambodia	840,000	95	Afghanistan	126,000	148	Dominica	10,100
43	Taiwan	808,000	96	Liberia	122,000	149	Tonga	10,100
44	Ghana	805,000	97	Netherlands	110,000	150	Slovakia	10,000
45	France	735,000	98	Switzerland	108,000	151	Saint Vincent and the Grenadines	9,000
46	Niger	699,000	99	Mauritania	100,000			
47	Haiti	667,000	100	Fiji	95,000	152	Grenada	8,000
48	Guatemala	600,000	101	Oman	95,000	153	Iceland	7,000
49	Yemen	591,000	102	Solomon Islands	92,000	154	Brunei	6,300
50	Germany	581,000	103	Botswana	90,300	155	Namibia	6,300
51	Croatia	569,000	104	Sweden	90,000	156	Lithuania	5,900
52	Mali	562,000	105	Guinea-Bissau	84,000	157	Mayotte	5,900
53	Côte d'Ivoire	550,000	106	Norway	83,200	158	French Polynesia	5,600
54	Bosnia and Herzegovina	540,000	107	Costa Rica	82,000	159	French Guiana	3,900
55	Zambia	520,000	108	Belgium	73,000	160	Romania	3,600
56	Bolivia	519,000	109	Gabon	71,000	161	Saint Kitts and Nevis	3,400
57	Ecuador	517,000	110	Denmark	68,800	162	Azerbaijan	3,200
58	Portugal	489,000	111	New Zealand	68,800	163	Hungary	3,200
59	Iraq	470,000	112	Latvia	64,300	164	Luxembourg	3,100
60	Syria	444,000	113	South Africa	62,000	165	Belarus	3,000
61	Guinea	431,000	114	Jordan	57,000	166	Tajikistan	2,800
62	Argentina	421,000	115	Uruguay	55,000	167	Kuwait	2,600
63	Benin	408,000	116	West Bank	55,000	168	Antigua and Barbuda	2,300
64	Dominican Republic	385,000	117	Israel	52,000	169	Bulgaria	2,200
65	Venezuela	381,000	118	Cyprus	48,000	170	Bahamas	1,800
66	Tunisia	376,000	119	Ukraine	34,800	171	Cuba	1,800
67	Chad	366,000	120	Mauritius	32,500	172	Tuvalu	1,500
68	Senegal	362,000	121	Cape Verde	32,200	173	Djibouti	1,200
69	Honduras	318,000	122	Vietnam	31,000	174	American Samoa	1,100
70	Armenia	316,000	123	Kazakhstan	30,800	175	Turkmenistan	1,000
71	Paraguay	307,000	124	Trinidad and Tobago	30,600	176	Seychelles	900
72	Chile	306,000	125	Czech Republic	26,900	177	Bahrain	800
73	Sierra Leone	286,000	126	Guyana	25,000	178	Isle of Man	800
74	Central African Republic	283,000	127	Kyrgyzstan	23,200	179	Papua New Guinea	800
75	Russia	280,000	128	Puerto Rico	22,000	180	Qatar	800
76	Canada	277,000	129	Suriname	22,000	181	San Marino	700
77	El Salvador	271,000	130	Vanuatu	22,000	182	Jersey	600
78	Austria	267,000	131	Uzbekistan	18,100	183	Albania	500
79	Togo	263,000	132	United Arab Emirates	17,900	184	Liechtenstein	400
80	United Kingdom	242,000	133	Barbados	17,200	185	Swaziland	400
81	Lesotho	229,000	134	Georgia	17,000	186	Mongolia	300
82	Panama	214,000	135	Moldova	16,100	187	Palau	300
83	Saudi Arabia	212,000	136	Singapore	16,000	188	Virgin Islands (U.S.)	300
84	Somalia	198,000	137	Guadeloupe	14,000	189	Guam	200
85	Jamaica	184,000	138	São Tomé and Príncipe	13,800	190	Northern Mariana Islands	100
86	Libya	176,000	139	Réunion	12,600	191	Guernsey	89
87	Macedonia	176,000	140	Malta	12,000	192	Bermuda	80
88	Finland	170,000	141	Saint Lucia	12,000			

Source: World Data

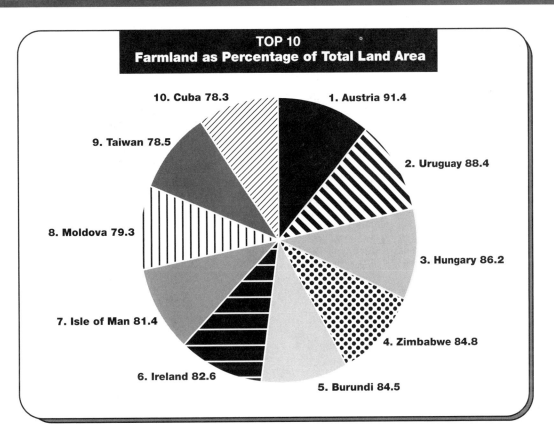

TOP 10
Farmland as Percentage of Total Land Area

10. Cuba 78.3
1. Austria 91.4
9. Taiwan 78.5
2. Uruguay 88.4
8. Moldova 79.3
3. Hungary 86.2
7. Isle of Man 81.4
4. Zimbabwe 84.8
6. Ireland 82.6
5. Burundi 84.5

Rank	Country/Entity	Farmland as Percentage of Total Land Area	Rank	Country/Entity	Farmland as Percentage of Total Land Area	Rank	Country/Entity	Farmland as Percentage of Total Land Area
11	South Africa	77.4	36	Afghanistan	58.4	61	Chad	45.8
12	San Marino	76.5	37	Netherlands	58.4	62	Belgium	45.6
13	United Kingdom	76.2	38	Croatia	57.0	63	Belarus	45.0
14	Mongolia	75.6	39	Costa Rica	56.2	64	Comoros	44.8
15	Italy	75.3	40	Jersey	56.2	65	Armenia	44.7
16	Turkmenistan	74.9	41	Bulgaria	55.8	66	Brazil	44.5
17	São Tomé and Príncipe	72.4	42	India	55.7	67	Mauritius	44.3
18	Bangladesh	70.2	43	Czech Republic	55.4	68	Jamaica	44.0
19	Ukraine	69.7	44	France	54.7	69	Georgia	43.2
20	Tonga	66.7	45	Lithuania	54.3	70	Finland	42.6
21	Kazakhstan	66.2	46	Luxembourg	53.3	71	Senegal	41.8
22	Argentina	64.8	47	Portugal	52.4	72	Guatemala	41.6
23	El Salvador	64.7	48	Mexico	52.0	73	Albania	41.1
24	Tunisia	64.6	49	Macedonia	51.3	74	United States	41.1
25	Denmark	64.2	50	Haiti	51.0	75	Malta	40.6
26	Romania	64.2	51	Kyrgyzstan	50.9	76	Panama	39.5
27	Iran	63.8	52	Barbados	50.2	77	Latvia	39.3
28	Maldives	63.5	53	Gaza Strip	50.0	78	Mayotte	39.0
29	Uzbekistan	63.2	54	Slovakia	49.9	79	Sierra Leone	38.3
30	New Zealand	61.9	55	Dominican Republic	49.8	80	Thailand	37.2
31	Spain	61.7	56	Germany	49.7	81	Grenada	36.8
32	Poland	61.3	57	Bosnia and Herzegovina	49.4	82	Puerto Rico	36.7
33	Yugoslavia	61.2	58	Azerbaijan	48.5	83	Slovenia	36.7
34	Australia	60.3	59	Nicaragua	47.7	84	Nigeria	35.9
35	Paraguay	59.9	60	Rwanda	47.4	85	Sri Lanka	35.9

Rank	Country/Entity	Farmland as Percentage of Total Land Area	Rank	Country/Entity	Farmland as Percentage of Total Land Area	Rank	Country/Entity	Farmland as Percentage of Total Land Area
86	Cyprus	35.6	124	Sweden	19.8	163	Botswana	5.9
87	Burkina Faso	35.0	125	Nepal	19.0	164	Antigua and Barbuda	5.7
88	Colombia	34.7	126	Western Sahara	18.8	165	Madagascar	5.3
89	Saint Lucia	34.4	127	Malawi	18.1	166	Bahrain	5.2
90	Venezuela	34.3	128	Mozambique	17.8	167	Egypt	5.2
91	Guadeloupe	31.7	129	China	17.4	168	Jordan	4.5
92	West Bank	31.4	130	Gambia	17.2	169	Bermuda	4.4
93	Turkey	31.0	131	New Caledonia	17.2	170	Liberia	3.9
94	Lebanon	30.9	132	Algeria	16.6	171	Eritrea	3.6
95	Philippines	30.8	133	Cambodia	16.5	172	Congo, Dem. Rep. of	3.5
96	Saint Vincent and the Grenadines	30.8	134	American Samoa	16.4	173	Bhutan	3.4
			135	Seychelles	15.6	174	Guinea-Bissau	3.4
97	Dominica	30.7	136	Uganda	15.3	175	Solomon Islands	3.4
98	Swaziland	30.6	137	Vanuatu	15.0	176	Cameroon	3.3
99	Ecuador	30.5	138	Fiji	14.2	177	Norway	3.3
100	Martinique	30.5	139	Japan	13.4	178	Guinea	3.0
101	Syria	30.1	140	Sudan	13.3	179	Yemen	2.9
102	Tajikistan	30.1	141	Iraq	13.1	180	Angola	2.8
103	Honduras	29.8	142	Russia	12.4	181	Brunei	2.8
104	Benin	29.3	143	Micronesia	12.2	182	Niger	2.8
105	Pakistan	28.7	144	Northern Mariana Islands	12.2	183	Andorra	2.0
106	Indonesia	28.2	145	Kenya	11.9	184	Bahamas	2.0
107	Guernsey	27.6	146	Chile	11.7	185	Mali	2.0
108	Vietnam	27.4	147	Peru	11.6	186	Guam	1.4
109	Switzerland	27.1	148	Ghana	10.8	187	Zambia	1.3
110	Guyana	26.2	149	Lesotho	10.5	188	Saudi Arabia	1.0
111	Greece	26.0	150	Myanmar (Burma)	10.5	189	Suriname	1.0
112	Trinidad and Tobago	25.9	151	French Polynesia	10.4	190	Papua New Guinea	0.9
113	Saint Kitts and Nevis	24.7	152	Cape Verde	10.2	191	Central African Republic	0.8
114	Liechtenstein	24.0	153	Belize	10.0	192	Namibia	0.8
115	Réunion	23.9	154	Singapore	9.0	193	Congo, Rep. of	0.7
116	Samoa	23.7	155	Libya	8.8	194	Qatar	0.7
117	Malaysia	23.1	156	Côte d'Ivoire	8.6	195	Djibouti	0.5
118	Estonia	22.7	157	Tanzania	8.5	196	United Arab Emirates	0.5
119	Virgin Islands (U.S.)	21.2	158	Hong Kong	8.1	197	Kuwait	0.4
120	Israel	21.1	159	Canada	7.4	198	Oman	0.4
121	Morocco	20.8	160	Laos	7.4	199	French Guiana	0.3
122	Bolivia	20.6	161	Togo	7.1	200	Gabon	0.3
123	South Korea	20.1	162	Ethiopia	6.4	201	Mauritania	0.2

Source: World Data

11.3 Average Farm Size

More than 100 countries in the world have what are generally described as agricultural economies. The vast majority of the farms are subsistence farms that provide little more than food for their owners and possibly something for the local market. At the next level are truck farms that supply surplus crops for the domestic market and cash crops for exports. Numerically, only a small portion are large mechanized farms, plantations, and estates, although they generate most of the crops and profits.

Rank	Country/Entity	Average Farm Size (hectares)	Rank	Country/Entity	Average Farm Size (hectares)	Rank	Country/Entity	Average Farm Size (hectares)
1	Mongolia	385,000.0	59	Iraq	13.3	117	Moldova	3.0
2	Romania	3,900.0	60	Finland	12.8	118	American Samoa	2.9
3	Australia	3,710.0	61	Israel	11.3	119	Jamaica	2.9
4	Bulgaria	2,467.0	62	Jersey	11.1	120	Guadeloupe	2.8
5	South Africa	1,319.0	63	Portugal	10.5	121	Brunei	2.6
6	Albania	1,182.0	64	Norway	10.2	122	Chad	2.6
7	Cuba	1,047.0	65	Saudi Arabia	10.1	123	Dominica	2.5
8	Papua New Guinea	483.0	66	Switzerland	9.9	124	Kenya	2.5
9	Argentina	469.0	67	Peru	9.5	125	Guinea	2.4
10	Kazakhstan	412.0	68	Pakistan	9.3	126	Kuwait	2.4
11	Uruguay	280.5	69	Syria	8.9	127	Congo, Dem. Rep. of	2.3
12	Canada	246.0	70	Liechtenstein	8.7	128	Martinique	2.3
13	Slovakia	245.0	71	São Tomé and Príncipe	8.7	129	Myanmar (Burma)	2.3
14	New Zealand	241.0	72	Bahamas	8.5	130	United Arab Emirates	2.3
15	United States	190.0	73	Poland	7.6	131	Yemen	2.3
16	United Kingdom	107.3	74	Italy	7.5	132	Malaysia	2.2
17	Barbados	95.8	75	Suriname	7.5	133	Philippines	2.2
18	Chile	94.1	76	Qatar	7.0	134	Antigua and Barbuda	2.1
19	Paraguay	88.0	77	San Marino	7.0	135	Mauritania	2.0
20	Kyrgyzstan	86.0	78	Senegal	7.0	136	Saint Lucia	2.0
21	Venezuela	82.0	79	Tajikistan	7.0	137	Sierra Leone	1.8
22	Bolivia	72.1	80	Vanuatu	6.9	138	Saint Vincent and the Grenadines	1.8
23	Brazil	64.5	81	Guatemala	6.8			
24	Isle of Man	59.7	82	Dominican Republic	6.3	139	Central African Republic	1.7
25	Swaziland	51.0	83	Jordan	6.3	140	Grenada	1.7
26	Mexico	50.0	84	Algeria	6.2	141	Mayotte	1.7
27	Northern Mariana Islands	49.1	85	Samoa	6.1	142	Tuvalu	1.7
28	Russia	43.0	86	Turkmenistan	6.0	143	Cameroon	1.6
29	Luxembourg	41.3	87	El Salvador	5.4	144	India	1.6
30	Zimbabwe	38.7	88	Botswana	5.0	145	Oman	1.6
31	Costa Rica	38.3	89	Côte d'Ivoire	5.0	146	Lesotho	1.5
32	Denmark	35.9	90	Niger	4.9	147	Togo	1.5
33	Sweden	29.5	91	Burkina Faso	4.8	148	Congo, Rep. of	1.4
34	Germany	28.0	92	French Guiana	4.6	149	Haiti	1.4
35	Vietnam	28.0	93	Bahrain	4.4	150	Cape Verde	1.3
36	Ireland	27.7	94	Lebanon	4.3	151	Ethiopia	1.3
37	Virgin Islands (U.S.)	27.0	95	Trinidad and Tobago	4.3	152	Madagascar	1.3
38	Belize	26.7	96	Fiji	4.2	153	Japan	1.2
39	France	26.6	97	Réunion	4.1	154	Malawi	1.2
40	Austria	26.4	98	Guam	4.0	155	Rwanda	1.2
41	Colombia	26.3	99	Mali	4.0	156	Malta	1.1
42	New Caledonia	23.0	100	Angola	3.9	157	Mauritius	1.1
43	Ukraine	23.0	101	Morocco	3.9	158	Nepal	1.1
44	Belarus	20.0	102	Uganda	3.9	159	Sri Lanka	1.1
45	Azerbaijan	19.0	103	Cyprus	3.8	160	Taiwan	1.1
46	Spain	19.0	104	South Korea	3.7	161	Armenia	1.0
47	Belgium	16.5	105	Cambodia	3.6	162	Gabon	1.0
48	Latvia	16.5	106	Somalia	3.6	163	Indonesia	1.0
49	Guernsey	16.2	107	Afghanistan	3.5	164	Solomon Islands	1.0
50	Lithuania	16.0	108	Thailand	3.4	165	Bangladesh	0.9
51	Netherlands	15.5	109	West Bank	3.4	166	Bhutan	0.8
52	Ecuador	15.4	110	Tonga	3.3	167	Greece	0.8
53	Uzbekistan	15.0	111	Ghana	3.2	168	Singapore	0.8
54	Puerto Rico	14.5	112	Bermuda	3.1	169	Egypt	0.7
55	Libya	14.0	113	Mozambique	3.1	170	Tanzania	0.5
56	Panama	13.8	114	Zambia	3.1	171	Djibouti	0.4
57	Tunisia	13.6	115	Guinea-Bissau	3.0	172	Hong Kong	0.3
58	Honduras	13.5	116	Liberia	3.0			

Source: World Data

Agricultural Crops

Worldwide agricultural production is more often underreported than overreported, which is probably one reason why people in countries with reported food shortages seldom starve. Agricultural statistics are notoriously inaccurate. Few farmers take the trouble to keep tabs on their output, even when they report sales, and most countries report only commercial sales of foodstuffs and ignore subsistence crops or barter. Almost all countries exclude the production of kitchen gardens and small plots even though they account for up to 25 percent of global output. Wild fruits and berries are completely ignored even by the Food and Agriculture Organization of the United Nations. In European and North American countries, millet and sorghum are used primarily as livestock or poultry feed and excluded from cereal totals, while in African countries they are used for human consumption and, therefore, reported as cereals. In many developed countries domestic production statistics are collected only for holdings above a certain size.

11.4 Grain Yield

Rank	Country/Entity	Grain Yield, 1998 (kilograms per hectare)	Rank	Country/Entity	Grain Yield, 1998 (kilograms per hectare)	Rank	Country/Entity	Grain Yield, 1998 (kilograms per hectare)
1	Belgium	7,620	38	Trinidad and Tobago	3,625	74	Lithuania	2,464
2	France	7,355	39	Dominican Republic	3,602	75	Lebanon	2,463
3	Netherlands	7,064	40	New Caledonia	3,596	76	Paraguay	2,459
4	Kuwait	6,950	41	Greece	3,526	77	Turkey	2,353
5	Egypt	6,877	42	Uruguay	3,513	78	São Tomé and Príncipe	2,263
6	Réunion	6,724	43	Spain	3,387	79	Philippines	2,241
7	Switzerland	6,676	44	French Guiana	3,376	80	Brunei	2,222
8	South Korea	6,631	45	Saint Vincent and the Grenadines	3,322	81	India	2,207
9	United Kingdom	6,618				82	Oman	2,173
10	Ireland	6,342	46	Finland	3,312	83	Pakistan	2,159
11	Germany	6,339	47	Sri Lanka	3,156	84	Ukraine	2,139
12	Denmark	6,135	48	Qatar	3,114	85	Belize	2,121
13	Mauritius	6,000	49	Poland	3,038	86	Bosnia and Herzegovina	2,121
14	Japan	5,849	50	Malta	3,000	87	Fiji	2,089
15	United States	5,682	51	Costa Rica	2,997	88	Latvia	2,073
16	Austria	5,656	52	Bulgaria	2,991	89	South Africa	2,066
17	Slovenia	5,569	53	Malaysia	2,957	90	Belarus	2,007
18	New Zealand	5,379	54	Myanmar (Burma)	2,910	91	Guam	2,000
19	Italy	5,064	55	North Korea	2,891	92	Cuba	1,973
20	China	4,811	56	Moldova	2,857	93	Nepal	1,968
21	Hungary	4,709	57	Laos	2,843	94	Australia	1,952
22	Croatia	4,672	58	Uzbekistan	2,835	95	Guatemala	1,951
23	Chile	4,592	59	Colombia	2,830	96	Iran	1,921
24	Maldives	4,400	60	Canada	2,785	97	El Salvador	1,902
25	Sweden	4,379	61	Venezuela	2,778	98	Armenia	1,883
26	Czech Republic	4,199	62	Peru	2,773	99	Madagascar	1,875
27	Papua New Guinea	4,170	63	Cyprus	2,735	100	Panama	1,875
28	Saudi Arabia	4,099	64	Mexico	2,728	101	Tajikistan	1,846
29	Slovakia	4,057	65	Kyrgyzstan	2,717	102	Bahamas	1,795
30	Guyana	4,053	66	Macedonia	2,696	103	Cambodia	1,781
31	Puerto Rico	4,000	67	Albania	2,679	104	Swaziland	1,780
32	Suriname	3,943	68	Bangladesh	2,669	105	Estonia	1,758
33	Norway	3,869	69	Romania	2,634	106	Gabon	1,728
34	Vietnam	3,838	70	Portugal	2,626	107	Georgia	1,725
35	Yugoslavia	3,825	71	Brazil	2,557	108	Azerbaijan	1,712
36	Indonesia	3,789	72	Barbados	2,500	109	Ecuador	1,695
37	Argentina	3,717	73	Thailand	2,466	110	Djibouti	1,625

Rank	Country/Entity	Grain Yield, 1998 (kilograms per hectare)	Rank	Country/Entity	Grain Yield, 1998 (kilograms per hectare)	Rank	Country/Entity	Grain Yield, 1998 (kilograms per hectare)
111	Antigua and Barbuda	1,607	134	Nigeria	1,211	157	Iraq	807
112	Israel	1,583	135	Sierra Leone	1,205	158	Western Sahara	774
113	Kenya	1,567	136	Rwanda	1,201	159	Mauritania	758
114	Syria	1,524	137	Jamaica	1,146	160	Congo, Dem. Rep. of	721
115	Nicaragua	1,511	138	Ethiopia	1,140	161	Saint Lucia	714
116	United Arab Emirates	1,442	139	Côte d'Ivoire	1,139	162	Burkina Faso	705
117	Honduras	1,434	140	Benin	1,134	163	Angola	703
118	Guinea-Bissau	1,425	141	Morocco	1,124	164	Senegal	699
119	Afghanistan	1,388	142	Zimbabwe	1,101	165	Chad	692
120	Ghana	1,384	143	Bhutan	1,097	166	Congo, Rep. of	687
121	Bolivia	1,367	144	Mali	1,094	167	Sudan	680
122	Zambia	1,363	145	Yemen	1,082	168	Mongolia	636
123	Tunisia	1,341	146	Central African Republic	1,035	169	Kazakhstan	562
124	Comoros	1,338	147	Grenada	1,000	170	Vanuatu	536
125	Guinea	1,321	148	Jordan	958	171	Gaza Strip	529
126	Uganda	1,320	149	Gambia	950	172	Eritrea	476
127	Malawi	1,317	150	Russia	927	173	Somalia	384
128	Dominica	1,308	151	Haiti	914	174	Niger	335
129	Liberia	1,293	152	Lesotho	878	175	Cape Verde	314
130	Tanzania	1,288	153	Togo	866	176	Namibia	190
131	Burundi	1,276	154	Libya	842	177	Botswana	146
132	Turkmenistan	1,258	155	Mozambique	839			
133	Cameroon	1,249	156	Algeria	821			

Source: FAO Production Statistics

11.5 Fruit

Rank	Country/Entity	Fruit Production, 1998 (thousand metric tons)	Rank	Country/Entity	Fruit Production, 1998 (thousand metric tons)	Rank	Country/Entity	Fruit Production, 1998 (thousand metric tons)
1	China	83,636	30	Russia	3,146	59	Moldova	1,426
2	India	38,685	31	Costa Rica	3,140	60	Dominican Republic	1,378
3	Brazil	38,035	32	Venezuela	3,119	61	Bulgaria	1,288
4	United States	34,410	33	Peru	2,976	62	Malaysia	1,246
5	Italy	18,784	34	Ukraine	2,906	63	Tunisia	1,227
6	Turkey	15,988	35	Australia	2,887	64	Myanmar (Burma)	1,143
7	Spain	15,089	36	Romania	2,523	65	Sudan	1,127
8	Iran	13,960	37	Poland	2,514	66	Kenya	1,062
9	Mexico	13,332	38	Rwanda	2,306	67	Guinea	996
10	France	11,152	39	Iraq	2,289	68	New Zealand	974
11	Philippines	10,246	40	Syria	2,217	69	Haiti	970
12	Uganda	9,882	41	Cameroon	2,214	70	Papua New Guinea	948
13	Ecuador	9,067	42	Tanzania	2,118	71	Georgia	946
14	Egypt	8,107	43	Ghana	2,050	72	Bolivia	923
15	Indonesia	7,450	44	Yugoslavia	1,918	73	Austria	861
16	Thailand	7,235	45	Uzbekistan	1,759	74	Madagascar	855
17	Argentina	7,141	46	Israel	1,744	75	Sri Lanka	825
18	Nigeria	7,075	47	Côte d'Ivoire	1,729	76	Canada	760
19	Pakistan	6,210	48	Algeria	1,660	77	Panama	735
20	Colombia	5,934	49	Saudi Arabia	1,635	78	Afghanistan	727
21	Japan	5,431	50	Hungary	1,621	79	Yemen	680
22	Germany	4,996	51	Honduras	1,578	80	Paraguay	670
23	Greece	4,170	52	Portugal	1,568	81	Switzerland	663
24	South Africa	4,150	53	Cuba	1,523	82	Netherlands	640
25	Vietnam	4,086	54	North Korea	1,500	83	Belgium	623
26	South Korea	3,912	55	Bangladesh	1,490	84	Uruguay	588
27	Chile	3,910	56	Burundi	1,484	85	Libya	576
28	Congo, Dem. Rep. of	3,443	57	Lebanon	1,459	86	Malawi	508
29	Morocco	3,402	58	Guatemala	1,434	87	Croatia	502

Rank	Country/Entity	Fruit Production, 1998 (thousand metric tons)	Rank	Country/Entity	Fruit Production, 1998 (thousand metric tons)	Rank	Country/Entity	Fruit Production, 1998 (thousand metric tons)
88	Azerbaijan	492	123	West Bank	163	157	Bahrain	21
89	Czech Republic	489	124	Sierra Leone	159	158	Vanuatu	19
90	Turkmenistan	489	125	Kyrgyzstan	150	159	Grenada	18
91	Macedonia	478	126	Benin	148	160	Ireland	18
92	Jordan	474	127	Gaza Strip	146	161	Malta	18
93	Angola	446	128	Lithuania	145	162	São Tomé and Príncipe	18
94	Tajikistan	446	129	Liberia	142	163	Estonia	17
95	Jamaica	431	130	Chad	115	164	Solomon Islands	16
96	Nepal	428	131	Saint Lucia	112	165	Cape Verde	15
97	Senegal	399	132	Sweden	112	166	Equatorial Guinea	15
98	Kazakhstan	380	133	Norway	103	167	Fiji	14
99	Mozambique	378	134	Zambia	96	168	French Guiana	14
100	Martinique	359	135	Bosnia and Herzegovina	89	169	Tonga	14
101	Cyprus	338	136	Dominica	86	170	Lesotho	13
102	Slovakia	338	137	Denmark	85	171	Mauritius	12
103	Albania	336	138	Trinidad and Tobago	78	172	Kuwait	10
104	United Arab Emirates	329	139	Burkina Faso	73	173	Antigua and Barbuda	9
105	Belarus	323	140	Suriname	73	174	French Polynesia	9
106	Cambodia	312	141	Guinea-Bissau	72	175	Maldives	9
107	Belize	296	142	Swaziland	69	176	Namibia	9
108	Armenia	293	143	Bhutan	64	177	Botswana	8
109	El Salvador	291	144	Saint Vincent and the Grenadines	61	178	Kiribati	6
110	Gabon	283				179	Brunei	5
111	United Kingdom	278	145	Comoros	60	180	Eritrea	5
112	Slovenia	267	146	Mali	52	181	Gambia	4
113	Central African Republic	245	147	Togo	49	182	Guam	4
114	Nicaragua	245	148	Niger	48	183	Barbados	3
115	Oman	242	149	Samoa	43	184	Hong Kong	3
116	Ethiopia	231	150	Guyana	40	185	New Caledonia	3
117	Somalia	230	151	Réunion	38	186	Seychelles	2
118	Laos	204	152	Latvia	36	187	Saint Kitts and Nevis	2
119	Zimbabwe	183	153	Bahamas	25	188	American Samoa	1
120	Puerto Rico	179	154	Finland	24	189	Tuvalu	1
121	Congo, Rep. of	172	155	Mauritania	23			
122	Guadeloupe	163	156	Qatar	22			

Source: FAO Production Statistics

Cattle and Milk

Of all the domesticated animals, cattle are the most numerous and the most productive. Throughout the world they are the principal sources of milk and meat, and in developing countries, they are used as draft animals. In primitive societies, wealth consisted chiefly of cattle (the words "cattle" and "capital" are etymologically related). The principal beef breeds are Angus and Hereford, and the principal dairy breeds are Ayrshire, Brown Swiss, Guernsey, Holstein-Friesian, and Jersey. Dual-purpose breeds include Devon, Red Poll, and Shorthorn.

11.6 Cattle

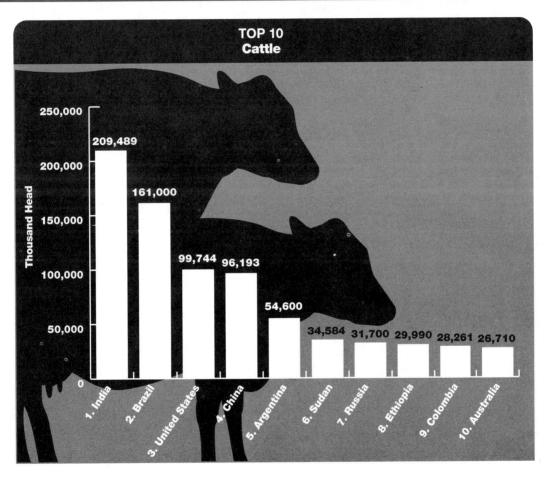

TOP 10 Cattle

Thousand Head

Rank	Country/Entity	Cattle, 1998 (thousand head)	Rank	Country/Entity	Cattle, 1998 (thousand head)	Rank	Country/Entity	Cattle, 1998 (thousand head)
11	Mexico	25,628	18	Tanzania	14,302	25	Turkey	11,185
12	Bangladesh	23,400	19	Kenya	14,116	26	Myanmar (Burma)	10,492
13	France	20,389	20	South Africa	13,800	27	Uruguay	10,475
14	Nigeria	19,610	21	Canada	13,357	28	Madagascar	10,335
15	Pakistan	18,000	22	Ukraine	12,759	29	Paraguay	9,794
16	Venezuela	15,367	23	Indonesia	12,239	30	New Zealand	8,772
17	Germany	15,277	24	United Kingdom	11,519	31	Iran	8,600

Rank	Country/Entity	Cattle, 1998 (thousand head)	Rank	Country/Entity	Cattle, 1998 (thousand head)	Rank	Country/Entity	Cattle, 1998 (thousand head)
32	Italy	7,166	87	Benin	1,400	142	Taiwan	165
33	Ireland	7,093	88	Iraq	1,350	143	Libya	155
34	Nepal	7,025	89	Eritrea	1,320	144	Vanuatu	151
35	Thailand	7,000	90	Côte d'Ivoire	1,312	145	Oman	146
36	Poland	6,955	91	Mauritania	1,312	146	New Caledonia	120
37	Bolivia	6,387	92	Haiti	1,300	147	Suriname	89
38	Cameroon	5,900	93	Mozambique	1,300	148	Papua New Guinea	86
39	Spain	5,839	94	Portugal	1,295	149	Guadeloupe	80
40	Mali	5,725	95	Yemen	1,263	150	Lebanon	80
41	Chad	5,582	96	Algeria	1,250	151	United Arab Emirates	76
42	Zimbabwe	5,450	97	El Salvador	1,157	152	Iceland	75
43	Uganda	5,370	98	Ghana	1,150	153	Congo, Rep. of	72
44	Ecuador	5,329	99	Finland	1,145	154	Jordan	65
45	Somalia	5,300	100	Laos	1,112	155	Cyprus	61
46	Uzbekistan	5,300	101	Lithuania	1,068	156	Belize	60
47	Belarus	4,801	102	Tajikistan	1,040	157	Comoros	50
48	Japan	4,700	103	Georgia	1,027	158	Gabon	39
49	Peru	4,657	104	Norway	1,018	159	Trinidad and Tobago	39
50	Cuba	4,650	105	Congo, Dem. Rep. of	1,000	160	Mauritius	37
51	Burkina Faso	4,522	106	Syria	900	161	Liberia	36
52	Netherlands	4,292	107	Turkmenistan	900	162	Martinique	30
53	Kazakhstan	4,000	108	Hungary	871	163	Réunion	26
54	Vietnam	3,984	109	Kyrgyzstan	830	164	Samoa	26
55	Chile	3,755	110	Slovakia	803	165	Barbados	22
56	Mongolia	3,613	111	Malawi	800	166	Cape Verde	22
57	Angola	3,500	112	Albania	780	167	Kuwait	22
58	South Korea	3,279	113	Tunisia	770	168	Malta	21
59	Romania	3,235	114	Malaysia	725	169	Antigua and Barbuda	16
60	Belgium	3,184	115	Swaziland	650	170	Micronesia	14
61	Egypt	3,022	116	Bulgaria	612	171	Qatar	14
62	Central African Republic	2,992	117	Greece	580	172	Bahrain	13
63	Senegal	2,913	118	Lesotho	580	173	Dominica	13
64	Cambodia	2,900	119	Guinea-Bissau	510	174	Saint Lucia	12
65	Morocco	2,600	120	Armenia	505	175	West Bank	12
66	Zambia	2,600	121	North Korea	500	176	Solomon Islands	10
67	Dominican Republic	2,528	122	Rwanda	500	177	French Guiana	9
68	Philippines	2,395	123	Moldova	485	178	French Polynesia	9
69	Guinea	2,337	124	Slovenia	445	179	Tonga	9
70	Botswana	2,330	125	Croatia	443	180	Virgin Islands (U.S.)	8
71	Guatemala	2,330	126	Bhutan	435	181	Liechtenstein	6
72	Austria	2,198	127	Latvia	434	182	Saint Vincent and the Grenadines	6
73	Namibia	2,192	128	Jamaica	400			
74	Niger	2,100	129	Sierra Leone	400	183	Equatorial Guinea	5
75	Denmark	1,974	130	Puerto Rico	388	184	Grenada	4
76	Honduras	1,945	131	Israel	370	185	São Tomé and Príncipe	4
77	Yugoslavia	1,894	132	Fiji	360	186	Saint Kitts and Nevis	4
78	Azerbaijan	1,843	133	Burundi	346	187	Gaza Strip	3
79	Sweden	1,706	134	Gambia	346	188	Brunei	2
80	Czech Republic	1,690	135	Estonia	312	189	Faroe Islands	2
81	Nicaragua	1,688	136	Macedonia	298	190	Hong Kong	2
82	Switzerland	1,637	137	Bosnia and Herzegovina	260	191	Bahamas	1
83	Sri Lanka	1,599	138	Togo	223	192	Bermuda	1
84	Costa Rica	1,527	139	Guyana	220	193	Netherlands Antilles	1
85	Afghanistan	1,500	140	Saudi Arabia	200	194	Seychelles	1
86	Panama	1,442	141	Djibouti	190			

Source: FAO Statistics

Rank	Country/Entity	Milk Yield, 1997 (kilograms per animal)	Rank	Country/Entity	Milk Yield, 1997 (kilograms per animal)	Rank	Country/Entity	Milk Yield, 1997 (kilograms per animal)
1	Israel	8,444	62	Paraguay	1,899	122	Cape Verde	683
2	United States	7,690	63	Uzbekistan	1,882	123	Solomon Islands	650
3	Saudi Arabia	7,282	64	Peru	1,801	124	Morocco	633
4	Sweden	6,922	65	Suriname	1,800	125	New Caledonia	600
5	South Korea	6,684	66	Uruguay	1,792	126	Yemen	600
6	Netherlands	6,581	67	Thailand	1,765	127	Réunion	524
7	Japan	6,552	68	Costa Rica	1,756	128	Cameroon	500
8	Denmark	6,385	69	Cuba	1,756	129	Comoros	500
9	Canada	6,225	70	Albania	1,721	130	Congo, Rep. of	500
10	Finland	6,195	71	Fiji	1,692	131	Angola	492
11	United Kingdom	5,713	72	Barbados	1,670	132	Kenya	491
12	Hungary	5,546	73	Qatar	1,647	133	Sudan	480
13	Germany	5,534	74	Kuwait	1,636	134	Malawi	465
14	France	5,476	75	Armenia	1,596	135	Zimbabwe	444
15	Norway	5,451	76	Turkey	1,586	136	Oman	420
16	Belgium	5,339	77	China	1,574	137	Malaysia	418
17	Switzerland	5,149	78	Macedonia	1,566	138	Somalia	412
18	Cyprus	4,844	79	Dominican Republic	1,562	139	Niger	400
19	Taiwan	4,802	80	Trinidad and Tobago	1,527	140	Namibia	399
20	Italy	4,800	81	Tunisia	1,465	141	Mongolia	398
21	Malta	4,767	82	Bolivia	1,419	142	Afghanistan	395
22	Portugal	4,670	83	Saint Vincent and the Grenadines	1,414	143	Myanmar (Burma)	392
23	Czech Republic	4,639				144	Nepal	380
24	Australia	4,547	84	Kazakhstan	1,413	145	Senegal	360
25	Spain	4,538	85	Chile	1,388	146	Botswana	350
26	Austria	4,474	86	Bosnia and Herzegovina	1,263	147	Burundi	350
27	Liechtenstein	4,444	87	El Salvador	1,255	148	Djibouti	350
28	Ireland	4,436	88	Netherlands Antilles	1,250	149	Mauritania	350
29	Argentina	4,081	89	Venezuela	1,250	150	Uganda	350
30	Estonia	4,070	90	Mexico	1,245	151	Zambia	300
31	Gaza Strip	4,000	91	Saint Lucia	1,236	152	Sri Lanka	298
32	Puerto Rico	3,933	92	Panama	1,233	153	Lesotho	290
33	Bermuda	3,857	93	Indonesia	1,217	154	Swaziland	285
34	Greece	3,750	94	Azerbaijan	1,214	155	Madagascar	276
35	Poland	3,506	95	Libya	1,214	156	Chad	270
36	Iceland	3,463	96	Iran	1,192	157	Central African Republic	261
37	New Zealand	3,414	97	Honduras	1,152	158	Bhutan	257
38	Slovakia	3,286	98	Belize	1,045	159	Gabon	250
39	Latvia	3,232	99	Colombia	1,040	160	Sierra Leone	250
40	Lithuania	3,087	100	Georgia	1,038	161	Haiti	249
41	Bulgaria	3,030	101	Pakistan	1,035	162	Mali	245
42	Jordan	3,000	102	Philippines	1,026	163	Nigeria	233
43	Romania	2,912	103	India	1,015	164	Togo	225
44	South Africa	2,863	104	Egypt	1,008	165	United Arab Emirates	210
45	Slovenia	2,795	105	Bahamas	1,000	166	Bangladesh	206
46	Virgin Islands (U.S.)	2,703	106	Jamaica	1,000	167	Vanuatu	203
47	Turkmenistan	2,685	107	Samoa	1,000	168	Laos	200
48	Lebanon	2,604	108	Antigua and Barbuda	968	169	Eritrea	196
49	Syria	2,584	109	Algeria	946	170	Guinea	185
50	Mauritius	2,500	110	Dominica	910	171	Tanzania	184
51	Belarus	2,425	111	Nicaragua	909	172	Burkina Faso	175
52	Ecuador	2,397	112	Congo, Dem. Rep. of	851	173	Gambia	175
53	North Korea	2,368	113	Guatemala	845	174	Cambodia	170
54	Russia	2,142	114	Guyana	828	175	Guinea-Bissau	170
55	Moldova	2,110	115	Brazil	809	176	Mozambique	170
56	Croatia	2,088	116	Grenada	800	177	Côte d'Ivoire	165
57	Ukraine	2,082	117	Vietnam	800	178	Benin	130
58	Kyrgyzstan	2,000	118	Martinique	763	179	Ghana	130
59	Bahrain	1,940	119	Tajikistan	753	180	Liberia	130
60	French Polynesia	1,905	120	Rwanda	727			
61	Yugoslavia	1,905	121	Iraq	690			

Source: FAO Statistics

11.8 Sheep

Sheep are found mostly in temperate climates. They are raised for their wool, meat (called mutton or lamb, according to age), and skins. In some countries their milk is drunk and made into cheese. Among the major breeds of wild sheep are the argali, the Barbary sheep, or the aoudad of North Africa, and the North American bighorn, or Rocky Mountain sheep. The more important breeds of domesticated sheep are Columbia, Cotswold, Dorset, Hampshire, Karakul, Leicester, Lincoln, Merino, Oxford, Rambouillet, Shropshire, Southdown, and Suffolk.

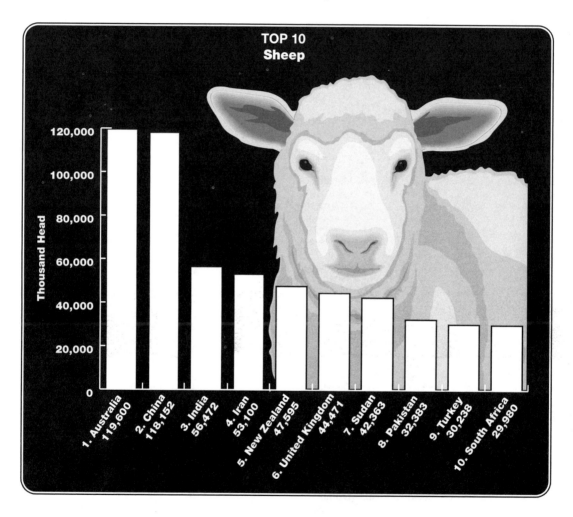

TOP 10
Sheep

1. Australia 119,600
2. China 118,152
3. India 56,472
4. Iran 53,100
5. New Zealand 47,595
6. United Kingdom 44,471
7. Sudan 42,363
8. Pakistan 32,383
9. Turkey 30,238
10. South Africa 29,980

Rank	Country/Entity	Sheep, 1998 (thousand head)	Rank	Country/Entity	Sheep, 1998 (thousand head)	Rank	Country/Entity	Sheep, 1998 (thousand head)
11	Spain	24,542	19	Afghanistan	14,300	27	Greece	9,516
12	Ethiopia	21,850	20	Mongolia	14,166	28	Romania	8,937
13	Brazil	18,300	21	Nigeria	14,000	29	Kazakhstan	8,908
14	Uruguay	17,800	22	Syria	14,000	30	Bolivia	8,409
15	Morocco	17,600	23	Peru	13,558	31	Indonesia	8,151
16	Russia	17,125	24	Somalia	13,500	32	Saudi Arabia	8,042
17	Algeria	16,750	25	Italy	10,890	33	Uzbekistan	8,000
18	Argentina	16,432	26	France	10,305	34	United States	7,616

Rank	Country/Entity	Sheep, 1998 (thousand head)	Rank	Country/Entity	Sheep, 1998 (thousand head)	Rank	Country/Entity	Sheep, 1998 (thousand head)
35	Iraq	6,900	85	Guatemala	551	135	Bhutan	59
36	Tunisia	6,600	86	Armenia	550	136	Martinique	42
37	Mexico	6,500	87	Georgia	543	137	Barbados	41
38	Portugal	6,300	88	Zimbabwe	520	138	Equatorial Guinea	36
39	Burkina Faso	6,207	89	Iceland	477	139	Estonia	34
40	Mauritania	6,200	90	Djibouti	470	140	Philippines	30
41	Mali	5,950	91	Poland	452	141	Latvia	29
42	Azerbaijan	5,867	92	Kuwait	445	142	Western Sahara	29
43	Kenya	5,700	93	Croatia	427	143	Slovenia	28
44	Libya	5,700	94	Switzerland	420	144	Lithuania	26
45	Ireland	5,624	95	Slovakia	417	145	Swaziland	25
46	Turkmenistan	5,400	96	Sweden	407	146	Gaza Strip	24
47	Yemen	4,527	97	Paraguay	387	147	Greenland	22
48	Egypt	4,300	98	United Arab Emirates	385	148	Comoros	20
49	Senegal	4,239	99	Austria	384	149	Bahrain	17
50	Niger	4,100	100	Myanmar (Burma)	369	150	Japan	16
51	Tanzania	3,960	101	Israel	360	151	Malta	16
52	Cameroon	3,800	102	West Bank	352	152	Honduras	14
53	Chile	3,754	103	Lebanon	350	153	Grenada	13
54	Kyrgyzstan	3,350	104	Sierra Leone	350	154	Saint Lucia	13
55	Bulgaria	2,848	105	Burundi	320	155	Saint Vincent and the Grenadines	13
56	Norway	2,447	106	Cuba	310			
57	Chad	2,432	107	Bosnia and Herzegovina	276	156	Antigua and Barbuda	12
58	Colombia	2,416	108	Guinea-Bissau	275	157	Sri Lanka	12
59	Yugoslavia	2,402	109	Rwanda	270	158	Trinidad and Tobago	12
60	Germany	2,302	110	Cyprus	262	159	Cape Verde	9
61	Ghana	2,100	111	Malaysia	255	160	Dominica	8
62	Namibia	2,086	112	Angola	245	161	Puerto Rico	8
63	Ecuador	2,056	113	Botswana	240	162	Saint Kitts and Nevis	8
64	Jordan	2,000	114	Liberia	210	163	Fiji	7
65	Uganda	1,960	115	Central African Republic	201	164	Mauritius	7
66	Albania	1,890	116	Qatar	200	165	Netherlands Antilles	7
67	Macedonia	1,805	117	Gambia	182	166	Suriname	7
68	Ukraine	1,700	118	Gabon	173	167	Bahamas	6
69	Netherlands	1,674	119	Belgium	155	168	Papua New Guinea	6
70	Tajikistan	1,600	120	Oman	155	169	El Salvador	5
71	Eritrea	1,530	121	North Korea	150	170	Guadeloupe	4
72	Côte d'Ivoire	1,347	122	Denmark	142	171	New Caledonia	4
73	Bangladesh	1,158	123	Haiti	138	172	Nicaragua	4
74	Lesotho	1,100	124	Dominican Republic	135	173	Belize	3
75	Congo, Dem. Rep. of	1,020	125	Guyana	130	174	Costa Rica	3
76	Moldova	1,017	126	Belarus	127	175	French Guiana	3
77	Nepal	870	127	Mozambique	123	176	Liechtenstein	3
78	Hungary	858	128	Malawi	120	177	São Tomé and Príncipe	3
79	Venezuela	820	129	Congo, Rep. of	114	178	Virgin Islands (U.S.)	3
80	Madagascar	765	130	Finland	103	179	Jamaica	2
81	Togo	740	131	Czech Republic	94	180	South Korea	2
82	Guinea	669	132	Faroe Islands	68	181	Réunion	2
83	Canada	634	133	Zambia	65			
84	Benin	605	134	Thailand	60			

Source: FAO Statistics

Pigs are sometimes known as swine or hogs. They are commonly grouped as meat-type, lard-type, and bacon-type. Meat-type breeds include Hereford and Berkshire; lard-type breeds include Poland, China, Duroc, and Spotted Swine; and bacon-type breeds include Tamworth, Yorkshire, and American Landrace. Male domestic swine suitable for breeding are known as boars.

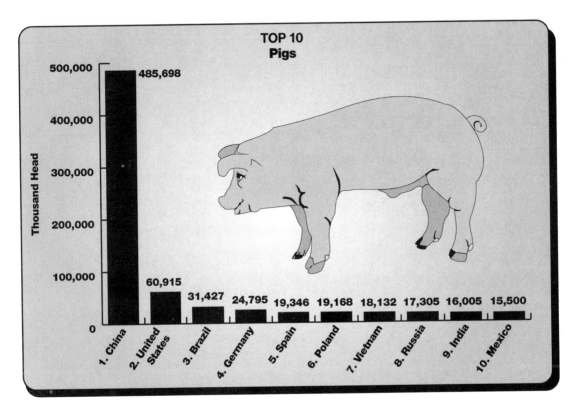

TOP 10 Pigs

Rank	Country	Thousand Head
1. China	485,698
2. United States	60,915
3. Brazil	31,427
4. Germany	24,795
5. Spain	19,346
6. Poland	19,168
7. Vietnam	18,132
8. Russia	17,305
9. India	16,005
10. Mexico	15,500

Rank	Country/Entity	Pigs, 1998 (thousand head)	Rank	Country/Entity	Pigs, 1998 (thousand head)	Rank	Country/Entity	Pigs, 1998 (thousand head)
11	France	15,430	29	Yugoslavia	4,150	47	Chile	1,771
12	Denmark	12,004	30	Czech Republic	3,995	48	Madagascar	1,670
13	Canada	11,843	31	Belarus	3,682	49	South Africa	1,641
14	Netherlands	11,438	32	Austria	3,680	50	North Korea	1,600
15	Taiwan	10,509	33	Myanmar (Burma)	3,501	51	Bulgaria	1,500
16	Philippines	10,210	34	Malaysia	3,400	52	Cuba	1,500
17	Indonesia	10,069	35	Argentina	3,200	53	Papua New Guinea	1,500
18	Japan	9,800	36	Ecuador	2,795	54	Switzerland	1,486
19	Ukraine	9,479	37	Australia	2,680	55	Laos	1,468
20	Italy	8,281	38	Bolivia	2,637	56	Finland	1,467
21	United Kingdom	8,146	39	Peru	2,547	57	Cameroon	1,410
22	Nigeria	7,600	40	Paraguay	2,525	58	Lithuania	1,205
23	Belgium	7,436	41	Colombia	2,480	59	Congo, Dem. Rep. of	1,170
24	Romania	7,097	42	Portugal	2,365	60	Croatia	1,166
25	South Korea	6,700	43	Sweden	2,309	61	Dominican Republic	960
26	Hungary	4,931	44	Cambodia	2,200	62	Uganda	950
27	Thailand	4,815	45	Slovakia	1,809	63	Greece	938
28	Venezuela	4,756	46	Ireland	1,801	64	Kazakhstan	860

Rank	Country/Entity	Pigs, 1998 (thousand head)	Rank	Country/Entity	Pigs, 1998 (thousand head)	Rank	Country/Entity	Pigs, 1998 (thousand head)
65	Togo	850	103	Puerto Rico	175	141	Azerbaijan	21
66	Guatemala	826	104	Israel	168	142	Mongolia	21
67	Angola	810	105	Fiji	145	143	Guyana	20
68	Haiti	800	106	Liberia	120	144	Suriname	20
69	Norway	770	107	Hong Kong	110	145	Mauritius	18
70	Moldova	762	108	Kenya	108	146	Seychelles	18
71	Nepal	725	109	Albania	98	147	Guadeloupe	15
72	Honduras	700	110	Réunion	87	148	Namibia	15
73	Cape Verde	636	111	Kyrgyzstan	85	149	Saint Lucia	15
74	Central African Republic	622	112	Tonga	81	150	Gambia	14
75	Burkina Faso	587	113	Rwanda	80	151	Tuvalu	13
76	Benin	580	114	Sri Lanka	76	152	American Samoa	11
77	Slovenia	578	115	Bhutan	75	153	French Guiana	11
78	Latvia	421	116	Burundi	73	154	Kiribati	10
79	Cyprus	415	117	Bosnia and Herzegovina	70	155	Saint Vincent and the Grenadines	9
80	Nicaragua	400	118	Malta	69	156	Morocco	8
81	Ghana	395	119	Lesotho	65	157	Algeria	6
82	New Zealand	340	120	Mali	65	158	Tunisia	6
83	Tanzania	340	121	Lebanon	60	159	Bahamas	5
84	Guinea-Bissau	335	122	Vanuatu	60	160	Brunei	5
85	Georgia	330	123	Solomon Islands	57	161	Dominica	5
86	Estonia	329	124	Guinea	53	162	Equatorial Guinea	5
87	Senegal	320	125	Armenia	52	163	Grenada	5
88	El Salvador	314	126	Sierra Leone	50	164	Turkey	5
89	Zambia	285	127	Congo, Rep. of	44	165	Botswana	4
90	Costa Rica	280	128	Iceland	43	166	Guam	4
91	Côte d'Ivoire	271	129	French Polynesia	42	167	Somalia	4
92	Uruguay	270	130	Niger	39	168	Liechtenstein	3
93	Zimbabwe	270	131	New Caledonia	38	169	Nauru	3
94	Panama	245	132	Turkmenistan	35	170	Saint Kitts and Nevis	3
95	Malawi	240	133	Martinique	33	171	Virgin Islands (U.S.)	3
96	Gabon	208	134	Barbados	30	172	Antigua and Barbuda	2
97	Uzbekistan	195	135	Swaziland	30	173	Netherlands Antilles	2
98	Macedonia	193	136	Egypt	29	174	São Tomé and Príncipe	2
99	Singapore	190	137	Trinidad and Tobago	28	175	Tajikistan	2
100	Jamaica	180	138	Belize	23	176	Bermuda	1
101	Samoa	179	139	Chad	23	177	Syria	1
102	Mozambique	176	140	Ethiopia	23			

Source: FAO Statistics

Although they have a short life and a high mortality rate, chickens outnumber humans worldwide at any given time. Most of them are raised in farms or broilers and they are specialized to produce either eggs or meat. These eggs and meat provide cheaper sources of protein than beef. The principal kinds of chickens are Rhode Island Red, White Leghorn, and Plymouth Rock.

11.10 Chickens

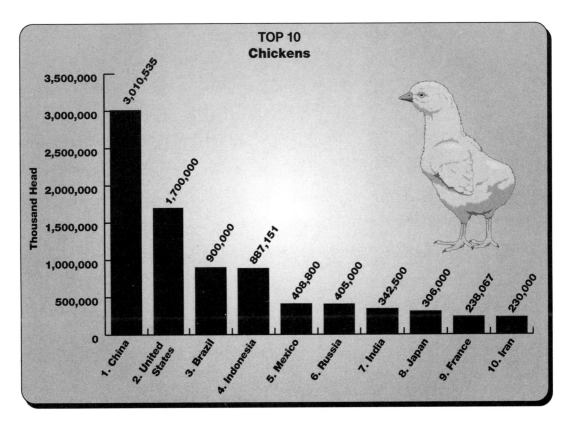

TOP 10 Chickens

Rank	Country/Entity	Chickens, 1998 (thousand head)	Rank	Country/Entity	Chickens, 1998 (thousand head)	Rank	Country/Entity	Chickens, 1998 (thousand head)
11	Pakistan	200,000	24	Germany	102,731	37	Romania	66,620
12	Turkey	166,273	25	Ukraine	102,000	38	Ecuador	64,736
13	Thailand	165,000	26	Taiwan	101,838	39	South Africa	59,000
14	United Kingdom	152,886	27	Morocco	100,000	40	Bolivia	58,796
15	Bangladesh	152,875	28	Venezuela	100,000	41	Argentina	55,000
16	Canada	139,000	29	Netherlands	98,692	42	Ethiopia	55,000
17	Italy	138,000	30	Saudi Arabia	95,000	43	Poland	51,120
18	Philippines	136,887	31	South Korea	88,000	44	Belgium	48,000
19	Algeria	132,000	32	Egypt	86,000	45	Senegal	44,100
20	Spain	127,000	33	Colombia	85,000	46	Sudan	40,500
21	Vietnam	126,361	34	Australia	83,000	47	Belarus	40,000
22	Nigeria	126,000	35	Peru	80,140	48	Dominican Republic	37,698
23	Malaysia	110,000	36	Chile	70,000	49	Tunisia	35,000

Rank	Country/Entity	Chickens, 1998 (thousand head)	Rank	Country/Entity	Chickens, 1998 (thousand head)	Rank	Country/Entity	Chickens, 1998 (thousand head)
50	Myanmar (Burma)	33,074	100	Puerto Rico	11,643	150	Namibia	2,300
51	Côte d'Ivoire	31,059	101	Guyana	11,500	151	Kyrgyzstan	2,000
52	Hungary	30,983	102	Ireland	11,233	152	Singapore	2,000
53	Lebanon	30,000	103	Réunion	11,000	153	Suriname	2,000
54	Kenya	29,000	104	Panama	10,000	154	Botswana	1,800
55	Greece	28,000	105	Croatia	9,959	155	Congo, Rep. of	1,800
56	Czech Republic	27,846	106	Sri Lanka	9,566	156	Lesotho	1,600
57	Benin	27,000	107	Jamaica	9,500	157	Belize	1,500
58	Portugal	27,000	108	Trinidad and Tobago	9,500	158	Rwanda	1,400
59	Tanzania	27,000	109	Nicaragua	9,000	159	Tajikistan	1,000
60	Zambia	27,000	110	Guinea	8,700	160	Swaziland	970
61	Kuwait	26,000	111	Slovenia	8,550	161	Guinea-Bissau	850
62	Yemen	25,200	112	North Korea	8,000	162	Malta	820
63	Congo, Dem. Rep. of	25,000	113	El Salvador	7,980	163	Gambia	740
64	Yugoslavia	24,018	114	Sweden	7,606	164	Seychelles	640
65	Guatemala	24,000	115	Togo	7,500	165	Bahrain	450
66	Libya	24,000	116	Afghanistan	7,200	166	Comoros	440
67	Mali	24,000	117	Lithuania	7,000	167	Cape Verde	430
68	Mozambique	23,500	118	Switzerland	6,570	168	Macau	420
69	Jordan	23,300	119	Angola	6,500	169	New Caledonia	390
70	Uganda	22,500	120	Sierra Leone	6,000	170	Samoa	350
71	Israel	22,000	121	Finland	5,230	171	Vanuatu	320
72	Burkina Faso	20,517	122	Haiti	5,000	172	Bhutan	310
73	Cameroon	20,000	123	Chad	4,700	173	Kiribati	300
74	Iraq	20,000	124	Albania	4,600	174	São Tomé and Príncipe	280
75	Niger	20,000	125	Burundi	4,600	175	Tonga	266
76	Syria	20,000	126	Eritrea	4,300	176	Saint Lucia	260
77	Denmark	18,156	127	Fiji	4,300	177	Martinique	250
78	Honduras	18,000	128	Mauritania	3,900	178	Equatorial Guinea	245
79	Costa Rica	17,000	129	Central African Republic	3,875	179	Grenada	220
80	Kazakhstan	16,920	130	Bosnia and Herzegovina	3,870	180	Guadeloupe	200
81	Madagascar	16,600	131	Qatar	3,850	181	Guam	200
82	Nepal	15,800	132	Bahamas	3,800	182	Saint Vincent and the Grenadines	200
83	Zimbabwe	15,500	133	Gaza Strip	3,600			
84	United Arab Emirates	15,000	134	Papua New Guinea	3,600	183	Dominica	190
85	Paraguay	14,835	135	Cyprus	3,500	184	French Guiana	190
86	Malawi	14,500	136	Liberia	3,500	185	Micronesia	185
87	Slovakia	14,222	137	Macedonia	3,500	186	Solomon Islands	185
88	Austria	13,950	138	Barbados	3,400	187	Iceland	179
89	Bulgaria	13,766	139	Norway	3,240	188	Netherlands Antilles	135
90	Georgia	13,500	140	Mauritius	3,200	189	French Polynesia	100
91	Ghana	13,300	141	Brunei	3,000	190	Antigua and Barbuda	90
92	Laos	13,097	142	Hong Kong	3,000	191	Saint Kitts and Nevis	70
93	Azerbaijan	13,000	143	Latvia	3,000	192	Mongolia	65
94	Cambodia	12,000	144	Oman	3,000	193	Bermuda	45
95	Cuba	12,000	145	Somalia	3,000	194	American Samoa	37
96	Moldova	12,000	146	Armenia	2,800	195	Virgin Islands (U.S.)	35
97	New Zealand	12,000	147	Turkmenistan	2,800	196	Tuvalu	27
98	Uruguay	12,000	148	Estonia	2,700	197	Nauru	5
99	Uzbekistan	12,000	149	Gabon	2,700			

Source: FAO Statistics

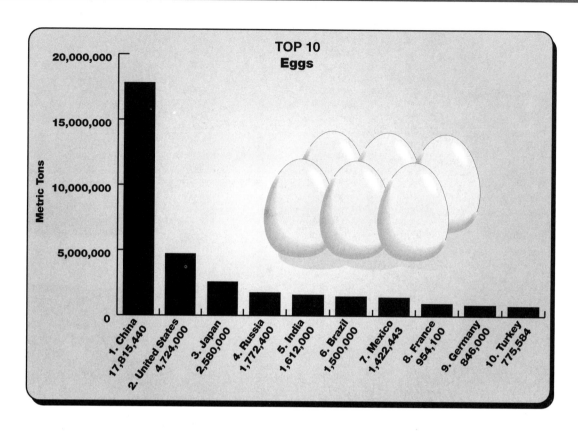

TOP 10
Eggs

1. China	17,815,440
2. United States	4,724,000
3. Japan	2,580,000
4. Russia	1,772,400
5. India	1,612,000
6. Brazil	1,500,000
7. Mexico	1,422,443
8. France	954,100
9. Germany	846,000
10. Turkey	775,584

Rank	Country/Entity	Eggs, 1998 (metric tons)	Rank	Country/Entity	Eggs, 1998 (metric tons)	Rank	Country/Entity	Eggs, 1998 (metric tons)
11	Italy	751,000	36	Hungary	162,000	61	Finland	63,000
12	United Kingdom	648,700	37	Vietnam	155,000	62	Ecuador	57,960
13	Iran	625,000	38	Peru	154,468	63	Cuba	56,000
14	Netherlands	624,000	39	Venezuela	137,329	64	Myanmar (Burma)	54,218
15	Spain	590,000	40	Saudi Arabia	130,000	65	Tanzania	52,000
16	Ukraine	491,303	41	Syria	125,650	66	Dominican Republic	50,349
17	Thailand	470,000	42	Algeria	117,000	67	Sri Lanka	49,657
18	South Korea	465,000	43	Greece	115,000	68	Kenya	48,720
19	Philippines	440,000	44	Guatemala	109,000	69	Norway	47,187
20	Indonesia	429,283	45	Sweden	107,000	70	Paraguay	47,000
21	Poland	403,895	46	Bangladesh	104,000	71	Libya	46,000
22	Malaysia	360,000	47	Portugal	103,000	72	Honduras	45,450
23	Nigeria	350,000	48	Austria	95,130	73	El Salvador	45,030
24	Canada	342,470	49	Chile	95,000	74	Croatia	45,024
25	Colombia	315,950	50	Israel	92,500	75	Jordan	44,000
26	Romania	292,300	51	Yugoslavia	90,650	76	Lebanon	44,000
27	South Africa	285,000	52	Bulgaria	87,360	77	Zambia	43,200
28	Pakistan	270,000	53	Slovakia	86,000	78	New Zealand	42,300
29	Argentina	256,030	54	Denmark	83,700	79	Sudan	42,000
30	Belgium	228,000	55	Uzbekistan	83,000	80	Lithuania	41,600
31	Czech Republic	200,000	56	North Korea	75,000	81	Switzerland	38,200
32	Belarus	194,000	57	Ethiopia	73,830	82	Senegal	32,500
33	Australia	190,000	58	Kazakhstan	70,000	83	Moldova	32,000
34	Morocco	180,000	59	Tunisia	70,000	84	Uruguay	31,900
35	Egypt	165,000	60	Bolivia	68,000	85	Ireland	30,800

Rank	Country/Entity	Eggs, 1998 (metric tons)	Rank	Country/Entity	Eggs, 1998 (metric tons)	Rank	Country/Entity	Eggs, 1998 (metric tons)
86	Nicaragua	30,270	124	Congo, Dem. Rep. of	8,400	162	Central African Republic	1,404
87	Azerbaijan	28,300	125	Gaza Strip	8,000	163	Lesotho	1,288
88	Jamaica	28,000	126	Guinea	7,770	164	Congo, Rep. of	1,080
89	Costa Rica	27,150	127	Laos	7,600	165	Bahamas	1,056
90	Yemen	25,500	128	Bosnia and Herzegovina	7,100	166	Grenada	920
91	Latvia	25,368	129	Sierra Leone	6,900	167	Hong Kong	900
92	Iraq	25,000	130	Guyana	6,800	168	Barbados	792
93	Slovenia	24,200	131	Malta	6,550	169	Comoros	720
94	Macedonia	21,500	132	Togo	6,325	170	Guam	700
95	Nepal	21,270	133	Oman	6,300	171	Macau	650
96	Georgia	20,600	134	Eritrea	5,934	172	Guinea-Bissau	648
97	Zimbabwe	20,100	135	Réunion	5,100	173	Saint Vincent and the Grenadines	640
98	Albania	20,000	136	Mauritius	4,900	174	Gambia	585
99	Estonia	19,919	137	Mauritania	4,590	175	Saint Lucia	516
100	Benin	19,800	138	Chad	4,230	176	Netherlands Antilles	510
101	Malawi	18,800	139	Angola	4,200	177	French Guiana	450
102	Panama	18,500	140	Papua New Guinea	3,900	178	Bhutan	380
103	Afghanistan	18,300	141	Haiti	3,750	179	Solomon Islands	372
104	Uganda	18,000	142	Liberia	3,600	180	Swaziland	340
105	Burkina Faso	17,000	143	Qatar	3,600	181	Mongolia	315
106	Côte d'Ivoire	16,000	144	Burundi	3,496	182	São Tomé and Príncipe	315
107	Singapore	15,710	145	Brunei	3,400	183	Saint Kitts and Nevis	300
108	Puerto Rico	15,143	146	Suriname	3,000	184	Bermuda	280
109	West Bank	15,000	147	Bahrain	2,965	185	Vanuatu	280
110	Turkmenistan	13,800	148	Fiji	2,900	186	Dominica	225
111	Ghana	13,780	149	Seychelles	2,660	187	Samoa	200
112	Madagascar	13,200	150	Somalia	2,300	188	Tajikistan	200
113	Cameroon	13,000	151	Iceland	2,200	189	Equatorial Guinea	190
114	Kuwait	12,710	152	Cape Verde	2,000	190	Micronesia	175
115	United Arab Emirates	12,500	153	New Caledonia	2,000	191	Virgin Islands (U.S.)	160
116	Mozambique	12,300	154	Rwanda	2,000	192	Antigua and Barbuda	150
117	Armenia	12,150	155	Gabon	1,750	193	Kiribati	140
118	Mali	11,880	156	Namibia	1,720	194	American Samoa	30
119	Cambodia	11,000	157	French Polynesia	1,670	195	Tonga	28
120	Cyprus	9,450	158	Botswana	1,656	196	Nauru	16
121	Niger	9,180	159	Guadeloupe	1,656	197	Tuvalu	12
122	Kyrgyzstan	9,000	160	Belize	1,581			
123	Trinidad and Tobago	9,000	161	Martinique	1,500			

Source: FAO Statistics

The three characteristic features of mechanized agriculture are the use of tractors, large-scale application of fertilizers, and access to irrigation. Tractors have reduced the labor-intensive nature of agriculture, fertilizers replenish the soil, and irrigation supplements rainfall and ground-water supplies. Some crops, such as rice, require enormous supplies of water. Three types of fertilizers are used, sometimes in combination according to the needs of the soil: nitrogenous fertilizers, phosphate fertilizers (such as super phosphates and ammonium phosphates), and potash fertilizers (such as muriate, nitrate, and sulfate of potash). The ranking does not include organic fertilizers.

11.12 Tractors

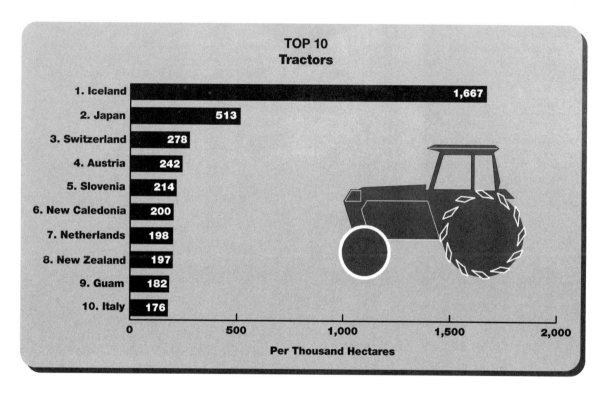

TOP 10 Tractors

Rank	Country	Per Thousand Hectares
1.	Iceland	1,667
2.	Japan	513
3.	Switzerland	278
4.	Austria	242
5.	Slovenia	214
6.	New Caledonia	200
7.	Netherlands	198
8.	New Zealand	197
9.	Guam	182
10.	Italy	176

Per Thousand Hectares

Rank	Country/Entity	Tractors, per Thousand Hectares	Rank	Country/Entity	Tractors, per Thousand Hectares	Rank	Country/Entity	Tractors, per Thousand Hectares
11	Norway	164.0	23	Finland	88.7	35	Bosnia and Herzegovina	48.3
12	Belgium	144.0	24	United Kingdom	84.1	36	North Korea	44.2
13	Cyprus	137.0	25	Gaza Strip	83.3	37	South Korea	42.6
14	Luxembourg	134.0	26	France	78.6	38	Uzbekistan	41.5
15	Ireland	127.0	27	Macedonia	77.3	39	Seychelles	40.0
16	Puerto Rico	126.7	28	Israel	73.2	40	Fiji	38.9
17	Martinique	117.0	29	Portugal	68.2	41	Réunion	38.9
18	Liechtenstein	112.0	30	Singapore	65.0	42	Guadeloupe	38.6
19	Yugoslavia	111.0	31	São Tomé and Príncipe	62.5	43	Barbados	38.0
20	Germany	110.1	32	Denmark	61.8	44	Malta	37.5
21	Greece	93.8	33	Sweden	61.3	45	Tajikistan	36.6
22	Poland	91.7	34	Spain	50.6	46	Sri Lanka	36.3

Rank	Country/Entity	Tractors, per Thousand Hectares	Rank	Country/Entity	Tractors, per Thousand Hectares	Rank	Country/Entity	Tractors, per Thousand Hectares
47	Turkmenistan	35.7	96	Algeria	13.2	146	Bolivia	2.5
48	Trinidad and Tobago	35.3	97	Ukraine	13.1	147	Netherlands Antilles	2.5
49	French Guiana	35.0	98	Dominica	12.9	148	Dominican Republic	2.4
50	Armenia	33.1	99	Argentina	11.2	149	Nicaragua	2.4
51	Latvia	32.5	100	Chile	10.4	150	Palau	2.2
52	French Polynesia	31.2	101	South Africa	10.2	151	Tanzania	2.2
53	Turkey	30.9	102	Panama	10.1	152	Philippines	2.1
54	Moldova	30.5	103	Colombia	9.4	153	Nepal	2.0
55	Antigua and Barbuda	30.0	104	Oman	9.4	154	Eritrea	1.9
56	Cuba	30.0	105	Bulgaria	9.2	155	Mozambique	1.9
57	Lithuania	28.6	106	Tunisia	9.2	156	Somalia	1.8
58	Papua New Guinea	28.5	107	Bermuda	9.0	157	Mauritania	1.6
59	Saint Kitts and Nevis	27.0	108	Russia	8.8	158	Côte d'Ivoire	1.5
60	Uruguay	26.2	109	Qatar	8.6	159	Ghana	1.5
61	United States	25.9	110	Mongolia	8.4	160	Samoa	1.4
62	Belize	25.6	111	China	7.7	161	Myanmar (Burma)	1.2
63	Egypt	25.1	112	Guyana	7.6	162	Laos	1.1
64	Costa Rica	24.6	113	Hungary	7.6	163	Madagascar	1.1
65	Jordan	24.2	114	India	7.6	164	Sierra Leone	1.1
66	Brunei	24.0	115	Paraguay	7.5	165	Zambia	1.1
67	Suriname	23.3	116	Mexico	7.4	166	Uganda	0.9
68	Georgia	22.9	117	Micronesia	7.4	167	Equatorial Guinea	0.8
69	Slovakia	22.1	118	Iran	7.1	168	Malawi	0.8
70	Northern Mariana Islands	22.0	119	Zimbabwe	7.1	169	Sudan	0.8
71	Swaziland	21.6	120	Thailand	6.9	170	Hong Kong	0.7
72	Malaysia	21.4	121	Australia	6.8	171	Bangladesh	0.6
73	Czech Republic	21.1	122	Tonga	6.8	172	Saudi Arabia	0.6
74	Azerbaijan	20.6	123	Vietnam	6.3	173	Guinea	0.5
75	Kuwait	20.0	124	El Salvador	6.1	174	Cambodia	0.4
76	Saint Vincent and the Grenadines	20.0	125	Grenada	6.0	175	Cape Verde	0.4
			126	Kazakhstan	6.0	176	Haiti	0.4
77	Belarus	19.9	127	Iraq	5.8	177	Nigeria	0.4
78	Jamaica	19.9	128	Lesotho	5.8	178	Congo, Dem. Rep. of	0.3
79	Libya	18.7	129	United Arab Emirates	5.7	179	Ethiopia	0.3
80	Saint Lucia	17.4	130	Ecuador	5.5	180	Gambia	0.3
81	Romania	17.3	131	Gabon	5.1	181	Mali	0.3
82	Brazil	17.0	132	Morocco	4.9	182	Burundi	0.2
83	Kyrgyzstan	16.4	133	Congo, Rep. of	4.8	183	Senegal	0.2
84	Canada	16.3	134	Namibia	4.8	184	Togo	0.2
85	Syria	16.1	135	Vanuatu	3.8	185	Afghanistan	0.1
86	Albania	15.6	136	Yemen	3.8	186	Benin	0.1
87	Virgin Islands (U.S.)	15.6	137	Mauritius	3.7	187	Cameroon	0.1
88	Venezuela	15.2	138	Croatia	3.6	188	Central African Republic	0.1
89	American Samoa	15.0	139	Kenya	3.5	189	Guinea-Bissau	0.1
90	Botswana	14.3	140	Peru	3.5	190	Rwanda	0.1
91	West Bank	14.1	141	Angola	3.4	191	Chad	0.05
92	Lebanon	13.9	142	Guatemala	3.2	192	Niger	0.05
93	Pakistan	13.6	143	Indonesia	3.2	193	Burkina Faso	0.04
94	Bahamas	13.3	144	Honduras	2.9			
95	Estonia	13.3	145	Liberia	2.6			

Source: World Data

Rank	Country/Entity	Percentage of Cropland Irrigated	Rank	Country/Entity	Percentage of Cropland Irrigated	Rank	Country/Entity	Percentage of Cropland Irrigated
1	Gaza Strip	133	58	Indonesia	27	114	Switzerland	6
2	Puerto Rico	118	59	Réunion	27	115	Venezuela	6
3	Egypt	112	60	Thailand	27	116	Australia	5
4	Suriname	105	61	Libya	26	117	Bolivia	5
5	Bahrain	100	62	Mexico	26	118	Slovakia	5
6	Kuwait	100	63	Dominican Republic	25	119	Tanzania	5
7	Qatar	100	64	Saint Vincent and the Grenadines	25	120	West Bank	5
8	Singapore	100				121	Belize	4
9	Uzbekistan	98	65	Mauritania	24	122	Cambodia	4
10	Turkmenistan	93	66	Jamaica	23	123	Germany	4
11	Oman	92	67	Spain	23	124	Honduras	4
12	Angola	89	68	Syria	22	125	Hungary	4
13	Tajikistan	88	69	El Salvador	21	126	Mozambique	4
14	North Korea	86	70	Guam	21	127	Russia	4
15	Pakistan	82	71	Bulgaria	20	128	Sweden	4
16	New Zealand	74	72	French Guiana	20	129	Zimbabwe	4
17	South Korea	71	73	Jordan	20	130	Côte d'Ivoire	3
18	Kyrgyzstan	71	74	Somalia	20	131	Finland	3
19	Japan	70	75	Saint Lucia	20	132	Mali	3
20	Azerbaijan	62	76	Colombia	19	133	Paraguay	3
21	Albania	61	77	Denmark	19	134	Senegal	3
22	Netherlands	61	78	French Polynesia	19	135	Belarus	2
23	Sri Lanka	61	79	Mauritius	19	136	Canada	2
24	Armenia	59	80	Laos	18	137	Ethiopia	2
25	Georgia	59	81	Moldova	18	138	Fiji	2
26	Greece	55	82	Turkey	17	139	Kenya	2
27	Israel	55	83	United Arab Emirates	17	140	Liberia	2
28	China	53	84	Guinea	15	141	Malawi	2
29	Martinique	50	85	Morocco	15	142	Niger	2
30	Iraq	46	86	Sudan	15	143	United Kingdom	2
31	Peru	45	87	Guadeloupe	14	144	Yugoslavia	2
32	Costa Rica	44	88	Myanmar (Burma)	14	145	Burundi	1
33	Iran	44	89	Haiti	13	146	Gabon	1
34	Madagascar	42	90	Tunisia	13	147	Gambia	1
35	Lebanon	41	91	Saudi Arabia	12	148	Lesotho	0.9
36	Cyprus	40	92	United States	12	149	Namibia	0.9
37	Taiwan	38	93	Macedonia	11	150	Zambia	0.9
38	Nepal	37	94	Norway	11	151	Czech Republic	0.8
39	Swaziland	36	95	Uruguay	11	152	Nigeria	0.8
40	Afghanistan	35	96	Bahamas	10	153	Slovenia	0.8
41	Bangladesh	35	97	South Africa	10	154	Benin	0.7
42	Cuba	35	98	Guatemala	9	155	Burkina Faso	0.7
43	Bhutan	34	99	France	8	156	Congo, Rep. of	0.7
44	Ecuador	34	100	Malta	8	157	Poland	0.7
45	Brunei	33	101	Nicaragua	8	158	Rwanda	0.5
46	Hong Kong	33	102	Ukraine	8	159	Chad	0.4
47	Malaysia	33	103	Algeria	7	160	Austria	0.3
48	Romania	33	104	Argentina	7	161	Bosnia and Herzegovina	0.3
49	Yemen	33	105	Brazil	7	162	Cameroon	0.3
50	Chile	32	106	Cape Verde	7	163	Croatia	0.3
51	Italy	32	107	Barbados	6	164	Togo	0.3
52	Vietnam	31	108	Eritrea	6	165	Botswana	0.2
53	India	29	109	Guinea-Bissau	6	166	Ghana	0.2
54	Philippines	29	110	Kazakhstan	6	167	Uganda	0.2
55	Portugal	29	111	Mongolia	6	168	Belgium	0.1
56	Trinidad and Tobago	29	112	Panama	6	169	Congo, Dem. Rep. of	0.1
57	Guyana	27	113	Sierra Leone	6	170	Micronesia	0

Source: World Data

11.14 Fertilizer

Rank	Country/Entity	Artificial Fertilizer (kilograms per hectare)	Rank	Country/Entity	Artificial Fertilizer (kilograms per hectare)	Rank	Country/Entity	Artificial Fertilizer (kilograms per hectare)
1	Singapore	5,600	53	Spain	101	105	Kazakhstan	19
2	Iceland	2,529	54	Hong Kong	100	106	Honduras	18
3	Martinique	945	55	United States	99	107	Russia	17
4	Ireland	741	56	Bangladesh	98	108	Zambia	15
5	New Zealand	741	57	Czech Republic	97	109	Lesotho	14
6	Netherlands	628	58	Fiji	96	110	Algeria	13
7	Belgium	496	59	Barbados	91	111	Mauritania	12
8	South Korea	454	60	Pakistan	91	112	Mongolia	12
9	Switzerland	430	61	Belize	88	113	Nigeria	12
10	Japan	414	62	Oman	83	114	Yemen	12
11	North Korea	407	63	Vietnam	82	115	Côte d'Ivoire	11
12	Taiwan	400	64	Iran	80	116	Gambia	11
13	Saudi Arabia	398	65	Lebanon	79	117	Mali	9
14	Egypt	384	66	India	75	118	Paraguay	9
15	Germany	384	67	Portugal	73	119	Tanzania	9
16	United Kingdom	376	68	Mexico	70	120	Myanmar (Burma)	8
17	Bahrain	333	69	Chile	69	121	Togo	8
18	France	319	70	Philippines	67	122	Afghanistan	7
19	Guadeloupe	307	71	Guatemala	66	123	Angola	7
20	Mauritius	304	72	French Guiana	64	124	Ethiopia	7
21	Réunion	282	73	Turkey	64	125	Liberia	7
22	Slovenia	270	74	Jordan	63	126	Burkina Faso	6
23	China	261	75	New Caledonia	60	127	Cameroon	6
24	Dominica	259	76	South Africa	59	128	Argentina	4
25	Denmark	255	77	Panama	58	129	Burundi	4
26	Israel	252	78	Brunei	57	130	Gibraltar	4
27	Norway	242	79	Trinidad and Tobago	57	131	Haiti	4
28	Hungary	231	80	Uruguay	54	132	Sudan	4
29	Yugoslavia	221	81	Zimbabwe	53	133	Bolivia	3
30	Poland	219	82	Dominican Republic	50	134	Congo, Rep. of	3
31	Finland	210	83	Kenya	48	135	Gabon	3
32	Costa Rica	203	84	Canada	47	136	Ghana	3
33	Austria	201	85	Swaziland	46	137	Guinea-Bissau	3
34	Qatar	200	86	Syria	46	138	Somalia	3
35	Cuba	199	87	Slovakia	45	139	Benin	2
36	Bulgaria	195	88	Brazil	43	140	Central African Republic	2
37	Greece	175	89	Peru	41	141	Chad	2
38	Malaysia	170	90	Papua New Guinea	40	142	Laos	2
39	Kuwait	167	91	Iraq	39	143	Madagascar	2
40	Albania	158	92	Libya	39	144	Senegal	2
41	Italy	151	93	Malta	39	145	Tonga	2
42	Cyprus	144	94	Morocco	36	146	Bhutan	1
43	Venezuela	138	95	Thailand	36	147	Botswana	1
44	Romania	133	96	French Polynesia	33	148	Cambodia	1
45	Sweden	127	97	Guyana	33	149	Congo, Dem. Rep. of	1
46	United Arab Emirates	120	98	Ecuador	29	150	Guinea	1
47	Belarus	119	99	Australia	28	151	Mozambique	1
48	Jamaica	116	100	Nicaragua	28	152	Niger	1
49	Sri Lanka	111	101	Suriname	26	153	Rwanda	1
50	Indonesia	110	102	Nepal	25	154	Sierra Leone	1
51	El Salvador	106	103	Malawi	23			
52	Colombia	101	104	Tunisia	20			

Source: Fertilizer Yearbook

Food Production

The natural process in food production is decline rather than growth. First, there are more mouths to feed, so there is less food per capita. Second, nutrients in the soil are being constantly depleted. Third, more of agricultural land is being converted to industrial and residential use, so there is less cropland today than there was in the twentieth and earlier centuries. As a result, agriculture has to depend more on technology and chemical fertilizers to produce the same amount of food. It seems a safe prediction that as a result of better fertilizers and technology, food production will continue to increase until the end of the twenty-first century, but will decline thereafter.

11.15 Food Production Index

Rank	Country/Entity	Food Production Index, 1996–1998 (1989–1991=100)	Rank	Country/Entity	Food Production Index, 1996–1998 (1989–1991=100)	Rank	Country/Entity	Food Production Index, 1996–1998 (1989–1991=100)
1	United Arab Emirates	222.7	42	Ethiopia	123.7	83	Dominican Republic	105.4
2	Kuwait	161.2	43	Namibia	123.5	84	France	105.4
3	Sudan	156.0	44	Nicaragua	122.7	85	Kenya	104.9
4	China	153.5	45	South Korea	122.2	86	Mauritania	104.7
5	Jordan	152.5	46	Tunisia	121.4	87	Zambia	104.5
6	Syria	148.7	47	Yemen	120.7	88	Denmark	103.0
7	Iran	144.7	48	Indonesia	120.4	89	Yugoslavia	102.4
8	Ghana	144.1	49	Cameroon	120.2	90	Austria	102.3
9	Ecuador	143.6	50	Mexico	120.2	91	Kyrgyzstan	102.0
10	Nigeria	142.5	51	Jamaica	120.1	92	Zimbabwe	101.9
11	Benin	140.6	52	Paraguay	120.0	93	Turkmenistan	101.7
12	Peru	140.5	53	India	119.9	94	Italy	101.2
13	Vietnam	140.5	54	United States	117.9	95	Norway	100.9
14	Egypt	139.7	55	Canada	117.7	96	South Africa	100.8
15	Chad	139.1	56	Nepal	117.2	97	Sweden	100.8
16	Lebanon	138.2	57	Guinea-Bissau	117.1	98	Senegal	100.4
17	Myanmar (Burma)	138.1	58	Eritrea	114.6	99	Slovenia	100.3
18	Guinea	137.4	59	Mali	114.5	100	Tanzania	100.0
19	Pakistan	136.2	60	Venezuela	114.4	101	Trinidad and Tobago	99.9
20	Togo	135.9	61	Belgium	113.0	102	United Kingdom	99.7
21	Bolivia	134.1	62	Honduras	113.0	103	Panama	99.6
22	Mozambique	130.9	63	Thailand	112.6	104	Sierra Leone	99.5
23	Uruguay	130.8	64	Congo, Rep. of	112.1	105	Greece	99.0
24	Cambodia	130.6	65	El Salvador	111.3	106	Netherlands	99.0
25	Australia	130.4	66	Turkey	111.3	107	Botswana	98.7
26	Libya	130.1	67	Lesotho	111.1	108	Iraq	98.7
27	Angola	130.0	68	Oman	111.1	109	Macedonia	97.0
28	Chile	129.6	69	Mauritius	111.0	110	Portugal	97.0
29	Algeria	129.4	70	Bangladesh	110.8	111	Congo, Dem. Rep. of	95.9
30	Costa Rica	128.6	71	Spain	110.1	112	Romania	95.9
31	Côte d'Ivoire	128.5	72	Uzbekistan	109.8	113	Burundi	95.8
32	Central African Republic	127.9	73	Colombia	109.7	114	Switzerland	95.8
33	Burkina Faso	127.8	74	Malawi	109.7	115	Japan	95.2
34	Niger	127.8	75	Sri Lanka	109.1	116	Haiti	94.4
35	Laos	126.7	76	Gabon	108.7	117	Germany	92.3
36	Argentina	125.9	77	Madagascar	108.7	118	Finland	90.7
37	Philippines	125.8	78	Papua New Guinea	107.8	119	Mongolia	88.5
38	Brazil	125.7	79	Morocco	107.2	120	Poland	88.2
39	Malaysia	125.2	80	Uganda	107.1	121	Georgia	85.2
40	New Zealand	124.6	81	Israel	107.0	122	Gambia	84.9
41	Guatemala	124.1	82	Ireland	106.2	123	Puerto Rico	82.0

Rank	Country/Entity	Food Production Index, 1996–1998 (1989–1991=100)	Rank	Country/Entity	Food Production Index, 1996–1998 (1989–1991=100)	Rank	Country/Entity	Food Production Index, 1996–1998 (1989–1991=100)
124	Czech Republic	79.7	131	Bulgaria	67.8	138	Kazakhstan	57.2
125	Rwanda	79.1	132	Belarus	65.9	139	Moldova	53.2
126	Saudi Arabia	78.8	133	Russia	64.4	140	Ukraine	52.3
127	Armenia	76.8	134	Cuba	63.8	141	Latvia	48.1
128	Hungary	76.3	135	Azerbaijan	60.6	142	Estonia	47.0
129	Slovakia	74.7	136	Croatia	59.4	143	Singapore	31.8
130	Lithuania	69.2	137	Tajikistan	59.0	144	Hong Kong	25.9

Source: FAO Production Statistics

11.16 Agricultural Productivity per Worker

Rank	Country/Entity	Agricultural Value Added per Worker, 1996–1998 (in U.S. Dollars)	Rank	Country/Entity	Agricultural Value Added per Worker, 1996–1998 (in U.S. Dollars)	Rank	Country/Entity	Agricultural Value Added per Worker, 1996–1998 (in U.S. Dollars)
1	Singapore	42,851	40	Dominican Republic	2,599	79	Laos	546
2	United States	39,523	41	Ukraine	2,544	80	Togo	539
3	France	36,889	42	Panama	2,512	81	Benin	534
4	Norway	32,600	43	Russia	2,476	82	Congo, Rep. of	492
5	Australia	30,904	44	Uzbekistan	2,128	83	Central African Republic	462
6	Japan	30,272	45	Georgia	2,120	84	Mauritania	449
7	Finland	28,231	46	Trinidad and Tobago	2,102	85	Sierra Leone	411
8	Lebanon	27,409	47	Guatemala	2,075	86	Cambodia	408
9	Slovenia	26,521	48	Algeria	1,943	87	India	406
10	Germany	22,452	49	Turkey	1,851	88	Haiti	396
11	Italy	20,031	50	Albania	1,847	89	Tajikistan	396
12	Austria	16,070	51	Gabon	1,839	90	Lesotho	393
13	Argentina	13,715	52	Morocco	1,836	91	Zimbabwe	347
14	Spain	13,499	53	Macedonia	1,826	92	Uganda	345
15	South Korea	11,760	54	Nicaragua	1,821	93	Senegal	320
16	Saudi Arabia	10,742	55	Ecuador	1,795	94	Guinea-Bissau	315
17	Uruguay	9,826	56	Poland	1,752	95	China	307
18	Croatia	8,521	57	Mexico	1,704	96	Yemen	302
19	Malaysia	6,061	58	El Salvador	1,679	97	Ghana	286
20	Mauritius	5,630	59	Peru	1,663	98	Congo, Dem. Rep. of	285
21	Bulgaria	5,135	60	Moldova	1,474	99	Guinea	271
22	Chile	5,039	61	Kazakhstan	1,450	100	Mali	263
23	Venezuela	5,036	62	Jordan	1,431	101	Kenya	228
24	Armenia	4,828	63	Philippines	1,352	102	Bangladesh	227
25	Hungary	4,770	64	Jamaica	1,291	103	Chad	217
26	Costa Rica	4,409	65	Namibia	1,190	104	Rwanda	212
27	Iran	4,089	66	Egypt	1,189	105	Zambia	209
28	Brazil	4,081	67	Mongolia	1,151	106	Gambia	203
29	South Africa	3,884	68	Côte d'Ivoire	1,028	107	Niger	195
30	Estonia	3,519	69	Honduras	1,018	108	Nepal	189
31	Belarus	3,509	70	Cameroon	1,015	109	Madagascar	186
32	Paraguay	3,448	71	Thailand	924	110	Tanzania	174
33	Slovakia	3,379	72	Papua New Guinea	799	111	Burkina Faso	161
34	Lithuania	3,228	73	Azerbaijan	776	112	Burundi	141
35	Romania	3,193	74	Indonesia	749	113	Malawi	136
36	Latvia	3,191	75	Sri Lanka	726	114	Mozambique	127
37	Kyrgyzstan	3,144	76	Botswana	676	115	Angola	123
38	Tunisia	2,959	77	Nigeria	624			
39	Colombia	2,693	78	Pakistan	623			

Source: FAO Yearbook

Rank	Country/Entity	Agricultural Value Added per Agricultural Worker, 1995– 1997 (in U.S. Dollars)	Rank	Country/Entity	Agricultural Value Added per Agricultural Worker, 1995– 1997 (in U.S. Dollars)	Rank	Country/Entity	Agricultural Value Added per Agricultural Worker, 1995– 1997 (in U.S. Dollars)
1	Denmark	46,621	39	Lithuania	2,907	77	Pakistan	585
2	Netherlands	43,836	40	Colombia	2,890	78	Nigeria	541
3	Singapore	39,851	41	Tunisia	2,750	79	Ghana	533
4	France	34,760	42	Russia	2,540	80	Laos	526
5	United States	34,727	43	Panama	2,463	81	Togo	510
6	Norway	31,577	44	Dominican Republic	2,454	82	Benin	504
7	Australia	29,044	45	Ukraine	2,259	83	Congo, Rep. of	470
8	Japan	28,665	46	Uzbekistan	2,085	84	Central African Republic	439
9	Finland	28,296	47	Algeria	1,903	85	Mauritania	439
10	Slovenia	26,006	48	Guatemala	1,902	86	Cambodia	407
11	Germany	19,930	49	Georgia	1,838	87	Haiti	407
12	Italy	19,001	50	Turkey	1,835	88	Sierra Leone	404
13	Austria	15,474	51	Ecuador	1,764	89	India	343
14	Argentina	13,833	52	Albania	1,717	90	Uganda	326
15	Greece	12,611	53	El Salvador	1,705	91	Senegal	321
16	Spain	12,022	54	Mexico	1,690	92	Lesotho	319
17	South Korea	10,962	55	Poland	1,647	93	Zimbabwe	316
18	Saudi Arabia	10,507	56	Jordan	1,634	94	Yemen	305
19	Uruguay	9,384	57	Peru	1,619	95	China	296
20	Croatia	7,144	58	Morocco	1,593	96	Congo, Dem. Rep. of	285
21	Malaysia	6,267	59	Macedonia	1,528	97	Guinea	262
22	Portugal	5,574	60	Kazakhstan	1,477	98	Mali	241
23	Chile	5,211	61	Moldova	1,473	99	Kenya	230
24	Venezuela	4,931	62	Nicaragua	1,407	100	Vietnam	226
25	Hungary	4,655	63	Philippines	1,379	101	Zambia	226
26	Costa Rica	4,627	64	Jamaica	1,294	102	Bangladesh	221
27	Armenia	4,477	65	Namibia	1,235	103	Chad	212
28	Bulgaria	4,351	66	Egypt	1,163	104	Rwanda	201
29	Brazil	3,931	67	Mongolia	1,085	105	Niger	190
30	Iran	3,831	68	Honduras	1,018	106	Nepal	187
31	Belarus	3,461	69	Côte d'Ivoire	1,005	107	Madagascar	180
32	South Africa	3,355	70	Cameroon	958	108	Burkina Faso	159
33	Slovakia	3,347	71	Thailand	928	109	Tanzania	159
34	Estonia	3,342	72	Azerbaijan	847	110	Burundi	139
35	Paraguay	3,295	73	Papua New Guinea	827	111	Malawi	122
36	Romania	3,170	74	Indonesia	745	112	Angola	117
37	Latvia	3,125	75	Sri Lanka	732	113	Mozambique	76
38	Kyrgyzstan	2,917	76	Botswana	647			

Source: FAO Production Statistics

Roundwood is wood felled and stripped of bark but not cut into logs. There is a strong correspondence between this ranking and the ranking of forest area. (See Table 16.7.) The production of roundwood is driven by the demand for and consumption of lumber for construction, furniture, and newsprint. The major constraint on the production of roundwood is a concern for the environment. In fact, the tree has become one of the icons of the environmentalist movement. Most of the top producers have strong afforestation programs to sustain their current forest yields.

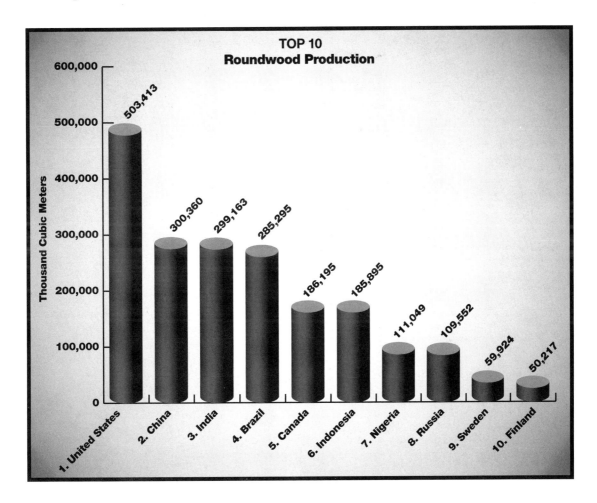

Rank	Country/Entity	Roundwood Production (1,000 cubic meters)	Rank	Country/Entity	Roundwood Production (1,000 cubic meters)	Rank	Country/Entity	Roundwood Production (1,000 cubic meters)
11	Ethiopia	47,337	20	Vietnam	34,913	29	Mexico	22,474
12	Congo, Dem. Rep. of	47,189	21	Bangladesh	32,044	30	Australia	22,458
13	France	46,345	22	Chile	31,365	31	Nepal	20,822
14	Malaysia	45,573	23	Pakistan	29,665	32	Colombia	20,491
15	Kenya	41,696	24	Ghana	26,473	33	Poland	19,334
16	Philippines	39,857	25	Sudan	25,410	34	Turkey	19,279
17	Thailand	39,288	26	South Africa	25,332	35	Mozambique	18,390
18	Germany	38,970	27	Myanmar (Burma)	23,281	36	Uganda	17,226
19	Tanzania	36,747	28	Japan	23,257	37	New Zealand	17,155

Rank	Country/Entity	Roundwood Production (1,000 cubic meters)	Rank	Country/Entity	Roundwood Production (1,000 cubic meters)	Rank	Country/Entity	Roundwood Production (1,000 cubic meters)
38	Cameroon	15,710	78	Bosnia and Herzegovina	5,379	118	Solomon Islands	872
39	Spain	15,121	79	Slovakia	5,323	119	Equatorial Guinea	811
40	Côte d'Ivoire	14,782	80	Senegal	5,219	120	Lesotho	709
41	Zambia	14,613	81	Burundi	4,969	121	Libya	651
42	Austria	14,405	82	North Korea	4,923	122	Fiji	598
43	Guatemala	14,123	83	Gabon	4,882	123	Guinea-Bissau	579
44	Czech Republic	12,906	84	Costa Rica	4,806	124	Jamaica	577
45	Romania	12,856	85	Guinea	4,788	125	Mongolia	541
46	Peru	12,580	86	Switzerland	4,748	126	Lebanon	515
47	Argentina	11,792	87	Chad	4,531	127	Guyana	508
48	Madagascar	10,893	88	Hungary	4,415	128	Albania	409
49	Malawi	10,475	89	Belgium	4,185	129	Yemen	324
50	Paraguay	10,401	90	Uruguay	4,093	130	Brunei	295
51	Ecuador	10,361	91	Central African Republic	3,864	131	Belize	188
52	Burkina Faso	10,033	92	Congo, Rep. of	3,830	132	Iraq	161
53	Belarus	10,015	93	Nicaragua	3,809	133	Macedonia	151
54	Italy	9,802	94	Estonia	3,730	134	French Guiana	132
55	Sri Lanka	9,625	95	Tunisia	3,562	135	Samoa	131
56	Portugal	9,448	96	Sierra Leone	3,328	136	Suriname	122
57	Norway	9,035	97	Cuba	3,152	137	Singapore	120
58	Somalia	8,794	98	Bulgaria	2,856	138	Bahamas	117
59	Papua New Guinea	8,772	99	Egypt	2,698	139	Israel	113
60	United Kingdom	8,299	100	Croatia	2,670	140	Trinidad and Tobago	68
61	Zimbabwe	8,102	101	Bolivia	2,567	141	Vanuatu	63
62	Cambodia	7,765	102	Algeria	2,517	142	Syria	55
63	Afghanistan	7,680	103	Togo	2,401	143	Cyprus	54
64	Iran	7,463	104	Morocco	2,346	144	Taiwan	48
65	Angola	7,005	105	Greece	2,306	145	Réunion	36
66	Latvia	6,907	106	Denmark	2,288	146	Hong Kong	19
67	El Salvador	6,804	107	Venezuela	2,267	147	Guadeloupe	15
68	Mali	6,540	108	Ireland	2,204	148	Mauritania	14
69	South Korea	6,485	109	Slovenia	1,944	149	Martinique	12
70	Honduras	6,459	110	Botswana	1,584	150	Mauritius	12
71	Haiti	6,417	111	Swaziland	1,424	151	Jordan	11
72	Liberia	6,267	112	Bhutan	1,399	152	São Tomé and Príncipe	9
73	Benin	5,899	113	Yugoslavia	1,320	153	Barbados	5
74	Niger	5,866	114	Gambia	1,221	154	New Caledonia	5
75	Rwanda	5,660	115	Netherlands	1,103	155	Tonga	5
76	Laos	5,508	116	Panama	1,070			
77	Lithuania	5,499	117	Dominican Republic	982			

Source: Forestry Statistics

Fishing was until recently a cottage industry in which anyone with a small boat and net could engage. Because of this ease of entry, there are few maritime nations in the world without fishers or a rudimentary fishing industry. But by the late twentieth century, fishing—especially ocean fishing—had become a complicated industry requiring substantial long-term investments in vessels, refrigeration, and equipment. Fishers also face tough international competition and require familiarity with the hundreds of laws and environmental regulations regarding the maximum catch for each type of fish. Certain varieties of fish are protected under international agreements because they are being depleted faster than they can reproduce and certain types of fishing practices are prohibited. Conflicts between nations over fishing rights, such as the "Cod War" between Great Britain and Iceland, are common.

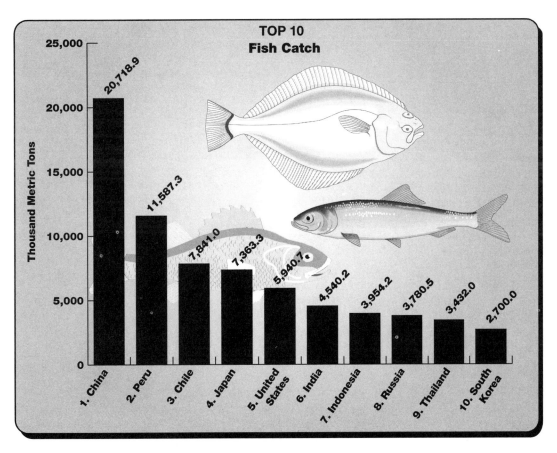

Rank	Country/Entity	Fish Catch (thousand metric tons)	Rank	Country/Entity	Fish Catch (thousand metric tons)	Rank	Country/Entity	Fish Catch (thousand metric tons)
11	Norway	2,551.5	18	Mexico	1,260.0	25	France	838.3
12	Philippines	2,276.2	19	Malaysia	1,173.5	26	Myanmar (Burma)	824.5
13	Denmark	1,886.9	20	Vietnam	1,150.0	27	Brazil	820.0
14	North Korea	1,800.0	21	Bangladesh	1,090.6	28	Morocco	750.1
15	Iceland	1,560.2	22	Canada	1,010.6	29	Turkey	604.1
16	Spain	1,380.0	23	United Kingdom	953.9	30	Pakistan	551.9
17	Taiwan	1,286.8	24	Argentina	949.3	31	Italy	547.3

Rank	Country/Entity	Fish Catch (thousand metric tons)	Rank	Country/Entity	Fish Catch (thousand metric tons)	Rank	Country/Entity	Fish Catch (thousand metric tons)
32	Netherlands	526.1	92	Benin	37.0	152	Brunei	4.5
33	South Africa	521.1	93	Congo, Rep. of	37.0	153	Réunion	4.5
34	New Zealand	493.2	94	Azerbaijan	35.0	154	Jersey	4.3
35	Poland	460.2	95	Georgia	35.0	155	Armenia	4.1
36	Venezuela	424.0	96	Laos	35.0	156	New Caledonia	3.9
37	Sweden	394.2	97	Belgium	34.6	157	Tajikistan	3.8
38	Senegal	388.0	98	Fiji	32.0	158	Equatorial Guinea	3.7
39	Tanzania	342.9	99	Mozambique	30.0	159	Isle of Man	3.6
40	Ecuador	339.9	100	Kiribati	29.0	160	Rwanda	3.5
41	Ghana	336.3	101	Papua New Guinea	27.0	161	Slovakia	3.5
42	Iran	314.3	102	Dominican Republic	25.9	162	Albania	3.2
43	Ireland	314.1	103	Gabon	24.4	163	Cyprus	3.1
44	Ukraine	310.7	104	Hungary	24.0	164	Slovenia	3.1
45	Egypt	305.7	105	Honduras	23.2	165	Eritrea	3.0
46	Namibia	300.9	106	Burundi	23.1	166	São Tomé and Príncipe	3.0
47	Nigeria	282.1	107	Gambia	22.3	167	Vanuatu	2.8
48	Germany	270.8	108	Bulgaria	22.0	168	Switzerland	2.7
49	Portugal	253.9	109	Iraq	22.0	169	Barbados	2.6
50	Faroe Islands	249.9	110	Czech Republic	21.8	170	Tonga	2.5
51	Sri Lanka	224.0	111	Croatia	21.4	171	Bosnia and Herzegovina	2.4
52	Greece	223.1	112	Costa Rica	20.8	172	Lebanon	2.4
53	Hong Kong	220.1	113	Israel	20.4	173	Niger	2.2
54	Uganda	213.1	114	Zimbabwe	20.3	174	Puerto Rico	2.2
55	Australia	210.5	115	Mauritius	19.0	175	Botswana	2.0
56	Kenya	203.5	116	Uzbekistan	17.7	176	Belize	1.9
57	Congo, Dem. Rep. of	194.0	117	Nepal	17.0	177	Macau	1.9
58	Finland	167.2	118	Somalia	16.3	178	Malta	1.8
59	Panama	165.4	119	Belarus	14.5	179	Micronesia	1.7
60	Latvia	138.7	120	Suriname	14.5	180	Saint Vincent and the Grenadines	1.7
61	Algeria	135.4	121	Paraguay	13.9			
62	Estonia	124.1	122	Singapore	13.7	181	Grenada	1.6
63	Colombia	122.7	123	Comoros	13.5	182	Palau	1.5
64	Uruguay	120.7	124	Togo	13.2	183	Samoa	1.5
65	Oman	118.6	125	El Salvador	13.1	184	Afghanistan	1.3
66	Greenland	112.6	126	Central African Republic	13.0	185	Macedonia	1.2
67	United Arab Emirates	108.0	127	Nicaragua	12.3	186	Netherlands Antilles	1.1
68	Madagascar	104.8	128	Guatemala	11.6	187	Dominica	0.9
69	Maldives	104.1	129	Jamaica	11.0	188	Saint Lucia	0.9
70	Cambodia	103.2	130	Trinidad and Tobago	11.0	189	Virgin Islands (U.S.)	0.9
71	Cuba	87.7	131	Bahamas	10.0	190	Guam	0.7
72	Tunisia	86.6	132	Guadeloupe	8.7	191	Antigua and Barbuda	0.6
73	Mauritania	85.0	133	French Polynesia	8.6	192	Tuvalu	0.6
74	Yemen	82.8	134	Libya	8.5	193	Mayotte	0.5
75	Chad	80.0	135	Burkina Faso	8.0	194	Nauru	0.5
76	Angola	77.9	136	Kuwait	7.8	195	Bermuda	0.4
77	Côte d'Ivoire	74.1	137	Liberia	7.7	196	Aruba	0.3
78	Zambia	70.1	138	Bahrain	7.6	197	Bhutan	0.3
79	Cameroon	66.0	139	French Guiana	7.5	198	Djibouti	0.3
80	Sierra Leone	63.9	140	Syria	7.3	199	Kyrgyzstan	0.3
81	Mali	63.0	141	Yugoslavia	6.8	200	Marshall Islands	0.3
82	Malawi	58.8	142	Bolivia	6.0	201	Saint Kitts and Nevis	0.2
83	Saudi Arabia	58.0	143	Cape Verde	5.9	202	Jordan	0.1
84	Lithuania	51.0	144	Martinique	5.9	203	Mongolia	0.1
85	Solomon Islands	49.2	145	Seychelles	5.4	204	Northern Mariana Islands	0.1
86	Guyana	46.4	146	Ethiopia	5.3	205	Swaziland	0.1
87	Kazakhstan	45.6	147	Guinea-Bissau	5.3	206	American Samoa	0.04
88	Sudan	44.2	148	Haiti	5.2	207	Lesotho	0.04
89	Guinea	44.0	149	Qatar	5.1	208	Monaco	0.03
90	Romania	42.7	150	Moldova	4.8			
91	Turkmenistan	38.0	151	Austria	4.6			

Source: Yearbook of Fisheries Statistics

Despite the importance of food production in a hungry world, agriculture remains labor intensive, agricultural prices fluctuate markedly, and agricultural productivity is low. As a result, agriculture's share of the Gross Domestic Product (GDP) in relation to other sectors has been declining in most technologically advanced countries of the world, but remains high in the least developed countries. National policy in almost all countries deliberately favors industry over agriculture, and even short-term growth prospects in the sector are unlikely due to the ongoing migration of rural people to towns and cities, thereby depleting the agricultural labor force.

Rank	Country/Entity	Agriculture's Share of GDP (Percentage)	Rank	Country/Entity	Agriculture's Share of GDP (Percentage)	Rank	Country/Entity	Agriculture's Share of GDP (Percentage)
1	Somalia	65	46	Syria	29	91	Namibia	14
2	Myanmar (Burma)	61	47	Vietnam	29	92	Peru	14
3	Laos	56	48	Uzbekistan	28	93	Suriname	14
4	Albania	55	49	Papua New Guinea	27	94	Colombia	13
5	Ethiopia	54	50	Paraguay	26	95	Dominican Republic	13
6	Central African Republic	53	51	Zambia	26	96	Tunisia	13
7	Guinea-Bissau	52	52	São Tomé and Príncipe	25	97	Angola	12
8	Cambodia	51	53	Guatemala	24	98	Bulgaria	12
9	Tanzania	50	54	Guinea	24	99	Grenada	12
10	Afghanistan	48	55	Honduras	24	100	Kazakhstan	12
11	Moldova	48	56	Sri Lanka	24	101	Croatia	11
12	Burundi	47	57	Kiribati	23	102	Lesotho	11
13	Equatorial Guinea	47	58	Mauritania	23	103	Algeria	10
14	Ghana	47	59	Pakistan	23	104	Jamaica	10
15	Uganda	45	60	Yugoslavia	23	105	Panama	10
16	Armenia	43	61	Fiji	22	106	Swaziland	10
17	Niger	43	62	Senegal	22	107	Thailand	10
18	Nepal	42	63	Philippines	22	108	Zimbabwe	10
19	Samoa	42	64	Tuvalu	22	109	Estonia	10
20	Haiti	41	65	Vanuatu	22	110	Gabon	9
21	Mali	41	66	Ukraine	22	111	Iceland	9
22	Rwanda	40	67	Chad	21	112	Ireland	9
23	Cameroon	39	68	China	21	113	Mauritius	9
24	Nigeria	39	69	Gambia	21	114	New Zealand	9
25	Sierra Leone	39	70	Iran	21	115	Saint Vincent and the Grenadines	9
26	Bhutan	38	71	Romania	20	116	Turkmenistan	9
27	Kyrgyzstan	38	72	Belize	19	117	Uruguay	9
28	Madagascar	37	73	Macedonia	19	118	Chile	8
29	Sudan	37	74	Morocco	19	119	Lebanon	8
30	Iraq	35	75	Tajikistan	19	120	Jordan	8
31	Mongolia	34	76	Cape Verde	18	121	Maldives	8
32	Togo	34	77	Eritrea	18	122	Saint Lucia	8
33	Benin	33	78	Yemen	18	123	Slovakia	8
34	Nicaragua	33	79	Dominica	17	124	Libya	7
35	Solomon Islands	33	80	Ecuador	17	125	South Korea	7
36	Tonga	33	81	Indonesia	17	126	Mexico	7
37	Guyana	31	82	Belarus	16	127	Russia	7
38	India	31	83	Bolivia	16	128	Argentina	6
39	Malawi	31	84	Turkey	16	129	Hungary	6
40	Mozambique	31	85	Egypt	15	130	Latvia	6
41	Azerbaijan	30	86	Greece	15	131	Poland	6
42	Bangladesh	30	87	Lithuania	15	132	Portugal	6
43	Burkina Faso	30	88	Malaysia	15	133	Saudi Arabia	6
44	Georgia	29	89	Brazil	14	134	Saint Kitts and Nevis	6
45	Kenya	29	90	El Salvador	14			

Rank	Country/Entity	Agriculture's Share of GDP (Percentage)	Rank	Country/Entity	Agriculture's Share of GDP (Percentage)	Rank	Country/Entity	Agriculture's Share of GDP (Percentage)
135	Botswana	5	149	Australia	3	163	Belgium	2
136	Cyprus	5	150	Brunei	3	164	Japan	2
137	Czech Republic	5	151	Canada	3	165	Sweden	2
138	Finland	5	152	Djibouti	3	166	Trinidad and Tobago	2
139	Slovenia	5	153	France	3	167	United Kingdom	2
140	South Africa	5	154	Israel	3	168	United States	2
141	Venezuela	5	155	Italy	3	169	Bahamas	1
142	Antigua and Barbuda	4	156	Malta	3	170	Bahrain	1
143	Barbados	4	157	Norway	3	171	Germany	1
144	Denmark	4	158	Oman	3	172	Luxembourg	1
145	Netherlands	4	159	Spain	3	173	Qatar	1
146	Reunion	4	160	Switzerland	3	174	Puerto Rico	1
147	Seychelles	4	161	United Arab Emirates	3			
148	Taiwan	4	162	Austria	2			

Source: World Development Report

Chapter 12

Industry

Industry and Manufacturing

Only some forty nations of the world can be described as industrial nations, defined as nations in which manufacturing provides the bulk of the Gross Domestic Product. Industrial progress requires the conjunction of a variety of factors, such as a pool of technological expertise, good infrastructure, access to capital and skilled labor, supply of raw materials, and good export markets. Industrial strength may not always ensure economic independence, as was once thought. In fact, it may have the opposite effect of reinforcing dependence because of the need to find reliable suppliers and profitable export markets.

Developing nations are experiencing a late version of the industrial revolution. In many countries, the terms industrialization and modernization are used as synonyms. On the one hand, industrialization creates demand for all kinds of products and thus elevates the standard of living, reduces unemployment, increases energy consumption, enhances vocational skills, and promotes improvements in the infrastructure, including the building of roads. There is also a flip side, as developing countries are discovering. Industrialization leads to environmental degradation, urban overcrowding, and social dislocation.

12.1 Industrial Growth Rate

Rank	Country/Entity	Percentage Growth Rate	Rank	Country/Entity	Percentage Growth Rate	Rank	Country/Entity	Percentage Growth Rate
1	Lebanon	25.0	37	El Salvador	7.0	73	Ghana	4.2
2	Lesotho	19.7	38	Hungary	7.0	74	Nigeria	4.1
3	Uganda	19.7	39	North Korea	7.0	75	Bolivia	4.0
4	Belarus	17.0	40	Singapore	7.0	76	Brunei	4.0
5	Saudi Arabia	16.0	41	Taiwan	7.0	77	France	4.0
6	Nepal	14.7	42	Czech Republic	6.9	78	Seychelles	4.0
7	Malaysia	14.4	43	India	6.7	79	United States	3.9
8	Samoa	14.0	44	Comoros	6.5	80	Kenya	3.8
9	Togo	13.6	45	Sri Lanka	6.5	81	Madagascar	3.8
10	China	13.0	46	Suriname	6.5	82	Lithuania	3.7
11	Vietnam	12.0	47	Vanuatu	6.4	83	Netherlands	3.7
12	Poland	11.2	48	Dominican Republic	6.3	84	Swaziland	3.7
13	Kyrgyzstan	10.8	49	Maldives	6.3	85	Tunisia	3.5
14	Turkey	10.8	50	Philippines	6.3	86	Zambia	3.5
15	Costa Rica	10.5	51	United Arab Emirates	6.1	87	Bahrain	3.4
16	Indonesia	10.5	52	Albania	6.0	88	Macedonia	3.4
17	Ireland	10.1	53	Cuba	6.0	89	Luxembourg	3.3
18	Honduras	10.0	54	Uzbekistan	6.0	90	Pakistan	3.3
19	Namibia	10.0	55	Romania	5.9	91	Guinea	3.2
20	Zimbabwe	10.0	56	Mauritius	5.8	92	Djibouti	3.0
21	Belgium	9.7	57	Iran	5.7	93	Germany	3.0
22	Mexico	9.3	58	Guyana	5.6	94	Kazakhstan	3.0
23	Myanmar (Burma)	9.2	59	Uruguay	5.6	95	Norway	3.0
24	Côte d'Ivoire	9.0	60	Israel	5.4	96	Oman	3.0
25	Argentina	8.7	61	Bangladesh	5.3	97	Slovakia	3.0
26	Egypt	8.5	62	Paraguay	5.1	98	Estonia	3.0
27	South Korea	8.2	63	Chad	5.0	99	Fiji	2.9
28	Georgia	8.1	64	Puerto Rico	5.0	100	Saint Lucia	2.8
29	Yugoslavia	8.0	65	Sudan	5.0	101	Guinea-Bissau	2.6
30	Bhutan	7.6	66	Rwanda	4.9	102	Sweden	2.6
31	Trinidad and Tobago	7.5	67	Botswana	4.6	103	Haiti	2.5
32	Equatorial Guinea	7.4	68	Brazil	4.5	104	Ecuador	2.4
33	Finland	7.4	69	Mongolia	4.5	105	Gabon	2.3
34	Senegal	7.4	70	Morocco	4.5	106	Portugal	2.2
35	Mauritania	7.2	71	Japan	4.3	107	Latvia	2.0
36	Cambodia	7.0	72	Burkina Faso	4.2	108	United Kingdom	2.0

Rank	Country/Entity	Percentage Growth Rate	Rank	Country/Entity	Percentage Growth Rate	Rank	Country/Entity	Percentage Growth Rate
109	Guatemala	1.9	124	Armenia	0.7	138	Switzerland	0.0
110	Russia	1.9	125	Kiribati	0.7	139	Dominica	−0.4
111	Tonga	1.9	126	Mali	0.6	140	Spain	−0.8
112	Grenada	1.8	127	Greece	0.5	141	Colombia	−1.2
113	Canada	1.7	128	Italy	0.5	142	Ukraine	−1.8
114	Nicaragua	1.4	129	Niger	0.5	143	Moldova	−2.0
115	Denmark	1.3	130	Venezuela	0.5	144	Jordan	−3.4
116	Australia	1.2	131	Panama	0.4	145	Cyprus	−4.0
117	Peru	1.2	132	Tanzania	0.4	146	Qatar	−4.0
118	South Africa	1.2	133	Azerbaijan	0.3	147	Chile	−4.2
119	Austria	1.0	134	Saint Vincent and	0.3	148	Bulgaria	−7.4
120	Kuwait	1.0		the Grenadines		149	Thailand	−15.0
121	Malawi	0.9	135	Belize	0.2	150	Tajikistan	−20.0
122	Barbados	0.8	136	Syria	0.2			
123	Slovenia	0.8	137	Croatia	0.0			

Source: UN Statistical Yearbook

12.2 Manufacturing

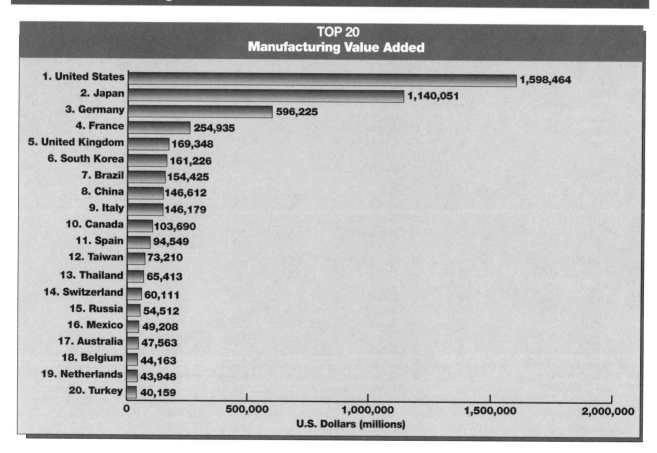

TOP 20
Manufacturing Value Added

Rank	Country	U.S. Dollars (millions)
1.	United States	1,598,464
2.	Japan	1,140,051
3.	Germany	596,225
4.	France	254,935
5.	United Kingdom	169,348
6.	South Korea	161,226
7.	Brazil	154,425
8.	China	146,612
9.	Italy	146,179
10.	Canada	103,690
11.	Spain	94,549
12.	Taiwan	73,210
13.	Thailand	65,413
14.	Switzerland	60,111
15.	Russia	54,512
16.	Mexico	49,208
17.	Australia	47,563
18.	Belgium	44,163
19.	Netherlands	43,948
20.	Turkey	40,159

U.S. Dollars (millions)

Rank	Country/Entity	Manufacturing Value Added in U.S. Dollars (millions)	Rank	Country/Entity	Manufacturing Value Added in U.S. Dollars (millions)	Rank	Country/Entity	Manufacturing Value Added in U.S. Dollars (millions)
21	Sweden	35,125	24	Ukraine	28,630	27	South Africa	25,669
22	Austria	33,371	25	Indonesia	27,701	28	Puerto Rico	22,737
23	Argentina	29,622	26	Denmark	26,633	29	Poland	22,523

Rank	Country/Entity	Manufacturing Value Added in U.S. Dollars (millions)	Rank	Country/Entity	Manufacturing Value Added in U.S. Dollars (millions)	Rank	Country/Entity	Manufacturing Value Added in U.S. Dollars (millions)
30	India	22,176	90	Tajikistan	862	150	Netherlands Antilles	101
31	Finland	20,972	91	Myanmar (Burma)	858	151	Tanzania	101
32	Singapore	20,593	92	Jamaica	819	152	Chad	98
33	Portugal	17,025	93	Qatar	810	153	Isle of Man	98
34	Malaysia	16,287	94	Congo, Dem. Rep. of	808	154	Mali	96
35	Ireland	14,780	95	Turkmenistan	801	155	Bahamas	95
36	Norway	13,472	96	Iceland	795	156	Barbados	95
37	Chile	11,841	97	Libya	784	157	Burundi	94
38	Venezuela	11,292	98	Paraguay	782	158	Malawi	92
39	Hong Kong	11,198	99	Macedonia	768	159	Sierra Leone	92
40	Colombia	10,846	100	Latvia	714	160	Togo	90
41	Greece	10,660	101	Kenya	703	161	Mongolia	86
42	Israel	10,624	102	Suriname	700	162	Guinea	83
43	Philippines	10,548	103	Panama	694	163	Guadeloupe	77
44	Czech Republic	9,896	104	Oman	669	164	Congo, Rep. of	75
45	New Zealand	8,251	105	Mauritius	658	165	Haiti	73
46	Hungary	8,062	106	Nicaragua	653	166	Laos	66
47	Peru	6,895	107	Ghana	610	167	Liberia	64
48	Kazakhstan	6,867	108	Iraq	606	168	Guernsey	61
49	Saudi Arabia	6,780	109	Trinidad and Tobago	593	169	Belize	59
50	Romania	6,651	110	Ethiopia	529	170	Benin	59
51	United Arab Emirates	6,621	111	Honduras	526	171	Eritrea	58
52	Bulgaria	5,889	112	El Salvador	521	172	Northern Mariana Islands	58
53	Iran	5,839	113	Azerbaijan	512	173	Gaza Strip	50
54	Pakistan	5,719	114	Malta	499	174	Saint Lucia	46
55	Cuba	5,560	115	Cameroon	470	175	French Guiana	45
56	Egypt	5,486	116	Kyrgyzstan	452	176	Jersey	45
57	Vietnam	5,472	117	Papua New Guinea	451	177	Andorra	38
58	Croatia	5,227	118	Macau	448	178	Somalia	36
59	Slovenia	4,837	119	Afghanistan	435	179	Mauritania	35
60	Yugoslavia	4,506	120	Réunion	371	180	Central African Republic	27
61	Morocco	4,165	121	Armenia	368	181	Greenland	27
62	Algeria	4,084	122	Nepal	356	182	Seychelles	26
63	Bosnia and Herzegovina	4,021	123	Swaziland	344	183	Djibouti	23
64	Tunisia	3,696	124	New Caledonia	341	184	Gambia	22
65	Guatemala	3,674	125	American Samoa	326	185	Bhutan	21
66	Yemen	3,541	126	Angola	319	186	Guyana	20
67	Nigeria	3,165	127	Senegal	310	187	Grenada	19
68	Ecuador	3,095	128	Brunei	305	188	Saint Kitts and Nevis	19
69	Belarus	3,006	129	Zambia	305	189	Guinea-Bissau	16
70	Syria	2,990	130	Moldova	254	190	Samoa	15
71	Uruguay	2,962	131	Mozambique	238	191	Cape Verde	14
72	Slovakia	2,720	132	Namibia	234	192	Saint Vincent and the Grenadines	14
73	Lithuania	2,667	133	Albania	224			
74	Kuwait	2,232	134	French Polynesia	214	193	Dominica	13
75	Uzbekistan	2,147	135	Botswana	186	194	Tonga	13
76	Luxembourg	2,035	136	Rwanda	178	195	Palau	12
77	Bangladesh	1,899	137	Gabon	174	196	Maldives	11
78	Bahrain	1,730	138	Bermuda	173	197	Vanuatu	10
79	Zimbabwe	1,479	139	Fiji	156	198	Comoros	9.9
80	Dominican Republic	1,298	140	Uganda	155	199	Guam	9.1
81	Costa Rica	1,285	141	Niger	153	200	Antigua and Barbuda	8.4
82	Sri Lanka	1,267	142	Georgia	150	201	Solomon Islands	7.8
83	Estonia	1,254	143	Martinique	145	202	São Tomé and Príncipe	4.6
84	Sudan	1,179	144	West Bank	132	203	Marshall Islands	2.7
85	Côte d'Ivoire	1,022	145	Burkina Faso	131	204	Micronesia	2.2
86	Jordan	987	146	Cambodia	128	205	Equatorial Guinea	1.9
87	Cyprus	899	147	Lesotho	128	206	Kiribati	0.68
88	Bolivia	880	148	Madagascar	121	207	Tuvalu	0.31
89	Lebanon	870	149	Faroe Islands	120			

Source: World Development Report

12.3 Mineral Production

Mining appears in most statistical compilations, along with manufacturing, under the rubric of industry. Mining statistics, like manufacturing statistics, tend to be very reliable because they are reported at various stages to the authorities: first during mining; then during transport, trade, and industrial processing. Metals are ferrous and nonferrous metallic ores, concentrates, and scrap; nonmetals include nonmetallic minerals.

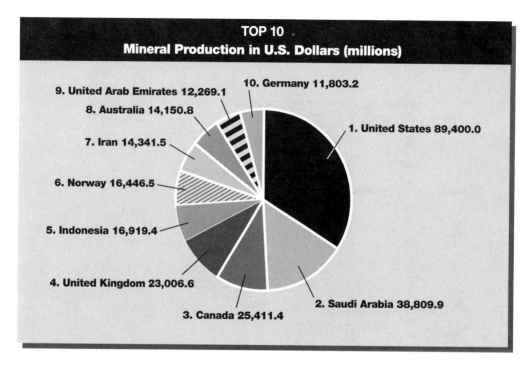

TOP 10
Mineral Production in U.S. Dollars (millions)

- 9. United Arab Emirates 12,269.1
- 10. Germany 11,803.2
- 8. Australia 14,150.8
- 7. Iran 14,341.5
- 1. United States 89,400.0
- 6. Norway 16,446.5
- 5. Indonesia 16,919.4
- 4. United Kingdom 23,006.6
- 3. Canada 25,411.4
- 2. Saudi Arabia 38,809.9

Rank	Country/Entity	Mineral Production Value Added in U.S. Dollars (millions)	Rank	Country/Entity	Mineral Production Value Added in U.S. Dollars (millions)	Rank	Country/Entity	Mineral Production Value Added in U.S. Dollars (millions)
11	France	11,521.0	31	Angola	2,610.9	51	Papua New Guinea	944.9
12	Nigeria	11,361.0	32	Syria	2,594.1	52	Greece	922.1
13	Algeria	10,628.8	33	Italy	2,554.5	53	Taiwan	791.6
14	Kuwait	10,513.4	34	Qatar	2,445.1	54	Bahrain	763.8
15	Japan	10,047.9	35	Chile	2,440.0	55	Iraq	739.9
16	China	9,885.2	36	Thailand	2,231.6	56	Tunisia	704.5
17	Netherlands	9,620.1	37	Ecuador	1,883.6	57	Portugal	704.2
18	South Africa	9,182.3	38	Turkey	1,882.4	58	Cameroon	681.6
19	Venezuela	9,156.9	39	Yemen	1,788.2	59	Philippines	668.9
20	Libya	7,212.2	40	Botswana	1,478.7	60	Congo, Rep. of	659.9
21	Brazil	7,171.9	41	Brunei	1,437.7	61	Sweden	634.3
22	Malaysia	6,103.8	42	Romania	1,315.6	62	New Zealand	621.0
23	India	6,065.9	43	Trinidad and Tobago	1,300.8	63	Bulgaria	582.1
24	Mexico	5,526.5	44	Denmark	1,289.7	64	Morocco	574.2
25	Oman	5,300.9	45	Gabon	1,214.1	65	Belgium	541.0
26	Egypt	5,151.3	46	South Korea	1,103.6	66	Austria	515.1
27	Poland	4,964.0	47	Peru	1,098.1	67	Ireland	512.1
28	Argentina	4,383.3	48	Vietnam	1,062.9	68	Myanmar (Burma)	497.4
29	Colombia	4,045.4	49	Czech Republic	1,050.3	69	Finland	424.1
30	Spain	3,786.9	50	Yugoslavia	981.7	70	Zambia	371.5

Rank	Country/Entity	Mineral Production Value Added in U.S. Dollars (millions)	Rank	Country/Entity	Mineral Production Value Added in U.S. Dollars (millions)	Rank	Country/Entity	Mineral Production Value Added in U.S. Dollars (millions)
71	Bolivia	369.6	100	Senegal	42.3	129	Bhutan	6.0
72	Israel	352.6	101	El Salvador	40.3	130	Burundi	5.4
73	Guinea	336.5	102	Hong Kong	34.7	131	Bangladesh	5.27
74	Zimbabwe	336.1	103	Puerto Rico	31.0	132	Chad	5.0
75	Hungary	335.0	104	Latvia	30.9	133	Mauritius	4.9
76	Namibia	302.4	105	Uruguay	30.8	134	Cambodia	4.4
77	Pakistan	284.4	106	Luxembourg	29.2	135	Costa Rica	3.8
78	Jamaica	271.4	107	Burkina Faso	28.4	136	Laos	3.6
79	New Caledonia	262.4	108	Equatorial Guinea	26.0	137	Belize	3.5
80	Congo, Dem. Rep. of	226.5	109	Paraguay	25.6	138	Maldives	3.3
81	Slovenia	195.1	110	Singapore	25.6	139	Saint Lucia	3.1
82	Jordan	194.7	111	Cyprus	23.7	140	Belarus	2.0
83	Sri Lanka	157.3	112	Tanzania	22.0	141	Macau	1.8
84	Dominican Republic	126.0	113	Nepal	20.6	142	Fiji	1.7
85	Liberia	122.3	114	Afghanistan	16.2	143	Dominica	1.5
86	Croatia	119.7	115	Uganda	15.8	144	Grenada	1.4
87	Sierra Leone	117.7	116	Benin	14.4	145	Somalia	1.0
88	Ghana	109.8	117	Kenya	14.1	146	Faroe Islands	0.9
89	Guyana	105.8	118	Ethiopia	13.9	147	Cape Verde	0.8
90	Mauritania	104.1	119	Côte d'Ivoire	13.3	148	Lesotho	0.8
91	Sudan	95.4	120	Malawi	12.8	149	Saint Vincent and the Grenadines	0.8
92	Albania	81.4	121	Nicaragua	11.3			
93	Togo	73.3	122	Swaziland	10.6	150	Saint Kitts and Nevis	0.6
94	Honduras	69.2	123	Barbados	10.47	151	Tonga	0.4
95	Mali	68.4	124	Panama	8.6	152	Eritrea	0.3
96	Central African Republic	65.5	125	Mozambique	8.2	153	Marshall Islands	0.3
97	Suriname	63.9	126	Madagascar	8.1	154	Rwanda	0.3
98	Niger	62.5	127	Antigua and Barbuda	7.6	155	Haiti	0.2
99	Estonia	58.3	128	Malta	6.7	156	Tuvalu	0.1

Source: World Development Report

12.4 Industry's Share of Gross Domestic Product (GDP)

The industrial sector comprises mining, manufacturing, construction, and utilities. Until the 1970s this sector dominated the economies of all developed countries, but since then it has been pushed back by services. The share of manufacturing and mining, particularly, has fallen considerably in what is now described as the post-industrial economy. Even so, industry makes substantial contributions to export earnings in most countries.

Rank	Country/Entity	Industry's Share of GDP (Percentage)	Rank	Country/Entity	Industry's Share of GDP (Percentage)	Rank	Country/Entity	Industry's Share of GDP (Percentage)
1	Belarus	45	12	Malaysia	31	23	Croatia	28
2	Puerto Rico	42	13	Ukraine	31	24	Czech Republic	28
3	Brunei	41	14	Slovenia	30	25	Singapore	28
4	China	41	15	Zambia	30	26	Thailand	28
5	Yugoslavia	41	16	Armenia	29	27	Afghanistan	26
6	Zimbabwe	41	17	Bulgaria	29	28	Kazakhstan	26
7	Ireland	38	18	South Korea	29	29	Lithuania	26
8	Macedonia	38	19	Poland	29	30	Azerbaijan	25
9	Tajikistan	35	20	Portugal	29	31	Egypt	25
10	Mongolia	32	21	Russia	29	32	Finland	25
11	Romania	32	22	Taiwan	29	33	Japan	25

Rank	Country/Entity	Industry's Share of GDP (Percentage)	Rank	Country/Entity	Industry's Share of GDP (Percentage)	Rank	Country/Entity	Industry's Share of GDP (Percentage)
34	Philippines	25	83	Nicaragua	16	132	Togo	9
35	Slovakia	25	84	Pakistan	16	133	Trinidad and Tobago	9
36	Austria	24	85	Uzbekistan	16	134	Benin	8
37	Indonesia	24	86	Venezuela	16	135	Congo, Dem. Rep. of	8
38	Luxembourg	24	87	Bahrain	15	136	Ethiopia	8
39	Malta	24	88	Ecuador	15	137	Libya	8
40	Mauritius	24	89	Greece	15	138	Mozambique	8
41	Moldova	24	90	Latvia	15	139	Myanmar (Burma)	8
42	Brazil	23	91	Sri Lanka	15	140	Panama	8
43	Germany	23	92	Paraguay	15	141	Papua New Guinea	8
44	South Africa	23	93	Belize	14	142	Saint Vincent and the Grenadines	8
45	Spain	23	94	Bolivia	14			
46	Switzerland	23	95	Guatemala	14	143	Saudi Arabia	8
47	Argentina	22	96	Jordan	14	144	United Arab Emirates	8
48	Belgium	22	97	Lesotho	14	145	Central African Republic	7
49	Israel	22	98	Malawi	14	146	Niger	7
50	Mexico	22	99	Mauritania	14	147	Tanzania	7
51	Peru	22	100	Rwanda	14	148	Turkmenistan	7
52	Sweden	22	101	Albania	13	149	Barbados	6
53	Swaziland	29	102	Cyprus	13	150	Cape Verde	6
54	El Salvador	21	103	Iceland	13	151	Chad	6
55	Equatorial Guinea	21	104	Iran	13	152	Dominica	6
56	Georgia	21	105	Laos	13	153	Gambia	6
57	Italy	21	106	Norway	13	154	Grenada	6
58	Kyrgyzstan	21	107	Qatar	13	155	Maldives	6
59	United Kingdom	21	108	Yemen	13	156	Nigeria	6
60	France	20	109	Senegal	13	157	Uganda	6
61	Hungary	20	110	Eritrea	12	158	Cambodia	5
62	Jamaica	20	111	Fiji	12	159	Congo, Rep. of	5
63	Turkey	20	112	Lebanon	12	160	Djibouti	5
64	Canada	19	113	Samoa	12	161	Gabon	5
65	Colombia	19	114	Burundi	11	162	Guinea	5
66	Costa Rica	19	115	Guinea-Bissau	11	163	Oman	5
67	Denmark	19	116	Haiti	11	164	Saint Lucia	5
68	Netherlands	19	117	Kenya	11	165	São Tomé and Príncipe	5
69	Burkina	18	118	Kuwait	11	166	Syria	5
70	Cote d'Ivoire	18	119	Saint Kitts and Nevis	11	167	Vanuatu	5
71	Dominican Republic	18	120	Bangladesh	10	168	Botswana	4
72	Honduras	18	121	Bhutan	10	169	Comoros	4
73	New Zealand	18	122	Cameroon	10	170	Seychelles	4
74	Tunisia	18	123	Guyana	10	171	Solomon Islands	4
75	United States	18	124	Suriname	10	172	Somalia	4
76	Uruguay	18	125	Algeria	9	173	Tonga	4
77	Bahamas	17	126	China	9	174	Angola	3
78	Chile	17	127	Iraq	9	175	Tuvalu	3
79	Estonia	17	128	Namibia	9	176	Antigua and Barbuda	2
80	India	17	129	Nepal	9	177	Kiribati	1
81	Morocco	17	130	Sierra Leone	9			
82	Australia	16	131	Sudan	9			

Source: World Development Report

Energy

The term energy encompasses a wide range of sources of power, including fossil fuels, natural gas, electricity, coal, nuclear power, and alternate sources of power. Different sources of power have different scales of efficiency and benefits. Some sources of energy are renewable, but most are not; ironically, nonrenewable sources are exploited more thoroughly than renewable ones. Energy rankings are critical in assessing the future prospects of industrial civilization because modern civilization cannot survive without adequate sources of power. The two most troubling aspects of energy production are the uneven distribution of fossil fuels among countries (and its heavy concentration in certain Middle Eastern countries, giving them an extraordinary influence over the global economy) and the finite nature of the supply in relation to unrestrained demand.

Rank	Country/Entity	Energy Production, 1997 (oil equivalent, thousand metric tons)	Rank	Country/Entity	Energy Production, 1997 (oil equivalent, thousand metric tons)	Rank	Country/Entity	Energy Production, 1997 (oil equivalent, thousand metric tons)
1	United States	1,683,810	40	Syria	32,794	80	Bolivia	5,953
2	China	1,097,210	41	Czech Republic	31,539	81	Ghana	5,843
3	Russia	927,341	42	Spain	31,358	82	Zambia	5,556
4	Saudi Arabia	487,095	43	Romania	31,013	83	Côte d'Ivoire	4,908
5	India	404,503	44	Italy	29,311	84	Slovakia	4,688
6	Canada	362,701	45	Turkey	27,556	85	Guatemala	4,433
7	United Kingdom	268,985	46	South Korea	24,037	86	Sri Lanka	4,345
8	Iran	224,935	47	Ecuador	22,792	87	Croatia	4,011
9	Mexico	223,132	49	Denmark	20,274	88	Lithuania	3,970
10	Indonesia	221,549	50	Gabon	19,786	89	Estonia	3,788
11	Norway	212,653	51	Yemen	19,105	90	Belarus	3,275
12	Venezuela	203,979	52	Turkmenistan	18,739	91	Ireland	2,871
13	Australia	199,167	53	Philippines	16,616	92	Slovenia	2,870
14	Nigeria	191,034	54	Ethiopia	16,316	93	El Salvador	2,649
15	United Arab Emirates	153,555	55	Finland	15,059	94	Portugal	2,317
16	South Africa	142,139	56	Congo, Dem. Rep. of	14,364	95	Honduras	2,003
17	Germany	139,734	57	New Zealand	14,158	96	Benin	1,897
18	France	127,843	58	Azerbaijan	14,027	97	Senegal	1,654
19	Algeria	125,576	59	Trinidad and Tobago	13,579	98	Latvia	1,636
20	Brazil	120,236	60	Congo, Rep. of	13,540	99	Nicaragua	1,529
21	Kuwait	116,087	61	Tanzania	13,529	100	Dominican Republic	1,423
22	Japan	106,978	62	Belgium	13,153	101	Kyrgyzstan	1,408
23	Poland	100,935	63	Hungary	12,747	102	Haiti	1,298
24	Ukraine	81,175	64	Myanmar (Burma)	12,249	103	Tajikistan	1,253
25	Argentina	80,134	65	Peru	12,225	104	Costa Rica	1,157
26	Libya	78,942	66	Kenya	11,651	105	Uruguay	1,086
27	Malaysia	73,979	67	Cameroon	11,250	106	Morocco	1,067
28	Colombia	67,524	68	Switzerland	10,993	107	Albania	912
29	Netherlands	65,298	69	Bulgaria	9,981	108	Panama	808
30	Kazakhstan	64,784	70	Sudan	9,881	109	Georgia	694
31	Iraq	62,088	71	Greece	9,645	110	Bosnia and Herzegovina	626
32	Egypt	57,997	72	Chile	8,168	111	Israel	601
33	Oman	51,620	73	Zimbabwe	8,152	112	Jamaica	595
34	Uzbekistan	49,054	74	Austria	8,007	113	Armenia	537
35	Thailand	46,166	75	Cuba	7,255	114	Lebanon	207
36	Vietnam	43,525	76	Mozambique	6,994	115	Jordan	193
37	Pakistan	42,048	77	Paraguay	6,960	116	Moldova	98
38	Angola	41,430	78	Tunisia	6,655	117	Singapore	61
39	Sweden	33,067	79	Nepal	6,559	118	Hong Kong	48

Source: World Energy Statistics

Energy Use

What is wrong with energy is that both its production and its consumption are lopsided. While production is monopolized by members of the Organization of Petroleum Exporting Countries (OPEC), consumption is monopolized by Western nations, especially the United States. During the 1970s many Western countries adopted energy policies designed to reduce consumption by mandating the production of cars that can travel more miles per gallon, improving home heating through better insulation, and making energy conservation fashionable. In the 1980s and 1990s, some of these energy policies were abandoned as oil became more affordable. Thus, by the beginning of the twenty-first century, the world was once again returning to the insecurities of the 1970s. The plight of oil-consuming countries may get worse before it gets better.

13.2 Commercial Energy Use

Rank	Country/Entity	Energy Use (oil equivalent, thousand metric tons)	Rank	Country/Entity	Energy Use (oil equivalent, thousand metric tons)	Rank	Country/Entity	Energy Use (oil equivalent, thousand metric tons)
1	United States	2,162,190	41	Colombia	30,481	81	Nepal	7,160
2	China	1,113,050	42	Austria	27,761	82	Sri Lanka	7,159
3	Russia	591,982	43	Iraq	27,091	83	Ghana	6,896
4	Japan	514,898	44	Singapore	26,878	84	Angola	6,848
5	India	461,032	45	Algeria	26,497	85	Tunisia	6,805
6	Germany	347,272	46	Switzerland	26,218	86	Oman	6,775
7	France	247,534	47	Greece	25,556	87	Slovenia	6,380
8	Canada	237,983	48	Hungary	25,311	88	Zambia	5,987
9	United Kingdom	227,977	49	Belarus	25,142	89	Cameroon	5,756
10	South Korea	176,351	50	Bangladesh	24,327	90	Guatemala	5,633
11	Brazil	172,030	51	Norway	24,226	91	Côte d'Ivoire	5,597
12	Italy	163,315	52	Chile	23,012	92	Estonia	5,556
13	Ukraine	150,059	53	Denmark	21,107	93	Dominican Republic	5,453
14	Mexico	141,520	54	Bulgaria	20,616	94	Lebanon	5,244
15	Indonesia	138,779	55	Portugal	20,400	95	Jordan	4,795
16	Iran	108,289	56	Israel	17,591	96	Latvia	4,460
17	Spain	107,328	57	Slovakia	17,216	97	Moldova	4,436
18	South Africa	107,220	58	Ethiopia	17,131	98	Bolivia	4,254
19	Poland	105,155	59	New Zealand	16,679	99	Paraguay	4,191
20	Australia	101,626	60	Kuwait	16,165	100	El Salvador	4,095
21	Saudi Arabia	98,449	61	Peru	15,127	101	Jamaica	3,963
22	Nigeria	88,652	62	Libya	15,090	102	Tajikistan	3,384
23	Thailand	79,963	63	Syria	14,642	103	Yemen	3,355
24	Netherlands	74,910	64	Congo, Dem. Rep. of	14,539	104	Honduras	3,182
25	Turkey	71,273	65	Cuba	14,273	105	Uruguay	2,883
26	Argentina	61,710	66	Tanzania	14,258	106	Kyrgyzstan	2,793
27	Venezuela	57,530	67	Kenya	14,138	107	Senegal	2,770
28	Belgium	57,125	68	Hong Kong	14,121	108	Costa Rica	2,663
29	Pakistan	56,818	69	Myanmar (Burma)	13,009	109	Nicaragua	2,573
30	Sweden	51,934	70	Ireland	12,491	110	Panama	2,328
31	Malaysia	48,473	71	Turkmenistan	12,181	111	Georgia	2,295
32	Romania	44,135	72	Azerbaijan	11,987	112	Benin	2,182
33	Uzebekistan	42,553	73	Sudan	11,480	113	Armenia	1,804
34	Czech Republic	40,576	74	Zimbabwe	9,926	114	Haiti	1,779
35	Egypt	39,581	75	Morocco	9,275	115	Bosnia and Herzegovina	1,750
36	Vietnam	39,306	76	Lithuania	8,806	116	Gabon	1,635
37	Kazakhstan	38,418	77	Ecuador	8,513	117	Congo, Rep. of	1,242
38	Philippines	38,251	78	Trinidad and Tobago	8,196	118	Albania	1,048
39	Finland	33,075	79	Mozambique	7,664			
40	United Arab Emirates	30,874	80	Croatia	7,650			

Source: World Energy Statistics

13.3 Commercial Energy Use per Capita

Rank	Country/Entity	Energy Use per Capita (oil equivalent, kilograms)	Rank	Country/Entity	Energy Use per Capita (oil equivalent, kilograms)	Rank	Country/Entity	Energy Use per Capita (oil equivalent, kilograms)
1	Qatar	12,597	59	Romania	1,733	117	Paraguay	299
2	Brunei	10,839	60	Malaysia	1,699	118	Grenada	293
3	United Arab Emirates	10,531	61	Seychelles	1,691	119	Dominica	290
4	Bahrain	10,268	62	Latvia	1,569	120	Vanuatu	279
5	Luxembourg	9,361	63	Mexico	1,561	121	Swaziland	264
6	Kuwait	8,622	64	Iran	1,505	122	Pakistan	254
7	Singapore	8,103	65	Argentina	1,504	123	India	248
8	Iceland	7,932	66	Croatia	1,395	124	Papua New Guinea	236
9	Canada	7,854	67	Barbados	1,375	125	Guatemala	210
10	United States	7,819	68	Macedonia	1,279	126	Yemen	206
11	Bahamas	6,864	69	Iraq	1,213	127	Honduras	204
12	Finland	5,997	70	North Korea	1,129	128	Saint Vincent and the Grenadines	199
13	Sweden	5,723	71	Moldova	1,095			
14	Trinidad and Tobago	5,436	72	Jamaica	1,083	129	São Tomé and Príncipe	184
15	Australia	5,341	73	Jordan	1,067	130	Nigeria	162
16	Norway	5,318	74	Mongolia	1,058	131	Solomon Islands	159
17	Belgium	5,120	75	Chile	1,012	132	Zambia	149
18	Netherlands	4,580	76	Syria	997	133	Maldives	139
19	Saudi Arabia	4,566	77	Lebanon	964	134	Kenya	110
20	New Zealand	4,245	78	Turkey	957	135	Côte d'Ivoire	103
21	Germany	4,128	79	Cuba	923	136	Cameroon	103
22	France	4,042	80	Djibouti	909	137	Mauritania	103
23	Russia	4,014	81	Algeria	906	138	Vietnam	101
24	Denmark	3,977	82	Thailand	769	139	Senegal	97
25	Czech Republic	3,868	83	Brazil	718	140	Sri Lanka	97
26	Japan	3,856	84	China	664	141	Ghana	93
27	United Kingdom	3,772	85	Gabon	652	142	Angola	89
28	Estonia	3,709	86	Colombia	622	143	Equatorial Guinea	80
29	Switzerland	3,629	87	Uruguay	622	144	Sierra Leone	77
30	Kazakhstan	3,371	88	Panama	618	145	Sudan	66
31	Austria	3,301	89	Kyrgyzstan	616	146	Guinea	65
32	Slovakia	3,243	90	Tajikistan	616	147	Bangladesh	64
33	Ukraine	3,180	91	Georgia	614	148	Gambia	56
34	Ireland	3,137	92	Egypt	600	149	Cambodia	52
35	South Korea	2,982	93	Tunisia	595	150	Myanmar (Burma)	49
36	Israel	2,717	94	Ecuador	565	151	Togo	46
37	Italy	2,707	95	Costa Rica	558	152	Congo, Dem. Rep. of	45
38	Cyprus	2,701	96	Fiji	527	153	Mozambique	40
39	Slovenia	2,612	97	Saint Kitts and Nevis	486	154	Malawi	39
40	Malta	2,511	98	Zimbabwe	438	155	Laos	38
41	Libya	2,499	99	Samoa	433	156	Comoros	37
42	Spain	2,458	100	Belize	417	157	Guinea-Bissau	37
43	Bulgaria	2,438	101	Botswana	387	158	Niger	37
44	Poland	2,401	102	Mauritius	387	159	Madagascar	36
45	Belarus	2,392	103	Armenia	384	160	Tanzania	34
46	Oman	2,392	104	Bolivia	373	161	Bhutan	33
47	Hungary	2,383	105	El Salvador	370	162	Central African Republic	29
48	Turkmenistan	2,361	106	Peru	367	163	Haiti	29
49	Greece	2,260	107	Indonesia	366	164	Nepal	28
50	Venezuela	2,186	108	Guyana	350	165	Burundi	23
51	Hong Kong	2,185	109	Albania	341	166	Uganda	23
52	Azerbaijan	2,182	110	Saint Lucia	338	167	Ethiopia	22
53	South Africa	2,146	111	Dominican Republic	337	168	Mali	22
54	Lithuania	2,030	112	Congo, Rep. of	331	169	Benin	20
55	Antigua and Barbuda	2,017	113	Morocco	327	170	Burkina Faso	16
56	Suriname	1,926	114	Philippines	316	171	Chad	16
57	Uzbekistan	1,869	115	Cape Verde	307			
58	Portugal	1,827	116	Nicaragua	300			

Source: World Energy Statistics

13.4 Commercial Energy Use Growth Rate per Capita

Rank	Country/Entity	Annual Energy Use Growth Rate per Capita, 1980–1996 (percentage)	Rank	Country/Entity	Annual Energy Use Growth Rate per Capita, 1980–1996 (percentage)	Rank	Country/Entity	Annual Energy Use Growth Rate per Capita, 1980–1996 (percentage)
1	South Korea	8.1	36	Philippines	1.1	71	Ethiopia	-0.1
2	Singapore	8.1	37	Algeria	1.0	72	Nicaragua	-0.1
3	Belarus	7.5	38	Brazil	1.0	73	Nigeria	-0.1
4	Thailand	7.3	39	Colombia	1.0	74	Congo, Dem. Rep. of	-0.2
5	Uzbekistan	7.0	40	El Salvador	1.0	75	Honduras	-0.2
6	Malaysia	6.0	41	Slovenia	1.0	76	Panama	-0.3
7	Tajikistan	5.1	42	Ukraine	1.0	77	South Africa	-0.4
8	Portugal	4.5	43	Australia	0.9	78	Venezuela	-0.4
9	Hong Kong	4.4	44	Austria	0.9	79	Germany	-0.5
10	Kyrgyzstan	4.1	45	Bangladesh	0.9	80	Côte d'Ivoire	-0.6
11	Chile	3.7	46	Netherlands	0.9	81	Congo, Rep. of	-0.6
12	Indonesia	3.5	47	Sweden	0.9	82	Senegal	-0.7
13	Iran	3.2	48	Denmark	0.8	83	Hungary	-0.8
14	New Zealand	2.9	49	Switzerland	0.8	84	Benin	-1.0
15	Spain	2.8	50	United Kingdom	0.8	85	Cameroon	-1.1
16	China	2.6	51	Argentina	0.7	86	Kenya	-1.1
17	Egypt	2.6	52	Costa Rica	0.7	87	Tanzania	-1.1
18	Israel	2.6	53	Kuwait	0.7	88	Angola	-1.2
19	Turkey	2.6	54	Sri Lanka	0.7	89	Peru	-1.2
20	Greece	2.5	55	Vietnam	0.7	90	Czech Republic	-1.7
21	Japan	2.4	56	Jordan	0.6	91	Zambia	-1.7
22	Syria	2.4	57	Yemen	0.6	92	Slovakia	-1.8
23	Jamaica	2.3	58	Ghana	0.4	93	Bulgaria	-2.0
24	Pakistan	2.3	59	Saudi Arabia	0.4	94	Mozambique	-2.0
25	Morocco	2.1	60	United States	0.4	95	Poland	-2.0
26	Ireland	2.0	61	Zimbabwe	0.4	96	Haiti	-2.8
27	India	1.9	62	Canada	0.3	97	Romania	-2.9
28	Lebanon	1.7	63	Myanmar (Burma)	0.3	98	Russia	-3.6
29	France	1.6	64	Ecuador	0.2	99	Lithuania	-4.0
30	Paraguay	1.5	65	Mexico	0.2	100	Armenia	-4.9
31	Belgium	1.4	66	Uruguay	0.2	101	Kazakhstan	-4.9
32	Tunisia	1.4	67	Dominican Republic	0.1	102	Azerbaijan	-5.6
33	Italy	1.3	68	Nepal	0.1	103	Georgia	-5.8
34	Norway	1.2	69	Bolivia	0.0	104	Albania	-7.8
35	Finland	1.1	70	Guatemala	0.0	105	Turkmenistan	-10.5

Source: World Energy Statistics

13.5 Net Commercial Energy Imports

Rank	Country/Entity	Energy Imports as Percentage of Energy Consumption	Rank	Country/Entity	Energy Imports as Percentage of Energy Consumption	Rank	Country/Entity	Energy Imports as Percentage of Energy Consumption
1	Antigua and Barbuda	100	13	Guyana	100	25	Singapore	100
2	Bahamas	100	14	Hong Kong	100	26	Solomon Islands	100
3	Belize	100	15	Jamaica	100	27	Togo	100
4	Burkina Faso	100	16	Malta	100	28	Vanuatu	100
5	Cape Verde	100	17	Mauritania	100	29	Luxembourg	99
6	Chad	100	18	Moldova	100	30	Lebanon	98
7	Comoros	100	19	Saint Kitts and Nevis	100	31	Burundi	97
8	Cyprus	100	20	Saint Lucia	100	32	Equatorial Guinea	97
9	Djibouti	100	21	Samoa	100	33	Cambodia	96
10	Gambia	100	22	Senegal	100	34	Israel	96
11	Grenada	100	23	Seychelles	100	35	Jordan	96
12	Guinea-Bissau	100	24	Sierra Leone	100	36	Bhutan	95

Rank	Country/Entity	Energy Imports as Percentage of Energy Consumption	Rank	Country/Entity	Energy Imports as Percentage of Energy Consumption	Rank	Country/Entity	Energy Imports as Percentage of Energy Consumption
37	France	95	82	Uruguay	67	128	Uzbekistan	0
38	Morocco	95	83	Austria	66	129	China	-1
39	Sudan	95	84	Ghana	66	130	Poland	-2
40	Dominican Republic	94	85	Nicaragua	63	131	United Kingdom	-10
41	Haiti	93	86	Greece	62	132	Argentina	-18
42	Mauritius	92	87	Thailand	61	133	Laos	-18
43	Latvia	90	88	Malawi	59	134	Iraq	-25
44	Belarus	88	89	Finland	58	135	Kazakhstan	-25
45	Cuba	88	90	Germany	58	136	Bahrain	-26
46	Nepal	88	91	Uganda	58	137	South Africa	-35
47	Portugal	88	92	Switzerland	57	138	Canada	-47
48	Ethiopia	87	93	Bulgaria	56	139	Mexico	-48
49	Panama	87	94	Botswana	55	140	Russia	-53
50	São Tomé and Príncipe	87	95	Tajikistan	53	141	Vietnam	-55
51	Guinea	86	96	Turkey	53	142	Bolivia	-61
52	South Korea	86	97	Slovenia	51	143	Malaysia	-71
53	Georgia	85	98	Ukraine	48	144	Egypt	-79
54	Kenya	83	99	Hungary	47	145	Australia	-83
55	Madagascar	83	100	Kyrgyzstan	47	146	Trinidad and Tobago	-87
56	Niger	83	101	Macedonia	44	147	Colombia	-99
57	Tanzania	83	102	Croatia	43	148	Indonesia	-120
58	Honduras	82	103	Pakistan	40	149	Paraguay	-123
59	Italy	81	104	Brazil	39	150	Syria	-130
60	Japan	81	105	Estonia	39	151	Iran	-136
61	Mali	80	106	Sweden	38	152	Papua New Guinea	-150
62	Sri Lanka	80	107	Iceland	37	153	Turkmenistan	-191
63	Armenia	79	108	Zambia	31	154	Benin	-194
64	Belgium	78	109	Bangladesh	28	155	Ecuador	-231
65	Central African Republic	76	110	Denmark	28	156	Qatar	-267
66	Fiji	76	111	Romania	27	157	Venezuela	-269
67	Guatemala	74	112	Maldives	24	158	Algeria	-318
68	Mozambique	74	113	Zimbabwe	24	159	Cameroon	-333
69	Saint Vincent and the Grenadines	73	114	Swaziland	22	160	United Arab Emirates	-454
70	Slovakia	72	115	India	21	161	Saudi Arabia	-463
71	Dominica	71	116	United States	19	162	Yemen	-463
72	Philippines	71	117	Mongolia	15	163	Libya	-473
73	Côte d'Ivoire	70	118	New Zealand	15	164	Nigeria	-484
74	El Salvador	70	119	North Korea	12	165	Brunei	-515
75	Lithuania	70	120	Tunisia	9	166	Norway	-638
76	Suriname	70	121	Czech Republic	7	167	Kuwait	-693
77	Barbados	69	122	Netherlands	7	168	Oman	-787
78	Spain	69	123	Albania	3	169	Congo, Rep. of	-1,013
79	Chile	68	124	Azerbaijan	1	170	Gabon	-2,212
80	Ireland	68	125	Congo, Dem. Rep. of	1	171	Angola	-2,576
81	Costa Rica	67	126	Myanmar (Burma)	1			
			127	Peru	0			

Source: World Development Report

Petroleum is at the core of the energy crisis. It is the most efficient of the fuels that drive the world and, for a time, it was also the cheapest. The petroleum industry is the largest in the world in terms of value of output, estimated at between $1.5 trillion and $2 trillion per year. It is significant that of the top Fortune 40 companies of the world, seventeen are in the petroleum sector and each of these companies has an annual revenue that exceeds the Gross Domestic Product of half the nations of the world. While production is concentrated in OPEC countries, downstream facilities, including refining, are spread around the world. Generally, crude oil is pumped to the nearest port, which may or may not have refineries. If the crude is carried by tankers, it is taken to several strategic refinery facilities, where it is then distributed to the consuming countries. Before the oil reaches the gas pump, it passes through at least six intermediaries. Despite official discouragement of excessive oil consumption, governments are among the principal beneficiaries of the oil industry, collecting nearly half a trillion dollars in taxes annually. One of the most dreaded questions is: How long will the oil reserves last? At the rate of current production, Saudi Arabia may still be producing oil at the end of the twenty-first century, but in almost all other nations, oil may run out. However, estimates of oil reserves have been revised upward almost every year since the 1960s, and it is possible that as a result of new and intense exploration, unknown fields may be discovered on land or in sea in the coming decades.

13.6 Crude Petroleum Production

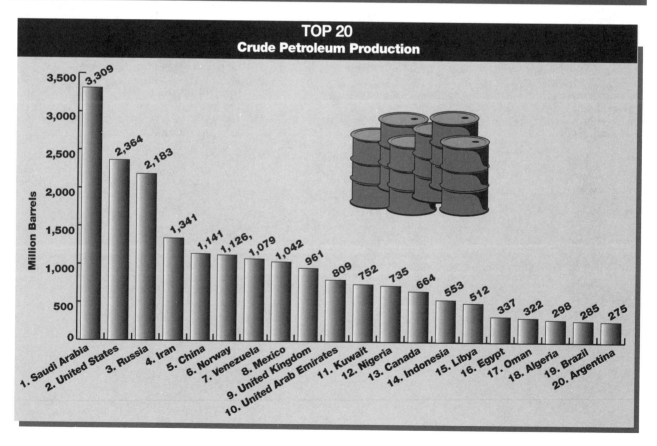

TOP 20
Crude Petroleum Production

(Million Barrels)

1. Saudi Arabia — 3,309
2. United States — 2,364
3. Russia — 2,183
4. Iran — 1,341
5. China — 1,141
6. Norway — 1,126
7. Venezuela — 1,079
8. Mexico — 1,042
9. United Kingdom — 961
10. United Arab Emirates — 809
11. Kuwait — 752
12. Nigeria — 735
13. Canada — 664
14. Indonesia — 553
15. Libya — 512
16. Egypt — 337
17. Oman — 322
18. Algeria — 298
19. Brazil — 285
20. Argentina — 275

Rank	Country/Entity	Petroleum Production, 1996 (million barrels)	Rank	Country/Entity	Petroleum Production, 1996 (million barrels)	Rank	Country/Entity	Petroleum Production, 1996 (million barrels)
21	Angola	258	46	Cameroon	33	71	Chile	3
22	Malaysia	237	47	Tunisia	32	72	Equatorial Guinea	3
23	India	235	48	Turkmenistan	32	73	Georgia	3
24	Colombia	227	49	Turkey	25	74	Greece	3
25	Syria	220	50	Ukraine	25	75	Suriname	3
26	Iraq	219	51	Netherlands	22	76	Ghana	2
27	Australia	195	52	Thailand	22	77	Poland	2
28	Azerbaijan	190	53	Germany	21	78	Lithuania	1.20
29	Qatar	175	54	Pakistan	20	79	Benin	0.70
30	Kazakhstan	169	55	France	16	80	Czech Republic	0.70
31	Ecuador	141	56	New Zealand	13	81	Kyrgyzstan	0.70
32	Gabon	135	57	Croatia	12	82	Tajikistan	0.70
33	Yemen	123	58	Bolivia	11	83	Bangladesh	0.50
34	Denmark	75	59	Congo, Dem. Rep. of	11	84	Sudan	0.50
35	Congo, Rep. of	74	60	Hungary	11	85	Barbados	0.40
36	Uzbekistan	63	61	Cuba	10	86	Bulgaria	0.40
37	Vietnam	62	62	Austria	8	87	Philippines	0.40
38	Brunei	55	63	Côte d'Ivoire	7	88	Slovakia	0.40
39	Romania	50	64	Yugoslavia	7	89	Taiwan	0.40
40	Trinidad and Tobago	47	65	Spain	6	90	Israel	0.04
41	Peru	44	66	Guatemala	5	91	Jordan	0.04
42	Papua New Guinea	39	67	Japan	5	92	Morocco	0.04
43	Bahrain	38	68	Myanmar (Burma)	5	93	Slovenia	0.01
44	Belarus	37	69	South Africa	4			
45	Italy	37	70	Albania	3			

Source: World Energy Statistics

13.7 Crude Petroleum Refining Capacity

Rank	Country/Entity	Petroleum Refining Capacity, 1997 (thousand barrels per day)	Rank	Country/Entity	Petroleum Refining Capacity, 1997 (thousand barrels per day)	Rank	Country/Entity	Petroleum Refining Capacity, 1997 (thousand barrels per day)
1	United States	15,459	26	Argentina	665	51	Bahrain	249
2	Russia	6,733	27	Belgium	630	52	Colombia	249
3	Japan	4,989	28	Romania	559	53	Syria	246
4	China	2,867	29	Thailand	558	54	Trinidad and Tobago	245
5	Italy	2,262	30	Egypt	546	55	Lithuania	240
6	South Korea	2,211	31	Virgin Islands (U.S.)	545	56	Turkmenistan	237
7	Germany	2,108	32	Netherlands Antilles	525	57	Hungary	232
8	United Kingdom	1,941	33	Belarus	473	58	Israel	220
9	Canada	1,852	34	Algeria	465	59	United Arab Emirates	213
10	France	1,786	35	Azerbaijan	442	60	Austria	210
11	Saudi Arabia	1,651	36	Nigeria	433	61	Finland	200
12	Mexico	1,520	37	Kazakhstan	427	62	Chile	192
13	Spain	1,296	38	Sweden	427	63	Denmark	189
14	Brazil	1,256	39	South Africa	414	64	Czech Republic	187
15	Ukraine	1,246	40	Greece	396	65	Peru	182
16	Iran	1,242	41	Poland	352	66	Uzbekistan	175
17	Netherlands	1,187	42	Iraq	348	67	Yugoslavia	167
18	Venezuela	1,177	43	Libya	348	68	Morocco	156
19	Singapore	1,157	44	Malaysia	330	69	Ecuador	148
20	India	1,086	45	Philippines	323	70	Pakistan	137
21	Kuwait	824	46	Norway	307	71	Puerto Rico	134
22	Indonesia	805	47	Portugal	304	72	Switzerland	132
23	Australia	771	48	Cuba	301	73	Yemen	120
24	Taiwan	770	49	Bulgaria	300	74	Slovakia	115
25	Turkey	683	50	Croatia	294	75	Georgia	106

Rank	Country/Entity	Petroleum Refining Capacity, 1997 (thousand barrels per day)	Rank	Country/Entity	Petroleum Refining Capacity, 1997 (thousand barrels per day)	Rank	Country/Entity	Petroleum Refining Capacity, 1997 (thousand barrels per day)
76	Jordan	100	92	Lebanon	38	108	Nicaragua	17
77	New Zealand	91	93	Jamaica	36	109	Senegal	17
78	Kenya	86	94	Tunisia	34	110	Martinique	16
79	Oman	85	95	Angola	32	111	Tanzania	16
80	North Korea	71	96	Myanmar (Burma)	32	112	Costa Rica	15
81	Ireland	65	97	Bangladesh	31	113	Liberia	15
82	Côte d'Ivoire	64	98	Ghana	27	114	Madagascar	15
83	Panama	60	99	Cyprus	26	115	Honduras	14
84	Qatar	58	100	Zambia	25	116	Slovenia	12
85	Macedonia	51	101	Sudan	22	117	Kyrgyzstan	10
86	Dominican Republic	50	102	Congo, Rep. of	21	118	Sierra Leone	10
87	Bolivia	48	103	El Salvador	21	119	Somalia	10
88	Sri Lanka	48	104	Guatemala	20	120	Brunei	9
89	Cameroon	42	105	Eritrea	18	121	Paraguay	8
90	Albania	40	106	Congo, Dem. Rep. of	17	122	Barbados	4
91	Uruguay	40	107	Gabon	17			

Source: World Energy Statistics

13.8 Crude Petroleum Consumption

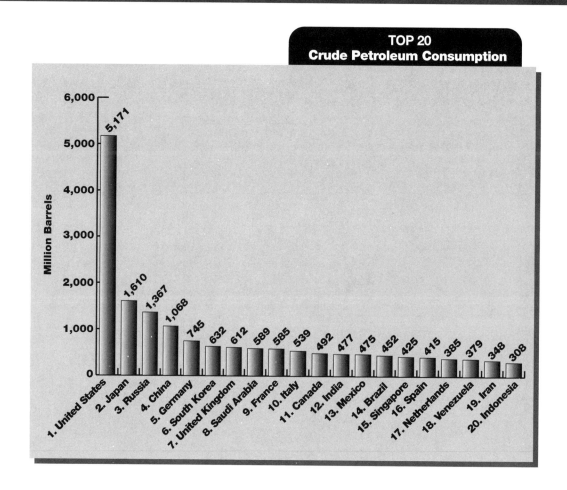

TOP 20
Crude Petroleum Consumption

Rank	Country/Entity	Petroleum Consumption, 1995 (million barrels)	Rank	Country/Entity	Petroleum Consumption, 1995 (million barrels)	Rank	Country/Entity	Petroleum Consumption, 1995 (million barrels)
21	Kuwait	289	57	Chile	58	93	Sudan	8
22	Iraq	208	58	Ecuador	53	94	Gabon	7
23	Australia	205	59	Hungary	51	95	Ghana	7
24	Belgium	192	60	Uzbekistan	51	96	Jamaica	7
25	Egypt	192	61	Morocco	47	97	Mauritania	7
26	Turkey	186	62	Pakistan	47	98	Myanmar (Burma)	7
27	Thailand	165	63	Puerto Rico	45	99	Cyprus	6
28	Algeria	164	64	Czech Republic	43	100	Ethiopia	6
29	Argentina	163	65	Cuba	40	101	Martinique	6
30	South Africa	136	66	Trinidad and Tobago	38	102	Senegal	6
31	Ukraine	125	67	Croatia	37	103	El Salvador	5
32	Sweden	124	68	New Zealand	35	104	Nicaragua	5
33	Virgin Islands (U.S.)	118	69	Yemen	35	105	Costa Rica	4
34	Malaysia	116	70	Slovakia	34	106	Tanzania	4
35	Romania	116	71	Switzerland	33	107	Zambia	4
36	Philippines	114	72	Turkmenistan	29	108	Albania	3
37	Libya	113	73	Oman	26	109	Congo, Rep. of	3
38	Greece	107	74	Côte d'Ivoire	25	110	Georgia	3
39	Poland	100	75	Jordan	23	111	Honduras	3
40	Netherlands Antilles	99	76	Lithuania	23	112	Lebanon	3
41	Colombia	98	77	Qatar	22	113	Slovenia	3
42	Belarus	97	78	Ireland	16	114	Aruba	2
43	Portugal	94	79	North Korea	16	115	Barbados	2
44	Norway	93	80	Bosnia and Herzegovina	15	116	Brunei	2
45	Bahrain	91	81	Dominican Republic	15	117	Paraguay	2
46	Israel	89	82	Sri Lanka	14	118	Sierra Leone	2
47	Syria	86	83	Tunisia	14	119	Madagascar	1.40
48	Azerbaijan	74	84	Kenya	12	120	Suriname	1.40
49	Denmark	74	85	Angola	11	121	Armenia	1
50	United Arab Emirates	74	86	Bangladesh	10	122	Tajikistan	1
51	Kazakhstan	69	87	Bolivia	10	123	Macedonia	0.90
52	Nigeria	65	88	Uruguay	10	124	Papua New Guinea	0.60
53	Finland	63	89	Yugoslavia	10	125	Kyrgyzstan	0.50
54	Peru	62	90	Cameroon	9	126	Congo, Dem. Rep. of	0.40
55	Austria	61	91	Panama	9	127	Vietnam	0.30
56	Bulgaria	59	92	Guatemala	8	128	Equatorial Guinea	0.01

Source: World Energy Statistics

13.9 Crude Petroleum Reserves

Rank	Country/Entity	Petroleum Reserves (million barrels)	Rank	Country/Entity	Petroleum Reserves (million barrels)	Rank	Country/Entity	Petroleum Reserves (million barrels)
1	Saudi Arabia	261,500	19	United Kingdom	4,517	37	Peru	808
2	Russia	155,146	20	India	4,333	38	Italy	685
3	Iraq	112,000	21	Malaysia	4,000	39	Vietnam	600
4	Kuwait	96,500	22	Yemen	4,000	40	Trinidad and Tobago	551
5	United Arab Emirates	93,800	23	Qatar	3,700	41	Cameroon	400
6	Iran	93,000	24	Egypt	3,696	42	Germany	385
7	Venezuela	64,878	25	Azerbaijan	3,300	43	Tunisia	308
8	Mexico	48,796	26	Turkmenistan	3,000	44	Chile	300
9	Libya	29,500	27	Colombia	2,800	45	Sudan	300
10	United States	22,351	28	Syria	2,500	46	Thailand	295
11	Nigeria	15,521	29	Argentina	2,386	47	Papua New Guinea	275
12	Norway	11,234	30	Ecuador	2,115	48	Turkey	260
13	Algeria	9,200	31	Australia	1,800	49	Philippines	213
14	Angola	5,412	32	Romania	1,606	50	Bahrain	210
15	Oman	5,138	33	Congo, Rep. of	1,506	51	Pakistan	208
16	Indonesia	4,980	34	Brunei	1,350	52	Guatemala	200
17	Canada	4,894	35	Gabon	1,340	53	Congo, Dem. Rep. of	187
18	Brazil	4,800	36	Denmark	957	54	Albania	165

Rank	Country/Entity	Petroleum Reserves (million barrels)	Rank	Country/Entity	Petroleum Reserves (million barrels)	Rank	Country/Entity	Petroleum Reserves (million barrels)
55	New Zealand	135	66	Japan	50	77	Slovakia	9
56	Bolivia	132	67	Myanmar (Burma)	50	78	Slovenia	7
57	Hungary	120	68	Poland	40	79	Czech Republic	6
58	France	117	69	Spain	30	80	Bangladesh	5
59	Côte d'Ivoire	100	70	Benin	29	81	Israel	4
60	Cuba	100	71	South Africa	27	82	Taiwan	4
61	Netherlands	88	72	China	24	83	Barbados	2
62	Yugoslavia	78	73	Ghana	17	84	Morocco	1.2
63	Austria	76	74	Bulgaria	15	85	Ethiopia	0.4
64	Suriname	74	75	Equatorial Guinea	12	86	Jordan	0.3
65	Croatia	55	76	Greece	12			

Source: World Energy Statistics

Natural Gas

Natural gas is used in industrialized countries both as a fuel and as an illuminant. The main constraint is the cost of building long pipelines, until recently the only means of transporting natural gas. Because of the short lifespan of proved resources, the construction of new pipelines is not commercially viable. Since its boiling point is very low, natural gas is not easy to liquefy or maintain in its liquid state. But cryogenic technology has now advanced to the point where such liquefaction is technologically possible, although the weight of containers made of stainless steel to transport liquefied natural gas limits its usefulness.

13.10 Natural Gas Production

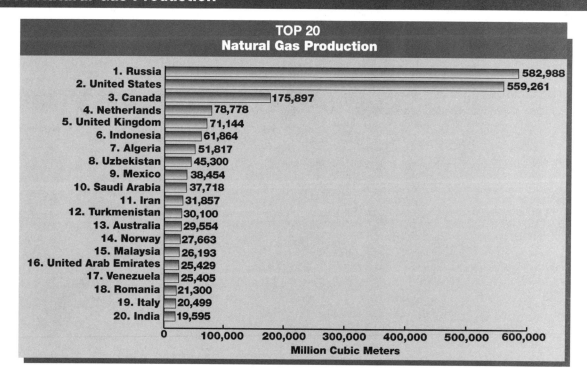

TOP 20
Natural Gas Production

Rank	Country	Million Cubic Meters
1.	Russia	582,988
2.	United States	559,261
3.	Canada	175,897
4.	Netherlands	78,778
5.	United Kingdom	71,144
6.	Indonesia	61,864
7.	Algeria	51,817
8.	Uzbekistan	45,300
9.	Mexico	38,454
10.	Saudi Arabia	37,718
11.	Iran	31,857
12.	Turkmenistan	30,100
13.	Australia	29,554
14.	Norway	27,663
15.	Malaysia	26,193
16.	United Arab Emirates	25,429
17.	Venezuela	25,405
18.	Romania	21,300
19.	Italy	20,499
20.	India	19,595

Rank	Country/Entity	Natural Gas Production, 1995 (million cubic meters)	Rank	Country/Entity	Natural Gas Production, 1995 (million cubic meters)	Rank	Country/Entity	Natural Gas Production, 1995 (million cubic meters)
21	Germany	18,998	42	Oman	4,361	63	Czech Republic	290
22	Pakistan	17,840	43	Nigeria	4,131	64	Belarus	262
23	Argentina	17,336	44	Azerbaijan	3,896	65	Slovakia	241
24	China	17,300	45	Iraq	3,426	66	Turkey	201
25	Ukraine	16,900	46	France	3,395	67	Spain	178
26	Qatar	13,499	47	Bolivia	3,279	68	Albania	136
27	Egypt	12,233	48	Brazil	2,880	69	Greece	119
28	Thailand	10,477	49	Ireland	2,500	70	Ecuador	102
29	Brunei	9,922	50	Japan	2,192	71	Gabon	102
30	Bangladesh	7,365	51	Croatia	1,869	72	Papua New Guinea	99
31	Libya	6,298	52	Austria	1,475	73	Georgia	45
32	Trinidad and Tobago	6,071	53	Myanmar (Burma)	1,430	74	Kyrgyzstan	34
33	Kuwait	5,975	54	Peru	1,303	75	Tajikistan	34
34	Kazakhstan	5,500	55	Chile	1,164	76	Israel	23
35	Hungary	5,479	56	Taiwan	841	77	Barbados	17
36	Bahrain	5,250	57	Yugoslavia	765	78	Morocco	17
37	Denmark	4,936	58	Vietnam	697	79	Bulgaria	11
38	New Zealand	4,763	59	Angola	561	80	Slovenia	11
39	Poland	4,593	60	Tunisia	337	81	Guatemala	8
40	Colombia	4,437	61	Afghanistan	294	82	Congo, Rep. of	2
41	Syria	4,412	62	Jordan	294	83	Belgium	1

Source: World Energy Statistics

13.11 Natural Gas Reserves

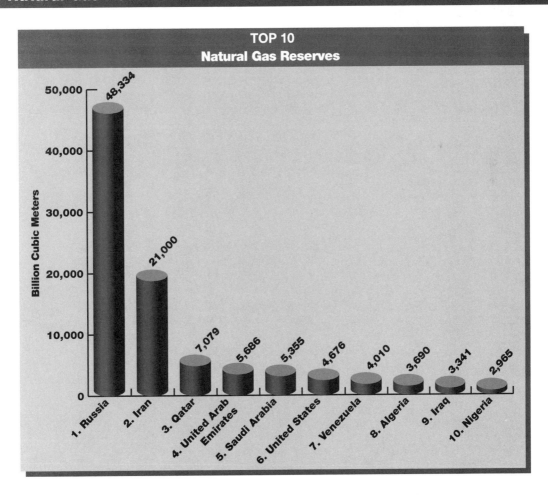

Rank	Country/Entity	Natural Gas Reserves (billion cubic meters)	Rank	Country/Entity	Natural Gas Reserves (billion cubic meters)	Rank	Country/Entity	Natural Gas Reserves (billion cubic meters)
11	Turkmenistan	2,900	40	Colombia	234	69	Ethiopia	25
12	Malaysia	2,271	41	Thailand	202	70	South Africa	25
13	Indonesia	2,046	42	Peru	200	71	Guinea	24
14	Canada	1,929	43	Brazil	154	72	Côte d'Ivoire	23
15	Mexico	1,916	44	Poland	149	73	Austria	22
16	Uzbekistan	1,900	45	Bahrain	147	74	Croatia	22
17	Netherlands	1,815	46	Vietnam	142	75	Tanzania	21
18	Kazakhstan	1,800	47	Bolivia	128	76	France	19
19	Kuwait	1,498	48	Cameroon	110	77	Spain	17
20	Norway	1,352	49	Denmark	109	78	Slovakia	15
21	Libya	1,311	50	Philippines	109	79	Gabon	14
22	China	1,171	51	Ecuador	105	80	Ireland	11
23	Ukraine	1,100	52	Chile	102	81	Turkey	9
24	Oman	850	53	Azerbaijan	100	82	Greece	8
25	United Kingdom	700	54	Afghanistan	99	83	Ghana	6
26	India	685	55	Hungary	94	84	Jordan	6
27	Pakistan	623	56	Congo, Rep. of	91	85	Somalia	6
28	Argentina	619	57	Namibia	85	86	Bulgaria	4
29	Egypt	576	58	Sudan	85	87	Czech Republic	4
30	Australia	550	59	Taiwan	76	88	Slovenia	4
31	Yemen	479	60	New Zealand	68	89	Cuba	3
32	Brunei	399	61	Tunisia	68	90	Albania	2
33	Romania	396	62	Mozambique	57	91	Madagascar	2
34	Trinidad and Tobago	350	63	Rwanda	57	92	Benin	1.2
35	Germany	329	64	Angola	48	93	Morocco	1.1
36	Myanmar (Burma)	311	65	Yugoslavia	45	94	Congo, Dem. Rep. of	1.0
37	Italy	297	66	Papua New Guinea	42	95	Guatemala	0.3
38	Bangladesh	288	67	Equatorial Guinea	37	96	Israel	0.3
39	Syria	235	68	Japan	30	97	Barbados	0.1

Source: World Energy Statistics

Electricity

Electricity has the broadest range of uses as a source of energy. Electricity is produced in many ways: thermal/fossil fuels (such as coal and oil), hydro, and nuclear. Measured in millions of kilowatt-hours, annual production of electricity ranges generally between 50 percent and 60 percent of total production capacity. Total consumption (residential and nonresidential) is equal to the total electricity requirement less transformation and distribution losses. Most advanced countries have electricity available to 100 percent of their national territories, but in the majority of the developing world, electricity is available only in urban areas.

13.12 Electricity Production

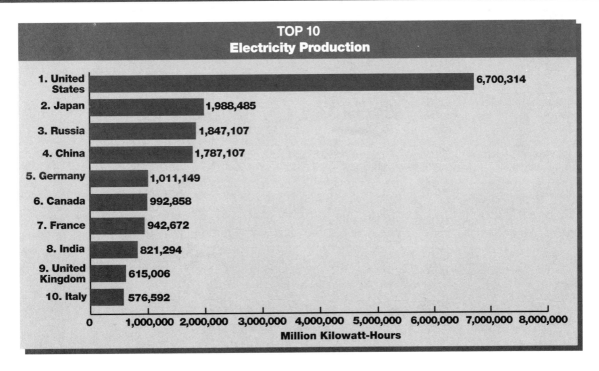

TOP 10
Electricity Production

Rank	Country	Million Kilowatt-Hours
1.	United States	6,700,314
2.	Japan	1,988,485
3.	Russia	1,847,107
4.	China	1,787,107
5.	Germany	1,011,149
6.	Canada	992,858
7.	France	942,672
8.	India	821,294
9.	United Kingdom	615,006
10.	Italy	576,592

Rank	Country/Entity	Electricity Production (million kilowatt-hours)	Rank	Country/Entity	Electricity Production (million kilowatt-hours)	Rank	Country/Entity	Electricity Production (million kilowatt-hours)
11	Brazil	517,155	25	Saudi Arabia	183,382	39	Bulgaria	105,882
12	Ukraine	475,169	26	Indonesia	177,793	40	Yugoslavia	103,184
13	Spain	400,893	27	Venezuela	174,981	41	Uzbekistan	100,057
14	Mexico	387,691	28	Argentina	171,784	42	Denmark	97,621
15	Australia	347,711	29	Netherlands	166,545	43	Colombia	94,240
16	South Africa	314,458	30	Kazakhstan	166,072	44	Malaysia	92,856
17	South Korea	309,710	31	Thailand	153,685	45	Hong Kong	88,441
18	Sweden	294,537	32	Austria	152,774	46	Iraq	83,220
19	Poland	258,113	33	Switzerland	145,915	47	North Korea	83,220
20	Norway	242,424	34	Egypt	140,291	48	Portugal	82,151
21	Iran	230,011	35	Belgium	130,664	49	Greece	78,332
22	Romania	195,138	36	Finland	126,381	50	Philippines	67,645
23	Taiwan	191,826	37	Pakistan	122,859	51	New Zealand	65,875
24	Turkey	183,548	38	Czech Republic	121,344	52	Belarus	64,736

Rank	Country/Entity	Electricity Production (million kilowatt-hours)	Rank	Country/Entity	Electricity Production (million kilowatt-hours)	Rank	Country/Entity	Electricity Production (million kilowatt-hours)
53	Slovakia	62,327	103	Côte d'Ivoire	10,275	153	Sierra Leone	1,104
54	Hungary	61,425	104	Costa Rica	10,205	154	Congo, Rep. of	1,034
55	Kuwait	61,215	105	Trinidad and Tobago	10,074	155	Martinique	1,007
56	Paraguay	57,229	106	Jordan	9,864	156	Guyana	999
57	Lithuania	55,495	107	Iceland	9,470	157	Northern Mariana Islands	999
58	Algeria	52,621	108	Bahrain	9,461	158	Greenland	929
59	Chile	52,157	109	Panama	8,383	159	Mauritania	920
60	Nigeria	51,518	110	Mongolia	7,893	160	Faroe Islands	806
61	United Arab Emirates	47,216	111	Yemen	7,096	161	Aruba	788
62	Azerbaijan	45,894	112	Kenya	7,087	162	French Polynesia	780
63	Libya	40,296	113	Bolivia	7,052	163	Mali	762
64	Puerto Rico	40,077	114	Guatemala	6,710	164	Djibouti	745
65	Georgia	39,928	115	El Salvador	6,579	165	Burkina Faso	683
66	Singapore	39,534	116	Cyprus	6,123	166	Somalia	613
67	Vietnam	39,420	117	Cameroon	5,493	167	Niger	552
68	Israel	39,245	118	Angola	5,405	168	Palau	543
69	Tajikistan	38,921	119	Tanzania	4,757	169	Western Sahara	491
70	Ireland	38,535	120	Sudan	4,380	170	Burundi	377
71	Syria	37,931	121	Afghanistan	4,327	171	Central African Republic	377
72	Cuba	34,935	122	Papua New Guinea	4,292	172	Cambodia	307
73	Turkmenistan	34,602	123	Brunei	4,143	173	Rwanda	298
74	Peru	33,560	124	Ethiopia	4,065	174	Togo	298
75	Morocco	33,244	125	Nicaragua	4,003	175	American Samoa	289
76	Kyrgyzstan	32,359	126	Suriname	3,723	176	Gibraltar	263
77	Croatia	31,825	127	Bahamas	3,513	177	Chad	254
78	Armenia	31,387	128	Guadeloupe	3,399	178	Gambia	254
79	Estonia	28,794	129	Bhutan	3,206	179	Seychelles	245
80	Bangladesh	28,768	130	Mauritius	3,189	180	Antigua and Barbuda	228
81	Congo, Dem. Rep. of	27,971	131	Liberia	2,908	181	Belize	219
82	Moldova	23,083	132	Virgin Islands (U.S.)	2,829	182	Saint Lucia	193
83	Ecuador	22,242	133	Macau	2,733	183	Samoa	166
84	Slovenia	22,058	134	Gabon	2,716	184	Maldives	149
85	Zambia	21,339	135	Honduras	2,672	185	Saint Kitts and Nevis	140
86	Bosnia and Herzegovina	21,085	136	Guam	2,646	186	Benin	131
87	Mozambique	20,875	137	Réunion	2,619	187	Saint Vincent and the Grenadines	123
88	Zimbabwe	18,816	138	Nepal	2,558			
89	Latvia	18,098	139	Laos	2,243	188	Solomon Islands	105
90	Uruguay	17,976	140	New Caledonia	2,216	189	Guinea-Bissau	96
91	Albania	16,574	141	Malta	2,190	190	Mayotte	96
92	Oman	15,277	142	Senegal	2,024	191	Vanuatu	96
93	Tunisia	15,207	143	Madagascar	1,927	192	Nauru	88
94	Sri Lanka	13,622	144	Netherlands Antilles	1,927	193	Grenada	79
95	Macedonia	13,087	145	Fiji	1,752	194	Dominica	70
96	Dominican Republic	12,702	146	Malawi	1,621	195	Cape Verde	61
97	Qatar	11,957	147	Guinea	1,542	196	Tonga	61
98	Myanmar (Burma)	11,773	148	French Guiana	1,445	197	São Tomé and Príncipe	53
99	Luxembourg	11,011	149	Uganda	1,419	198	Comoros	44
100	Lebanon	10,687	150	Haiti	1,340	199	Equatorial Guinea	44
101	Ghana	10,398	151	Bermuda	1,279	200	Kiribati	18
102	Jamaica	10,354	152	Barbados	1,226			

Source: World Energy Statistics

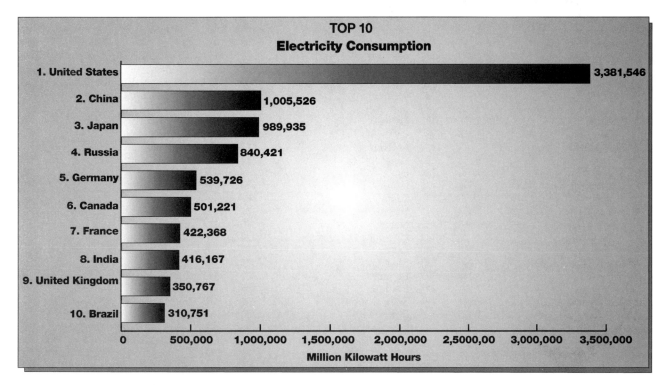

TOP 10 Electricity Consumption

Rank	Country	Million Kilowatt Hours
1. United States		3,381,546
2. China		1,005,526
3. Japan		989,935
4. Russia		840,421
5. Germany		539,726
6. Canada		501,221
7. France		422,368
8. India		416,167
9. United Kingdom		350,767
10. Brazil		310,751

Rank	Country/Entity	Electricity Consumption (million kilowatt-hours)	Rank	Country/Entity	Electricity Consumption (million kilowatt-hours)	Rank	Country/Entity	Electricity Consumption (million kilowatt-hours)
11	Italy	278,533	39	Malaysia	46,609	67	Croatia	13,359
12	South Korea	205,102	40	Colombia	45,619	68	Morocco	12,724
13	Ukraine	191,200	41	Greece	42,348	69	Bangladesh	11,689
14	South Africa	188,975	42	Bulgaria	41,629	70	Lithuania	11,220
15	Australia	173,404	43	Hungary	36,422	71	Cuba	11,189
16	Spain	170,866	44	North Korea	36,000	72	Slovenia	10,996
17	Mexico	150,039	45	Denmark	35,996	73	Kyrgyzstan	10,981
18	Sweden	145,334	46	New Zealand	34,375	74	Zimbabwe	10,350
19	Poland	136,192	47	Portugal	34,177	75	Moldova	8,892
20	Norway	116,774	48	Hong Kong	33,979	76	Ecuador	8,349
21	Saudi Arabia	99,833	49	Philippines	33,426	77	Oman	8,258
22	Netherlands	92,224	50	Belarus	32,077	78	Turkmenistan	7,780
23	Thailand	84,280	51	Chile	29,906	79	Tunisia	7,620
24	Iran	81,330	52	Iraq	29,000	80	Georgia	7,570
25	Turkey	81,038	53	Israel	28,790	81	Uruguay	7,536
26	Belgium	78,500	54	Slovakia	24,415	82	Estonia	6,847
27	Venezuela	74,752	55	Kuwait	24,126	83	Dominican Republic	6,506
28	Kazakhstan	73,496	56	Singapore	22,057	84	Zambia	6,310
29	Finland	70,859	57	Algeria	19,441	85	Luxembourg	6,243
30	Argentina	69,291	58	United Arab Emirates	19,070	86	Latvia	6,235
31	Indonesia	68,804	59	Libya	18,000	87	Macedonia	6,114
32	Pakistan	60,155	60	Ireland	17,863	88	Ghana	5,935
33	Romania	59,565	61	Azerbaijan	17,200	89	Jamaica	5,829
34	Czech Republic	58,047	62	Peru	16,759	90	Qatar	5,738
35	Switzerland	55,803	63	Syria	15,300	91	Jordan	5,616
36	Austria	54,117	64	Vietnam	14,867	92	Armenia	5,574
37	Egypt	48,864	65	Nigeria	14,810	93	Lebanon	5,573
38	Uzbekistan	46,800	66	Tajikistan	13,960	94	Iceland	4,981

Rank	Country/Entity	Electricity Consumption (million kilowatt-hours)	Rank	Country/Entity	Electricity Consumption (million kilowatt-hours)	Rank	Country/Entity	Electricity Consumption (million kilowatt-hours)
95	Congo, Dem. Rep. of	4,898	121	Sudan	1,331	147	Djibouti	184
96	Costa Rica	4,868	122	Ethiopia	1,265	148	Mauritania	152
97	Sri Lanka	4,800	123	Mozambique	1,164	149	Burundi	149
98	Bahrain	4,750	124	Mauritius	1,120	150	Belize	148
99	Albania	4,479	125	Nepal	1,075	151	Seychelles	128
100	Trinidad and Tobago	4,229	126	Bahamas	1,028	152	Saint Lucia	113
101	Kenya	3,919	127	Gabon	940	153	Central African Republic	102
102	Myanmar (Burma)	3,780	128	Malawi	803	154	Antigua and Barbuda	98
103	Paraguay	3,692	129	Senegal	774	155	Chad	89
104	Panama	3,606	130	Uganda	677	156	Saint Kitts and Nevis	86
105	El Salvador	3,370	131	Barbados	613	157	Gambia	74
106	Guatemala	3,229	132	Madagascar	611	158	Grenada	71
107	Bolivia	3,030	133	Congo, Rep. of	547	159	Saint Vincent and the Grenadines	65
108	Mongolia	3,010	134	Fiji	544			
109	Cameroon	2,746	135	Guinea	543	160	Samoa	65
110	Honduras	2,746	136	Togo	408	161	Maldives	57
111	Cyprus	2,473	137	Haiti	407	162	Guinea-Bissau	43
112	Yemen	1,980	138	Niger	370	163	Cape Verde	39
113	Côte d'Ivoire	1,913	139	Guyana	334	164	Dominica	37
114	Angola	1,870	140	Laos	295	165	Solomon Islands	32
115	Papua New Guinea	1,790	141	Mali	290	166	Vanuatu	30
116	Tanzania	1,738	142	Benin	269	167	Equatorial Guinea	20
117	Nicaragua	1,699	143	Bhutan	246	168	Comoros	16
118	Suriname	1,614	144	Sierra Leone	241	169	São Tomé and Príncipe	15
119	Brunei	1,560	145	Burkina Faso	220			
120	Malta	1,512	146	Cambodia	194			

Source: World Energy Statistics

13.14 Electricity Consumption per Capita

Rank	Country/Entity	Electricity Consumption per Capita, 1995 (kilowatt-hours)	Rank	Country/Entity	Electricity Consumption per Capita, 1995 (kilowatt-hours)	Rank	Country/Entity	Electricity Consumption per Capita, 1995 (kilowatt-hours)
1	Norway	26,956	27	New Caledonia	6,492	53	Suriname	3,780
2	Iceland	18,517	28	United Kingdom	6,016	54	Oman	3,742
3	Canada	17,047	29	Netherlands	5,957	55	Faroe Islands	3,723
4	Sweden	16,538	30	Slovenia	5,712	56	Ukraine	3,694
5	Luxembourg	15,339	31	Russia	5,661	57	Bahamas	3,685
6	Kuwait	14,267	32	Czech Republic	5,656	58	Yugoslavia	3,627
7	Finland	13,875	33	Hong Kong	5,549	59	Hungary	3,604
8	United States	12,663	34	Guam	5,500	60	Poland	3,533
9	Qatar	10,471	35	Saudi Arabia	5,469	61	Portugal	3,482
10	Virgin Islands (U.S.)	10,200	36	Brunei	5,324	62	Venezuela	3,422
11	Australia	9,706	37	Israel	5,211	63	Macau	3,370
12	New Zealand	9,653	38	Puerto Rico	5,143	64	Libya	3,329
13	United Arab Emirates	8,629	39	Ireland	5,038	65	Cyprus	3,319
14	Bahrain	8,528	40	Guernsey	4,997	66	Trinidad and Tobago	3,286
15	Bermuda	8,270	41	Taiwan	4,946	67	Gibraltar	3,143
16	Japan	7,915	42	Bulgaria	4,892	68	Belarus	3,099
17	Switzerland	7,754	43	Italy	4,867	69	French Guiana	3,061
18	Belgium	7,752	44	Estonia	4,601	70	Lithuania	3,003
19	Netherlands Antilles	7,577	45	Slovakia	4,574	71	Croatia	2,965
20	France	7,282	46	South Korea	4,567	72	Nauru	2,909
21	Denmark	6,892	47	Greenland	4,431	73	Macedonia	2,836
22	Austria	6,727	48	Kazakhstan	4,370	74	Romania	2,621
23	Singapore	6,630	49	Spain	4,312	75	Kyrgyzstan	2,462
24	Germany	6,615	50	Malta	4,120	76	Latvia	2,459
25	Aruba	6,614	51	Greece	4,051	77	Tajikistan	2,395
26	Jersey	6,579	52	South Africa	3,992	78	Guadeloupe	2,392

Rank	Country/Entity	Electricity Consumption per Capita, 1995 (kilowatt-hours)	Rank	Country/Entity	Electricity Consumption per Capita, 1995 (kilowatt-hours)	Rank	Country/Entity	Electricity Consumption per Capita, 1995 (kilowatt-hours)
79	Martinique	2,382	121	Saint Lucia	796	162	Bhutan	139
80	Uruguay	2,365	122	Egypt	787	163	Nigeria	133
81	Jamaica	2,362	123	Zambia	781	164	Yemen	132
82	Barbados	2,349	124	Grenada	772	165	São Tomé and Príncipe	113
83	Malaysia	2,314	125	Paraguay	765	166	Congo, Dem. Rep. of	108
84	Azerbaijan	2,284	126	Ecuador	729	167	Cape Verde	101
85	Chile	2,105	127	Peru	712	168	Togo	100
86	Saint Kitts and Nevis	2,098	128	Belize	695	169	Bangladesh	99
87	Uzbekistan	2,056	129	Fiji	694	170	Senegal	93
88	American Samoa	2,037	130	Algeria	692	171	Kiribati	90
89	Moldova	2,004	131	Bosnia and Herzegovina	675	172	Solomon Islands	85
90	Argentina	1,993	132	El Salvador	595	173	Myanmar (Burma)	84
91	Brazil	1,954	133	Saint Vincent and the Grenadines	580	174	Malawi	83
92	Turkmenistan	1,909				175	Guinea	74
93	Lebanon	1,852	134	Dominica	521	176	Gambia	67
94	Seychelles	1,753	135	Philippines	493	177	Mauritania	67
95	Réunion	1,722	136	Honduras	486	178	Mozambique	67
96	Mexico	1,646	137	Morocco	480	179	Laos	60
97	North Korea	1,629	138	India	448	180	Tanzania	58
98	French Polynesia	1,594	139	Pakistan	441	181	Haiti	57
99	Armenia	1,535	140	Papua New Guinea	416	182	Sierra Leone	57
100	Antigua and Barbuda	1,485	141	Nicaragua	412	183	Benin	50
101	Thailand	1,447	142	Bolivia	409	184	Equatorial Guinea	50
102	Iraq	1,443	143	Guyana	402	185	Nepal	50
103	Costa Rica	1,422	144	Samoa	394	186	Sudan	50
104	Georgia	1,389	145	Western Sahara	351	187	Madagascar	41
105	Panama	1,371	146	Indonesia	348	188	Guinea-Bissau	40
106	Turkey	1,332	147	Ghana	342	189	Niger	40
107	Albania	1,324	148	Djibouti	306	190	Afghanistan	38
108	Colombia	1,274	149	Guatemala	304	191	Rwanda	34
109	Mongolia	1,222	150	Tonga	296	192	Uganda	34
110	Iran	1,190	151	Mayotte	276	193	Central African Republic	31
111	Syria	1,077	152	Sri Lanka	268	194	Somalia	29
112	Jordan	1,045	153	Liberia	229	195	Mali	27
113	Cuba	1,021	154	Maldives	224	196	Comoros	26
114	Mauritius	1,003	155	Congo, Rep. of	211	197	Burundi	25
115	Zimbabwe	925	156	Cameroon	208	198	Ethiopia	24
116	Gabon	874	157	Vietnam	201	199	Burkina Faso	21
117	Palau	856	158	Vanuatu	178	200	Cambodia	19
118	Tunisia	848	159	Angola	173	201	Chad	14
119	China	839	160	Kenya	144			
120	Dominican Republic	832	161	Côte d'Ivoire	140			

Source: World Energy Statistics

13.15 Nuclear Reactors

With a membership between six and twelve countries, the Nuclear Club is one of the most exclusive clubs in the world. Most nuclear reactors are designed for the production of electricity. At one point in the 1960s, nuclear energy was regarded as the wave of the future, but rising environmental activism in the 1980s and 1990s placed advocates of nuclear power on the defensive. Further, major nuclear accidents or meltdowns in facilities such as Three-Mile Island in the United States in 1979 and Chernobyl in the Soviet Union (now Ukraine) in 1986 have had a chilling effect on the nuclear industry's plans for expansion. Nuclear plants currently in operation are getting old, and political opposition may prevent new ones from being built.

Rank	Country/Entity	Nuclear Power Reactors	Rank	Country/Entity	Nuclear Power Reactors	Rank	Country/Entity	Nuclear Power Reactors
1	United States	107	12	Spain	9	23	Lithuania	2
2	France	56	13	Belgium	7	24	Mexico	2
3	Japan	53	14	Bulgaria	6	25	South Africa	2
4	United Kingdom	35	15	Taiwan	6	26	Armenia	1
5	Russia	29	16	Switzerland	5	27	Brazil	1
6	Canada	21	17	Czech Republic	4	28	Netherlands	1
7	Germany	20	18	Finland	4	29	Pakistan	1
8	South Korea	14	19	Hungary	4	30	Romania	1
9	Ukraine	14	20	Slovakia	4	31	Slovenia	1
10	Sweden	12	21	Argentina	2			
11	India	10	22	China	2			

Source: World Data

13.16 Pipelines

There are three types of pipelines: those carrying crude petroleum, those carrying refined products, and those carrying natural gas. The construction of pipelines involves complex engineering problems and is very expensive. Therefore, new pipelines are built only where the reserves of natural gas or oil to be transported are large enough to justify the cost. But once constructed, pipelines are among the most efficient and cheapest form of transportation for oil and gas.

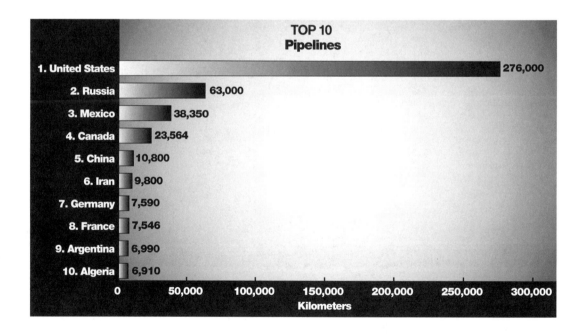

TOP 10 Pipelines

Rank	Country	Kilometers
1.	United States	276,000
2.	Russia	63,000
3.	Mexico	38,350
4.	Canada	23,564
5.	China	10,800
6.	Iran	9,800
7.	Germany	7,590
8.	France	7,546
9.	Argentina	6,990
10.	Algeria	6,910

Rank	Country/Entity	Pipelines (kilometers)	Rank	Country/Entity	Pipelines (kilometers)	Rank	Country/Entity	Pipelines (kilometers)
11	Venezuela	6,850	15	Iraq	5,075	19	Kazakhstan	4,350
12	Saudi Arabia	6,550	16	Nigeria	5,042	20	Romania	4,229
13	Brazil	5,804	17	Colombia	4,935	21	Turkey	4,059
14	India	5,692	18	Libya	4,826	22	Ukraine	3,930

Rank	Country/Entity	Pipelines (kilometers)	Rank	Country/Entity	Pipelines (kilometers)	Rank	Country/Entity	Pipelines (kilometers)
23	United Kingdom	3,926	50	Tunisia	883	77	Qatar	235
24	Italy	3,851	51	United Arab Emirates	830	78	Zimbabwe	212
25	Australia	3,000	52	Sudan	815	79	Jordan	209
26	Indonesia	2,961	53	Peru	800	80	Albania	200
27	South Africa	2,679	54	Austria	725	81	Angola	179
28	Belarus	2,570	55	Bulgaria	718	82	Costa Rica	176
29	Bolivia	2,380	56	Croatia	690	83	Bosnia and Herzegovina	174
30	Poland	2,346	57	Denmark	688	84	New Zealand	160
31	Ecuador	2,158	58	Yemen	676	85	Vietnam	150
32	Spain	2,059	59	Georgia	670	86	Laos	136
33	Syria	1,819	60	Taiwan	615	87	Panama	130
34	Egypt	1,767	61	Mozambique	595	88	Lithuania	105
35	Azerbaijan	1,760	62	Greece	573	89	Dominican Republic	104
36	Zambia	1,724	63	Brunei	553	90	Portugal	80
37	Chile	1,540	64	Yugoslavia	545	91	Bahrain	72
38	Latvia	1,530	65	Kenya	483	92	Lebanon	72
39	Netherlands	1,383	66	South Korea	455	93	Thailand	67
40	Myanmar (Burma)	1,343	67	Japan	406	94	Sri Lanka	62
41	Belgium	1,328	68	Congo, Dem. Rep. of	390	95	Nicaragua	56
42	Malaysia	1,307	69	Morocco	362	96	Norway	53
43	Oman	1,300	70	Philippines	357	97	Luxembourg	48
44	Hungary	1,204	71	Switzerland	314	98	North Korea	37
45	Pakistan	1,135	72	Slovenia	290	99	Congo, Rep. of	25
46	Trinidad and Tobago	1,051	73	Uzbekistan	290	100	Somalia	15
47	Israel	998	74	Gabon	284	101	Jamaica	10
48	Tanzania	982	75	Guatemala	275			
49	Kuwait	917	76	Turkmenistan	250			

Source: World Energy Statistics

13.17 Coal Production

Coal is the least efficient and ecologically the most harmful of all fossil fuels. Its production, especially through strip mining, often disfigures the landscape and leaves permanent scars. Its burning adds to air pollution. Nevertheless, it is the most plentiful of all fossil fuels and, as such, may be the most significant source of energy after other sources have been depleted. Most coal reserves are located in the consuming coun-tries, where it provides a viable alternative to oil.

Rank	Country/Entity	Coal Production, 1995 (thousand metric tons)	Rank	Country/Entity	Coal Production, 1995 (thousand metric tons)	Rank	Country/Entity	Coal Production, 1995 (thousand metric tons)
1	China	1,360,730	14	Greece	57,662	27	Mexico	8,886
2	United States	937,099	15	Turkey	55,073	28	Vietnam	7,452
3	Russia	326,828	16	United Kingdom	52,630	29	Macedonia	7,249
4	India	287,682	17	Romania	41,121	30	Japan	6,277
5	Germany	251,615	18	Yugoslavia	40,010	31	South Korea	5,720
6	Australia	241,806	19	Indonesia	36,104	32	Brazil	5,173
7	Poland	200,713	20	Bulgaria	30,830	33	Slovenia	4,884
8	South Africa	197,001	21	Spain	28,403	34	Mongolia	4,871
9	North Korea	97,000	22	Colombia	26,020	35	Venezuela	4,640
10	Kazakhstan	87,011	23	Thailand	18,421	36	New Zealand	3,517
11	Ukraine	83,600	24	Hungary	14,588	37	Uzbekistan	3,100
12	Canada	74,942	25	Estonia	13,310	38	Pakistan	3,043
13	Czech Republic	70,947	26	France	9,045	39	Slovakia	2,310

Rank	Country/Entity	Coal Production, 1995 (thousand metric tons)	Rank	Country/Entity	Coal Production, 1995 (thousand metric tons)	Rank	Country/Entity	Coal Production, 1995 (thousand metric tons)
40	Zimbabwe	2,120	51	Argentina	305	62	Nigeria	50
41	Bosnia and Herzegovina	1,640	52	Norway	292	63	Georgia	40
42	Philippines	1,321	53	Taiwan	235	64	Mozambique	38
43	Austria	1,297	54	Niger	173	65	Tajikistan	30
44	Chile	1,078	55	Portugal	147	66	Algeria	22
45	Iran	1,000	56	Peru	143	67	Afghanistan	5
46	Kyrgyzstan	743	57	Albania	130	68	Tanzania	5
47	Morocco	649	58	Malaysia	112	69	Bhutan	2
48	Belgium	637	59	Croatia	108	70	Cameroon	1
49	Italy	380	60	Congo, Dem. Rep. of	95	71	Ireland	1
50	Zambia	360	61	Myanmar (Burma)	79	72	Laos	1

Source: World Energy Statistics

Chapter 14

Labor

14.1 Economically Active Population

Labor Force is the conventional term often used in lieu of the more complex concept of economically active population. According to the International Labor Organization, economically active population is defined as persons of all ages who are either employed or looking for work. It does not include students, people at home engaged in purely domestic duties, retired persons, persons wholly dependent on others, or persons living entirely on their own income. Persons engaged in illegal activities, such as smugglers, prostitutes, and drug dealers, are also excluded. Some countries exclude prisoners and persons in mental institutions, members of the armed forces, the unemployed, migrant workers, and persons holding part-time jobs. Poor countries with a large population, where there is substantial unemployment or a smaller female participation rate, may have a smaller labor force than countries with a smaller population but a higher participation and activity rate.

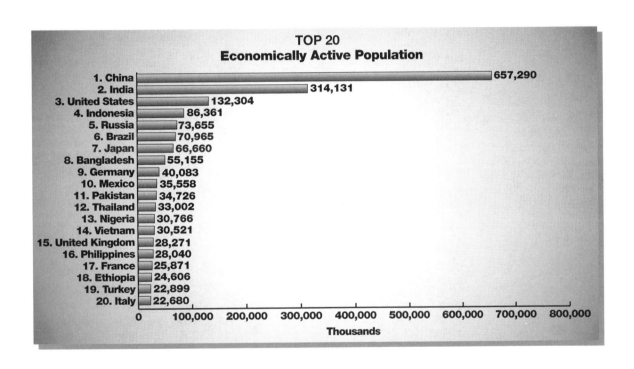

TOP 20 Economically Active Population

Rank	Country/Entity	Economically Active Population (thousands)
1. China		657,290
2. India		314,131
3. United States		132,304
4. Indonesia		86,361
5. Russia		73,655
6. Brazil		70,965
7. Japan		66,660
8. Bangladesh		55,155
9. Germany		40,083
10. Mexico		35,558
11. Pakistan		34,726
12. Thailand		33,002
13. Nigeria		30,766
14. Vietnam		30,521
15. United Kingdom		28,271
16. Philippines		28,040
17. France		25,871
18. Ethiopia		24,606
19. Turkey		22,899
20. Italy		22,680

Rank	Country/Entity	Econimically Active Population (thousands)	Rank	Country/Entity	Econimically Active Population (thousands)	Rank	Country/Entity	Econimically Active Population (thousands)
21	Ukraine	22,270	32	Romania	12,120	43	Malaysia	7,869
22	South Korea	20,797	33	South Africa	11,624	44	Netherlands	7,358
23	Egypt	17,572	34	Kenya	10,260	45	Nepal	7,340
24	Myanmar (Burma)	17,358	35	Colombia	9,558	46	Kazakhstan	6,976
25	Poland	17,004	36	Taiwan	9,310	47	Sudan	6,343
26	Spain	15,625	37	North Korea	9,084	48	Sri Lanka	6,115
27	Canada	14,928	38	Australia	9,066	49	Morocco	5,999
28	Iran	14,737	39	Peru	8,906	50	Mozambique	5,671
29	Argentina	14,345	40	Venezuela	8,611	51	Ghana	5,580
30	Congo, Dem. Rep. of	13,848	41	Uganda	8,365	52	Saudi Arabia	5,369
31	Tanzania	13,123	42	Uzbekistan	8,235	53	Algeria	5,341

Rank	Country/Entity	Econimically Active Population (thousands)	Rank	Country/Entity	Econimically Active Population (thousands)	Rank	Country/Entity	Econimically Active Population (thousands)
54	Madagascar	5,311	108	Guinea	1,823	162	Gaza Strip	173
55	Czech Republic	5,283	109	Singapore	1,748	163	Guadeloupe	172
56	Chile	5,274	110	New Zealand	1,742	164	Luxembourg	168
57	Portugal	4,806	111	Moldova	1,699	165	Martinique	165
58	Belarus	4,798	112	Kyrgyzstan	1,691	166	Iceland	149
59	Cameroon	4,740	113	Turkmenistan	1,680	167	Bahamas	139
60	Burkina Faso	4,679	114	Armenia	1,618	168	Barbados	137
61	Cuba	4,570	115	Sierra Leone	1,532	169	Malta	132
62	Sweden	4,319	116	Nicaragua	1,459	170	Cape Verde	121
63	Côte d'Ivoire	4,263	117	Ireland	1,443	171	Brunei	112
64	Greece	4,249	118	Togo	1,432	172	Equatorial Guinea	103
65	Belgium	4,237	119	Uruguay	1,344	173	Suriname	90
66	Angola	4,166	120	Albania	1,340	174	Netherlands Antilles	88
67	Iraq	4,127	121	Latvia	1,272	175	Belize	76
68	Hungary	4,095	122	Costa Rica	1,232	176	French Polynesia	75
69	Cambodia	4,010	123	Puerto Rico	1,228	177	Vanuatu	67
70	Afghanistan	3,941	124	Central African Republic	1,187	178	Guam	66
71	Austria	3,881	125	Libya	1,169	179	New Caledonia	66
72	Switzerland	3,860	126	Jamaica	1,091	180	Maldives	56
73	Bulgaria	3,738	127	Paraguay	1,039	181	Saint Lucia	53
74	Rwanda	3,649	128	Bosnia and Herzegovina	1,026	182	French Guiana	49
75	Zimbabwe	3,601	129	Panama	967	183	Jersey	48
76	Syria	3,485	130	Slovenia	952	184	Virgin Islands (U.S.)	47
77	Malawi	3,458	131	Macedonia	937	185	Samoa	46
78	Mali	3,438	132	Lebanon	904	186	Saint Vincent and the Grenadines	42
79	Ecuador	3,360	133	Jordan	859			
80	Senegal	3,249	134	Mongolia	845	187	Grenada	39
81	Somalia	3,215	135	Kuwait	746	188	São Tomé and Príncipe	35
82	Yugoslavia	3,182	136	Papua New Guinea	733	189	Bermuda	34
83	Hong Kong	3,068	137	Estonia	730	190	Isle of Man	33
84	Yemen	3,029	138	Oman	705	191	Kiribati	33
85	Zambia	2,928	139	Liberia	704	192	Tonga	32
86	Guatemala	2,898	140	United Arab Emirates	690	193	Aruba	31
87	Denmark	2,812	141	Mauritania	638	194	Micronesia	31
88	Burundi	2,780	142	Congo, Rep. of	563	195	Guernsey	30
89	Azerbaijan	2,698	143	Trinidad and Tobago	521	196	Solomon Islands	30
90	Haiti	2,679	144	Gabon	504	197	Seychelles	28
91	Bolivia	2,530	145	Lesotho	504	198	Mayotte	27
92	Finland	2,521	146	Namibia	494	199	Antigua and Barbuda	27
93	Slovakia	2,481	147	Guinea-Bissau	464	200	Northern Mariana Islands	27
94	Tunisia	2,361	148	Mauritius	463	201	Dominica	26
95	Niger	2,316	149	Botswana	441	202	Andorra	25
96	Norway	2,186	150	West Bank	357	203	Greenland	21
97	El Salvador	2,136	151	Gambia	326	204	Faroe Islands	18
98	Israel	2,100	152	Swaziland	326	205	Saint Kitts and Nevis	17
99	Benin	2,085	153	Cyprus	303	206	San Marino	17
100	Croatia	2,040	154	Qatar	293	207	Liechtenstein	16
101	Chad	2,016	155	Djibouti	282	208	American Samoa	14
102	Laos	2,014	156	Guyana	278	209	Gibraltar	13
103	Tajikistan	1,984	157	Fiji	241	210	Monaco	13
104	Lithuania	1,937	158	Réunion	234	211	Marshall Islands	12
105	Georgia	1,920	159	Bahrain	226	212	Palau	6
106	Dominican Republic	1,915	160	Comoros	215	213	Tuvalu	6
107	Honduras	1,866	161	Macau	187	214	Nauru	2

Source: Yearbook of Labor Statistics

Activity and Female Participation Rates

Two important structural concepts relating to the labor force of a country are the activity rate and the female participation rate. The former expresses the total number of gainfully employed persons as a percentage of the total population. Generally only between one-third and one-half of the total population are working for wages at any given time: the rest include children under legal working age, parents at home raising children, retired persons, persons in institutions, and so on. The female participation rate is the percentage of women in the working population. Modern societies have a greater female participation rate than more traditional ones and this ranking provides a clue to the degree of modernization in every society. However, unlike males, females have a highly volatile participation rate. Many tend to opt out of the employment market for domestic and personal reasons, and some go back and forth because they have no compelling reasons to keep working. No country counts housewives among working women, nor are they regarded as contributing to the Gross Domestic Product.

14.2 Activity Rate

Rank	Country/Entity	Activity Rate (percentage)	Rank	Country/Entity	Activity Rate (percentage)	Rank	Country/Entity	Activity Rate (percentage)
1	Tuvalu	65.3	37	Germany	49.1	73	Antigua and Barbuda	45.1
2	Djibouti	61.5	38	Estonia	48.9	74	Kiribati	45.1
3	Northern Mariana Islands	61.3	39	Laos	48.9	75	France	44.8
4	Singapore	58.5	40	Sweden	48.9	76	Mali	44.7
5	China	57.9	41	Portugal	48.8	77	Bahrain	44.6
6	Albania	57.4	42	New Zealand	48.7	78	North Korea	44.6
7	San Marino	57.2	43	Mozambique	48.6	79	Guadeloupe	44.5
8	Jersey	56.5	44	Austria	48.3	80	Mauritius	44.5
9	Bermuda	55.8	45	Central African Republic	48.2	81	Comoros	44.4
10	Iceland	55.6	46	Brazil	47.9	82	Cuba	44.2
11	Thailand	55.5	47	Slovenia	47.9	83	Macau	44.1
12	Andorra	55.1	48	Isle of Man	47.6	84	Poland	44.0
13	Switzerland	55.0	49	Gibraltar	47.5	85	Gabon	43.9
14	Qatar	53.7	50	Netherlands	47.5	86	Jamaica	43.6
15	Denmark	53.4	51	Kuwait	47.4	87	Uganda	43.6
16	Romania	53.4	52	Vietnam	47.4	88	Luxembourg	43.5
17	Japan	53.2	53	Gambia	47.3	89	Ukraine	43.5
18	Burundi	52.5	54	Cyprus	47.0	90	Taiwan	43.4
19	Lithuania	52.1	55	United Arab Emirates	47.0	91	Ethiopia	43.3
20	Liechtenstein	52.0	56	Vanuatu	47.0	92	Malawi	43.3
21	Barbados	51.8	57	Uruguay	46.8	93	Armenia	43.1
22	Guernsey	51.2	58	Aruba	46.7	94	Cambodia	43.1
23	Czech Republic	51.1	59	Virgin Islands (U.S.)	46.6	95	Greenland	43.1
24	Burkina Faso	50.9	60	Belarus	46.5	96	Benin	43.0
25	Hong Kong	50.8	61	South Korea	46.4	97	Brunei	43.0
26	Latvia	50.8	62	Bulgaria	46.3	98	Indonesia	42.9
27	Bahamas	50.7	63	Netherlands Antilles	46.3	99	Madagascar	42.8
28	Canada	50.4	64	Slovakia	46.2	100	Senegal	42.6
29	Norway	50.2	65	Bangladesh	46.0	101	French Guiana	42.5
30	Rwanda	50.2	66	Tanzania	46.0	102	Belgium	42.2
31	United States	50.1	67	Guinea-Bissau	45.9	103	Monaco	42.0
32	Australia	49.9	68	Martinique	45.9	104	Faroe Islands	41.9
33	Russia	49.8	69	Ghana	45.4	105	Argentina	41.5
34	Guam	49.7	70	Croatia	45.3	106	Greece	41.5
35	Finland	49.4	71	Macedonia	45.2	107	Trinidad and Tobago	41.3
36	United Kingdom	49.4	72	Suriname	45.2	108	Haiti	41.1

Rank	Country/Entity	Activity Rate (percentage)	Rank	Country/Entity	Activity Rate (percentage)	Rank	Country/Entity	Activity Rate (percentage)
109	Somalia	40.9	144	Chile	37.8	180	Botswana	33.3
110	Kazakhstan	40.8	145	Peru	37.8	181	Puerto Rico	32.2
111	Sri Lanka	40.5	146	India	37.5	182	Niger	31.9
112	Angola	40.3	147	Kyrgyzstan	37.5	183	Lesotho	31.6
113	Ireland	40.3	148	Panama	37.5	184	Nigeria	31.1
114	Myanmar (Burma)	40.2	149	South Africa	37.5	185	Mauritania	30.8
115	New Caledonia	40.2	150	Uzbekistan	37.3	186	Nauru	30.5
116	Palau	40.2	151	Malta	37.2	187	American Samoa	30.4
117	Spain	40.2	152	Turkey	37.1	188	Egypt	30.4
118	Hungary	40.1	153	Costa Rica	36.9	189	Afghanistan	30.3
119	Italy	40.1	154	Saudi Arabia	36.3	190	Micronesia	30.3
120	Cameroon	40.0	155	Azerbaijan	36.2	191	São Tomé and Príncipe	30.1
121	Nepal	40.0	156	Congo, Dem. Rep. of	36.1	192	Yugoslavia	30.1
122	Togo	40.0	157	Turkmenistan	36.1	193	Tunisia	29.8
123	French Polynesia	39.9	158	Sierra Leone	35.9	194	Congo, Rep. of	29.5
124	Grenada	39.9	159	Georgia	35.7	195	Morocco	29.3
125	Saint Lucia	39.9	160	Cape Verde	35.3	196	Samoa	29.0
126	Swaziland	39.8	161	Chad	35.3	197	Mayotte	28.9
127	Saint Kitts and Nevis	39.5	162	Namibia	35.2	198	Pakistan	27.9
128	Bolivia	39.4	163	Nicaragua	35.2	199	Syria	27.8
129	Côte d'Ivoire	39.4	164	Malaysia	35.1	200	Lebanon	26.5
130	Mexico	39.4	165	Sudan	35.1	201	Maldives	26.5
131	Venezuela	39.4	166	Honduras	35.0	202	Marshall Islands	26.5
132	Mongolia	39.3	167	Oman	34.9	203	Iran	26.4
133	Equatorial Guinea	39.2	168	Ecuador	34.8	204	Yemen	26.4
134	El Salvador	39.1	169	Zimbabwe	34.6	205	Libya	24.8
135	Guinea	39.1	170	Tajikistan	34.4	206	Iraq	24.7
136	Moldova	39.1	171	Colombia	34.3	207	Papua New Guinea	24.6
137	Réunion	39.1	172	Paraguay	34.3	208	Algeria	23.6
138	Saint Vincent and the Grenadines	39.1	173	Belize	34.1	209	Bosnia and Herzegovina	22.7
			174	Dominican Republic	33.9	210	West Bank	22.7
139	Kenya	39.0	175	Fiji	33.7	211	Jordan	22.2
140	Seychelles	38.9	176	Tonga	33.6	212	Gaza Strip	18.0
141	Guyana	38.8	177	Guatemala	33.5	213	Solomon Islands	13.7
142	Dominica	38.0	178	Liberia	33.5			
143	Israel	37.9	179	Zambia	33.4			

Source: Yearbook of Labor Statistics

14.3 Female Participation Rate

Rank	Country/Entity	Female Participation Rate (percentage)	Rank	Country/Entity	Female Participation Rate (percentage)	Rank	Country/Entity	Female Participation Rate (percentage)
1	Cambodia	55.8	16	Estonia	47.6	31	Slovenia	46.2
2	Burundi	52.6	17	Bahamas	47.5	32	North Korea	46.0
3	Mozambique	52.4	18	Martinique	47.5	33	United States	46.0
4	Vietnam	51.7	19	Rwanda	47.5	34	Poland	45.9
5	Tuvalu	51.3	20	Jamaica	47.4	35	Norway	45.7
6	Ghana	51.2	21	Mongolia	47.2	36	Andorra	45.6
7	Malawi	51.0	22	Albania	47.0	37	Antigua and Barbuda	45.6
8	Bermuda	50.0	23	Finland	47.0	38	Congo, Rep. of	45.6
9	Barbados	49.5	24	Central African Republic	46.8	39	Thailand	45.6
10	Burkina Faso	49.4	25	Iceland	46.7	40	Guadeloupe	45.5
11	Latvia	49.1	26	Kiribati	46.4	41	Denmark	45.3
12	Grenada	48.6	27	Gambia	46.3	42	Laos	45.3
13	Bulgaria	48.4	28	Romania	46.3	43	Canada	45.1
14	Sweden	47.9	29	Vanuatu	46.3	44	Netherlands Antilles	45.1
15	Virgin Islands (U.S.)	47.8	30	Czech Republic	46.2	45	China	44.9

Rank	Country/Entity	Female Participation Rate (percentage)	Rank	Country/Entity	Female Participation Rate (percentage)	Rank	Country/Entity	Female Participation Rate (percentage)
46	France	44.9	98	San Marino	39.3	149	Brunei	32.9
47	Slovakia	44.9	99	Taiwan	39.2	150	Colombia	32.8
48	Portugal	44.6	100	Senegal	39.1	151	Chile	32.4
49	New Zealand	44.1	101	Swaziland	39.0	152	Sierra Leone	32.4
50	United Kingdom	43.8	102	Singapore	38.7	153	Côte d'Ivoire	32.3
51	Hungary	43.6	103	Cyprus	38.6	154	Mexico	32.1
52	Namibia	43.6	104	Botswana	38.5	155	Yemen	31.6
53	Yugoslavia	43.4	105	Angola	38.4	156	Belize	30.8
54	Guernsey	43.2	106	Spain	38.3	157	Costa Rica	30.5
55	Israel	43.2	107	Bolivia	38.2	158	Turkey	30.4
56	Jersey	43.2	108	French Guiana	38.2	159	Marshall Islands	30.1
57	Macau	43.2	109	Indonesia	38.2	160	Honduras	29.9
58	Northern Mariana Islands	43.2	110	Greece	38.1	161	Micronesia	29.8
59	Switzerland	43.2	111	Gibraltar	38.0	162	Zambia	29.6
60	Australia	42.9	112	Hong Kong	37.9	163	Mayotte	29.4
61	Croatia	42.9	113	Ireland	37.8	164	Sudan	29.1
62	Austria	42.8	114	New Caledonia	37.5	165	Dominican Republic	28.9
63	Germany	42.8	115	Guam	37.4	166	India	28.6
64	Uruguay	42.8	116	Mali	37.4	167	Faroe Islands	27.2
65	Benin	42.6	117	Philippines	37.4	168	Lesotho	27.0
66	Aruba	42.5	118	Trinidad and Tobago	37.2	169	Ecuador	26.4
67	Belgium	42.3	119	Cape Verde	37.1	170	Kuwait	26.1
68	Isle of Man	42.3	120	El Salvador	37.1	171	Solomon Islands	25.6
69	Netherlands	41.5	121	French Polynesia	37.1	172	Guatemala	25.5
70	American Samoa	41.1	122	Bosnia and Herzegovina	36.9	173	Malta	25.4
71	Ethiopia	41.1	123	Gabon	36.9	174	Egypt	23.0
72	Réunion	41.1	124	Italy	36.9	175	Mauritania	22.3
73	Liberia	41.0	125	Palau	36.9	176	Fiji	21.2
74	Saint Kitts and Nevis	41.0	126	Argentina	36.7	177	Tunisia	20.9
75	Djibouti	40.8	127	Luxembourg	36.5	178	Niger	20.4
76	Uganda	40.8	128	Togo	36.2	179	Maldives	19.9
77	Guinea-Bissau	40.5	129	Cuba	36.1	180	Morocco	19.7
78	Japan	40.5	130	Saint Vincent and the Grenadines	35.9	181	Paraguay	19.7
79	Somalia	40.5				182	Samoa	18.8
80	Nepal	40.4	131	Equatorial Guinea	35.7	183	Chad	18.2
81	Liechtenstein	40.3	132	Myanmar (Burma)	35.3	184	Syria	18.0
82	Saint Lucia	40.3	133	Congo, Dem. Rep. of	35.2	185	Bahrain	17.5
83	South Korea	40.2	134	Mauritius	35.2	186	Lebanon	16.6
84	Comoros	40.0	135	Suriname	35.1	187	West Bank	16.1
85	Haiti	40.0	136	Peru	34.7	188	Pakistan	15.4
86	Tanzania	40.0	137	Dominica	34.5	189	Iraq	12.0
87	Turkmenistan	40.0	138	Panama	34.3	190	Jordan	11.4
88	Papua New Guinea	39.8	139	Guyana	34.1	191	Qatar	11.2
89	Monaco	39.7	140	Malaysia	33.9	192	Iran	11.1
90	Brazil	39.6	141	São Tomé and Príncipe	33.6	193	United Arab Emirates	10.4
91	Zimbabwe	39.6	142	Venezuela	33.6	194	Oman	9.7
92	Guinea	39.4	143	Greenland	33.4	195	Libya	9.3
93	Kenya	39.4	144	Nigeria	33.3	196	Algeria	9.2
94	Puerto Rico	39.4	145	Sri Lanka	33.3	197	Gaza Strip	9.0
95	South Africa	39.4	146	Cameroon	33.2	198	Afghanistan	7.9
96	Bangladesh	39.3	147	Nicaragua	33.2	199	Saudi Arabia	3.6
97	Madagascar	39.3	148	Tonga	33.0			

Source: Yearbook of Labor Statistics

The distinction between employers and the self-employed on one hand and employees on the other has existed from ancient times. In agricultural societies there were small farmers who were independent, managed their own affairs, and regulated their own activities, while there were renters and sharecroppers who worked for owners and received a share of the produce in return. In the industrial age of the nineteenth and twentieth centuries, there were small craftworkers who worked on their own, but the vast majority of laborers were employees who worked for capitalists and corporations in return for acceptable wages. In the new information age, the capitalist tradition continues but a greater number of people have the opportunity, although not always the desire, to become entrepreneurs on their own and manage small home-office businesses. The following ranking illustrates this trend. One anomaly that may be noted is the high percentage of self-employed in countries like the Central African Republic, Togo, and Nigeria. This may be explained by the large number of small farmers who own and run their own plots of land.

Rank	Country/Entity	Percentage of Employers and Self-Employed in Labor Force	Rank	Country/Entity	Percentage of Employers and Self-Employed in Labor Force	Rank	Country/Entity	Percentage of Employers and Self-Employed in Labor Force
1	Central African Republic	75.3	42	North Korea	44.6	83	Georgia	35.7
2	Papua New Guinea	72.7	43	Guadeloupe	44.5	84	Namibia	35.2
3	Togo	70.3	44	Mauritius	44.5	85	Nicaragua	35.2
4	Nigeria	64.6	45	Macau	44.1	86	Malaysia	35.1
5	Congo, Rep. of	64.3	46	Gabon	43.9	87	Honduras	35.0
6	Burundi	62.8	47	Jamaica	43.6	88	Fiji	33.7
7	Cameroon	60.2	48	Luxembourg	43.5	89	Tonga	33.7
8	Ethiopia	58.5	49	Malawi	43.3	90	Guatemala	33.5
9	Benin	58.4	50	Greenland	43.1	91	Liberia	33.5
10	Jersey	56.5	51	Paraguay	43.1	92	El Salvador	31.7
11	Iceland	55.6	52	Indonesia	42.9	93	Lesotho	31.6
12	Japan	53.2	53	Madagascar	42.8	94	Thailand	31.2
13	Afghanistan	52.2	54	French Guiana	42.5	95	Syria	31.0
14	Lithuania	52.1	55	Monaco	42.0	96	Mauritania	30.8
15	Liechtenstein	52.0	56	Faroe Islands	41.9	97	Nauru	30.5
16	Niger	51.4	57	Greece	41.5	98	Micronesia	30.3
17	Guernsey	51.2	58	Bolivia	41.2	99	Venezuela	30.2
18	Hong Kong	50.8	59	Pakistan	41.2	100	Solomon Islands	29.6
19	Latvia	50.8	60	Haiti	41.1	101	Morocco	29.3
20	Guam	49.7	61	Kazakhstan	40.8	102	Dominica	29.2
21	Finland	49.4	62	Ireland	40.3	103	Equatorial Guinea	29.0
22	Germany	49.1	63	Myanmar (Burma)	40.2	104	Mayotte	28.9
23	Laos	48.9	64	New Caledonia	40.2	105	Argentina	28.0
24	New Zealand	48.7	65	Hungary	40.1	106	Turkey	27.6
25	Mozambique	48.6	66	Italy	40.1	107	Lebanon	26.5
26	Comoros	47.6	67	Nepal	40.0	108	Maldives	26.5
27	Isle of Man	47.6	68	French Polynesia	39.9	109	Marshall Islands	26.5
28	Gibraltar	47.5	69	Grenada	39.9	110	Chile	26.4
29	Netherlands	47.5	70	Peru	39.8	111	Iran	26.4
30	Kuwait	47.4	71	Mexico	39.4	112	Bangladesh	26.3
31	Gambia	47.3	72	Mongolia	39.3	113	Brazil	26.3
32	South Korea	46.4	73	Guinea	39.1	114	Belize	26.2
33	Netherlands Antilles	46.3	74	Moldova	39.1	115	São Tomé and Príncipe	25.8
34	Guinea-Bissau	45.9	75	Kenya	39.0	116	Sri Lanka	24.9
35	Martinique	45.9	76	Guyana	38.8	117	Libya	24.8
36	Ecuador	45.7	77	Israel	37.9	118	Cape Verde	24.7
37	Ghana	45.4	78	India	37.5	119	Egypt	24.7
38	Macedonia	45.2	79	Kyrgyzstan	37.5	120	Iraq	24.7
39	Kiribati	45.1	80	Malta	37.2	121	West Bank	24.5
40	France	44.8	81	Dominican Republic	36.5	122	Panama	24.1
41	Mali	44.7	82	Philippines	36.2	123	Zimbabwe	24.1

Rank	Country/Entity	Percentage of Employers and Self-Employed in Labor Force	Rank	Country/Entity	Percentage of Employers and Self-Employed in Labor Force	Rank	Country/Entity	Percentage of Employers and Self-Employed in Labor Force
124	Costa Rica	24.0	142	Puerto Rico	13.6	161	Réunion	8.4
125	Portugal	23.1	143	Australia	13.4	162	United States	8.3
126	Uruguay	22.9	144	Switzerland	12.8	163	Norway	8.1
127	Zambia	22.9	145	Belgium	12.7	164	Virgin Islands (U.S.)	7.6
128	Romania	22.8	146	Croatia	12.7	165	Aruba	7.0
129	Jordan	22.2	147	Czech Republic	12.7	166	South Africa	7.0
130	Taiwan	21.7	148	Antigua and Barbuda	12.1	167	United Arab Emirates	6.8
131	Samoa	21.1	149	Bahamas	11.6	168	Botswana	6.5
132	Saint Lucia	21.0	150	Slovenia	11.3	169	Cuba	5.7
133	Tunisia	20.9	151	United Kingdom	11.2	170	Slovakia	5.6
134	Poland	20.1	152	Singapore	10.6	171	Oman	5.2
135	Cyprus	18.7	153	Sweden	9.9	172	Bahrain	5.1
136	Saint Vincent and the Grenadines	18.2	154	Austria	9.7	173	Estonia	4.8
			155	Bermuda	9.7	174	Brunei	3.5
137	Gaza Strip	18.0	156	Saint Kitts and Nevis	9.7	175	Palau	2.5
138	Trinidad and Tobago	17.8	157	Canada	9.6	176	American Samoa	2.1
139	Algeria	16.8	158	Barbados	8.8	177	Qatar	1.8
140	Spain	16.7	159	Denmark	8.8	178	Northern Mariana Islands	1.4
141	San Marino	15.3	160	Bulgaria	8.4	179	Tuvalu	0.3

Source: Yearbook of Labor Statistics

Labor Force

The structure of the economically active population is an indicator of the relative importance of three principal sectors in a country: agriculture, industry, and services. These three sectors represent chronologically the principal eras of human civilization. The existence of a large percentage of the population in a labor-intensive field such as agriculture is an indication that the country is still lagging or has yet to make the transition to a modern economy. In most countries, agricultural workers are excluded from the purview of labor laws, have no guaranteed minimum wage, and receive no social security. They work for longer hours each day than workers in industrial or service establishments. Work may be seasonal resulting in serious underemployment or long periods of inactivity. Agricultural labor is also characterized by a greater proportion of women, most of whom serve as unpaid family workers. In most countries, the trend is shifting toward industry as the principal employer. Unlike agricultural workers, industrial workers require specialized skills that require continuous training and are covered by an array of regulations and laws governing wages, work periods, occupational health, and fringe benefits. Industrial workers constitute the core of the labor force in almost all countries. In postindustrial economies, the trend is shifting away from both agriculture and industry toward services. Services provide a broad spectrum of social needs. Service workers may range from highly trained specialists in the so-called information and knowledge industries to retail clerks, who require less specialized skills.

14.5 Percentage of Labor Force in Agriculture

Rank	Country/Entity	Percentage of Labor Force in Agriculture	Rank	Country/Entity	Percentage of Labor Force in Agriculture	Rank	Country/Entity	Percentage of Labor Force in Agriculture
1	Bhutan	94	8	Ethiopia	86	15	Gambia	82
2	Nepal	94	9	Mali	86	16	Central African Republic	80
3	Burkina Faso	92	10	Guinea-Bissau	85	17	Eritrea	80
4	Burundi	92	11	Uganda	85	18	Kenya	80
5	Niger	90	12	Tanzania	84	19	Laos	78
6	Guinea	87	13	Chad	83	20	Madagascar	78
7	Malawi	87	14	Mozambique	83	21	Comoros	77

Rank	Country/Entity	Percentage of Labor Force in Agriculture	Rank	Country/Entity	Percentage of Labor Force in Agriculture	Rank	Country/Entity	Percentage of Labor Force in Agriculture
22	Senegal	77	68	Turkmenistan	37	114	Jordan	15
23	Solomon Islands	77	69	El Salvador	36	115	Cyprus	14
24	Angola	75	70	Peru	36	116	Estonia	14
25	Zambia	75	71	Uzbekistan	35	117	Ireland	14
26	Cambodia	74	72	Belize	34	118	Russia	14
27	Myanmar (Burma)	73	73	Ecuador	33	119	South Africa	14
28	China	72	74	Moldova	33	120	Uruguay	14
29	Vietnam	71	75	Syria	33	121	Bulgaria	13
30	Cameroon	70	76	Iran	32	122	Argentina	12
31	Sudan	69	77	Kyrgyzstan	32	123	Slovakia	12
32	Congo, Dem. Rep. of	68	78	Maldives	32	124	Spain	12
33	Haiti	68	79	Mongolia	32	125	Venezuela	12
34	Zimbabwe	68	80	Azerbaijan	31	126	Czech Republic	11
35	Sierra Leone	67	81	Cape Verde	31	127	Iceland	11
36	Togo	66	82	Nicaragua	29	128	Libya	11
37	Bangladesh	65	83	Mexico	28	129	New Zealand	10
38	Benin	64	84	Tunisia	28	130	Italy	9
39	India	64	85	Colombia	27	131	Austria	8
40	Thailand	64	86	Malaysia	27	132	Finland	8
41	Yemen	61	87	Poland	27	133	United Arab Emirates	8
42	Côte d'Ivoire	60	88	Algeria	26	134	Barbados	7
43	Ghana	59	89	Costa Rica	26	135	Japan	7
44	Albania	55	90	Georgia	26	136	Lebanon	7
45	Indonesia	55	91	Panama	26	137	Australia	6
46	Mauritania	55	92	Dominican Republic	25	138	Denmark	6
47	Turkey	54	93	Jamaica	25	139	Norway	6
48	Gabon	52	94	Romania	24	140	Slovenia	6
49	Guatemala	52	95	Brazil	23	141	Switzerland	6
50	Pakistan	52	96	Greece	23	142	Bahamas	5
51	Congo	49	97	Guyana	22	143	France	5
52	Namibia	49	98	Kazakhstan	22	144	Netherlands	5
53	Sri Lanka	49	99	Macedonia	22	145	Germany	4
54	Bolivia	47	100	Suriname	21	146	Israel	4
55	Botswana	46	101	Belarus	20	147	Luxembourg	4
56	Fiji	46	102	Ukraine	20	148	Sweden	4
57	Philippines	46	103	Chile	19	149	Belgium	3
58	Morocco	45	104	Armenia	18	150	Canada	3
59	Oman	45	105	Cuba	18	151	Malta	3
60	Nigeria	43	106	South Korea	18	152	Qatar	3
61	Honduras	41	107	Lithuania	18	153	United States	3
62	Tajikistan	41	108	Portugal	18	154	Bahrain	2
63	Egypt	40	109	Mauritius	17	155	Brunei	2
64	Lesotho	40	110	Croatia	16	156	United Kingdom	2
65	Paraguay	39	111	Iraq	16	157	Hong Kong	1
66	Swaziland	39	112	Latvia	16	158	Kuwait	1
67	North Korea	38	113	Hungary	15	159	Singapore	0

Source: Yearbook of Labor Statistics

14.6 Percentage of Labor Force in Industry

Rank	Country/Entity	Percentage of Labor Force in Industry	Rank	Country/Entity	Percentage of Labor Force in Industry	Rank	Country/Entity	Percentage of Labor Force in Industry
1	Bulgaria	48	9	Lithuania	41	17	Hong Kong	37
2	Romania	47	10	Belarus	40	18	Poland	36
3	Slovenia	46	11	Latvia	40	19	Singapore	36
4	Czech Republic	45	12	Macedonia	40	20	South Korea	35
5	Armenia	43	13	Ukraine	40	21	Malta	35
6	Mauritius	43	14	Austria	38	22	Switzerland	35
7	Russia	42	15	Germany	38	23	Croatia	34
8	Estonia	41	16	Hungary	38	24	Japan	34

Rank	Country/Entity	Percentage of Labor Force in Industry	Rank	Country/Entity	Percentage of Labor Force in Industry	Rank	Country/Entity	Percentage of Labor Force in Industry
25	Portugal	34	70	Iran	25	115	Fiji	15
26	Slovakia	33	71	Kuwait	25	116	Namibia	15
27	Spain	33	72	Morocco	25	117	Philippines	15
28	Tunisia	33	73	New Zealand	25	118	Sierra Leone	15
29	Argentina	32	74	Norway	25	119	Indonesia	14
30	Kazakhstan	32	75	Uzbekistan	25	120	Thailand	14
31	North Korea	32	76	Brunei	24	121	Vietnam	14
32	Qatar	32	77	Mexico	24	122	Congo, Dem. Rep. of	13
33	South Africa	32	78	Oman	24	123	Ghana	13
34	Algeria	31	79	Syria	24	124	Côte d'Ivoire	10
35	Finland	31	80	Albania	23	125	Mauritania	10
36	Georgia	31	81	Barbados	23	126	Myanmar (Burma)	10
37	Italy	31	82	Brazil	23	127	Togo	10
38	Lebanon	31	83	Colombia	23	128	Cameroon	9
39	Maldives	31	84	Jamaica	23	129	Comoros	9
40	Bahrain	30	85	Jordan	23	130	Haiti	9
41	Cape Verde	30	86	Libya	23	131	Angola	8
42	Cuba	30	87	Malaysia	23	132	Benin	8
43	Cyprus	30	88	Mongolia	23	133	Cambodia	8
44	Moldova	30	89	Tajikistan	23	134	Gambia	8
45	Sweden	30	90	Turkmenistan	23	135	Mozambique	8
46	Azerbaijan	29	91	Egypt	22	136	Senegal	8
47	Dominican Republic	29	92	Paraguay	22	137	Sudan	8
48	France	29	93	Swaziland	22	138	Zambia	8
49	Ireland	29	94	El Salvador	21	139	Zimbabwe	8
50	Israel	29	95	Sri Lanka	21	140	Kenya	7
51	United Kingdom	29	96	Botswana	20	141	Madagascar	7
52	Belgium	28	97	Honduras	20	142	Nigeria	7
53	Denmark	28	98	Belize	19	143	Solomon Islands	7
54	Lesotho	28	99	Ecuador	19	144	Laos	6
55	Costa Rica	27	100	Pakistan	19	145	Eritrea	5
56	Greece	27	101	Bolivia	18	146	Malawi	5
57	Iceland	27	102	Iraq	18	147	Tanzania	5
58	Kyrgyzstan	27	103	Peru	18	148	Uganda	5
59	Luxembourg	27	104	Suriname	18	149	Chad	4
60	United Arab Emirates	27	105	Turkey	18	150	Niger	4
61	Uruguay	27	106	Guatemala	17	151	Burundi	3
62	Venezuela	27	107	Yemen	17	152	Central African Republic	3
63	Australia	26	108	Bangladesh	16	153	Burkina Faso	2
64	Netherlands	26	109	Gabon	16	154	Ethiopia	2
65	Nicaragua	26	110	India	16	155	Guinea	2
66	United States	26	111	Panama	16	156	Guinea-Bissau	2
67	Canada	25	112	Bahamas	15	157	Mali	2
68	Chile	25	113	China	15	158	Bhutan	1
69	Guyana	25	114	Congo, Rep. of	15	159	Nepal	0

Source: Yearbook of Labor Statistics

14.7 Percentage of Labor Force in Services

Rank	Country/Entity	Percentage of Labor Force in Services	Rank	Country/Entity	Percentage of Labor Force in Services	Rank	Country/Entity	Percentage of Labor Force in Services
1	Bahamas	79	9	Luxembourg	69	17	Iraq	66
2	Brunei	74	10	United Kingdom	69	18	Libya	66
3	Kuwait	74	11	Australia	68	19	Sweden	66
4	Canada	71	12	Bahrain	68	20	New Zealand	65
5	United States	71	13	Norway	68	21	Qatar	65
6	Barbados	70	14	Israel	67	22	United Arab Emirates	65
7	Belgium	70	15	Denmark	66	23	Singapore	64
8	Netherlands	70	16	France	66	24	Iceland	63

Rank	Country/Entity	Percentage of Labor Force in Services	Rank	Country/Entity	Percentage of Labor Force in Services	Rank	Country/Entity	Percentage of Labor Force in Services
25	Malta	63	70	Latvia	44	115	Romania	29
26	Hong Kong	62	71	Algeria	43	116	Benin	28
27	Lebanon	62	72	Czech Republic	43	117	Ghana	28
28	Finland	61	73	El Salvador	43	118	Turkey	28
29	Jordan	61	74	Georgia	43	119	Togo	24
30	Suriname	61	75	Iran	43	120	Zimbabwe	24
31	Venezuela	61	76	Syria	43	121	Haiti	23
32	Italy	60	77	Kyrgyzstan	41	122	Albania	22
33	Switzerland	60	78	Lithuania	41	123	Sudan	22
34	Japan	59	79	Azerbaijan	40	124	Thailand	22
35	Uruguay	59	80	Belarus	40	125	Yemen	22
36	Germany	58	81	Cape Verde	40	126	Cameroon	21
37	Panama	58	82	Mauritius	40	127	India	20
38	Ireland	57	83	Turkmenistan	40	128	Cambodia	19
39	Chile	56	84	Ukraine	40	129	Congo, Dem. Rep. of	19
40	Cyprus	56	85	Uzbekistan	40	130	Bangladesh	18
41	Argentina	55	86	Armenia	39	131	Angola	17
42	Austria	55	87	Fiji	39	132	Myanmar (Burma)	17
43	Slovakia	55	88	Honduras	39	133	Sierra Leone	17
44	South Africa	55	89	Paraguay	39	134	Zambia	17
45	Spain	55	90	Philippines	39	135	Central African Republic	16
46	Brazil	54	91	Tunisia	39	136	Laos	16
47	Guyana	53	92	Bulgaria	38	137	Senegal	16
48	Jamaica	52	93	Egypt	38	138	Solomon Islands	16
49	Cuba	51	94	Macedonia	38	139	Eritrea	15
50	Colombia	50	95	Swaziland	38	140	Madagascar	15
51	Croatia	50	96	Congo, Rep. of	37	141	Vietnam	15
52	Greece	50	97	Maldives	37	142	Chad	13
53	Malaysia	50	98	Moldova	37	143	China	13
54	Nigeria	50	99	Poland	37	144	Comoros	13
55	Belize	48	100	Bolivia	36	145	Guinea-Bissau	13
56	Ecuador	48	101	Namibia	36	146	Kenya	13
57	Mexico	48	102	Tajikistan	36	147	Ethiopia	12
58	Portugal	48	103	Mauritania	34	148	Mali	12
59	Slovenia	48	104	Botswana	33	149	Gambia	11
60	Costa Rica	47	105	Gabon	33	150	Guinea	11
61	Hungary	47	106	Lesotho	32	151	Tanzania	11
62	South Korea	47	107	Oman	32	152	Uganda	11
63	Peru	47	108	Indonesia	31	153	Mozambique	9
64	Dominican Republic	46	109	Morocco	31	154	Malawi	8
65	Kazakhstan	46	110	Sri Lanka	31	155	Burkina Faso	6
66	Mongolia	45	111	Côte d'Ivoire	30	156	Burundi	6
67	Nicaragua	45	112	Guatemala	30	157	Nepal	6
68	Russia	45	113	North Korea	30	158	Niger	6
69	Estonia	44	114	Pakistan	30	159	Bhutan	5

Source: Yearbook of Labor Statistics

14.8 Union Membership

As much of the world moves beyond the industrial age, one significant trend is the decline of labor (or trade) unions. Such organizations of laborers long proved effective in poorly regulated classical capitalist systems where they fought for decent wages, better working conditions, and a more economically just society. Today, the strength of organized labor varies from country to country. It is still strong in democratic countries, such as the United Kingdom, where it operates either as a pressure group or as an overt political party and where it influences legislation through intensive lobbying. In many Western European countries, and to a certain extent in the United States, the labor movement has attached itself to the political party that best serves its goals and leverages its mem-

bership as a vote-getting mechanism. Most labor unions, at least in the West, have become less radical and more conservative in the past two generations.

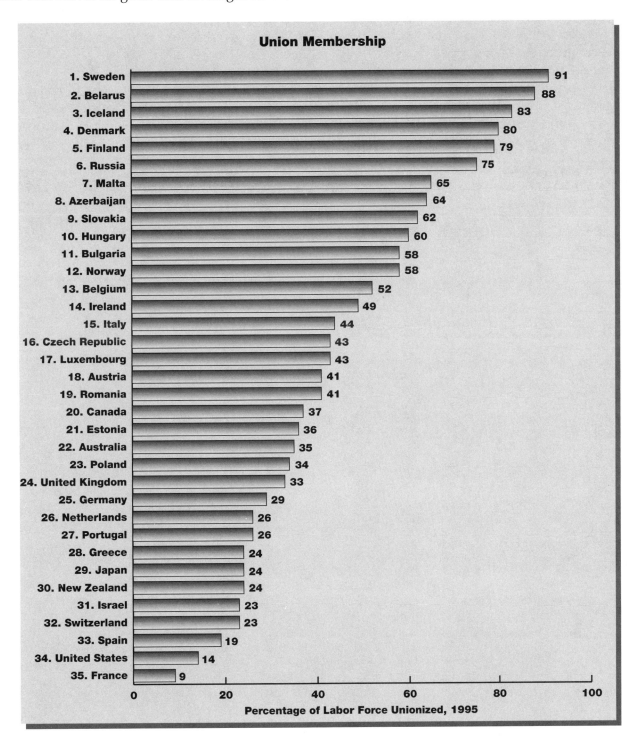

Union Membership

Rank	Country	Percentage
1.	Sweden	91
2.	Belarus	88
3.	Iceland	83
4.	Denmark	80
5.	Finland	79
6.	Russia	75
7.	Malta	65
8.	Azerbaijan	64
9.	Slovakia	62
10.	Hungary	60
11.	Bulgaria	58
12.	Norway	58
13.	Belgium	52
14.	Ireland	49
15.	Italy	44
16.	Czech Republic	43
17.	Luxembourg	43
18.	Austria	41
19.	Romania	41
20.	Canada	37
21.	Estonia	36
22.	Australia	35
23.	Poland	34
24.	United Kingdom	33
25.	Germany	29
26.	Netherlands	26
27.	Portugal	26
28.	Greece	24
29.	Japan	24
30.	New Zealand	24
31.	Israel	23
32.	Switzerland	23
33.	Spain	19
34.	United States	14
35.	France	9

Percentage of Labor Force Unionized, 1995

Source: *World Factbook*

Labor Cost and Value

Under the capitalist system, workers are expected to produce more wealth than they earn. Each worker thus adds a certain value to the product and receives a certain share of that value as wages. The ratio between the value added and the labor cost to the employer is a critical element determining the viability of the industry. Employers are interested in keeping the labor cost as low as possible and the value added as high as possible. When the ratio becomes skewed in favor of the employer, workers generally strike or engage in other concerted measures to restore the balance. If, on the other hand, workers do not produce as much to justify their wages, employers generally shut down the business or move to countries where wages are lower and value added is higher. This helps explain the constant migration of industries from the developed world to the developing world.

14.9 Annual Labor Cost per Worker in Manufacturing

Rank	Country/Entity	Annual Labor Cost per Worker in U.S. Dollars, 1995–1999	Rank	Country/Entity	Annual Labor Cost per Worker in U.S. Dollars, 1995–1999	Rank	Country/Entity	Annual Labor Cost per Worker in U.S. Dollars, 1995–1999
1	Netherlands	39,865	27	South Africa	8,475	53	Philippines	2,450
2	Norway	38,415	28	Turkey	7,958	54	Bolivia	2,343
3	Italy	35,138	29	Senegal	7,754	55	Jordan	2,082
4	Germany	33,226	30	Mexico	7,607	56	Mauritius	1,973
5	Japan	31,687	31	Portugal	7,577	57	Czech Republic	1,876
6	Denmark	29,235	32	Argentina	7,338	58	Egypt	1,863
7	Sweden	29,043	33	Panama	6,351	59	Dominican Republic	1,806
8	United States	28,907	34	Chile	5,822	60	Guatemala	1,802
9	Canada	28,424	35	Venezuela	4,667	61	Poland	1,714
10	Austria	28,342	36	Syria	4,338	62	Ethiopia	1,596
11	Israel	26,635	37	Zambia	4,292	63	Russia	1,528
12	Finland	26,615	38	Ecuador	3,738	64	Yemen	1,291
13	Australia	26,087	39	Uruguay	3,738	65	India	1,192
14	Ireland	25,414	40	Jamaica	3,655	66	Romania	1,190
15	Belgium	24,132	41	Tunisia	3,599	67	Bulgaria	1,179
16	United Kingdom	23,843	42	Malaysia	3,429	68	Indonesia	1,008
17	New Zealand	23,767	43	Zimbabwe	3,422	69	Belarus	754
18	Singapore	21,534	44	Morocco	3,391	70	China	729
19	Spain	19,329	45	Paraguay	3,241	71	Vietnam	711
20	Greece	15,899	46	Oman	3,099	72	Kyrgyzstan	687
21	Brazil	14,134	47	Botswana	2,884	73	Bangladesh	671
22	Hong Kong	13,539	48	Costa Rica	2,829	74	Sri Lanka	604
23	Iraq	13,288	49	Hungary	2,777	75	Latvia	366
24	South Korea	10,743	50	Thailand	2,705	76	Kenya	94
25	Côte d'Ivoire	9,995	51	Honduras	2,658			
26	Slovenia	9,632	52	Colombia	2,507			

Source: Yearbook of Labor Statistics

14.10 Value Added per Worker in Manufacturing

Rank	Country/Entity	Annual Value Added per Worker in Manufacturing in U.S. Dollars, 1995–1999	Rank	Country/Entity	Annual Value Added per Worker in Manufacturing in U.S. Dollars, 1995–1999	Rank	Country/Entity	Annual Value Added per Worker in Manufacturing in U.S. Dollars, 1995–1999
1	Japan	92,582	23	Israel	35,526	45	Jamaica	11,091
2	Ireland	86,036	24	Iraq	34,316	46	Philippines	10,781
3	United States	81,353	25	Chile	32,977	47	Syria	9,918
4	Germany	79,616	26	Turkey	32,961	48	Ecuador	9,747
5	Switzerland	61,848	27	New Zealand	32,723	49	Guatemala	9,235
6	Brazil	61,595	28	Greece	30,429	50	Morocco	9,089
7	Oman	61,422	29	Bolivia	26,282	51	Poland	7,637
8	France	61,019	30	Mexico	25,931	52	Honduras	7,427
9	Canada	60,712	31	Venezuela	24,867	53	Costa Rica	7,184
10	Belgium	58,678	32	Thailand	19,946	54	Ethiopia	7,094
11	Australia	57,857	33	Hong Kong	19,533	55	Hungary	6,106
12	Netherlands	56,801	34	Panama	17,320	56	Egypt	5,976
13	Sweden	56,675	35	Portugal	17,273	57	Yemen	5,782
14	United Kingdom	55,060	36	Colombia	17,061	58	Indonesia	5,139
15	Finland	55,037	37	Zambia	16,615	59	Czech Republic	5,094
16	Austria	53,061	38	South Africa	16,612	60	Mauritius	4,217
17	Norway	51,510	39	Uruguay	16,028	61	Romania	3,482
18	Denmark	49,273	40	Paraguay	14,873	62	Sri Lanka	3,405
19	Spain	47,016	41	Malaysia	12,661	63	India	3,118
20	South Korea	40,916	42	Slovenia	12,536	64	China	2,885
21	Singapore	40,674	43	Zimbabwe	11,944	65	Bangladesh	1,711
22	Argentina	37,480	44	Jordan	11,906	66	Kenya	228

Source: Yearbook of Labor Statistics

Chapter 15

Transportation and Communication

Railroads

Railroads are the oldest form of modern transportation and, before the invention of the automobile, the most popular and convenient. The nineteenth century was the age of the railroad and it witnessed the construction of railways in most of the countries of the world, under the aegis of mostly British engineers. Railroads declined to become the third of the three primary forms of transportation in the twentieth century–trailing both motor vehicles and airplanes–but with the projected rise in gasoline prices they might see a resurgence in the twenty-first century. In the West, steam trains are only a nostalgic memory for railroad buffs, and almost all the major rail systems are electrified. Double tracks are now the rule rather than the exception. Track length is one of the elements in determining the accessibility of railroads and their ability to provide transit to the maximum number of people and freight. Total track length has been declining worldwide for the past fifty years, of the celebrated transcontinental railroads, such as the Orient Express, have disappeared. Many, however, but many have survived, such as the Trans-Siberian, the Trans-Australian from Sydney to Freemantle; the Trans-Andean from Buenos Aires, Argentina, to Valparaiso, Chile; the Beijing-Canton; the Tanzam from Zambia, to Dar-es-Salaam, Tanzania; and the four major transcontinental routes in the United States. In most countries, railroads still make money on freight but face intense competition from trucks and barges.

15.1 Railroad Tracks

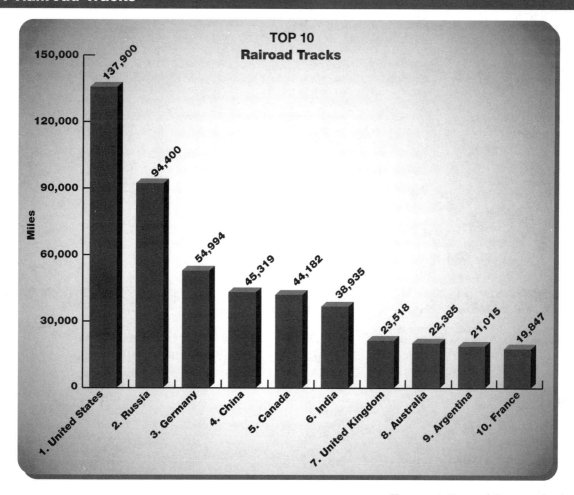

TOP 10 Rairoad Tracks

Rank	Country	Miles
1	United States	137,900
2	Russia	94,400
3	Germany	54,994
4	China	45,319
5	Canada	44,182
6	India	38,935
7	United Kingdom	23,518
8	Australia	22,385
9	Argentina	21,015
10	France	19,847

Rank	Country/Entity	Railroad Tracks (miles)	Rank	Country/Entity	Railroad Tracks (miles)	Rank	Country/Entity	Railroad Tracks (miles)
11	Brazil	18,578	55	Portugal	1,909	99	Guatemala	549
12	Mexico	16,432	56	Kenya	1,885	100	Armenia	515
13	Poland	14,904	57	Lithuania	1,862	101	Congo, Rep. of	494
14	Ukraine	14,100	58	Denmark	1,780	102	Malawi	490
15	Kazakhstan	13,422	59	Angola	1,739	103	Ethiopia	486
16	South Africa	13,418	60	Zimbabwe	1,714	104	Mauritania	437
17	Japan	12,511	61	Netherlands	1,702	105	Jordan	421
18	Italy	9,944	62	Bangladesh	1,681	106	Albania	419
19	Spain	8,252	63	Croatia	1,676	107	Gabon	415
20	Hungary	8,190	64	Vietnam	1,619	108	Guinea	411
21	Romania	7,062	65	Greece	1,537	109	Côte d'Ivoire	405
22	Sweden	6,744	66	Latvia	1,499	110	Mali	398
23	Czech Republic	5,860	67	Namibia	1,480	111	Venezuela	390
24	Pakistan	5,453	68	Turkmenistan	1,359	112	Burkina Faso	386
25	North Korea	5,302	69	Tunisia	1,337	113	Cambodia	380
26	Turkey	5,252	70	Peru	1,318	114	Israel	379
27	Iran	4,527	71	Azerbaijan	1,305	115	Fiji	370
28	Indonesia	4,090	72	Mongolia	1,294	116	Benin	359
29	Chile	4,084	73	Uruguay	1,288	117	El Salvador	349
30	South Korea	4,072	74	Iraq	1,263	118	Liberia	306
31	Bulgaria	4,043	75	Ireland	1,210	119	Tajikistan	300
32	Finland	3,641	76	Malaysia	1,113	120	Paraguay	274
33	Austria	3,524	77	Morocco	1,099	121	Kyrgyzstan	249
34	Belarus	3,480	78	Syria	1,097	122	Togo	245
35	Congo, Dem. Rep. of	3,162	79	Dominican Republic	1,083	123	Panama	220
36	Myanmar (Burma)	3,144	80	Georgia	983	124	Suriname	187
37	Switzerland	3,125	81	Sri Lanka	928	125	Swaziland	187
38	Cuba	3,033	82	Saudi Arabia	864	126	Luxembourg	171
39	Egypt	2,989	83	Zambia	791	127	Lebanon	138
40	Algeria	2,965	84	Uganda	771	128	Jamaica	129
41	Sudan	2,960	85	Moldova	746	129	Guyana	116
42	Yugoslavia	2,505	86	Slovenia	746	130	Djibouti	66
43	Norway	2,485	87	Cameroon	686	131	Nepal	63
44	Thailand	2,471	88	Madagascar	640	132	Sierra Leone	52
45	New Zealand	2,433	89	Estonia	636	133	Singapore	52
46	Taiwan	2,410	90	Bosnia and Herzegovina	634	134	Isle of Man	37
47	Bolivia	2,295	91	Honduras	614	135	Hong Kong	21
48	Slovakia	2,277	92	Botswana	603	136	Afghanistan	16
49	Tanzania	2,218	93	Ecuador	600	137	Brunei	12
50	Nigeria	2,178	94	Ghana	592	138	Liechtenstein	12
51	Uzbekistan	2,100	95	Costa Rica	590	139	Nauru	3
52	Belgium	2,093	96	Macedonia	573	140	Lesotho	2
53	Colombia	2,007	97	Senegal	562	141	Monaco	1
54	Mozambique	1,940	98	Philippines	557			

Source: International Railway Statistics

15.2 Railroad Passengers

Rank	Country/Entity	Railroad Passengers (million miles)	Rank	Country/Entity	Railroad Passengers (million miles)	Rank	Country/Entity	Railroad Passengers (million miles)
1	Japan	248,584	10	South Korea	18,201	19	Netherlands	8,685
2	China	220,319	11	United Kingdom	18,154	20	Thailand	8,062
3	India	198,500	12	Poland	16,550	21	Belarus	7,770
4	Russia	163,900	13	United States	13,897	22	Australia	7,152
5	Ukraine	42,900	14	Romania	11,731	23	Switzerland	7,084
6	Germany	39,830	15	Pakistan	10,908	24	Austria	6,509
7	France	34,467	16	Indonesia	9,895	25	Tajikistan	6,094
8	Italy	30,882	17	Spain	9,526	26	Hungary	5,814
9	Egypt	29,821	18	Brazil	9,009	27	Taiwan	5,577

Rank	Country/Entity	Railroad Passengers (million miles)	Rank	Country/Entity	Railroad Passengers (million miles)	Rank	Country/Entity	Railroad Passengers (million miles)
28	Czech Republic	4,985	61	Georgia	792	94	Albania	139
29	Belgium	4,199	62	Swaziland	752	95	Senegal	128
30	Argentina	4,014	63	Sudan	735	96	Burkina Faso	126
31	Iran	3,990	64	Latvia	734	97	Côte d'Ivoire	117
32	Turkey	3,967	65	Lithuania	702	98	Peru	103
33	Sweden	3,942	66	Tunisia	636	99	Uruguay	87
34	Uzbekistan	3,300	67	Moldova	633	100	Saudi Arabia	86
35	Bulgaria	3,147	68	Croatia	598	101	Kyrgyzstan	82
36	Myanmar (Burma)	3,041	69	South Africa	556	102	Ghana	73
37	Portugal	3,025	70	Syria	531	103	Benin	66
38	Denmark	3,004	71	Azerbaijan	516	104	Botswana	53
39	Slovakia	2,611	72	Mongolia	516	105	Philippines	43
40	Bangladesh	2,508	73	Chile	428	106	Macedonia	40
41	Mexico	2,382	74	Slovenia	370	107	Cambodia	34
42	Tanzania	2,324	75	Congo, Dem. Rep. of	360	108	Madagascar	29
43	Hong Kong	2,231	76	Nigeria	345	109	Guinea	26
44	North Korea	2,100	77	Bosnia and Herzegovina	344	110	Gabon	21
45	Sri Lanka	2,028	78	Zimbabwe	339	111	Venezuela	20
46	Cuba	1,880	79	Mali	304	112	Ecuador	17
47	Finland	1,626	80	Kenya	288	113	Uganda	17
48	Algeria	1,568	81	New Zealand	285	114	Jamaica	12
49	Norway	1,479	82	Estonia	262	115	Malawi	12
50	Kazakhstan	1,355	83	Cameroon	247	116	Colombia	9.6
51	Vietnam	1,305	84	Bolivia	217	117	Togo	9.0
52	Turkmenistan	1,300	85	Angola	203	118	Guatemala	7.8
53	Namibia	1,248	86	Armenia	196	119	Lebanon	5.3
54	Yugoslavia	1,137	87	Mozambique	194	120	Honduras	4.8
55	Iraq	973	88	Luxembourg	176	121	Costa Rica	3.7
56	Morocco	951	89	Djibouti	173	122	Jordan	3.7
57	Canada	889	90	Ethiopia	172	123	El Salvador	3.4
58	Greece	869	91	Israel	166	124	Paraguay	1.9
59	Ireland	828	92	Zambia	166			
60	Malaysia	798	93	Congo, Rep. of	141			

Source: International Railway Statistics

15.3 Railroad Cargo

Rank	Country/Entity	Railroad Cargo (million short ton miles)	Rank	Country/Entity	Railroad Cargo (million short ton miles)	Rank	Country/Entity	Railroad Cargo (million short ton miles)
1	United States	1,305,685	20	Sweden	13,280	39	Armenia	3,345
2	China	881,539	21	Austria	9,526	40	Morocco	3,165
3	Canada	185,641	22	South Korea	9,478	41	Indonesia	2,679
4	India	173,268	23	Slovakia	9,366	42	Estonia	2,634
5	Brazil	93,455	24	Latvia	8,502	43	New Zealand	2,277
6	Ukraine	85,600	25	Tajikistan	7,617	44	Thailand	2,221
7	Australia	67,593	26	Spain	6,624	45	Moldova	2,147
8	South Africa	65,248	27	Finland	6,551	46	Netherlands	2,121
9	Uzbekistan	48,400	28	Iran	6,249	47	United Kingdom	1,997
10	Poland	47,341	29	North Korea	6,200	48	Swaziland	1,993
11	Germany	45,649	30	Turkey	5,654	49	Slovenia	1,973
12	France	32,466	31	Switzerland	5,586	50	Norway	1,860
13	Italy	28,499	32	Belgium	5,334	51	Algeria	1,644
14	Mexico	24,042	33	Lithuania	5,264	52	Egypt	1,600
15	Romania	18,617	34	Argentina	5,214	53	Chile	1,595
16	Belarus	17,473	35	Hungary	5,200	54	Sudan	1,534
17	Czech Republic	17,439	36	Bulgaria	5,171	55	Tunisia	1,524
18	Japan	17,193	37	Mauritania	4,719	56	Yugoslavia	1,412
19	Turkmenistan	13,600	38	Pakistan	3,877	57	Portugal	1,382

Rank	Country/Entity	Railroad Cargo (million short ton miles)	Rank	Country/Entity	Railroad Cargo (million short ton miles)	Rank	Country/Entity	Railroad Cargo (million short ton miles)
58	Denmark	1,360	82	Saudi Arabia	559	106	Hong Kong	68
59	Bosnia and Herzegovina	1,333	83	Bolivia	522	107	Madagascar	64
60	Congo, Dem. Rep. of	1,258	84	Bangladesh	521	108	Costa Rica	46
61	Angola	1,178	85	Senegal	476	109	Malawi	39
62	Botswana	1,171	86	Cameroon	405	110	Guatemala	32
63	Iraq	1,129	87	Kyrgyzstan	394	111	Venezuela	32
64	Taiwan	1,086	88	Ireland	392	112	Burkina Faso	31
65	Croatia	1,071	89	Luxembourg	388	113	Lebanon	29
66	Azerbaijan	1,055	90	Zambia	316	114	Honduras	21
67	Tanzania	1,021	91	Greece	210	115	El Salvador	20
68	Malaysia	970	92	Mali	187	116	Cambodia	6.9
69	Cuba	937	93	Djibouti	187	117	Ecuador	6.0
70	Jordan	915	94	Côte d'Ivoire	182	118	Guinea	5.0
71	Kenya	899	95	Benin	173	119	Nauru	4.7
72	Israel	805	96	Colombia	166	120	Paraguay	3.8
73	Syria	751	97	Congo, Rep. of	152	121	Togo	3.8
74	Namibia	741	98	Liberia	137	122	Zimbabwe	3.2
75	Vietnam	727	99	Uruguay	129	123	Jamaica	1.7
76	Georgia	705	100	Uganda	128	124	Nigeria	1.5
77	Russia	704	101	Gabon	126	125	Mongolia	1.4
78	Kazakhstan	661	102	Macedonia	116	126	Philippines	1.0
79	Mozambique	612	103	Sri Lanka	99	127	Panama	0.5
80	Peru	606	104	Ghana	94	128	Albania	0.3
81	Myanmar (Burma)	603	105	Ethiopia	86			

Source: International Railway Statistics

Motor Vehicles

The automobile is one of the icons of the industrial age. Once considered a sign of affluence, it is now deemed a necessity that in developed countries is available to practically everyone. There are half a billion cars on the road in the world, one for every twelve persons. In the United States alone there is one car for every two persons. But the world is paying a heavy price for the convenience of auto travel. More than half a million people die annually in road accidents, 22.653 billion tons of carbon dioxide are pumped into the atmosphere, and the world's dwindling petroleum and iron reserves are being depleted. Because its future is tied to the availability of petroleum, the future of the oil-powered automobile is in serious doubt. Mass transit has made a comeback in recent years as an alternative to automobile travel, but it is now used generally by the poor or by urban commuters. Commercial vehicles include vans, trucks, buses, tractors, and semitrailer combinations.

15.4 Automobiles

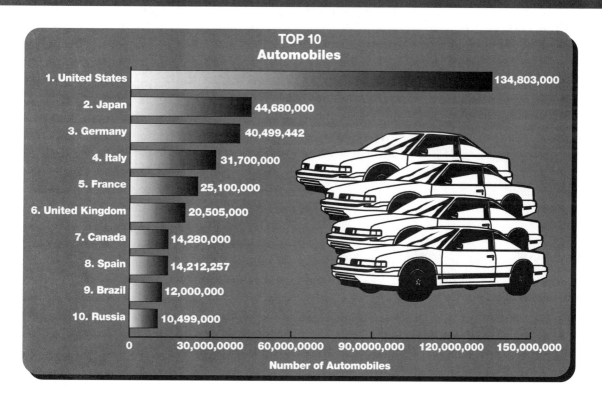

TOP 10
Automobiles

Rank	Country/Entity	Automobiles
1. United States		134,803,000
2. Japan		44,680,000
3. Germany		40,499,442
4. Italy		31,700,000
5. France		25,100,000
6. United Kingdom		20,505,000
7. Canada		14,280,000
8. Spain		14,212,257
9. Brazil		12,000,000
10. Russia		10,499,000

Number of Automobiles

Rank	Country/Entity	Automobiles	Rank	Country/Entity	Automobiles	Rank	Country/Entity	Automobiles
11	Mexico	8,449,969	20	Taiwan	4,146,500	29	Portugal	2,560,000
12	Australia	8,370,000	21	South Africa	3,810,000	30	Hungary	2,264,165
13	Poland	7,517,266	22	Sweden	3,630,760	31	Greece	2,204,761
14	South Korea	6,006,290	23	Austria	3,593,588	32	Romania	2,197,477
15	Netherlands	5,740,000	24	Turkey	3,231,562	33	Indonesia	2,107,299
16	Argentina	4,665,329	25	Switzerland	3,229,169	34	Finland	1,900,855
17	Ukraine	4,510,000	26	Czech Republic	3,113,476	35	Denmark	1,729,405
18	Belgium	4,339,231	27	India	2,720,000	36	Saudi Arabia	1,710,000
19	China	4,179,000	28	Malaysia	2,588,641	37	Norway	1,684,664

Rank	Country/Entity	Automobiles	Rank	Country/Entity	Automobiles	Rank	Country/Entity	Automobiles
38	New Zealand	1,650,112	97	Turkmenistan	170,600	156	Uganda	24,400
39	Bulgaria	1,647,571	98	Jordan	167,828	157	Guyana	24,000
40	Iran	1,630,000	99	Moldova	165,941	158	Gabon	23,800
41	Venezuela	1,485,221	100	Kyrgyzstan	164,000	159	San Marino	23,561
42	Thailand	1,440,000	101	Réunion	157,700	160	Benin	22,200
43	Puerto Rico	1,432,000	102	Zambia	142,000	161	Gaza Strip	21,206
44	Yugoslavia	1,400,000	103	Bahrain	141,901	162	Mongolia	21,200
45	Egypt	1,280,000	104	Brunei	141,371	163	Sierra Leone	20,860
46	Lebanon	1,197,521	105	Panama	140,900	164	Monaco	20,715
47	Colombia	1,150,000	106	Martinique	135,269	165	Bermuda	20,700
48	Israel	1,121,730	107	Syria	134,000	166	Cuba	20,000
49	Kazakhstan	1,030,000	108	Qatar	125,700	167	Liechtenstein	18,820
50	Morocco	1,030,000	109	Iceland	124,909	168	Gibraltar	18,404
51	Slovakia	1,015,794	110	Trinidad and Tobago	123,500	169	Mauritania	17,300
52	Ireland	990,384	111	El Salvador	102,000	170	Laos	17,200
53	Belarus	955,526	112	Guatemala	102,000	171	Burkina Faso	16,800
54	Pakistan	955,098	113	Guadeloupe	94,700	172	Burundi	16,800
55	Chile	888,645	114	Cameroon	92,200	173	Guinea	13,700
56	Algeria	871,000	115	Jamaica	86,791	174	Antigua and Barbuda	13,588
57	Uzbekistan	865,300	116	Ghana	86,200	175	Papua New Guinea	13,000
58	Congo, Dem. Rep. of	762,000	117	Mozambique	84,000	176	Northern Mariana Islands	12,113
59	Lithuania	718,469	118	Bangladesh	82,198	177	Rwanda	11,900
60	Croatia	710,910	119	Honduras	81,439	178	Somalia	11,800
61	Slovenia	698,211	120	Senegal	80,600	179	Faroe Islands	11,528
62	Iraq	672,000	121	Guam	74,728	180	Lesotho	11,100
63	Nigeria	663,000	122	Togo	74,662	181	Belize	10,667
64	Philippines	609,000	123	Nicaragua	72,413	182	Liberia	10,300
65	Libya	592,000	124	Netherlands Antilles	69,321	183	Saint Lucia	10,000
66	Kuwait	545,000	125	West Bank	69,200	184	Chad	9,630
67	Peru	505,766	126	Namibia	62,500	185	Central African Republic	9,500
68	Zimbabwe	492,000	127	Albania	58,682	186	Djibouti	8,550
69	Uruguay	444,835	128	New Caledonia	58,500	187	Gambia	7,950
70	Georgia	441,828	129	Jersey	58,491	188	Comoros	7,080
71	Bosnia and Herzegovina	438,080	130	Madagascar	58,100	189	Equatorial Guinea	6,500
72	Ecuador	395,000	131	Fiji	49,712	190	Cape Verde	6,479
73	Singapore	384,450	132	Tanzania	47,500	191	Guinea-Bissau	6,300
74	Estonia	383,444	133	Virgin Islands (U.S.)	47,255	192	Western Sahara	6,284
75	Latvia	379,895	134	Bahamas	46,089	193	Saint Vincent and the Grenadines	5,473
76	Hong Kong	325,131	135	Ethiopia	45,559			
77	Azerbaijan	289,000	136	Suriname	44,300	194	Eritrea	5,350
78	Macedonia	285,907	137	Myanmar (Burma)	44,000	195	Seychelles	5,100
79	Côte d'Ivoire	271,000	138	Barbados	43,711	196	Nepal	4,949
80	Kenya	271,000	139	Cambodia	42,210	197	Grenada	4,739
81	Sudan	263,000	140	Macau	41,403	198	American Samoa	4,628
82	Costa Rica	259,000	141	Isle of Man	38,917	199	Saint Kitts and Nevis	4,000
83	North Korea	248,000	142	French Polynesia	38,900	200	Vanuatu	4,000
84	Tunisia	248,000	143	Mauritius	37,766	201	São Tomé and Príncipe	3,810
85	Luxembourg	231,666	144	Niger	37,500	202	Dominica	2,770
86	Yemen	229,084	145	Congo, Rep. of	36,100	203	Bhutan	2,590
87	Sri Lanka	220,000	146	Andorra	35,941	204	Solomon Islands	2,052
88	Cyprus	219,749	147	Aruba	35,679	205	Greenland	1,944
89	Bolivia	213,666	148	Guernsey	33,037	206	Armenia	1,590
90	Dominican Republic	209,000	149	Haiti	32,000	207	Marshall Islands	1,418
91	Oman	202,741	150	Afghanistan	31,000	208	Tonga	1,136
92	Angola	197,000	151	French Guiana	27,700	209	Samoa	1,068
93	United Arab Emirates	197,000	152	Swaziland	27,300	210	Maldives	938
94	Tajikistan	184,900	153	Botswana	27,058	211	Kiribati	307
95	Paraguay	174,212	154	Malawi	25,400			
96	Malta	173,259	155	Mali	24,700			

Source: World Motor Vehicle Data

15.5 Persons per Automobile

Rank	Country/Entity	Persons per Automobile	Rank	Country/Entity	Persons per Automobile	Rank	Country/Entity	Persons per Automobile
1	Nepal	2,259	60	Syria	40	118	Chile	10.0
2	Ethiopia	842	61	Sri Lanka	39	119	Saint Kitts and Nevis	10.0
3	Bangladesh	634	62	Equatorial Guinea	37	120	United Arab Emirates	9.7
4	Myanmar (Burma)	525	63	Egypt	35	121	Fiji	9.4
5	Armenia	499	64	Albania	34	122	Macau	9.2
6	Uganda	397	65	Côte d'Ivoire	34	123	Bosnia and Herzegovina	8.9
7	Bhutan	348	66	Marshall Islands	34	124	Romania	8.8
8	Afghanistan	332	67	Congo, Dem. Rep. of	33	125	Costa Rica	8.5
9	Tanzania	323	68	Nicaragua	31	126	Trinidad and Tobago	8.5
10	Burkina Faso	304	69	Yemen	31	127	South Africa	7.6
11	Somalia	278	70	Tajikistan	30	128	Saint Lucia	7.3
12	Chad	265	71	Gabon	29	129	Mexico	7.2
13	Mali	224	72	Gaza Strip	29	130	Suriname	7.0
14	Guinea	217	73	Peru	28	131	Yugoslavia	6.9
15	Rwanda	216	74	Iran	26	132	Malaysia	6.8
16	Laos	208	75	Vanuatu	26	133	Oman	6.8
17	Cuba	205	76	Ecuador	25	134	Uruguay	6.4
18	Cambodia	197	77	São Tomé and Príncipe	25	135	Nauru	6.3
19	Central African Republic	195	78	Uzbekistan	25	136	Macedonia	6.2
20	India	190	79	Mauritius	23	137	Saudi Arabia	6.2
21	Burundi	186	80	Guyana	22	138	Croatia	6.0
22	Madagascar	181	81	Honduras	22	139	Argentina	5.9
23	Malawi	174	82	Bolivia	21	140	Libya	5.8
24	Niger	171	83	Colombia	21	141	Singapore	5.8
25	Benin	160	84	Dominican Republic	21	142	South Korea	5.3
26	Mozambique	155	85	El Salvador	21	143	Latvia	5.3
27	Kiribati	147	86	Algeria	20	144	Barbados	4.9
28	Sierra Leone	141	87	Azerbaijan	20	145	Slovakia	4.8
29	Nigeria	134	88	Botswana	20	146	Bahamas	4.7
30	China	128	89	Iraq	20	147	Bulgaria	4.5
31	Maldives	123	90	Morocco	20	148	Lithuania	4.4
32	Haiti	121	91	Western Sahara	20	149	Antigua and Barbuda	4.3
33	Pakistan	107	92	Greenland	19	150	Poland	4.3
34	Guinea-Bissau	100	93	Jamaica	19	151	Taiwan	4.3
35	Sudan	98	94	Zimbabwe	19	152	French Polynesia	3.9
36	Papua New Guinea	93	95	Moldova	18	153	Hungary	3.9
37	Cameroon	91	96	Paraguay	18	154	Israel	3.9
38	Mauritania	85	97	Swaziland	18	155	Palau	3.8
39	Philippines	82	98	Tunisia	17	156	Portugal	3.6
40	Ghana	80	99	Jordan	16	157	French Guiana	3.5
41	Kenya	80	100	Turkey	15	158	Bahrain	3.4
42	Senegal	78	101	Russia	14	159	Greece	3.4
43	Solomon Islands	75	102	Dominica	13	160	Réunion	3.4
44	Samoa	74	103	Hong Kong	13	161	Estonia	3.3
45	Gambia	72	104	Namibia	13	162	Czech Republic	3.1
46	Liberia	59	105	Saint Vincent and the Grenadines	13	163	Guadeloupe	3.1
47	Lesotho	58				164	Ireland	3.1
48	Djibouti	56	106	Thailand	13	165	Faroe Islands	3.0
49	Tonga	53	107	West Bank	13	166	Northern Mariana Islands	3.0
50	Angola	52	108	Belize	12	167	Qatar	3.0
51	Guatemala	52	109	Grenada	12	168	Lebanon	2.9
52	Congo, Rep. of	48	110	Panama	12	169	Slovenia	2.7
53	Indonesia	47	111	American Samoa	11	170	Cyprus	2.6
54	Zambia	44	112	Belarus	11	171	Denmark	2.6
55	Cape Verde	43	113	Georgia	11	172	Bermuda	2.5
56	Mongolia	42	114	Kazakhstan	11	173	United Kingdom	2.5
57	Comoros	41	115	Seychelles	11	174	Finland	2.4
58	Togo	41	116	Venezuela	11	175	Kuwait	2.4
59	Mayotte	40	117	Brazil	10	176	Netherlands	2.4

Rank	Country/Entity	Persons per Automobile	Rank	Country/Entity	Persons per Automobile	Rank	Country/Entity	Persons per Automobile
177	Martinique	2.3	188	Brunei	1.9	199	Isle of Man	1.6
178	New Caledonia	2.3	189	France	1.9	200	Italy	1.6
179	Spain	2.3	190	Germany	1.9	201	Luxembourg	1.6
180	Aruba	2.2	191	Iceland	1.9	202	Virgin Islands (U.S.)	1.6
181	Netherlands Antilles	2.2	192	Japan	1.9	203	Liechtenstein	1.5
182	Puerto Rico	2.2	193	New Zealand	1.8	204	Gibraltar	1.4
183	Sweden	2.2	194	Malta	1.7	205	Guam	1.4
184	Austria	2.1	195	Andorra	1.6	206	Jersey	1.3
185	Belgium	2.1	196	Australia	1.6	207	Monaco	1.3
186	Norway	2.1	197	Canada	1.6	208	United States	1.3
187	Switzerland	2.0	198	Guernsey	1.6	209	San Marino	0.9

Source: World Motor Vehicle Data

15.6 Trucks and Buses

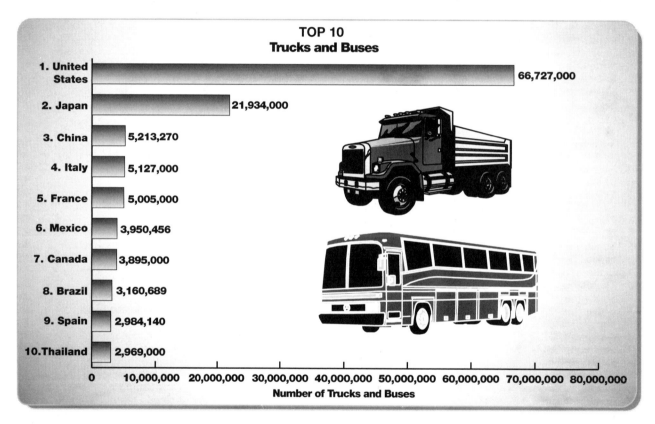

TOP 10
Trucks and Buses

Rank	Country	Number
1. United States		66,727,000
2. Japan		21,934,000
3. China		5,213,270
4. Italy		5,127,000
5. France		5,005,000
6. Mexico		3,950,456
7. Canada		3,895,000
8. Brazil		3,160,689
9. Spain		2,984,140
10. Thailand		2,969,000

Number of Trucks and Buses

Rank	Country/Entity	Trucks and Buses	Rank	Country/Entity	Trucks and Buses	Rank	Country/Entity	Trucks and Buses
11	United Kingdom	2,712,000	20	Saudi Arabia	1,172,600	29	Kazakhstan	516,000
12	Australia	2,640,300	21	Greece	908,423	30	Venezuela	511,809
13	South Korea	2,462,611	22	Turkey	809,361	31	Chile	469,142
14	Germany	2,336,760	23	Taiwan	799,600	32	Malaysia	465,940
15	India	2,207,000	24	Netherlands	680,000	33	Belgium	431,376
16	Indonesia	2,024,702	25	Iran	609,000	34	Egypt	423,300
17	South Africa	1,640,000	26	Algeria	566,000	35	Russia	407,000
18	Poland	1,472,278	27	Colombia	550,000	36	Romania	385,111
19	Argentina	1,181,569	28	Congo, Dem. Rep. of	550,000	37	Norway	382,017

Rank	Country/Entity	Trucks and Buses	Rank	Country/Entity	Trucks and Buses	Rank	Country/Entity	Trucks and Buses
38	Iraq	368,000	95	Ecuador	58,650	152	Bahamas	11,858
39	New Zealand	351,494	96	Bosnia and Herzegovina	50,578	153	Sierra Leone	11,014
40	Peru	338,871	97	Georgia	50,220	154	Mauritius	10,625
41	Sweden	322,286	98	United Arab Emirates	49,150	155	Barbados	10,583
42	Hungary	322,000	99	Sudan	47,800	156	French Guiana	10,400
43	Libya	312,000	100	Uruguay	46,245	157	Jersey	9,922
44	Austria	300,042	101	Botswana	42,696	158	Belarus	9,289
45	Denmark	288,464	102	Myanmar (Burma)	42,000	159	Mauritania	9,210
46	Tunisia	283,000	103	Malta	41,849	160	Saint Lucia	9,200
47	Yemen	282,615	104	Jamaica	41,312	161	Cambodia	9,005
48	Switzerland	277,399	105	Slovenia	40,206	162	Guyana	9,000
49	Morocco	273,100	106	Réunion	38,600	163	Gambia	8,240
50	Israel	272,593	107	Tanzania	38,000	164	Guernsey	7,522
51	Finland	260,115	108	Guadeloupe	36,000	165	Martinique	7,328
52	Sri Lanka	248,900	109	Albania	34,441	166	Central African Republic	7,000
53	Puerto Rico	229,000	110	Afghanistan	34,000	167	Northern Mariana Islands	6,479
54	Pakistan	225,829	111	Fiji	33,928	168	Belize	6,108
55	Philippines	221,900	112	Mongolia	33,420	169	Laos	6,020
56	Portugal	219,696	113	Togo	33,061	170	Armenia	5,950
57	Syria	218,900	114	Cuba	33,000	171	Isle of Man	4,925
58	Bulgaria	204,950	115	Senegal	32,410	172	Guinea-Bissau	4,900
59	Czech Republic	204,238	116	Papua New Guinea	32,000	173	Comoros	4,870
60	Honduras	170,006	117	Guam	30,739	174	Gaza Strip	4,639
61	El Salvador	159,700	118	Bahrain	29,584	175	Andorra	4,186
62	Ireland	155,153	119	Macedonia	29,197	176	San Marino	4,013
63	Kuwait	155,000	120	Malawi	28,900	177	Bermuda	4,000
64	Côte d'Ivoire	150,000	121	Liberia	28,300	178	Equatorial Guinea	4,000
65	Hong Kong	142,446	122	Mozambique	26,800	179	Macau	3,803
66	Dominican Republic	141,400	123	Swaziland	26,340	180	Tajikistan	3,600
67	Singapore	139,113	124	Angola	26,000	181	Nepal	3,363
68	Bolivia	133,984	125	Luxembourg	25,529	182	Grenada	3,068
69	Costa Rica	132,940	126	Uganda	25,300	183	Faroe Islands	2,895
70	Yugoslavia	132,000	127	Trinidad and Tobago	24,500	184	Saint Vincent and the Grenadines	2,878
71	Ghana	130,000	128	New Caledonia	22,600			
72	Lithuania	118,474	129	Lesotho	22,200	185	Dominica	2,839
73	Oman	108,600	130	Netherlands Antilles	21,194	186	Monaco	2,702
74	Zimbabwe	108,000	131	Haiti	21,000	187	Solomon Islands	2,574
75	Bangladesh	104,860	132	West Bank	20,723	188	Vanuatu	2,300
76	Cyprus	103,852	133	Ethiopia	20,462	189	Cape Verde	2,099
77	Slovakia	97,516	134	Guinea	19,300	190	Seychelles	2,000
78	Guatemala	96,800	135	Burkina Faso	17,222	191	Liechtenstein	1,949
79	Latvia	90,184	136	Mali	17,100	192	Djibouti	1,870
80	Azerbaijan	88,800	137	Suriname	17,050	193	São Tomé and Príncipe	1,470
81	Lebanon	84,736	138	Iceland	16,623	194	Bhutan	1,367
82	Jordan	82,516	139	Brunei	16,557	195	Antigua and Barbuda	1,342
83	Panama	79,000	140	French Polynesia	16,500	196	Samoa	1,169
84	Croatia	77,394	141	Rwanda	15,900	197	Maldives	1,117
85	Paraguay	76,565	142	Gabon	15,700	198	Gibraltar	1,064
86	Kenya	75,900	143	Congo, Rep. of	15,600	199	Greenland	1,039
87	Zambia	73,500	144	Madagascar	15,340	200	Aruba	935
88	Estonia	72,607	145	Burundi	15,000	201	Tonga	766
89	Moldova	69,069	146	Virgin Islands (U.S.)	14,868	202	Saint Kitts and Nevis	700
90	Nigeria	68,300	147	Uzbekistan	14,500	203	American Samoa	489
91	Nicaragua	68,090	148	Chad	14,360	204	Western Sahara	424
92	Namibia	66,500	149	Niger	14,100	205	Marshall Islands	193
93	Qatar	63,800	150	Benin	12,400	206	Kiribati	130
94	Cameroon	60,000	151	Somalia	12,200			

Source: World Motor Vehicle Data

Roads

In terms of length and intensity of use, roads dwarf both railroads and waterways. Ranging from the great national highways in every country which are engineering marvels—the German autobahns being a classic example—to small dusty trails and paths, they form arterial networks for every conceivable form of traffic. Historically designed for use by pedestrians, they are now designed solely for vehicular traffic in Western countries, although in many African and Asian nations pedestrians still outnumber vehicles. Ironically, growth of traffic on most highways tends to create congestion and long delays at critical points, thus extending travel time and defeating the purpose of roads. The percentage of paved roads is a major distinction between the developed and developing worlds. In most developing countries, only urban roads are paved and the unpaved rural roads are virtually impassable in rainy weather.

15.7 Roads

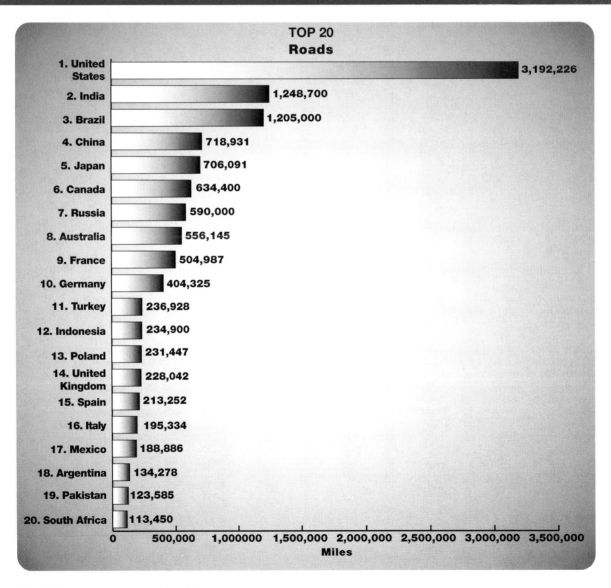

TOP 20
Roads

Rank	Country	Miles
1.	United States	3,192,226
2.	India	1,248,700
3.	Brazil	1,205,000
4.	China	718,931
5.	Japan	706,091
6.	Canada	634,400
7.	Russia	590,000
8.	Australia	556,145
9.	France	504,987
10.	Germany	404,325
11.	Turkey	236,928
12.	Indonesia	234,900
13.	Poland	231,447
14.	United Kingdom	228,042
15.	Spain	213,252
16.	Italy	195,334
17.	Mexico	188,886
18.	Argentina	134,278
19.	Pakistan	123,585
20.	South Africa	113,450

Rank	Country/Entity	Roads (miles)	Rank	Country/Entity	Roads (miles)	Rank	Country/Entity	Roads (miles)
21	Ukraine	107,035	85	Mozambique	18,523	149	Lesotho	3,079
22	Bangladesh	104,709	86	Paraguay	17,956	150	United Arab Emirates	2,952
23	Philippines	100,062	87	Ethiopia	17,622	151	Suriname	2,778
24	Saudi Arabia	98,798	88	Malawi	17,324	152	Kuwait	2,704
25	Kazakhstan	98,583	89	Myanmar (Burma)	17,100	153	Guinea-Bissau	2,703
26	Iran	98,200	90	Cuba	16,839	154	Haiti	2,535
27	Congo, Dem. Rep. of	95,708	91	Croatia	16,732	155	Eritrea	2,442
28	Romania	95,175	92	Uganda	16,653	156	Swaziland	2,377
29	Belgium	88,579	93	Central African Republic	14,795	157	Guadeloupe	2,000
30	Sweden	84,645	94	Turkmenistan	14,600	158	Bhutan	1,998
31	Austria	80,792	95	Puerto Rico	14,379	159	Singapore	1,886
32	Czech Republic	77,528	96	Somalia	14,300	160	Djibouti	1,796
33	Netherlands	77,090	97	Tunisia	13,975	161	Bahrain	1,762
34	Greece	72,350	98	Bosnia and Herzegovina	13,153	162	Belize	1,721
35	Colombia	66,238	99	Georgia	13,049	163	Réunion	1,711
36	Vietnam	65,895	100	Afghanistan	13,000	164	Equatorial Guinea	1,667
37	Sri Lanka	63,753	101	Papua New Guinea	12,263	165	Gambia	1,640
38	Algeria	63,643	102	Taiwan	11,830	166	Brunei	1,527
39	Malaysia	58,393	103	Jamaica	11,600	167	Bahamas	1,522
40	Ireland	57,377	104	Kyrgyzstan	11,533	168	Martinique	1,286
41	New Zealand	57,081	105	Botswana	11,388	169	Mauritius	1,138
42	Zimbabwe	57,048	106	Laos	11,280	170	Hong Kong	1,083
43	Norway	56,086	107	Slovakia	11,103	171	Barbados	1,000
44	Venezuela	55,737	108	Nicaragua	10,654	172	Malta	997
45	Tanzania	54,743	109	Albania	9,631	173	Solomon Islands	826
46	Libya	50,704	110	Honduras	9,383	174	Qatar	752
47	Chile	49,550	111	Estonia	9,316	175	Antigua and Barbuda	721
48	Uzbekistan	48,715	112	Mali	9,181	176	French Guiana	706
49	Finland	48,294	113	Slovenia	9,158	177	Grenada	700
50	South Korea	46,127	114	Israel	9,134	178	Cape Verde	680
51	Angola	45,128	115	Senegal	9,060	179	Vanuatu	652
52	Peru	44,400	116	Rwanda	9,050	180	Saint Vincent and the Grenadines	634
53	Denmark	44,378	117	Burundi	8,997			
54	Switzerland	44,151	118	Tajikistan	8,000	181	French Polynesia	584
55	Portugal	42,708	119	Guatemala	7,950	182	Guam	550
56	Latvia	40,198	120	Congo, Rep. of	7,929	183	Comoros	544
57	Yemen	40,144	121	Burkina Faso	7,771	184	Virgin Islands (U.S.)	532
58	Kenya	39,558	122	Iceland	7,691	185	Saint Lucia	500
59	Lithuania	38,178	123	El Salvador	7,655	186	Samoa	485
60	Thailand	38,000	124	Cambodia	7,643	187	Dominica	475
61	Morocco	37,601	125	Dominican Republic	7,643	188	Tonga	419
62	Egypt	36,000	126	Moldova	7,617	189	Kiribati	407
63	Azerbaijan	35,897	127	Sierra Leone	7,254	190	Netherlands Antilles	368
64	Bolivia	34,478	128	Sudan	7,214	191	Isle of Man	357
65	Belarus	32,030	129	Mongolia	6,947	192	Northern Mariana Islands	307
66	Uruguay	31,600	130	Panama	6,706	193	Faroe Islands	285
67	Côte d'Ivoire	31,168	131	Liberia	6,400	194	Aruba	236
68	Madagascar	30,967	132	Cyprus	6,307	195	American Samoa	217
69	Yugoslavia	30,832	133	Niger	6,129	196	Seychelles	214
70	Iraq	28,900	134	Macedonia	5,302	197	Liechtenstein	201
71	Ecuador	26,785	135	Benin	5,257	198	Mayotte	195
72	Namibia	25,134	136	Trinidad and Tobago	5,070	199	São Tomé and Príncipe	193
73	Syria	24,384	137	Guyana	4,859	200	Saint Kitts and Nevis	193
74	Zambia	24,170	138	Armenia	4,797	201	Andorra	167
75	Ghana	23,339	139	Gabon	4,743	202	Bermuda	149
76	Bulgaria	23,190	140	Mauritania	4,700	203	San Marino	147
77	Costa Rica	22,121	141	Nepal	4,691	204	Micronesia	140
78	Cameroon	21,300	142	Togo	4,672	205	Macau	80
79	Nigeria	20,387	143	Jordan	4,194	206	Greenland	50
80	Chad	20,319	144	Lebanon	3,951	207	Palau	40
81	Oman	19,160	145	Western Sahara	3,900	208	Gibraltar	27
82	Guinea	18,809	146	New Caledonia	3,580	209	Monaco	27
83	Hungary	18,640	147	Luxembourg	3,206	210	Nauru	17
84	North Korea	18,600	148	Fiji	3,200	211	Tuvalu	5

Source: World Road Statistics

15.8 Density of Road Networks

Rank	Country/Entity	Kilometers of Road Per Square Kilometer	Rank	Country/Entity	Kilometers of Road Per Square Kilometer	Rank	Country/Entity	Kilometers of Road Per Square Kilometer
1	Singapore	4.71	14	Hong Kong	1.64	27	Mauritius	0.91
2	Belgium	4.69	15	Trinidad and Tobago	1.62	28	Greece	0.89
3	Bahrain	4.36	16	Puerto Rico	1.58	29	South Korea	0.84
4	Barbados	3.84	17	Bangladesh	1.55	30	Portugal	0.77
5	Netherlands	3.06	18	Austria	1.54	31	Slovakia	0.75
6	Japan	3.03	19	United Kingdom	1.53	32	Slovenia	0.74
7	Luxembourg	2.00	20	Sri Lanka	1.51	33	Israel	0.73
8	Germany	1.77	21	Ireland	1.32	34	Czech Republic	0.70
9	Jamaica	1.73	22	Poland	1.20	35	Costa Rica	0.70
10	Switzerland	1.72	23	Cyprus	1.13	36	United States	0.68
11	Hungary	1.71	24	Italy	1.05	37	Spain	0.68
12	Denmark	1.66	25	Lithuania	1.00	38	Romania	0.65
13	France	1.64	26	Latvia	0.94	39	India	0.63

Source: World Road Statistics

Air Traffic

Air traffic is the main global means of travel. Worldwide it now far exceeds 1 trillion passenger miles (1.6 trillion passenger kilometers) and 29 billion freight miles (46 billion freight kilometers). The growth in air traffic, both passenger and freight, has been phenomenal since the 1960s. Air travel has become cheaper, faster, and safer.

Further, airlines have become more profitable because of the heavier traffic. More cities now have modern airports, and more commuter flights are scheduled between large cities. More than 100 nations of the world have national airways, some of them directly owned by their governments.

15.9 Air Passangers

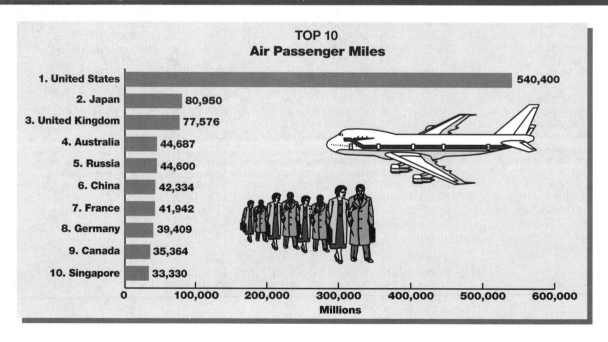

TOP 10
Air Passenger Miles

Rank	Country	Air Passenger Miles (Millions)
1.	United States	540,400
2.	Japan	80,950
3.	United Kingdom	77,576
4.	Australia	44,687
5.	Russia	44,600
6.	China	42,334
7.	France	41,942
8.	Germany	39,409
9.	Canada	35,364
10.	Singapore	33,330

Rank	Country/Entity	Air Passenger Miles (millions)	Rank	Country/Entity	Air Passenger Miles (millions)	Rank	Country/Entity	Air Passenger Miles (millions)
11	South Korea	30,139	67	Cuba	1,648	123	Dominican Republic	145
12	Netherlands	28,292	68	Algeria	1,643	124	New Caledonia	145
13	Taiwan	25,230	69	Cyprus	1,588	125	Antigua and Barbuda	140
14	Brazil	22,471	70	Peru	1,535	126	Benin	140
15	Spain	21,154	71	Czech Republic	1,469	127	Central African Republic	140
16	Italy	18,429	72	Moldova	1,461	128	Mali	140
17	Thailand	18,160	73	Tajikistan	1,386	129	Mauritania	140
18	Malaysia	14,017	74	Tunisia	1,338	130	Niger	140
19	Mexico	12,902	75	Azerbaijan	1,259	131	Senegal	140
20	India	12,563	76	El Salvador	1,229	132	Côte d'Ivoire	139
21	Switzerland	12,257	77	Jamaica	1,204	133	Congo, Rep. of	139
22	Saudi Arabia	11,500	78	Lebanon	1,174	134	Guyana	139
23	New Zealand	11,090	79	Ethiopia	1,142	135	Chad	138
24	Indonesia	8,904	80	Kenya	1,142	136	Burkina Faso	135
25	South Africa	8,595	81	Costa Rica	1,135	137	Congo, Dem. Rep. of	135
26	Philippines	7,987	82	Romania	1,126	138	Togo	134
27	Turkey	7,646	83	Malta	1,070	139	Vietnam	130
28	Israel	7,430	84	Iraq	976	140	Nauru	128
29	Argentina	7,323	85	Turkmenistan	971	141	Afghanistan	122
30	Pakistan	6,911	86	Bolivia	912	142	Bahamas	119
31	Finland	6,654	87	Ecuador	876	143	Isle of Man	116
32	Belgium	5,599	88	Belarus	864	144	Tanzania	114
33	Norway	5,439	89	Paraguay	767	145	Cape Verde	106
34	Egypt	5,432	90	Fiji	742	146	Barbados	93
35	Sweden	5,236	91	Yemen	735	147	Vanuatu	93
36	Portugal	4,957	92	Syria	692	148	Somalia	81
37	Greece	4,937	93	Nigeria	612	149	Luxembourg	80
38	Austria	4,701	94	Yugoslavia	598	150	Sierra Leone	68
39	Venezuela	4,581	95	Angola	589	151	Estonia	67
40	Chile	3,935	96	Suriname	549	152	North Korea	52
41	Iran	3,808	97	Panama	542	153	Nicaragua	45
42	Armenia	3,453	98	Zimbabwe	522	154	Djibouti	42
43	Denmark	3,340	99	Nepal	478	155	Solomon Islands	40
44	Georgia	3,291	100	Namibia	470	156	Slovakia	38
45	Ireland	3,186	101	Papua New Guinea	459	157	Botswana	36
46	Kuwait	3,184	102	Madagascar	409	158	Uganda	32
47	Uzbekistan	3,017	103	Ghana	407	159	Gambia	31
48	Morocco	2,992	104	Sudan	404	160	Swaziland	31
49	Poland	2,879	105	Uruguay	401	161	Marshall Islands	30
50	Kazakhstan	2,858	106	Seychelles	389	162	Bhutan	29
51	Colombia	2,837	107	Slovenia	382	163	Laos	29
52	Kyrgyzstan	2,739	108	Gabon	354	164	Guinea	20
53	Jordan	2,731	109	Croatia	306	165	Greenland	16
54	Trinidad and Tobago	2,538	110	Mongolia	305	166	Kiribati	6.0
55	Sri Lanka	2,403	111	Myanmar (Burma)	272	167	Tonga	5.8
56	Mauritius	2,115	112	Libya	248	168	São Tomé and Príncipe	5.0
57	Iceland	1,850	113	Guatemala	239	169	Maldives	4.8
58	Ukraine	1,775	114	Mozambique	239	170	Liberia	4.3
59	Bulgaria	1,765	115	Netherlands Antilles	234	171	Equatorial Guinea	4.0
60	Bangladesh	1,763	116	Lithuania	219	172	Lesotho	3.9
61	Hungary	1,716	117	Cameroon	196	173	Guinea-Bissau	3.7
62	Bahrain	1,714	118	Zambia	192	174	Comoros	1.9
63	Oman	1,714	119	Latvia	187	175	Burundi	1.2
64	Qatar	1,714	120	Macedonia	182	176	Rwanda	1.2
65	United Arab Emirates	1,714	121	Honduras	180			
66	Brunei	1,685	122	Malawi	180			

Source: World Air Transport Statistics

Rank	Country/Entity	Air Cargo (million short ton miles)	Rank	Country/Entity	Air Cargo (million short ton miles)	Rank	Country/Entity	Air Cargo (million short ton miles)
1	United States	14,568.0	58	Yemen	82.0	115	Central African Republic	11.2
2	Germany	8,611.0	59	Syria	81.0	116	Mali	11.2
3	France	7,740.0	60	Greece	80.0	117	Mauritania	11.2
4	Canada	4,824.0	61	Angola	77.0	118	Niger	11.2
5	Japan	4,487.0	62	Ethiopia	77.0	119	Senegal	11.2
6	South Korea	3,924.0	63	Iran	75.1	120	Romania	10.8
7	Yugoslavia	3,371.0	64	Brunei	74.0	121	Côte d'Ivoire	10.5
8	Singapore	2,871.0	65	Bahrain	72.5	122	Chad	10.5
9	United Kingdom	2,625.0	66	United Arab Emirates	72.5	123	Congo, Rep. of	10.5
10	Spain	2,578.0	67	Oman	72.4	124	Algeria	10.1
11	Netherlands	2,490.0	68	Qatar	72.4	125	El Salvador	9.8
12	Taiwan	2,444.0	69	Ireland	70.0	126	Malta	9.4
13	China	1,527.0	70	Kazakhstan	68.0	127	Paraguay	8.0
14	Mexico	1,348.0	71	Nepal	63.8	128	Nigeria	7.9
15	Australia	1,257.0	72	Madagascar	58.0	129	Afghanistan	7.5
16	Russia	1,200.0	73	Papua New Guinea	56.4	130	Belarus	7.0
17	Brazil	1,118.0	74	Gabon	56.0	131	Marshall Islands	7.0
18	Chile	923.0	75	Fiji	51.6	132	Zambia	6.8
19	Italy	914.3	76	Poland	51.0	133	Panama	6.4
20	Argentina	911.0	77	Seychelles	48.0	134	Mozambique	6.0
21	Thailand	904.0	78	Kyrgyzstan	44.7	135	Nicaragua	4.8
22	Israel	815.0	79	Uruguay	42.0	136	Djibouti	4.0
23	Malaysia	795.0	80	Iraq	37.4	137	Slovakia	3.8
24	Colombia	662.0	81	Iceland	36.2	138	Latvia	3.6
25	Norway	639.0	82	Armenia	34.0	139	New Caledonia	3.4
26	Saudi Arabia	613.0	83	Azerbaijan	34.0	140	Gambia	3.0
27	Luxembourg	606.9	84	Kenya	32.7	141	Laos	3.0
28	New Zealand	444.0	85	Lebanon	32.0	142	Solomon Islands	3.0
29	India	437.9	86	Bolivia	31.7	143	Somalia	3.0
30	Indonesia	415.6	87	Cuba	31.2	144	Uganda	3.0
31	South Africa	370.0	88	Mongolia	31.0	145	Croatia	2.4
32	Uzbekistan	306.0	89	Costa Rica	30.0	146	Slovenia	2.3
33	Pakistan	290.0	90	Congo, Dem. Rep. of	29.0	147	Myanmar (Burma)	2.2
34	Trinidad and Tobago	277.0	91	Cameroon	27.0	148	Tanzania	2.0
35	Morocco	268.0	92	Zimbabwe	27.0	149	Dominican Republic	1.7
36	Kuwait	225.8	93	Cyprus	26.0	150	North Korea	1.4
37	Philippines	225.2	94	Honduras	26.0	151	Sierra Leone	1.4
38	Belgium	221.9	95	Bulgaria	24.1	152	Netherlands Antilles	1.2
39	Ukraine	210.0	96	Burkina Faso	23.4	153	Switzerland	1.0
40	Jordan	181.6	97	Lithuania	23.0	154	Guinea	0.9
41	Peru	177.0	98	Togo	23.0	155	Barbados	0.8
42	Sweden	171.0	99	Hungary	22.5	156	Vanuatu	0.8
43	Finland	165.3	100	Sudan	21.0	157	Equatorial Guinea	0.7
44	Turkey	146.7	101	Ghana	20.0	158	Guinea-Bissau	0.7
45	Venezuela	144.0	102	Macedonia	20.0	159	Liberia	0.7
46	Portugal	143.6	103	Malawi	19.0	160	São Tomé and Príncipe	0.7
47	Tajikistan	140.0	104	Suriname	18.0	161	Kiribati	0.5
48	Tunisia	139.5	105	Czech Republic	16.0	162	Estonia	0.4
49	Egypt	136.0	106	Guyana	16.0	163	Lesotho	0.4
50	Jamaica	136.0	107	Namibia	16.0	164	Botswana	0.3
51	Austria	120.3	108	Antigua and Barbuda	14.0	165	Libya	0.3
52	Denmark	117.0	109	Guatemala	14.0	166	Greenland	0.2
53	Ecuador	111.0	110	Nauru	14.0	167	Isle of Man	0.2
54	Sri Lanka	109.0	111	Cape Verde	13.2	168	Swaziland	0.09
55	Turkmenistan	98.0	112	Moldova	13.0	169	Bahamas	0.01
56	Mauritius	93.4	113	Vietnam	13.0	170	Tonga	0.01
57	Bangladesh	82.0	114	Benin	11.2			

Source: World Air Transport Statistics

Airports

Worldwide, there are 65,000 airports and airfields in every country and city in the world. Some of them are large ones like O'Hare in Chicago that can handle hundreds of flights a day, but the majority are small airfields that can handle only small private biplanes. There are thousands of airstrips in remote jungles and deserts inaccessible by road, rail, or river. Only the larger airports have the sophisticated air traffic control equipment that commercial planes require for safe landing and takeoff. They also need security devices deterring terrorist entry into planes.

15.11 Airports with Scheduled Flights

Rank	Country/Entity	Airports with Scheduled Flights, 1996	Rank	Country/Entity	Airports with Scheduled Flights, 1996	Rank	Country/Entity	Airports with Scheduled Flights, 1996
1	Australia	400	45	Iran	19	89	Puerto Rico	7
2	Canada	301	46	Madagascar	19	90	Senegal	7
3	Brazil	139	47	Myanmar (Burma)	19	91	Zimbabwe	7
4	Papua New Guinea	129	48	Angola	17	92	Austria	6
5	China	113	49	Kiribati	17	93	Guadeloupe	6
6	Mexico	83	50	Portugal	16	94	Kazakhstan	6
7	United States	83*	51	Bolivia	14	95	Micronesia	6
8	Indonesia	81	52	Costa Rica	14	96	Netherlands	6
9	Japan	73	53	Cuba	14	97	Niger	6
10	India	66	54	Ecuador	14	98	Oman	6
11	France	61	55	South Korea	14	99	Tonga	6
12	Russia	58	56	Denmark	13	100	United Arab Emirates	6
13	United Kingdom	57	57	Fiji	13	101	Cameroon	5
14	Norway	50	58	Kenya	13	102	Congo, Rep. of	5
15	Sweden	48	59	Namibia	13	103	Croatia	5
16	Colombia	43	60	Taiwan	13	104	Greenland	5
17	Germany	40	61	Congo, Dem. Rep. of	12	105	Malawi	5
18	Argentina	39	62	Libya	12	106	Maldives	5
19	Malaysia	39	63	Morocco	12	107	Netherlands Antilles	5
20	French Polynesia	36	64	Nigeria	12	108	Paraguay	5
21	Greece	36	65	Romania	12	109	Switzerland	5
22	New Zealand	36	66	Vietnam	12	110	Syria	5
23	Italy	34	67	Côte d'Ivoire	11	111	Tunisia	5
24	Pakistan	34	68	Egypt	11	112	Botswana	4
25	Ethiopia	31	69	Laos	11	113	Chad	4
26	Vanuatu	29	70	Tanzania	11	114	Jamaica	4
27	Algeria	28	71	Yemen	11	115	Saint Vincent and the Grenadines	4
28	Peru	27	72	New Caledonia	10			
29	Turkey	26	73	Nicaragua	10	116	Virgin Islands (U.S.)	4
30	Saudi Arabia	25	74	Panama	10	117	Yugoslavia	4
31	Spain	25	75	Belize	9	118	Zambia	4
32	Thailand	25	76	Cape Verde	9	119	Afghanistan	3
33	Finland	24	77	Ireland	9	120	American Samoa	3
34	Iceland	24	78	Mali	9	121	Bulgaria	3
35	Nepal	24	79	Mauritania	9	122	Estonia	3
36	South Africa	24	80	Uzbekistan	9	123	Lithuania	3
37	Bahamas	23	81	Bangladesh	8	124	Northern Mariana Islands	3
38	Chile	23	82	Cambodia	8	125	Rwanda	3
39	Gabon	23	83	French Guiana	8	126	Samoa	3
40	Marshall Islands	23	84	Honduras	8	127	Sudan	3
41	Philippines	21	85	Poland	8	128	Suriname	3
42	Solomon Islands	21	86	Dominican Republic	7	129	Antigua and Barbuda	2
43	Ukraine	20	87	Israel	7	130	Belarus	2
44	Venezuela	20	88	Mozambique	7	131	Belgium	2

Rank	Country/Entity	Airports with Scheduled Flights, 1996	Rank	Country/Entity	Airports with Scheduled Flights, 1996	Rank	Country/Entity	Airports with Scheduled Flights, 1996
132	Burkina Faso	2	159	Benin	1	186	Liberia	1
133	Comoros	2	160	Bermuda	1	187	Luxembourg	1
134	Cyprus	2	161	Bhutan	1	188	Malta	1
135	Czech Republic	2	162	Bosnia and Herzegovina	1	189	Mauritius	1
136	Dominica	2	163	Brunei	1	190	Mayotte	1
137	Eritrea	2	164	Burundi	1	191	Moldova	1
138	Grenada	2	165	Central African Republic	1	192	Monaco	1
139	Guatemala	2	166	Djibouti	1	193	Mongolia	1
140	Guinea	2	167	El Salvador	1	194	Nauru	1
141	Guinea-Bissau	2	168	Equatorial Guinea	1	195	Palau	1
142	Haiti	2	169	Faroe Islands	1	196	Qatar	1
143	Jordan	2	170	Gambia	1	197	Réunion	1
144	Kyrgyzstan	2	171	Georgia	1	198	Sierra Leone	1
145	Macedonia	2	172	Ghana	1	199	Singapore	1
146	Martinique	2	173	Gibraltar	1	200	Slovenia	1
147	São Tomé and Príncipe	2	174	Guam	1	201	Somalia	1
148	Seychelles	2	175	Guernsey	1	202	Sri Lanka	1
149	Slovakia	2	176	Guyana	1	203	Swaziland	1
150	Saint Kitts and Nevis	2	177	Hong Kong	1	204	Tajikistan	1
151	Saint Lucia	2	178	Hungary	1	205	Togo	1
152	Trinidad and Tobago	2	179	Isle of Man	1	206	Turkmenistan	1
153	Albania	1	180	Jersey	1	207	Tuvalu	1
154	Armenia	1	181	North Korea	1	208	Uganda	1
155	Aruba	1	182	Kuwait	1	209	Uruguay	1
156	Azerbaijan	1	183	Latvia	1	210	Western Sahara	1
157	Bahrain	1	184	Lebanon	1			
158	Barbados	1	185	Lesotho	1			

Source: Official Airline Guide

Note: *U.S. figure covers only airports with scheduled international flights.

15.12 Busiest Airports

Rank	Country/Entity	Passengers (thousands)	Rank	Country/Entity	Passengers (thousands)	Rank	Country/Entity	Passengers (thousands)
1	Chicago O'Hare	69,154	8	Frankfurt	38,761	15	Singapore Changi	23,130
2	Atlanta Hartsfield	63,303	9	Seoul Kimpo	34,706	16	Tokyo Narita	22,666
3	Dallas	58,035	10	Miami International	33,505	17	London Gatwick	22,029
4	Los Angeles	57,975	11	Denver	32,296	18	New York Kennedy	17,453
5	London Heathrow	56,038	12	Hong Kong	29,543	19	Bangkok	16,380
6	Tokyo Hanido	48,631	13	Paris Charles de Gaulle	28,665	20	Zurich	14,783
7	San Francisco	39,252	14	Amsterdam Schipol	27,085			

Source: Official Airline Guide

There are 67,300 ships worldwide of which 27,052 ships are over 1,000 gross registered tonnage (GRT). Their total GRT is 477.514 million and includes 306 passenger ships, 5,623 bulk carriers, 8,426 cargo ships, 1,048 chemical tankers, 321 combination bulk carriers, 2,378 container ships, 768 liquefied gas tankers, 4,435 oil tankers, 1,084 roll-on/roll-off cargo ships, 491 short-sea passenger ships, and 21 barge carriers. Shipping statistics are among the most accurate in the world because of the care with which Lloyds of London compiles its Shipping Register. The data relating to the number of ships and their GRT must be interpreted with caution, however, because of the phenomenon known as flags of convenience. To avoid taxes and levies, many ships are registered with small countries such as Panama, Cyprus, and Liberia, even though the owners may be American or British. Over the latter half of the twentieth century, both the United Kingdom and the United States have lost their preeminence in shipping. British and U.S. shipyards produce very few ships because of the high labor costs in these countries. Much of international trade is seaborne, and a nation's share of this traffic is represented by the cargo handled (both loaded and unloaded) in its ports.

15.13 Merchant Marine Tonnage

Rank	Country/Entity	Merchant Marine Dead Weight Tonnage (thousands)	Rank	Country/Entity	Merchant Marine Dead Weight Tonnage (thousands)	Rank	Country/Entity	Merchant Marine Dead Weight Tonnage (thousands)
1	Liberia	97,374.0	34	Australia	3,857.3	68	Nigeria	733.3
2	Panama	79,255.6	35	Vanuatu	3,259.6	69	Israel	723.4
3	Greece	45,276.6	36	Kuwait	3,188.5	70	Estonia	680.4
4	Cyprus	36,198.1	37	Indonesia	3,130.2	71	Qatar	635.6
5	Bahamas	33,081.7	38	Malaysia	2,916.3	72	Peru	615.6
6	Japan	22,000.0	39	Canada	2,896.8	73	Switzerland	602.8
7	Norway	20,834.0	40	Sweden	2,881.0	74	Morocco	586.2
8	China	20,658.0	41	Netherlands	2,874.0	75	Bangladesh	566.8
9	United States	18,585.0	42	Isle of Man	2,836.5	76	Pakistan	513.8
10	Belarus	18,373.0	43	Luxembourg	2,603.6	77	Ecuador	504.1
11	Malta	17,073.2	44	Bulgaria	1,938.2	78	Sri Lanka	472.6
12	Russia	16,592.3	45	Egypt	1,685.2	79	Czech Republic	446.2
13	Singapore	14,929.2	46	Iraq	1,578.8	80	Tunisia	443.3
14	Philippines	13,807.1	47	Mexico	1,495.3	81	Lebanon	438.2
15	South Korea	11,724.9	48	United Arab Emirates	1,491.7	82	Colombia	403.0
16	Hong Kong	11,688.6	49	Honduras	1,437.3	83	Lithuania	373.9
17	India	10,365.9	50	Latvia	1,436.9	84	Brunei	349.7
18	Brazil	9,348.3	51	Saudi Arabia	1,361.7	85	Slovenia	346.5
19	Taiwan	9,241.3	52	Venezuela	1,355.4	86	South Africa	282.5
20	Iran	8,345.3	53	Myanmar (Burma)	1,354.0	87	New Zealand	279.8
21	Denmark	7,589.1	54	Libya	1,223.6	88	Belgium	218.5
22	Italy	7,149.5	55	Thailand	1,194.5	89	Syria	210.4
23	Turkey	7,114.3	56	Argentina	1,173.1	90	Ireland	208.6
24	Saint Vincent and the Grenadines	7,044.2	57	Gibraltar	1,136.1	91	Austria	208.5
			58	Portugal	1,129.3	92	Bahrain	192.5
25	Germany	6,832.3	59	Georgia	1,108.0	93	Uruguay	172.5
26	Bermuda	5,206.5	60	Algeria	1,093.4	94	Mauritius	152.2
27	Yugoslavia	5,173.1	61	Netherlands Antilles	1,053.6	95	Croatia	140.9
28	Spain	5,077.3	62	Antigua and Barbuda	997.4	96	Ghana	131.0
29	France	4,981.0	63	Finland	989.3	97	Angola	123.5
30	Romania	4,845.5	64	North Korea	951.2	98	Iceland	114.9
31	United Kingdom	4,355.0	65	Cuba	924.6	99	Jordan	113.6
32	Poland	4,314.3	66	Vietnam	872.8	100	Côte d'Ivoire	98.6
33	Marshall Islands	4,182.4	67	Chile	854.9	101	Hungary	93.2

Rank	Country/Entity	Merchant Marine Dead Weight Tonnage (thousands)
102	Ethiopia	84.3
103	Barbados	84.0
104	Madagascar	82.1
105	Albania	81.0
106	Maldives	79.0
107	Sudan	62.2
108	Fiji	60.4
109	Faroe Islands	59.8
110	Tanzania	48.5
111	Belize	45.7
112	Papua New Guinea	40.9
113	Cameroon	39.8
114	Paraguay	38.5
115	Réunion	33.5
116	Mozambique	31.6
117	Cape Verde	30.9
118	Congo, Dem. Rep. of	30.7
119	Gabon	30.2
120	Senegal	27.5
121	Mauritania	23.9
122	Togo	20.6
123	Somalia	18.5
124	Sierra Leone	18.4
125	New Caledonia	18.1
126	Trinidad and Tobago	17.5
127	Greenland	17.2
128	French Polynesia	16.5
129	Jamaica	16.2
130	Tuvalu	16.0
131	Bolivia	15.8
132	Suriname	15.7
133	Tonga	13.7
134	Yemen	13.7
135	Guyana	13.5
136	Oman	11.7
137	Kenya	11.6
138	Congo, Rep. of	10.8
139	Dominican Republic	10.4
140	Uganda	8.6
141	Costa Rica	8.4
142	Micronesia	6.9
143	Equatorial Guinea	6.7
144	Samoa	6.5
145	Namibia	5.9
146	Nauru	5.8
147	Solomon Islands	5.0
148	Guadeloupe	4.4
149	Djibouti	4.1
150	Cambodia	3.8
151	Comoros	3.6
152	Seychelles	3.3
153	Dominica	3.2
154	Kiribati	2.7
155	São Tomé and Príncipe	2.3
156	Saint Lucia	2.1
157	Gambia	2.0
158	Guinea-Bissau	1.8
159	Guinea	1.7
160	Laos	1.5
161	Nicaragua	1.3
162	Martinique	1.1
163	Mayotte	1.1
164	Northern Mariana Islands	0.9
165	French Guiana	0.7
166	Saint Kitts and Nevis	0.6
167	Grenada	0.5
168	Burundi	0.4
169	Guatemala	0.4
170	Haiti	0.4
171	Malawi	0.3
172	Benin	0.2
173	American Samoa	0.1
174	Guam	0.1
175	Macau	0.1

Source: Lloyd's Register of Shipping

15.14 Merchant Marine Vessels

Rank	Country/Entity	Merchant Marine Vessels Over 100 Gross Tons
1	Japan	7,165
2	Panama	5,217
3	Russia	4,543
4	China	2,390
5	Spain	2,190
6	South Korea	2,138
7	Indonesia	2,014
8	Italy	1,966
9	Greece	1,872
10	Liberia	1,672
11	United Kingdom	1,631
12	Norway	1,597
13	Philippines	1,499
14	Cyprus	1,416
15	Germany	1,375
16	Canada	1,185
17	Bahamas	1,061
18	Honduras	966
19	Singapore	946
20	Malta	889
21	India	888
22	Saint Vincent and the Grenadines	881
23	Turkey	880
24	France	729
25	Australia	695
26	Taiwan	649
27	Poland	644
28	Brazil	635
29	Mexico	635
30	Peru	623
31	Malaysia	552
32	United States	509
33	Morocco	492
34	Yugoslavia	462
35	Denmark	456
36	Egypt	444
37	Romania	439
38	Sweden	430
39	Argentina	423
40	Iran	403
41	Netherlands	399
42	Iceland	394
43	Cuba	393
44	Chile	392
45	Hong Kong	387
46	Thailand	351
47	Portugal	332
48	Bangladesh	301
49	Saudi Arabia	301
50	Antigua and Barbuda	292
51	Vanuatu	280
52	United Arab Emirates	276
53	Nigeria	271
54	Venezuela	271
55	Finland	263
56	Latvia	261
57	Estonia	234
58	Belgium	232
59	Vietnam	230
60	Bulgaria	222
61	South Africa	219
62	Kuwait	209
63	Croatia	203
64	Faroe Islands	191
65	Ireland	189
66	Senegal	183
67	Lebanon	163
68	Ghana	155
69	Ecuador	154
70	Netherlands Antilles	154
71	Libya	150
72	Algeria	149
73	Myanmar (Burma)	144
74	New Zealand	139
75	Iraq	131
76	Mauritania	126
77	Angola	113

Rank	Country/Entity	Merchant Marine Vessels Over 100 Gross Tons	Rank	Country/Entity	Merchant Marine Vessels Over 100 Gross Tons	Rank	Country/Entity	Merchant Marine Vessels Over 100 Gross Tons
78	Mozambique	107	112	Marshall Islands	35	146	Djibouti	10
79	Colombia	101	113	Mauritius	35	147	Seychelles	9
80	Isle of Man	101	114	Solomon Islands	33	148	Guatemala	8
81	North Korea	100	115	Belize	32	149	Togo	8
82	Bermuda	94	116	Namibia	30	150	Dominica	7
83	Syria	94	117	Gabon	29	151	French Guiana	7
84	Uruguay	93	118	Kenya	29	152	Kiribati	7
85	Bahrain	87	119	Dominican Republic	28	153	Réunion	7
86	Papua New Guinea	87	120	Somalia	28	154	Samoa	7
87	Madagascar	85	121	Congo, Dem. Rep. of	27	155	Saint Lucia	7
88	Greenland	82	122	Ethiopia	27	156	Comoros	6
89	Guyana	82	123	Austria	26	157	Macau	6
90	Tunisia	77	124	Oman	26	158	Martinique	6
91	Pakistan	73	125	Nicaragua	25	159	Tuvalu	6
92	Sri Lanka	66	126	Albania	24	160	Guam	5
93	Qatar	65	127	Costa Rica	24	161	Jordan	5
94	Fiji	64	128	Suriname	24	162	Haiti	4
95	Sierra Leone	62	129	Switzerland	24	163	Palau	4
96	Israel	58	130	Guinea	23	164	São Tomé and Príncipe	4
97	Georgia	54	131	Congo, Rep. of	22	165	American Samoa	3
98	Luxembourg	54	132	Czech Republic	22	166	Cambodia	3
99	Trinidad and Tobago	53	133	Guadeloupe	20	167	Equatorial Guinea	3
100	Lithuania	52	134	Guinea-Bissau	19	168	Grenada	3
101	Brunei	51	135	Micronesia	17	169	Nauru	2
102	Côte d'Ivoire	51	136	New Caledonia	17	170	Northern Mariana Islands	2
103	Gibraltar	49	137	Sudan	16	171	Uganda	2
104	Cameroon	47	138	El Salvador	15	172	Bolivia	1
105	Maldives	44	139	Hungary	15	173	Burundi	1
106	Tanzania	43	140	Tonga	15	174	Laos	1
107	Cape Verde	42	141	Puerto Rico	13	175	Malawi	1
108	French Polynesia	41	142	Slovenia	13	176	Mayotte	1
109	Yemen	40	143	Benin	12	177	Monaco	1
110	Paraguay	38	144	Jamaica	12	178	Saint Kitts and Nevis	1
111	Barbados	37	145	Gambia	11	179	Virgin Islands (U.S.)	1

Source: Lloyd's Register of Shipping

15.15 Shipping: International Cargo Loaded

Rank	Country/Entity	International Cargo Loaded (thousand metric tons)	Rank	Country/Entity	International Cargo Loaded (thousand metric tons)	Rank	Country/Entity	International Cargo Loaded (thousand metric tons)
1	United States	388,716	18	Venezuela	101,435	35	Latvia	36,012
2	Belgium	291,540	19	Iraq	97,830	36	Ukraine	34,200
3	Indonesia	216,396	20	United Arab Emirates	88,153	37	Oman	33,843
4	Saudi Arabia	214,070	21	Nigeria	86,993	38	Finland	33,336
5	United Kingdom	177,228	22	Netherlands	84,816	39	Poland	30,823
6	Canada	176,667	23	South Korea	74,736	40	Malaysia	23,472
7	Brazil	168,026	24	Germany	71,028	41	Angola	23,288
8	Colombia	159,084	25	Libya	62,491	42	Turkey	22,956
9	Taiwan	156,230	26	Algeria	57,607	43	Chile	21,768
10	Norway	152,604	27	Argentina	55,572	44	Liberia	21,653
11	Mexico	139,776	28	France	55,296	45	Thailand	21,192
12	Singapore	134,592	29	India	53,220	46	Greece	21,087
13	Panama	116,844	30	Sweden	52,812	47	Denmark	20,284
14	Japan	114,756	31	Italy	51,420	48	New Zealand	19,692
15	South Africa	114,331	32	Kuwait	51,400	49	Morocco	19,476
16	Iran	113,207	33	Spain	49,860	50	Netherlands Antilles	18,560
17	China	105,852	34	Hong Kong	41,512	51	Qatar	18,145

Rank	Country/Entity	International Cargo Loaded (thousand metric tons)	Rank	Country/Entity	International Cargo Loaded (thousand metric tons)	Rank	Country/Entity	International Cargo Loaded (thousand metric tons)
52	Guinea	16,760	91	Yemen	1,936	130	Guam	195
53	Egypt	14,808	92	Bangladesh	1,848	131	Gambia	185
54	Romania	14,676	93	Syria	1,788	132	Belize	178
55	Russia	14,124	94	Senegal	1,739	133	Haiti	170
56	Brunei	13,554	95	Guyana	1,730	134	Lebanon	152
57	Australia	13,536	96	Nauru	1,650	135	Saint Lucia	150
58	Bahrain	13,285	97	Kenya	1,596	136	Togo	148
59	Philippines	12,864	98	Suriname	1,595	137	Cape Verde	144
60	Gabon	12,828	99	Sudan	1,543	138	Slovenia	137
61	Ecuador	11,783	100	Honduras	1,316	139	Bermuda	130
62	Estonia	11,460	101	Austria	1,311	140	Faroe Islands	130
63	Israel	10,656	102	Cameroon	1,260	141	Equatorial Guinea	110
64	Mauritania	10,400	103	Tanzania	1,249	142	Virgin Islands (U.S.)	106
65	Peru	10,197	104	Iceland	1,162	143	Dominica	103
66	Lithuania	10,092	105	Namibia	1,132	144	Saint Vincent and the Grenadines	80
67	Portugal	9,672	106	Albania	1,065	145	Vanuatu	80
68	Trinidad and Tobago	9,622	107	New Caledonia	1,040	146	French Guiana	69
69	Congo, Rep. of	8,987	108	Mauritius	834	147	Central African Republic	53
70	Jamaica	8,802	109	Martinique	768	148	Guinea-Bissau	46
71	Cuba	8,092	110	Macau	755	149	Western Sahara	40
72	Jordan	7,392	111	Uruguay	710	150	Burundi	35
73	Tunisia	6,888	112	North Korea	635	151	Northern Mariana Islands	33
74	Ireland	6,367	113	Ethiopia	592	152	Marshall Islands	29
75	Bahamas	5,920	114	Fiji	568	153	Antigua and Barbuda	28
76	Sri Lanka	5,892	115	Madagascar	540	154	Maldives	27
77	Pakistan	5,625	116	Guadeloupe	431	155	Saint Kitts and Nevis	24
78	Bulgaria	5,290	117	Djibouti	414	156	Grenada	21
79	Côte d'Ivoire	4,173	118	Réunion	399	157	São Tomé and Príncipe	16
80	Croatia	3,948	119	American Samoa	380	158	French Polynesia	15
81	Mozambique	2,800	120	Benin	339	159	Kiribati	15
82	Costa Rica	2,643	121	Somalia	324	160	Tonga	15
83	Dominican Republic	2,550	122	Nicaragua	320	161	Comoros	12
84	Papua New Guinea	2,463	123	Malta	309	162	Samoa	12
85	Ghana	2,424	124	Vietnam	303	163	Cambodia	11
86	Congo, Dem. Rep. of	2,395	125	Greenland	298	164	Seychelles	11
87	Sierra Leone	2,310	126	Yugoslavia	288	165	Isle of Man	6
88	Cyprus	2,232	127	Solomon Islands	278	166	Gibraltar	5
89	Guatemala	2,096	128	El Salvador	221			
90	Myanmar (Burma)	2,040	129	Barbados	206			

Source: Maritime Transport

15.16 Shipping: International Cargo Unloaded

Rank	Country/Entity	Cargo Unloaded (thousand metric tons)	Rank	Country/Entity	Cargo Unloaded (thousand metric tons)	Rank	Country/Entity	Cargo Unloaded (thousand metric tons)
1	Japan	782,916	13	Germany	128,448	25	Malaysia	44,184
2	United States	602,436	14	China	101,688	26	Thailand	40,152
3	Colombia	456,636	15	Hong Kong	87,106	27	Denmark	37,314
4	Netherlands	293,304	16	Panama	84,312	28	Portugal	37,260
5	Belgium	292,476	17	Canada	83,287	29	Finland	36,948
6	South Korea	273,672	18	India	75,000	30	Philippines	34,128
7	Taiwan	263,938	19	Indonesia	64,656	31	Greece	33,048
8	Italy	222,060	20	Sweden	63,912	32	Egypt	22,860
9	Singapore	179,568	21	Mexico	61,956	33	Norway	22,776
10	United Kingdom	178,572	22	Turkey	61,728	34	Australia	22,740
11	France	177,696	23	Brazil	52,570	35	South Africa	22,203
12	Spain	147,804	24	Saudi Arabia	46,437	36	Romania	21,684

Rank	Country/Entity	Cargo Unloaded (thousand metric tons)	Rank	Country/Entity	Cargo Unloaded (thousand metric tons)	Rank	Country/Entity	Cargo Unloaded (thousand metric tons)
37	Morocco	21,120	81	Ethiopia	3,120	125	Albania	664
38	Bulgaria	20,080	82	Senegal	2,959	126	Virgin Islands (U.S.)	648
39	Israel	19,608	83	Ghana	2,904	127	Namibia	644
40	Netherlands Antilles	18,715	84	Tanzania	2,721	128	Fiji	625
41	Venezuela	17,932	85	Lithuania	2,628	129	Sierra Leone	589
42	Ireland	17,637	86	Qatar	2,588	130	American Samoa	581
43	Pakistan	17,526	87	Oman	2,492	131	Barbados	538
44	Argentina	17,316	88	Latvia	2,448	132	French Guiana	481
45	Poland	17,247	89	Mauritius	2,419	133	Bermuda	470
46	Iran	16,719	90	Cameroon	2,328	134	Gibraltar	400
47	Cuba	15,440	91	Slovenia	2,204	135	Faroe Islands	367
48	Algeria	14,284	92	Réunion	1,975	136	Solomon Islands	349
49	Chile	13,464	93	Ecuador	1,958	137	Seychelles	348
50	New Zealand	11,604	94	Guadeloupe	1,933	138	Cape Verde	299
51	Nigeria	11,346	95	Papua New Guinea	1,784	139	Greenland	288
52	Tunisia	11,136	96	Malta	1,781	140	Guinea-Bissau	283
53	Trinidad and Tobago	10,961	97	Benin	1,738	141	Belize	241
54	Bangladesh	10,608	98	Iceland	1,733	142	Gambia	240
55	United Arab Emirates	9,595	99	Nicaragua	1,629	143	Saint Lucia	234
56	Sri Lanka	9,588	100	Liberia	1,608	144	Gabon	212
57	Iraq	8,638	101	Guam	1,524	145	Northern Mariana Islands	205
58	Yemen	7,829	102	Martinique	1,524	146	Isle of Man	203
59	Libya	7,808	103	Vietnam	1,510	147	Grenada	193
60	Croatia	7,776	104	Congo, Dem. Rep. of	1,453	148	Samoa	192
61	Côte d'Ivoire	7,228	105	Uruguay	1,450	149	Burundi	188
62	Bahamas	5,705	106	Russia	1,428	150	Dominica	181
63	North Korea	5,520	107	Brunei	1,325	151	Saint Vincent and the Grenadines	140
64	Jamaica	5,285	108	Suriname	1,265			
65	Austria	5,122	109	Angola	1,261	152	Central African Republic	126
66	Peru	5,077	110	Yugoslavia	1,212	153	Marshall Islands	123
67	Cyprus	5,028	111	Lebanon	1,150	154	Antigua and Barbuda	113
68	Jordan	4,608	112	El Salvador	1,023	155	Comoros	107
69	Kuwait	4,522	113	Somalia	1,007	156	Tonga	104
70	Syria	4,512	114	Honduras	1,002	157	Cambodia	95
71	Sudan	4,300	115	Madagascar	984	158	Maldives	78
72	Dominican Republic	4,182	116	Djibouti	958	159	Equatorial Guinea	64
73	Costa Rica	4,054	117	New Caledonia	930	160	Palau	64
74	Estonia	3,996	118	Congo, Rep. of	736	161	Nauru	59
75	Macau	3,935	119	Guinea	734	162	Vanuatu	55
76	Guatemala	3,822	120	Mauritania	724	163	São Tomé and Príncipe	45
77	Myanmar (Burma)	3,624	121	Togo	709	164	Saint Kitts and Nevis	36
78	Bahrain	3,512	122	Haiti	704	165	Kiribati	26
79	Mozambique	3,400	123	Guyana	673	166	Western Sahara	15
80	Kenya	3,228	124	French Polynesia	666			

Source: Maritime Transport

Historically, waterways are among a nation's most important natural resources, but, as in other things, nations are not equally endowed in this respect. They differ not only in the length of the waterways, but also in their quality. Some, like the Amazon River in Brazil, are so deep that giant steamers can sail up the river for thousands of miles, while others may be so shallow that even canoes navigate with difficulty. Some are navigable year round while others dry up in the summer and are subject to floods in the rainy season. The usefulness of many of the largest rivers, such as the Nile and the Congo, is diminished by intervening rapids.

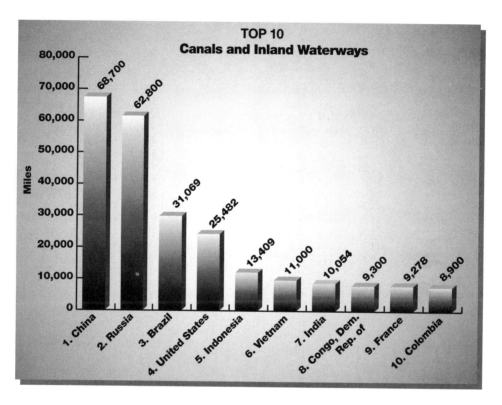

TOP 10 Canals and Inland Waterways

Rank	Country/Entity	Canals and Inland Waterways (miles)	Rank	Country/Entity	Canals and Inland Waterways (miles)	Rank	Country/Entity	Canals and Inland Waterways (miles)
11	Myanmar (Burma)	7,954	25	Sudan	3,300	39	Italy	1,500
12	Argentina	6,800	26	Laos	2,850	40	North Korea	1,400
13	Papua New Guinea	6,798	27	Kazakhstan	2,487	41	Zambia	1,398
14	Bolivia	6,214	28	Poland	2,484	42	Nicaragua	1,379
15	Nigeria	5,328	29	Mozambique	2,330	43	Cameroon	1,299
16	Peru	5,300	30	Cambodia	2,300	44	Sweden	1,275
17	Australia	5,200	31	Thailand	2,300	45	Belgium	1,269
18	Bangladesh	5,000	32	Egypt	2,175	46	Chad	1,240
19	Germany	4,686	33	Philippines	2,000	47	Mali	1,128
20	Malaysia	4,534	34	United Kingdom	1,990	48	Japan	1,100
21	Venezuela	4,400	35	Paraguay	1,900	49	Romania	1,071
22	Finland	4,148	36	Canada	1,860	50	Ukraine	1,039
23	Netherlands	3,939	37	Mexico	1,800	51	Hungary	1,008
24	Guyana	3,700	38	Yugoslavia	1,616	52	South Korea	1,000

Rank	Country/Entity	Canals and Inland Waterways (miles)	Rank	Country/Entity	Canals and Inland Waterways (miles)	Rank	Country/Entity	Canals and Inland Waterways (miles)
53	New Zealand	1,000	71	Syria	541	89	Denmark	259
54	Uruguay	1,000	72	Belize	513	90	Gambia	250
55	Gabon	994	73	Portugal	510	91	Mongolia	247
56	Norway	980	74	Central African Republic	500	92	Latvia	186
57	Ecuador	932	75	Sierra Leone	500	93	Niger	186
58	Malawi	891	76	Panama	497	94	Guatemala	162
59	Angola	805	77	Croatia	488	95	Cuba	149
60	Guinea	805	78	Costa Rica	454	96	Brunei	130
61	Ghana	803	79	Chile	450	97	Fiji	126
62	Afghanistan	750	80	Lithuania	373	98	Slovakia	107
63	Turkey	750	81	Estonia	311	99	Haiti	60
64	Suriname	746	82	Czech Republic	295	100	Greece	50
65	Congo, Rep. of	696	83	Bulgaria	292	101	Switzerland	40
66	Spain	649	84	Honduras	289	102	Togo	31
67	Iraq	631	85	French Guiana	286	103	Albania	27
68	Côte d'Ivoire	609	86	Austria	277	104	Luxembourg	23
69	Iran	562	87	Sri Lanka	267	105	Kiribati	3
70	Senegal	557	88	Moldova	263			

Source: World Data

Tourist Trade

Tourism is the most efficient redistribution of wealth among countries. For many developing nations as well as small islands, tourism provides more revenue than taxes or foreign aid. Tourism is of two kinds: domestic and foreign. Domestic or internal tourism is effective in sustaining facilities such as motels, shops, transportation, theme parks, and so on. The second, foreign tourism, is the major provider of hard currencies for most nations of the world. The big spenders in this respect are the Germans, Americans, Japanese, and British. Generally, tourism statistics do not distinguish between business travel and travel for pleasure. They also do not distinguish between travel by tourists and that by immigrants who are going away from or returning home. Commercial tour operators are encouraging new forms of tourism, such as environmental tourism, cultural tourism, adventure tourism, cruises, and so on.

15.18 Tourist Trade: Arrivals

Rank	Country/Entity	Tourist Arrivals, 1998 (thousands)	Rank	Country/Entity	Tourist Arrivals, 1998 (thousands)	Rank	Country/Entity	Tourist Arrivals, 1998 (thousands)
1	France	70,000	15	Portugal	11,295	29	Brazil	4,818
2	Spain	47,749	16	Greece	10,916	30	Tunisia	4,718
3	United States	46,395	17	Switzerland	10,900	31	Indonesia	4,606
4	Italy	34,829	18	Hong Kong	9,575	32	South Korea	4,250
5	United Kingdom	25,745	19	Netherlands	9,320	33	Australia	4,167
6	China	25,073	20	Turkey	8,960	34	Croatia	4,112
7	Mexico	19,810	21	Thailand	7,843	35	Japan	4,106
8	Canada	18,837	22	Ukraine	6,208	36	Saudi Arabia	3,700
9	Poland	18,780	23	Belgium	6,179	37	Puerto Rico	3,396
10	Austria	17,352	24	Ireland	6,064	38	Morocco	3,243
11	Germany	16,511	25	South Africa	5,898	39	Egypt	3,213
12	Czech Republic	16,325	26	Singapore	5,631	40	Bulgaria	3,000
13	Russia	15,805	27	Malaysia	5,551	41	Romania	2,966
14	Hungary	15,000	28	Argentina	4,860	42	Norway	2,829

Rank	Country/Entity	Tourist Arrivals, 1998 (thousands)	Rank	Country/Entity	Tourist Arrivals, 1998 (thousands)	Rank	Country/Entity	Tourist Arrivals, 1998 (thousands)
43	Sweden	2,568	77	Latvia	567	111	Haiti	150
44	India	2,359	78	Namibia	560	112	Lesotho	150
45	Dominican Republic	2,309	79	Mauritius	558	113	Burkina Faso	140
46	United Arab Emirates	2,184	80	El Salvador	542	114	Cameroon	135
47	Uruguay	2,163	81	Ecuador	511	115	Mongolia	135
48	Philippines	2,149	82	Tajikistan	511	116	North Korea	130
49	Denmark	2,073	83	Tanzania	450	117	Madagascar	121
50	Zimbabwe	1,984	84	Nepal	435	118	Bosnia and Herzegovina	100
51	Israel	1,942	85	Bolivia	434	119	Guinea	99
52	Finland	1,858	86	Panama	431	120	Togo	94
53	Chile	1,757	87	Pakistan	429	121	Ethiopia	91
54	Vietnam	1,520	88	Nicaragua	406	122	Gambia	91
55	New Zealand	1,485	89	Sri Lanka	381	123	Yemen	88
56	Lithuania	1,416	90	Zambia	362	124	Mali	83
57	Cuba	1,390	91	Belarus	355	125	Kuwait	79
58	Syria	1,267	92	Senegal	352	126	Papua New Guinea	67
59	Jordan	1,256	93	Paraguay	350	127	Kyrgyzstan	59
60	Jamaica	1,225	94	Trinidad and Tobago	347	128	Angola	52
61	Iran	1,008	95	Ghana	335	129	Iraq	51
62	Slovenia	977	96	Honduras	318	130	Sierra Leone	50
63	Costa Rica	943	97	Georgia	317	131	Congo, Rep. of	44
64	Slovakia	896	98	Côte d'Ivoire	301	132	Sudan	39
65	Kenya	894	99	Turkmenistan	300	133	Armenia	32
66	Colombia	841	100	Yugoslavia	283	134	Congo, Dem. Rep. of	32
67	Venezuela	837	101	Uzbekistan	272	135	Libya	32
68	Peru	833	102	Uganda	238	136	Albania	27
69	Estonia	825	103	Malawi	205	137	Central African Republic	20
70	Botswana	740	104	Myanmar	201	138	Moldova	20
71	Nigeria	739	105	Laos	200	139	Niger	19
72	Algeria	678	106	Gabon	192	140	Burundi	14
73	Guatemala	636	107	Eritrea	188	141	Chad	11
74	Lebanon	631	108	Bangladesh	172	142	Rwanda	2
75	Oman	612	109	Azerbaijan	170			
76	Cambodia	576	110	Benin	152			

Source: Compendium of Tourist Statistics

15.19 Tourist Trade: Departures

Rank	Country/Entity	Tourist Departures, 1998 (thousands)	Rank	Country/Entity	Tourist Departures, 1998 (thousands)	Rank	Country/Entity	Tourist Departures, 1998 (thousands)
1	Germany	82,975	19	China	8,426	37	Israel	2,983
2	United States	52,735	20	Belgium	7,773	38	Egypt	2,921
3	United Kingdom	50,872	21	Romania	6,893	39	Syria	2,750
4	Poland	49,328	22	Argentina	5,522	40	Portugal	2,425
5	Malaysia	25,631	23	Denmark	4,972	41	Indonesia	2,200
6	France	18,077	24	Finland	4,743	42	Latvia	1,961
7	Canada	17,648	25	Turkey	4,601	43	Greece	1,935
8	Japan	15,806	26	Brazil	4,598	44	Philippines	1,817
9	Italy	14,327	27	Hong Kong	4,197	45	Estonia	1,659
10	Austria	13,263	28	India	3,811	46	Lebanon	1,650
11	Spain	13,203	29	Singapore	3,745	47	Tunisia	1,526
12	Netherlands	12,860	30	Lithuania	3,241	48	Thailand	1,412
13	Hungary	12,317	31	Australia	3,161	49	Algeria	1,377
14	Switzerland	12,213	32	Norway	3,120	50	Morocco	1,359
15	Russia	11,711	33	South Africa	3,080	51	Iran	1,354
16	Sweden	11,422	34	South Korea	3,067	52	Chile	1,351
17	Ukraine	10,326	35	Bulgaria	3,059	53	Jordan	1,347
18	Mexico	9,803	36	Ireland	3,053	54	Puerto Rico	1,250

Rank	Country/Entity	Tourist Departures, 1998 (thousands)	Rank	Country/Entity	Tourist Departures, 1998 (thousands)	Rank	Country/Entity	Tourist Departures, 1998 (thousands)
55	New Zealand	1,166	71	Guatemala	391	87	Zimbabwe	123
56	Colombia	1,140	72	Turkmenistan	357	88	Nepal	110
57	Bangladesh	992	73	Dominican Republic	354	89	Papua New Guinea	63
58	Belarus	969	74	Kenya	350	90	Cuba	55
59	El Salvador	868	75	Costa Rica	330	91	Cambodia	41
60	Uruguay	654	76	Ecuador	330	92	Madagascar	35
61	Libya	650	77	Bolivia	298	93	Moldova	35
62	Peru	577	78	Trinidad and Tobago	250	94	Kyrgyzstan	32
63	Venezuela	524	79	Azerbaijan	232	95	Albania	18
64	Sri Lanka	518	80	Panama	211	96	Burundi	16
65	Paraguay	498	81	Honduras	202	97	Chad	10
66	Botswana	460	82	Sudan	200	98	Niger	10
67	Georgia	433	83	Vietnam	168	99	Côte d'Ivoire	5
68	Nicaragua	422	84	Tanzania	150	100	Angola	3
69	Benin	420	85	Mauritius	143			
70	Slovakia	414	86	Ethiopia	140			

Source: Tourism Annual Statistics

15.20 Tourist Trade: Expenditures by Nationals Abroad

Rank	Country/Entity	Tourist Expenditures by Nationals Abroad, 1995, in U.S. Dollars (millions)	Rank	Country/Entity	Tourist Expenditures by Nationals Abroad, 1995, in U.S. Dollars (millions)	Rank	Country/Entity	Tourist Expenditures by Nationals Abroad, 1995, in U.S. Dollars (millions)
1	Germany	50,675	36	Czech Republic	1,630	71	Guatemala	174
2	United States	45,855	37	Greece	1,322	72	Bahrain	163
3	Japan	36,792	38	New Zealand	1,283	73	Côte d'Ivoire	159
4	United Kingdom	24,737	39	Egypt	1,278	74	Mauritius	159
5	France	16,328	40	Hungary	1,070	75	Libya	154
6	Italy	12,419	41	Turkey	912	76	Bolivia	148
7	Austria	11,687	42	Iran	862	77	Jamaica	148
8	Russia	11,599	43	Puerto Rico	833	78	Botswana	145
9	Netherlands	11,455	44	Colombia	822	79	Nigeria	144
10	Canada	10,220	45	Chile	774	80	Bermuda	140
11	Belgium	9,215	46	Croatia	771	81	Lithuania	138
12	Taiwan	8,457	47	Romania	695	82	Nepal	136
13	Switzerland	7,636	48	India	470	83	Algeria	135
14	South Korea	5,903	49	Pakistan	449	84	Kenya	135
15	Poland	5,500	50	Philippines	422	85	Panama	128
16	Sweden	5,422	51	Jordan	420	86	Macau	117
17	Singapore	5,134	52	Slovenia	413	87	Gabon	112
18	Australia	4,604	53	Syria	398	88	Zimbabwe	106
19	Spain	4,540	54	Tanzania	360	89	Uganda	93
20	Denmark	4,280	55	Slovakia	330	90	Estonia	90
21	Brazil	4,245	56	Costa Rica	312	91	Dominican Republic	85
22	Norway	4,221	57	Morocco	302	92	Namibia	82
23	China	3,688	58	Peru	302	93	Trinidad and Tobago	79
24	Thailand	3,372	59	Cyprus	293	94	Yemen	76
25	Mexico	3,153	60	Iceland	282	95	Papua New Guinea	75
26	Israel	3,148	61	Tunisia	251	96	Senegal	75
27	Finland	2,383	62	Uruguay	236	97	Aruba	73
28	Kuwait	2,322	63	Ecuador	235	98	El Salvador	72
29	Indonesia	2,172	64	Bangladesh	229	99	Azerbaijan	70
30	Portugal	2,155	65	Cameroon	225	100	Angola	66
31	Argentina	2,067	66	Bahamas	213	101	Madagascar	59
32	Ireland	2,030	67	Bulgaria	195	102	Honduras	57
33	Venezuela	1,865	68	Sri Lanka	186	103	Mali	56
34	South Africa	1,749	69	Malta	184	104	Moldova	56
35	Malaysia	1,737	70	Paraguay	181	105	Zambia	56

Rank	Country/Entity	Tourist Expenditures by Nationals Abroad, 1995, in U.S. Dollars (millions)
106	Fiji	55
107	Barbados	52
108	Oman	47
109	Central African Republic	43
110	Nicaragua	40
111	Congo, Rep. of	39
112	Swaziland	37
113	Haiti	35
114	Sudan	33
115	Maldives	32
116	Mauritania	31
117	Laos	30
118	Chad	26
119	Burundi	25
120	Ethiopia	25
121	Antigua and Barbuda	24
122	Latvia	24
123	Macedonia	24
124	Seychelles	24
125	Burkina Faso	23
126	Saint Lucia	23
127	Togo	23
128	Belize	21
129	Guinea	21
130	Guyana	21
131	Niger	21
132	Ghana	20
133	Rwanda	17
134	Congo, Dem. Rep. of	16
135	Gambia	16
136	Myanmar (Burma)	16
137	Malawi	15
138	Cape Verde	12
139	Solomon Islands	11
140	Cambodia	8
141	Djibouti	7
142	Lesotho	7
143	Benin	6
144	Comoros	6
145	Kyrgyzstan	6
146	Albania	5
147	Dominica	5
148	Saint Kitts and Nevis	5
149	Vanuatu	5
150	Grenada	4
151	Kiribati	3
152	Samoa	3
153	Saint Vincent and the Grenadines	3
154	Suriname	3
155	São Tomé and Príncipe	2
156	Sierra Leone	2
157	Afghanistan	1
158	Tonga	1

Source: Compendium of Tourist Statistics

15.21 Tourist Trade: Receipts from Foreign Nationals

Rank	Country/Entity	Tourist Receipts from Foreign Nationals, 1995, in U.S. Dollars (millions)
1	United States	61,137
2	France	27,527
3	Italy	27,451
4	Spain	25,701
5	United Kingdom	19,073
6	Germany	16,221
7	Austria	14,618
8	Hong Kong	9,604
9	Switzerland	9,364
10	China	8,733
11	Singapore	8,212
12	Canada	8,012
13	Thailand	7,664
14	Australia	7,100
15	Poland	6,700
16	Mexico	6,164
17	Netherlands	5,762
18	Belgium	5,719
19	South Korea	5,587
20	Indonesia	5,228
21	Turkey	4,957
22	Portugal	4,402
23	Russia	4,312
24	Argentina	4,306
25	Greece	4,106
26	Malaysia	3,910
27	Denmark	3,672
28	Sweden	3,447
29	Taiwan	3,286
30	Japan	3,226
31	Macau	3,117
32	Czech Republic	2,875
33	Egypt	2,800
34	Israel	2,784
35	Ireland	2,688
36	India	2,574
37	Philippines	2,450
38	Norway	2,386
39	Brazil	2,171
40	New Zealand	2,163
41	Saudi Arabia	1,884
42	Puerto Rico	1,826
43	Cyprus	1,783
44	Hungary	1,723
45	Finland	1,716
46	Dominican Republic	1,604
47	South Africa	1,595
48	Croatia	1,584
49	Bahamas	1,346
50	Syria	1,325
51	Tunisia	1,325
52	Morocco	1,163
53	Cuba	1,100
54	Slovenia	1,079
55	Jamaica	1,069
56	Chile	990
57	Guam	950
58	Colombia	851
59	Virgin Islands (U.S.)	821
60	Venezuela	811
61	Jordan	696
62	Barbados	680
63	Lebanon	672
64	Costa Rica	660
65	Northern Mariana Islands	655
66	Netherlands Antilles	639
67	Slovakia	620
68	Uruguay	611
69	Malta	606
70	Romania	574
71	Jersey	526
72	Aruba	521
73	Peru	520
74	Bermuda	488
75	Bulgaria	473
76	Guadeloupe	458
77	Kenya	454
78	Mauritius	430
79	Martinique	384
80	Estonia	353
81	Antigua and Barbuda	329
82	Fiji	312
83	Panama	310
84	Luxembourg	290
85	Bahrain	288
86	Guatemala	277
87	Saint Lucia	268
88	Namibia	263
89	French Polynesia	260
90	Tanzania	259
91	Ecuador	255
92	Ghana	233
93	Sri Lanka	224
94	Paraguay	213
95	Maldives	210
96	Iceland	167
97	Botswana	162
98	Iran	160
99	Réunion	157
100	Zimbabwe	154
101	Azerbaijan	146
102	Bolivia	146

Rank	Country/Entity	Tourist Receipts from Foreign Nationals, 1995, in U.S. Dollars (millions)	Rank	Country/Entity	Tourist Receipts from Foreign Nationals, 1995, in U.S. Dollars (millions)	Rank	Country/Entity	Tourist Receipts from Foreign Nationals, 1995, in U.S. Dollars (millions)
103	Guernsey	146	129	Iraq	55	156	Angola	13
104	Senegal	130	130	Nigeria	54	157	Djibouti	13
105	Lithuania	124	131	Laos	51	158	Tonga	11
106	Nepal	117	132	Nicaragua	50	159	American Samoa	10
107	Pakistan	114	133	Cameroon	47	160	Cape Verde	10
108	Kuwait	107	134	Guyana	47	161	Comoros	8
109	New Caledonia	102	135	Zambia	47	162	Togo	8
110	Cambodia	100	136	Yugoslavia	42	163	Albania	7
111	Seychelles	100	137	Myanmar (Burma)	38	164	Libya	7
112	Oman	92	138	Yemen	38	165	Central African Republic	6
113	Gibraltar	90	139	Chad	36	166	Congo, Dem. Rep. of	6
114	Vietnam	85	140	Ethiopia	36	167	Malawi	6
115	Haiti	81	141	Samoa	36	168	Sierra Leone	6
116	Honduras	80	142	Swaziland	35	169	Solomon Islands	6
117	Uganda	79	143	Dominica	33	170	Bhutan	5
118	Belize	78	144	Algeria	27	171	Kyrgyzstan	5
119	El Salvador	75	145	Benin	27	172	Congo, Rep. of	4
120	Trinidad and Tobago	73	146	Bangladesh	23	173	Gabon	4
121	Côte d'Ivoire	72	147	Gambia	23	174	Sudan	3
122	Saint Kitts and Nevis	65	148	Burkina Faso	22	175	Marshall Islands	2
123	Madagascar	60	149	Latvia	20	176	Rwanda	2
124	Papua New Guinea	60	150	Macedonia	19	177	Afghanistan	1
125	Grenada	58	151	Lesotho	17	178	Burundi	1
126	Vanuatu	58	152	Mali	17	179	Guinea	1
127	Moldova	57	153	Mauritania	15	180	Kiribati	1
128	Saint Vincent and the Grenadines	57	154	Niger	15	181	São Tomé and Príncipe	1
			155	Suriname	14	182	Tuvalu	0.3

Source: Compendium of Tourist Statistics

Postal Service

In almost all countries the postal service is a state monopoly and it has thus acquired some of the characteristics of a public, rather than commercial, service. Despite various short-comings, the postal service is generally smooth and efficient. However, the telecommunications revolution of the 1990s has in some respects sidelined, if not displaced, the post office. Its parcel shipments face severe competition from overnight carriers, such as United Parcel Service and Federal Express, and its letter delivery system—nicknamed "snail mail"—appears antiquated in comparison to fax, phone, and Internet. Nevertheless, the volume of mail has been increasing in all countries, helped by the growth in "junk" mail, direct mail, greeting cards, newspapers, and magazines. Worldwide, the volume of mail is estimated at 2 trillion pieces. The share of personal communications is dwindling while the reverse is true of business communications.

15.22 Postal Service: Pieces Handled per Capita

Rank	Country/Entity	Pieces of Mail per Capita, 1995	Rank	Country/Entity	Pieces of Mail per Capita, 1995	Rank	Country/Entity	Pieces of Mail per Capita, 1995
1	Samoa	5,871	7	France	419	13	Isle of Man	281
2	Switzerland	601	8	Luxembourg	378	14	Australia	252
3	Jersey	594	9	Malta	373	15	Guernsey	251
4	Sweden	513	10	Canada	370	16	Germany	244
5	Norway	499	11	Belgium	352	17	Bermuda	240
6	Austria	425	12	Denmark	350	18	Finland	224

Rank	Country/Entity	Pieces of Mail per Capita, 1995	Rank	Country/Entity	Pieces of Mail per Capita, 1995	Rank	Country/Entity	Pieces of Mail per Capita, 1995
19	Bahamas	216	70	Trinidad and Tobago	23	121	Nicaragua	2.6
20	Singapore	216	71	Chile	21	122	Bangladesh	2.2
21	Gibraltar	214	72	Thailand	21	123	Pakistan	2.0
22	Faroe Islands	198	73	Algeria	20	124	Myanmar (Burma)	1.9
23	Japan	197	74	Bulgaria	19	125	Mongolia	1.8
24	Georgia	188	75	Belize	18	126	Ecuador	1.6
25	Hong Kong	187	76	Namibia	18	127	Tajikistan	1.6
26	Ireland	172	77	Philippines	16	128	Benin	1.5
27	Slovenia	135	78	India	15	129	Burkina Faso	1.5
28	New Caledonia	131	79	Oman	15	130	Comoros	1.5
29	Bahrain	122	80	Moldova	13	131	Guinea	1.4
30	Greenland	120	81	Romania	13	132	Burundi	1.3
31	Hungary	116	82	Tunisia	13	133	Chad	1.3
32	Spain	110	83	Argentina	12	134	Dominican Republic	1.3
33	Italy	100	84	Kenya	12	135	Bhutan	1.2
34	Slovakia	98	85	Jordan	11	136	Haiti	1.2
35	French Polynesia	95	86	Kyrgyzstan	11	137	Syria	1.2
36	Portugal	93	87	Solomon Islands	11	138	Cambodia	1.1
37	Israel	92	88	Ukraine	11	139	Albania	1.0
38	Cyprus	79	89	Lithuania	10	140	Azerbaijan	1.0
39	South Korea	77	90	Malawi	10	141	Paraguay	1.0
40	Czech Republic	71	91	Mexico	10	142	Togo	1.0
41	United Arab Emirates	70	92	Papua New Guinea	10	143	Uganda	1.0
42	Barbados	68	93	Maldives	9.6	144	Peru	0.9
43	Kuwait	68	94	Latvia	9.0	145	Belarus	0.7
44	Seychelles	64	95	Costa Rica	8.5	146	Congo, Rep. of	0.7
45	South Africa	59	96	Guatemala	7.7	147	Senegal	0.7
46	Saint Kitts and Nevis	59	97	Nigeria	7.3	148	United States	0.7
47	Croatia	58	98	Ghana	6.9	149	Liechtenstein	0.6
48	Malaysia	52	99	China	6.5	150	Armenia	0.5
49	Saudi Arabia	50	100	Honduras	5.9	151	Eritrea	0.5
50	Russia	48	101	Libya	5.8	152	Ethiopia	0.5
51	Brunei	45	102	Guyana	5.3	153	Mozambique	0.5
52	Dominica	42	103	Egypt	5.2	154	Yemen	0.5
53	Tonga	40	104	Nepal	4.9	155	Cameroon	0.4
54	Mauritius	38	105	Kiribati	4.7	156	Mali	0.4
55	Macau	37	106	Uruguay	4.7	157	Niger	0.4
56	Brazil	36	107	Cape Verde	4.5	158	Guinea-Bissau	0.3
57	Lesotho	36	108	Gabon	4.3	159	Laos	0.3
58	Qatar	36	109	Venezuela	4.3	160	Mauritania	0.3
59	Greece	35	110	Indonesia	4.0	161	Angola	0.2
60	Estonia	32	111	Colombia	3.9	162	Sierra Leone	0.2
61	Poland	32	112	Panama	3.9	163	Sudan	0.2
62	Fiji	31	113	El Salvador	3.6	164	Tanzania	0.2
63	Djibouti	28	114	Iran	3.3	165	Virgin Islands (U.S.)	0.2
64	Jamaica	28	115	Côte d'Ivoire	3.2	166	Bosnia and Herzegovina	0.1
65	Swaziland	27	116	Iraq	3.1	167	São Tomé and Príncipe	0.02
66	Sri Lanka	26	117	Bolivia	2.8	168	Yugoslavia	0.02
67	Zimbabwe	26	118	Zambia	2.8	169	Kazakhstan	0.01
68	Botswana	25	119	Cuba	2.6			
69	Turkey	24	120	Madagascar	2.6			

Source: Postal Statistics

15.23 Postal Service: Persons per Post Office

Rank	Country/Entity	Persons per Post Office, 1995	Rank	Country/Entity	Persons per Post Office, 1995	Rank	Country/Entity	Persons per Post Office, 1995
1	Rwanda	6,018,000	59	Namibia	18,900	117	Germany	4,760
2	Cambodia	328,000	60	Qatar	18,600	118	Albania	4,600
3	Burundi	219,000	61	El Salvador	18,500	119	Australia	4,560
4	Chad	200,000	62	Equatorial Guinea	18,300	120	Sri Lanka	4,440
5	Angola	162,000	63	China	17,500	121	Samoa	4,360
6	Burkina Faso	157,000	64	Ghana	17,300	122	Bermuda	4,350
7	Congo, Dem. Rep. of	144,000	65	Madagascar	16,300	123	Romania	4,330
8	Niger	134,000	66	Barbados	15,500	124	Jordan	4,190
9	Central African Republic	104,000	67	Paraguay	15,000	125	Guernsey	4,120
10	Ethiopia	97,500	68	Seychelles	15,000	126	Italy	4,050
11	Eritrea	95,300	69	Swaziland	14,900	127	Azerbaijan	4,040
12	Togo	88,200	70	Brazil	14,300	128	Croatia	4,010
13	Guinea	86,300	71	Malaysia	14,000	129	Luxembourg	3,860
14	Sierra Leone	85,000	72	Saudi Arabia	13,900	130	Slovenia	3,860
15	Denmark	81,800	73	Thailand	13,900	131	Kazakhstan	3,810
16	Mali	75,600	74	Libya	13,700	132	Jersey	3,700
17	Sudan	74,300	75	Comoros	13,611	133	Lithuania	3,680
18	Uganda	64,500	76	United Arab Emirates	13,200	134	France	3,440
19	Afghanistan	61,300	77	São Tomé and Príncipe	13,100	135	Moldova	3,320
20	Senegal	61,100	78	South Korea	13,000	136	Kiribati	3,310
21	Djibouti	58,600	79	Honduras	12,700	137	New Caledonia	3,280
22	Tonga	55,600	80	Lesotho	12,500	138	Russia	3,250
23	Tanzania	54,400	81	Mexico	12,300	139	Hungary	3,170
24	Haiti	53,200	82	Laos	11,600	140	Jamaica	3,140
25	Cameroon	53,100	83	Mauritius	10,900	141	Ukraine	3,140
26	Hong Kong	50,000	84	Virgin Islands (U.S.)	10,800	142	Slovakia	3,100
27	Venezuela	49,200	85	Uruguay	10,600	143	Austria	3,050
28	Brunei	48,700	86	Pakistan	9,750	144	Czech Republic	2,940
29	Bahrain	48,100	87	Tunisia	9,390	145	Fiji	2,930
30	Bolivia	46,600	88	Gibraltar	9,040	146	Finland	2,850
31	Zambia	44,200	89	Algeria	8,950	147	Solomon Islands	2,730
32	Guinea-Bissau	43,300	90	Guyana	8,950	148	Saint Vincent and the Grenadines	2,680
33	Ecuador	42,900	91	Spain	8,660	149	Belarus	2,650
34	Mozambique	40,400	92	Egypt	8,280	150	Singapore	2,570
35	Zimbabwe	39,900	93	Greece	8,260	151	Estonia	2,550
36	Papua New Guinea	39,800	94	Israel	8,160	152	San Marino	2,488
37	Côte d'Ivoire	38,900	95	Bhutan	7,990	153	Latvia	2,470
38	Mauritania	37,700	96	Tajikistan	7,930	154	Bulgaria	2,340
39	Myanmar (Burma)	37,400	97	Netherlands	7,690	155	French Polynesia	2,250
40	Dominican Republic	35,000	98	Panama	7,670	156	Congo, Rep. of	2,170
41	Benin	34,700	99	Botswana	7,520	157	Bahamas	2,040
42	Macau	34,500	100	Malta	7,420	158	Isle of Man	2,040
43	Yemen	34,000	101	Cuba	7,150	159	Turkey	1,970
44	Malawi	30,800	102	Nepal	7,080	160	Switzerland	1,920
45	Peru	28,100	103	Cape Verde	6,930	161	Belize	1,900
46	Nigeria	26,900	104	Yugoslavia	6,722	162	Ireland	1,860
47	Kenya	26,000	105	Mongolia	6,430	163	Norway	1,850
48	Chile	24,200	106	Belgium	6,200	164	Grenada	1,680
49	Indonesia	23,800	107	India	6,130	165	Canada	1,590
50	Oman	23,400	108	Argentina	6,100	166	Portugal	1,490
51	Philippines	22,600	109	Iran	5,700	167	Cyprus	1,130
52	Bosnia and Herzegovina	21,800	110	Saint Kitts and Nevis	5,630	168	Faroe Islands	1,010
53	Syria	21,800	111	United States	5,300	169	Greenland	744
54	Nicaragua	21,600	112	Trinidad and Tobago	5,190	170	Maldives	700
55	Colombia	21,207	113	Japan	5,090	171	Dominica	566
56	Aruba	20,500	114	Sweden	5,060	172	Nauru	406
57	Guatemala	19,700	115	Kyrgyzstan	4,920			
58	Gabon	19,300	116	Poland	4,920			

Source: Postal Statistics

The telephone, like the aircraft, is an American invention that has changed modern life. Worldwide, there are over 718 million telephone access lines of which 40 percent are in the United States. Every year more than 200 trillion telephone calls are made, at the rate of 550 million a day. For most people, phones take up a considerable portion of every workday. In every country without exception, telephone companies are among the biggest and the most powerful, and the industry is poised to grow even larger in the twenty-first century because of the emergence of computer, fax, and cellular technologies. About 78 percent of all telephone companies are privately owned, and with deregulation there is intense competition in the communications marketplace. Costs have plummeted as the rankings for cost of a local call show. Through the use of communications satellites, international telephone calls have become easier, clearer, cheaper, and faster.

15.24 Telephones

Rank	Country/Entity	Telephones (Thousands)	Rank	Country/Entity	Telephones (Thousands)	Rank	Country/Entity	Telephones (Thousands)
1	United States	164,624	44	Yugoslavia	2,017	87	Libya	318
2	Japan	61,106	45	Belarus	1,968	88	Jordan	317
3	China	40,706	46	Kazakhstan	1,963	89	Panama	304
4	Germany	40,400	47	Hungary	1,893	90	Jamaica	292
5	France	32,400	48	Philippines	1,787	91	Guatemala	290
6	United Kingdom	29,409	49	Uzbekistan	1,738	92	Bangladesh	287
7	Russia	25,019	50	New Zealand	1,719	93	El Salvador	285
8	Italy	24,854	51	Saudi Arabia	1,719	94	Tajikistan	263
9	South Korea	18,600	52	Singapore	1,429	95	Kenya	240
10	Canada	17,457	53	Ireland	1,310	96	Bosnia	238
11	Spain	15,095	54	Croatia	1,287	97	Luxembourg	222
12	Turkey	13,228	55	Puerto Rico	1,196	98	Trinidad and Tobago	209
13	Brazil	12,083	56	Algeria	1,176	99	Sri Lanka	204
14	India	11,978	57	Morocco	1,158	100	Yemen	187
15	Taiwan	10,011	58	Slovakia	1,119	101	Malta	171
16	Australia	9,200	59	Peru	1,109	102	Oman	170
17	Mexico	8,801	60	North Korea	1,100	103	Paraguay	167
18	Ukraine	8,311	61	Lithuania	941	104	Honduras	161
19	Netherlands	8,120	62	Syria	930	105	Iceland	149
20	Sweden	6,010	63	Vietnam	775	106	Mauritius	148
21	Poland	5,729	64	Ecuador	748	107	Zimbabwe	155
22	Argentina	5,532	65	Latvia	705	108	Myanmar (Burma)	147
23	Greece	5,163	66	Iraq	675	109	Ethiopia	143
24	Iran	5,090	67	United Arab Emirates	672	110	Bahrain	141
25	Belgium	4,632	68	Azerbaijan	640	111	Qatar	123
26	Switzerland	4,319	69	Uruguay	622	112	Côte d'Ivoire	116
27	South Africa	3,919	70	Slovenia	615	113	Nicaragua	97
28	Colombia	3,873	71	Armenia	583	114	Barbados	90
29	Austria	3,749	72	Moldova	567	115	Tanzania	90
30	Portugal	3,566	73	Costa Rica	557	116	Senegal	82
31	Thailand	3,482	74	Georgia	554	117	Namibia	79
32	Malaysia	3,332	75	Dominican Republic	569	118	Mongolia	78
33	Indonesia	3,291	76	Tunisia	523	119	Bahamas	77
34	Denmark	3,203	77	Estonia	412	120	Nepal	77
35	Romania	2,968	78	Nigeria	405	121	Zambia	77
36	Finland	2,796	79	Kuwait	382	122	Sudan	75
37	Egypt	2,716	80	Kyrgyzstan	357	123	Brunei	68
38	Bulgaria	2,563	81	Cuba	353	124	Fiji	65
39	Venezuela	2,463	82	Macedonia	349	125	Angola	60
40	Czech Republic	2,444	83	Bolivia	348	126	Botswana	60
41	Norway	2,431	84	Cyprus	347	127	Cameroon	60
42	Israel	2,343	85	Lebanon	330	128	Ghana	60
43	Pakistan	2,127	86	Turkmenistan	320	129	Haiti	60

Rank	Country/Entity	Telephones (Thousands)	Rank	Country/Entity	Telephones (Thousands)	Rank	Country/Entity	Telephones (Thousands)
130	Mozambique	60	148	Togo	22	166	Guinea-Bissau	9.4
131	Suriname	53	149	Congo, Rep. of	21	167	Mauritania	9.2
132	Guyana	45	150	Antigua and Barbuda	20	168	Micronesia	7.2
133	Papua New Guinea	44	151	Laos	20	169	Central African Republic	7.8
134	Uganda	43	152.	Swaziland	20	170	Samoa	7.8
135	Albania	42	153	Gambia	19	171	Djibouti	7.6
136.	Vanuatu	42	154	Dominica	18	172	Tonga	6.6
137	Congo, Rep. of	36	155	Lesotho	18	173	Solomon Islands	6.5
138	Malawi	34	156	Burundi	17	174	Cambodia	5.4
139	Madagascar	33	157	Eritrea	17	175	Chad	5.3
140	Gabon	32	158	Mali	17	176	Bhutan	5.2
141	Andorra	30	159	Sierra Leone	17	177	Comoros	4.5
142	Burkina	30	160	Rwanda	15	178	Liberia	4.5
143	Afghanistan	29	161	Somalia	15	179	Equatorial Guinea	2.5
144	Belize	29	162	Maldives	14	180	São Tomé and Príncipe	2.5
145	Benin	28	163	Seychelles	14	181	Kiribati	2.0
146	Grenada	23	164	Niger	13			
147	Cape Verde	22	165	Guinea	11			

Source: The World's Telephones

15.25 Telephone Lines per Capita

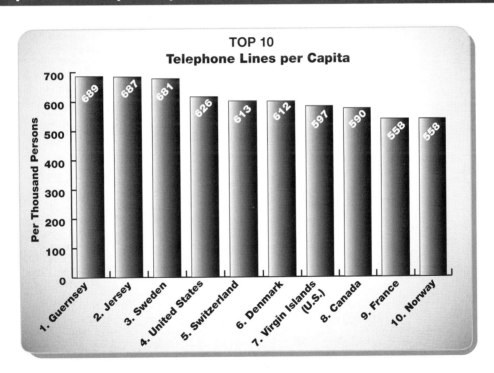

Rank	Country/Entity	Telephone Lines per Thousand Persons, 1995	Rank	Country/Entity	Telephone Lines per Thousand Persons, 1995	Rank	Country/Entity	Telephone Lines per Thousand Persons, 1995
11	Hong Kong	556	18	Germany	494	25	Austria	466
12	Iceland	556	19	Greece	493	26	Guam	461
13	Luxembourg	550	20	Japan	488	27	Malta	459
14	Finland	547	21	New Zealand	479	28	Belgium	458
15	Netherlands	525	22	Singapore	478	29	Andorra	438
16	Australia	510	23	Cyprus	474	30	Italy	433
17	United Kingdom	502	24	Taiwan	467	31	Israel	418

Rank	Country/Entity	Telephone Lines per Thousand Persons, 1995	Rank	Country/Entity	Telephone Lines per Thousand Persons, 1995	Rank	Country/Entity	Telephone Lines per Thousand Persons, 1995
32	South Korea	415	88	Panama	116	144	Indonesia	17
33	Aruba	390	89	Venezuela	111	145	Solomon Islands	17
34	Spain	385	90	Georgia	103	146	Pakistan	16
35	Martinique	381	91	Colombia	100	147	Zimbabwe	14
36	Guadeloupe	378	92	Mexico	96	148	Djibouti	13
37	Netherlands Antilles	374	93	Saudi Arabia	96	149	India	13
38	Ireland	365	94	South Africa	95	150	Albania	12
39	Portugal	362	95	Lebanon	89	151	Yemen	12
40	Macau	361	96	Azerbaijan	85	152	Sri Lanka	11
41	Barbados	345	97	Iran	85	153	Vietnam	11
42	Réunion	329	98	Fiji	83	154	Papua New Guinea	10
43	Puerto Rico	321	99	Oman	79	155	Senegal	9.8
44	Antigua and Barbuda	311	100	Brazil	78	156	Kenya	9.0
45	Slovenia	309	101	Kyrgyzstan	77	157	Lesotho	9.0
46	Bulgaria	306	102	Dominican Republic	76	158	Guinea-Bissau	8.8
47	French Guiana	288	103	Uzbekistan	76	159	Haiti	8.4
48	United Arab Emirates	283	104	Micronesia	74	160	Comoros	8.2
49	Latvia	280	105	Jordan	73	161	Zambia	8.2
50	Bahamas	277	106	Turkmenistan	71	162	Côte d'Ivoire	8.1
51	Estonia	277	107	Bosnia and Herzegovina	69	163	Congo, Rep. of	8.1
52	Croatia	269	108	Tonga	67	164	Bhutan	6.3
53	Grenada	255	109	Ecuador	65	165	Equatorial Guinea	6.3
54	Lithuania	254	110	Guyana	63	166	Angola	5.6
55	Vanuatu	250	111	Syria	63	167	Benin	5.2
56	Bahrain	242	112	West Bank	63	168	Togo	5.2
57	Brunei	240	113	Libya	59	169	Eritrea	4.8
58	Dominica	240	114	Thailand	59	170	Cameroon	4.5
59	Czech Republic	237	115	Tunisia	58	171	Laos	4.1
60	New Caledonia	236	116	Maldives	57	172	Mauritania	4.1
61	Kuwait	226	117	Cape Verde	55	173	Sierra Leone	3.7
62	French Polynesia	219	118	El Salvador	53	174	Malawi	3.6
63	Turkey	215	119	Namibia	51	175	Nepal	3.6
64	Qatar	212	120	Mayotte	48	176	Nigeria	3.6
65	Slovakia	208	121	Bolivia	47	177	Ghana	3.5
66	Uruguay	199	122	Peru	47	178	Mozambique	3.4
67	Yugoslavia	192	123	Egypt	46	179	Myanmar (Burma)	3.3
68	Belarus	190	124	North Korea	46	180	Tanzania	3.0
69	Seychelles	187	125	Samoa	46	181	Burkina Faso	2.9
70	Hungary	185	126	Tajikistan	45	182	Burundi	2.7
71	Macedonia	179	127	Morocco	43	183	Sudan	2.7
72	Russia	170	128	Algeria	42	184	Ethiopia	2.5
73	Costa Rica	167	129	Botswana	41	185	Rwanda	2.5
74	Malaysia	166	130	China	34	186	Bangladesh	2.4
75	Trinidad and Tobago	166	131	Paraguay	34	187	Madagascar	2.4
76	Ukraine	161	132	Iraq	33	188	Central African Republic	2.3
77	Argentina	160	133	Cuba	32	189	Uganda	2.3
78	Armenia	155	134	Mongolia	32	190	Liberia	2.1
79	Poland	148	135	Honduras	29	191	Mali	1.7
80	Belize	134	136	Guatemala	27	192	Somalia	1.7
81	Chile	132	137	Kiribati	26	193	Guinea	1.6
82	Mauritius	131	138	Philippines	25	194	Niger	1.5
83	Moldova	131	139	Gabon	24	195	Afghanistan	1.4
84	Romania	131	140	Nicaragua	23	196	Chad	0.8
85	Suriname	123	141	Swaziland	21	197	Congo, Dem. Rep. of	0.8
86	Kazakhstan	118	142	São Tomé and Príncipe	19	198	Cambodia	0.5
87	Jamaica	116	143	Gambia	17			

Source: The World's Telephones

Rank	Country/Entity	International Calls (minutes per capita)	Rank	Country/Entity	International Calls (minutes per capita)	Rank	Country/Entity	International Calls (minutes per capita)
1	Luxembourg	569.1	54	Czech Rep.	17.7	107	Peru	2.7
2	Hong Kong	274.8	55	Mauritius	17.7	108	Philippines	2.6
3	Singapore	258.8	56	Latvia	17.4	109	Senegal	2.4
4	Switzerland	247.1	57	Jordan	16.5	110	Côte d'Ivoire	2.3
5	United Arab Emirates	211.8	58	Vanuatu	16.3	111	Mauritania	2.2
6	Saint Kitts and Nevis	196.1	59	Uruguay	16.2	112	Guinea-Bissau	2.1
7	Cyprus	160.3	60	Costa Rica	15.5	113	Togo	2.1
8	Bahrain	152.6	61	Moldova	15.2	114	Equatorial Guinea	2.0
9	Qatar	137.6	62	Lithuania	14.9	115	Comoros	1.9
10	Barbados	122.6	63	Panama	14.9	116	Brazil	1.8
11	Ireland	113.5	64	Armenia	13.9	117	Cameroon	1.8
12	Austria	111.9	65	Suriname	13.5	118	Angola	1.7
13	Belgium	109.2	66	Japan	13.0	119	Egypt	1.7
14	Sweden	108.2	67	Belarus	12.8	120	Russia	1.6
15	Brunei	108.0	68	Maldives	12.6	121	Sri Lanka	1.5
16	Iceland	107.9	69	South Korea	12.4	122	Yemen	1.5
17	Denmark	100.7	70	Gabon	12.1	123	Zambia	1.3
18	Norway	100.0	71	El Salvador	11.9	124	China	1.1
19	Canada	99.9	72	Slovakia	11.0	125	Indonesia	1.1
20	Netherlands	94.4	73	Mexico	10.3	126	Benin	1.0
21	New Zealand	85.6	74	Bulgaria	10.0	127	Cuba	1.0
22	Grenada	81.6	75	Cape Verde	10.0	128	Ghana	1.0
23	Malta	76.6	76	Poland	9.9	129	Laos	1.0
24	Saint Lucia	76.4	77	Chile	9.5	130	Kazakhstan	0.9
25	Kuwait	74.5	78	Tunisia	8.7	131	Mozambique	0.9
26	United Kingdom	69.5	79	Libya	8.6	132	Nigeria	0.9
27	Germany	64.1	80	Lebanon	8.5	133	Kenya	0.8
28	Finland	61.7	81	South Africa	7.4	134	Malawi	0.8
29	United States	59.5	82	Nicaragua	7.1	135	Mongolia	0.8
30	Australia	52.6	83	Solomon Islands	7.1	136	Bhutan	0.7
31	Slovenia	50.5	84	Djibouti	7.0	137	Central African Republic	0.7
32	France	48.3	85	Albania	6.3	138	Mali	0.7
33	Israel	45.0	86	Honduras	6.1	139	Nepal	0.7
34	Trinidad and Tobago	44.9	87	Turkey	6.1	140	Burkina Faso	0.6
35	Greece	44.3	88	Venezuela	5.8	141	Cambodia	0.5
36	Croatia	44.1	89	Papua New Guinea	5.6	142	Guinea	0.5
37	Estonia	35.7	90	Zimbabwe	5.1	143	Pakistan	0.5
38	Italy	33.3	91	Kyrgyzstan	5.0	144	Sierra Leone	0.5
39	Namibia	31.5	92	Morocco	4.9	145	Vietnam	0.5
40	Portugal	30.2	93	Argentina	4.4	146	Burundi	0.4
41	Saudi Arabia	30.0	94	Gambia	4.3	147	India	0.4
42	Seychelles	28.6	95	Paraguay	4.2	148	Niger	0.4
43	Belize	27.1	96	São Tomé and Principe	4.2	149	Chad	0.3
44	Spain	27.1	97	Syria	4.1	150	Madagascar	0.3
45	Swaziland	26.6	98	Azerbaijan	4.0	151	Myanmar (Burma)	0.3
46	Oman	25.2	99	Romania	3.9	152	Sudan	0.3
47	Guyana	24.4	100	Thailand	3.7	153	Uganda	0.3
48	Hungary	24.2	101	Guatemala	3.4	154	Bangladesh	0.2
49	Jamaica	21.8	102	Colombia	3.3	155	Eritrea	0.2
50	Macedonia	21.2	103	Ecuador	3.2	156	Ethiopia	0.2
51	Botswana	20.4	104	Bolivia	3.1	157	Tanzania	0.2
52	Fiji	19.3	105	Iran	3.1	158	Tajikistan	0.1
53	Malaysia	18.3	106	Algeria	2.8	159	Georgia	0

Source: The World's Telephones

Chapter 16

Environment

16.1 Nationally Protected Areas

Conservation is one of the ideas that have found easy acceptance throughout the world. One of the key ingredients of conservation is the setting apart of certain environmentally significant areas and their exclusion from development and despoliation. Nationally protected are areas of at least 1,000 hectares (2,500 acres) that fall into one of five categories defined by the World Conservation Monitoring Center: (1) scientific reserves and strict nature reserves with limited public access; (2) national parks of international significance where human activity may be permitted; (3) natural monuments and natural landscapes with unique aspects; (4) managed nature reserves and wildlife sanctuaries; and (5) protected landscapes and seascapes, including cultural landscapes. Designating land as protected area does not necessarily mean that protection is in force. In many corrupt countries, the law is more often circumvented than not. The total data may also be affected by the fact that many small countries have only protected areas of less than 1,000 hectares. The coverage also excludes sites protected under local or provincial law.

Rank	Country/Entity	Protected Area as Percentage of Total Land Area, 1996	Rank	Country/Entity	Protected Area as Percentage of Total Land Area, 1996	Rank	Country/Entity	Protected Area as Percentage of Total Land Area, 1996
1	Ecuador	43.1	45	Spain	8.4	89	Belarus	4.1
2	Hong Kong	40.4	46	Central African Republic	8.2	90	Mali	3.7
3	Venezuela	36.3	47	Togo	7.9	91	Mexico	3.7
4	Denmark	32.3	48	Zimbabwe	7.9	92	Kyrgyzstan	3.6
5	Norway	30.5	49	Nepal	7.8	93	Paraguay	3.5
6	Austria	28.3	50	Niger	7.6	94	Jordan	3.4
7	Germany	27.0	51	Armenia	7.4	95	Nigeria	3.3
8	Dominican Republic	25.2	52	Nicaragua	7.4	96	Russia	3.1
9	New Zealand	23.6	53	Australia	7.3	97	Vietnam	3.0
10	Slovakia	21.8	54	Italy	7.3	98	Albania	2.9
11	United Kingdom	20.9	55	Benin	7.1	99	Georgia	2.7
12	Panama	19.1	56	Macedonia	7.1	100	Kazakhstan	2.7
13	Chile	18.9	57	Netherlands	7.1	101	Peru	2.7
14	Botswana	18.5	58	South Korea	6.9	102	Algeria	2.5
15	Switzerland	18.0	59	Hungary	6.8	103	Greece	2.4
16	Guatemala	16.8	60	Japan	6.8	104	Saudi Arabia	2.3
17	Cambodia	16.2	61	Angola	6.6	105	Uzbekistan	2.0
18	Czech Republic	15.8	62	Croatia	6.6	106	Madagascar	1.9
19	Tanzania	15.6	63	China	6.4	107	Argentina	1.7
20	Israel	15.0	64	Portugal	6.4	108	Kuwait	1.7
21	Rwanda	14.6	65	Côte d'Ivoire	6.3	109	Mauritania	1.7
22	Bolivia	14.4	66	Kenya	6.1	110	Ukraine	1.6
23	Thailand	13.8	67	Mozambique	6.1	111	Turkey	1.4
24	Costa Rica	13.7	68	Finland	6.0	112	Moldova	1.2
25	United States	13.4	69	Azerbaijan	5.5	113	Sierra Leone	1.1
26	Sri Lanka	13.3	70	Burundi	5.5	114	Ireland	0.9
27	Namibia	12.9	71	Ethiopia	5.5	115	Bangladesh	0.8
28	Latvia	12.6	72	Slovenia	5.5	116	Egypt	0.8
29	Estonia	12.1	73	South Africa	5.4	117	Guinea	0.7
30	Malawi	11.3	74	Iran	5.1	118	Morocco	0.7
31	Senegal	11.3	75	Eritrea	5.0	119	El Salvador	0.5
32	France	10.7	76	Philippines	4.9	120	Haiti	0.4
33	Indonesia	10.6	77	Ghana	4.8	121	Lesotho	0.3
34	Burkina Faso	10.5	78	India	4.8	122	Myanmar (Burma)	0.3
35	Mongolia	10.3	79	Pakistan	4.8	123	Tunisia	0.3
36	Canada	10.0	80	Romania	4.6	124	Uruguay	0.3
37	Lithuania	10.0	81	Cameroon	4.5	125	Jamaica	0.0
38	Honduras	9.9	82	Congo, Dem. Rep. of	4.5	126	Laos	0.0
39	Poland	9.6	83	Congo, Rep. of	4.5	127	Lebanon	0.0
40	Uganda	9.6	84	Malaysia	4.5	128	Papua New Guinea	0.0
41	Chad	9.1	85	Bulgaria	4.4	129	Singapore	0.0
42	Colombia	9.0	86	Brazil	4.2	130	Syria	0.0
43	Sweden	8.8	87	Tajikistan	4.2	131	Yemen	0.0
44	Zambia	8.6	88	Turkmenistan	4.2			

Source: World Resources

Human societies generate several types of waste simply through routine activities but the amount of waste is multiplied several fold through industrial activities. The principal forms of waste are polluted water and sewage, hazardous wastes, medical wastes, and municipal wastes. Prosperous societies generate more waste than poor ones. Almost all forms of waste, except hazardous waste, are recyclable although the cost of recovery in some cases may not make it commercially viable. Hazardous waste generation occurs almost entirely in developed countries, where it is a byproduct of nuclear and chemical industries. The disposal of such hazardous wastes is a problem for which no clear solution has yet emerged. In some cases they are buried underground or under the ocean floor, but these sites have a potential for leaks at a later time. The United States is believed to produce about 25 percent of all hazardous wastes in the world. Certain nuclear wastes present hazards to human life for several millennia to come. In the United States, the superfund has been established to meet the enormous costs involved in both the transport of nuclear wastes from the nuclear plants to the disposal sites, and their burial in containers to withstand radiation and prevent leakage. Most recycling programs, especially those handled by municipalities, concentrate on waste water and domestic waste, including paper, glass, and metal.

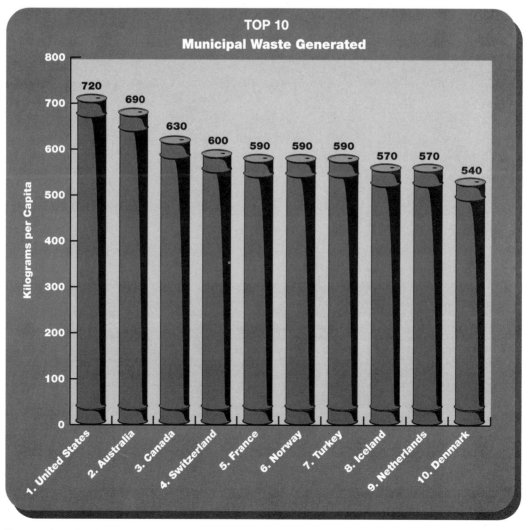

Rank	Country/Entity	Municipal Waste Generated (kilograms per capita)	Rank	Country/Entity	Municipal Waste Generated (kilograms per capita)	Rank	Country/Entity	Municipal Waste Generated (kilograms per capita)
11	Austria	510	18	Ireland	430	25	Portugal	350
12	Hungary	500	19	Finland	410	26	Greece	340
13	Belgium	480	20	Germany	400	27	Poland	320
14	United Kingdom	480	21	Japan	400	28	Czech Republic	310
15	Italy	470	22	South Korea	400	29	Mexico	300
16	Luxembourg	460	23	Spain	370			
17	Sweden	440	24	New Zealand	350			

Source: The State of the Environment

Pollution

The principal sources of pollution are carbon monoxide, sulfur dioxide (SO_2), and nitrogen. Carbon monoxide is one of the principal air pollutants in urban areas. It is one of the principal culprits in global warming and the depletion of the ozone layer. The Kyoto Protocol, negotiated in 1997, calls for a global reduction in all pollutants in land, air, and water over a period of time that varies according to the developmental status of nations.

16.3 Carbon Dioxide Emissions

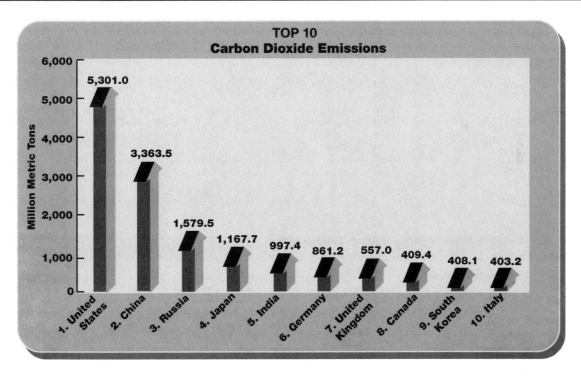

TOP 10
Carbon Dioxide Emissions

Million Metric Tons

- 1. United States — 5,301.0
- 2. China — 3,363.5
- 3. Russia — 1,579.5
- 4. Japan — 1,167.7
- 5. India — 997.4
- 6. Germany — 861.2
- 7. United Kingdom — 557.0
- 8. Canada — 409.4
- 9. South Korea — 408.1
- 10. Italy — 403.2

Rank	Country/Entity	Carbon Dioxide Emissions, 1996 (million metric tons)	Rank	Country/Entity	Carbon Dioxide Emissions, 1996 (million metric tons)	Rank	Country/Entity	Carbon Dioxide Emissions, 1996 (million metric tons)
11	Ukraine	397.3	14	Mexico	348.1	17	Brazil	273.4
12	France	361.8	15	Australia	306.6	18	Saudi Arabia	267.8
13	Poland	356.8	16	South Africa	292.7	19	Iran	266.7

Rank	Country/Entity	Carbon Dioxide Emissions, 1996 (million metric tons)	Rank	Country/Entity	Carbon Dioxide Emissions, 1996 (million metric tons)	Rank	Country/Entity	Carbon Dioxide Emissions, 1996 (million metric tons)
20	North Korea	254.3	61	Turkmenistan	34.2	102	Armenia	3.7
21	Indonesia	245.1	62	Cuba	31.2	103	Gabon	3.7
22	Spain	232.5	63	Azerbaijan	30.0	104	Paraguay	3.7
23	Thailand	205.4	64	New Zealand	29.8	105	Cameroon	3.5
24	Turkey	178.3	65	Morocco	27.9	106	Sudan	3.5
25	Kazakhstan	173.8	66	Peru	26.2	107	Ethiopia	3.4
26	Netherlands	155.2	67	Ecuador	24.5	108	Bosnia and Herzegovina	3.1
27	Venezuela	144.5	68	Hong Kong	23.1	109	Senegal	3.1
28	Argentina	129.9	69	Bangladesh	23.0	110	Georgia	3.0
29	Czech Republic	126.7	70	Trinidad and Tobago	22.2	111	Mauritania	2.9
30	Romania	119.3	71	Zimbabwe	18.4	112	Nicaragua	2.9
31	Malaysia	119.1	72	Croatia	17.5	113	Papua New Guinea	2.4
32	Belgium	106.0	73	Estonia	16.4	114	Tanzania	2.4
33	Egypt	97.9	74	Tunisia	16.2	115	Zambia	2.4
34	Uzbekistan	95.0	75	Puerto Rico	15.8	116	Congo, Dem. Rep. of	2.3
35	Algeria	94.3	76	Oman	15.1	117	Botswana	2.1
36	Pakistan	94.3	77	Lebanon	14.2	118	Albania	1.9
37	Iraq	91.4	78	Lithuania	13.8	119	Mauritius	1.7
38	Nigeria	83.3	79	Côte d'Ivoire	13.1	120	Nepal	1.6
39	United Arab Emirates	81.8	80	Slovenia	13.0	121	Madagascar	1.2
40	Greece	80.6	81	Dominican Republic	12.9	122	Guinea	1.1
41	Norway	67.0	82	Macedonia	12.7	123	Haiti	1.1
42	Singapore	65.8	83	Moldova	12.1	124	Niger	1.1
43	Colombia	65.3	84	Bolivia	10.1	125	Burkina Faso	1.0
44	Philippines	63.2	85	Jamaica	10.1	126	Mozambique	1.0
45	Belarus	61.7	86	Latvia	9.3	127	Uganda	1.0
46	Hungary	59.5	87	Mongolia	8.9	128	Togo	0.8
47	Austria	59.3	88	Myanmar (Burma)	7.3	129	Benin	0.7
48	Finland	59.2	89	Sri Lanka	7.1	130	Malawi	0.7
49	Denmark	56.6	90	Guatemala	6.8	131	Cambodia	0.5
50	Bulgaria	55.3	91	Kenya	6.8	132	Mali	0.5
51	Sweden	54.1	92	Panama	6.7	133	Rwanda	0.5
52	Israel	52.3	93	Kyrgyzstan	6.1	134	Sierra Leone	0.4
53	Chile	48.8	94	Tajikistan	5.8	135	Laos	0.3
54	Portugal	47.9	95	Uruguay	5.6	136	Burundi	0.2
55	Syria	44.3	96	Angola	5.1	137	Central African Republic	0.2
56	Switzerland	44.2	97	Congo, Rep. of	5.0	138	Gambia	0.2
57	Libya	40.6	98	Costa Rica	4.7	139	Guinea-Bissau	0.2
58	Slovakia	39.6	99	El Salvador	4.0	140	Chad	0.1
59	Vietnam	37.6	100	Ghana	4.0			
60	Ireland	34.9	101	Honduras	4.0			

Source: World Resources

16.4 Carbon Dioxide Emissions per Capita

Rank	Country/Entity	Carbon Dioxide Emissions per Capita, 1996 (metric tons)	Rank	Country/Entity	Carbon Dioxide Emissions per Capita, 1996 (metric tons)	Rank	Country/Entity	Carbon Dioxide Emissions per Capita, 1996 (metric tons)
1	Singapore	21.6	12	Russia	10.7	23	Ukraine	7.8
2	United States	20.0	13	Germany	10.5	24	Greece	7.7
3	Australia	16.7	14	Belgium	10.4	25	Austria	7.4
4	Norway	15.3	15	Netherlands	10.0	26	Slovakia	7.4
5	Saudi Arabia	13.8	16	Ireland	9.6	27	Turkmenistan	7.4
6	Canada	13.7	17	United Kingdom	9.5	28	South Africa	7.3
7	Czech Republic	12.3	18	Japan	9.3	29	Italy	7.0
8	Finland	11.5	19	Israel	9.2	30	Bulgaria	6.6
9	Estonia	11.2	20	Poland	9.2	31	Slovenia	6.5
10	Kazakhstan	10.9	21	South Korea	9.0	32	Venezuela	6.5
11	Denmark	10.7	22	New Zealand	8.0	33	Macedonia	6.4

Rank	Country/Entity	Carbon Dioxide Emissions per Capita, 1996 (metric tons)	Rank	Country/Entity	Carbon Dioxide Emissions per Capita, 1996 (metric tons)	Rank	Country/Entity	Carbon Dioxide Emissions per Capita, 1996 (metric tons)
34	Switzerland	6.3	65	Tunisia	1.8	96	Vietnam	0.5
35	France	6.2	66	Brazil	1.7	97	Senegal	0.4
36	Sweden	6.1	67	Colombia	1.7	98	Sri Lanka	0.4
37	Belarus	6.0	68	Egypt	1.7	99	Cameroon	0.3
38	Spain	5.9	69	Uruguay	1.7	100	Zambia	0.3
39	Hungary	5.8	70	Dominican Republic	1.6	101	Bangladesh	0.2
40	Malaysia	5.6	71	Zimbabwe	1.6	102	Ghana	0.2
41	Romania	5.3	72	Botswana	1.4	103	Guinea	0.2
42	Portugal	4.8	73	Costa Rica	1.4	104	Kenya	0.2
43	Iran	4.4	74	Bolivia	1.3	105	Myanmar (Burma)	0.2
44	Uzbekistan	4.1	75	Kyrgyzstan	1.3	106	Togo	0.2
45	Azerbaijan	4.0	76	Indonesia	1.2	107	Benin	0.1
46	Jamaica	4.0	77	Mauritania	1.2	108	Burkina Faso	0.1
47	Mexico	3.8	78	India	1.1	109	Central African Republic	0.1
48	Argentina	3.7	79	Peru	1.1	110	Congo, Dem. Rep. of	0.1
49	Croatia	3.7	80	Armenia	1.0	111	Ethiopia	0.1
50	Hong Kong	3.7	81	Morocco	1.0	112	Haiti	0.1
51	Latvia	3.7	82	Tajikistan	1.0	113	Laos	0.1
52	Lithuania	3.7	83	Côte d'Ivoire	0.9	114	Madagascar	0.1
53	Mongolia	3.6	84	Philippines	0.9	115	Malawi	0.1
54	Lebanon	3.5	85	Pakistan	0.8	116	Mozambique	0.1
55	Chile	3.4	86	El Salvador	0.7	117	Nepal	0.1
56	Thailand	3.4	87	Guatemala	0.7	118	Niger	0.1
57	Algeria	3.3	88	Honduras	0.7	119	Rwanda	0.1
58	Syria	3.1	89	Nigeria	0.7	120	Sierra Leone	0.1
59	China	2.8	90	Paraguay	0.7	121	Tanzania	0.1
60	Moldova	2.8	91	Albania	0.6	122	Uganda	0.1
61	Turkey	2.8	92	Nicaragua	0.6	123	Burundi	0.0
62	Panama	2.5	93	Angola	0.5	124	Cambodia	0.0
63	Ecuador	2.1	94	Georgia	0.5	125	Chad	0.0
64	Congo, Rep. of	1.9	95	Papua New Guinea	0.5	126	Mali	0.0

Source: World Resources

16.5 Sulfuric Oxide Emissions per Capita

Rank	Country/Entity	SO$_2$ Emissions per Capita (thousand metric tons)	Rank	Country/Entity	SO$_2$ Emissions per Capita (thousand metric tons)	Rank	Country/Entity	SO$_2$ Emissions per Capita (thousand metric tons)
1	Czech Republic	149.5	11	United Kingdom	55.0	21	Luxembourg	25.3
2	Bulgaria	120.0	12	Ukraine	53.6	22	France	21.2
3	Canada	105.2	13	Ireland	53.1	23	Albania	14.9
4	Hungary	81.0	14	Greece	49.2	24	Sweden	11.6
5	United States	78.7	15	Germany	48.2	25	Netherlands	10.7
6	Romania	78.4	16	Iceland	32.7	26	Belgium	9.4
7	Poland	70.9	17	Denmark	30.5	27	Austria	9.0
8	Slovakia	70.4	18	Italy	29.4	28	Norway	8.4
9	Belarus	56.5	19	Portugal	29.1	29	Switzerland	8.2
10	Spain	55.8	20	Finland	27.5	30	Japan	7.0

Source: Environmental Almanac

Freshwater resources refer to total renewable water resources, which include flows of rivers and groundwater from rainfall in the country, and river flows that originate or flow through other countries. Water resources vary considerably from one year to the next. Data for small countries and countries in arid and semiarid zones are less reliable than those for larger countries and countries with higher rainfall. Not all freshwater is necessarily safe water, and even treated water may not be safe to drink. These qualifications must be considered in evaluating this ranking.

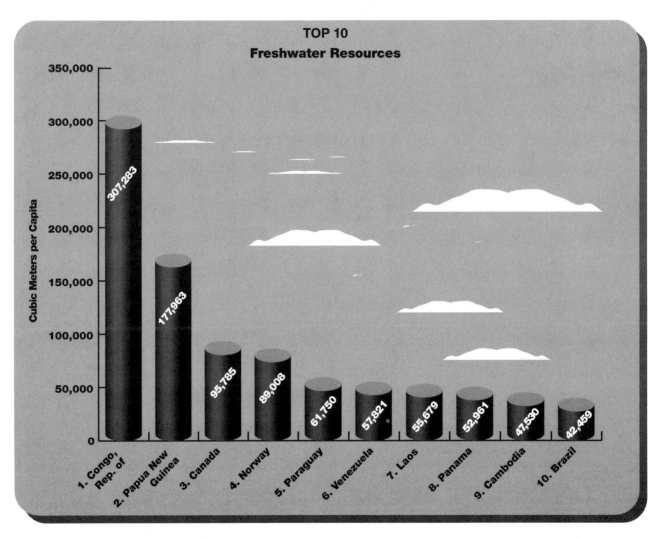

TOP 10
Freshwater Resources

Cubic Meters per Capita

Rank	Country/Entity	Freshwater Resources, 1996 (cubic meters per capita)	Rank	Country/Entity	Freshwater Resources, 1996 (cubic meters per capita)	Rank	Country/Entity	Freshwater Resources, 1996 (cubic meters per capita)
11	Central African Republic	41,250	16	Guinea	32,661	21	Costa Rica	27,425
12	Bolivia	38,625	17	Chile	32,007	22	Colombia	26,722
13	Uruguay	37,966	18	Russia	30,168	23	Ecuador	26,305
14	Nicaragua	37,420	19	Namibia	28,042	24	Bulgaria	24,663
15	Sierra Leone	33,698	20	Argentina	27,861	25	Myanmar (Burma)	24,651

Rank	Country/Entity	Freshwater Resources, 1996 (cubic meters per capita)	Rank	Country/Entity	Freshwater Resources, 1996 (cubic meters per capita)	Rank	Country/Entity	Freshwater Resources, 1996 (cubic meters per capita)
26	Madagascar	23,819	61	Czech Republic	5,649	96	India	2,167
27	Finland	21,985	62	Uzbekistan	5,476	97	Armenia	2,136
28	Congo, Dem. Rep. of	21,816	63	Côte d'Ivoire	5,468	98	Germany	2,084
29	Malaysia	21,046	64	Greece	5,289	99	Belarus	1,841
30	Sweden	20,340	65	Vietnam	4,902	100	Ethiopia	1,841
31	Cameroon	19,231	66	Mauritania	4,632	101	Malawi	1,814
32	Bangladesh	19,065	67	Ukraine	4,556	102	Zimbabwe	1,744
33	Australia	18,508	68	Senegal	4,482	103	Burkina Faso	1,671
34	Albania	16,785	69	Benin	4,451	104	Peru	1,641
35	Angola	15,782	70	Philippines	4,393	105	Haiti	1,468
36	Latvia	13,793	71	Azerbaijan	4,339	106	Poland	1,454
37	Ireland	13,657	72	Japan	4,338	107	South Korea	1,438
38	Mozambique	12,989	73	Turkmenistan	3,950	108	Iran	1,339
39	Croatia	12,879	74	Mexico	3,788	109	South Africa	1,231
40	Indonesia	12,625	75	Niger	3,317	110	Belgium	1,227
41	Zambia	12,284	76	Pakistan	3,256	111	United Kingdom	1,203
42	Estonia	12,071	77	Jamaica	3,250	112	Morocco	1,088
43	Hungary	11,817	78	Uganda	3,248	113	Kenya	1,056
44	Austria	11,187	79	El Salvador	3,197	114	Egypt	966
45	Guatemala	11,028	80	France	3,029	115	Lebanon	941
46	Mali	9,718	81	Ghana	2,958	116	Syria	859
47	Mongolia	9,677	82	Thailand	2,954	117	Rwanda	798
48	Botswana	9,589	83	Italy	2,903	118	Burundi	559
49	Honduras	9,259	84	Tanzania	2,842	119	New Zealand	532
50	United States	9,259	85	Togo	2,762	120	Algeria	463
51	Romania	9,222	86	Lesotho	2,597	121	Tunisia	447
52	Kazakhstan	8,696	87	Kyrgyzstan	2,509	122	Moldova	397
53	Georgia	8,291	88	Dominican Republic	2,467	123	Israel	377
54	Nepal	7,616	89	Denmark	2,460	124	Yemen	255
55	Switzerland	7,054	90	Spain	2,398	125	Jordan	198
56	Portugal	6,998	91	Nigeria	2,375	126	Singapore	193
57	Lithuania	6,531	92	Eritrea	2,332	127	Saudi Arabia	120
58	Chad	6,011	93	Sri Lanka	2,329	128	Kuwait	11
59	Netherlands	5,767	94	China	2,282			
60	Slovakia	5,720	95	Turkey	2,246			

Source: World Resources

Forests are the lungs of the planet. As part of the ecosystem, they are the principal mechanism for maintaining the circulatory system on which living things depend for their survival. Like all green plants, forests help renew the atmosphere by giving off oxygen and removing carbon dioxide from the air. They also provide a home for many forms of wildlife and plants and trees that cannot exist elsewhere. However, the past 500 years have witnessed progressive deforestation throughout the world for purposes of agriculture and human settlement. Of the many types of forests, the most important are tropical rain forests, which are tropical woodlands with an annual rainfall of 100 inches or more. The largest of these forests grow in the Amazon River Basin of South America, the Congo River Basin of Africa, and throughout Southeast Asia. The Brazilian rain forest and the Indonesian rain forest make up one-fifth of all forests in the world. Russia, however, with its vast expanse of Siberia, contains the most forest area of any country.

Rank	Country/Entity	Forest Area in Square Kilometers (thousands)	Rank	Country/Entity	Forest Area in Square Kilometers (thousands)	Rank	Country/Entity	Forest Area in Square Kilometers (thousands)
1	Russia	7,635	41	Chad	110	81	Portugal	29
2	Brazil	3,511	42	Germany	107	82	Panama	28
3	Canada	2,446	43	Kazakhstan	105	83	Bosnia	27
4	United States	2,125	44	Cambodia	98	84	Czech Republic	26
5	Congo, Dem. Rep. of	1,746	45	Mongolia	94	85	Niger	26
6	China	1,333	46	Ukraine	92	86	United Kingdom	24
7	Indonesia	1,098	47	Uzbekistan	91	87	Guinea-Bissau	23
8	Peru	676	48	Vietnam	91	88	Estonia	20
9	India	650	49	Ghana	90	89	Lithuania	20
10	Mexico	554	50	Turkey	89	90	Slovakia	20
11	Colombia	539	51	Poland	87	91	Algeria	19
12	Bolivia	483	52	Zimbabwe	87	92	Croatia	18
13	Venezuela	440	53	Spain	84	93	Sri Lanka	18
14	Sudan	416	54	Norway	81	94	Yugoslavia	18
15	Australia	409	55	Chile	79	95	Hungary	17
16	Papua New Guinea	369	56	New Zealand	79	96	Pakistan	17
17	Argentina	339	57	South Korea	76	97	Dominican Republic	16
18	Tanzania	325	58	Senegal	74	98	Iran	15
19	Zambia	314	59	Belarus	74	99	Kenya	13
20	Central African Republic	299	60	Philippines	68	100	Sierra Leone	13
21	Myanmar (Burma)	272	61	Greece	65	101	Costa Rica	12
22	Japan	251	62	Italy	65	102	Togo	12
23	Sweden	244	63	Guinea	64	103	Slovenia	11
24	Angola	222	64	North Korea	62	104	Switzerland	11
25	Finland	200	65	Romania	62	105	Albania	11
26	Cameroon	196	66	Uganda	61	106	Azerbaijan	10
27	Congo, Rep. of	195	67	Nicaragua	56	107	Bangladesh	10
28	Gabon	179	68	Côte d'Ivoire	55	108	Macedonia	10
29	Mozambique	169	69	Nepal	48	109	Uruguay	8
30	Malaysia	155	70	Benin	46	110	Kyrgyzstan	7
31	Madagascar	151	71	Burkina	43	111	Ireland	6
32	France	150	72	Honduras	41	112	Mauritania	6
33	Botswana	139	73	Austria	39	113	Tunisia	6
34	Nigeria	138	74	Guatemala	38	114	Denmark	4
35	Ethiopia	136	75	Morocco	38	115	Libya	4
36	Namibia	124	76	Turkmenistan	38	116	Moldova	4
37	Mali	116	77	Malawi	33	117	Tajikistan	4
38	Thailand	116	78	Bulgaria	32	118	Armenia	3
39	Paraguay	115	79	Georgia	30	119	Burundi	3
40	Ecuador	111	80	Latvia	29	120	Eritrea	3

Rank	Country/Entity	Forest Area in Square Kilometers (thousands)	Rank	Country/Entity	Forest Area in Square Kilometers (thousands)	Rank	Country/Entity	Forest Area in Square Kilometers (thousands)
121	Netherlands	3	125	Syria	2	129	Iraq	1
122	Puerto Rico	3	126	Trinidad and Tobago	2	130	Israel	1
123	Jamaica	2	127	El Salvador	1	131	Lebanon	1
124	Saudi Arabia	2	128	Gambia	1	132	United Arab Emirates	1

Source: Forestry Statistics

16.8 Deforestation Rate

Deforestation is a major cause of loss of biodiversity and thus a key issue for conservationists. The data on which this ranking is based do not distinguish between natural forest and plantation. For this reason, deforestation data may underestimate the rate at which natural forests are permanently disappearing from the ecological horizon. Deforestation occurs in all countries but in most developed countries is offset by reforestation programs that reestablish forests so that the extent of forest cover is not seriously upset. The major exceptions are in the rain forests of Brazil and Indonesia, where logging and clearcutting operations destroy the forest cover permanently. Shrinking rain forests also affect the oxygen supply of the world and cause other ecological damage. Permanent losses also occur in many African countries where trees are cut down for firewood. Air pollution, desertification, and soil erosion also cause irreversible loss of forests. As a result, there is a continuing global deficit in forests and biodiversity every year.

Rank	Country/Entity	Deforestation Rate by Percentage, 1990–1995	Rank	Country/Entity	Deforestation Rate by Percentage, 1990–1995	Rank	Country/Entity	Deforestation Rate by Percentage, 1990–1995
1	Lebanon	7.8	29	Ghana	1.3	57	Congo, Dem. Rep. of	0.7
2	Jamaica	7.2	30	Algeria	1.2	58	Mozambique	0.7
3	Comoros	5.6	31	Benin	1.2	59	Senegal	0.7
4	Saint Lucia	3.6	32	Bolivia	1.2	60	Brunei	0.6
5	Philippines	3.5	33	Cuba	1.2	61	Côte d'Ivoire	0.6
6	Haiti	3.4	34	Laos	1.2	62	Cameroon	0.6
7	El Salvador	3.3	35	Guinea	1.1	63	Zimbabwe	0.6
8	Belize	3.0	36	Nepal	1.1	64	Botswana	0.5
9	Costa Rica	3.0	37	Sri Lanka	1.1	65	Brazil	0.5
10	Sierra Leone	3.0	38	Venezuela	1.1	66	Colombia	0.5
11	Pakistan	2.9	39	Angola	1.0	67	Equatorial Guinea	0.5
12	Bahamas	2.6	40	Indonesia	1.0	68	Ethiopia	0.5
13	Paraguay	2.6	41	Mali	1.0	69	Gabon	0.5
14	Thailand	2.6	42	Samoa	1.0	70	Tunisia	0.5
15	Jordan	2.5	43	Tanzania	1.0	71	Burundi	0.4
16	Nicaragua	2.5	44	Vietnam	1.0	72	Central African Republic	0.4
17	Malaysia	2.4	45	Gambia	0.9	73	Chile	0.4
18	Honduras	2.3	46	Mexico	0.9	74	Fiji	0.4
19	Syria	2.2	47	Nigeria	0.9	75	Guinea-Bissau	0.4
20	Panama	2.1	48	Uganda	0.9	76	Argentina	0.3
21	Guatemala	2.0	49	Bangladesh	0.8	77	Bhutan	0.3
22	Iran	1.7	50	Chad	0.8	78	Kenya	0.3
23	Cambodia	1.6	51	Madagascar	0.8	79	Morocco	0.3
24	Dominican Republic	1.6	52	Saudi Arabia	0.8	80	Namibia	0.3
25	Ecuador	1.6	53	Sudan	0.8	81	Peru	0.3
26	Malawi	1.6	54	Vanuatu	0.8	82	Congo, Rep. of	0.2
27	Trinidad and Tobago	1.5	55	Zambia	0.8	83	South Korea	0.2
28	Myanmar (Burma)	1.4	56	Burkina Faso	0.7	84	Solomon Islands	0.2

Rank	Country/Entity	Deforestation Rate by Percentage, 1990–1995	Rank	Country/Entity	Deforestation Rate by Percentage, 1990–1995	Rank	Country/Entity	Deforestation Rate by Percentage, 1990–1995
85	South Africa	0.2	111	Lesotho	0.0	136	United Arab Emirates	0.0
86	China	0.1	112	Libya	0.0	137	Yemen	0.0
87	Finland	0.1	113	Malta	0.0	138	Canada	-0.1
88	Japan	0.1	114	Mauritania	0.0	139	Italy	-0.1
89	Suriname	0.1	115	Mauritius	0.0	140	Poland	-0.1
90	Albania	0.0	116	Moldova	0.0	141	Slovakia	-0.1
91	Antigua and Barbuda	0.0	117	Mongolia	0.0	142	Ukraine	-0.1
92	Austria	0.0	118	Netherlands	0.0	143	Norway	-0.3
93	Azerbaijan	0.0	119	Niger	0.0	144	United States	-0.3
94	Bahrain	0.0	120	North Korea	0.0	145	Hungary	-0.5
95	Barbados	0.0	121	Oman	0.0	146	United Kingdom	-0.5
96	Croatia	0.0	122	Papua New Guinea	0.0	147	Lithuania	-0.6
97	Cyprus	0.0	123	Qatar	0.0	148	New Zealand	-0.6
98	Denmark	0.0	124	São Tomé and Príncipe	0.0	149	Latvia	-0.9
99	Djibouti	0.0	125	Saint Kitts and Nevis	0.0	150	Portugal	-0.9
100	Dominica	0.0	126	Saint Vincent and the Grenadines	0.0	151	Belarus	-1.0
101	Egypt	0.0				152	Estonia	-1.0
102	Eritrea	0.0	127	Seychelles	0.0	153	France	-1.1
103	Georgia	0.0	128	Singapore	0.0	154	Kazakhstan	-1.9
104	Germany	0.0	129	Slovenia	0.0	155	Greece	-2.3
105	Grenada	0.0	130	Spain	0.0	156	Armenia	-2.7
106	Iceland	0.0	131	Swaziland	0.0	157	Ireland	-2.7
107	Iraq	0.0	132	Switzerland	0.0	158	Uzbekistan	-2.7
108	Israel	0.0	133	Tajikistan	0.0	159	Cape Verde	-24.0
109	Kuwait	0.0	134	Turkey	0.0			
110	Kyrgyzstan	0.0	135	Turkmenistan	0.0			

Source: Environmental Almanac

Mammals, Birds, and Plants

Every nation has its own stock of mammals, birds, and higher (vascular) plant species that reflect its ecological history, climate, and other habitat characteristics. Some of them are common to the globe, and some to the region, but some are peculiar to the country. In every case, a few species are endangered or are vulnerable to extinction because of human predatory practices and destruction of habitats. Because taxonomic concepts and categories vary, the figures are not necessarily comparable across national borders. While the number of birds and mammals is fairly well known, that is not the case with plants. In fact, despite intense botanical explorations during the last several centuries, thousands of plants have still not been identified or classified. Together, these mammals, birds, and higher plants, along with other species, such as insects, constitute the core elements of biodiversity, any diminution of which would cause an impoverishment of the vitality of the biosphere.

16.9 Mammal Species

Rank	Country/Entity	Mammals Species, 1996	Rank	Country/Entity	Mammals Species, 1996	Rank	Country/Entity	Mammals Species, 1996
1	Mexico	450	11	Argentina	320	21	Nigeria	274
2	Indonesia	436	12	Bolivia	316	22	Zimbabwe	270
3	United States	428	13	India	316	23	Russia	269
4	Congo, Dem. Rep. of	415	14	Tanzania	316	24	Sudan	267
5	Brazil	394	15	Paraguay	305	25	Thailand	265
6	China	394	16	Venezuela	305	26	Ethiopia	255
7	Colombia	359	17	Ecuador	302	27	Australia	252
8	Kenya	359	18	Cameroon	297	28	Myanmar (Burma)	251
9	Peru	344	19	Malaysia	286	29	Guatemala	250
10	Uganda	338	20	Angola	276	30	South Africa	247

Rank	Country/Entity	Mammals Species, 1996	Rank	Country/Entity	Mammals Species, 1996	Rank	Country/Entity	Mammals Species, 1996
31	Côte d'Ivoire	230	65	Niger	131	99	Slovenia	69
32	Zambia	229	66	Cambodia	123	100	Albania	68
33	Ghana	222	67	Turkey	116	101	Lithuania	68
34	Panama	218	68	Eritrea	112	102	Moldova	68
35	Papua New Guinea	214	69	Bangladesh	109	103	Yemen	66
36	Vietnam	213	70	Gambia	108	104	Estonia	65
37	Central African Republic	209	71	Guinea-Bissau	108	105	Portugal	63
38	Costa Rica	205	72	Burundi	107	106	Syria	63
39	Congo, Rep. of	200	73	Madagascar	105	107	Mauritania	61
40	Nicaragua	200	74	Morocco	105	108	Finland	60
41	Togo	196	75	Trinidad and Tobago	100	109	Sweden	60
42	Malawi	195	76	Egypt	98	110	Belgium	58
43	Canada	193	77	Greece	95	111	Oman	56
44	Gabon	190	78	France	93	112	Netherlands	55
45	Guinea	190	79	Algeria	92	113	Lebanon	54
46	Benin	188	80	Israel	92	114	Norway	54
47	Mozambique	179	81	Chile	91	115	United Kingdom	50
48	Honduras	173	82	Italy	90	116	South Korea	49
49	Laos	172	83	Sri Lanka	88	117	Singapore	45
50	Nepal	167	84	Poland	84	118	Denmark	43
51	Botswana	164	85	Romania	84	119	Lesotho	33
52	Senegal	155	86	Austria	83	120	Cuba	31
53	Namibia	154	87	Latvia	83	121	Ireland	25
54	Philippines	153	88	Spain	82	122	United Arab Emirates	25
55	Pakistan	151	89	Bulgaria	81	123	Hong Kong	24
56	Rwanda	151	90	Iraq	81	124	Jamaica	24
57	Burkina Faso	147	91	Uruguay	81	125	Kuwait	21
58	Sierra Leone	147	92	Tunisia	78	126	Dominican Republic	20
59	Iran	140	93	Saudi Arabia	77	127	Puerto Rico	16
60	Mali	137	94	Germany	76	128	New Zealand	10
61	El Salvador	135	95	Libya	76	129	Mauritius	4
62	Chad	134	96	Switzerland	75	130	Haiti	3
63	Mongolia	134	97	Hungary	72			
64	Japan	132	98	Jordan	71			

Source: World Data

16.10 Bird Species

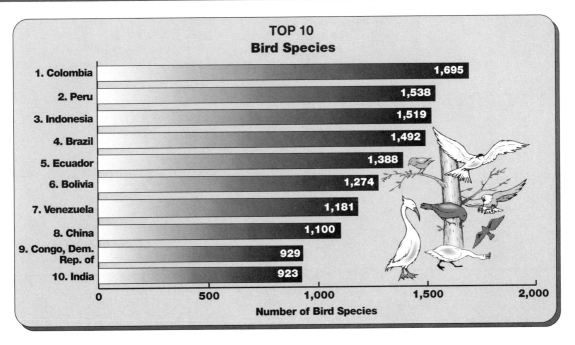

TOP 10
Bird Species

1. Colombia — 1,695
2. Peru — 1,538
3. Indonesia — 1,519
4. Brazil — 1,492
5. Ecuador — 1,388
6. Bolivia — 1,274
7. Venezuela — 1,181
8. China — 1,100
9. Congo, Dem. Rep. of — 929
10. India — 923

Number of Bird Species

Rank	Country/Entity	Bird Species, 1996	Rank	Country/Entity	Bird Species, 1996	Rank	Country/Entity	Bird Species, 1996
11	Argentina	897	53	Mali	397	95	Austria	213
12	Myanmar (Burma)	867	54	Philippines	395	96	Estonia	213
13	Kenya	844	55	Togo	391	97	Morocco	210
14	Uganda	830	56	Mongolia	390	98	Slovakia	209
15	Tanzania	822	57	Botswana	386	99	Portugal	207
16	Mexico	769	58	Senegal	384	100	Slovenia	207
17	Angola	765	59	Pakistan	375	101	Hungary	205
18	Panama	732	60	Chad	370	102	Syria	204
19	Cameroon	690	61	Burkina Faso	335	103	Lithuania	202
20	Nigeria	681	62	Iran	323	104	Madagascar	202
21	Sudan	680	63	Eritrea	319	105	Czech Republic	199
22	United States	650	64	Benin	307	106	Denmark	196
23	Australia	649	65	Cambodia	307	107	Switzerland	193
24	Papua New Guinea	644	66	Turkey	302	108	Algeria	192
25	Russia	628	67	Niger	299	109	Netherlands	191
26	Ethiopia	626	68	Chile	296	110	Belgium	180
27	Thailand	616	69	Bangladesh	295	111	Israel	180
28	Nepal	611	70	Gambia	280	112	Moldova	177
29	Zambia	605	71	Spain	278	113	Tunisia	173
30	Costa Rica	600	72	Mauritania	273	114	Iraq	172
31	South Africa	596	73	France	269	115	Saudi Arabia	155
32	Paraguay	556	74	Ukraine	263	116	Lebanon	154
33	Central African Republic	537	75	Trinidad and Tobago	260	117	Egypt	153
34	Côte d'Ivoire	535	76	El Salvador	251	118	New Zealand	150
35	Vietnam	535	77	Greece	251	119	Yemen	143
36	Zimbabwe	532	78	Japan	250	120	Ireland	142
37	Ghana	529	79	Sri Lanka	250	121	Jordan	141
38	Malawi	521	80	Sweden	249	122	Cuba	137
39	Rwanda	513	81	Finland	248	123	Dominican Republic	136
40	Malaysia	501	82	Romania	247	124	Singapore	118
41	Mozambique	498	83	Guinea-Bissau	243	125	North Korea	115
42	Laos	487	84	Norway	243	126	Jamaica	113
43	Nicaragua	482	85	Bulgaria	240	127	South Korea	112
44	Namibia	469	86	Germany	239	128	Oman	107
45	Gabon	466	87	Uruguay	237	129	Puerto Rico	105
46	Sierra Leone	466	88	Italy	234	130	Libya	91
47	Guatemala	458	89	Albania	230	131	Hong Kong	76
48	Burundi	451	90	United Kingdom	230	132	Haiti	75
49	Congo, Rep. of	449	91	Poland	227	133	United Arab Emirates	67
50	Canada	426	92	Croatia	224	134	Lesotho	58
51	Honduras	422	93	Belarus	221	135	Mauritius	27
52	Guinea	409	94	Latvia	217	136	Kuwait	20

Source: World Development Report

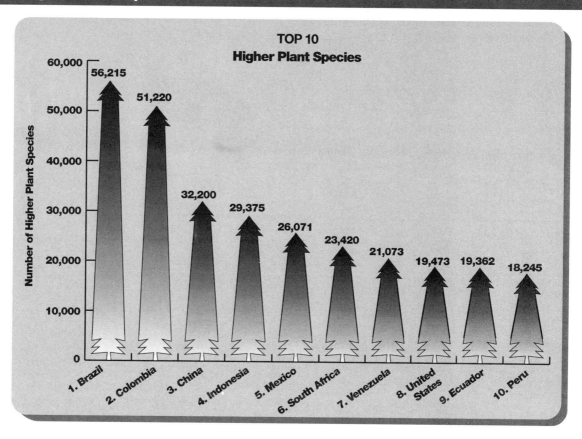

TOP 10
Higher Plant Species

Rank	Country/Entity	Plant Species, 1997	Rank	Country/Entity	Plant Species, 1997	Rank	Country/Entity	Plant Species, 1997
11	Bolivia	17,367	36	Kenya	6,506	61	Bulgaria	3,572
12	India	16,000	37	Congo, Rep. of	6,000	62	Romania	3,400
13	Australia	15,638	38	Mozambique	5,692	63	Sri Lanka	3,314
14	Malaysia	15,500	39	Honduras	5,680	64	Jamaica	3,308
15	Costa Rica	12,119	40	Dominican Republic	5,657	65	Canada	3,270
16	Thailand	11,625	41	Italy	5,599	66	Namibia	3,174
17	Papua New Guinea	11,544	42	Japan	5,565	67	Algeria	3,164
18	Congo, Dem. Rep. of	11,007	43	Uganda	5,406	68	Sudan	3,137
19	Vietnam	10,500	44	Chile	5,284	69	Austria	3,100
20	Tanzania	10,008	45	Haiti	5,242	70	Albania	3,031
21	Panama	9,915	46	Angola	5,185	71	Switzerland	3,030
22	Madagascar	9,505	47	Portugal	5,050	72	Guinea	3,000
23	Argentina	9,372	48	Spain	5,050	73	Lebanon	3,000
24	Philippines	8,931	49	Bangladesh	5,000	74	Syria	3,000
25	Guatemala	8,681	50	Greece	4,992	75	El Salvador	2,911
26	Turkey	8,650	51	Pakistan	4,950	76	North Korea	2,898
27	Cameroon	8,260	52	Zambia	4,747	77	South Korea	2,898
28	Iran	8,000	53	Nigeria	4,715	78	Germany	2,682
29	Paraguay	7,851	54	France	4,630	79	Burundi	2,500
30	Nicaragua	7,590	55	Zimbabwe	4,440	80	Puerto Rico	2,493
31	Myanmar (Burma)	7,000	56	Malawi	3,765	81	Poland	2,450
32	Nepal	6,973	57	Ghana	3,725	82	New Zealand	2,382
33	Gabon	6,651	58	Morocco	3,675	83	Israel	2,317
34	Ethiopia	6,603	59	Côte d'Ivoire	3,660	84	Rwanda	2,288
35	Cuba	6,522	60	Central African Republic	3,602	85	Uruguay	2,278

Rank	Country/Entity	Plant Species, 1997	Rank	Country/Entity	Plant Species, 1997	Rank	Country/Entity	Plant Species, 1997
86	Mongolia	2,272	98	Saudi Arabia	2,028	110	Oman	1,204
87	Trinidad and Tobago	2,259	99	Hong Kong	1,984	111	Niger	1,170
88	Hungary	2,214	100	Libya	1,825	112	Latvia	1,153
89	Benin	2,201	101	Sweden	1,750	113	Finland	1,102
90	Togo	2,201	102	Mali	1,741	114	Burkina Faso	1,100
91	Tunisia	2,196	103	Norway	1,715	115	Mauritania	1,100
92	Singapore	2,168	104	United Kingdom	1,623	116	Guinea-Bissau	1,000
93	Botswana	2,151	105	Chad	1,600	117	Gambia	974
94	Jordan	2,100	106	Lesotho	1,591	118	Ireland	950
95	Sierra Leone	2,090	107	Belgium	1,550	119	Mauritius	750
96	Senegal	2,086	108	Denmark	1,450	120	Kuwait	234
97	Egypt	2,076	109	Netherlands	1,221			

Source: World Development Report

Chapter 17

Consumption and Housing

Consumption Expenditures and the Household Budget

Consumption expenditures are defined as the purchase of goods and services to satisfy current needs and wants. It excludes income spent on taxes, debts, savings and investments, and insurance policies. In most developing countries, food often constitutes by a wide margin the largest share of consumer spending. As incomes rise, the share spent on food decreases and up to three-fourths of the income may be spent on clothing, recreation, luxuries, healthcare, and so on. Consumer expenditures also reflect the com-plexities of social habits, necessity and aspiration, gender, and age. In developed societies, advertising creates demand even where there is no legitimate need. Consumer expenditures are also important in macroeconomics because they are almost everywhere the principal component of Gross Domestic Product expenditures and help to sustain the economy. Decline in consumer expenditures is generally followed by a decline in production and factory orders, which, in turn, causes a slide in personal income and corporate profits. Most consumption statistics are published by marketing research organizations rather than public agencies. The little UN data that are available relate to what is called apparent consumption, which is production minus exports plus imports.

17.1 Consumption Expenditures per Capita

Rank	Country/Entity	Consumption Expenditures per Capita, 1995, in U.S. Dollars	Rank	Country/Entity	Consumption Expenditures per Capita, 1995, in U.S. Dollars	Rank	Country/Entity	Consumption Expenditures per Capita, 1995, in U.S. Dollars
1	Switzerland	26,060	36	Puerto Rico	5,640	71	Malaysia	2,090
2	Japan	24,670	37	Macau	5,480	72	Trinidad and Tobago	2,050
3	United States	18,840	38	Slovenia	5,460	73	South Africa	1,970
4	Denmark	17,730	39	New Caledonia	5,410	74	Poland	1,940
5	Germany	16,850	40	South Korea	5,390	75	Turkey	1,940
6	Norway	16,570	41	Malta	5,380	76	Lithuania	1,910
7	Belgium	16,550	42	Barbados	4,860	77	Bosnia and Herzegovina	1,890
8	Austria	16,020	43	Martinique	4,840	78	American Samoa	1,880
9	Iceland	15,850	44	Réunion	4,820	79	Peru	1,820
10	France	15,810	45	Brazil	4,420	80	Belize	1,780
11	Netherlands	15,290	46	French Polynesia	4,310	81	Jamaica	1,770
12	Luxembourg	15,140	47	Hungary	4,270	82	Iraq	1,710
13	Hong Kong	13,880	48	Uruguay	4,140	83	Saint Vincent and the Grenadines	1,700
14	Sweden	13,680	49	Guadeloupe	4,080			
15	Finland	13,260	50	Gabon	4,060	84	Grenada	1,650
16	Bermuda	12,690	51	Antigua and Barbuda	4,050	85	Costa Rica	1,600
17	Taiwan	12,230	52	Bahamas	3,950	86	Paraguay	1,590
18	Australia	12,040	53	Croatia	3,790	87	Slovakia	1,580
19	United Kingdom	12,020	54	Qatar	3,600	88	Panama	1,570
20	Italy	11,860	55	Seychelles	3,410	89	Romania	1,570
21	Singapore	11,710	56	Lebanon	3,010	90	Colombia	1,540
22	Canada	11,460	57	Oman	3,000	91	Thailand	1,540
23	Aruba	11,190	58	Saudi Arabia	2,980	92	El Salvador	1,520
24	Greenland	11,110	59	Chile	2,940	93	Cuba	1,510
25	New Zealand	10,300	60	Czech Republic	2,620	94	Bulgaria	1,470
26	Israel	9,930	61	Venezuela	2,490	95	Fiji	1,430
27	Ireland	9,650	62	Saint Kitts and Nevis	2,480	96	Estonia	1,390
28	Spain	8,840	63	Yugoslavia	2,480	97	West Bank	1,380
29	Cyprus	8,300	64	Latvia	2,400	98	Kazakhstan	1,290
30	Greece	8,140	65	Libya	2,330	99	Tunisia	1,260
31	United Arab Emirates	7,940	66	Mauritius	2,290	100	Guatemala	1,180
32	Portugal	6,860	67	Bahrain	2,240	101	Russia	1,180
33	Argentina	6,620	68	Syria	2,210	102	Dominican Republic	1,150
34	Netherlands Antilles	6,050	69	Dominica	2,110	103	Papua New Guinea	1,140
35	Suriname	5,960	70	Mexico	2,110	104	Namibia	1,050

Rank	Country/Entity	Consumption Expenditures per Capita, 1995, in U.S. Dollars	Rank	Country/Entity	Consumption Expenditures per Capita, 1995, in U.S. Dollars	Rank	Country/Entity	Consumption Expenditures per Capita, 1995, in U.S. Dollars
105	Sudan	1,050	134	Guinea	510	163	Uganda	260
106	Ecuador	1,040	135	Swaziland	500	164	Benin	240
107	Iran	1,040	136	Ukraine	490	165	Guinea-Bissau	230
108	Botswana	1,030	137	Côte d'Ivoire	480	166	Mongolia	230
109	Jordan	1,020	138	Mauritania	470	167	Burkina Faso	220
110	Macedonia	1,010	139	Azerbaijan	460	168	Kenya	220
111	Uzbekistan	950	140	Honduras	450	169	Madagascar	220
112	Cape Verde	920	141	Georgia	430	170	Moldova	220
113	Gaza Strip	910	142	Senegal	380	171	Zambia	220
114	Morocco	900	143	Angola	370	172	India	210
115	Congo, Rep. of	870	144	Kiribati	370	173	Niger	210
116	Solomon Islands	820	145	Armenia	360	174	Togo	210
117	Algeria	810	146	Nicaragua	360	175	Mali	200
118	Philippines	800	147	Central African Republic	350	176	Burundi	190
119	Myanmar (Burma)	750	148	Comoros	350	177	Congo, Dem. Rep. of	190
120	Egypt	740	149	Nigeria	350	178	Sierra Leone	190
121	Samoa	710	150	Tajikistan	340	179	Bangladesh	170
122	Bolivia	690	151	Gambia	330	180	Bhutan	170
123	Albania	680	152	Liberia	330	181	Chad	170
124	Vanuatu	680	153	Haiti	320	182	Eritrea	170
125	Kyrgyzstan	670	154	Equatorial Guinea	310	183	Nepal	170
126	Indonesia	640	155	Yemen	310	184	Tanzania	150
127	Belarus	610	156	Pakistan	300	185	Laos	140
128	Djibouti	590	157	Ghana	290	186	Rwanda	130
129	Zimbabwe	580	158	Cambodia	280	187	Malawi	109
130	Cameroon	570	159	Vietnam	280	188	Ethiopia	87
131	Turkmenistan	570	160	Maldives	270	189	Mozambique	57
132	Lesotho	530	161	São Tomé and Príncipe	270	190	Somalia	17
133	Sri Lanka	520	162	China	260			

Source: International Marketing Statistics

17.2 Percentage of Household Budget on Food

Rank	Country/Entity	Percentage of Household Budget on Food	Rank	Country/Entity	Percentage of Household Budget on Food	Rank	Country/Entity	Percentage of Household Budget on Food
1	Mozambique	74.6	24	Samoa	58.8	48	China	49.9
2	Angola	74.1	25	Syria	58.8	49	Saint Lucia	49.6
3	Mauritania	73.1	26	Gambia	58.0	50	Tonga	49.3
4	Bhutan	72.3	27	Ghana	57.4	51	Cameroon	49.1
5	Central African Republic	70.5	28	Maldives	57.4	52	Myanmar (Burma)	49.1
6	Comoros	67.3	29	Uganda	57.1	53	Senegal	49.0
7	Tanzania	66.7	30	Mali	57.0	54	Ethiopia	49.0
8	Tajikistan	65.3	31	Philippines	56.8	55	Paraguay	48.7
9	Guatemala	64.4	32	Saint Kitts and Nevis	55.6	56	Lesotho	48.0
10	Sierra Leone	63.8	33	Gabon	54.7	57	Nigeria	48.0
11	Sudan	63.6	34	Seychelles	53.9	58	Côte d'Ivoire	48.0
12	Bangladesh	63.3	35	Algeria	52.3	59	Sri Lanka	48.0
13	Vietnam	62.4	36	India	52.2	60	Indonesia	47.5
14	Somalia	62.3	37	Saudi Arabia	52.2	61	Armenia	47.3
15	Equatorial Guinea	62.0	38	Latvia	51.6	62	Bulgaria	47.0
16	Congo, Rep. of	61.7	39	Yugoslavia	51.6	63	Solomon Islands	46.8
17	Guinea	61.5	40	Haiti	51.1	64	Bolivia	46.6
18	Nepal	61.2	41	Romania	51.1	65	Kenya	46.5
19	Yemen	61.0	42	Niger	50.5	66	North Korea	46.5
20	Cape Verde	60.0	43	Lithuania	50.3	67	Dominican Republic	46.0
21	Saint Vincent and the Grenadines	59.8	44	Djibouti	50.3	68	Barbados	45.8
			45	Egypt	50.2	69	Tuvalu	45.5
22	Burundi	59.6	46	Iraq	50.2	70	Chad	45.3
23	Madagascar	59.0	47	Kiribati	50.0	71	Brunei	45.1

Rank	Country/Entity	Percentage of Household Budget on Food	Rank	Country/Entity	Percentage of Household Budget on Food	Rank	Country/Entity	Percentage of Household Budget on Food
72	Colombia	45.0	107	El Salvador	37.0	142	Slovakia	26.8
73	Bosnia	44.7	108	Pakistan	37.0	143	Taiwan	26.8
74	Honduras	44.4	109	Mexico	36.6	144	Cuba	26.7
75	Peru	44.1	110	Ecuador	36.1	145	Czech Republic	26.7
76	Dominica	43.1	111	Zambia	36.0	146	Trinidad and Tobago	25.5
77	Antigua and Barbuda	42.9	112	Jamaica	35.7	147	Brazil	25.3
78	Lebanon	42.8	113	Panama	34.9	148	Qatar	24.5
79	Iran	42.6	114	Portugal	34.8	149	United Arab Emirates	24.1
80	Guyana	42.5	115	Russia	34.8	150	Israel	23.8
81	Togo	42.5	116	Fiji	34.7	151	Norway	23.5
82	Azerbaijan	42.2	117	Liberia	34.4	152	Cyprus	22.7
83	Mauritius	41.9	118	Belize	34.0	153	Japan	22.6
84	Ukraine	41.3	119	Afghanistan	33.9	154	Finland	22.5
85	Poland	41.2	120	Kyrgyzstan	33.5	155	San Marino	22.1
86	Estonia	41.0	121	Swaziland	33.5	156	Spain	21.6
87	Papua New Guinea	40.9	122	Bahrain	32.4	157	Liechtenstein	21.3
88	Grenada	40.7	123	Iceland	31.3	158	Sweden	21.3
89	Jordan	40.6	124	Malta	31.2	159	Puerto Rico	20.6
90	Macedonia	40.6	125	Slovenia	30.8	160	New Zealand	20.0
91	Oman	40.6	126	Ireland	30.5	161	Italy	19.5
92	Argentina	40.1	127	Vanuatu	30.5	162	Germany	19.0
93	Suriname	39.9	128	Venezuela	30.4	163	Australia	18.7
94	Uruguay	39.9	129	Zimbabwe	30.1	164	Singapore	18.7
95	Botswana	39.5	130	Malawi	30.0	165	Belgium	18.3
96	Costa Rica	39.1	131	Greece	29.9	166	Denmark	17.9
97	Mongolia	39.1	132	South Korea	29.7	167	France	17.4
98	Tunisia	39.0	133	Kazakhstan	29.6	168	United Kingdom	17.1
99	Burkina Faso	38.7	134	South Africa	29.3	169	United States	15.4
100	Turkey	38.5	135	Belarus	29.0	170	Bermuda	14.6
101	Georgia	38.3	136	Thailand	29.0	171	Bahamas	13.8
102	Morocco	38.0	137	Malaysia	28.7	172	Netherlands	13.6
103	Croatia	37.8	138	Austria	28.1	173	Canada	13.4
104	Libya	37.2	139	Kuwait	28.1	174	Luxembourg	12.8
105	Benin	37.0	140	Chile	27.9			
106	Congo, Dem. Rep. of	37.0	141	Switzerland	27.0			

Source: FAO Food Balance Sheet

17.3 Percentage of Household Budget on Housing

Rank	Country/Entity	Percentage of Household Budget on Housing	Rank	Country/Entity	Percentage of Household Budget on Housing	Rank	Country/Entity	Percentage of Household Budget on Housing
1	Qatar	35.1	19	Brazil	21.3	37	Barbados	16.8
2	Bahamas	32.8	20	Bahrain	21.2	38	Lebanon	16.8
3	Libya	32.2	21	San Marino	20.9	39	Paraguay	16.4
4	Vanuatu	29.0	22	Indonesia	20.1	40	Romania	16.4
5	Bermuda	27.7	23	Iraq	19.9	41	France	16.2
6	Iran	24.9	24	Sweden	19.9	42	Dominica	16.0
7	Oman	24.6	25	Israel	19.8	43	Guatemala	16.0
8	Canada	24.5	26	New Zealand	19.4	44	Iceland	16.0
9	United Arab Emirates	23.7	27	Niger	19.1	45	Syria	16.0
10	Antigua and Barbuda	23.3	28	Australia	18.5	46	Jordan	15.8
11	Denmark	22.9	29	Slovenia	18.3	47	Kuwait	15.5
12	Turkey	22.8	30	Cameroon	18.0	48	Somalia	15.3
13	Taiwan	22.5	31	Liechtenstein	18.0	49	Chile	15.2
14	Honduras	22.4	32	Uruguay	17.6	50	Fiji	15.2
15	Solomon Islands	21.9	33	Nepal	17.3	51	Liberia	14.9
16	United Kingdom	21.7	34	Sweden	17.2	52	Netherlands	14.9
17	Trinidad and Tobago	21.6	35	Finland	16.9	53	United States	14.9
18	Guyana	21.4	36	Germany	16.9	54	Austria	14.5

Rank	Country/Entity	Percentage of Household Budget on Housing
55	Greece	14.1
56	Luxembourg	13.7
57	Norway	13.7
58	Seychelles	13.6
59	Saint Lucia	13.5
60	Swaziland	13.4
61	Togo	13.4
62	Mexico	13.3
63	Yemen	13.2
64	Rwanda	13.1
65	Switzerland	13.1
66	Gabon	13.0
67	Panama	12.6
68	South Africa	12.6
69	Spain	12.6
70	Papua New Guinea	12.5
71	Costa Rica	12.1
72	El Salvador	12.0
73	Grenada	11.9
74	Botswana	11.8
75	Puerto Rico	11.8
76	Mozambique	11.7
77	Congo, Rep. of	11.5
78	Ghana	11.5
79	Sudan	11.5
80	Tuvalu	11.5
81	Venezuela	11.5
82	Belgium	11.4
83	Pakistan	11.0
84	Tunisia	10.7
85	Egypt	10.5
86	Tonga	10.5
87	Myanmar (Burma)	10.4
88	Angola	10.2
89	Malaysia	10.2
90	Singapore	10.2
91	Lesotho	10.1

Rank	Country/Entity	Percentage of Household Budget on Housing
92	Benin	10.0
93	Dominican Republic	10.0
94	Italy	10.0
95	Kenya	10.0
96	Estonia	9.6
97	Argentina	9.3
98	Belize	9.0
99	Ecuador	9.0
100	Bangladesh	8.8
101	Mauritius	8.8
102	Cape Verde	8.5
103	Tanzania	8.3
104	Bolivia	7.8
105	Colombia	7.8
106	Côte d'Ivoire	7.8
107	Saint Kitts and Nevis	7.6
108	Slovakia	7.6
109	Kiribati	7.5
110	Guinea	7.3
111	Ireland	7.1
112	Ethiopia	7.0
113	Morocco	7.0
114	Senegal	7.0
115	Zambia	7.0
116	China	6.8
117	Peru	6.8
118	Algeria	6.7
119	Japan	6.7
120	Zimbabwe	6.5
121	Djibouti	6.4
122	Saint Vincent and the Grenadines	6.3
123	Thailand	6.3
124	India	6.1
125	Congo, Dem. Rep. of	6.0
126	Madagascar	6.0
127	Mongolia	5.9

Rank	Country/Entity	Percentage of Household Budget on Housing
128	Sierra Leone	5.8
129	Hungary	5.7
130	Jamaica	5.7
131	Cyprus	5.5
132	Czech Republic	5.5
133	Burkina Faso	5.1
134	Gambia	5.1
135	Samoa	5.1
136	Burundi	4.4
137	Suriname	4.4
138	Haiti	4.3
139	Bulgaria	4.1
140	South Korea	4.1
141	Philippines	4.1
142	Malawi	4.0
143	Malta	3.5
144	Afghanistan	3.0
145	Nigeria	3.0
146	Croatia	2.9
147	Poland	2.8
148	Belarus	2.7
149	Russia	2.7
150	Brunei	2.6
151	Kazakhstan	2.6
152	Mauritania	2.5
153	Vietnam	2.5
154	Comoros	2.3
155	Kyrgyzstan	2.2
156	Mali	2.0
157	Portugal	2.0
158	Macedonia	1.9
159	Sri Lanka	1.9
160	Ukraine	1.7
161	Bosnia	1.6
162	Maldives	1.6
163	Yugoslavia	1.4
164	North Korea	0.8

Source: World Data

17.4 Percentage of Household Budget on Clothing

Rank	Country/Entity	Percentage of Household Budget on Clothing
1	North Korea	29.9
2	Mongolia	23.4
3	Chile	22.5
4	Russia	22.3
5	Bhutan	21.2
6	Gabon	17.5
7	Gambia	17.5
8	Armenia	17.4
9	Lesotho	16.4
10	Romania	15.7
11	Myanmar (Burma)	15.3
12	Georgia	14.8
13	Ghana	14.3
14	Benin	14.0
15	Liberia	13.8

Rank	Country/Entity	Percentage of Household Budget on Clothing
16	China	13.7
17	Azerbaijan	13.6
18	Brazil	12.9
19	Iran	11.8
20	Nepal	11.7
21	Comoros	11.6
22	Thailand	11.6
23	Togo	11.5
24	Burundi	11.1
25	Morocco	11.0
26	Senegal	11.0
27	Suriname	11.0
28	Egypt	10.9
29	Poland	10.9
30	Iraq	10.6

Rank	Country/Entity	Percentage of Household Budget on Clothing
31	Venezuela	10.6
32	Trinidad and Tobago	10.4
33	Portugal	10.3
34	Zimbabwe	10.3
35	Ecuador	10.1
36	Peru	10.1
37	Sri Lanka	10.1
38	Côte d'Ivoire	10.0
39	Cyprus	10.0
40	Equatorial Guinea	10.0
41	India	10.0
42	Zambia	10.0
43	Tanzania	9.9
44	Italy	9.8
45	Congo, Rep. of	9.7

Rank	Country/Entity	Percentage of Household Budget on Clothing
46	Paraguay	9.7
47	Central African Republic	9.5
48	Costa Rica	9.4
49	Rwanda	9.4
50	Fiji	9.3
51	Honduras	9.1
52	Qatar	9.1
53	United Arab Emirates	9.1
54	Malawi	9.0
55	Turkey	9.0
56	Slovakia	8.9
57	Belize	8.8
58	Haiti	8.7
59	Algeria	8.6
60	Croatia	8.6
61	Guyana	8.6
62	Lebanon	8.6
63	Spain	8.6
64	Sweden	8.6
65	Austria	8.5
66	Slovenia	8.5
67	Estonia	8.4
68	Mexico	8.4
69	Mauritius	8.4
70	Bosnia	8.3
71	Kuwait	8.1
72	Mauritania	8.1
73	Argentina	8.0
74	Kiribati	8.0
75	Maldives	8.0
76	San Marino	8.0
77	Germany	7.9
78	Guinea	7.9
79	Macedonia	7.8
80	Kenya	7.7
81	South Korea	7.7
82	Saint Vincent and the Grenadines	7.7
83	Cameroon	7.6
84	Malta	7.6
85	Ireland	7.5
86	Saint Kitts and Nevis	7.5
87	South Africa	7.5
88	Syria	7.5
89	Tuvalu	7.5
90	Bulgaria	7.4
91	Hungary	7.4
92	Ireland	7.4
93	Puerto Rico	7.4
94	Yugoslavia	7.4
95	Czech Republic	7.3
96	Niger	7.3
97	Sierra Leone	7.3
98	Netherlands	7.1
99	Singapore	7.1
100	Belgium	7.0
101	Norway	7.0
102	Uruguay	7.0
103	Libya	6.9
104	United States	6.9
105	El Salvador	6.7
105	Jordan	6.7
106	Liechtenstein	6.6
107	Saudi Arabia	6.6
108	Dominica	6.5
109	Greece	6.5
110	Saint Lucia	6.5
111	Papua New Guinea	6.2
112	Brunei	6.1
113	France	6.1
114	Congo, Dem. Rep. of	6.0
115	Ethiopia	6.0
116	Japan	6.0
117	Madagascar	6.0
118	Mali	6.0
119	Pakistan	6.0
120	Swaziland	6.0
121	Tunisia	6.0
122	United Kingdom	6.0
123	Bahamas	5.9
124	Bangladesh	5.9
125	Bahrain	5.9
126	Luxembourg	5.9
127	Solomon Islands	5.7
128	Australia	5.6
129	Botswana	5.6
130	Somalia	5.6
131	Taiwan	5.6
132	Tonga	5.6
133	Angola	5.5
134	Antigua and Barbuda	5.5
135	Indonesia	5.5
136	Uganda	5.5
137	Canada	5.3
138	Israel	5.3
139	Sudan	5.3
140	Denmark	5.2
141	Grenada	5.2
142	Barbados	5.1
143	Bolivia	5.1
144	Oman	5.1
145	Panama	5.1
146	Finland	5.0
147	Nigeria	5.0
148	Vietnam	5.0
149	Bermuda	4.9
150	Vanuatu	4.7
151	Jamaica	4.6
152	Colombia	4.5
153	Burkina	4.4
154	New Zealand	4.4
155	Switzerland	4.4
156	Malaysia	4.3
157	Samoa	4.2
158	Seychelles	4.2
159	Philippines	3.9
160	Mozambique	3.7
161	Chad	3.5
162	Guatemala	3.1
163	Dominican Republic	3.0
164	Cape Verde	2.5
165	Djibouti	1.7

Source: World Data

17.5 Percentage of Household Budget on Healthcare

Rank	Country/Entity	Percentage of Household Budget on Healthcare
1	United States	17.0
2	Netherlands	12.9
3	Chad	11.9
4	Puerto Rico	11.6
5	Guinea	11.1
6	Belgium	10.5
7	Switzerland	9.9
8	France	9.8
9	Uruguay	9.3
10	Brazil	9.1
11	Poland	8.1
12	Dominican Republic	8.0
13	Thailand	8.0
14	Zambia	8.0
15	Argentina	7.9
16	Taiwan	7.8
17	Liechtenstein	7.7
18	Burundi	7.6
19	Luxembourg	7.3
20	Lebanon	7.2
21	Australia	7.1
22	Zimbabwe	7.1
23	Honduras	7.0
24	Italy	6.7
25	Cameroon	6.6
26	Colombia	6.4
27	Israel	6.2
28	Congo, Dem. Rep. of	6.0
29	Equatorial Guinea	6.0
30	Austria	5.8
31	Norway	5.4
32	Burkina Faso	5.2
33	Yugoslavia	5.2

Rank	Country/Entity	Percentage of Household Budget on Healthcare	Rank	Country/Entity	Percentage of Household Budget on Healthcare	Rank	Country/Entity	Percentage of Household Budget on Healthcare
34	Benin	5.0	68	Sweden	3.2	102	Jordan	2.2
35	South Korea	5.0	69	Cyprus	3.1	103	Bolivia	2.1
36	Morocco	5.0	70	Greece	3.1	104	Saudi Arabia	2.1
37	Slovenia	5.0	71	Ethiopia	3.1	105	Madagascar	2.0
38	Togo	5.0	72	Macedonia	3.0	106	Mali	2.0
39	Azerbaijan	4.8	73	Mauritius	3.0	107	Senegal	2.0
40	Finland	4.8	74	Nigeria	3.0	108	Gabon	1.9
41	Canada	4.7	75	Tunisia	3.0	109	Angola	1.8
42	Spain	4.7	76	China	2.9	110	Antigua and Barbuda	1.8
43	Singapore	4.6	77	New Zealand	2.9	111	Sri Lanka	1.8
44	Portugal	4.5	78	Venezuela	2.9	112	Swaziland	1.8
45	Sierra Leone	4.5	79	Algeria	2.8	113	Belize	1.6
46	South Africa	4.5	80	Jamaica	2.8	114	Iraq	1.6
47	Bahamas	4.4	81	Egypt	2.7	115	Ghana	1.3
48	Croatia	4.3	82	Japan	2.7	116	Rwanda	1.3
49	El Salvador	4.2	83	Peru	2.7	117	Taiwan	1.3
50	Ecuador	4.2	84	Congo, Rep. of	2.6	118	Romania	1.2
51	Sweden	4.1	85	San Marino	2.6	119	Bangladesh	1.1
52	Malawi	4.0	86	Turkey	2.6	120	United Arab Emirates	1.1
53	Iran	3.9	87	Malaysia	2.5	121	Yemen	1.1
54	Barbados	3.8	88	Maldives	2.5	122	Central African Republic	1.0
55	Costa Rica	3.7	89	Djibouti	2.4	123	Pakistan	1.0
56	Nepal	3.7	90	Fiji	2.4	124	Qatar	1.0
57	Suriname	3.6	91	India	2.4	125	Mauritania	0.9
58	Germany	3.5	92	Myanmar (Burma)	2.4	126	Mozambique	0.8
59	Malta	3.5	93	Oman	2.4	127	Afghanistan	0.7
60	Panama	3.5	94	Bahrain	2.3	128	Côte d'Ivoire	0.7
61	Bosnia	3.4	95	Botswana	2.3	129	Kuwait	0.7
62	Mexico	3.4	96	Iceland	2.3	130	Guatemala	0.6
63	Paraguay	3.4	97	Saint Lucia	2.3	131	Cape Verde	0.5
64	Libya	3.3	98	Hungary	1.5	132	Mongolia	0.5
65	Belgium	3.2	99	Denmark	2.2	133	Seychelles	0.4
66	Comoros	3.2	100	Haiti	2.2	134	Tonga	0.3
67	Ireland	3.2	101	Kenya	2.2			

Source: World Data

Alcohol and Cigarettes

These rankings explore two items about which there is a social stigma as well as a medical concern, because their consumption can harm not merely the user, but also other innocent people. The consumption of alcoholic beverages is one of the oldest social traditions in the world, as prevalent in primitive as in modern societies. As a stimulant of undoubted potency, it produces temporary elation (hence the custom of "happy hour" in bars), but, like all other stimulants, it can be habituating, can create dependence and withdrawal symptoms, and can impair motor and cognitive functions. Its association with highway deaths has made alcohol consumption a matter of legal concern. Cigarette smoking, similarly, is a personal habit that has reverberations in the public arena because it is one of the leading killers in the modern world. Despite antismoking legislation and litigation, there has been no significant decline in total cigarette consumption worldwide, although per capita consumption has slipped below its all-time high of nearly 1,000 cigarettes. In the course of a year, tobacco kills three million people.

17.6 Alcohol Consumption

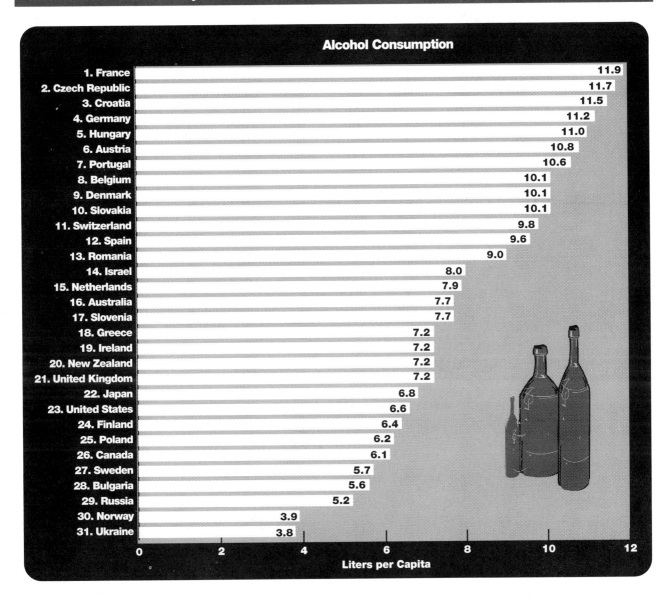

Alcohol Consumption

Rank	Country	Liters per Capita
1. France		11.9
2. Czech Republic		11.7
3. Croatia		11.5
4. Germany		11.2
5. Hungary		11.0
6. Austria		10.8
7. Portugal		10.6
8. Belgium		10.1
9. Denmark		10.1
10. Slovakia		10.1
11. Switzerland		9.8
12. Spain		9.6
13. Romania		9.0
14. Israel		8.0
15. Netherlands		7.9
16. Australia		7.7
17. Slovenia		7.7
18. Greece		7.2
19. Ireland		7.2
20. New Zealand		7.2
21. United Kingdom		7.2
22. Japan		6.8
23. United States		6.6
24. Finland		6.4
25. Poland		6.2
26. Canada		6.1
27. Sweden		5.7
28. Bulgaria		5.6
29. Russia		5.2
30. Norway		3.9
31. Ukraine		3.8

Liters per Capita

Source: International Marketing Statistics

17.7 Cigarette Consumption

Rank	Country/Entity	Cigarette Consumption per Smoker per Year, 1988–1998	Rank	Country/Entity	Cigarette Consumption per Smoker per Year, 1988–1998	Rank	Country/Entity	Cigarette Consumption per Smoker per Year, 1988–1998
1	Iraq	5,751	9	Singapore	4,250	17	Czech Republic	3,187
2	Belgium	5,300	10	Japan	4,126	18	Netherlands	3,169
3	Australia	4,951	11	Ireland	4,013	19	Italy	3,101
4	Hungary	4,949	12	Germany	3,927	20	France	3,088
5	United States	4,938	13	Saudi Arabia	3,800	21	Canada	3,081
6	Greece	4,877	14	United Kingdom	3,706	22	Bulgaria	3,058
7	Switzerland	4,618	15	Spain	3,384	23	Austria	3,041
8	Poland	4,544	16	Israel	3,331	24	Slovakia	2,973

Rank	Country/Entity	Cigarette Consumption per Smoker per Year, 1988–1998	Rank	Country/Entity	Cigarette Consumption per Smoker per Year, 1988–1998	Rank	Country/Entity	Cigarette Consumption per Smoker per Year, 1988–1998
25	New Zealand	2,927	36	South Africa	2,276	47	Jamaica	1,446
26	Finland	2,906	37	Russia	2,256	48	Kuwait	1,403
27	Argentina	2,771	38	Romania	2,162	49	Dominican Republic	1,303
28	Hong Kong	2,679	39	Thailand	2,140	50	Nigeria	1,131
29	Sweden	2,641	40	Morocco	2,022	51	Laos	949
30	Cuba	2,566	41	Honduras	1,978	52	Cambodia	912
31	Denmark	2,532	42	Mexico	1,940	53	Sri Lanka	786
32	Lithuania	2,509	43	Estonia	1,819	54	Nepal	750
33	Ukraine	2,471	44	Chile	1,718	55	Vietnam	730
34	Pakistan	2,354	45	Venezuela	1,699	56	Guatemala	646
35	Turkey	2,319	46	Colombia	1,684	57	Bangladesh	351

Source: International Marketing Statistics

Housing

Housing censuses are carried out periodically under UN auspices and yield a wealth of data on the number of dwellings, particularly with reference to their habitability. These include not only the five basic amenities of a proper dwelling—piped water, electric light, kitchen, toilet, and bath–but also the number of homes, time living, and space in each home per inhabitant. The trend in these rankings is toward better housing—more spacious than older ones, improved construction, and widespread home ownership. The data do not cover shanty towns or slums where extremely crowded conditions prevail.

17.8 Housing Stock

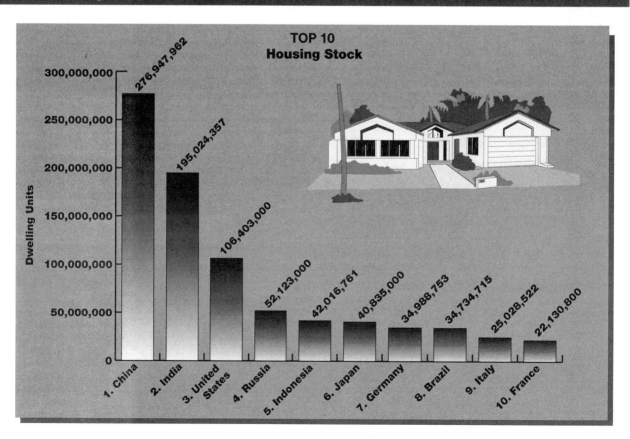

TOP 10 Housing Stock

Country	Dwelling Units
1. China	276,947,962
2. India	195,024,357
3. United States	106,403,000
4. Russia	52,123,000
5. Indonesia	42,016,761
6. Japan	40,835,000
7. Germany	34,988,753
8. Brazil	34,734,715
9. Italy	25,028,522
10. France	22,130,800

Rank	Country/Entity	Dwelling Units	Rank	Country/Entity	Dwelling Units	Rank	Country/Entity	Dwelling Units
11	United Kingdom	21,897,322	78	Yemen	1,701,203	145	Luxembourg	144,683
12	Bangladesh	19,020,489	79	Slovakia	1,617,829	146	Fiji	124,098
13	Mexico	16,197,802	80	Bolivia	1,614,995	147	Guinea-Bissau	123,936
14	Ukraine	14,057,000	81	Croatia	1,575,644	148	Swaziland	122,369
15	Turkey	13,341,000	82	Azerbaijan	1,473,100	149	West Bank	119,165
16	Vietnam	12,958,041	83	Mali	1,364,079	150	Guadeloupe	112,478
17	Pakistan	12,597,000	84	Zambia	1,327,098	151	Martinique	106,536
18	Thailand	12,305,197	85	Burkina Faso	1,274,546	152	Malta	101,509
19	Poland	11,967,021	86	Guatemala	1,259,598	153	Macau	89,193
20	Spain	11,736,000	87	Georgia	1,244,000	154	Bahrain	83,470
21	Philippines	11,395,304	88	El Salvador	1,236,866	155	Comoros	81,791
22	Canada	10,018,625	89	Chad	1,228,862	156	Suriname	77,744
23	Egypt	9,732,728	90	Lithuania	1,225,800	157	Barbados	75,211
24	Ethiopia	9,300,000	91	Bosnia and Herzegovina	1,203,000	158	Iceland	70,777
25	South Korea	9,204,929	92	Puerto Rico	1,188,985	159	Cape Verde	67,619
26	Argentina	8,515,441	93	New Zealand	1,185,396	160	Gaza Strip	66,819
27	Iran	8,211,375	94	Haiti	1,164,136	161	Qatar	64,543
28	Romania	7,632,000	95	Niger	1,163,424	162	Netherlands Antilles	57,608
29	Myanmar (Burma)	6,750,884	96	Dominican Republic	1,125,785	163	Bahamas	54,308
30	Australia	6,677,900	97	Moldova	1,112,800	164	Western Sahara	46,120
31	Netherlands	6,195,100	98	Israel	1,104,270	165	Solomon Islands	43,842
32	Colombia	5,824,857	99	Rwanda	1,055,950	166	Brunei	40,351
33	Congo, Dem. Rep. of	5,669,600	100	Ireland	1,006,506	167	New Caledonia	40,266
34	Morocco	4,444,271	101	Latvia	953,000	168	French Polynesia	39,513
35	Peru	4,427,517	102	Burundi	938,000	169	Virgin Islands (U.S.)	39,290
36	Kazakhstan	4,410,000	103	Paraguay	868,284	170	French Guiana	38,324
37	Kenya	4,352,751	104	Kyrgyzstan	856,000	171	Belize	37,658
38	Taiwan	4,237,174	105	Uruguay	852,400	172	Maldives	37,114
39	North Korea	4,054,027	106	Benin	832,526	173	Guam	35,223
40	Hungary	3,971,000	107	Honduras	809,263	174	Samoa	33,402
41	Sweden	3,830,037	108	Tajikistan	799,000	175	Saint Lucia	33,079
42	Belgium	3,748,165	109	Nicaragua	794,093	176	Jersey	32,463
43	Czech Republic	3,705,691	110	Singapore	744,203	177	Vanuatu	28,252
44	Belarus	3,679,600	111	Guinea	716,378	178	São Tomé and Príncipe	27,449
45	South Africa	3,599,518	112	Jordan	683,000	179	Isle of Man	27,316
46	Tanzania	3,554,793	113	Albania	674,633	180	Saint Vincent and	27,110
47	Venezuela	3,534,507	114	Slovenia	640,000		the Grenadines	
48	Malaysia	3,447,597	115	Estonia	618,300	181	Djibouti	25,000
49	Uganda	3,434,177	116	Laos	601,797	182	Bermuda	22,061
50	Bulgaria	3,419,937	117	Turkmenistan	598,000	183	Grenada	21,974
51	Uzbekistan	3,415,000	118	Libya	569,679	184	Guernsey	21,215
52	Austria	3,393,271	119	Armenia	559,000	185	Greenland	19,847
53	Chile	3,369,849	120	Papua New Guinea	556,519	186	Dominica	19,374
54	Ghana	3,320,000	121	Panama	524,284	187	Mayotte	19,227
55	Greece	3,167,152	122	Central African Republic	519,314	188	Aruba	19,224
56	Portugal	3,059,300	123	Jamaica	517,297	189	Antigua and Barbuda	18,476
57	Algeria	3,050,812	124	Macedonia	511,300	190	Andorra	17,881
58	Yugoslavia	3,039,000	125	Costa Rica	500,788	191	Monaco	16,122
59	Sri Lanka	2,811,406	126	Sierra Leone	486,550	192	Gabon	15,886
60	Switzerland	2,800,953	127	Lebanon	483,908	193	Tonga	15,091
61	Mozambique	2,712,439	128	Togo	462,694	194	Seychelles	15,050
62	Madagascar	2,688,951	129	Congo, Rep. of	363,140	195	Senegal	13,000
63	Nepal	2,585,154	130	Oman	344,846	196	Saint Kitts and Nevis	11,615
64	Denmark	2,426,503	131	Lesotho	312,655	197	Micronesia	11,562
65	Cuba	2,363,364	132	Botswana	276,209	198	Kiribati	11,301
66	Finland	2,331,406	133	Trinidad and Tobago	271,871	199	Faroe Islands	11,172
67	Afghanistan	2,260,000	134	Liberia	263,333	200	Liechtenstein	10,386
68	Zimbabwe	2,163,289	135	Namibia	254,389	201	San Marino	8,518
69	Ecuador	2,111,121	136	Kuwait	251,682	202	Northern Mariana Islands	8,210
70	Malawi	1,859,572	137	Mauritania	246,462	203	Gibraltar	7,604
71	Syria	1,836,195	138	Mongolia	242,000	204	American Samoa	6,959
72	Côte d'Ivoire	1,798,799	139	Mauritius	236,885	205	Marshall Islands	4,923
73	Cameroon	1,787,835	140	Gambia	202,199	206	Palau	3,312
74	Norway	1,769,000	141	Cyprus	185,459	207	Tuvalu	1,079
75	Iraq	1,759,176	142	Réunion	184,500	208	Nauru	508
76	Hong Kong	1,735,500	143	United Arab Emirates	153,009			
77	Tunisia	1,703,279	144	Guyana	149,734			

Source: *Human Settlements Basic Statistics*

17.9 Housing Space

Rank	Country/Entity	Persons per Room	Rank	Country/Entity	Persons per Room	Rank	Country/Entity	Persons per Room
1	Djibouti	6.9	55	São Tomé and Príncipe	1.8	108	Saint Kitts and Nevis	1.1
2	Guinea-Bissau	4.5	56	Saint Vincent and	1.8	109	Benin	1.0
3	Jamaica	4.3		the Grenadines		110	Bosnia and Herzegovina	1.0
4	Togo	3.4	57	United Arab Emirates	1.8	111	Chile	1.0
5	El Salvador	3.3	58	Congo, Rep. of	1.7	112	Cuba	1.0
6	Pakistan	3.3	59	Ecuador	1.7	113	Czech Republic	1.0
7	Bangladesh	2.9	60	Indonesia	1.7	114	Hungary	1.0
8	Oman	2.9	61	Liberia	1.7	115	Netherlands Antilles	1.0
9	Cape Verde	2.8	62	Malawi	1.7	116	Poland	1.0
10	Hong Kong	2.8	63	Uruguay	1.7	117	Slovenia	1.0
11	Yemen	2.8	64	American Samoa	1.6	118	Antigua and Barbuda	0.9
12	India	2.7	65	Brunei	1.6	119	Brazil	0.9
13	Thailand	2.7	66	Colombia	1.6	120	Bulgaria	0.9
14	West Bank	2.7	67	Grenada	1.6	121	Estonia	0.9
15	Albania	2.6	68	Nauru	1.6	122	Guadeloupe	0.9
16	Algeria	2.6	69	Panama	1.6	123	Iceland	0.9
17	Malaysia	2.6	70	Egypt	1.5	124	Martinique	0.9
18	Zambia	2.6	71	Iraq	1.5	125	Réunion	0.9
19	Gaza Strip	2.5	72	Maldives	1.5	126	Barbados	0.8
20	Singapore	2.5	73	Mexico	1.5	127	Cyprus	0.8
21	Sudan	2.5	74	Senegal	1.5	128	Greece	0.8
22	Ethiopia	2.4	75	Bahrain	1.4	129	Guam	0.8
23	Ghana	2.4	76	Costa Rica	1.4	130	Monaco	0.8
24	Lesotho	2.4	77	Mauritius	1.4	131	Portugal	0.8
25	Paraguay	2.4	78	Namibia	1.4	132	Puerto Rico	0.8
26	Tunisia	2.4	79	Romania	1.4	133	Aruba	0.7
27	Honduras	2.3	80	Trinidad and Tobago	1.4	134	Bermuda	0.7
28	Philippines	2.3	81	Argentina	1.3	135	France	0.7
29	Guatemala	2.2	82	French Polynesia	1.3	136	Italy	0.7
30	Mali	2.2	83	Gabon	1.3	137	Japan	0.7
31	Mayotte	2.2	84	Macau	1.3	138	Netherlands	0.7
32	Morocco	2.2	85	Malta	1.3	139	San Marino	0.7
33	Turkey	2.2	86	Qatar	1.3	140	Australia	0.6
34	Afghanistan	2.1	87	Venezuela	1.3	141	Austria	0.6
35	Comoros	2.1	88	Yugoslavia	1.3	142	Belgium	0.6
36	Haiti	2.1	89	Bahamas	1.2	143	Burundi	0.6
37	Nicaragua	2.1	90	Cambodia	1.2	144	Denmark	0.6
38	Sri Lanka	2.1	91	Cameroon	1.2	145	Finland	0.6
39	Gambia	2.0	92	French Guiana	1.2	146	Ireland	0.6
40	Peru	2.0	93	Israel	1.2	147	Liechtenstein	0.6
41	Solomon Islands	2.0	94	New Caledonia	1.2	148	Norway	0.6
42	Syria	2.0	95	Saint Lucia	1.2	149	Sweden	0.6
43	Botswana	1.9	96	Taiwan	1.2	150	Switzerland	0.6
44	Nepal	1.9	97	Western Sahara	1.2	151	Virgin Islands (U.S.)	0.6
45	Suriname	1.9	98	Croatia	1.1	152	Canada	0.5
46	Tanzania	1.9	99	Dominica	1.1	153	Germany	0.5
47	Zimbabwe	1.9	100	Faroe Islands	1.1	154	Guernsey	0.5
48	China	1.8	101	Gibraltar	1.1	155	Jersey	0.5
49	Fiji	1.8	102	Greenland	1.1	156	Luxembourg	0.5
50	Guyana	1.8	103	South Korea	1.1	157	New Zealand	0.5
51	Iran	1.8	104	Nigeria	1.1	158	United Kingdom	0.5
52	Kuwait	1.8	105	Northern Mariana Islands	1.1	159	United States	0.5
53	Libya	1.8	106	Seychelles	1.1	160	Isle of Man	0.4
54	Palau	1.8	107	Slovakia	1.1			

Source: Human Settlements Basic Statistics

Chapter 18

Health and Social Services

Health Expenditures

Health and education are two social functions that most governments take seriously. In most national budgets, combined expenditures on these two functions are larger than that for defense. Still, health expenditures vary widely from country to country based on the existence or absence of a national health service. Health expenditures also have a tendency to rise faster than the cost of living index, the reason being the high cost of drugs and medical personnel compensation. In most countries, there is a dual private–public health establishment, the private sector comprising both religious, philanthropic institutions, and commercial profit-making ones. Public intervention in the healthcare field consists primarily—in the absence of a national health service—of disease control centers, collection and dissemination of statistics, promotion of family planning, and subsidization of university-based medical research. Ministries or departments of health often employ a surgeon-general to monitor the overall health of the population and initiate measures to counter epidemics. A large part of the resources for healthcare is allocated for preventive rather than curative programs. Many developing nations receive direct aid from international organizations to maintain a reasonable level of healthcare for their people. In the case of some countries, such as Cape Verde, such international aid is more than the budgetary allocation.

18.1 Health Expenditures per Capita

Rank	Country/Entity	Health Expenditures per Capita in U.S. Dollars	Rank	Country/Entity	Health Expenditures per Capita in U.S. Dollars	Rank	Country/Entity	Health Expenditures per Capita in U.S. Dollars
1	United States	2,765	32	Bahrain	324	63	Grenada	133
2	Switzerland	2,520	33	Barbados	323	64	Costa Rica	132
3	Sweden	2,343	34	Taiwan	323	65	Ukraine	131
4	Finland	2,046	35	Seychelles	289	66	Turkmenistan	125
5	Canada	1,945	36	Yugoslavia	264	67	Uruguay	123
6	Iceland	1,884	37	Saudi Arabia	260	68	Bulgaria	121
7	France	1,869	38	Iran	244	69	Kyrgyzstan	118
8	Norway	1,835	39	Antigua and Barbuda	241	70	Solomon Islands	117
9	Austria	1,711	40	Estonia	228	71	Uzbekistan	116
10	Luxembourg	1,662	41	Latvia	220	72	Saint Vincent and the Grenadines	102
11	Denmark	1,588	42	Singapore	215			
12	Japan	1,538	43	Saint Kitts and Nevis	212	73	Chile	100
13	Germany	1,511	44	Oman	209	74	Mauritius	100
14	Netherlands	1,501	45	Dominica	192	75	Tajikistan	100
15	Belgium	1,449	46	Hungary	185	76	Azerbaijan	99
16	Italy	1,449	47	Trinidad and Tobago	180	77	Suriname	93
17	Australia	1,294	48	Czech Republic	169	78	Mexico	89
18	United Kingdom	1,039	49	Saint Lucia	169	79	Venezuela	88
19	New Zealand	925	50	Gabon	164	80	Poland	84
20	Ireland	876	51	Lithuania	159	81	Jamaica	83
21	Spain	831	52	Russia	159	82	South Africa	77
22	Hong Kong	687	53	Belarus	157	83	Tunisia	76
23	Qatar	630	54	Kazakhstan	154	84	Turkey	76
24	Kuwait	541	55	Armenia	152	85	Thailand	72
25	Israel	480	56	Georgia	152	86	Malaysia	71
26	Tuvalu	472	57	Algeria	149	87	Fiji	70
27	United Arab Emirates	472	58	Brazil	146	88	Vanuatu	67
28	Portugal	383	59	Moldova	143	89	Cape Verde	64
29	South Korea	365	60	Panama	142	90	Cyprus	64
30	Greece	359	61	Botswana	139	91	Swaziland	64
31	Malta	349	62	Argentina	137	92	Tonga	63

Rank	Country/Entity	Health Expenditures per Capita in U.S. Dollars	Rank	Country/Entity	Health Expenditures per Capita in U.S. Dollars	Rank	Country/Entity	Health Expenditures per Capita in U.S. Dollars
93	Peru	61	117	Equatorial Guinea	28	141	Ghana	15
94	El Salvador	58	118	Cameroon	27	142	Mali	15
95	Mongolia	58	119	Guatemala	27	143	Chad	12
96	Romania	58	120	Haiti	27	144	Indonesia	12
97	Jordan	55	121	Albania	26	145	Pakistan	12
98	Honduras	52	122	Lesotho	26	146	China	11
99	Colombia	51	123	Morocco	26	147	Malawi	11
100	Congo, Rep. of	50	124	Bolivia	25	148	Bhutan	10
101	Namibia	45	125	Belize	23	149	Nigeria	10
102	Ecuador	44	126	Gambia	22	150	Rwanda	10
103	Guyana	42	127	India	21	151	Somalia	8
104	Syria	41	128	Samoa	20	152	Uganda	8
105	Zimbabwe	39	129	Yemen	20	153	Burkina Faso	7
106	Dominican Republic	38	130	Benin	19	154	Madagascar	7
107	São Tomé and Príncipe	38	131	Central African Republic	18	155	Nepal	7
108	Papua New Guinea	37	132	Mauritania	18	156	Bangladesh	6
109	Paraguay	35	133	Sri Lanka	18	157	Congo, Dem. Rep. of	5
110	Nicaragua	34	134	Togo	18	158	Laos	5
111	Sudan	34	135	Guinea	17	159	Mozambique	5
112	Burundi	30	136	Zambia	17	160	Ethiopia	4
113	Senegal	29	137	Guinea-Bissau	16	161	Liberia	4
114	Côte d'Ivoire	28	138	Kenya	16	162	Sierra Leone	4
115	Comoros	28	139	Niger	16	163	Tanzania	4
116	Egypt	28	140	Philippines	16	164	Vietnam	3

Source: World Health Statistics Annual

18.2 Health Expenditures as Percentage of Gross Domestic Product (GDP)

Rank	Country/Entity	Health Expenditures as Percentage of GDP	Rank	Country/Entity	Health Expenditures as Percentage of GDP	Rank	Country/Entity	Health Expenditures as Percentage of GDP
1	United States	12.71	29	Panama	7.13	57	Hong Kong	5.69
2	Guyana	10.37	30	Haiti	6.99	58	Saint Vincent and the Grenadines	5.69
3	France	9.40	31	Portugal	6.99			
4	São Tomé and Príncipe	9.22	32	Algeria	6.95	59	Vanuatu	5.68
5	Canada	9.05	33	Mongolia	6.63	60	South Africa	5.56
6	Sweden	8.79	34	South Korea	6.61	61	Comoros	5.40
7	Germany	8.73	35	Spain	6.59	62	Greece	5.39
8	Nicaragua	8.61	36	Luxembourg	6.56	63	Malta	5.38
9	Burkina Faso	8.46	37	Costa Rica	6.51	64	Bulgaria	5.36
10	Austria	8.38	38	Tonga	6.46	65	Mali	5.19
11	Iceland	8.34	39	Japan	6.45	66	Yugoslavia	5.11
12	Lesotho	8.32	40	Cape Verde	6.32	67	Poland	5.07
13	Liberia	8.24	41	Denmark	6.30	68	Bhutan	5.05
14	Guinea-Bissau	8.15	42	Zimbabwe	6.23	69	Barbados	5.04
15	Dominica	8.06	43	Chad	6.22	70	Jamaica	5.04
16	Netherlands	8.03	44	Botswana	6.19	71	Turkmenistan	4.99
17	Finland	7.82	45	United Kingdom	6.11	72	Malawi	4.98
18	Australia	7.67	46	Seychelles	6.03	73	Niger	4.98
19	Equatorial Guinea	7.60	47	India	6.00	74	Thailand	4.98
20	Italy	7.54	48	Saint Kitts and Nevis	5.99	75	Kyrgyzstan	4.97
21	Gambia	7.53	49	Tajikistan	5.98	76	Tunisia	4.91
22	Switzerland	7.52	50	Grenada	5.96	77	Kuwait	4.86
23	Belgium	7.50	51	Hungary	5.95	78	Saudi Arabia	4.76
24	New Zealand	7.37	52	Czech Republic	5.94	79	Chile	4.73
25	Norway	7.35	53	Uzbekistan	5.90	80	Qatar	4.73
26	Ireland	7.22	54	Belize	5.88	81	Tanzania	4.73
27	Swaziland	7.22	55	El Salvador	5.86	82	Bahrain	4.62
28	Saint Lucia	7.18	56	Mozambique	5.86	83	Uruguay	4.62

Rank	Country/Entity	Health Expenditures as Percentage of GDP	Rank	Country/Entity	Health Expenditures as Percentage of GDP	Rank	Country/Entity	Health Expenditures as Percentage of GDP
84	Antigua and Barbuda	4.55	111	Namibia	3.92	138	Belarus	3.19
85	Honduras	4.54	112	Moldova	3.91	139	Yemen	3.19
86	Nepal	4.54	113	Guinea	3.90	140	Mexico	3.17
87	Trinidad and Tobago	4.54	114	Latvia	3.87	141	Zambia	3.16
88	Georgia	4.45	115	Romania	3.87	142	Russia	3.02
89	Kazakhstan	4.44	116	Ethiopia	3.80	143	Paraguay	2.97
90	Papua New Guinea	4.44	117	Mauritania	3.80	144	Malaysia	2.96
91	Mauritius	4.40	118	Jordan	3.77	145	Samoa	2.94
92	Kenya	4.33	119	Fiji	3.76	146	Suriname	2.88
93	Benin	4.32	120	Sri Lanka	3.74	147	Nigeria	2.72
94	Taiwan	4.30	121	Dominican Republic	3.72	148	Tuvalu	2.66
95	Azerbaijan	4.27	122	Guatemala	3.70	149	United Arab Emirates	2.66
96	Oman	4.22	123	Senegal	3.66	150	Cameroon	2.62
97	Argentina	4.21	124	Estonia	3.62	151	Egypt	2.61
98	Brazil	4.20	125	Venezuela	3.60	152	Madagascar	2.56
99	Israel	4.20	126	Lithuania	3.58	153	Morocco	2.55
100	Central African Republic	4.19	127	China	3.51	154	Iran	2.54
101	Armenia	4.17	128	Ghana	3.50	155	Laos	2.53
102	Ecuador	4.14	129	Pakistan	3.48	156	Sierra Leone	2.43
103	Gabon	4.10	130	Rwanda	3.44	157	Congo, Dem. Rep. of	2.38
104	Togo	4.10	131	Uganda	3.40	158	Solomon Islands	2.18
105	Bolivia	4.01	132	Côte d'Ivoire	3.35	159	Philippines	2.15
106	Albania	4.00	133	Sudan	3.33	160	Vietnam	2.11
107	Congo, Rep. of	3.99	134	Ukraine	3.30	161	Syria	2.07
108	Colombia	3.98	135	Burundi	3.28	162	Indonesia	2.01
109	Cyprus	3.96	136	Peru	3.21	163	Singapore	1.87
110	Turkey	3.94	137	Bangladesh	3.19	164	Somalia	1.51

Source: World Health Statistics Annual

18.3 Social Security Expenditures as Percentage of National Budget

Government expenditures on social security and welfare provide an important yardstick for measuring social progress. Because social welfare programs must compete with other sectors for funds and for their share of finite national revenues, such expenditures reveal the extent of a government's commitment to the general welfare of people in need. Such expenditures are generally in addition to Social Security programs and are carried out through programs targeted to specific groups, such as widows and widowers, children, drug addicts, unemployed, homeless, and alcoholics. Government-sponsored social services are supplemented by philanthropic and religious groups who, in many cases, receive direct government subsidies for their work.

Rank	Country/Entity	Social Security Expenditures as Percentage of National Budget, 1994	Rank	Country/Entity	Social Security Expenditures as Percentage of National Budget, 1994	Rank	Country/Entity	Social Security Expenditures as Percentage of National Budget, 1994
1	Uruguay	60.6	10	Belgium	42.3	19	Japan	36.8
2	Luxembourg	51.1	11	Canada	39.8	20	Latvia	36.7
3	Argentina	50.7	12	Spain	39.6	21	Norway	36.7
4	Sweden	48.2	13	France	39.3	22	Lithuania	35.6
5	Switzerland	48.2	14	Netherlands Antilles	38.1	23	Australia	33.9
6	Austria	46.4	15	Italy	38.0	24	Malta	33.6
7	Germany	45.3	16	New Zealand	38.0	25	Chile	33.3
8	Finland	44.4	17	Netherlands	37.2	26	United Kingdom	31.3
9	Denmark	43.2	18	Isle of Man	37.0	27	Croatia	30.5

Rank	Country/Entity	Social Security Expenditures as Percentage of National Budget, 1994	Rank	Country/Entity	Social Security Expenditures as Percentage of National Budget, 1994	Rank	Country/Entity	Social Security Expenditures as Percentage of National Budget, 1994
28	Estonia	30.0	67	Benin	8.7	105	Oman	3.2
29	United States	29.2	68	Colombia	7.8	106	Gambia	3.0
30	Romania	28.8	69	Saint Vincent and	7.7	107	Mali	3.0
31	Russia	28.5		the Grenadines		108	Philippines	2.9
32	Czech Republic	28.2	70	Grenada	7.6	109	Rwanda	2.9
33	Bulgaria	28.0	71	El Salvador	7.3	110	Singapore	2.9
34	Hungary	27.7	72	Ghana	7.1	111	Senegal	2.6
35	Ireland	27.6	73	Ethiopia	6.9	112	Nigeria	2.5
36	Portugal	27.3	74	Venezuela	6.9	113	Sierra Leone	2.3
37	Brazil	27.1	75	Namibia	6.8	114	Syria	2.1
38	Israel	24.5	76	Malaysia	6.6	115	Uganda	2.1
39	Cyprus	23.2	77	Togo	6.5	116	Chad	1.9
40	Mexico	22.8	78	Central African Republic	6.2	117	Ecuador	1.9
41	Iceland	22.5	79	Djibouti	6.2	118	Madagascar	1.9
42	Albania	21.7	80	Suriname	6.0	119	Niger	1.7
43	Mongolia	21.6	81	Yugoslavia	6.0	120	Somalia	1.7
44	Panama	21.4	82	Morocco	5.9	121	Dominica	1.4
45	Barbados	19.8	83	Indonesia	5.3	122	Lesotho	1.2
46	Costa Rica	17.7	84	Trinidad and Tobago	5.3	123	Congo, Dem. Rep. of	1.1
47	Sri Lanka	16.7	85	Guatemala	5.2	124	Cameroon	1.0
48	Kuwait	16.6	86	Haiti	5.1	125	Liberia	1.0
49	Mauritius	16.6	87	Fiji	4.7	126	Vanuatu	0.9
50	Paraguay	16.2	88	Belize	4.6	127	Tonga	0.8
51	Nicaragua	14.9	89	Honduras	4.5	128	Burundi	0.7
52	Bolivia	14.6	90	Bahamas	4.1	129	Nepal	0.7
53	Jordan	14.3	91	Bahrain	3.9	130	Papua New Guinea	0.7
54	Tunisia	14.3	92	Turkey	3.9	131	Solomon Islands	0.7
55	Taiwan	13.8	93	Zambia	3.9	132	Bhutan	0.5
56	Greece	13.4	94	Botswana	3.8	133	Tanzania	0.5
57	Seychelles	12.8	95	Dominican Republic	3.8	134	Congo, Rep. of	0.4
58	Aruba	11.0	96	Guyana	3.7	135	Sudan	0.4
59	Belarus	11.0	97	Mauritania	3.7	136	Swaziland	0.4
60	Egypt	11.0	98	Côte d'Ivoire	3.6	137	Pakistan	0.2
61	Iran	10.3	99	Myanmar (Burma)	3.6	138	Peru	0.2
62	South Korea	9.9	100	Thailand	3.5	139	Burkina Faso	0.1
63	Bangladesh	9.8	101	United Arab Emirates	3.4	140	China	0.1
64	Jersey	9.5	102	Zimbabwe	3.4	141	Kenya	0.1
65	Saint Kitts and Nevis	9.4	103	Jamaica	3.2	142	Malawi	0.1
66	Guinea-Bissau	8.8	104	Maldives	3.2			

Source: World Bank

18.4 People with Disabilities

Included in the category of people with disabilities are those who are blind, deaf, lame, paralyzed, mentally retarded, or use prosthetic devices of various kinds. In most modern nations, such people receive legislative protection and also preferential treatment for jobs. Transportation and building codes mandate facilities for their access and egress.

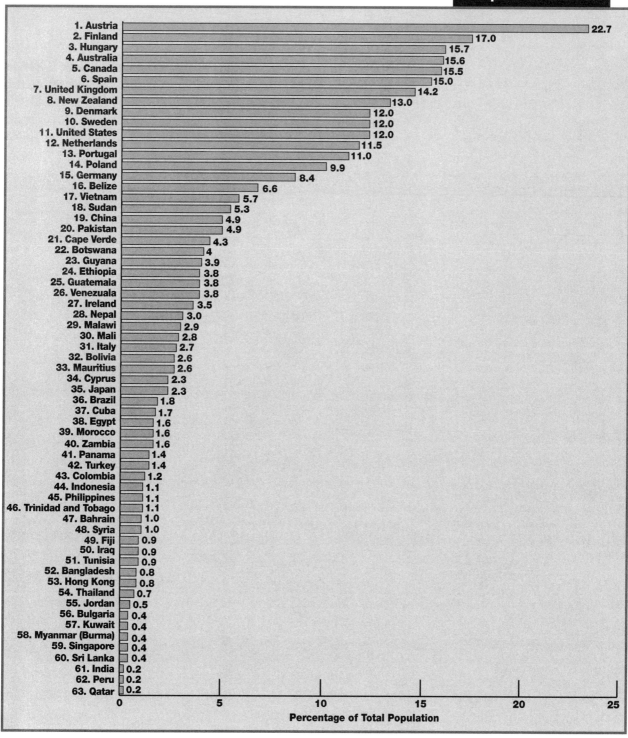

Rank	Country	Percentage
1.	Austria	22.7
2.	Finland	17.0
3.	Hungary	15.7
4.	Australia	15.6
5.	Canada	15.5
6.	Spain	15.0
7.	United Kingdom	14.2
8.	New Zealand	13.0
9.	Denmark	12.0
10.	Sweden	12.0
11.	United States	12.0
12.	Netherlands	11.5
13.	Portugal	11.0
14.	Poland	9.9
15.	Germany	8.4
16.	Belize	6.6
17.	Vietnam	5.7
18.	Sudan	5.3
19.	China	4.9
20.	Pakistan	4.9
21.	Cape Verde	4.3
22.	Botswana	4
23.	Guyana	3.9
24.	Ethiopia	3.8
25.	Guatemala	3.8
26.	Venezuala	3.8
27.	Ireland	3.5
28.	Nepal	3.0
29.	Malawi	2.9
30.	Mali	2.8
31.	Italy	2.7
32.	Bolivia	2.6
33.	Mauritius	2.6
34.	Cyprus	2.3
35.	Japan	2.3
36.	Brazil	1.8
37.	Cuba	1.7
38.	Egypt	1.6
39.	Morocco	1.6
40.	Zambia	1.6
41.	Panama	1.4
42.	Turkey	1.4
43.	Colombia	1.2
44.	Indonesia	1.1
45.	Philippines	1.1
46.	Trinidad and Tobago	1.1
47.	Bahrain	1.0
48.	Syria	1.0
49.	Fiji	0.9
50.	Iraq	0.9
51.	Tunisia	0.9
52.	Bangladesh	0.8
53.	Hong Kong	0.8
54.	Thailand	0.7
55.	Jordan	0.5
56.	Bulgaria	0.4
57.	Kuwait	0.4
58.	Myanmar (Burma)	0.4
59.	Singapore	0.4
60.	Sri Lanka	0.4
61.	India	0.2
62.	Peru	0.2
63.	Qatar	0.2

Percentage of Total Population

Source: World Health Statistics Annual

Survival Rate

While rankings on life expectancy look at length of life, these rankings look at the population in each country at greatest risk of an early death. The gap between rich and poor nations is clearly illustrated in these rankings, because a greater percentage of the population in the developing world does not even reach the average life expectancy assigned to them. Among the factors contributing to this state of affairs are poor medical attention, poor nutrition, AIDS, and water pollution. In the developed world, factors militating against longer life are car accidents, air pollution, suicide, and heart disease.

18.5 People in Developed Countries Not Expected to Survive to Age 60

Rank	Country/Entity	Percentage of Population Not Expected to Survive to Age 60	Rank	Country/Entity	Percentage of Population Not Expected to Survive to Age 60	Rank	Country/Entity	Percentage of Population Not Expected to Survive to Age 60
1	Russia	32	18	Slovakia	19	35	New Zealand	10
2	Turkmenistan	29	19	Bulgaria	18	36	Spain	10
3	Armenia	26	20	Georgia	17	37	Australia	9
4	Kazakhstan	26	21	Albania	16	38	Canada	9
5	Moldova	26	22	Croatia	16	39	Greece	9
6	Kyrgyzstan	25	23	Slovenia	15	40	Ireland	9
7	Latvia	25	24	Czech Republic	14	41	Israel	9
8	Tajikistan	25	25	Macedonia	14	42	Italy	9
9	Uzbekistan	25	26	United States	13	43	Malta	9
10	Belarus	24	27	Denmark	12	44	Netherlands	9
11	Hungary	24	28	Portugal	12	45	Norway	9
12	Ukraine	24	29	Austria	11	46	Switzerland	9
13	Estonia	23	30	Finland	11	47	United Kingdom	9
14	Lithuania	23	31	France	11	48	Iceland	8
15	Azerbaijan	21	32	Germany	11	49	Japan	8
16	Romania	21	33	Luxembourg	11	50	Sweden	8
17	Poland	20	34	Belgium	10			

Source: Human Development Report

18.6 People in Developed Countries Not Expected to Survive to Age 40

Rank	Country/Entity	Percentage of Population Not Expected to Survive to Age 40	Rank	Country/Entity	Percentage of Population Not Expected to Survive to Age 40	Rank	Country/Entity	Percentage of Population Not Expected to Survive to Age 40
1	Sierra Leone	50	15	Central African Republic	35	29	Mauritania	29
2	Malawi	46	16	Equatorial Guinea	34	30	Bhutan	28
3	Uganda	44	17	Ethiopia	34	31	Laos	28
4	Guinea-Bissau	42	18	Zimbabwe	34	32	Benin	27
5	Zambia	42	19	Djibouti	33	33	Cambodia	27
6	Angola	38	20	Eritrea	33	34	Kenya	27
7	Burkina Faso	38	21	Togo	33	35	Sudan	27
8	Gambia	38	22	Côte d'Ivoire	32	36	Cameroon	26
9	Guinea	38	23	Congo, Rep. of	32	37	Gabon	26
10	Mozambique	38	24	Senegal	32	38	Namibia	26
11	Burundi	37	25	Botswana	31	39	Haiti	25
12	Chad	37	26	Nigeria	31	40	Ghana	23
13	Mali	36	27	Tanzania	31	41	Lesotho	23
14	Niger	36	28	Congo, Dem. Rep. of	30	42	Comoros	22

Rank	Country/Entity	Percentage of Population Not Expected to Survive to Age 40	Rank	Country/Entity	Percentage of Population Not Expected to Survive to Age 40	Rank	Country/Entity	Percentage of Population Not Expected to Survive to Age 40
43	Nepal	22	68	Ecuador	11	93	Solomon Islands	6
44	Yemen	22	69	Mongolia	11	94	Sri Lanka	6
45	Bangladesh	21	70	Vietnam	11	95	Suriname	6
46	Madagascar	21	71	Iran	10	96	Venezuela	6
47	Swaziland	21	72	Samoa	10	97	Bahrain	5
48	Myanmar (Burma)	19	73	Thailand	10	98	Fiji	5
49	Papua New Guinea	19	74	Turkey	10	99	Jamaica	5
50	Bolivia	18	75	Vanuatu	10	100	North Korea	5
51	Iraq	17	76	Algeria	9	101	Malaysia	5
52	India	16	77	Colombia	9	102	Qatar	5
53	Pakistan	15	78	Dominican Republic	9	103	Uruguay	5
54	Guatemala	14	79	Paraguay	9	104	Chile	4
55	Guyana	14	80	Philippines	9	105	Costa Rica	4
56	Cape Verde	13	81	Jordan	8	106	Cuba	4
57	Egypt	13	82	Mexico	8	107	South Korea	4
58	Indonesia	13	83	Syria	8	108	Mauritius	4
59	Libya	13	84	Tunisia	8	109	Trinidad and Tobago	4
60	Maldives	13	85	China	7	110	Barbados	3
61	South Africa	13	86	Lebanon	7	111	Brunei	3
62	El Salvador	12	87	Argentina	6	112	Cyprus	3
63	Honduras	12	88	Bahamas	6	113	Kuwait	3
64	Morocco	12	89	Belize	6	114	United Arab Emirates	3
65	Nicaragua	12	90	Oman	6	115	Hong Kong	2
66	Peru	12	91	Panama	6	116	Singapore	2
67	Brazil	11	92	Saudi Arabia	6			

Source: Human Development Report

Mortality and Health of Infants, Children, and Mothers

Four measures that health professionals consider as reliable indicators of the general level of health in a country are the three key mortality rates—infant, children under five, and maternal—and the percentage of low birthweight infants. Healthy babies and healthy mothers are the primary goals of maternity hospitals and specialists in obstetrics and childhood disorders. Early prevention and resistance to disease, care of pregnant and nursing mothers, and support services during gestation and delivery help to reduce the mortality of mothers, infants, and children under five. Low birthweight indicates nutritional deficiencies in both mother and child or exposure to problems like drug addiction and emotional trauma. Premature births increase the possibility of low birthweight and infant mortality. Infant mortality may also be caused by complications during pregnancy or childbirth, the puerperium (the period immediately following birth), or abortion.

18.7 Infant Mortality Rate

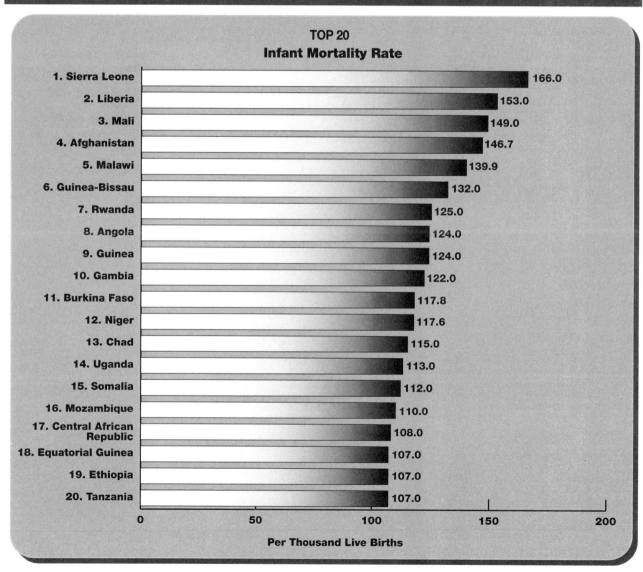

TOP 20
Infant Mortality Rate

Rank	Country	Per Thousand Live Births
1.	Sierra Leone	166.0
2.	Liberia	153.0
3.	Mali	149.0
4.	Afghanistan	146.7
5.	Malawi	139.9
6.	Guinea-Bissau	132.0
7.	Rwanda	125.0
8.	Angola	124.0
9.	Guinea	124.0
10.	Gambia	122.0
11.	Burkina Faso	117.8
12.	Niger	117.6
13.	Chad	115.0
14.	Uganda	113.0
15.	Somalia	112.0
16.	Mozambique	110.0
17.	Central African Republic	108.0
18.	Equatorial Guinea	107.0
19.	Ethiopia	107.0
20.	Tanzania	107.0

Per Thousand Live Births

Rank	Country/Entity	Infant Mortality Rate per 1,000 Live Births	Rank	Country/Entity	Infant Mortality Rate per 1,000 Live Births	Rank	Country/Entity	Infant Mortality Rate per 1,000 Live Births
21	Cambodia	106.0	87	Vanuatu	39.0	152	Virgin Islands (U.S.)	12.3
22	Djibouti	106.0	88	China	38.0	153	Puerto Rico	11.5
23	Haiti	105.1	89	Mayotte	38.0	154	Chile	11.1
24	Bhutan	105.0	90	Vietnam	38.0	155	Kuwait	11.1
25	Burundi	104.8	91	Gaza Strip	37.0	156	American Samoa	11.0
26	Benin	103.0	92	Tunisia	37.0	157	Malaysia	11.0
27	Zambia	103.0	93	Philippines	36.0	158	Hungary	10.9
28	Eritrea	98.0	94	Uzbekistan	35.0	159	Estonia	10.5
29	Iraq	91.9	95	Jordan	34.0	160	Malta	10.5
30	Congo, Rep. of	90.0	96	Belize	33.9	161	French Polynesia	10.2
31	Congo, Dem. Rep. of	89.0	97	Azerbaijan	33.0	162	Slovakia	10.2
32	Swaziland	88.4	98	Albania	32.0	163	Lithuania	10.1
33	Laos	87.0	99	Thailand	32.0	164	South Korea	10.0
34	Côte d'Ivoire	86.0	100	El Salvador	31.5	165	Aruba	9.6
35	Togo	86.0	101	Ecuador	30.5	166	Dominica	9.6
36	Gabon	85.0	102	Suriname	30.2	167	Brunei	9.0
37	Nigeria	84.2	103	Syria	29.6	168	Monaco	9.0
38	Nepal	83.0	104	Jamaica	28.6	169	Northern Mariana Islands	9.0
39	Mauritania	81.7	105	Oman	28.2	170	Croatia	8.9
40	Yemen	80.0	106	Lebanon	28.0	171	Bermuda	8.8
41	Bangladesh	79.0	107	Kazakhstan	27.9	172	Faroe Islands	8.5
42	Myanmar (Burma)	79.0	108	Kyrgyzstan	27.7	173	Greece	8.1
43	Madagascar	77.0	109	Colombia	26.9	174	Cuba	8.0
44	Comoros	75.3	110	Marshall Islands	26.0	175	Guadeloupe	8.0
45	Pakistan	75.0	111	Nauru	26.0	176	Guam	8.0
46	Ghana	73.0	112	Panama	25.3	177	New Caledonia	7.8
47	Lesotho	72.0	113	Saint Kitts and Nevis	25.1	178	Andorra	7.7
48	India	71.1	114	Armenia	25.0	179	Guernsey	7.6
49	Egypt	71.0	115	North Korea	23.0	180	United States	7.5
50	Sudan	71.0	116	Saudi Arabia	23.0	181	Réunion	7.3
51	Bolivia	66.0	117	Solomon Islands	23.0	182	San Marino	7.1
52	Senegal	64.0	118	Macedonia	22.7	183	Martinique	7.0
53	Western Sahara	64.0	119	Argentina	22.0	184	Portugal	6.9
54	Zimbabwe	62.3	120	Romania	21.2	185	New Zealand	6.7
55	São Tomé and Príncipe	62.1	121	Palau	21.0	186	Taiwan	6.4
56	Papua New Guinea	62.0	122	Moldova	20.4	187	Netherlands Antilles	6.3
57	Namibia	60.0	123	Fiji	20.0	188	United Kingdom	6.2
58	Samoa	60.0	124	Qatar	20.0	189	Canada	6.1
59	Cameroon	58.0	125	Mauritius	19.7	190	Czech Republic	6.0
60	Libya	56.0	126	Uruguay	19.6	191	Italy	6.0
61	Brazil	55.3	127	Bahamas	19.0	192	Jersey	6.0
62	Kenya	55.2	128	Trinidad and Tobago	18.2	193	Ireland	5.9
63	Kiribati	54.0	129	Bahrain	18.0	194	Israel	5.8
64	Guatemala	53.9	130	Russia	18.0	195	Australia	5.7
65	Iran	52.7	131	Saint Lucia	18.0	196	Denmark	5.7
66	South Africa	52.4	132	Mexico	17.5	197	Gibraltar	5.7
67	Guyana	51.4	133	Georgia	17.4	198	Isle of Man	5.7
68	Indonesia	51.0	134	Antigua and Barbuda	17.2	199	Belgium	5.6
69	Morocco	51.0	135	Seychelles	17.0	200	Germany	5.6
70	Peru	50.1	136	Venezuela	16.8	201	Macau	5.6
71	Maldives	50.0	137	Latvia	15.9	202	Spain	5.6
72	Micronesia	49.0	138	Bulgaria	15.6	203	Liechtenstein	5.5
73	Algeria	48.7	139	French Guiana	15.4	204	Slovenia	5.5
74	Dominican Republic	47.7	140	Sri Lanka	15.0	205	Netherlands	5.1
75	Honduras	47.2	141	Tonga	15.0	206	Austria	5.0
76	Nicaragua	45.8	142	United Arab Emirates	15.0	207	Switzerland	5.0
77	Turkmenistan	45.0	143	Grenada	14.3	208	Cyprus	4.9
78	Bosnia and Herzegovina	43.2	144	Barbados	14.2	209	France	4.9
79	Turkey	43.2	145	Saint Vincent and the Grenadines	14.1	210	Luxembourg	4.9
80	Tajikistan	42.4	146	Ukraine	14.1	211	Iceland	4.6
81	Cape Verde	41.0	147	Yugoslavia	14.1	212	Japan	4.2
82	Tuvalu	41.0	148	Poland	14.0	213	Hong Kong	4.1
83	Mongolia	40.5	149	Costa Rica	13.3	214	Norway	4.1
84	West Bank	40.0	150	Greenland	13.0	215	Finland	3.9
85	Botswana	39.0	151	Belarus	12.6	216	Singapore	3.8
86	Paraguay	39.0				217	Sweden	3.5

Source: UN Statistical Yearbook

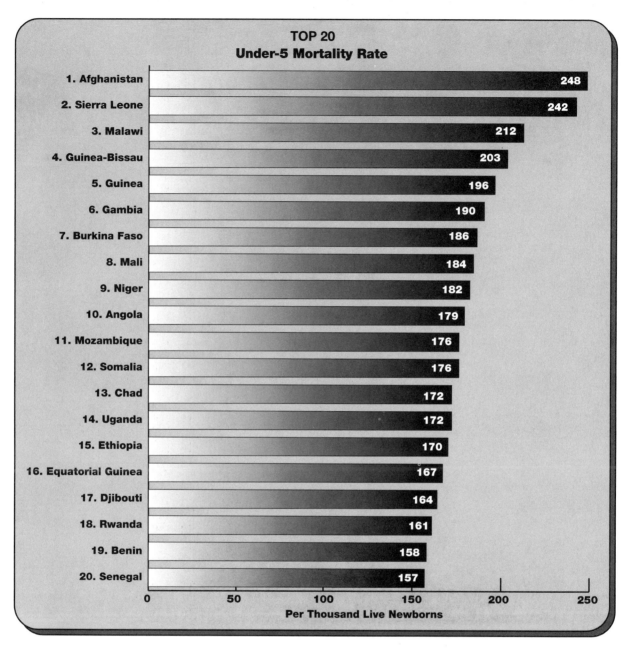

TOP 20
Under-5 Mortality Rate

Rank	Country	Rate
1. Afghanistan		248
2. Sierra Leone		242
3. Malawi		212
4. Guinea-Bissau		203
5. Guinea		196
6. Gambia		190
7. Burkina Faso		186
8. Mali		184
9. Niger		182
10. Angola		179
11. Mozambique		176
12. Somalia		176
13. Chad		172
14. Uganda		172
15. Ethiopia		170
16. Equatorial Guinea		167
17. Djibouti		164
18. Rwanda		161
19. Benin		158
20. Senegal		157

Per Thousand Live Newborns

Rank	Country/Entity	Under-5 Mortality Rate per 1,000 Live Newborns,1996	Rank	Country/Entity	Under-5 Mortality Rate per 1,000 Live Newborns,1996	Rank	Country/Entity	Under-5 Mortality Rate per 1,000 Live Newborns,1996
21	Yemen	155	30	Mauritania	142	39	Madagascar	121
22	Liberia	151	31	Zambia	140	40	Togo	118
23	Central African Republic	149	32	Côte d'Ivoire	137	41	Sudan	112
24	Eritrea	146	33	Cambodia	137	42	Comoros	111
25	Nigeria	146	34	Congo, Rep. of	133	43	Ghana	111
26	Bhutan	145	35	Congo, Dem. Rep. of	131	44	Cameroon	109
27	Bangladesh	144	36	Gabon	130	45	Kenya	106
28	Burundi	143	37	Tanzania	126	46	Haiti	104
29	Laos	143	38	Nepal	122	47	Pakistan	104

Under-5 Mortality Rate per 1,000 Live Newborns, 1996

Rank	Country/Entity	Under-5 Mortality Rate per 1,000 Live Newborns,1996
48	Zimbabwe	103
49	India	99
50	Swaziland	99
51	Myanmar (Burma)	95
52	Marshall Islands	92
53	Namibia	91
54	Bolivia	88
55	Papua New Guinea	82
56	Lesotho	81
57	São Tomé and Príncipe	81
58	Libya	80
59	Kiribati	78
60	Morocco	76
61	South Africa	73
62	Peru	71
63	Samoa	71
64	Egypt	70
65	Brazil	69
66	Maldives	68
67	Mongolia	68
68	Guatemala	67
69	Nicaragua	66
70	Turkmenistan	66
71	Turkey	65
72	El Salvador	64
73	Indonesia	63
74	Cape Verde	60
75	Guyana	60
76	Iran	59
77	Iraq	59
78	Botswana	57
79	Ecuador	57
80	Tajikistan	56
81	Tuvalu	56
82	Vietnam	56
83	Algeria	54
84	Honduras	50
85	Tunisia	49
86	Vanuatu	48
87	Paraguay	47
88	Uzbekistan	47
89	Dominican Republic	46
90	Philippines	45
91	China	43
92	Syria	43
93	Thailand	43
94	Colombia	40
95	Mexico	40
96	Saint Kitts and Nevis	40
97	Jordan	39
98	Kyrgyzstan	39
99	Albania	38
100	Azerbaijan	37
101	Belize	37
102	Macedonia	37
103	Lebanon	36
104	Palau	35
105	Grenada	33
106	Oman	32
107	Kazakhstan	31
108	Romania	30
109	Saudi Arabia	30
110	Micronesia	29
111	Solomon Islands	29
112	Moldova	28
113	Panama	28
114	Russia	27
115	North Korea	26
116	Suriname	26
117	Argentina	25
118	Venezuela	25
119	Bahamas	24
120	Tonga	24
121	Armenia	23
122	Bahrain	23
123	Fiji	23
124	Qatar	23
125	Saint Vincent and the Grenadines	23
126	Antigua and Barbuda	22
127	Malaysia	22
128	Saint Lucia	22
129	Dominica	21
130	Georgia	21
131	Ukraine	21
132	Bosnia and Herzegovina	20
133	Jamaica	20
134	Latvia	20
135	Seychelles	20
136	Uruguay	20
137	Belarus	19
138	Estonia	19
139	Sri Lanka	19
140	United Arab Emirates	19
141	Bulgaria	18
142	Poland	18
143	Chile	17
144	Hungary	17
145	Lithuania	17
146	Mauritius	17
147	Trinidad and Tobago	17
148	Croatia	16
149	Kuwait	16
150	Barbados	15
151	Costa Rica	14
152	Slovakia	14
153	Brunei	13
154	Cuba	13
155	South Korea	13
156	Slovenia	12
157	Malta	11
158	Portugal	11
159	Czech Republic	10
160	Greece	10
161	New Zealand	10
162	Cyprus	9
163	France	9
164	Israel	9
165	Italy	9
166	Norway	9
167	Singapore	9
168	United States	9
169	Australia	8
170	Austria	8
171	Canada	8
172	Denmark	8
173	Luxembourg	8
174	Netherlands	8
175	Spain	8
176	Taiwan	8
177	United Kingdom	8
178	Belgium	7
179	Germany	7
180	Ireland	7
181	Switzerland	7
182	Finland	6
183	Hong Kong	6
184	Japan	6
185	Sweden	6
186	Iceland	4

Source: World Development Report

18.9 Low Birthweight Infants

Rank	Country/Entity	Low Birthweight Infants as Percentage of Births, 1992–1998
1	Bangladesh	50
2	India	33
3	Pakistan	25
4	Iraq	24
5	Papua New Guinea	23
6	Nepal	23
7	Burkina Faso	21
8	Togo	20
9	Mozambique	20
10	Malawi	20
11	Guinea-Bissau	20
12	Yemen	19
13	Lebanon	19
14	Sri Lanka	18
15	Laos	18
16	Cambodia	18
17	Vietnam	17
18	Rwanda	17
19	Mali	17
20	Ghana	17
21	Tunisia	16
22	Nigeria	16
23	Myanmar (Burma)	16
24	Kenya	16
25	Ethiopia	16
26	Congo, Rep. of	16
27	Burundi	16

Rank	Country/Entity	Low Birthweight Infants as Percentage of Births, 1992–1998	Rank	Country/Entity	Low Birthweight Infants as Percentage of Births, 1992–1998	Rank	Country/Entity	Low Birthweight Infants as Percentage of Births, 1992–1998
28	Sudan	15	60	Honduras	9	92	Slovenia	6
29	Niger	15	61	Greece	9	93	Slovakia	6
30	Nicaragua	15	62	El Salvador	9	94	New Zealand	6
31	Madagascar	15	63	Colombia	9	95	Kyrgyzstan	6
32	Haiti	15	64	Algeria	9	96	Kuwait	6
33	Central African Republic	15	65	Uruguay	8	97	Japan	6
34	Zimbabwe	14	66	United States	8	98	France	6
35	Tanzania	14	67	United Arab Emirates	8	99	Czech Republic	6
36	Guatemala	14	68	Ukraine	8	100	China	6
37	Côte d'Ivoire	14	69	Turkey	8	101	Canada	6
38	Zambia	13	70	Tajikistan	8	102	Belgium	6
39	Guinea	13	71	Romania	8	103	Azerbaijan	6
40	Ecuador	13	72	Panama	8	104	Austria	6
41	Cameroon	13	73	Oman	8	105	Australia	6
42	Egypt	12	74	Mexico	8	106	Turkmenistan	5
43	Philippines	11	75	Malaysia	8	107	Switzerland	5
44	Peru	11	76	Macedonia	8	108	Sweden	5
45	Lesotho	11	77	Israel	8	109	Portugal	5
46	Indonesia	11	78	Cuba	8	110	Norway	5
47	Dominican Republic	11	79	Croatia	8	111	Libya	5
48	Trinidad and Tobago	10	80	Botswana	8	112	Hong Kong	5
49	Mongolia	10	81	Thailand	7	113	Finland	5
50	Jamaica	10	82	Syria	7	114	Denmark	5
51	Iran	10	83	Moldova	7	115	Belarus	5
52	Gabon	10	84	Italy	7	116	Netherlands	4
53	Bolivia	10	85	Costa Rica	7	117	Morocco	4
54	Venezuela	9	86	Chile	7	118	Lithuania	4
55	Poland	9	87	Bulgaria	7	119	Latvia	4
56	Paraguay	9	88	Argentina	7	120	South Korea	4
57	Mauritania	9	89	Albania	7	121	Ireland	4
58	Kazakhstan	9	90	Uzbekistan	6	122	Jordan	2
59	Hungary	9	91	United Kingdom	6	123	Spain	1

Source: State of the World's Children

18.10 Maternal Mortality Rate

Rank	Country/Entity	Maternal Mortality Rate per 100,000 Live Births, 1990	Rank	Country/Entity	Maternal Mortality Rate per 100,000 Live Births, 1990	Rank	Country/Entity	Maternal Mortality Rate per 100,000 Live Births, 1990
1	Sierra Leone	1,800	20	Benin	990	39	Togo	640
2	Bhutan	1,600	21	Zambia	940	40	Lesotho	610
3	Guinea	1,600	22	Burkina Faso	930	41	Morocco	610
4	Angola	1,500	23	Mauritania	930	42	Myanmar (Burma)	580
5	Chad	1,500	24	Papua New Guinea	930	43	India	570
6	Mozambique	1,500	25	Guinea-Bissau	910	44	Zimbabwe	570
7	Nepal	1,500	26	Cambodia	900	45	Malawi	560
8	Eritrea	1,400	27	Congo, Rep. of	890	46	Cameroon	550
9	Ethiopia	1,400	28	Congo, Dem. Rep. of	870	47	Gabon	500
10	Yemen	1,400	29	Bangladesh	850	48	Madagascar	490
11	Burundi	1,300	30	Côte d'Ivoire	810	49	Namibia	370
12	Rwanda	1,300	31	Tanzania	770	50	Pakistan	340
13	Mali	1,200	32	Ghana	740	51	Iraq	310
14	Niger	1,200	33	Central African Republic	700	52	El Salvador	300
15	Senegal	1,200	34	Sudan	660	53	Lebanon	300
16	Uganda	1,200	35	Bolivia	650	54	Peru	280
17	Gambia	1,100	36	Indonesia	650	55	Philippines	280
18	Haiti	1,000	37	Kenya	650	56	Botswana	250
19	Nigeria	1,000	38	Laos	650	57	South Africa	230

Rank	Country/Entity	Maternal Mortality Rate per 100,000 Live Births, 1990	Rank	Country/Entity	Maternal Mortality Rate per 100,000 Live Births, 1990	Rank	Country/Entity	Maternal Mortality Rate per 100,000 Live Births, 1990
58	Brazil	220	87	Colombia	100	116	Azerbaijan	22
59	Honduras	220	88	China	95	117	Germany	22
60	Libya	220	89	Cuba	95	118	Poland	19
61	Guatemala	200	90	Trinidad and Tobago	90	119	Japan	18
62	Thailand	200	91	Uruguay	85	120	Czech Republic	15
63	Oman	190	92	Kazakhstan	80	121	France	15
64	Syria	180	93	Malaysia	80	122	Portugal	15
65	Turkey	180	94	Russia	75	123	Slovenia	13
66	Egypt	170	95	North Korea	70	124	Italy	12
67	Tunisia	170	96	Albania	65	125	Netherlands	12
68	Algeria	160	97	Chile	65	126	United States	12
69	Nicaragua	160	98	Mongolia	65	127	Finland	11
70	Paraguay	160	99	Costa Rica	60	128	Austria	10
71	Vietnam	160	100	Moldova	60	129	Belgium	10
72	Ecuador	150	101	Panama	55	130	Greece	10
73	Jordan	150	102	Turkmenistan	55	131	Ireland	10
74	Sri Lanka	140	103	Uzbekistan	55	132	Singapore	10
75	South Korea	130	104	Armenia	50	133	Australia	9
76	Romania	130	105	Ukraine	50	134	Denmark	9
77	Saudi Arabia	130	106	Estonia	41	135	United Kingdom	9
78	Tajikistan	130	107	Latvia	40	136	Taiwan	8
79	Iran	120	108	Belarus	37	137	Hong Kong	7
80	Jamaica	120	109	Lithuania	36	138	Israel	7
81	Mauritius	120	110	Georgia	33	139	Spain	7
82	Venezuela	120	111	Hungary	30	140	Sweden	7
83	Dominican Republic	110	112	Kuwait	29	141	Canada	6
84	Kyrgyzstan	110	113	Bulgaria	27	142	Norway	6
85	Mexico	110	114	United Arab Emirates	26	143	Switzerland	6
86	Argentina	100	115	New Zealand	25			

Source: State of the World's Children

Hospitals

There are various types of hospitals in the world—teaching hospitals, general hospitals, specialized hospitals, children's hospitals, research hospitals, medical centers, clinics, and so on —but they are combined in this ranking. Hospitals are only one of the many factors in the evaluation of the quality of medical care in a country. But since they combine all forms of medical, nursing, and custodial care, they form the principal channel of healthcare in every country. The availability of hospital beds is no longer as important an indicator as it was a few decades ago. Many types of medical procedures, including surgery, are handled as ambulatory cases requiring no overnight stay, and even in the case of those required to stay overnight, most are discharged within days.

18.11 Hospitals

Rank	Country/Entity	Hospitals	Rank	Country/Entity	Hospitals	Rank	Country/Entity	Hospitals
1	China	67,807	10	Brazil	6,372	19	Thailand	1,097
2	India	15,067	11	Ukraine	3,900	20	Canada	1,079
3	Vietnam	12,500	12	France	3,810	21	Laos	1,074
4	Russia	12,265	13	Germany	2,354	22	Australia	1,071
5	Nigeria	11,588	14	Italy	1,874	23	Indonesia	1,039
6	Pakistan	10,667	15	Kazakhstan	1,805	24	Turkey	982
7	Japan	9,844	16	Philippines	1,723	25	Zambia	965
8	United States	6,580	17	Mexico	1,539	26	Colombia	947
9	Egypt	6,418	18	Zimbabwe	1,378	27	Bangladesh	919

Rank	Country/Entity	Hospitals	Rank	Country/Entity	Hospitals	Rank	Country/Entity	Hospitals
28	Albania	895	79	Latvia	170	130	Swaziland	24
29	Belarus	880	80	Denmark	163	131	Mauritius	23
30	Kenya	877	81	Tunisia	163	132	Lesotho	22
31	Spain	813	82	Lebanon	153	133	Senegal	17
32	Azerbaijan	787	83	Central African Republic	133	134	West Bank	17
33	Taiwan	787	84	Ghana	121	135	Greenland	16
34	Poland	753	85	Uruguay	112	136	Guinea-Bissau	16
35	Dominican Republic	723	86	Slovakia	111	137	Mauritania	16
36	Myanmar (Burma)	710	87	Cyprus	110	138	Gambia	13
37	South Africa	698	88	Estonia	107	139	Bahrain	12
38	Iran	653	89	Liberia	92	140	Netherlands Antilles	12
39	Cameroon	629	90	Vanuatu	90	141	Barbados	10
40	Venezuela	610	91	Hong Kong	88	142	Brunei	10
41	Mongolia	475	92	Ethiopia	86	143	Eritrea	10
42	Tajikistan	449	93	Croatia	84	144	Saint Vincent and	9
43	Ecuador	429	94	Nepal	84		the Grenadines	
44	Peru	427	95	Uganda	81	145	Djibouti	8
45	Sri Lanka	426	96	Yemen	81	146	New Caledonia	8
46	Georgia	422	97	Burkina Faso	78	147	Solomon Islands	8
47	Congo, Dem. Rep. of	400	98	El Salvador	78	148	Tuvalu	8
48	Turkmenistan	398	99	Cape Verde	75	149	Belize	7
49	Kyrgyzstan	396	100	Puerto Rico	72	150	Malta	7
50	Malawi	395	101	Ireland	63	151	Seychelles	7
51	Finland	380	102	Jordan	63	152	Gaza Strip	6
52	Greece	368	103	Macedonia	62	153	Jersey	6
53	Belgium	363	104	Honduras	61	154	Bahamas	5
54	Moldova	339	105	Panama	59	155	Maldives	5
55	Bolivia	336	106	Angola	58	156	Micronesia	4
56	Portugal	335	107	Nicaragua	56	157	Qatar	4
57	Austria	330	108	Dominica	53	158	Saint Kitts and Nevis	4
58	New Zealand	330	109	Oman	53	159	Saint Lucia	4
59	Malaysia	315	110	Haiti	50	160	Tonga	4
60	Czech Republic	299	111	Namibia	47	161	Faroe Islands	3
61	Bulgaria	289	112	United Arab Emirates	47	162	Grenada	3
62	Saudi Arabia	279	113	Guinea	38	163	Isle of Man	3
63	Syria	264	114	Samoa	36	164	Antigua and Barbuda	2
64	Israel	259	115	French Polynesia	34	165	Aruba	2
65	Cuba	244	116	Luxembourg	34	166	Bermuda	2
66	Mozambique	238	117	Costa Rica	33	167	Gibraltar	2
67	Netherlands	231	118	Botswana	30	168	Marshall Islands	2
68	Rwanda	220	119	Guadeloupe	30	169	Mayotte	2
69	Sierra Leone	219	120	Guyana	30	170	American Samoa	1
70	Morocco	201	121	Jamaica	30	171	Andorra	1
71	Chile	198	122	Macau	30	172	Guernsey	1
72	Lithuania	195	123	Bhutan	27	173	Kiribati	1
73	Uzbekistan	192	124	Gabon	27	174	Liechtenstein	1
74	Cambodia	188	125	Iceland	26	175	Monaco	1
75	Iraq	185	126	Fiji	25	176	Northern Mariana Islands	1
76	Armenia	183	127	Kuwait	24	177	Palau	1
77	Algeria	181	128	Singapore	24			
78	Tanzania	173	129	Slovenia	24			

Source: World Health Statistics Annual

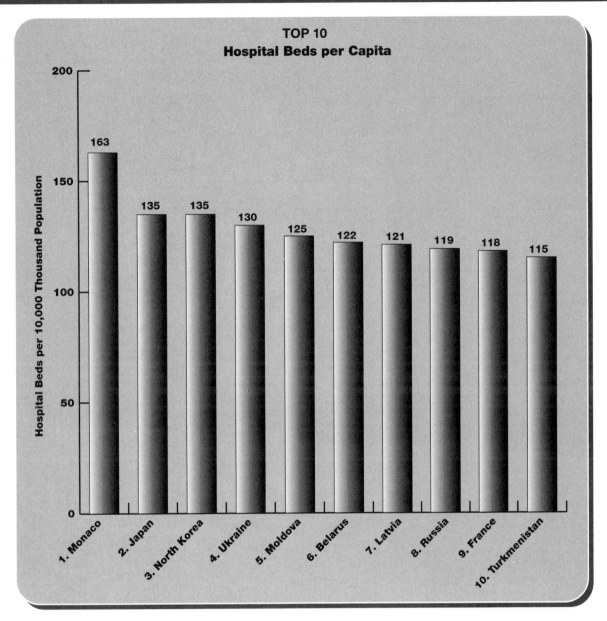

TOP 10
Hospital Beds per Capita

Hospital Beds per 10,000 Thousand Population

Rank	Country	Hospital Beds per 10,000
1. Monaco		163
2. Japan		135
3. North Korea		135
4. Ukraine		130
5. Moldova		125
6. Belarus		122
7. Latvia		121
8. Russia		119
9. France		118
10. Turkmenistan		115

Rank	Country/Entity	Hospital Beds per 10,000 Population	Rank	Country/Entity	Hospital Beds per 10,000 Population	Rank	Country/Entity	Hospital Beds per 10,000 Population
11	Luxembourg	109	22	Hungary	91	33	Germany	77
12	Georgia	105	23	Australia	89	34	Martinique	77
13	Iceland	105	24	Czech Republic	89	35	Romania	77
14	Mongolia	105	25	Gibraltar	88	36	Belgium	76
15	Bulgaria	103	26	Jersey	88	37	Barbados	75
16	Kyrgyzstan	99	27	Tajikistan	88	38	Greenland	75
17	Finland	98	28	Kazakhstan	86	39	Netherlands Antilles	70
18	Azerbaijan	96	29	Estonia	84	40	Switzerland	69
19	Austria	93	30	Uzbekistan	84	41	New Zealand	68
20	Lithuania	92	31	Armenia	82	42	Saint Kitts and Nevis	67
21	Slovakia	92	32	Guadeloupe	80	43	San Marino	66

Rank	Country/Entity	Hospital Beds per 10,000 Population	Rank	Country/Entity	Hospital Beds per 10,000 Population	Rank	Country/Entity	Hospital Beds per 10,000 Population
44	Cuba	65	99	Congo, Rep. of	33	155	Togo	16
45	Italy	65	100	Ireland	33	156	Cape Verde	15
46	Faroe Islands	64	101	Suriname	33	157	Central African Republic	15
47	Poland	63	102	Chile	31	158	Iran	15
48	New Caledonia	62	103	Kuwait	31	159	Lesotho	15
49	Israel	61	104	Micronesia	31	160	Colombia	14
50	Croatia	59	105	Guyana	30	161	Iraq	14
51	Antigua and Barbuda	58	106	Belize	29	162	Kenya	14
52	Albania	57	107	Equatorial Guinea	29	163	Guinea-Bissau	13
53	Malta	57	108	Trinidad and Tobago	29	164	Angola	12
54	Slovenia	57	109	Zambia	29	165	Bhutan	12
55	French Guiana	56	110	Bahrain	28	166	Dominican Republic	12
56	Macedonia	56	111	Mauritius	28	167	Paraguay	12
57	Netherlands	55	112	Sri Lanka	28	168	Uganda	12
58	Canada	54	113	Tonga	28	169	Mayotte	11
59	Seychelles	54	114	United Arab Emirates	28	170	Nicaragua	11
60	Solomon Islands	53	115	American Samoa	27	171	Philippines	11
61	Taiwan	53	116	Cameroon	27	172	Syria	11
62	Cyprus	52	117	Djibouti	27	173	Bolivia	10
63	Sweden	52	118	Panama	27	174	Haiti	10
64	Yugoslavia	52	119	Vietnam	27	175	Mexico	10
65	Gabon	51	120	Puerto Rico	26	176	Morocco	10
66	Norway	51	121	Venezuela	26	177	Senegal	10
67	Greece	50	122	Comoros	25	178	Sierra Leone	10
68	Palau	50	123	Dominica	25	179	Tanzania	10
69	United Kingdom	49	124	Laos	25	180	Eritrea	9
70	Virgin Islands (U.S.)	49	125	China	24	181	Gaza Strip	9
71	French Polynesia	48	126	Botswana	23	182	Honduras	9
72	Hong Kong	47	127	Saudi Arabia	23	183	Madagascar	9
73	Bosnia and Herzegovina	46	128	Fiji	22	184	Rwanda	9
74	Namibia	45	129	Jamaica	22	185	West Bank	9
75	Uruguay	45	130	Lebanon	22	186	Côte d'Ivoire	8
76	Argentina	44	131	Macau	22	187	Maldives	8
77	Aruba	44	132	Turkey	22	188	Mozambique	8
78	Réunion	44	133	Vanuatu	22	189	Sudan	8
79	Saint Vincent and the Grenadines	44	134	Congo, Dem. Rep. of	21	190	Burundi	7
80	Bermuda	43	135	Oman	21	191	Chad	7
81	Portugal	42	136	Malaysia	20	192	Gambia	7
82	South Africa	42	137	Algeria	19	193	India	7
83	Spain	42	138	Egypt	19	194	Mauritania	7
84	Libya	41	139	Marshall Islands	19	195	Nigeria	7
85	United States	41	140	Northern Mariana Islands	19	196	Somalia	7
86	Bahamas	40	141	Zimbabwe	19	197	Yemen	7
87	Kiribati	40	142	Andorra	18	198	Guinea	6
88	Grenada	38	143	Costa Rica	18	199	Indonesia	6
89	Saint Lucia	37	144	Jordan	18	200	Myanmar (Burma)	6
90	Tuvalu	36	145	Qatar	18	201	Pakistan	6
91	Denmark	35	146	Tunisia	18	202	Burkina Faso	5
92	Liechtenstein	35	147	El Salvador	17	203	Niger	5
93	Singapore	35	148	Peru	17	204	Mali	4
94	Brazil	34	149	Thailand	17	205	Afghanistan	3
95	South Korea	34	150	Cambodia	16	206	Bangladesh	3
96	Papua New Guinea	34	151	Ecuador	16	207	Ethiopia	3
97	Samoa	34	152	Ghana	16	208	Benin	2
98	Brunei	33	153	Guatemala	16	209	Nepal	2
			154	Malawi	16			

Source: World Health Statistics Annual

Health Professionals

The number of health professionals in a country has become skewed in the past fifty years because of a constant skills drain from the developing to the developed world, or from those who need it most to those who need it least. There are countries in Africa that have only one physician per 27,000 persons, but the few who graduate in this field from there eventually emigrate to France or the United States, thus depriving their compatriots of the benefit of their skills. The same lopsided flow of professionals also takes place within countries. In the United States, for example, the availability of physicians ranges from about one per 730 persons in the least well-served states to one per 150 persons in the best-served states. The rural-urban disparity in healthcare services is universal. Even when trained personnel and facilities exist in rural areas, limited financial resources may leave those facilities underserved, and a lack of good transportation may prevent those most in need from reaching the right clinic or hospital. However, "medivac" services exist in many remote areas of the world helping people to receive medical attention in time. Dental care is virtually nonexistent for most Africans and Asians except in the larger cities. In most developing countries nurses receive little professional training, especially for handling sophisticated medical instruments, and they have only little time to devote to the large number of patients for whom they have to care. Drug costs are spiraling in both developed and developing countries, but in the latter they are beyond the reach of all but the wealthiest.

18.13 Physicians

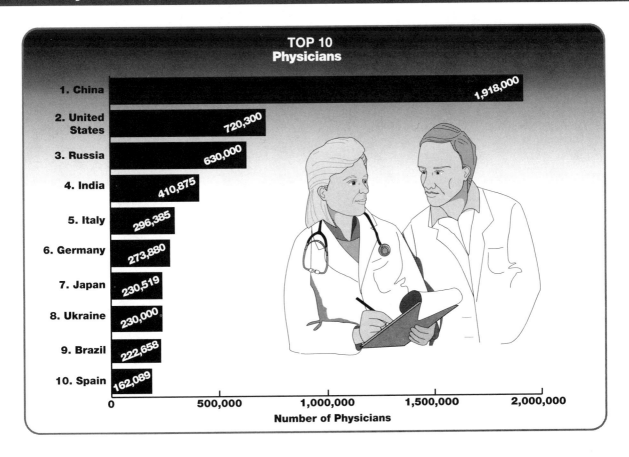

TOP 10
Physicians

1. China — 1,918,000
2. United States — 720,300
3. Russia — 630,000
4. India — 410,875
5. Italy — 296,385
6. Germany — 273,880
7. Japan — 230,519
8. Ukraine — 230,000
9. Brazil — 222,658
10. Spain — 162,089

Number of Physicians

Rank	Country/Entity	Physicians	Rank	Country/Entity	Physicians	Rank	Country/Entity	Physicians
11	France	160,235	76	Morocco	8,838	141	Macau	467
12	Mexico	146,021	77	Iraq	8,787	142	Somalia	450
13	Egypt	129,000	78	Latvia	7,714	143	Gabon	448
14	United Kingdom	91,100	79	Guatemala	7,601	144	Fiji	426
15	Argentina	88,800	80	Jordan	7,322	145	Sierra Leone	404
16	Poland	88,523	81	Lebanon	6,987	146	Mozambique	387
17	Philippines	78,445	82	Puerto Rico	6,269	147	Bahamas	373
18	Uzbekistan	76,200	83	Ireland	6,200	148	Benin	363
19	Pakistan	69,694	84	Mongolia	5,911	149	New Caledonia	358
20	Turkey	65,832	85	Cambodia	5,642	150	Burundi	354
21	Canada	63,700	86	Tunisia	5,344	151	French Polynesia	353
22	Kazakhstan	62,290	87	Libya	4,749	152	Burkina Faso	341
23	North Korea	61,200	88	Estonia	4,680	153	Botswana	339
24	South Korea	57,188	89	Singapore	4,661	154	Namibia	324
25	Cuba	46,860	90	Kenya	4,558	155	Togo	319
26	Australia	45,800	91	El Salvador	4,525	156	Netherlands Antilles	314
27	Belarus	45,000	92	Macedonia	4,516	157	Barbados	312
28	Romania	41,827	93	Bosnia and Herzegovina	4,500	158	Guinea-Bissau	274
29	Greece	40,487	94	Albania	4,467	159	Rwanda	272
30	Belgium	38,363	95	Costa Rica	4,422	160	Brunei	251
31	Netherlands	37,493	96	United Arab Emirates	4,095	161	Suriname	251
32	Hungary	37,420	97	Slovenia	4,086	162	Guyana	244
33	Iran	37,000	98	Honduras	3,803	163	Niger	237
34	Colombia	36,551	99	Sri Lanka	3,713	164	Chad	217
35	Venezuela	32,616	100	Bolivia	3,392	165	French Guiana	213
36	Czech Republic	32,195	101	Paraguay	3,341	166	Malawi	186
37	Georgia	29,900	102	Kuwait	3,077	167	Monaco	186
38	Vietnam	29,700	103	Panama	3,074	168	Virgin Islands (U.S.)	167
39	Bulgaria	29,529	104	Yemen	2,785	169	Central African Republic	157
40	Azerbaijan	29,300	105	Sudan	2,600	170	Guam	147
41	Saudi Arabia	29,227	106	Nicaragua	2,577	171	Belize	139
42	Indonesia	28,989	107	Oman	2,476	172	Lesotho	136
43	Austria	27,869	108	Congo, Dem. Rep. of	2,469	173	Mauritania	135
44	Taiwan	27,782	109	Afghanistan	2,233	174	Andorra	132
45	South Africa	26,452	110	Côte d'Ivoire	2,020	175	Cape Verde	112
46	Algeria	25,796	111	Jamaica	1,589	176	Bermuda	100
47	Bangladesh	24,911	112	Zimbabwe	1,551	177	Bhutan	100
48	Portugal	24,499	113	Nepal	1,478	178	Maldives	100
49	Israel	24,344	114	Ethiopia	1,466	179	Western Sahara	100
50	Peru	23,771	115	Cyprus	1,455	180	Equatorial Guinea	99
51	Sweden	23,000	116	Madagascar	1,392	181	Djibouti	97
52	Nigeria	21,739	117	Tanzania	1,365	182	Jersey	95
53	Switzerland	21,680	118	West Bank	1,344	183	Liberia	89
54	Yugoslavia	21,313	119	Trinidad and Tobago	1,183	184	Isle of Man	86
55	Armenia	19,000	120	Laos	1,173	185	Seychelles	84
56	Moldova	17,400	121	Réunion	1,164	186	Greenland	83
57	Chile	16,000	122	Mauritius	960	187	Swaziland	83
58	Syria	15,391	123	Cameroon	945	188	Faroe Islands	81
59	Norway	15,368	124	Malta	925	189	Guernsey	79
60	Kyrgyzstan	15,000	125	Guinea	920	190	Comoros	77
61	Lithuania	14,737	126	Luxembourg	908	191	Aruba	74
62	Denmark	14,497	127	Uganda	840	192	Eritrea	68
63	Slovakia	14,447	128	Iceland	797	193	Grenada	64
64	Turkmenistan	14,100	129	Ghana	753	194	Saint Lucia	64
65	Thailand	14,098	130	Papua New Guinea	736	195	Gambia	61
66	Finland	13,771	131	Qatar	715	196	São Tomé and Príncipe	61
67	Tajikistan	13,084	132	Zambia	713	197	Samoa	60
68	Myanmar (Burma)	12,950	133	Angola	662	198	San Marino	60
69	Ecuador	12,149	134	Martinique	652	199	Antigua and Barbuda	59
70	New Zealand	11,889	135	Haiti	641	200	Solomon Islands	52
71	Uruguay	11,241	136	Congo, Rep. of	613	201	Micronesia	45
72	Dominican Republic	11,130	137	Guadeloupe	590	202	Tonga	45
73	Malaysia	9,608	138	Senegal	520	203	Saint Vincent and the Grenadines	40
74	Hong Kong	9,196	139	Mali	483			
75	Croatia	9,138	140	Bahrain	482	204	Saint Kitts and Nevis	39

Rank	Country/Entity	Physicians	Rank	Country/Entity	Physicians	Rank	Country/Entity	Physicians
205	Liechtenstein	32	209	Northern Mariana Islands	23	213	Palau	10
206	Gibraltar	29	210	Marshall Islands	17	214	Mayotte	9
207	American Samoa	26	211	Vanuatu	12	215	Tuvalu	8
208	Dominica	23	212	Kiribati	10			

Source: World Health Statistics Annual

18.14 Population per Physician

Rank	Country/Entity	Population per Physician	Rank	Country/Entity	Population per Physician	Rank	Country/Entity	Population per Physician
1	Malawi	49,118	50	Yemen	4,549	98	Brunei	1,164
2	Eritrea	46,200	51	Botswana	4,395	99	Tuvalu	1,152
3	Mozambique	36,320	52	Nigeria	4,257	100	Bahrain	1,115
4	Niger	35,141	53	Thailand	4,165	101	Antigua and Barbuda	1,083
5	Ethiopia	30,195	54	Congo, Rep. of	4,028	102	Trinidad and Tobago	1,067
6	Chad	27,765	55	Laos	3,555	103	Algeria	1,066
7	Burkina Faso	27,158	56	Equatorial Guinea	3,532	104	Saint Kitts and Nevis	1,057
8	Rwanda	24,697	57	Myanmar (Burma)	3,485	105	Liechtenstein	966
9	Liberia	24,600	58	Marshall Islands	3,269	106	Gibraltar	951
10	Ghana	22,970	59	Guinea-Bissau	3,245	107	Peru	944
11	Uganda	22,399	60	Dominica	3,200	108	Aruba	936
12	Tanzania	20,511	61	Guyana	3,148	109	Syria	922
13	Central African Republic	18,660	62	Cape Verde	2,931	110	Turkey	917
14	Mali	18,376	63	Morocco	2,923	111	Colombia	914
15	Burundi	17,153	64	Saint Vincent and	2,708	112	Seychelles	906
16	Congo, Dem. Rep. of	15,584		the Grenadines		113	Ecuador	904
17	Angola	15,136	65	Samoa	2,682	114	Jersey	895
18	Senegal	14,825	66	Maldives	2,533	115	Macau	876
19	Gambia	14,536	67	Gabon	2,504	116	Chile	875
20	Lesotho	14,306	68	Western Sahara	2,504	117	Panama	856
21	Mauritania	14,259	69	Vietnam	2,411	118	Oman	852
22	Benin	14,216	70	Micronesia	2,311	119	Philippines	849
23	Vanuatu	14,025	71	Saint Lucia	2,235	120	Barbados	842
24	Nepal	13,777	72	Iraq	2,181	121	Guam	823
25	Somalia	13,315	73	India	2,173	122	Guernsey	804
26	Cameroon	11,848	74	Malaysia	2,153	123	Qatar	787
27	Zambia	11,414	75	Tonga	2,139	124	South Korea	784
28	Sudan	11,300	76	Bolivia	2,083	125	Taiwan	775
29	Togo	11,270	77	American Samoa	1,885	126	Costa Rica	763
30	Sierra Leone	10,832	78	São Tomé and Príncipe	1,881	127	Isle of Man	745
31	Haiti	9,846	79	Pakistan	1,863	128	Albania	729
32	Swaziland	9,265	80	Fiji	1,829	129	Bahamas	709
33	Madagascar	8,628	81	Suriname	1,685	130	Bosnia and Herzegovina	703
34	Bhutan	8,000	82	Cambodia	1,650	131	Guadeloupe	692
35	Kiribati	7,687	83	Tunisia	1,640	132	Libya	690
36	Mayotte	7,427	84	Iran	1,600	133	Hong Kong	686
37	Zimbabwe	6,909	85	Nicaragua	1,566	134	Brazil	681
38	Afghanistan	6,701	86	Belize	1,546	135	Greenland	672
39	Comoros	6,600	87	Jamaica	1,541	136	Dominican Republic	671
40	Indonesia	6,570	88	West Bank	1,536	137	French Guiana	669
41	Guinea	6,448	89	South Africa	1,529	138	Netherlands Antilles	669
42	Solomon Islands	6,154	90	Grenada	1,523	139	Singapore	653
43	Kenya	5,954	91	Palau	1,518	140	United Kingdom	641
44	Côte d'Ivoire	5,931	92	Paraguay	1,406	141	China	633
45	Papua New Guinea	5,584	93	Honduras	1,358	142	Venezuela	626
46	Djibouti	5,258	94	Northern Mariana Islands	1,324	143	Mexico	623
47	Bangladesh	4,759	95	Guatemala	1,282	144	Virgin Islands (U.S.)	622
48	Sri Lanka	4,745	96	El Salvador	1,219	145	Saudi Arabia	612
49	Namibia	4,594	97	Mauritius	1,169	146	Bermuda	609

Rank	Country/Entity	Population per Physician	Rank	Country/Entity	Population per Physician	Rank	Country/Entity	Population per Physician
147	Jordan	607	170	Macedonia	432	193	Uzbekistan	299
148	French Polynesia	595	171	Netherlands	412	194	Germany	298
149	Martinique	588	172	Malta	403	195	Austria	289
150	Ireland	580	173	Portugal	403	196	Norway	285
151	Réunion	571	174	Australia	400	197	Bulgaria	283
152	Puerto Rico	558	175	Sweden	382	198	Uruguay	282
153	Faroe Islands	550	176	Argentina	376	199	Hungary	273
154	Kuwait	549	177	Mongolia	376	200	Kazakhstan	265
155	United Arab Emirates	545	178	San Marino	375	201	Belgium	264
156	Romania	544	179	Finland	371	202	Greece	258
157	Japan	542	180	Slovakia	371	203	Azerbaijan	256
158	Lebanon	529	181	North Korea	370	204	Lithuania	252
159	Croatia	524	182	United States	365	205	Moldova	251
160	New Caledonia	513	183	France	361	206	Spain	241
161	Yugoslavia	495	184	Denmark	358	207	Russia	235
162	Andorra	491	185	Iceland	335	208	Cuba	231
163	Slovenia	489	186	Latvia	330	209	Ukraine	224
164	Egypt	472	187	Switzerland	323	210	Belarus	222
165	Canada	465	188	Czech Republic	321	211	Israel	214
166	Luxembourg	454	189	Turkmenistan	320	212	Armenia	198
167	Tajikistan	439	190	Estonia	319	213	Italy	193
168	Poland	436	191	Kyrgyzstan	301	214	Georgia	182
169	Cyprus	433	192	New Zealand	301	215	Monaco	169

Source: World Health Statistics Annual

18.15 Dentists

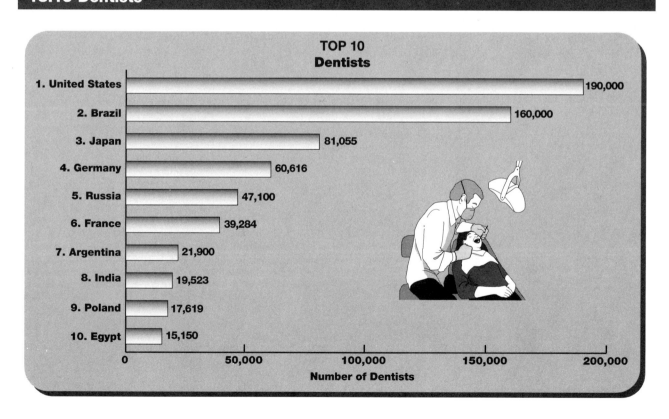

TOP 10
Dentists

Rank	Country	Number of Dentists
1. United States		190,000
2. Brazil		160,000
3. Japan		81,055
4. Germany		60,616
5. Russia		47,100
6. France		39,284
7. Argentina		21,900
8. India		19,523
9. Poland		17,619
10. Egypt		15,150

Number of Dentists

Rank	Country/Entity	Dentists	Rank	Country/Entity	Dentists	Rank	Country/Entity	Dentists
11	Canada	14,621	66	El Salvador	1,182	121	Fiji	40
12	Colombia	13,815	67	Paraguay	1,160	122	Ghana	39
13	South Korea	13,681	68	Kyrgyzstan	1,100	123	Barbados	38
14	Spain	13,242	69	Albania	1,099	124	Brunei	38
15	Turkey	11,457	70	Macedonia	1,087	125	French Guiana	38
16	Greece	10,865	71	Guatemala	1,065	126	Cambodia	36
17	Italy	10,814	72	Tunisia	1,004	127	Congo, Rep. of	35
18	Australia	9,100	73	Latvia	968	128	Guyana	34
19	Cuba	8,057	74	Tajikistan	926	129	Gabon	32
20	Syria	8,025	75	Puerto Rico	902	130	Greenland	31
21	Peru	7,945	76	Myanmar (Burma)	860	131	Zambia	26
22	Venezuela	7,945	77	Singapore	835	132	Bermuda	22
23	Algeria	7,763	78	Estonia	820	133	Macau	22
24	Taiwan	7,332	79	Bangladesh	812	134	Monaco	22
25	Netherlands	7,328	80	Libya	686	135	Togo	22
26	Kazakhstan	7,075	81	Panama	656	136	Mauritania	20
27	Belgium	6,983	82	Kenya	630	137	Aruba	19
28	Israel	6,956	83	Honduras	622	138	Burkina Faso	19
29	Czech Republic	6,267	84	United Arab Emirates	563	139	Benin	16
30	Romania	6,163	85	Bosnia and Herzegovina	550	140	Antigua and Barbuda	13
31	Iran	6,080	86	Cyprus	498	141	Guinea-Bissau	13
32	Mexico	5,612	87	West Bank	445	142	Mali	13
33	Bulgaria	5,467	88	Kuwait	437	143	Belize	12
34	Norway	5,222	89	Sri Lanka	333	144	Liechtenstein	12
35	Chile	5,200	90	Nicaragua	321	145	Angola	10
36	Denmark	5,088	91	Mongolia	299	146	Djibouti	10
37	Hungary	5,069	92	Réunion	295	147	Bhutan	9
38	Sweden	4,700	93	Iceland	273	148	Burundi	9
39	Finland	4,696	94	Jamaica	270	149	Seychelles	9
40	Switzerland	4,400	95	Afghanistan	267	150	Tonga	9
41	Uzbekistan	4,300	96	Côte d'Ivoire	219	151	Central African Republic	8
42	Yugoslavia	4,075	97	Luxembourg	203	152	Grenada	8
43	South Africa	4,029	98	Zimbabwe	194	153	Saint Kitts and Nevis	8
44	Uruguay	3,740	99	Yemen	167	154	American Samoa	7
45	Austria	3,687	100	Mauritius	152	155	Micronesia	7
46	Lebanon	3,100	101	Oman	152	156	Rwanda	7
47	Thailand	2,984	102	Trinidad and Tobago	134	157	Samoa	7
48	Pakistan	2,753	103	Malta	122	158	Swaziland	7
49	Slovakia	2,236	104	Guadeloupe	119	159	Comoros	6
50	Jordan	2,180	105	Martinique	112	160	Dominica	6
51	New Zealand	1,959	106	Mozambique	108	161	Saint Lucia	6
52	Dominican Republic	1,898	107	New Caledonia	97	162	Saint Vincent and the Grenadines	6
53	Croatia	1,798	108	Haiti	95			
54	Malaysia	1,750	109	Madagascar	89	163	Chad	5
55	Lithuania	1,742	110	Qatar	88	164	Liberia	5
56	Iraq	1,656	111	French Polynesia	81	165	Niger	5
57	Hong Kong	1,654	112	Netherlands Antilles	67	166	São Tomé and Príncipe	5
58	Bolivia	1,643	113	Bahamas	58	167	Marshall Islands	4
59	Philippines	1,614	114	Senegal	58	168	Northern Mariana Islands	4
60	Ecuador	1,524	115	Cameroon	55	169	Vanuatu	3
61	Portugal	1,509	116	Namibia	51	170	Somalia	2
62	Nigeria	1,335	117	Nepal	45	171	Tuvalu	2
63	Costa Rica	1,332	118	Congo, Dem. Rep. of	41	172	Mayotte	1
64	Morocco	1,204	119	Bahrain	40			
65	Slovenia	1,194	120	Faroe Islands	40			

Source: World Health Statistics Annual

18.16 Nurses

Rank	Country/Entity	Nurses	Rank	Country/Entity	Nurses	Rank	Country/Entity	Nurses
1	United States	2,044,000	63	Libya	13,849	125	Zambia	1,503
2	China	1,125,000	64	Morocco	13,358	126	Guadeloupe	1,470
3	Russia	1,008,800	65	Iraq	13,206	127	Martinique	1,460
4	Japan	891,021	66	Singapore	13,193	128	Afghanistan	1,451
5	Germany	708,000	67	Latvia	12,559	129	Netherlands Antilles	1,441
6	Ukraine	598,000	68	Tunisia	12,195	130	Central African Republic	1,353
7	India	449,351	69	Bosnia and Herzegovina	11,900	131	Brunei	1,288
8	France	330,943	70	Sri Lanka	11,818	132	Burundi	1,270
9	United Kingdom	284,578	71	Ghana	11,808	133	Swaziland	1,264
10	Canada	262,288	72	Cambodia	9,950	134	Benin	1,236
11	Uzbekistan	249,600	73	Myanmar (Burma)	9,851	135	Togo	1,187
12	Kazakhstan	213,320	74	Bangladesh	9,630	136	Bahamas	1,067
13	Poland	210,425	75	Angola	9,334	137	Suriname	995
14	Italy	170,409	76	Mongolia	9,183	138	Liberia	908
15	Mexico	166,644	77	United Arab Emirates	8,506	139	Barbados	889
16	Spain	161,852	78	Kuwait	8,337	140	Chad	878
17	Australia	160,500	79	Estonia	7,302	141	Lesotho	874
18	South Africa	158,538	80	Albania	6,801	142	Macau	861
19	Indonesia	138,816	81	Honduras	6,288	143	Rwanda	835
20	Finland	131,829	82	Cameroon	6,053	144	Mauritania	819
21	Netherlands	124,000	83	Oman	6,036	145	Gabon	759
22	South Korea	120,415	84	Dominican Republic	6,035	146	Guyana	681
23	Belarus	117,000	85	Yemen	5,772	147	New Caledonia	669
24	Thailand	94,103	86	Chile	5,653	148	Guam	594
25	Sweden	91,400	87	Macedonia	5,638	149	French Polynesia	586
26	Nigeria	80,186	88	Laos	5,593	150	Bermuda	553
27	Cuba	73,943	89	El Salvador	5,094	151	Greenland	539
28	Azerbaijan	70,100	90	Nepal	5,015	152	Aruba	515
29	Norway	68,308	91	Paraguay	4,558	153	French Guiana	495
30	Georgia	64,100	92	Namibia	4,471	154	Eritrea	488
31	Denmark	63,841	93	Jordan	4,304	155	Solomon Islands	447
32	Taiwan	61,494	94	Ecuador	4,215	156	Gambia	430
33	Saudi Arabia	61,246	95	Malta	4,000	157	Faroe Islands	385
34	Turkey	56,280	96	Côte d'Ivoire	3,691	158	Grenada	365
35	Hungary	54,792	97	Mozambique	3,533	159	Seychelles	346
36	Vietnam	53,700	98	Lebanon	3,500	160	Gibraltar	302
37	Venezuela	52,260	99	Ethiopia	3,496	161	Belize	300
38	Bulgaria	51,269	100	Botswana	3,329	162	Samoa	298
39	Iran	48,639	101	Madagascar	3,124	163	Monaco	293
40	Moldova	48,400	102	Panama	2,823	164	Tonga	292
41	Colombia	46,376	103	Réunion	2,785	165	Malawi	284
42	New Zealand	45,107	104	Uganda	2,782	166	Maldives	281
43	Turkmenistan	43,000	105	Haiti	2,725	167	Dominica	265
44	Kyrgyzstan	42,300	106	Mauritius	2,629	168	Saint Kitts and Nevis	260
45	Austria	40,756	107	Burkina Faso	2,627	169	Vanuatu	259
46	Tajikistan	38,852	108	Papua New Guinea	2,614	170	Saint Lucia	256
47	Hong Kong	36,395	109	Costa Rica	2,600	171	Bhutan	233
48	Malaysia	34,996	110	Cyprus	2,536	172	Micronesia	230
49	Armenia	34,900	111	West Bank	2,279	173	Saint Vincent and the Grenadines	224
50	Greece	34,314	112	Trinidad and Tobago	2,260			
51	Portugal	30,975	113	Niger	2,213	174	São Tomé and Príncipe	223
52	Lithuania	29,259	114	Nicaragua	2,144	175	Cape Verde	205
53	Congo, Dem. Rep. of	27,601	115	Uruguay	2,139	176	Antigua and Barbuda	179
54	Kenya	27,143	116	Iceland	1,952	177	Comoros	155
55	Syria	23,151	117	Bolivia	1,869	178	Equatorial Guinea	154
56	Zimbabwe	22,590	118	Jamaica	1,836	179	Kiribati	147
57	Pakistan	22,531	119	Qatar	1,834	180	American Samoa	140
58	Puerto Rico	19,666	120	Somalia	1,834	181	Marshall Islands	124
59	Argentina	18,000	121	Mali	1,674	182	Northern Mariana Islands	103
60	Peru	15,026	122	Fiji	1,631	183	Palau	84
61	Philippines	14,853	123	Congo, Rep. of	1,624	184	Mayotte	51
62	Guatemala	14,401	124	Bahrain	1,608	185	Tuvalu	39

Source: World Health Statistics Annual

18.17 Pharmacists

Rank	Country/Entity	Pharmacists	Rank	Country/Entity	Pharmacists	Rank	Country/Entity	Pharmacists
1	China	418,000	54	Costa Rica	1,254	107	New Caledonia	78
2	United States	184,000	55	Kyrgyzstan	1,122	108	Gabon	71
3	Japan	176,871	56	Mongolia	1,113	109	Ghana	67
4	Brazil	57,047	57	Hong Kong	1,067	110	Togo	65
5	Italy	53,948	58	Slovenia	1,019	111	Monaco	64
6	France	53,085	59	Honduras	975	112	Lesotho	60
7	Germany	44,696	60	Kuwait	969	113	Congo, Dem. Rep. of	59
8	South Korea	43,269	61	Estonia	930	114	Mali	57
9	Spain	40,323	62	Uruguay	922	115	Burundi	55
10	United Kingdom	37,832	63	Ecuador	906	116	Bahamas	52
11	Egypt	34,700	64	Singapore	858	117	French Guiana	47
12	Canada	22,121	65	Albania	772	118	French Polynesia	47
13	Taiwan	19,667	66	Tajikistan	709	119	Macau	41
14	Poland	19,450	67	United Arab Emirates	686	120	Jamaica	37
15	Turkey	18,366	68	Malta	648	121	Netherlands Antilles	37
16	Belgium	13,926	69	Kenya	605	122	Niger	29
17	Australia	12,900	70	Finland	584	123	Grenada	28
18	South Africa	9,447	71	Trinidad and Tobago	534	124	Bermuda	27
19	Kazakhstan	8,722	72	Sri Lanka	520	125	Dominica	27
20	Greece	8,147	73	Afghanistan	510	126	Saint Vincent and the Grenadines	27
21	Bangladesh	7,485	74	Cyprus	423			
22	Russia	7,300	75	Zimbabwe	411	127	Rwanda	25
23	Vietnam	6,500	76	Oman	370	128	Western Sahara	24
24	Nigeria	6,474	77	Ethiopia	364	129	Zambia	24
25	Romania	6,432	78	Macedonia	357	130	Central African Republic	22
26	Portugal	5,950	79	Mozambique	353	131	Guyana	22
27	Sweden	5,945	80	Luxembourg	336	132	Madagascar	19
28	Peru	5,940	81	Slovakia	322	133	Nepal	18
29	Syria	5,919	82	Yemen	295	134	Belize	17
30	Venezuela	5,615	83	Latvia	292	135	Brunei	15
31	Thailand	5,575	84	Réunion	266	136	Djibouti	14
32	Iran	4,185	85	Cambodia	262	137	Saint Kitts and Nevis	14
33	Israel	4,127	86	Chile	230	138	Antigua and Barbuda	13
34	Czech Republic	4,032	87	Martinique	225	139	Aruba	13
35	Indonesia	3,988	88	Mauritius	223	140	Swaziland	13
36	Pakistan	3,772	89	Cameroon	206	141	Guinea-Bissau	12
37	New Zealand	3,532	90	Guadeloupe	206	142	Chad	10
38	Algeria	3,425	91	Senegal	200	143	Faroe Islands	10
39	Jordan	3,265	92	Guinea	197	144	Greenland	10
40	Lithuania	3,203	93	Qatar	187	145	Cape Verde	9
41	Netherlands	2,484	94	Somalia	180	146	Micronesia	7
42	Morocco	2,470	95	Iceland	176	147	Comoros	6
43	Lebanon	2,369	96	Congo, Rep. of	175	148	Mauritania	6
44	Puerto Rico	2,111	97	West Bank	149	149	Samoa	6
45	Austria	2,068	98	Barbados	138	150	Vanuatu	6
46	Hungary	2,024	99	Côte d'Ivoire	135	151	Bhutan	5
47	Yugoslavia	2,016	100	Maldives	134	152	Malawi	5
48	Bulgaria	1,736	101	Dominican Republic	115	153	Seychelles	4
49	Uzbekistan	1,700	102	Panama	115	154	American Samoa	2
50	Tunisia	1,685	103	Burkina Faso	113	155	Liechtenstein	2
51	Croatia	1,598	104	Bahrain	101	156	Northern Mariana Islands	2
52	Switzerland	1,591	105	Namibia	91	157	Mayotte	1
53	Iraq	1,561	106	Benin	86	158	São Tomé and Príncipe	1

Source: World Health Statistics Annual

Certain deadly diseases are peculiar to the developed world and certain others to the developing world. Deaths from cancer and heart disease are ones that are apparently more prevalent in the developed world. Although the cause and origin of these diseases have not been settled, it is commonly believed that richer diet and pollution are contributing factors. Causes of death can be determined only imprecisely. Even in a developed country such determinations are left to nonmedical personnel, but in a developing country with only one physician for 10,000 persons, there are few physicians to perform autopsies to assess accurately the cause of death after the fact or infer the cause of death from records based on prior diagnosis. Statistics on causes of death seek to identify the underlying cause (that which sets the final train of events leading to death) but often must settle for the most immediate cause or symptom. Thus if a diabetic dies of a cardiovascular disease, the cause of death may be noted as a heart attack, but the ultimate cause would have been diabetes.

18.18 Deaths from Cancer

Rank	Country/Entity	Deaths from Cancer per 100,000 Population	Rank	Country/Entity	Deaths from Cancer per 100,000 Population	Rank	Country/Entity	Deaths from Cancer per 100,000 Population
1	Hungary	318.7	41	Malta	187.8	80	French Polynesia	83.0
2	Denmark	296.6	42	Greenland	186.3	81	Grenada	82.8
3	Guernsey	282.3	43	Belarus	184.5	82	Bahamas	80.4
4	Czech Republic	277.1	44	Bermuda	181.5	83	Costa Rica	80.0
5	United Kingdom	275.4	45	Barbados	178.5	84	Turkey	80.0
6	Italy	270.5	46	Yugoslavia	167.7	85	Virgin Islands (U.S.)	78.9
7	Belgium	270.1	47	Iceland	166.5	86	Macau	76.6
8	Germany	260.2	48	Romania	163.4	87	Peru	73.0
9	France	247.5	49	Thailand	162.0	88	Northern Mariana Islands	70.2
10	Austria	243.5	50	Hong Kong	156.1	89	Tuvalu	70.0
11	Switzerland	238.7	51	Netherlands Antilles	149.0	90	North Korea	69.0
12	Netherlands	237.1	52	Argentina	143.0	91	Marshall Islands	68.4
13	Norway	237.0	53	Moldova	138.0	92	Suriname	68.0
14	Slovenia	235.6	54	Israel	137.6	93	Azerbaijan	67.4
15	Luxembourg	234.5	55	Palau	136.9	94	Kyrgyzstan	67.3
16	Sweden	229.8	56	Martinique	135.5	95	Saint Lucia	64.4
17	San Marino	229.4	57	Liechtenstein	134.6	96	Colombia	62.9
18	Spain	224.3	58	Kazakhstan	133.5	97	Iran	61.0
19	Uruguay	222.8	59	New Caledonia	129.0	98	Mauritius	60.2
20	Latvia	220.1	60	Cuba	128.7	99	Guam	60.0
21	Estonia	218.1	61	Seychelles	128.6	100	French Guiana	58.1
22	Isle of Man	217.4	62	Singapore	128.2	101	Panama	57.3
23	Croatia	216.1	63	Aruba	124.9	102	Nicaragua	56.0
24	Greece	206.7	64	Bosnia and Herzegovina	122.6	103	Turkmenistan	55.4
25	Slovakia	206.5	65	Puerto Rico	122.2	104	Tonga	54.9
26	Ireland	205.6	66	Guadeloupe	121.2	105	Vietnam	54.0
27	New Zealand	205.1	67	China	117.7	106	Albania	53.8
28	United States	204.5	68	Dominica	116.6	107	Paraguay	53.0
29	Gibraltar	203.9	69	Chile	111.5	108	Belize	52.4
30	Russia	203.0	70	South Korea	110.3	109	Venezuela	51.1
31	Lithuania	200.7	71	Taiwan	101.5	110	Ecuador	50.0
32	Ukraine	198.9	72	Georgia	100.8	111	Mexico	49.9
33	Poland	198.2	73	Réunion	99.7	112	El Salvador	49.0
34	Canada	196.7	74	Saint Kitts and Nevis	95.5	113	Uzbekistan	48.2
35	Japan	196.4	75	Brazil	94.0	114	South Africa	48.0
36	Portugal	193.6	76	Saint Vincent and the Grenadines	94.0	115	American Samoa	46.8
37	Bulgaria	192.4				116	Dominican Republic	45.0
38	Finland	192.3	77	Armenia	93.8	117	Antigua and Barbuda	44.5
39	Faroe Islands	191.3	78	Trinidad and Tobago	86.4	118	Cape Verde	43.8
40	Australia	190.0	79	Jamaica	84.1	119	Tajikistan	40.7

Rank	Country/Entity	Deaths from Cancer per 100,000 Population	Rank	Country/Entity	Deaths from Cancer per 100,000 Population	Rank	Country/Entity	Deaths from Cancer per 100,000 Population
120	Nauru	38.0	128	Micronesia	27.1	136	São Tomé and Príncipe	19.6
121	Guyana	37.1	129	Brunei	27.0	137	Morocco	14.0
122	Fiji	35.5	130	Malawi	27.0	138	Honduras	12.4
123	Philippines	35.2	131	Sri Lanka	26.7	139	Syria	12.0
124	Bahrain	32.3	132	Kuwait	22.6	140	Samoa	11.2
125	Guatemala	29.8	133	Egypt	22.0	141	Macedonia	6.2
126	Vanuatu	29.2	134	Qatar	21.4			
127	Zimbabwe	28.4	135	Malaysia	20.4			

Source: World Health Statistics Annual

18.19 Deaths from Heart Disease

Rank	Country/Entity	Deaths from Heart Disease per 100,000 Population	Rank	Country/Entity	Deaths from Heart Disease per 100,000 Population	Rank	Country/Entity	Deaths from Heart Disease per 100,000 Population
1	Latvia	915.9	49	Azerbaijan	336.3	96	Tonga	158.5
2	Bulgaria	869.8	50	Netherlands	335.9	97	Chile	157.4
3	Estonia	815.7	51	Spain	334.2	98	Marshall Islands	155.1
4	Russia	784.0	52	Kyrgyzstan	333.0	99	South Korea	155.0
5	Ukraine	782.6	53	Liechtenstein	328.2	100	Fiji	153.4
6	Hungary	722.9	54	San Marino	324.8	101	Tuvalu	150.0
7	Romania	707.7	55	Malta	324.2	102	Colombia	144.7
8	Lithuania	654.3	56	Egypt	314.4	103	São Tomé and Príncipe	143.5
9	Czech Republic	638.4	57	Iran	304.0	104	Nicaragua	142.0
10	Belarus	624.7	58	France	302.0	105	Guam	141.8
11	Gibraltar	601.4	59	Iceland	300.4	106	Taiwan	140.1
12	Yugoslavia	573.7	60	Uzbekistan	300.3	107	Cape Verde	135.8
13	Isle of Man	552.7	61	Australia	296.0	108	Northern Mariana Islands	135.7
14	Georgia	548.4	62	Cuba	294.7	109	Hong Kong	131.3
15	Slovakia	541.1	63	Mauritius	288.6	110	American Samoa	131.1
16	Austria	539.9	64	Seychelles	288.4	111	Costa Rica	126.6
17	Germany	527.4	65	Canada	274.4	112	Bahamas	126.3
18	Croatia	517.4	66	Dominica	273.5	113	Vietnam	123.8
19	Sweden	514.8	67	Trinidad and Tobago	270.0	114	El Salvador	120.0
20	Poland	512.7	68	Israel	268.8	115	Macau	119.5
21	Moldova	504.4	69	Grenada	264.3	116	Panama	118.4
22	Norway	483.7	70	Thailand	250.0	117	French Polynesia	118.0
23	Greece	478.5	71	Puerto Rico	242.3	118	New Caledonia	115.3
24	United Kingdom	473.3	72	Saint Vincent and the Grenadines	239.2	119	Peru	115.0
25	Denmark	471.3				120	Venezuela	115.0
26	Kazakhstan	456.6	73	Japan	239.1	121	French Guiana	114.3
27	Finland	448.6	74	Brazil	238.0	122	Sri Lanka	101.4
28	Saint Kitts and Nevis	443.2	75	Antigua and Barbuda	237.5	123	Mexico	100.7
29	Guernsey	441.1	76	Virgin Islands (U.S.)	232.7	124	Ecuador	93.1
30	Portugal	431.2	77	North Korea	224.9	125	South Africa	91.2
31	Italy	423.7	78	Tajikistan	222.8	126	Nauru	89.0
32	Slovenia	408.1	79	Martinique	208.0	127	Bahrain	86.6
33	Belgium	398.9	80	China	206.4	128	Syria	86.0
34	Ireland	392.1	81	Saint Lucia	205.6	129	Philippines	82.2
35	Luxembourg	391.1	82	Guyana	202.5	130	Brunei	80.0
36	Macedonia	385.8	83	Suriname	193.0	131	Kuwait	76.5
37	Switzerland	381.5	84	Palau	192.9	132	Netherlands Antilles	71.6
38	Uruguay	378.4	85	Aruba	189.5	133	Qatar	59.9
39	Armenia	369.7	86	Jamaica	189.5	134	Guatemala	57.2
40	Turkey	369.0	87	Greenland	188.2	135	Malaysia	54.0
41	Barbados	366.8	88	Albania	187.0	136	Micronesia	53.2
42	United States	355.1	89	Guadeloupe	186.8	137	Malawi	50.0
43	Faroe Islands	352.8	90	Singapore	186.2	138	Honduras	48.4
44	New Zealand	346.7	91	Maldives	170.1	139	Zimbabwe	40.8
45	Bermuda	344.4	92	Réunion	170.1	140	Vanuatu	39.0
46	Bosnia and Herzegovina	344.1	93	Dominican Republic	165.0	141	Morocco	35.5
47	Argentina	337.3	94	Belize	164.0	142	Samoa	24.2
48	Turkmenistan	337.2	95	Paraguay	162.0			

Source: World Health Statistics Annual

The war against tobacco, like the war against drugs, appears to be an unwinnable war. Despite social and legal sanctions against smoking, and despite medical evidence as to the toxicity of tobacco smoke, the number of cigarettes sold throughout the world has continued to rise, although per capita use has declined slightly. This ranking examines the prevalence of smoking. With a few exceptions more men smoke than women. However, the most disturbing trend is the popularity of smoking by teenagers.

Rank	Country/Entity	Percentage of Men Smokers, 1985–1988	Percentage of Women Smokers, 1985–1988	Rank	Country/Entity	Percentage of Men Smokers, 1985–1988	Percentage of Women Smokers, 1985–1988
1	Vietnam	73	4	41	Hungary	40	27
2	India	70	—	42	Brazil	40	25
3	Cambodia	70	10	43	Argentina	40	23
4	Nepal	69	13	44	Morocco	40	9
5	South Korea	68	—	45	Mongolia	40	7
6	Romania	68	32	46	Iraq	40	5
7	Russia	67	30	47	Italy	38	26
8	Latvia	67	12	48	Chile	38	25
9	Dominican Republic	66	14	49	Guatemala	38	18
10	Togo	65	14	50	Portugal	38	15
11	Turkey	63	24	51	Mexico	38	14
12	Laos	62	8	52	El Salvador	38	12
13	Bangladesh	60	15	53	Lesotho	38	1
14	Japan	59	15	54	Denmark	37	37
15	Myanmar (Burma)	58	2	55	Germany	37	22
16	Ukraine	57	22	56	Norway	36	36
17	Sri Lanka	55	1	57	Netherlands	36	29
18	Saudi Arabia	53	—	58	Switzerland	36	26
19	Estonia	52	24	59	Zimbabwe	36	15
20	South Africa	52	17	60	Honduras	36	11
21	Kuwait	52	12	61	Slovenia	35	23
22	Lithuania	52	10	62	Costa Rica	35	20
23	Poland	51	29	63	Colombia	35	19
24	Bolivia	50	21	64	Singapore	32	3
25	Albania	50	8	65	Canada	31	29
26	Cuba	49	25	66	Belgium	31	19
27	Bulgaria	49	17	67	Ireland	29	28
28	Thailand	49	4	68	Australia	29	21
29	Spain	48	25	69	Venezuela	29	12
30	Mauritius	47	4	70	Hong Kong	29	3
31	Greece	46	28	71	United Kingdom	28	26
32	Papua New Guinea	46	28	72	United States	28	23
33	Israel	45	30	73	Finland	27	19
34	Czech Republic	43	31	74	Pakistan	27	4
35	Slovakia	43	26	75	Turkmenistan	27	1
36	Jamaica	43	13	76	New Zealand	24	22
37	Austria	42	27	77	Nigeria	24	7
38	Uruguay	41	27	78	Paraguay	24	6
39	Peru	41	13	79	Sweden	22	24
40	France	40	27				

Source: World Development Report

AIDS, or acquired immunodeficiency syndrome, has been described as the Black Plague of the late twentieth and twenty-first centuries. Almost all countries have been affected by AIDS to some degree, and the toll has been heavy in many countries, especially in Africa, the home of the disease. The disease has not only challenged the ability of medical researchers to find a cure, but also has changed sexual and social mores drastically. The number of reported cases in the following table is only the tip of the iceberg. More cases are unreported because of social stigma, and the country and global totals may be considerably higher than indicated on the list.

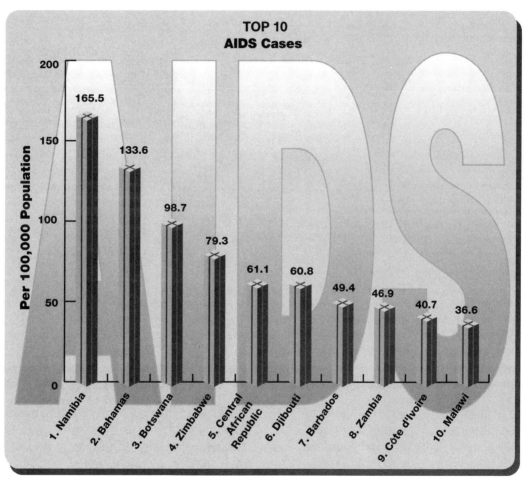

TOP 10
AIDS Cases

Per 100,000 Population

Rank	Country/Entity	AIDS Cases per 100,000 Population	Rank	Country/Entity	AIDS Cases per 100,000 Population	Rank	Country/Entity	AIDS Cases per 100,000 Population
11	Togo	35.8	19	Antigua and Barbuda	19.7	27	Lesotho	16.4
12	Trinidad and Tobago	31.2	20	Dominica	19.7	28	Suriname	14.6
13	Thailand	30.2	21	Grenada	19.6	29	Spain	14.3
14	Swaziland	28.3	22	Chad	19.0	30	Uganda	13.8
15	Eritrea	24.7	23	Equatorial Guinea	18.1	31	United States	13.8
16	Gabon	23.4	24	Belize	17.2	32	Honduras	13.7
17	Kenya	22.4	25	Guyana	17.1	33	Guinea	13.4
18	Jamaica	21.4	26	Saint Lucia	16.8	34	Mozambique	12.6

Rank	Country/Entity	AIDS Cases per 100,000 Population	Rank	Country/Entity	AIDS Cases per 100,000 Population	Rank	Country/Entity	AIDS Cases per 100,000 Population
35	Cameroon	10.9	72	Chile	2.2	109	Saint Vincent and the Grenadines	0.5
36	Brazil	10.0	73	United Kingdom	2.1	110	Saudi Arabia	0.5
37	Saint Kitts and Nevis	9.7	74	Greece	2.0	111	Vietnam	0.5
38	Burkina Faso	9.2	75	Senegal	1.7	112	Bolivia	0.4
39	Panama	9.1	76	South Africa	1.7	113	Croatia	0.4
40	Benin	9.0	77	Austria	1.6	114	Finland	0.4
41	Cape Verde	8.9	78	New Zealand	1.6	115	Qatar	0.4
42	Burundi	8.8	79	Papua New Guinea	1.6	116	Slovenia	0.4
43	Italy	8.6	80	Belgium	1.5	117	Yemen	0.4
44	Guatemala	7.6	81	Ethiopia	1.5	118	Kuwait	0.3
45	Portugal	7.3	82	Malaysia	1.5	119	Laos	0.3
46	El Salvador	7.1	83	Myanmar (Burma)	1.5	120	Nigeria	0.3
47	Niger	6.9	84	Sweden	1.5	121	Poland	0.3
48	Gambia	6.8	85	Germany	1.4	122	Ukraine	0.3
49	Ghana	6.5	86	Ireland	1.4	123	Algeria	0.2
50	France	6.3	87	Hong Kong	1.2	124	Armenia	0.2
51	Argentina	5.9	88	Norway	1.2	125	Czech Republic	0.2
52	Costa Rica	5.5	89	Samoa	1.2	126	Japan	0.2
53	Mali	5.3	90	Iceland	1.1	127	Latvia	0.2
54	Uruguay	4.9	91	Malta	1.1	128	Lebanon	0.2
55	Dominican Republic	4.6	92	Angola	1.0	129	Morocco	0.2
56	Mexico	4.4	93	Paraguay	1.0	130	Nepal	0.2
57	Switzerland	4.4	94	Bahrain	0.9	131	Bulgaria	0.1
58	Peru	4.1	95	Cuba	0.9	132	India	0.1
59	Guinea-Bissau	3.4	96	Sierra Leone	0.9	133	Iran	0.1
60	Singapore	3.2	97	Maldives	0.8	134	Iraq	0.1
61	Australia	3.1	98	Sudan	0.8	135	Jordan	0.1
62	Denmark	3.0	99	Brunei	0.7	136	South Korea	0.1
63	São Tomé and Príncipe	3.0	100	Israel	0.7	137	Lithuania	0.1
64	Cambodia	2.9	101	Ecuador	0.6	138	Macedonia	0.1
65	Colombia	2.9	102	Mauritania	0.6	139	Philippines	0.1
66	Luxembourg	2.9	103	Nicaragua	0.6	140	Sri Lanka	0.1
67	Venezuela	2.8	104	Tunisia	0.6	141	Syria	0.1
68	Canada	2.7	105	Cyprus	0.5	142	Turkey	0.1
69	Seychelles	2.7	106	Estonia	0.5			
70	Netherlands	2.4	107	Hungary	0.5			
71	Romania	2.4	108	Oman	0.5			

Source: World Health Statistics Annual

18.22 Suicides

Suicide is a leading cause of death in many developed countries, and it is the only one that is not classifiable as a medical malady, and one for which there is no cure. Apparently, it is related to the stress of life and consequent manic depression, but the exact progression is not clear. Certain age groups (especially adolescents) and social classes are more prone than others to suicide.

Rank	Country/Entity	Suicides per 100,000 Population	Rank	Country/Entity	Suicides per 100,000 Population	Rank	Country/Entity	Suicides per 100,000 Population
1	Hungary	38.2	9	Sweden	17.8	17	Canada	13.1
2	Finland	27.5	10	United Kingdom	17.6	18	New Zealand	12.6
3	Denmark	22.4	11	Japan	15.4	19	United States	12.2
4	Austria	21.7	12	Norway	15.3	20	Netherlands	10.0
5	Belgium	21.0	13	Germany	14.5	21	Portugal	8.5
6	Switzerland	20.1	14	Bulgaria	14.1	22	Spain	7.1
7	France	19.6	15	Poland	13.8	23	Italy	7.0
8	Czechoslovakia	18.3	16	Australia	13.3			

Source: World Health Statistics Annual

Water, like air, is easily subject to contamination, particularly in communities where there are no filtration or water purification systems and water and sewage are not separated. In many countries in the Third World, people bathe in the river or lake from which they draw their drinking water, and they also use the same source for doing their laundry and cooking. In the absence of a septic system, sewage flows into the same rivers and lakes and then is used for household purposes. In many Western countries, the problem is less severe although of a different order. Chemicals and toxic substances leach into underground reservoirs and contaminate well springs. Ensuring safe water is essential for maintaining public health, a task that is becoming more difficult in the absence of proper environmental controls.

Rank	Country/Entity	Percentage of Population with Access to Safe Water, 1994–1995	Rank	Country/Entity	Percentage of Population with Access to Safe Water, 1994–1995	Rank	Country/Entity	Percentage of Population with Access to Safe Water, 1994–1995
1	Austria	100	45	Bahamas	97	89	Kyrgyzstan	75
2	Bahrain	100	46	Seychelles	97	90	Zimbabwe	74
3	Barbados	100	47	Ukraine	97	91	Mauritania	72
4	Belgium	100	48	Chile	96	92	Suriname	72
5	Canada	100	49	Colombia	96	93	Vanuatu	72
6	Costa Rica	100	50	Croatia	96	94	Benin	70
7	Cyprus	100	51	Antigua and Barbuda	95	95	Botswana	70
8	Czech Republic	100	52	Australia	95	96	Ecuador	70
9	Denmark	100	53	Equatorial Guinea	95	97	Honduras	70
10	Finland	100	54	Japan	95	98	Jamaica	70
11	France	100	55	Cuba	94	99	São Tomé and Príncipe	70
12	Germany	100	56	Hungary	94	100	South Africa	70
13	Hong Kong	100	57	Saudi Arabia	93	101	Gabon	67
14	Iceland	100	58	Brazil	92	102	Togo	67
15	Ireland	100	59	Turkey	92	103	Rwanda	66
16	Italy	100	60	Brunei	90	104	Guyana	65
17	North Korea	100	61	Djibouti	90	105	Argentina	64
18	Kuwait	100	62	Malaysia	90	106	Guatemala	64
19	Lebanon	100	63	Samoa	90	107	India	63
20	Luxembourg	100	64	United States	90	108	Indonesia	63
21	Malta	100	65	Iran	89	109	El Salvador	62
22	Mauritius	100	66	Jordan	89	110	Gambia	61
23	Micronesia	100	67	South Korea	89	111	Bolivia	60
24	Netherlands	100	68	Maldives	88	112	Congo, Rep. of	60
25	New Zealand	100	69	Venezuela	88	113	Pakistan	60
26	Norway	100	70	Mexico	87	114	Peru	60
27	Poland	100	71	Syria	87	115	Morocco	59
28	Portugal	100	72	Tunisia	86	116	Burundi	58
29	Qatar	100	73	Grenada	85	117	Guinea-Bissau	57
30	Romania	100	74	Turkmenistan	85	118	Lesotho	57
31	San Marino	100	75	Egypt	84	119	Namibia	57
32	Singapore	100	76	Philippines	84	120	Nicaragua	57
33	Saint Kitts and Nevis	100	77	Bangladesh	83	121	Niger	57
34	Sweden	100	78	Belize	82	122	Sri Lanka	57
35	Switzerland	100	79	Côte d'Ivoire	82	123	Ghana	56
36	Tonga	100	80	Panama	82	124	Oman	56
37	Tuvalu	100	81	Trinidad and Tobago	82	125	Malawi	54
38	United Kingdom	100	82	Thailand	81	126	Mongolia	54
39	Bulgaria	99	83	Dominican Republic	79	127	Yemen	52
40	Greece	99	84	Algeria	78	128	Cape Verde	51
41	Israel	99	85	Burkina Faso	78	129	Senegal	50
42	Kiribati	99	86	Dominica	77	130	Guinea	49
43	Spain	99	87	Fiji	77	131	Kenya	49
44	United Arab Emirates	98	88	Sudan	77	132	Tanzania	49

Rank	Country/Entity	Percentage of Population with Access to Safe Water, 1994–1995	Rank	Country/Entity	Percentage of Population with Access to Safe Water, 1994–1995	Rank	Country/Entity	Percentage of Population with Access to Safe Water, 1994–1995
133	Comoros	48	144	Liberia	40	155	Haiti	28
134	Nepal	48	145	Myanmar (Burma)	39	156	Mozambique	28
135	Zambia	47	146	Vietnam	38	157	Ethiopia	27
136	China	46	147	Sierra Leone	34	158	Congo, Dem. Rep. of	25
137	Iraq	45	148	Uruguay	34	159	Bhutan	21
138	Mali	44	149	Angola	32	160	Central African Republic	18
139	Nigeria	43	150	Madagascar	32	161	Cambodia	13
140	Swaziland	43	151	Marshall Islands	31	162	Afghanistan	10
141	Uganda	42	152	Papua New Guinea	31	163	Paraguay	8
142	Cameroon	41	153	Libya	30			
143	Laos	41	154	Chad	29			

Source: World Health Statistics Annual

18.24 Deaths from Accidents, Violence, and Poisoning

This category brings together a motley group of causes of death and includes deaths that result from natural disasters, traffic accidents, domestic accidents, crime, food poisoning, and so forth. The category excludes suicide. Few of these causes of death have medical origins, although some may be ascribed to social pathology.

Rank	Country/Entity	Deaths from Accidents, Violence, and Poisoning per 100,000	Rank	Country/Entity	Deaths from Accidents, Violence, and Poisoning per 100,000	Rank	Country/Entity	Deaths from Accidents, Violence, and Poisoning per 100,000
1	Russia	234.0	31	Romania	74.3	61	Guatemala	52.0
2	Latvia	233.8	32	South Korea	72.0	62	Argentina	51.6
3	Estonia	233.1	33	Philippines	71.8	63	New Zealand	50.3
4	Tajikistan	181.3	34	Suriname	71.0	64	Germany	50.1
5	Sri Lanka	135.7	35	Denmark	70.8	65	Mauritius	49.9
6	El Salvador	140.0	36	Switzerland	69.3	66	Italy	49.8
7	Belarus	132.6	37	Slovakia	67.9	67	Costa Rica	49.7
8	Colombia	132.3	38	Peru	67.0	68	Uzbekistan	49.5
9	Ukraine	131.2	39	Ecuador	66.7	69	Japan	49.1
10	Kazakhstan	125.0	40	Chile	66.1	70	Canada	47.2
11	Nauru	116.0	41	Bulgaria	66.0	71	Bosnia	47.1
12	Hungary	115.6	42	Belgium	65.1	72	San Marino	45.2
13	Moldova	112.8	43	Mexico	64.6	73	Paraguay	45.0
14	Palau	112.0	44	Taiwan	63.7	74	Zimbabwe	44.9
15	Iran	108.0	45	Armenia	62.8	75	Seychelles	43.3
16	Azerbaijan	106.4	46	Luxembourg	62.7	76	Greece	42.4
17	Brazil	104.0	47	Ireland	62.2	77	Honduras	42.2
18	Thailand	104.0	48	Uruguay	61.7	78	Yugoslavia	42.2
19	South Africa	99.3	49	Venezuela	61.4	79	Albania	41.7
20	Kyrgyzstan	96.3	50	Austria	60.8	80	Spain	41.1
21	Nicaragua	93.0	51	Turkmenistan	60.1	81	Australia	41.0
22	Belize	92.6	52	Panama	58.0	82	Bahamas	40.8
23	Slovenia	87.6	53	Portugal	57.2	83	Barbados	40.3
24	Finland	85.0	54	China	56.6	84	Brunei	39.8
25	Czech Republic	82.3	55	Guyana	56.5	85	Saint Vincent and the Grenadines	39.3
26	France	81.0	56	Norway	56.5			
27	Cuba	79.9	57	Georgia	56.1	86	Egypt	39.1
28	Malawi	78.0	58	Trinidad and Tobago	56.1	87	Bermuda	38.6
29	Croatia	77.8	59	Dominican Republic	56.0	88	North Korea	38.2
30	Poland	75.4	60	United States	54.4	89	Singapore	37.5

Rank	Country/Entity	Deaths from Accidents, Violence, and Poisoning per 100,000	Rank	Country/Entity	Deaths from Accidents, Violence, and Poisoning per 100,000	Rank	Country/Entity	Deaths from Accidents, Violence, and Poisoning per 100,000
90	Israel	36.7	100	United Kingdom	32.8	110	Bahrain	19.0
91	Liechtenstein	36.1	101	Sweden	32.6	111	Dominica	18.0
92	Qatar	36.0	102	Fiji	32.2	112	São Tomé and Príncipe	14.3
93	Iceland	35.7	103	Cape Verde	30.1	113	Maldives	9.9
94	Macedonia	35.3	104	Saint Kitts and Nevis	29.5	114	Vanuatu	9.1
95	Kuwait	35.2	105	Malaysia	29.0	115	Jamaica	8.4
96	Saint Lucia	34.7	106	Syria	27.0	116	Antigua and Barbuda	5.1
97	Netherlands	34.3	107	Malta	25.5	117	Tonga	4.1
98	Puerto Rico	34.1	108	Micronesia	23.8	118	Samoa	2.5
99	Turkey	33.0	109	Morocco	19.2			

Source: World Health Statistics

Chapter 19

Food

Daily food intake is based on many factors, including age, climate, type of work, and average body weight. The Food and Agriculture Organization of the United Nations (FAO) has broadly determined the average minimum daily nutritional requirements for each major geographical region as follows: Africa, 2,320 calories; Russia and the Commonwealth of Independent States, 2,300; East and South Asia, 2,240; Latin America, 2,360; Middle East, 2,440; and the developed countries of Europe and North America, 2,600 calories. Generally, food consumption varies according to social class more than anything else. The rich may eat well, but they are still bound by the culinary traditions of their country, which may dictate the percentage of calories available from carbohydrates and animal products.

Rank	Country/Entity	Percentage of FAO Requirement, 1995	Rank	Country/Entity	Percentage of FAO Requirement, 1995	Rank	Country/Entity	Percentage of FAO Requirement, 1995
1	Cyprus	150	45	New Caledonia	126	89	Paraguay	111
2	Portugal	149	46	Poland	126	90	Vanuatu	111
3	Réunion	146	47	Dominica	125	91	Côte d'Ivoire	109
4	Ireland	145	48	French Guiana	125	92	Guyana	108
5	Hong Kong	143	49	United Kingdom	125	93	India	108
6	Turkey	143	50	Belize	123	94	Nepal	108
7	France	142	51	Germany	123	95	Panama	108
8	Greece	142	52	Iran	123	96	Gabon	107
9	South Korea	139	53	Japan	123	97	Pakistan	107
10	United Arab Emirates	139	54	Yugoslavia	123	98	Ecuador	106
11	Denmark	138	55	Kiribati	122	99	Nigeria	106
12	Italy	137	56	Norway	122	100	Philippines	106
13	Malta	137	57	Bermuda	121	101	Trinidad and Tobago	106
14	Spain	136	58	Netherlands	120	102	Uruguay	106
15	United States	136	59	Switzerland	120	103	Benin	105
16	Fiji	135	60	Brazil	119	104	Guatemala	105
17	Macau	135	61	Colombia	119	105	Guinea-Bissau	105
18	Mexico	135	62	Iceland	119	106	Sri Lanka	105
19	Belgium	134	63	Romania	119	107	Honduras	104
20	Luxembourg	134	64	Jamaica	118	108	Seychelles	104
21	Slovenia	134	65	Martinique	118	109	Bahamas	103
22	Barbados	133	66	South Africa	118	110	Dominican Republic	103
23	Egypt	133	67	Slovakia	117	111	Nicaragua	103
24	Syria	133	68	Bulgaria	116	112	Thailand	103
25	Tunisia	133	69	Canada	116	113	Antigua and Barbuda	102
26	Argentina	132	70	China	116	114	Papua New Guinea	102
27	Lebanon	132	71	Saint Lucia	116	115	Senegal	102
28	Libya	132	72	Sweden	116	116	North Korea	101
29	Kuwait	131	73	Australia	115	117	Saint Vincent and the Grenadines	100
30	Austria	130	74	Swaziland	115			
31	Mauritius	130	75	Ghana	114	118	Cuba	99
32	Morocco	130	76	Netherlands Antilles	114	119	Venezuela	99
33	Cape Verde	129	77	Russia	114	120	Sudan	98
34	Czech Republic	129	78	Vietnam	114	121	Peru	97
35	Costa Rica	128	79	Chile	113	122	Uganda	97
36	New Zealand	128	80	El Salvador	113	123	Albania	96
37	Algeria	127	81	Guadeloupe	113	124	Congo, Rep. of	96
38	Brunei	127	82	Saudi Arabia	113	125	Burkina Faso	95
39	French Polynesia	127	83	Suriname	113	126	Cameroon	95
40	Israel	127	84	Finland	112	127	Croatia	95
41	Myanmar (Burma)	127	85	Grenada	112	128	Laos	95
42	Hungary	126	86	Maldives	112	129	Guinea	94
43	Indonesia	126	87	Mauritania	112	130	Iraq	94
44	Malaysia	126	88	Jordan	111	131	Botswana	93

Rank	Country/Entity	Percentage of FAO Requirement, 1995	Rank	Country/Entity	Percentage of FAO Requirement, 1995	Rank	Country/Entity	Percentage of FAO Requirement, 1995
132	Solomon Islands	93	142	Madagascar	89	152	Central African Republic	83
133	Bolivia	92	143	Malawi	88	153	Angola	82
134	Macedonia	92	144	Sierra Leone	88	154	Zimbabwe	82
135	Namibia	92	145	Bangladesh	87	155	Chad	80
136	São Tomé and Príncipe	92	146	Tanzania	87	156	Comoros	79
137	Saint Kitts and Nevis	92	147	Kenya	86	157	Djibouti	79
138	Cambodia	91	148	Lesotho	86	158	Mongolia	78
139	Gambia	91	149	Congo, Dem. Rep. of	85	159	Togo	76
140	Mali	91	150	Yemen	84	160	Burundi	75
141	Niger	91	151	Zambia	84	161	Mozambique	72

Source: FAO Yearbook

Calories

The total number of calories consumed daily per capita varies from 1,800 in poor countries to 3,600 in the United States. But the sources from which these calories are obtained vary as widely. In poorer countries, cereals constitute more than half the daily intake and can be as high as 76 percent. In richer countries, the diet is more balanced, but the intake of meat and poultry, as well as of oils and fats, is much higher. Dietary patterns have medical consequences as well, reflected in the table on causes of death, as well as relative life expectancy.

19.2 Daily Calories Available per Capita

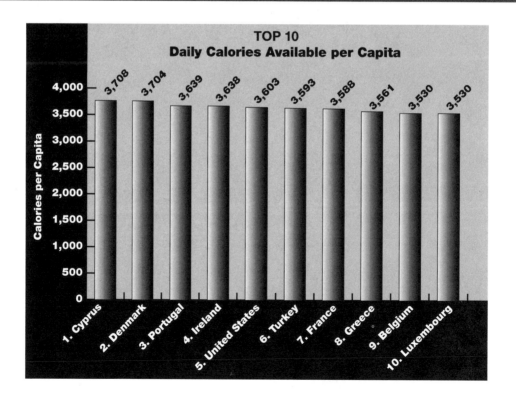

Rank	Country/Entity	Calories per Capita	Rank	Country/Entity	Calories per Capita	Rank	Country/Entity	Calories per Capita
11	Italy	3,458	62	Costa Rica	2,865	112	North Korea	2,360
12	Austria	3,417	63	Martinique	2,865	113	Honduras	2,359
13	Slovenia	3,396	64	Brunei	2,849	114	Macedonia	2,340
14	Malta	3,387	65	Brazil	2,834	115	Sri Lanka	2,334
15	New Zealand	3,379	66	Uruguay	2,826	116	Albania	2,324
16	United Arab Emirates	3,361	67	French Guiana	2,818	117	Dominican Republic	2,323
17	Spain	3,338	68	Malaysia	2,807	118	Papua New Guinea	2,323
18	Egypt	3,327	69	Saint Lucia	2,801	119	Sudan	2,313
19	Réunion	3,308	70	Belize	2,791	120	Nicaragua	2,311
20	Poland	3,307	71	Kiribati	2,772	121	Guatemala	2,300
21	Hungary	3,302	72	Chile	2,769	122	Thailand	2,296
22	Syria	3,296	73	Netherlands Antilles	2,759	123	Cuba	2,291
23	Hong Kong	3,285	74	Colombia	2,758	124	Peru	2,277
24	Norway	3,274	75	Myanmar (Burma)	2,752	125	Iraq	2,268
25	Israel	3,271	76	Saudi Arabia	2,746	126	Uganda	2,268
26	Lebanon	3,270	77	China	2,741	127	Burkina Faso	2,250
27	South Korea	3,268	78	Jordan	2,734	128	Saint Kitts and Nevis	2,234
28	Germany	3,265	79	Guadeloupe	2,732	129	Cameroon	2,214
29	Netherlands	3,230	80	Indonesia	2,732	130	Bolivia	2,192
30	Switzerland	3,220	81	Grenada	2,713	131	Guinea	2,161
31	Barbados	3,207	82	Swaziland	2,658	132	Gambia	2,157
32	Tunisia	3,187	83	Jamaica	2,647	133	São Tomé and Príncipe	2,156
33	Czech Republic	3,175	84	Ghana	2,622	134	Botswana	2,153
34	Romania	3,166	85	Mauritania	2,592	135	Mali	2,149
35	Kuwait	3,160	86	El Salvador	2,577	136	Congo, Rep. of	2,141
36	Iceland	3,159	87	Trinidad and Tobago	2,566	137	Niger	2,136
37	Morocco	3,157	88	Paraguay	2,560	138	Solomon Islands	2,131
38	United Kingdom	3,149	89	Suriname	2,556	139	Laos	2,117
39	Mexico	3,136	90	Vanuatu	2,542	140	Namibia	2,107
40	Yugoslavia	3,134	91	Côte d'Ivoire	2,517	141	Malawi	2,038
41	Libya	3,126	92	Gabon	2,511	142	Sierra Leone	2,029
42	Sweden	3,117	93	Nigeria	2,508	143	Yemen	2,025
43	Argentina	3,110	94	Bahamas	2,498	144	Tanzania	2,024
44	Macau	3,094	95	Panama	2,490	145	Bangladesh	2,017
45	Canada	3,093	96	Maldives	2,485	146	Cambodia	2,012
46	Fiji	3,078	97	Pakistan	2,475	147	Madagascar	2,009
47	Australia	3,068	98	Vietnam	2,463	148	Kenya	1,991
48	Bermuda	3,050	99	Guyana	2,460	149	Lesotho	1,972
49	Algeria	3,042	100	Venezuela	2,442	150	Zimbabwe	1,965
50	Dominica	3,032	101	Ecuador	2,436	151	Zambia	1,931
51	Cape Verde	3,031	102	Guinea-Bissau	2,433	152	Angola	1,927
52	Finland	3,022	103	Seychelles	2,428	153	Chad	1,913
53	Iran	2,955	104	Saint Vincent and the Grenadines	2,427	154	Mongolia	1,897
54	Mauritius	2,943				155	Central African Republic	1,885
55	Russia	2,926	105	Senegal	2,416	156	Congo, Dem. Rep. of	1,879
56	Bulgaria	2,907	106	Croatia	2,413	157	Comoros	1,850
57	French Polynesia	2,906	107	Antigua and Barbuda	2,406	158	Djibouti	1,831
58	Slovakia	2,892	108	Benin	2,405	159	Togo	1,754
59	South Africa	2,890	109	Philippines	2,395	160	Burundi	1,749
60	Japan	2,887	110	India	2,388	161	Mozambique	1,678
61	New Caledonia	2,867	111	Nepal	2,367			

Source: World Data

19.3 Percentage of Total Calories from Cereals

Rank	Country/Entity	Percentage of Calories from Cereal	Rank	Country/Entity	Percentage of Calories from Cereal	Rank	Country/Entity	Percentage of Calories from Cereal
1	Bangladesh	82.4	55	South Korea	47.6	108	Slovenia	32.2
2	Cambodia	81.2	56	Jordan	47.0	109	Netherlands Antilles	31.6
3	Nepal	77.9	57	Swaziland	47.0	110	Brazil	31.4
4	Myanmar (Burma)	77.6	58	Guinea	46.7	111	Dominican Republic	31.4
5	Mali	76.1	59	Mongolia	46.4	112	Belize	31.2
6	Burkina Faso	75.6	60	Mexico	46.2	113	Hong Kong	31.1
7	Laos	75.6	61	Mauritius	45.8	114	Slovakia	30.9
8	Lesotho	73.2	62	Bolivia	44.4	115	Argentina	30.6
9	Vietnam	73.1	63	Comoros	44.3	116	Croatia	30.2
10	Niger	71.0	64	Macedonia	44.1	117	Martinique	30.0
11	Malawi	68.4	65	Brunei	43.6	118	Papua New Guinea	29.1
12	Yemen	66.7	66	Togo	42.7	119	Bahamas	29.0
13	Zambia	66.7	67	Cameroon	42.4	120	Greece	29.0
14	Egypt	66.3	68	Russia	42.2	121	Malta	29.0
15	Indonesia	63.7	69	Nigeria	42.1	122	Uruguay	28.5
16	Guinea-Bissau	63.2	70	Mozambique	41.8	123	Ghana	28.4
17	Morocco	62.6	71	Panama	41.7	124	Portugal	28.3
18	India	62.1	72	Côte d'Ivoire	41.5	125	Angola	28.1
19	North Korea	62.1	73	Réunion	41.4	126	Barbados	28.1
20	Guatemala	60.3	74	Maldives	41.3	127	Grenada	27.9
21	Algeria	59.3	75	São Tomé and Príncipe	40.4	128	Saint Kitts and Nevis	27.7
22	Iran	59.2	76	Bulgaria	40.3	129	Ireland	27.3
23	Zimbabwe	58.9	77	Malaysia	40.3	130	Dominica	27.2
24	Sri Lanka	58.7	78	Peru	40.1	131	Norway	27.2
25	Sudan	58.5	79	Japan	40.0	132	Bermuda	27.0
26	China	57.6	80	Seychelles	39.9	133	Hungary	27.0
27	El Salvador	55.9	81	Chile	39.4	134	Antigua and Barbuda	26.7
28	Madagascar	55.8	82	Albania	38.6	135	Czech Republic	26.7
29	Syria	55.7	83	Fiji	38.1	136	Paraguay	26.5
30	Pakistan	55.2	84	Guadeloupe	37.8	137	Gabon	26.0
31	Senegal	55.2	85	Macau	37.7	138	Australia	24.6
32	South Africa	54.3	86	Venezuela	37.6	139	Cyprus	24.1
33	Chad	54.0	87	Trinidad and Tobago	37.3	140	Iceland	24.1
34	Mauritania	53.6	88	Cuba	36.5	141	Sweden	23.9
35	Gambia	53.5	89	Kiribati	36.2	142	France	23.7
36	Sierra Leone	53.5	90	Solomon Islands	35.9	143	United States	23.5
37	Botswana	52.9	91	Yugoslavia	35.8	144	New Zealand	23.2
38	Kenya	52.9	92	Kuwait	35.6	145	Spain	22.8
39	Philippines	51.4	93	Poland	35.6	146	United Kingdom	22.6
40	Iraq	51.2	94	New Caledonia	35.5	147	Congo, Rep. of	22.3
41	Suriname	51.1	95	Benin	35.1	148	Austria	22.2
42	Thailand	51.0	96	Lebanon	34.6	149	Canada	22.1
43	Nicaragua	50.7	97	Costa Rica	34.4	150	Switzerland	22.0
44	Saudi Arabia	50.7	98	Saint Vincent and the Grenadines	34.4	151	Denmark	21.7
45	Tunisia	50.3				152	Central African Republic	21.3
46	Guyana	50.1	99	Israel	34.2	153	Belgium	21.2
47	Turkey	49.5	100	United Arab Emirates	34.1	154	Finland	21.2
48	Tanzania	49.4	101	French Polynesia	33.6	155	Luxembourg	21.2
49	Romania	49.1	102	Saint Lucia	33.3	156	Uganda	21.0
50	Cape Verde	48.6	103	Italy	33.0	157	Germany	20.9
51	Djibouti	48.6	104	Jamaica	32.8	158	Vanuatu	17.9
52	Namibia	48.6	105	Colombia	32.5	159	Burundi	17.0
53	Honduras	48.5	106	Ecuador	32.4	160	Netherlands	16.7
54	Libya	47.8	107	French Guiana	32.4	161	Congo, Dem. Rep. of	16.6

Source: World Data

19.4 Percentage of Total Calories from Potatoes and Cassava

Rank	Country/Entity	Percentage of Calories from Potatoes and Cassava	Rank	Country/Entity	Percentage of Calories from Potatoes and Cassava	Rank	Country/Entity	Percentage of Calories from Potatoes and Cassava
1	Congo, Dem. Rep. of	55.3	54	Luxembourg	5.4	108	Cyprus	2.1
2	Ghana	45.6	55	Saint Lucia	5.4	109	El Salvador	2.0
3	Congo, Rep. of	39.3	56	Netherlands	5.0	110	Italy	2.0
4	Benin	37.2	57	Vietnam	5.0	111	Sri Lanka	2.0
5	Mozambique	35.6	58	Lesotho	4.8	112	Bulgaria	1.9
6	Angola	35.3	59	Czech Republic	4.7	113	Cape Verde	1.9
7	Solomon Islands	34.4	60	French Polynesia	4.6	114	South Africa	1.9
8	Central African Republic	31.5	61	Guyana	4.6	115	Albania	1.8
9	Togo	31.1	62	Norway	4.5	116	Bermuda	1.8
10	Vanuatu	28.0	63	Finland	4.3	117	India	1.8
11	Burundi	27.4	64	Malawi	4.3	118	Panama	1.8
12	Papua New Guinea	26.6	65	Barbados	4.2	119	Cambodia	1.7
13	Côte d'Ivoire	26.1	66	Germany	4.2	120	Réunion	1.7
14	Nigeria	24.3	67	Greece	4.2	121	Tunisia	1.7
15	Uganda	22.0	68	Laos	4.2	122	Belize	1.6
16	Madagascar	20.9	69	Martinique	4.2	123	Botswana	1.6
17	Gabon	20.3	70	Netherlands Antilles	4.2	124	Egypt	1.6
18	Tanzania	20.1	71	Philippines	4.1	125	Hong Kong	1.6
19	Cameroon	16.0	72	Romania	4.1	126	Saudi Arabia	1.6
20	Paraguay	15.5	73	Sweden	3.8	127	United Arab Emirates	1.6
21	Comoros	15.4	74	Argentina	3.7	128	Algeria	1.5
22	Namibia	13.9	75	Malta	3.7	129	Bahamas	1.5
23	Guinea	13.3	76	Chile	3.6	130	Jordan	1.5
24	Chad	12.1	77	France	3.6	131	Libya	1.5
25	Zambia	10.4	78	Lebanon	3.6	132	Nicaragua	1.5
26	Peru	9.0	79	Niger	3.6	133	Bangladesh	1.4
27	Sierra Leone	8.9	80	Canada	3.5	134	Iraq	1.4
28	Kiribati	8.5	81	Maldives	3.5	135	Costa Rica	1.3
29	São Tomé and Príncipe	8.3	82	Hungary	3.4	136	Kuwait	1.3
30	Saint Vincent and the Grenadines	8.0	83	Austria	3.3	137	Mauritius	1.3
31	French Guiana	7.9	84	Macedonia	3.3	138	Brunei	1.2
32	Dominica	7.8	85	Turkey	3.3	139	Mongolia	1.2
33	Slovenia	7.8	86	Denmark	3.2	140	Morocco	1.2
34	Kenya	7.7	87	Dominican Republic	3.2	141	Swaziland	1.2
35	Poland	7.7	88	Uruguay	3.2	142	Syria	1.2
36	Portugal	7.6	89	Australia	3.0	143	Seychelles	1.1
37	Russia	7.6	90	Ecuador	3.0	144	Yemen	1.1
38	Colombia	7.4	91	Iceland	3.0	145	Antigua and Barbuda	1.0
39	Bolivia	7.0	92	New Zealand	3.0	146	Jamaica	1.0
40	Croatia	7.0	93	Switzerland	3.0	147	Senegal	1.0
41	United Kingdom	6.3	94	Nepal	2.9	148	Thailand	1.0
42	Guinea-Bissau	6.2	95	United States	2.8	149	South Korea	0.9
43	Indonesia	6.2	96	Venezuela	2.8	150	Gambia	0.8
44	Ireland	6.0	97	Trinidad and Tobago	2.7	151	Mexico	0.8
45	Cuba	5.9	98	Guadeloupe	2.6	152	Pakistan	0.8
46	New Caledonia	5.9	99	Iran	2.6	153	Burkina Faso	0.7
47	Slovakia	5.9	100	Grenada	2.4	154	Macau	0.6
48	Fiji	5.6	101	Japan	2.4	155	Sudan	0.6
49	Brazil	5.5	102	Malaysia	2.4	156	Guatemala	0.4
50	China	5.5	103	Saint Kitts and Nevis	2.4	157	Mauritania	0.4
51	Spain	5.5	104	Yugoslavia	2.4	158	Myanmar (Burma)	0.4
52	Belgium	5.4	105	Israel	2.3	159	Djibouti	0.3
53	North Korea	5.4	106	Suriname	2.3	160	Honduras	0.3
			107	Zimbabwe	2.2	161	Mali	0.3

Source: World Data

Rank	Country/Entity	Percentage of Calories from Meat and Poultry	Rank	Country/Entity	Percentage of Calories from Meat and Poultry	Rank	Country/Entity	Percentage of Calories from Meat and Poultry
1	Mongolia	26.3	54	Malaysia	9.6	108	Cambodia	4.2
2	Uruguay	22.6	55	Vanuatu	9.5	109	Mauritania	4.2
3	Denmark	22.5	56	Brazil	9.4	110	Libya	4.0
4	Cyprus	20.6	57	Russia	9.3	111	Kenya	3.8
5	Hong Kong	20.3	58	Sweden	9.3	112	Mali	3.8
6	Bahamas	17.5	59	Bulgaria	9.0	113	North Korea	3.7
7	Finland	16.4	60	Malta	8.9	114	Angola	3.6
8	Argentina	16.3	61	Fiji	8.8	115	Senegal	3.6
9	France	15.9	62	Albania	8.7	116	Iran	3.5
10	New Zealand	15.9	63	Greece	8.7	117	Laos	3.5
11	Netherlands Antilles	15.5	64	South Korea	8.6	118	Congo, Rep. of	3.4
12	Switzerland	15.5	65	Macedonia	8.6	119	Cameroon	3.3
13	Saint Lucia	15.4	66	Slovakia	8.4	120	Solomon Islands	3.2
14	Australia	15.3	67	Israel	8.3	121	Syria	3.1
15	Macau	14.8	68	Belize	8.2	122	Togo	3.1
16	Antigua and Barbuda	14.5	69	Gabon	8.2	123	Uganda	3.1
17	Iceland	14.4	70	Philippines	8.2	124	Algeria	3.0
18	Brunei	14.2	71	Venezuela	7.9	125	Yemen	3.0
19	French Polynesia	14.2	72	Grenada	7.6	126	Tunisia	2.9
20	United Kingdom	14.1	73	Cape Verde	7.5	127	Guatemala	2.8
21	Bermuda	13.9	74	Mexico	7.5	128	Zambia	2.8
22	Barbados	13.7	75	Dominican Republic	7.3	129	Chad	2.7
23	China	13.6	76	Saudi Arabia	7.3	130	El Salvador	2.7
24	Austria	13.4	77	South Africa	7.1	131	Honduras	2.7
25	Netherlands	13.4	78	Romania	7.0	132	Morocco	2.7
26	Spain	13.4	79	Colombia	6.8	133	Pakistan	2.7
27	French Guiana	13.2	80	Panama	6.8	134	Nicaragua	2.6
28	Paraguay	13.2	81	Costa Rica	6.7	135	Tanzania	2.6
29	Ireland	12.8	82	Papua New Guinea	6.6	136	Niger	2.5
30	Martinique	12.1	83	Vietnam	6.5	137	Burkina Faso	2.4
31	United Arab Emirates	12.0	84	Ecuador	6.4	138	Egypt	2.4
32	United States	12.0	85	Jamaica	6.4	139	Turkey	2.4
33	Réunion	11.9	86	Central African Republic	6.3	140	Benin	2.3
34	Chile	11.8	87	Japan	6.2	141	Indonesia	2.3
35	Slovenia	11.8	88	Botswana	5.9	142	Côte d'Ivoire	2.0
36	Czech Republic	11.7	89	Croatia	5.9	143	Comoros	1.9
37	Italy	11.6	90	Swaziland	5.8	144	Congo, Dem. Rep. of	1.9
38	Canada	11.5	91	Namibia	5.6	145	Maldives	1.8
39	Germany	11.3	92	Peru	5.5	146	Myanmar (Burma)	1.8
40	New Caledonia	11.3	93	Jordan	5.4	147	Nigeria	1.8
41	Saint Kitts and Nevis	11.2	94	Cuba	5.3	148	São Tomé and Príncipe	1.8
42	Norway	11.1	95	Kiribati	5.3	149	Zimbabwe	1.8
43	Yugoslavia	11.1	96	Madagascar	5.2	150	Mozambique	1.7
44	Kuwait	11.0	97	Suriname	5.2	151	Iraq	1.6
45	Guadeloupe	10.8	98	Djibouti	5.1	152	Gambia	1.4
46	Poland	10.6	99	Seychelles	5.1	153	Ghana	1.4
47	Hungary	10.5	100	Trinidad and Tobago	5.0	154	Nepal	1.4
48	Bolivia	10.4	101	Lebanon	4.6	155	Burundi	1.3
49	Portugal	10.1	102	Mauritius	4.6	156	Malawi	1.3
50	Saint Vincent and the Grenadines	10.1	103	Thailand	4.6	157	Sierra Leone	1.1
			104	Guinea-Bissau	4.5	158	Guinea	0.9
51	Belgium	9.9	105	Sudan	4.5	159	India	0.9
52	Dominica	9.9	106	Guyana	4.4	160	Sri Lanka	0.9
53	Luxembourg	9.9	107	Lesotho	4.4	161	Bangladesh	0.8

Source: World Data

19.6 Percentage of Total Calories from Fish

Rank	Country/Entity	Percentage of Calories from Fish	Rank	Country/Entity	Percentage of Calories from Fish	Rank	Country/Entity	Percentage of Calories from Fish
1	Maldives	10.9	53	Saint Vincent and the Grenadines	1.3	104	Mexico	0.6
2	Japan	6.3	54	Venezuela	1.3	105	Namibia	0.6
3	Iceland	6.1	55	Angola	1.2	106	Trinidad and Tobago	0.6
4	Kiribati	5.1	56	Belgium	1.2	107	Yemen	0.6
5	Seychelles	4.9	57	Indonesia	1.2	108	Congo, Dem. Rep. of	0.5
6	Antigua and Barbuda	4.4	58	Jamaica	1.2	109	Kenya	0.5
7	Norway	3.5	59	Luxembourg	1.2	110	Kuwait	0.5
8	Saint Kitts and Nevis	3.5	60	Malta	1.2	111	Morocco	0.5
9	North Korea	3.3	61	Netherlands	1.2	112	South Africa	0.5
10	Philippines	3.2	62	Canada	1.1	113	Tunisia	0.5
11	Grenada	3.1	63	France	1.1	114	Argentina	0.4
12	Comoros	3.0	64	Greece	1.1	115	Belize	0.4
13	Guyana	3.0	65	Italy	1.1	116	Burundi	0.4
14	Hong Kong	3.0	66	Panama	1.1	117	Central African Republic	0.4
15	Martinique	2.9	67	Australia	1.0	118	Czech Republic	0.4
16	South Korea	2.8	68	Brunei	1.0	119	Egypt	0.4
17	Congo, Rep. of	2.7	69	Côte d'Ivoire	1.0	120	Guinea-Bissau	0.4
18	Gabon	2.7	70	Tanzania	1.0	121	Lesotho	0.4
19	French Polynesia	2.6	71	Togo	1.0	122	Nigeria	0.4
20	Guadeloupe	2.6	72	United Arab Emirates	1.0	123	Saudi Arabia	0.4
21	Portugal	2.4	73	United Kingdom	1.0	124	Turkey	0.4
22	Sweden	2.4	74	Vietnam	1.0	125	Uruguay	0.4
23	Papua New Guinea	2.2	75	Germany	0.9	126	Algeria	0.3
24	Solomon Islands	2.2	76	Ireland	0.9	127	Brazil	0.3
25	Denmark	2.1	77	Israel	0.9	128	Colombia	0.3
26	Finland	2.1	78	Mauritania	0.9	129	Costa Rica	0.3
27	French Guiana	2.1	79	Myanmar (Burma)	0.9	130	India	0.3
28	Senegal	2.1	80	Bangladesh	0.8	131	Iran	0.3
29	Spain	2.1	81	Benin	0.8	132	Jordan	0.3
30	Thailand	2.1	82	Cambodia	0.8	133	Libya	0.3
31	Bermuda	2.0	83	Cape Verde	0.8	134	Paraguay	0.3
32	Chile	2.0	84	China	0.8	135	Slovenia	0.3
33	Fiji	2.0	85	Cyprus	0.8	136	Croatia	0.2
34	Macau	2.0	86	New Zealand	0.8	137	Djibouti	0.2
35	Mauritius	2.0	87	Poland	0.8	138	El Salvador	0.2
36	Ghana	1.9	88	Switzerland	0.8	139	Hungary	0.2
37	Barbados	1.8	89	Uganda	0.8	140	Macedonia	0.2
38	Sierra Leone	1.8	90	United States	0.8	141	Mozambique	0.2
39	Bahamas	1.7	91	Zambia	0.8	142	Pakistan	0.2
40	Dominica	1.6	92	Austria	0.7	143	Romania	0.2
41	Gambia	1.6	93	Cameroon	0.7	144	Zimbabwe	0.2
42	São Tomé and Príncipe	1.6	94	Dominican Republic	0.7	145	Bolivia	0.1
43	Malaysia	1.5	95	Ecuador	0.7	146	Bulgaria	0.1
44	Netherlands Antilles	1.5	96	Botswana	0.6	147	Burkina Faso	0.1
45	Peru	1.5	97	Chad	0.6	148	Guatemala	0.1
46	Réunion	1.5	98	Cuba	0.6	149	Iraq	0.1
47	Saint Lucia	1.5	99	Guinea	0.6	150	Mongolia	0.1
48	Vanuatu	1.5	100	Laos	0.6	151	Nicaragua	0.1
49	Sri Lanka	1.4	101	Madagascar	0.6	152	Sudan	0.1
50	Suriname	1.4	102	Malawi	0.6	153	Yugoslavia	0.1
51	New Caledonia	1.3	103	Mali	0.6			
52	Russia	1.3						

Source: World Data

19.7 Percentage of Total Calories from Eggs and Milk

Rank	Country/Entity	Percentage of Calories from Eggs and Milk	Rank	Country/Entity	Percentage of Calories from Eggs and Milk	Rank	Country/Entity	Percentage of Calories from Eggs and Milk
1	Albania	22.9	55	Panama	8.0	108	Iran	3.4
2	Finland	16.1	56	Cuba	7.9	109	Namibia	3.4
3	Sweden	15.1	57	Saint Kitts and Nevis	7.9	110	Nepal	3.2
4	Netherlands	14.5	58	Colombia	7.7	111	Bolivia	3.1
5	Uruguay	14.4	59	Bermuda	7.6	112	Madagascar	2.9
6	Australia	14.2	60	Mauritius	7.6	113	Sri Lanka	2.8
7	Iceland	13.9	61	Portugal	7.6	114	Thailand	2.6
8	Switzerland	12.8	62	Brazil	7.5	115	Chad	2.5
9	France	12.7	63	French Guiana	7.5	116	China	2.4
10	Norway	12.6	64	Turkey	7.4	117	Senegal	2.3
11	Sudan	12.6	65	Bahamas	7.3	118	Zimbabwe	2.3
12	Cyprus	12.5	66	Chile	7.0	119	Niger	2.2
13	Ireland	12.1	67	Ecuador	7.0	120	Tanzania	2.2
14	Austria	12.0	68	Kenya	7.0	121	Gabon	2.1
15	Croatia	12.0	69	Honduras	6.8	122	South Korea	2.0
16	United Kingdom	11.6	70	French Polynesia	6.7	123	Morocco	2.0
17	United States	11.6	71	Japan	6.6	124	Philippines	2.0
18	Romania	11.2	72	Trinidad and Tobago	6.6	125	Egypt	1.8
19	Mauritania	11.1	73	Venezuela	6.5	126	Uganda	1.8
20	Antigua and Barbuda	11.0	74	Dominican Republic	6.4	127	Vanuatu	1.8
21	Malta	11.0	75	Barbados	6.3	128	Angola	1.7
22	Greece	10.8	76	Malaysia	6.2	129	Laos	1.7
23	Czech Republic	10.6	77	Paraguay	6.2	130	Yemen	1.7
24	Kuwait	10.5	78	Brunei	6.1	131	Iraq	1.6
25	New Zealand	10.5	79	Djibouti	6.0	132	Central African Republic	1.5
26	Germany	10.4	80	El Salvador	6.0	133	Gambia	1.5
27	Argentina	10.2	81	Macedonia	6.0	134	Bangladesh	1.4
28	Yugoslavia	10.2	82	Mexico	5.9	135	Burkina Faso	1.4
29	Slovenia	10.0	83	Suriname	5.9	136	Cameroon	1.4
30	Canada	9.7	84	Jamaica	5.8	137	Guinea-Bissau	1.4
31	Grenada	9.7	85	Lebanon	5.8	138	Lesotho	1.4
32	Bulgaria	9.6	86	Seychelles	5.7	139	Kiribati	1.3
33	New Caledonia	9.6	87	Syria	5.3	140	Zambia	1.3
34	Spain	9.4	88	Hong Kong	5.2	141	North Korea	1.2
35	Belgium	9.3	89	Réunion	5.2	142	Comoros	1.1
36	Costa Rica	9.3	90	Algeria	5.1	143	Congo, Rep. of	1.1
37	Luxembourg	9.3	91	Tunisia	4.9	144	Guinea	1.1
38	United Arab Emirates	9.3	92	Guyana	4.7	145	Myanmar (Burma)	1.1
39	Russia	9.2	93	India	4.6	146	Benin	0.9
40	Slovakia	9.2	94	Jordan	4.6	147	Togo	0.9
41	Denmark	9.1	95	Libya	4.6	148	Côte d'Ivoire	0.8
42	Dominica	9.1	96	Macau	4.6	149	São Tomé and Príncipe	0.8
43	Netherlands Antilles	9.1	97	Saint Vincent and the Grenadines	4.6	150	Burundi	0.7
44	Mongolia	9.0				151	Indonesia	0.7
45	Poland	9.0	98	Cape Verde	4.5	152	Mozambique	0.7
46	Belize	8.8	99	Peru	4.5	153	Papua New Guinea	0.7
47	Israel	8.7	100	Nicaragua	4.3	154	Sierra Leone	0.7
48	Hungary	8.6	101	Maldives	4.2	155	Solomon Islands	0.7
49	Italy	8.6	102	Mali	4.1	156	Cambodia	0.6
50	Guadeloupe	8.5	103	Saudi Arabia	4.1	157	Malawi	0.6
51	Martinique	8.5	104	Fiji	3.9	158	Nigeria	0.6
52	Saint Lucia	8.2	105	Guatemala	3.8	159	Vietnam	0.6
53	Botswana	8.1	106	South Africa	3.8	160	Ghana	0.2
54	Pakistan	8.0	107	Swaziland	3.8	161	Congo, Dem. Rep. of	0.1

Source: World Data

19.8 Percentage of Total Calories from Fruits and Vegetables

Rank	Country/Entity	Percentage of Calories from Fruits and Vegetables	Rank	Country/Entity	Percentage of Calories from Fruits and Vegetables	Rank	Country/Entity	Percentage of Calories from Fruits and Vegetables
1	Uganda	24.2	55	Belgium	6.3	108	Hungary	4.0
2	Papua New Guinea	17.3	56	Bulgaria	6.3	109	Iceland	4.0
3	Gabon	16.3	57	Luxembourg	6.3	110	Vietnam	4.0
4	Lebanon	14.2	58	Egypt	6.2	111	Algeria	3.8
5	United Arab Emirates	14.1	59	North Korea	6.2	112	Denmark	3.8
6	Cameroon	13.7	60	Thailand	6.1	113	French Polynesia	3.8
7	Guinea	13.1	61	Austria	6.0	114	Malaysia	3.8
8	Martinique	11.0	62	Chile	6.0	115	New Caledonia	3.8
9	Saudi Arabia	10.6	63	Tunisia	6.0	116	Trinidad and Tobago	3.8
10	Bermuda	10.3	64	Albania	5.8	117	Guinea-Bissau	3.7
11	Dominican Republic	10.2	65	Costa Rica	5.8	118	India	3.7
12	Côte d'Ivoire	10.0	66	Germany	5.7	119	Ireland	3.7
13	Burundi	9.9	67	Maldives	5.7	120	Madagascar	3.5
14	Dominica	9.8	68	Panama	5.7	121	Uruguay	3.5
15	Ecuador	9.4	69	Switzerland	5.6	122	Saint Kitts and Nevis	3.4
16	Greece	9.1	70	Australia	5.5	123	Yemen	3.4
17	Israel	9.0	71	Jordan	5.5	124	Angola	3.3
18	Saint Lucia	9.0	72	Libya	5.5	125	El Salvador	3.2
19	Ghana	8.9	73	Netherlands Antilles	5.4	126	Russia	3.2
20	Iraq	8.6	74	France	5.3	127	Sierra Leone	3.2
21	Guadeloupe	8.4	75	Syria	5.3	128	Kenya	3.1
22	Comoros	8.3	76	Brazil	5.2	129	Cambodia	2.9
23	Turkey	8.2	77	Norway	5.2	130	Pakistan	2.9
24	Grenada	8.1	78	United States	5.2	131	Benin	2.8
25	Iran	8.0	79	Seychelles	5.1	132	Sudan	2.8
26	São Tomé and Príncipe	8.0	80	Saint Vincent and the Grenadines	5.1	133	Solomon Islands	2.7
27	Bahamas	7.9				134	Botswana	2.6
28	Malta	7.9	81	Réunion	5.0	135	Cape Verde	2.6
29	Congo, Dem. Rep. of	7.8	82	Slovenia	5.0	136	Guatemala	2.6
30	Macedonia	7.8	83	Tanzania	5.0	137	Nepal	2.6
31	Kuwait	7.7	84	United Kingdom	5.0	138	Indonesia	2.5
32	Colombia	7.6	85	China	4.9	139	Mauritius	2.5
33	Belize	7.5	86	Malawi	4.9	140	Mauritania	2.4
34	Bolivia	7.5	87	Yugoslavia	4.9	141	Nicaragua	2.4
35	Congo, Rep. of	7.5	88	Kiribati	4.8	142	Swaziland	2.4
36	Venezuela	7.4	89	Macau	4.8	143	Laos	2.3
37	Antigua and Barbuda	7.2	90	Romania	4.8	144	Myanmar (Burma)	2.3
38	Suriname	7.2	91	Hong Kong	4.7	145	South Africa	2.3
39	French Guiana	7.0	92	Paraguay	4.7	146	Togo	2.1
40	Italy	7.0	93	Sweden	4.7	147	Chad	1.9
41	Vanuatu	7.0	94	Barbados	4.6	148	Namibia	1.9
42	New Zealand	6.9	95	Brunei	4.6	149	Djibouti	1.8
43	Croatia	6.8	96	Japan	4.6	150	Fiji	1.7
44	Peru	6.8	97	Nigeria	4.5	151	Zambia	1.7
45	Canada	6.7	98	Guyana	4.4	152	Lesotho	1.6
46	Honduras	6.7	99	Czech Republic	4.3	153	Niger	1.6
47	South Korea	6.7	100	Morocco	4.3	154	Mozambique	1.5
48	Jamaica	6.6	101	Argentina	4.2	155	Gambia	1.3
49	Philippines	6.6	102	Sri Lanka	4.2	156	Bangladesh	1.1
50	Spain	6.6	103	Finland	4.1	157	Senegal	1.1
51	Central African Republic	6.5	104	Mexico	4.1	158	Zimbabwe	1.1
52	Netherlands	6.5	105	Poland	4.1	159	Burkina Faso	1.0
53	Portugal	6.5	106	Slovakia	4.1	160	Mali	0.8
54	Cyprus	6.4	107	Cuba	4.0	161	Mongolia	0.5

Source: World Data

Rank	Country/Entity	Percentage of Calories from Oils and Fats	Rank	Country/Entity	Percentage of Calories from Oils and Fats	Rank	Country/Entity	Percentage of Calories from Oils and Fats
1	Iraq	27.4	55	Panama	14.5	109	Romania	9.7
2	Belgium	26.2	56	Finland	14.2	110	Bahamas	9.6
3	Luxembourg	26.2	57	Guinea	13.9	111	Comoros	9.4
4	Libya	23.2	58	Kuwait	13.8	112	Kenya	9.3
5	Hungary	23.1	59	Turkey	13.8	113	Myanmar (Burma)	8.9
6	Ecuador	22.7	60	Barbados	13.7	114	Martinique	8.7
7	Germany	22.1	61	Malta	13.7	115	Dominica	8.6
8	Spain	22.1	62	Costa Rica	13.6	116	Indonesia	8.4
9	Italy	20.9	63	Nigeria	13.6	117	India	8.2
10	Austria	20.7	64	Grenada	13.3	118	Saint Vincent and the Grenadines	8.1
11	Sweden	20.6	65	French Polynesia	13.2			
12	Greece	20.4	66	Netherlands Antilles	13.2	119	Cameroon	7.9
13	Canada	19.8	67	Seychelles	13.2	120	Kiribati	7.9
14	Czech Republic	19.4	68	Syria	13.2	121	Suriname	7.9
15	France	19.4	69	Brazil	13.1	122	Egypt	7.7
16	Tunisia	19.4	70	Cuba	13.1	123	El Salvador	7.7
17	Yugoslavia	19.4	71	Guadeloupe	13.1	124	Papua New Guinea	7.7
18	United Kingdom	19.0	72	Malaysia	13.1	125	Sudan	7.7
19	United States	18.4	73	Gambia	13.0	126	Gabon	7.6
20	Portugal	18.2	74	Croatia	12.8	127	Botswana	7.5
21	Sierra Leone	18.1	75	South Africa	12.8	128	Brunei	7.4
22	Switzerland	18.0	76	Honduras	12.5	129	Côte d'Ivoire	7.4
23	Hong Kong	17.9	77	Saudi Arabia	12.4	130	Mali	7.4
24	Netherlands	17.8	78	Morocco	12.3	131	Philippines	6.9
25	Macau	17.7	79	Vanuatu	12.2	132	Congo, Dem. Rep. of	6.7
26	Slovenia	17.5	80	Australia	11.9	133	Thailand	6.5
27	Fiji	17.2	81	Mauritania	11.9	134	China	6.3
28	Cape Verde	17.1	82	Zimbabwe	11.9	135	Chad	6.2
29	Norway	17.1	83	Peru	11.7	136	Tanzania	6.1
30	Algeria	16.9	84	Congo, Rep. of	11.6	137	Mongolia	5.9
31	Israel	16.8	85	São Tomé and Príncipe	11.6	138	Bangladesh	5.8
32	Senegal	16.8	86	Nicaragua	11.3	139	Saint Lucia	5.8
33	Mauritius	16.7	87	Iran	11.2	140	North Korea	5.7
34	Ireland	16.2	88	Belize	11.1	141	Maldives	5.7
35	Central African Republic	16.1	89	Japan	11.0	142	Ghana	5.6
36	Jordan	16.1	90	Mexico	11.0	143	Swaziland	5.6
37	Slovakia	16.1	91	Paraguay	11.0	144	Nepal	5.5
38	Antigua and Barbuda	16.0	92	Angola	10.8	145	Benin	5.4
39	Dominican Republic	16.0	93	Chile	10.8	146	Guatemala	5.2
40	New Caledonia	15.8	94	Colombia	10.8	147	Namibia	5.1
41	Djibouti	15.7	95	Togo	10.8	148	Niger	4.6
42	Lebanon	15.7	96	United Arab Emirates	10.6	149	Guyana	4.5
43	Bulgaria	15.6	97	French Guiana	10.5	150	Burkina Faso	4.1
44	Pakistan	15.6	98	Russia	10.5	151	Cambodia	3.9
45	Poland	15.6	99	Iceland	10.4	152	Madagascar	3.9
46	Denmark	15.4	100	South Korea	10.3	153	Lesotho	3.7
47	Cyprus	15.3	101	Uruguay	10.3	154	Malawi	3.4
48	Venezuela	15.3	102	Albania	10.2	155	Zambia	3.4
49	Argentina	14.8	103	Yemen	10.2	156	Solomon Islands	3.2
50	Trinidad and Tobago	14.8	104	Bolivia	9.9	157	Uganda	2.9
51	Bermuda	14.7	105	Macedonia	9.8	158	Vietnam	2.8
52	Guinea-Bissau	14.7	106	Réunion	9.8	159	Laos	2.1
53	Saint Kitts and Nevis	14.7	107	Jamaica	9.7	160	Sri Lanka	1.8
54	New Zealand	14.6	108	Mozambique	9.7	161	Burundi	1.3

Source: World Data

19.10 Child Malnutrition

It has been found that children in poorer countries, in general, and poorer families, in particular, tend to receive the least amount of food supply and therefore suffer from severe malnutrition in their growing years. Such malnutrition is evidenced by low weight, developmental problems, susceptibility to disease, and inability to study or concentrate. The effects of child nutrition are long lasting and may permanently debilitate the affected person.

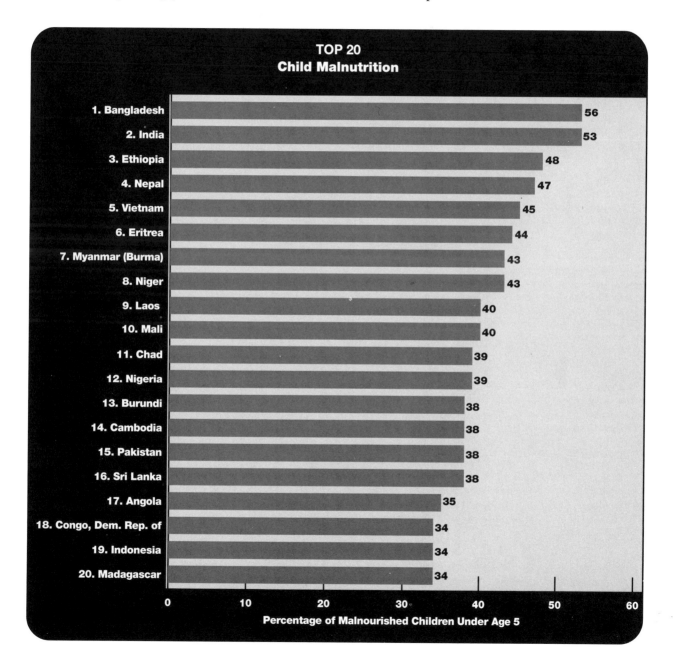

TOP 20
Child Malnutrition

Rank	Country	Percentage
1.	Bangladesh	56
2.	India	53
3.	Ethiopia	48
4.	Nepal	47
5.	Vietnam	45
6.	Eritrea	44
7.	Myanmar (Burma)	43
8.	Niger	43
9.	Laos	40
10.	Mali	40
11.	Chad	39
12.	Nigeria	39
13.	Burundi	38
14.	Cambodia	38
15.	Pakistan	38
16.	Sri Lanka	38
17.	Angola	35
18.	Congo, Dem. Rep. of	34
19.	Indonesia	34
20.	Madagascar	34

Percentage of Malnourished Children Under Age 5

Rank	Country/Entity	Percentage of Malnourished Children Under Age 5, 1992–1997	Rank	Country/Entity	Percentage of Malnourished Children Under Age 5, 1992–1997	Rank	Country/Entity	Percentage of Malnourished Children Under Age 5, 1992–1997
21	Burkina Faso	33	44	Malaysia	20	67	South Africa	9
22	Tanzania	31	45	Togo	19	68	Tunisia	9
23	Malawi	30	46	Uzbekistan	19	69	Bolivia	8
24	Papua New Guinea	30	47	Honduras	18	70	Colombia	8
25	Philippines	30	48	Ecuador	17	71	Kazakhstan	8
26	Benin	29	49	China	16	72	Peru	8
27	Rwanda	29	50	Iran	16	73	Brazil	6
28	Yemen	29	51	Lesotho	16	74	Dominican Republic	6
29	Haiti	28	52	Zimbabwe	16	75	Panama	6
30	Botswana	27	53	Egypt	15	76	Romania	6
31	Ghana	27	54	Mexico	14	77	Costa Rica	5
32	Guatemala	27	55	Algeria	13	78	Venezuela	5
33	Mozambique	26	56	Syria	13	79	Uruguay	4
34	Namibia	26	57	Mongolia	12	80	Lebanon	3
35	Uganda	26	58	Nicaragua	12	81	Russia	3
36	Côte d'Ivoire	24	59	El Salvador	11	82	Argentina	2
37	Congo, Rep. of	24	60	Kuwait	11	83	Chile	1
38	Guinea	24	61	Kyrgyzstan	11	84	Croatia	1
39	Zambia	24	62	Azerbaijan	10	85	Czech Republic	1
40	Central African Republic	23	63	Jamaica	10	86	United States	1
41	Kenya	23	64	Jordan	10	87	Australia	0
42	Mauritania	23	65	Morocco	10			
43	Senegal	22	66	Turkey	10			

Source: World Data

Chapter 20

Education

Literacy

Literacy has conflicting definitions in different countries. UNESCO defines literacy as the ability to read and write a simple sentence. In some countries, such as Japan, Sudan, Uganda, and Zambia, illiteracy is defined as never having attended school. In Tunisia, literacy is defined as the ability to read but not necessarily to write. In developed countries, literacy is defined in functional terms as the ability to fill out a simple application form. Literacy figures are also qualified by the age groups to which they refer. Data for most countries relate to populations aged fifteen and over but in others, such as Italy, the figures are based on the population over six. Other kinds of bias and error include exclusion of segments of the population, such as nomads in the Middle East and Africa, and Native Americans in South America. Further, because of the great prestige attached to literacy, governments in developing countries have shown a tendency to inflate, distort, and even fabricate literacy ratios. Even in developed countries, such as the United States, literacy rates may be far lower than noted in the ranking below. Female literacy rate is presented separately because the wide disparities between the rates for males and females in developing countries– sometimes as high as thirty to forty percentage points. Female education is deliberately discouraged in some Islamic societies because religious authorities fear that education might make women independent and rebellious.

20.1 Literacy

Rank	Country/Entity	Literacy Rate	Rank	Country/Entity	Literacy Rate	Rank	Country/Entity	Literacy Rate
1	Andorra	100.0	33	Guam	99.0	65	Malta	96.0
2	Austria	100.0	34	Nauru	99.0	66	Saint Vincent and	96.0
3	Belgium	100.0	35	Hungary	98.9		the Grenadines	
4	Czech Republic	100.0	36	Armenia	98.8	67	American Samoa	95.9
5	Denmark	100.0	37	France	98.8	68	Cuba	95.7
6	Finland	100.0	38	Poland	98.7	69	Israel	95.6
7	Germany	100.0	39	Ukraine	98.4	70	United States	95.5
8	Greenland	100.0	40	Bahamas	98.2	71	Chile	95.2
9	Guernsey	100.0	41	Guyana	98.1	72	Cyprus	95.2
10	Iceland	100.0	42	South Korea	98.0	73	Greece	95.2
11	Ireland	100.0	43	Russia	98.0	74	Aruba	95.0
12	Japan	100.0	44	Belarus	97.9	75	French Polynesia	95.0
13	Jersey	100.0	45	Bulgaria	97.9	76	North Korea	95.0
14	Liechtenstein	100.0	46	Trinidad and Tobago	97.9	77	Tuvalu	95.0
15	Luxembourg	100.0	47	Tajikistan	97.7	78	Costa Rica	94.8
16	Netherlands	100.0	48	Turkmenistan	97.7	79	Philippines	94.6
17	New Zealand	100.0	49	Palau	97.6	80	Taiwan	94.0
18	Norway	100.0	50	Kazakhstan	97.5	81	Netherlands Antilles	93.8
19	Samoa	100.0	51	Barbados	97.4	82	Thailand	93.8
20	Slovakia	100.0	52	Azerbaijan	97.3	83	Vietnam	93.7
21	Slovenia	100.0	53	Uruguay	97.3	84	Yugoslavia	93.3
22	Sweden	100.0	54	Uzbekistan	97.2	85	Maldives	93.2
23	Switzerland	100.0	55	Italy	97.1	86	Suriname	93.0
24	United Kingdom	100.0	56	Kyrgyzstan	97.0	87	Tonga	92.8
25	Estonia	99.7	57	Bermuda	96.9	88	Martinique	92.5
26	Australia	99.5	58	Croatia	96.7	89	Lebanon	92.4
27	Georgia	99.5	59	Moldova	96.7	90	Hong Kong	92.2
28	Latvia	99.5	60	Romania	96.7	91	Paraguay	92.1
29	Lithuania	99.5	61	Canada	96.6	92	Mayotte	91.9
30	San Marino	99.1	62	Spain	96.5	93	Albania	91.8
31	Faroe Islands	99.0	63	Northern Mariana Islands	96.3	94	Fiji	91.6
32	Gibraltar	99.0	64	Argentina	96.2	95	Colombia	91.3

Rank	Country/Entity	Literacy Rate	Rank	Country/Entity	Literacy Rate	Rank	Country/Entity	Literacy Rate
96	Marshall Islands	91.2	135	Qatar	79.4	174	Laos	56.6
97	Venezuela	91.1	136	United Arab Emirates	79.2	175	Malawi	56.4
98	Saint Kitts and Nevis	90.9	137	Kuwait	78.6	176	Guatemala	55.6
99	Panama	90.8	138	Equatorial Guinea	78.5	177	Guinea-Bissau	54.9
100	Sri Lanka	90.2	139	Réunion	78.2	178	São Tomé and Príncipe	54.2
101	Ecuador	90.1	140	Zambia	78.2	179	Solomon Islands	54.1
102	Guadeloupe	90.1	141	Kenya	78.1	180	Vanuatu	52.9
103	Antigua and Barbuda	90.0	142	Congo, Dem. Rep. of	77.3	181	India	52.0
104	Dominica	90.0	143	Micronesia	76.7	182	Togo	51.7
105	Kiribati	90.0	144	Swaziland	76.7	183	Egypt	51.4
106	Puerto Rico	89.7	145	Libya	76.2	184	Chad	48.1
107	Mexico	89.6	146	Namibia	75.8	185	Djibouti	46.2
108	Portugal	89.6	147	Congo, Rep. of	74.9	186	Sudan	46.1
109	Macau	89.5	148	El Salvador	74.1	187	Haiti	45.0
110	Macedonia	89.1	149	Honduras	72.7	188	Morocco	43.7
111	Singapore	89.1	150	Papua New Guinea	72.2	189	Yemen	43.2
112	Peru	88.7	151	Iran	72.1	190	Bhutan	42.2
113	Brunei	87.8	152	Cape Verde	71.6	191	Angola	41.7
114	Jordan	86.6	153	Lesotho	71.3	192	Côte d'Ivoire	40.1
115	Bosnia and Herzegovina	85.5	154	Syria	70.8	193	Mozambique	40.1
116	Bahrain	85.2	155	Belize	70.3	194	Gambia	38.6
117	Zimbabwe	85.1	156	Botswana	69.8	195	Liberia	38.3
118	Grenada	85.0	157	Tanzania	67.8	196	Bangladesh	38.1
119	Jamaica	85.0	158	Tunisia	66.7	197	Pakistan	37.8
120	Seychelles	84.2	159	Nicaragua	65.7	198	Mauritania	37.7
121	Indonesia	83.8	160	Cambodia	65.3	199	Benin	37.0
122	Malaysia	83.5	161	Ghana	64.5	200	Guinea	35.9
123	Brazil	83.3	162	Cameroon	63.4	201	Ethiopia	35.5
124	Bolivia	83.1	163	Gabon	63.2	202	Burundi	35.3
125	Myanmar (Burma)	83.1	164	Saudi Arabia	62.8	203	Senegal	33.1
126	French Guiana	83.0	165	Uganda	61.8	204	Afghanistan	31.5
127	Mauritius	82.9	166	Algeria	61.6	205	Sierra Leone	31.4
128	Mongolia	82.9	167	Rwanda	60.5	206	Mali	31.0
129	Turkey	82.3	168	Central African Republic	60.0	207	Nepal	27.5
130	Dominican Republic	82.1	169	Oman	58.8	208	Somalia	24.0
131	Saint Lucia	82.0	170	Iraq	58.0	209	Eritrea	20.0
132	South Africa	81.8	171	New Caledonia	57.9	210	Burkina Faso	19.2
133	China	81.5	172	Comoros	57.3	211	Niger	13.6
134	Madagascar	80.2	173	Nigeria	57.1			

Source: UNESCO Statistical Yearbook

20.2 Female Literacy

Rank	Country/Entity	Female Literacy Rate	Rank	Country/Entity	Female Literacy Rate	Rank	Country/Entity	Female Literacy Rate
1	Andorra	100.0	15	Luxembourg	100.0	29	Faroe Islands	99.0
2	Austria	100.0	16	Netherlands	100.0	30	Gibraltar	99.0
3	Belgium	100.0	17	New Zealand	100.0	31	Guam	99.0
4	Czech Republic	100.0	18	Norway	100.0	32	San Marino	98.8
5	Denmark	100.0	19	Samoa	100.0	33	France	98.7
6	Finland	100.0	20	Slovakia	100.0	34	Hungary	98.6
7	Germany	100.0	21	Slovenia	100.0	35	Poland	98.3
8	Greenland	100.0	22	Sweden	100.0	36	Armenia	98.1
9	Guernsey	100.0	23	Switzerland	100.0	37	Bahamas	98.0
10	Iceland	100.0	24	United Kingdom	100.0	38	Uruguay	97.7
11	Ireland	100.0	25	Estonia	99.6	39	Guyana	97.5
12	Japan	100.0	26	Georgia	99.4	40	Ukraine	97.4
13	Jersey	100.0	27	Lithuania	99.3	41	Bulgaria	97.1
14	Liechtenstein	100.0	28	Latvia	99.2	42	Bermuda	97.0

Rank	Country/Entity	Female Literacy Rate	Rank	Country/Entity	Female Literacy Rate	Rank	Country/Entity	Female Literacy Rate
43	Trinidad and Tobago	97.0	95	Albania	88.0	147	Ghana	53.5
44	Barbados	96.8	96	Mexico	87.4	148	Cambodia	53.4
45	Russia	96.8	97	Micronesia	87.2	149	Gabon	53.3
46	South Korea	96.7	98	Sri Lanka	87.2	150	Central African Republic	52.4
47	Belarus	96.6	99	Portugal	87.0	151	Cameroon	52.1
48	Palau	96.6	100	Seychelles	85.7	152	Rwanda	51.6
49	Tajikistan	96.6	101	Macau	85.3	153	Comoros	50.4
50	Turkmenistan	96.6	102	Macedonia	83.8	154	Saudi Arabia	50.2
51	Italy	96.4	103	Brazil	83.2	155	Uganda	50.2
52	American Samoa	96.3	104	Peru	83.0	156	Algeria	49.0
53	Argentina	96.2	105	Singapore	83.0	157	Guatemala	48.6
54	Kazakhstan	96.1	106	Brunei	82.5	158	Vanuatu	47.8
55	Uzbekistan	96.0	107	French Guiana	82.3	159	Nigeria	47.3
56	Azerbaijan	95.9	108	Dominican Republic	82.2	160	Oman	46.2
57	Malta	95.9	109	South Africa	81.7	161	Iraq	45.0
58	Northern Mariana Islands	95.6	110	Réunion	80.3	162	Solomon Islands	44.9
59	Kyrgyzstan	95.5	111	Qatar	79.9	163	Laos	44.4
60	Cuba	95.3	112	Zimbabwe	79.9	164	Guinea-Bissau	42.5
61	United States	95.3	113	United Arab Emirates	79.8	165	Haiti	42.2
62	Spain	95.1	114	Bahrain	79.4	166	Malawi	41.8
63	Chile	95.0	115	Jordan	79.4	167	São Tomé and Príncipe	39.1
64	Costa Rica	95.0	116	Mauritius	78.8	168	Egypt	38.8
65	French Polynesia	95.0	117	Malaysia	78.1	169	India	37.7
66	Romania	95.0	118	Indonesia	78.0	170	Togo	37.0
67	Croatia	94.8	119	Myanmar (Burma)	77.7	171	Chad	34.7
68	Moldova	94.4	120	Mongolia	77.2	172	Sudan	34.6
69	Philippines	94.3	121	Bosnia and Herzegovina	76.6	173	Djibouti	32.7
70	Israel	93.6	122	Bolivia	76.0	174	Morocco	31.0
71	Netherlands Antilles	93.4	123	Swaziland	75.6	175	Côte d'Ivoire	30.0
72	Martinique	93.2	124	Kuwait	74.9	176	Angola	28.5
73	Greece	93.0	125	Namibia	74.0	177	Bhutan	28.1
74	Maldives	93.0	126	Madagascar	72.9	178	Mauritania	26.3
75	Cyprus	92.8	127	China	72.7	179	Bangladesh	26.1
76	Tonga	92.8	128	Honduras	72.7	180	Benin	25.8
77	Thailand	91.6	129	Turkey	72.4	181	Ethiopia	25.3
78	Colombia	91.4	130	El Salvador	71.3	182	Gambia	24.9
79	Vietnam	91.2	131	Zambia	71.3	183	Pakistan	24.4
80	Suriname	91.0	132	Kenya	70.0	184	Mozambique	23.3
81	Paraguay	90.6	133	Equatorial Guinea	68.1	185	Senegal	23.2
82	Guadeloupe	90.5	134	Congo, Dem. Rep. of	67.7	186	Mali	23.1
83	Lebanon	90.3	135	Congo, Rep. of	67.2	187	Yemen	23.1
84	Venezuela	90.3	136	Nicaragua	66.6	188	Burundi	22.5
85	Panama	90.2	137	Iran	65.8	189	Liberia	22.4
86	Taiwan	90.2	138	Cape Verde	63.8	190	Guinea	21.9
87	Marshall Islands	90.0	139	Libya	63.0	191	Sierra Leone	18.2
88	Saint Kitts and Nevis	90.0	140	Papua New Guinea	62.7	192	Afghanistan	15.0
89	Puerto Rico	89.7	141	Lesotho	62.3	193	Nepal	14.0
90	Fiji	89.3	142	Botswana	59.9	194	Somalia	14.0
91	Yugoslavia	89.2	143	New Caledonia	58.3	195	Burkina Faso	9.2
92	Jamaica	89.1	144	Tanzania	56.8	196	Niger	6.6
93	Ecuador	88.2	145	Syria	55.8			
94	Hong Kong	88.2	146	Tunisia	54.6			

Source: UNESCO Statistical Yearbook

Public Expenditures on Education

A progressive government is distinguished by its commitment to education as an investment rather than as an expenditure. Reactionary governments generally tend to jettison educational programs in hard times and spend as little as possible on improving the quality of education. In many countries, especially those with federal systems, such as the United States and Australia, education is more a state or provincial subject, but the national government provides extensive financial support. Actual oversight of the school systems falls on municipalities and local school boards specially appointed or elected for the purpose. The data in these rankings include expenditures at the local and state or provincial levels but exclude expenditures by private schools at all levels. Private schools are a significant segment of the educational system, especially at the kindergarten and college and university levels.

20.3 Public Expenditures on Education as Percentage of Gross National Product (GNP)

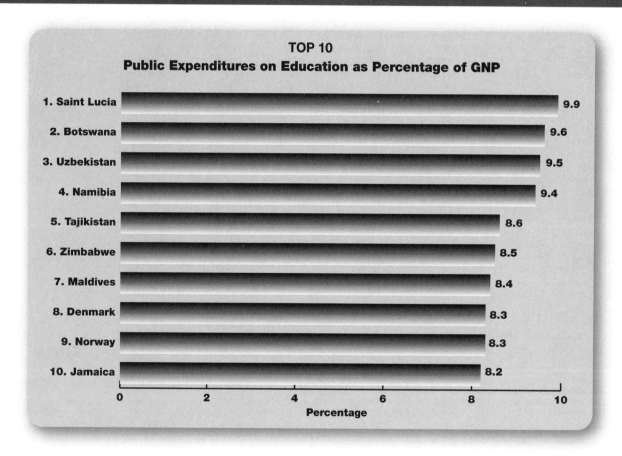

TOP 10
Public Expenditures on Education as Percentage of GNP

Rank	Country	Percentage
1.	Saint Lucia	9.9
2.	Botswana	9.6
3.	Uzbekistan	9.5
4.	Namibia	9.4
5.	Tajikistan	8.6
6.	Zimbabwe	8.5
7.	Maldives	8.4
8.	Denmark	8.3
9.	Norway	8.3
10.	Jamaica	8.2

Rank	Country/Entity	Public Expenditures on Education as Percentage of GNP	Rank	Country/Entity	Public Expenditures on Education as Percentage of GNP	Rank	Country/Entity	Public Expenditures on Education as Percentage of GNP
11	Swaziland	8.1	14	Finland	7.6	17	Kenya	7.4
12	Sweden	8.0	15	Seychelles	7.5	18	Canada	7.3
13	Ukraine	7.7	16	Yemen	7.5	19	Armenia	7.2

Rank	Country/Entity	Public Expenditures on Education as Percentage of GNP	Rank	Country/Entity	Public Expenditures on Education as Percentage of GNP	Rank	Country/Entity	Public Expenditures on Education as Percentage of GNP
20	Barbados	7.2	69	Panama	5.2	119	Senegal	3.6
21	Estonia	6.9	70	Taiwan	5.2	120	Colombia	3.5
22	Saint Vincent and the Grenadines	6.9	71	Venezuela	5.2	121	India	3.5
			72	Slovakia	5.1	122	Suriname	3.5
23	Kyrgyzstan	6.8	73	Iceland	5.0	123	Albania	3.4
24	South Africa	6.8	74	Mauritania	5.0	124	Ecuador	3.4
25	Tunisia	6.8	75	Spain	5.0	125	Qatar	3.4
26	New Zealand	6.7	76	Angola	4.9	126	Turkey	3.4
27	Bolivia	6.6	77	Italy	4.9	127	Saint Kitts and Nevis	3.3
28	Cuba	6.6	78	Morocco	4.9	128	Gabon	3.2
29	Hungary	6.6	79	Vanuatu	4.9	129	Benin	3.1
30	Israel	6.6	80	Bahrain	4.8	130	Brunei	3.1
31	Ireland	6.3	81	Côte d'Ivoire	4.7	131	Ghana	3.1
32	Jordan	6.3	82	Ethiopia	4.7	132	Niger	3.1
33	Kiribati	6.3	83	Germany	4.7	133	Sri Lanka	3.1
34	Latvia	6.3	84	Grenada	4.7	134	Azerbaijan	3.0
35	Mozambique	6.3	85	Tonga	4.7	135	Romania	3.0
36	Belize	6.1	86	Brazil	4.6	136	Singapore	3.0
37	Czech Republic	6.1	87	Poland	4.6	137	Cameroon	2.9
38	Lithuania	6.1	88	Argentina	4.5	138	Chile	2.9
39	Moldova	6.1	89	Aruba	4.5	139	Nepal	2.9
40	Congo, Rep. of	5.9	90	Costa Rica	4.5	140	Paraguay	2.9
41	France	5.9	91	Kazakhstan	4.5	141	Burundi	2.8
42	Lesotho	5.9	92	Trinidad and Tobago	4.5	142	Hong Kong	2.8
43	Slovenia	5.8	93	Cape Verde	4.4	143	Uruguay	2.8
44	Belgium	5.7	94	Cyprus	4.4	144	Bhutan	2.7
45	Malawi	5.7	95	Oman	4.4	145	Pakistan	2.7
46	Algeria	5.6	96	Mauritius	4.3	146	Vietnam	2.7
47	Australia	5.6	97	Syria	4.3	147	Central African Republic	2.5
48	Belarus	5.6	98	Bulgaria	4.2	148	Laos	2.4
49	Egypt	5.6	99	Samoa	4.2	149	Bangladesh	2.3
50	Kuwait	5.6	100	Thailand	4.2	150	China	2.3
51	Mongolia	5.6	101	Guyana	4.1	151	Chad	2.2
52	Togo	5.6	102	Russia	4.1	152	El Salvador	2.2
53	Austria	5.5	103	Bahamas	4.0	153	Mali	2.2
54	Dominica	5.5	104	Iran	4.0	154	Philippines	2.2
55	Gambia	5.5	105	Turkmenistan	4.0	155	Lebanon	2.0
56	Macedonia	5.5	106	Comoros	3.9	156	Dominican Republic	1.9
57	Saudi Arabia	5.5	107	Honduras	3.9	157	Eritrea	1.9
58	Switzerland	5.5	108	Nicaragua	3.9	158	Madagascar	1.9
59	United Kingdom	5.5	109	Djibouti	3.8	159	Uganda	1.9
60	Fiji	5.4	110	Japan	3.8	160	Equatorial Guinea	1.8
61	Portugal	5.4	111	Peru	3.8	161	Guinea	1.8
62	Croatia	5.3	112	Solomon Islands	3.8	162	United Arab Emirates	1.8
63	Malaysia	5.3	113	Bermuda	3.7	163	Zambia	1.8
64	Mexico	5.3	114	Greece	3.7	164	Guatemala	1.7
65	Netherlands	5.3	115	South Korea	3.7	165	Haiti	1.5
66	United States	5.3	116	Rwanda	3.7	166	Myanmar (Burma)	1.3
67	Georgia	5.2	117	Tanzania	3.7	167	Sierra Leone	0.9
68	Malta	5.2	118	Burkina Faso	3.6			

Source: UNESCO Statistical Yearbook

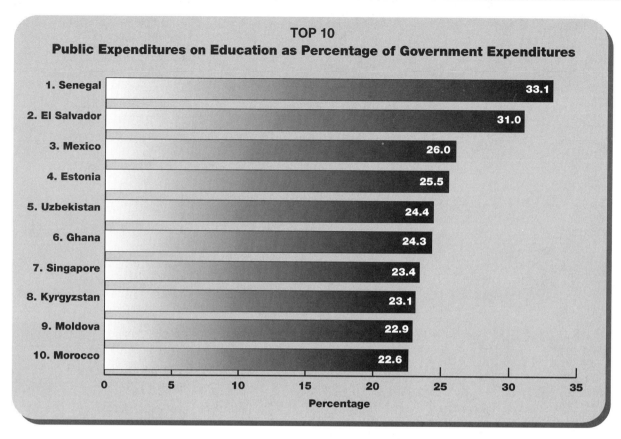

TOP 10
Public Expenditures on Education as Percentage of Government Expenditures

Rank	Country	Percentage
1. Senegal		33.1
2. El Salvador		31.0
3. Mexico		26.0
4. Estonia		25.5
5. Uzbekistan		24.4
6. Ghana		24.3
7. Singapore		23.4
8. Kyrgyzstan		23.1
9. Moldova		22.9
10. Morocco		22.6

Percentage

Rank	Country/Entity	Public Expenditures on Education as Percentage of Government Expenditures	Rank	Country/Entity	Public Expenditures on Education as Percentage of Government Expenditures	Rank	Country/Entity	Public Expenditures on Education as Percentage of Government Expenditures
11	Venezuela	22.4	33	Guatemala	18.2	55	United Arab Emirates	16.3
12	Saint Lucia	22.2	34	Iran	17.8	56	Cameroon	16.1
13	Lithuania	21.8	35	Saudi Arabia	17.8	57	Kenya	16.1
14	Swaziland	21.7	36	Algeria	17.6	58	Mauritania	16.1
15	Belize	21.3	37	Kazakhstan	17.6	59	Tajikistan	16.1
16	Namibia	21.3	38	Azerbaijan	17.5	60	Gambia	16.0
17	Central African Republic	20.9	39	Ecuador	17.5	61	Ukraine	15.7
18	Panama	20.9	40	South Korea	17.4	62	Switzerland	15.6
19	Yemen	20.8	41	Tunisia	17.4	63	Malaysia	15.5
20	Armenia	20.5	42	Mauritius	17.3	64	Benin	15.2
21	Botswana	20.5	43	Syria	17.3	65	Argentina	15.0
22	South Africa	20.5	44	Belarus	17.1	66	Malawi	15.0
23	Thailand	20.1	45	New Zealand	17.1	67	Norway	15.0
24	Haiti	20.0	46	Hong Kong	17.0	68	Uganda	15.0
25	Cape Verde	19.9	47	Czech Republic	16.9	69	Congo, Dem. Rep. of	14.7
26	Costa Rica	19.9	48	Paraguay	16.9	70	Myanmar (Burma)	14.4
27	Libya	19.8	49	Latvia	16.8	71	United States	14.1
28	Turkmenistan	19.7	50	Jordan	16.6	72	Chile	14.0
29	Barbados	19.0	51	Honduras	16.5	73	Poland	14.0
30	Macedonia	18.7	52	Bahamas	16.3	74	Egypt	13.8
31	Togo	18.7	53	Oman	16.3	75	Saint Vincent and the Grenadines	13.8
32	Fiji	18.6	54	Seychelles	16.3			

Rank	Country/Entity	Public Expenditures on Education as Percentage of Government Expenditures	Rank	Country/Entity	Public Expenditures on Education as Percentage of Government Expenditures	Rank	Country/Entity	Public Expenditures on Education as Percentage of Government Expenditures
76	Canada	13.7	96	Lesotho	12.2	116	Cuba	10.2
77	Australia	13.6	97	Nicaragua	12.2	117	Philippines	10.1
78	Madagascar	13.6	98	India	12.1	118	Saint Kitts and Nevis	9.8
79	Maldives	13.6	99	Iceland	12.0	119	Russia	9.6
80	Romania	13.6	100	Mozambique	12.0	120	Netherlands	9.5
81	Uruguay	13.3	101	Finland	11.9	121	Germany	9.4
82	Cyprus	13.2	102	Malta	11.8	122	Italy	8.8
83	Dominican Republic	13.2	103	Tanzania	11.4	123	Bangladesh	8.7
84	Ireland	13.2	104	United Kingdom	11.4	124	Bolivia	8.2
85	Mali	13.2	105	Burkina Faso	11.1	125	Guyana	8.1
86	Nepal	13.2	106	Djibouti	11.1	126	Sri Lanka	8.1
87	Ethiopia	13.0	107	Kuwait	11.0	127	Solomon Islands	7.9
88	Colombia	12.9	108	Sweden	11.0	128	Austria	7.7
89	Bahrain	12.8	109	France	10.8	129	Jamaica	7.7
90	Denmark	12.6	110	Japan	10.8	130	Vietnam	7.4
91	Slovenia	12.6	111	Niger	10.8	131	Greece	7.0
92	Spain	12.6	112	Angola	10.7	132	Georgia	6.9
93	Lebanon	12.5	113	Samoa	10.7	133	Hungary	6.9
94	Israel	12.3	114	Dominica	10.6	134	Equatorial Guinea	5.6
95	China	12.2	115	Belgium	10.2			

Source: UNESCO Statistical Yearbook

Primary Schools

These rankings deal with primary or elementary institutions. They cover the number of schools, as well as number of teachers and students and the student–teacher ratio. Because compulsory education laws apply at this stage, it is also the most universal educational level. The data reflect differences among countries in the age and duration of schooling. Most countries have social promotions at this level, where children automatically advance from grade to grade, but, nevertheless, dropout rates are quite high. Primary schools in some rural areas are quite rudimentary and teachers often have only low-level training.

20.5 Primary Schools

Rank	Country/Entity	Primary Schools	Rank	Country/Entity	Primary Schools	Rank	Country/Entity	Primary Schools
1	China	849,123	17	Philippines	35,671	33	Congo, Dem. Rep. of	14,885
2	India	590,421	18	Thailand	34,412	34	Romania	13,963
3	Brazil	195,545	19	United Kingdom	32,385	35	Madagascar	13,624
4	Indonesia	149,464	20	Argentina	25,448	36	Vietnam	13,092
5	Pakistan	115,744	21	Japan	24,548	37	Canada	12,700
6	Mexico	91,857	22	South Africa	22,260	38	Sudan	12,187
7	United States	85,393	23	Nepal	22,157	39	Portugal	12,069
8	Russia	70,200	24	Ukraine	21,900	40	Saudi Arabia	11,217
9	Bangladesh	66,168	25	Italy	20,442	41	Ghana	11,056
10	Iran	61,889	26	Poland	19,823	42	Yemen	11,013
11	Turkey	49,240	27	Germany	17,910	43	Tanzania	10,892
12	Colombia	46,707	28	Algeria	17,186	44	Guatemala	10,770
13	Peru	46,652	29	Spain	16,540	45	Syria	10,564
14	France	41,244	30	Egypt	16,188	46	Australia	9,865
15	Nigeria	38,649	31	Venezuela	15,894	47	Cuba	9,864
16	Myanmar (Burma)	35,856	32	Kenya	15,804	48	Sri Lanka	9,648

Rank	Country/Entity	Primary Schools	Rank	Country/Entity	Primary Schools	Rank	Country/Entity	Primary Schools
49	Uzbekistan	9,300	103	Chad	2,447	157	Comoros	275
50	Ethiopia	9,276	104	Uruguay	2,423	158	Vanuatu	272
51	Kazakhstan	8,700	105	New Zealand	2,397	159	Kuwait	251
52	Uganda	8,531	106	Lithuania	2,361	160	Gambia	250
53	Chile	8,323	107	Bosnia and Herzegovina	2,205	161	Belize	245
54	Honduras	8,186	108	Lebanon	2,100	162	Bhutan	235
55	Iraq	8,035	109	Mali	1,996	163	Iceland	205
56	Greece	7,634	110	Israel	1,937	164	Singapore	199
57	Laos	7,591	111	Croatia	1,928	165	Micronesia	177
58	Netherlands	7,411	112	Turkmenistan	1,900	166	Brunei	170
59	Côte d'Ivoire	7,185	113	Kyrgyzstan	1,885	167	Qatar	169
60	Malaysia	7,049	114	Albania	1,777	168	Maldives	134
61	Cameroon	6,801	115	Afghanistan	1,753	169	Bahrain	124
62	North Korea	6,122	116	Rwanda	1,710	170	Bahamas	115
63	Haiti	6,111	117	Moldova	1,700	171	Tonga	115
64	South Korea	5,732	118	Sierra Leone	1,643	172	Malta	111
65	Paraguay	5,318	119	Mauritania	1,635	173	Barbados	106
66	Nicaragua	4,993	120	Congo, Rep. of	1,612	174	Marshall Islands	103
67	Belarus	4,900	121	Puerto Rico	1,542	175	Kiribati	92
68	Sweden	4,900	122	Burundi	1,418	176	Greenland	88
69	Morocco	4,740	123	Armenia	1,400	177	Mayotte	88
70	Zimbabwe	4,633	124	Lesotho	1,234	178	Saint Lucia	88
71	Austria	4,557	125	West Bank	1,193	179	Netherlands Antilles	85
72	Cambodia	4,539	126	Somalia	1,125	180	Djibouti	81
73	Azerbaijan	4,502	127	Gabon	1,105	181	French Guiana	78
74	Finland	4,474	128	Macedonia	1,050	182	Saint Vincent and the Grenadines	65
75	Belgium	4,453	129	Namibia	933			
76	Yugoslavia	4,441	130	Central African Republic	930	183	Dominica	64
77	Tunisia	4,384	131	Hong Kong	856	184	São Tomé and Príncipe	64
78	Czech Republic	4,212	132	Slovenia	850	185	Faroe Islands	62
79	Mozambique	4,167	133	Jamaica	788	186	Virgin Islands (U.S.)	62
80	Dominican Republic	4,001	134	Equatorial Guinea	781	187	Macau	61
81	El Salvador	3,961	135	Estonia	741	188	Grenada	57
82	Zambia	3,883	136	Fiji	693	189	Antigua and Barbuda	43
83	Hungary	3,765	137	Botswana	669	190	Western Sahara	40
84	Costa Rica	3,544	138	Mongolia	650	191	Guam	36
85	Malawi	3,425	139	Latvia	643	192	Aruba	32
86	Tajikistan	3,400	140	Eritrea	537	193	Isle of Man	32
87	Georgia	3,378	141	Swaziland	535	194	Jersey	32
88	Bulgaria	3,325	142	Solomon Islands	520	195	Saint Kitts and Nevis	31
89	Ireland	3,319	143	United Arab Emirates	512	196	American Samoa	30
90	Norway	3,308	144	Trinidad and Tobago	475	197	Seychelles	27
91	Togo	3,283	145	Guyana	423	198	Bermuda	24
92	Guinea	3,237	146	Oman	415	199	Guernsey	22
93	Burkina Faso	2,971	147	Cyprus	383	200	Gibraltar	21
94	Benin	2,889	148	Cape Verde	370	201	Northern Mariana Islands	18
95	Panama	2,845	149	Réunion	345	202	Liechtenstein	14
96	Papua New Guinea	2,790	150	Guadeloupe	344	203	San Marino	14
97	Niger	2,656	151	Gaza Strip	339	204	Andorra	12
98	Denmark	2,536	152	New Caledonia	280	205	Tuvalu	11
99	Taiwan	2,523	153	Suriname	280	206	Monaco	7
100	Slovakia	2,485	154	Mauritius	279	207	Nauru	3
101	Jordan	2,482	155	French Polynesia	278			
102	Senegal	2,454	156	Martinique	276			

Source: UNESCO Statistical Yearbook

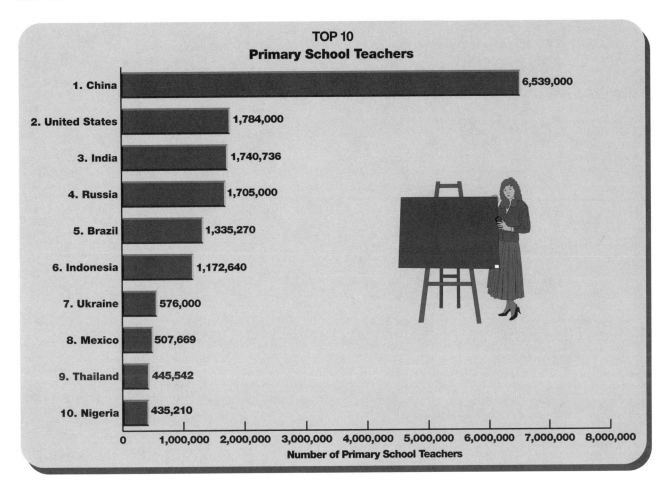

TOP 10
Primary School Teachers

Rank	Country	Number
1. China		6,539,000
2. United States		1,784,000
3. India		1,740,736
4. Russia		1,705,000
5. Brazil		1,335,270
6. Indonesia		1,172,640
7. Ukraine		576,000
8. Mexico		507,669
9. Thailand		445,542
10. Nigeria		435,210

Number of Primary School Teachers

Rank	Country/Entity	Primary School Teachers	Rank	Country/Entity	Primary School Teachers	Rank	Country/Entity	Primary School Teachers
11	Japan	431,000	32	Colombia	170,526	53	Taiwan	87,934
12	Uzbekistan	413,000	33	Myanmar (Burma)	169,748	54	Nepal	85,621
13	South Africa	349,436	34	Saudi Arabia	169,321	55	Tajikistan	84,000
14	Pakistan	337,400	35	Algeria	169,010	56	Hungary	83,658
15	Philippines	324,418	36	Romania	168,702	57	Sudan	83,306
16	Poland	323,500	37	Azerbaijan	156,000	58	Ethiopia	83,113
17	Iran	311,531	38	Canada	148,724	59	Chile	78,813
18	Egypt	302,916	39	Malaysia	144,937	60	Yemen	78,646
19	France	301,699	40	North Korea	138,945	61	Uganda	76,111
20	Vietnam	298,856	41	South Korea	137,912	62	Portugal	73,221
21	Italy	289,055	42	Spain	132,566	63	Turkmenistan	72,900
22	Argentina	286,885	43	Iraq	132,030	64	Belgium	72,589
23	Kazakhstan	262,000	44	Belarus	127,000	65	Bulgaria	70,763
24	Bangladesh	242,252	45	Congo, Dem. Rep. of	121,054	66	Sri Lanka	70,108
25	Turkey	232,000	46	Syria	113,530	67	Ghana	66,068
26	United Kingdom	231,659	47	Libya	103,791	68	Austria	65,977
27	Australia	202,401	48	Morocco	102,163	69	Zimbabwe	63,475
28	Germany	199,623	49	Tanzania	101,816	70	Ecuador	63,347
29	Venezuela	185,748	50	Netherlands	99,031	71	Czech Republic	63,019
30	Peru	176,173	51	Cuba	90,565	72	Tunisia	59,887
31	Kenya	173,002	52	Sweden	89,275	73	Denmark	58,500

Rank	Country/Entity	Primary School Teachers	Rank	Country/Entity	Primary School Teachers	Rank	Country/Entity	Primary School Teachers
74	Israel	57,618	118	Moldova	14,209	162	Malta	1,990
75	Armenia	54,000	119	Papua New Guinea	13,652	163	Belize	1,939
76	Bolivia	51,763	120	Macedonia	13,102	164	Bhutan	1,859
77	Yugoslavia	51,728	121	Senegal	12,711	165	New Caledonia	1,758
78	Jordan	48,158	122	Benin	12,343	166	Comoros	1,737
79	Lithuania	47,000	123	Niger	12,216	167	Luxembourg	1,732
80	Malawi	45,775	124	Guinea	11,875	168	Bahamas	1,581
81	Guatemala	44,220	125	Botswana	11,726	169	Barbados	1,553
82	Dominican Republic	42,135	126	Jamaica	11,283	170	Macau	1,482
83	Cameroon	40,970	127	Oman	11,158	171	Equatorial Guinea	1,381
84	Slovakia	39,224	128	Namibia	10,912	172	Saint Lucia	1,204
85	Zambia	38,528	129	Sierra Leone	10,595	173	Saint Vincent and	1,080
86	Cambodia	37,827	130	Burundi	10,400		the Grenadines	
87	Madagascar	37,676	131	Singapore	10,356	174	Netherlands Antilles	1,059
88	Norway	37,640	132	Burkina Faso	10,300	175	Greenland	1,021
89	Greece	37,549	133	Kuwait	9,414	176	Djibouti	1,005
90	Côte d'Ivoire	36,058	134	Chad	9,404	177	Western Sahara	925
91	Paraguay	34,580	135	Mali	8,738	178	Guam	898
92	Albania	32,098	136	Somalia	8,208	179	Vanuatu	852
93	Angola	31,062	137	Gaza Strip	7,941	180	Grenada	849
94	Honduras	28,978	138	Lesotho	7,433	181	French Guiana	802
95	Haiti	27,607	139	Trinidad and Tobago	7,210	182	Virgin Islands (U.S.)	790
96	El Salvador	26,259	140	Mongolia	7,088	183	Tonga	701
97	Laos	24,600	141	Congo, Rep. of	7,060	184	Marshall Islands	669
98	Mozambique	24,575	142	Mauritius	6,381	185	Dominica	641
99	Croatia	24,194	143	Swaziland	5,887	186	Seychelles	633
100	Kyrgyzstan	24,086	144	Qatar	5,853	187	São Tomé and Príncipe	559
101	Latvia	23,779	145	Eritrea	5,828	188	Mayotte	555
102	New Zealand	23,379	146	Mauritania	5,181	189	Kiribati	537
103	Bosnia and Herzegovina	23,369	147	Gabon	4,709	190	American Samoa	524
104	Ireland	20,901	148	Fiji	4,644	191	Antigua and Barbuda	439
105	Nicaragua	20,626	149	Central African Republic	4,004	192	Saint Kitts and Nevis	366
106	Afghanistan	20,055	150	Iceland	3,549	193	Aruba	331
107	Hong Kong	19,710	151	Bahrain	3,536	194	Gibraltar	305
108	Rwanda	18,937	152	Cyprus	3,498	195	Bermuda	294
109	Puerto Rico	18,359	153	Guyana	3,453	196	Northern Mariana Islands	240
110	Uruguay	16,821	154	Suriname	3,447	197	Guernsey	236
111	Togo	16,217	155	Brunei	3,380	198	San Marino	217
112	West Bank	15,912	156	Martinique	3,251	199	Liechtenstein	144
113	Costa Rica	15,806	157	Guadeloupe	3,167	200	Monaco	102
114	Slovenia	15,471	158	Gambia	3,158	201	Tuvalu	72
115	Estonia	15,453	159	French Polynesia	2,949	202	Nauru	61
116	United Arab Emirates	15,449	160	Cape Verde	2,657			
117	Panama	14,998	161	Solomon Islands	2,510			

Source: UNESCO Statistical Yearbook

20.7 Primary School Students

Rank	Country/Entity	Primary School Students	Rank	Country/Entity	Primary School Students	Rank	Country/Entity	Primary School Students
1	China	159,064,000	12	Philippines	10,903,529	23	Argentina	5,126,307
2	India	109,734,292	13	Vietnam	10,228,800	24	Poland	5,104,200
3	United States	33,410,000	14	Iran	9,745,600	25	Uzbekistan	5,090,000
4	Brazil	31,101,662	15	Thailand	8,583,525	26	United Kingdom	4,906,439
5	Indonesia	26,200,023	16	Japan	8,371,000	27	Peru	4,822,423
6	Russia	22,000,000	17	Egypt	7,470,437	28	Algeria	4,617,000
7	Nigeria	16,191,000	18	Ukraine	7,007,000	29	Colombia	4,327,507
8	Bangladesh	15,185,000	19	Turkey	6,403,000	30	Venezuela	4,217,283
9	Mexico	14,572,202	20	Myanmar (Burma)	5,711,202	31	France	4,012,600
10	South Africa	11,782,324	21	Kenya	5,428,600	32	South Korea	3,800,540
11	Pakistan	11,484,000	22	Congo, Dem. Rep. of	5,417,506	33	Tanzania	3,736,734

Rank	Country/Entity	Primary School Students	Rank	Country/Entity	Primary School Students	Rank	Country/Entity	Primary School Students
34	Germany	3,634,342	96	Laos	724,100	158	Equatorial Guinea	75,751
35	Nepal	3,191,600	97	Israel	691,800	159	Réunion	73,702
36	Australia	3,109,337	98	Slovakia	661,082	160	Solomon Islands	73,120
37	Kazakhstan	3,060,000	99	Burundi	651,086	161	Bahrain	72,329
38	Sudan	3,023,955	100	Austria	649,994	162	Cyprus	64,884
39	Iraq	2,977,800	101	Mali	608,444	163	Suriname	62,613
40	Uganda	2,912,473	102	Denmark	605,798	164	Bhutan	56,773
41	Morocco	2,895,737	103	Benin	602,069	165	Brunei	55,241
42	Malawi	2,860,819	104	Burkina Faso	600,032	166	Belize	52,994
43	Malaysia	2,843,663	105	Chad	591,784	167	Qatar	52,130
44	Italy	2,825,838	106	Finland	588,162	168	French Polynesia	48,160
45	Ethiopia	2,722,192	107	Guinea	584,161	169	Maldives	45,333
46	Syria	2,672,960	108	Armenia	574,500	170	Macau	45,153
47	Zimbabwe	2,655,564	109	Lithuania	562,000	171	Iceland	42,212
48	Romania	2,532,169	110	Bosnia and Herzegovina	539,875	172	Guadeloupe	38,092
49	Yemen	2,493,017	111	Albania	535,713	173	Samoa	37,833
50	Canada	2,413,126	112	Papua New Guinea	525,995	174	Malta	35,479
51	Spain	2,364,910	113	Costa Rica	508,923	175	New Caledonia	34,591
52	Saudi Arabia	2,248,122	114	Congo, Rep. of	497,305	176	Djibouti	33,960
53	Chile	2,119,737	115	Ireland	491,256	177	Martinique	33,532
54	Ecuador	1,986,753	116	Kyrgyzstan	473,077	178	Bahamas	33,343
55	Taiwan	1,971,439	117	Norway	470,936	179	Saint Lucia	32,545
56	Sri Lanka	1,960,495	118	Hong Kong	466,507	180	Western Sahara	32,257
57	Cameroon	1,896,722	119	New Zealand	455,671	181	Luxembourg	26,867
58	Ghana	1,796,490	120	Switzerland	452,789	182	Barbados	26,662
59	Cambodia	1,703,316	121	Croatia	431,795	183	Vanuatu	26,267
60	Côte d'Ivoire	1,609,929	122	West Bank	431,565	184	Micronesia	25,139
61	Belarus	1,561,000	123	Puerto Rico	427,582	185	Grenada	23,256
62	North Korea	1,543,000	124	Niger	414,296	186	Netherlands Antilles	22,735
63	Zambia	1,506,349	125	Lesotho	366,935	187	Mayotte	21,579
64	Madagascar	1,504,668	126	Namibia	366,666	188	Saint Vincent and	21,386
65	Azerbaijan	1,486,000	127	Lebanon	365,174		the Grenadines	
66	Netherlands	1,477,000	128	Panama	362,142	189	São Tomé and Príncipe	19,822
67	Tunisia	1,468,998	129	Uruguay	337,889	190	French Guiana	17,006
68	Dominican Republic	1,462,722	130	Moldova	320,055	191	Guam	16,816
69	Mozambique	1,415,428	131	Jamaica	319,298	192	Tonga	16,540
70	Guatemala	1,393,921	132	Botswana	310,050	193	Kiribati	16,316
71	Afghanistan	1,312,197	133	Central African Republic	308,409	194	Virgin Islands (U.S.)	14,544
72	Tajikistan	1,289,000	134	Oman	297,209	195	Marshall Islands	13,355
73	Bolivia	1,278,775	135	Gaza Strip	281,255	196	Dominica	12,627
74	Libya	1,254,242	136	Mauritania	268,216	197	Antigua and Barbuda	11,506
75	Rwanda	1,104,902	137	Sierra Leone	267,425	198	Seychelles	9,825
76	Cuba	1,074,153	138	United Arab Emirates	262,628	199	Greenland	9,056
77	El Salvador	1,042,256	139	Singapore	261,648	200	American Samoa	7,884
78	Jordan	1,036,079	140	Macedonia	258,955	201	Aruba	7,139
79	Honduras	1,008,092	141	Gabon	247,018	202	Saint Kitts and Nevis	7,101
80	Czech Republic	1,004,565	142	Eritrea	241,725	203	Faroe Islands	6,895
81	Angola	990,155	143	Estonia	218,600	204	Jersey	5,794
82	Hungary	966,000	144	Slovenia	210,989	205	Bermuda	5,793
83	Bulgaria	963,582	145	Trinidad and Tobago	195,013	206	Isle of Man	5,550
84	Turkmenistan	940,600	146	Swaziland	192,599	207	Andorra	5,424
85	Sweden	916,661	147	Mongolia	176,036	208	Northern Mariana Islands	4,882
86	Yugoslavia	914,532	148	Somalia	171,830	209	Guernsey	4,697
87	Portugal	910,650	149	Fiji	145,630	210	Gibraltar	2,936
88	Paraguay	835,089	150	Kuwait	140,979	211	Palau	2,635
89	Togo	824,626	151	Mauritius	122,895	212	Liechtenstein	1,998
90	Georgia	815,000	152	Gambia	105,471	213	Tuvalu	1,906
91	Haiti	787,553	153	Guyana	100,806	214	Monaco	1,893
92	Nicaragua	765,972	154	Guinea-Bissau	100,369	215	Nauru	1,367
93	Greece	745,666	155	Latvia	98,694	216	San Marino	1,134
94	Senegal	738,550	156	Cape Verde	78,173			
95	Belgium	731,527	157	Comoros	77,837			

Source: UNESCO Statistical Yearbook

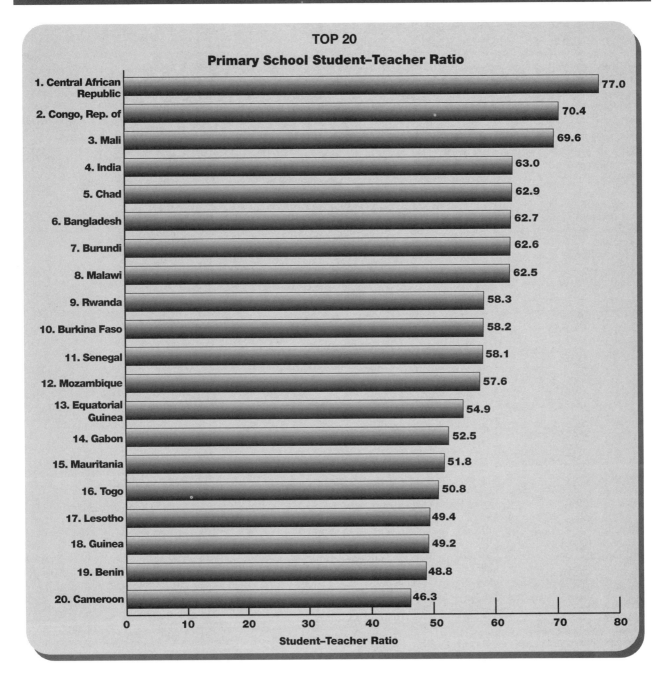

TOP 20

Primary School Student–Teacher Ratio

Rank / Country	Student–Teacher Ratio
1. Central African Republic	77.0
2. Congo, Rep. of	70.4
3. Mali	69.6
4. India	63.0
5. Chad	62.9
6. Bangladesh	62.7
7. Burundi	62.6
8. Malawi	62.5
9. Rwanda	58.3
10. Burkina Faso	58.2
11. Senegal	58.1
12. Mozambique	57.6
13. Equatorial Guinea	54.9
14. Gabon	52.5
15. Mauritania	51.8
16. Togo	50.8
17. Lesotho	49.4
18. Guinea	49.2
19. Benin	48.8
20. Cameroon	46.3

Student–Teacher Ratio

Rank	Country/Entity	Primary School Student–Teacher Ratio	Rank	Country/Entity	Primary School Student–Teacher Ratio	Rank	Country/Entity	Primary School Student–Teacher Ratio
21	Cambodia	45.0	27	Madagascar	39.9	33	Nepal	37.3
22	Congo, Dem. Rep. of	44.8	28	El Salvador	39.7	34	Nigeria	37.2
23	Côte d'Ivoire	44.6	29	Zambia	39.1	35	Nicaragua	37.1
24	Comoros	43.0	30	Mayotte	38.9	36	Tanzania	36.7
25	Zimbabwe	41.8	31	Papua New Guinea	38.5	37	Sudan	36.3
26	Eritrea	41.5	32	Uganda	38.3	38	South Africa	35.7

Rank	Country/Entity	Primary School Student–Teacher Ratio	Rank	Country/Entity	Primary School Student–Teacher Ratio	Rank	Country/Entity	Primary School Student–Teacher Ratio
39	São Tomé and Príncipe	35.5	92	Mongolia	24.8	144	Malta	17.8
40	Gaza Strip	35.4	93	Bolivia	24.7	145	Spain	17.8
41	Western Sahara	34.9	94	Egypt	24.7	146	Yugoslavia	17.7
42	Honduras	34.8	95	Tunisia	24.5	147	Barbados	17.2
43	Dominican Republic	34.7	96	China	24.3	148	United Arab Emirates	17.0
44	Vietnam	34.2	97	Panama	24.1	149	Albania	16.7
45	Pakistan	34.0	98	Paraguay	24.1	150	Slovakia	16.7
46	Niger	33.9	99	Hong Kong	23.7	151	Brunei	16.3
47	Myanmar (Burma)	33.6	100	Tonga	23.6	152	French Polynesia	16.3
48	Philippines	33.6	101	Ireland	23.5	153	Gibraltar	16.3
49	Gambia	33.4	102	Syria	23.5	154	Canada	16.2
50	Ethiopia	32.8	103	Brazil	23.3	155	Czech Republic	15.9
51	Swaziland	32.7	104	Puerto Rico	23.3	156	Poland	15.8
52	Namibia	32.0	105	Bosnia and Herzegovina	23.1	157	Netherlands	15.7
53	Angola	31.9	106	Venezuela	22.7	158	Luxembourg	15.5
54	Iran	31.7	107	Iraq	22.6	159	Seychelles	15.5
55	Yemen	31.7	108	Moldova	22.5	160	Australia	15.4
56	Guatemala	31.5	109	Nauru	22.4	161	Tajikistan	15.3
57	Costa Rica	31.4	110	Taiwan	22.4	162	American Samoa	15.0
58	Ecuador	31.4	111	Indonesia	22.3	163	Kuwait	15.0
59	Fiji	31.4	112	Aruba	21.6	164	Romania	15.0
60	Kenya	31.4	113	Jordan	21.5	165	Estonia	14.1
61	Vanuatu	30.8	114	Netherlands Antilles	21.5	166	Liechtenstein	13.9
62	Bhutan	30.5	115	French Guiana	21.2	167	Bulgaria	13.6
63	Macau	30.5	116	United Kingdom	21.2	168	Slovenia	13.6
64	Kiribati	30.4	117	Bahamas	21.1	169	Saudi Arabia	13.3
65	Dominica	29.8	118	Somalia	20.9	170	Russia	12.9
66	Cape Verde	29.4	119	Northern Mariana Islands	20.3	171	Turkmenistan	12.9
67	Laos	29.4	120	Uruguay	20.1	172	Norway	12.5
68	Guyana	29.2	121	Marshall Islands	20.0	173	Portugal	12.4
69	Solomon Islands	29.1	122	Greece	19.9	174	Ukraine	12.4
70	Mexico	28.7	123	Guernsey	19.9	175	Belarus	12.3
71	Haiti	28.5	124	Macedonia	19.9	176	Uzbekistan	12.3
72	Jamaica	28.3	125	Saint Vincent and the Grenadines	19.8	177	Libya	12.1
73	Morocco	28.3				178	Guadeloupe	12.0
74	Sri Lanka	28.0	126	Bermuda	19.7	179	Lithuania	12.0
75	South Korea	27.6	127	Kyrgyzstan	19.7	180	Cuba	11.9
76	Turkey	27.6	128	New Caledonia	19.7	181	Iceland	11.9
77	Grenada	27.4	129	Malaysia	19.6	182	Kazakhstan	11.7
78	Peru	27.4	130	New Zealand	19.5	183	Hungary	11.5
79	Algeria	27.3	131	Japan	19.4	184	North Korea	11.1
80	Ghana	27.2	132	Saint Kitts and Nevis	19.4	185	Armenia	11.0
81	West Bank	27.1	133	Mauritius	19.3	186	Greenland	10.5
82	Saint Lucia	27.0	134	Thailand	19.3	187	Denmark	10.4
83	Trinidad and Tobago	27.0	135	Guam	18.7	188	Martinique	10.3
84	Chile	26.9	136	United States	18.7	189	Sweden	10.3
85	Oman	26.6	137	Monaco	18.6	190	Austria	9.9
86	Botswana	26.4	138	Cyprus	18.5	191	Italy	9.8
87	Antigua and Barbuda	26.2	139	Virgin Islands (U.S.)	18.4	192	Azerbaijan	9.5
88	Belize	25.9	140	Germany	18.2	193	Qatar	8.9
89	Colombia	25.4	141	Suriname	18.2	194	San Marino	5.2
90	Singapore	25.3	142	Argentina	17.9			
91	Sierra Leone	25.2	143	Croatia	17.8			

Source: UNESCO Statistical Yearbook

Secondary Schools

In almost all countries, secondary schools mark the concluding stage of compulsory education and end with a school-leaving examination. Secondary schools may include what are called middle schools, which students attend between elementary school and high school. At the secondary level students generally tend to branch out into special fields of study. One of the principal functions of secondary schools is to prepare students for college; secondary curricula are therefore linked to college-level curricula. Secondary school teachers receive extensive professional training and their performance is closely monitored.

20.9 Secondary Schools

Rank	Country/Entity	Secondary Schools	Rank	Country/Entity	Secondary Schools	Rank	Country/Entity	Secondary Schools
1	India	265,869	44	Romania	1,276	87	Lesotho	187
2	China	81,020	45	Guatemala	1,274	88	Singapore	178
3	Indonesia	27,177	46	Yemen	1,224	89	Burkina Faso	173
4	Spain	25,775	47	Morocco	1,172	90	Sierra Leone	167
5	Mexico	22,255	48	Madagascar	1,142	91	Swaziland	165
6	Pakistan	20,243	49	Netherlands	1,124	92	Denmark	153
7	Iran	18,445	50	Paraguay	1,102	93	Benin	145
8	Germany	17,711	51	Hungary	980	94	Fiji	142
9	Japan	16,775	52	Taiwan	920	95	Papua New Guinea	135
10	Brazil	13,449	53	Afghanistan	819	96	Oman	128
11	France	11,212	54	Israel	797	97	Jamaica	126
12	Bangladesh	11,019	55	Laos	750	98	Mauritius	123
13	Turkey	10,689	56	Norway	746	99	Qatar	123
14	Italy	9,278	57	Jordan	741	100	Namibia	114
15	Colombia	8,161	58	Tunisia	712	101	Burundi	113
16	Peru	8,085	59	Austria	693	102	Cyprus	107
17	Nepal	7,582	60	Portugal	663	103	Niger	105
18	Egypt	7,307	61	Honduras	661	104	Réunion	104
19	Argentina	7,239	62	Haiti	630	105	Suriname	100
20	Saudi Arabia	6,346	63	Sweden	629	106	Macedonia	95
21	Vietnam	6,298	64	Yugoslavia	570	107	Malawi	94
22	Nigeria	6,074	65	Hong Kong	498	108	Guyana	93
23	Philippines	5,880	66	Tanzania	491	109	Eritrea	86
24	Sri Lanka	5,771	67	Croatia	482	110	Guadeloupe	84
25	Ghana	5,540	68	Finland	477	111	Somalia	82
26	Congo, Dem. Rep. of	4,276	69	Ireland	452	112	Martinique	76
27	Algeria	3,954	70	Nicaragua	451	113	Chad	66
28	South Korea	3,790	71	Cambodia	440	114	Malta	59
29	Canada	3,324	72	Kuwait	409	115	Mauritania	56
30	Greece	2,988	73	Puerto Rico	395	116	Albania	47
31	Myanmar (Burma)	2,916	74	Latvia	376	117	Central African Republic	46
32	Kenya	2,639	75	Czech Republic	361	118	New Caledonia	46
33	Iraq	2,635	76	Senegal	359	119	French Polynesia	38
34	Sudan	2,578	77	Uruguay	348	120	Tonga	38
35	Syria	2,526	78	New Zealand	339	121	Brunei	37
36	Thailand	2,318	79	Panama	339	122	Iceland	35
37	Cuba	2,175	80	Mali	307	123	Barbados	33
38	Belgium	1,950	81	Costa Rica	285	124	Gambia	32
39	Poland	1,705	82	Mozambique	239	125	Bhutan	31
40	Venezuela	1,621	83	Bosnia and Herzegovina	238	126	Belize	30
41	Zimbabwe	1,535	84	Slovenia	224	127	Netherlands Antilles	27
42	Kyrgyzstan	1,474	85	Slovakia	190	128	Djibouti	26
43	Malaysia	1,427	86	Botswana	188	129	Macau	25

Rank	Country/Entity	Secondary Schools	Rank	Country/Entity	Secondary Schools	Rank	Country/Entity	Secondary Schools
130	Guam	24	139	Dominica	13	149	American Samoa	7
131	Solomon Islands	23	140	Western Sahara	13	150	Isle of Man	7
132	French Guiana	22	141	Antigua and Barbuda	12	151	Saint Kitts and Nevis	7
133	Saint Vincent and the Grenadines	21	142	Bermuda	12	152	Andorra	6
			143	Marshall Islands	12	153	Faroe Islands	6
134	Seychelles	20	144	Aruba	10	154	Mayotte	5
135	Grenada	19	145	Kiribati	9	155	San Marino	3
136	Micronesia	16	146	Northern Mariana Islands	9	156	Nauru	2
137	Jersey	14	147	Guernsey	8	157	Tuvalu	1
138	Saint Lucia	14	148	Liechtenstein	8			

Source: UNESCO Statistical Yearbook

20.10 Secondary School Teachers

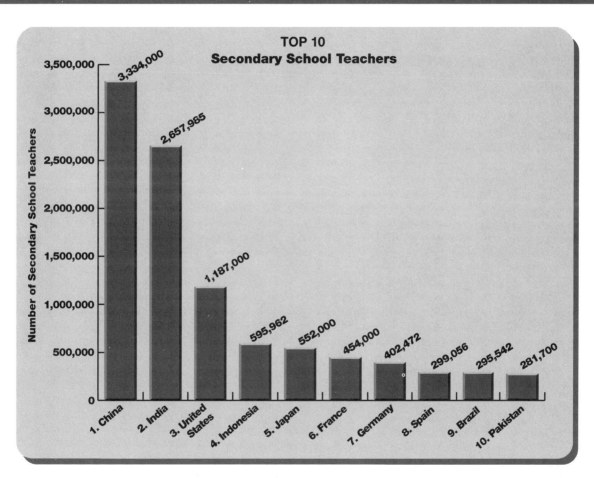

TOP 10
Secondary School Teachers

Rank	Country/Entity	Secondary School Teachers	Rank	Country/Entity	Secondary School Teachers	Rank	Country/Entity	Secondary School Teachers
11	Mexico	256,831	19	Nigeria	152,596	27	Belgium	110,599
12	Egypt	235,313	20	Algeria	150,397	28	Thailand	107,025
13	Argentina	233,564	21	Colombia	141,484	29	Sri Lanka	105,916
14	Iran	228,869	22	Turkey	138,000	30	Saudi Arabia	105,056
15	United Kingdom	228,187	23	Bangladesh	135,217	31	Peru	104,476
16	Italy	214,861	24	Canada	133,358	32	Netherlands	89,370
17	Vietnam	193,814	25	Philippines	131,831	33	Malaysia	86,891
18	South Korea	157,731	26	North Korea	111,000	34	Taiwan	76,562

Rank	Country/Entity	Secondary School Teachers	Rank	Country/Entity	Secondary School Teachers	Rank	Country/Entity	Secondary School Teachers
35	Morocco	73,726	84	Panama	11,627	134	Eritrea	2,031
36	Myanmar (Burma)	71,904	85	Yemen	11,130	135	Gabon	1,897
37	Portugal	69,095	86	Denmark	11,000	136	Guyana	1,828
38	Ecuador	62,630	87	Czech Republic	10,903	137	Mauritania	1,776
39	Romania	60,514	88	Dominican Republic	10,757	138	Bahamas	1,775
40	Congo, Dem. Rep. of	59,325	89	Tanzania	10,612	139	French Polynesia	1,745
41	Syria	51,483	90	Haiti	10,174	140	Luxembourg	1,686
42	Chile	50,187	91	Singapore	9,777	141	New Caledonia	1,669
43	Iraq	48,961	92	Slovenia	9,748	142	Iceland	1,454
44	Cuba	46,722	93	Côte d'Ivoire	9,505	143	Barbados	1,406
45	Greece	45,794	94	Oman	9,188	144	Western Sahara	1,267
46	Ghana	43,367	95	Bosnia and Herzegovina	9,030	145	Macau	1,205
47	Tunisia	41,885	96	Jamaica	8,377	146	Gambia	1,126
48	Latvia	41,029	97	Congo, Rep. of	5,710	147	Malawi	1,096
49	Austria	39,553	98	Senegal	5,509	148	French Guiana	875
50	Israel	39,093	99	Slovakia	5,457	149	Central African Republic	845
51	Kyrgyzstan	38,915	100	Nicaragua	5,356	150	Tonga	809
52	Laos	35,100	101	Angola	5,138	151	Guam	758
53	Poland	34,700	102	Trinidad and Tobago	4,844	152	Belize	740
54	Moldova	33,752	103	Togo	4,736	153	Bhutan	662
55	Venezuela	33,692	104	Botswana	4,712	154	Djibouti	628
56	Kenya	31,657	106	Jordan	4,597	155	Solomon Islands	618
57	Nepal	30,637	107	Réunion	4,591	156	Netherlands Antilles	617
58	Sweden	29,563	108	Mali	4,549	157	Comoros	613
59	Hungary	29,462	109	Macedonia	4,520	158	Virgin Islands (U.S.)	541
60	Sudan	29,208	110	Mozambique	4,376	159	Saint Lucia	524
61	Zimbabwe	27,320	111	Mauritius	4,375	160	Equatorial Guinea	466
62	Yugoslavia	26,954	112	Sierra Leone	4,313	161	Seychelles	440
63	Ethiopia	22,779	113	Albania	4,149	162	Cape Verde	438
64	Hong Kong	22,777	114	Guadeloupe	3,834	163	Saint Vincent and the Grenadines	395
65	Norway	21,197	115	Cyprus	3,832			
66	Guatemala	20,942	116	Qatar	3,738	164	Grenada	381
67	Paraguay	20,793	117	Martinique	3,736	165	Saint Kitts and Nevis	326
68	Uruguay	20,061	118	Rwanda	3,413	166	São Tomé and Príncipe	318
69	Kuwait	18,700	119	Burkina Faso	3,346	167	Antigua and Barbuda	277
70	Afghanistan	17,548	120	Fiji	3,045	168	Guernsey	276
71	Cambodia	16,349	121	Swaziland	2,872	169	Mayotte	246
72	Croatia	15,269	122	Malta	2,679	170	American Samoa	245
73	New Zealand	15,246	123	Lesotho	2,597	171	Vanuatu	220
74	Madagascar	15,118	124	Burundi	2,562	172	Bermuda	198
75	Libya	14,941	125	Namibia	2,534	173	Monaco	196
76	Cameroon	14,917	126	Papua New Guinea	2,415	174	Aruba	183
77	Uganda	14,447	127	Benin	2,384	175	Kiribati	179
78	Puerto Rico	13,612	128	Bahrain	2,305	176	Liechtenstein	164
79	Ireland	12,635	129	Niger	2,219	177	Northern Mariana Islands	163
80	Honduras	12,480	130	Brunei	2,157	178	Marshall Islands	144
81	Bolivia	12,434	131	Somalia	2,109	179	San Marino	134
82	United Arab Emirates	12,388	132	Suriname	2,056	180	Nauru	34
83	Mongolia	12,323	133	Chad	2,046	181	Tuvalu	21

Source: UNESCO Statistical Yearbook

20.11 Secondary School Students

Rank	Country/Entity	Secondary School Students	Rank	Country/Entity	Secondary School Students	Rank	Country/Entity	Secondary School Students
1	India	63,521,637	8	France	5,737,458	15	Mexico	4,493,173
2	China	53,710,000	9	Vietnam	5,332,400	16	Nigeria	4,451,000
3	United States	17,390,000	10	Bangladesh	4,884,000	17	Egypt	4,242,245
4	Japan	9,296,000	11	Pakistan	4,819,000	18	United Kingdom	3,779,262
5	Indonesia	8,864,001	12	Philippines	4,762,877	19	South Korea	3,683,857
6	Iran	7,284,611	13	Spain	4,744,829	20	Turkey	3,498,000
7	Germany	5,822,242	14	Brazil	4,510,199	21	Colombia	2,879,681

Rank	Country/Entity	Secondary School Students	Rank	Country/Entity	Secondary School Students	Rank	Country/Entity	Secondary School Students
22	Algeria	2,544,864	82	Bolivia	219,232	142	Malta	29,907
23	Canada	2,469,552	83	Panama	216,217	143	Suriname	29,554
24	North Korea	2,468,000	84	Nicaragua	211,606	144	El Salvador	29,527
25	Sri Lanka	2,315,541	85	Costa Rica	207,231	145	Bahamas	28,363
26	Argentina	2,238,091	86	Jamaica	207,035	146	Brunei	27,801
27	Thailand	2,118,767	87	Kuwait	204,194	147	Gambia	27,120
28	Peru	2,023,830	88	Singapore	203,662	148	French Polynesia	25,541
29	Italy	1,907,024	89	Zambia	199,081	149	Macau	21,813
30	Myanmar (Burma)	1,779,503	90	Croatia	196,740	150	Barbados	21,259
31	Malaysia	1,694,243	91	Haiti	193,624	151	Iceland	17,970
32	Taiwan	1,412,201	92	Congo, Rep. of	189,381	152	Guam	17,531
33	Saudi Arabia	1,375,753	93	Honduras	184,589	153	Comoros	17,474
34	Morocco	1,247,608	94	Uruguay	184,083	154	Bhutan	15,984
35	Iraq	1,062,204	95	Senegal	182,140	155	Maldives	15,933
36	Nepal	944,500	96	Libya	181,368	156	Tonga	15,702
37	Laos	886,500	97	Tanzania	180,899	157	New Caledonia	15,664
38	Netherlands	868,000	98	Bosnia and Herzegovina	172,063	158	Equatorial Guinea	14,511
39	Syria	846,778	99	Angola	166,812	159	French Guiana	13,585
40	Ghana	816,578	100	Mozambique	165,868	160	Virgin Islands (U.S.)	12,502
41	Ecuador	813,557	101	Togo	161,672	161	Cape Verde	11,808
42	Belgium	796,914	102	Oman	160,654	162	Djibouti	11,628
43	Tunisia	794,394	103	United Arab Emirates	158,625	163	Belize	10,648
44	Romania	757,673	104	Finland	134,851	164	Western Sahara	10,541
45	Portugal	749,838	105	Czech Republic	133,093	165	Saint Vincent and	9,870
46	Ethiopia	747,142	106	Guinea	127,517		the Grenadines	
47	Zimbabwe	711,094	107	Burkina Faso	116,033	166	Saint Lucia	9,550
48	Greece	700,488	108	Mali	112,670	167	Luxembourg	9,012
49	Sudan	683,982	109	Slovenia	102,117	168	Netherlands Antilles	8,801
50	Poland	683,000	110	Namibia	101,838	169	Solomon Islands	7,981
51	Chile	664,498	111	Trinidad and Tobago	100,609	170	São Tomé and Príncipe	7,446
52	Congo, Dem. Rep. of	640,298	112	Benin	97,480	171	Grenada	7,260
53	Kenya	517,577	113	Rwanda	94,586	172	Seychelles	6,548
54	Afghanistan	512,815	114	Jordan	93,773	173	Dominica	6,493
55	Kyrgyzstan	498,849	115	Mauritius	91,401	174	Guinea-Bissau	5,505
56	Israel	478,900	116	Niger	88,810	175	Micronesia	5,385
57	Hong Kong	477,708	117	Botswana	86,684	176	Saint Kitts and Nevis	4,541
58	Côte d'Ivoire	463,810	118	Chad	82,559	177	Isle of Man	4,458
59	Cuba	460,438	119	Eritrea	78,902	178	Jersey	4,405
60	Cameroon	459,068	120	Macedonia	77,754	179	Antigua and Barbuda	4,294
61	Moldova	412,679	121	Slovakia	76,380	180	Vanuatu	4,269
62	Switzerland	369,036	122	Denmark	75,793	181	Mayotte	3,973
63	Hungary	361,400	123	Albania	73,259	182	Guernsey	3,642
64	Yugoslavia	352,346	124	Réunion	71,694	183	Bermuda	3,610
65	Puerto Rico	334,661	125	Sierra Leone	70,900	184	American Samoa	3,483
66	Guatemala	334,383	126	Papua New Guinea	68,818	185	Aruba	3,247
67	Venezuela	311,209	127	Guyana	67,039	186	Kiribati	3,152
68	Sweden	309,952	128	Lesotho	61,615	187	Andorra	2,655
69	Madagascar	298,241	129	Fiji	60,237	188	Marshall Islands	2,400
70	Cambodia	297,555	130	Gabon	56,457	189	Monaco	2,387
71	Austria	295,473	131	Burundi	55,713	190	Northern Mariana Islands	2,075
72	Lebanon	277,646	132	Cyprus	53,738	191	Liechtenstein	1,887
73	Uganda	256,258	133	Swaziland	52,571	192	Gibraltar	1,805
74	Dominican Republic	240,441	134	Guadeloupe	51,366	193	Greenland	1,649
75	Latvia	235,952	135	Bahrain	48,944	194	Palau	1,021
76	Paraguay	235,914	136	Malawi	48,332	195	Faroe Islands	1,017
77	Yemen	232,506	137	Martinique	47,172	196	San Marino	771
78	New Zealand	227,934	138	Central African Republic	46,989	197	Nauru	629
79	Mongolia	227,811	139	Mauritania	43,861	198	Tuvalu	314
80	Norway	226,983	140	Somalia	42,764			
81	Ireland	225,490	141	Qatar	36,964			

Source: UNESCO Statistical Yearbook

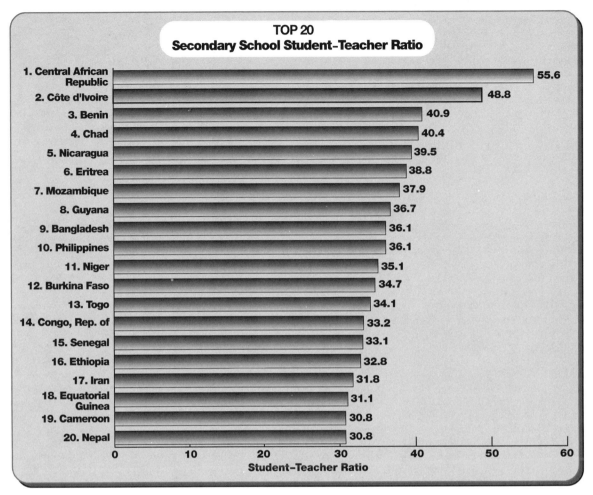

TOP 20
Secondary School Student–Teacher Ratio

Rank	Country	Student–Teacher Ratio
1. Central African Republic		55.6
2. Côte d'Ivoire		48.8
3. Benin		40.9
4. Chad		40.4
5. Nicaragua		39.5
6. Eritrea		38.8
7. Mozambique		37.9
8. Guyana		36.7
9. Bangladesh		36.1
10. Philippines		36.1
11. Niger		35.1
12. Burkina Faso		34.7
13. Togo		34.1
14. Congo, Rep. of		33.2
15. Senegal		33.1
16. Ethiopia		32.8
17. Iran		31.8
18. Equatorial Guinea		31.1
19. Cameroon		30.8
20. Nepal		30.8

Rank	Country/Entity	Secondary School Student–Teacher Ratio
21	Angola	30.2
22	Gabon	29.8
23	Namibia	29.3
24	Nigeria	29.2
25	Rwanda	27.7
26	Vietnam	27.5
27	Guinea	27.2
28	Cape Verde	27.0
29	Malawi	26.8
30	Zimbabwe	26.0
31	Comoros	25.5
32	Laos	25.3
33	Turkey	25.3
34	Saint Vincent and the Grenadines	25.0
35	Mali	24.8
36	Egypt	24.7
37	Jamaica	24.7
38	Mauritania	24.7
39	Myanmar (Burma)	24.7

Rank	Country/Entity	Secondary School Student–Teacher Ratio
40	Puerto Rico	24.6
41	Bhutan	24.1
42	Gambia	24.1
43	Papua New Guinea	24.1
44	India	23.9
45	Lesotho	23.7
46	South Korea	23.4
47	São Tomé and Príncipe	23.4
48	Sudan	23.4
49	Guam	23.1
50	Congo, Dem. Rep. of	22.6
51	Dominican Republic	22.4
52	North Korea	22.2
53	Sri Lanka	21.9
54	Burundi	21.7
55	Iraq	21.7
56	Hong Kong	21.2
57	Malta	20.9
58	Yemen	20.9
59	Mauritius	20.8

Rank	Country/Entity	Secondary School Student–Teacher Ratio
60	Singapore	20.8
61	Trinidad and Tobago	20.6
62	Jordan	20.4
63	Colombia	20.3
64	Somalia	20.3
65	Fiji	19.8
66	Thailand	19.8
67	Madagascar	19.7
68	Poland	19.7
69	Malaysia	19.5
70	Peru	19.4
71	Tonga	19.4
72	Vanuatu	19.4
73	Bosnia and Herzegovina	19.1
74	Grenada	19.1
75	Haiti	19.0
76	Tunisia	19.0
77	Tanzania	18.9
78	Ghana	18.8
79	Panama	18.6

Rank	Country/Entity	Secondary School Student–Teacher Ratio	Rank	Country/Entity	Secondary School Student–Teacher Ratio	Rank	Country/Entity	Secondary School Student–Teacher Ratio
80	Canada	18.5	112	Bahamas	16.0	144	Kyrgyzstan	12.8
81	Mongolia	18.5	113	Guatemala	16.0	145	Northern Mariana Islands	12.7
82	Nauru	18.5	114	Spain	15.9	146	France	12.6
83	Botswana	18.4	115	Antigua and Barbuda	15.5	147	Martinique	12.6
84	Taiwan	18.4	116	French Guiana	15.5	148	Romania	12.5
85	Swaziland	18.3	117	Brazil	15.3	149	Iceland	12.4
86	Bermuda	18.2	118	Greece	15.3	150	Hungary	12.3
87	Cambodia	18.2	119	Barbados	15.1	151	Czech Republic	12.2
88	Saint Lucia	18.2	120	Indonesia	14.9	152	Monaco	12.2
89	Macau	18.1	121	New Zealand	14.9	153	Libya	12.1
90	Ireland	17.8	122	Seychelles	14.9	154	United Arab Emirates	12.0
91	Albania	17.7	123	Honduras	14.8	155	Liechtenstein	11.5
92	Aruba	17.7	124	French Polynesia	14.6	156	Portugal	11.3
93	Uganda	17.7	125	United States	14.6	157	Kuwait	10.9
94	Bolivia	17.6	126	Suriname	14.4	158	Norway	10.7
95	Kiribati	17.6	127	Netherlands Antilles	14.3	159	Slovenia	10.5
96	Mexico	17.5	128	American Samoa	14.2	160	Sweden	10.5
97	Oman	17.5	129	Cyprus	14.0	161	Paraguay	10.3
98	Virgin Islands (U.S.)	17.2	130	Germany	14.0	162	Qatar	9.9
99	Pakistan	17.1	131	Slovakia	14.0	163	Cuba	9.8
100	Algeria	16.9	132	Saint Kitts and Nevis	13.9	164	Argentina	9.6
101	Morocco	16.9	133	Belize	13.7	165	Uruguay	9.2
102	Japan	16.8	134	Guadeloupe	13.4	166	Venezuela	9.2
103	Marshall Islands	16.7	135	Chile	13.2	167	Italy	8.9
104	United Kingdom	16.6	136	Guernsey	13.2	168	Western Sahara	8.3
105	Macedonia	16.5	137	New Caledonia	13.1	169	Netherlands	7.7
106	Sierra Leone	16.4	138	Saudi Arabia	13.1	170	Austria	7.5
107	Syria	16.4	139	Yugoslavia	13.1	171	Denmark	6.8
108	Kenya	16.3	140	Ecuador	13.0	172	San Marino	5.8
109	Réunion	16.3	141	Brunei	12.9	173	Luxembourg	5.3
110	Mayotte	16.2	142	Croatia	12.9			
111	China	16.1	143	Solomon Islands	12.9			

Source: UNESCO Statistical Yearbook

Colleges and Universities

Postsecondary institutions comprise undergraduate and graduate colleges and universities and postgraduate research institutions, both public and private. These institutions generally represent the culmination of a person's educational career ending with the award of degrees or certificates. It is also the stage at which there is a strong transnational flow of students, particularly from developing nations to the developed ones. Unlike primary and secondary schools, colleges are often prestigious institutions, and major universities constitute the flagships of the educational system. College studies generally take between four years for a basic degree to eight years for a professional degree. One of the most significant rankings relates to the educational attainment of the population. Despite the expansion of education throughout the world, only a minority of people have university education.

20.13 Colleges and Universities

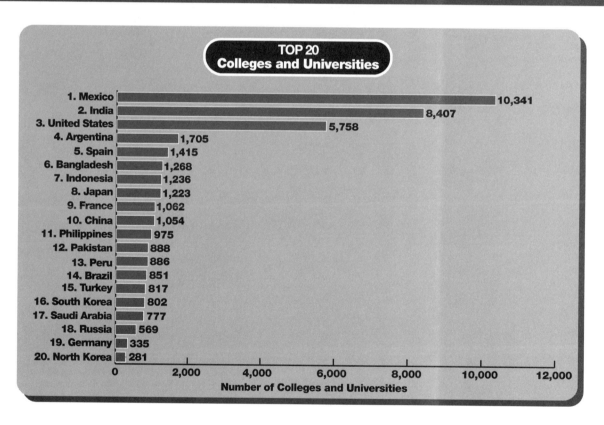

TOP 20
Colleges and Universities

Rank	Country	Number of Colleges and Universities
1. Mexico		10,341
2. India		8,407
3. United States		5,758
4. Argentina		1,705
5. Spain		1,415
6. Bangladesh		1,268
7. Indonesia		1,236
8. Japan		1,223
9. France		1,062
10. China		1,054
11. Philippines		975
12. Pakistan		888
13. Peru		886
14. Brazil		851
15. Turkey		817
16. South Korea		802
17. Saudi Arabia		777
18. Russia		569
19. Germany		335
20. North Korea		281

Number of Colleges and Universities

Rank	Country/Entity	Colleges and Universities	Rank	Country/Entity	Colleges and Universities	Rank	Country/Entity	Colleges and Universities
21	Portugal	273	27	Egypt	125	33	Hungary	89
22	Canada	265	28	Vietnam	104	34	Norway	89
23	Ukraine	255	29	Thailand	102	35	Bulgaria	88
24	Poland	179	30	Venezuela	99	36	Kazakhstan	69
25	Denmark	158	31	Australia	95	37	Romania	63
26	Taiwan	134	32	Yugoslavia	93	38	Croatia	61

Rank	Country/Entity	Colleges and Universities	Rank	Country/Entity	Colleges and Universities	Rank	Country/Entity	Colleges and Universities
39	Belarus	59	81	Iraq	12	123	Niger	2
40	Uzbekistan	58	82	Macau	12	124	Papua New Guinea	2
41	Jordan	55	83	Mongolia	12	125	Paraguay	2
42	Myanmar (Burma)	51	84	Belize	11	126	Senegal	2
43	Morocco	50	85	Libya	10	127	Sierra Leone	2
44	Italy	48	86	Nicaragua	10	128	Uruguay	2
45	Malaysia	48	87	Burkina Faso	9	129	Yemen	2
46	Puerto Rico	45	88	Cambodia	9	130	Angola	1
47	Austria	44	89	Laos	9	131	Aruba	1
48	Bosnia and Herzegovina	44	90	Panama	9	132	Bahamas	1
49	Macedonia	44	91	Albania	8	133	Barbados	1
50	Cuba	35	92	Burundi	8	134	Bermuda	1
51	Cyprus	32	93	Honduras	8	135	Botswana	1
52	Nigeria	31	94	Sri Lanka	8	136	Central African Republic	1
53	Costa Rica	29	95	Dominican Republic	7	137	Djibouti	1
54	Ireland	29	96	Israel	7	138	Eritrea	1
55	Latvia	28	97	Mali	7	139	Faroe Islands	1
56	Slovenia	28	98	Namibia	7	140	French Guiana	1
57	Zimbabwe	28	99	New Zealand	7	141	Grenada	1
58	Sudan	24	100	Singapore	7	142	Guadeloupe	1
59	Azerbaijan	23	101	New Caledonia	6	143	Guam	1
60	Czech Republic	23	102	Afghanistan	5	144	Kuwait	1
61	Kyrgyzstan	23	103	Gaza Strip	5	145	Lesotho	1
62	Estonia	22	104	Guatemala	5	146	Luxembourg	1
63	West Bank	22	105	Madagascar	5	147	Malta	1
64	Belgium	21	106	Oman	5	148	Martinique	1
65	Finland	21	107	Brunei	4	149	Nauru	1
66	Lebanon	20	108	Chad	4	150	Northern Mariana Islands	1
67	Moldova	20	109	French Polynesia	4	151	Qatar	1
68	Netherlands	20	110	Malawi	4	152	Réunion	1
69	Georgia	19	111	Mauritania	4	153	Solomon Islands	1
70	Greece	17	112	Tanzania	4	154	Somalia	1
71	Hong Kong	17	113	United Arab Emirates	4	155	Saint Kitts and Nevis	1
72	Benin	16	114	Mozambique	3	156	Saint Lucia	1
73	Ghana	16	115	Nepal	3	157	Suriname	1
74	Jamaica	15	116	American Samoa	2	158	Swaziland	1
75	Lithuania	15	117	Bhutan	2	159	Togo	1
76	Turkmenistan	15	118	Dominica	2	160	Tonga	1
77	Armenia	14	119	Gabon	2	161	Trinidad and Tobago	1
78	Iceland	14	120	Haiti	2	162	Vanuatu	1
79	Kenya	14	121	Mauritius	2	163	Virgin Islands (U.S.)	1
80	Slovakia	14	122	Netherlands Antilles	2			

Source: UNESCO Statistical Yearbook

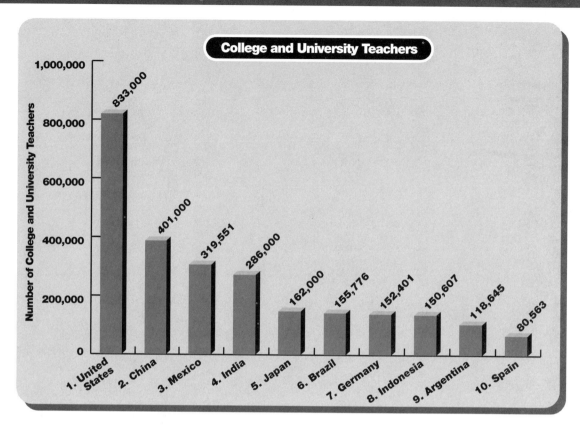

College and University Teachers

Rank	Country/Entity	College and University Teachers	Rank	Country/Entity	College and University Teachers	Rank	Country/Entity	College and University Teachers
11	Poland	71,300	39	Saudi Arabia	18,039	67	Ireland	4,889
12	Canada	64,100	40	Belarus	16,900	68	Syria	4,869
13	South Korea	60,883	41	Algeria	14,475	69	Panama	4,689
14	Italy	58,874	42	Austria	14,322	70	El Salvador	4,643
15	Philippines	56,880	43	Czech Republic	12,892	71	Kenya	4,392
16	Colombia	54,164	44	Ecuador	12,856	72	Guatemala	4,346
17	France	52,663	45	Malaysia	12,247	73	Jordan	4,280
18	Turkey	50,000	46	Nigeria	12,103	74	Bolivia	4,261
19	Peru	49,249	47	Iraq	11,847	75	Kyrgyzstan	3,691
20	United Kingdom	48,000	48	Yugoslavia	10,544	76	Honduras	3,676
21	Venezuela	43,833	49	Norway	10,366	77	Zimbabwe	3,581
22	Egypt	38,828	50	Myanmar (Burma)	9,147	78	Bosnia and Herzegovina	2,802
23	Iran	36,366	51	Greece	9,124	79	Slovenia	2,783
24	Taiwan	36,348	52	Puerto Rico	9,045	80	Macedonia	2,320
25	Bangladesh	36,000	53	Moldova	8,846	81	Uganda	2,029
26	Pakistan	33,654	54	Slovakia	8,014	82	Nicaragua	2,005
27	Portugal	30,998	55	Denmark	8,000	83	Yemen	1,991
28	Sweden	29,487	56	Israel	7,829	84	Sudan	1,943
29	Thailand	27,239	57	Finland	7,790	85	Ethiopia	1,937
30	South Africa	27,099	58	Lebanon	7,173	86	Sri Lanka	1,937
31	North Korea	27,000	59	Uruguay	7,157	87	Albania	1,774
32	Australia	25,916	60	Singapore	6,902	88	West Bank	1,598
33	Bulgaria	25,339	61	Morocco	6,877	89	Mongolia	1,341
34	Cuba	22,967	62	New Zealand	5,982	90	Laos	1,300
35	Vietnam	22,750	63	Croatia	5,814	91	Tanzania	1,206
36	Romania	20,452	64	Tunisia	5,655	92	Cameroon	1,086
37	Hungary	19,426	65	Dominican Republic	5,091	93	Kuwait	960
38	Chile	18,084	66	Nepal	4,925	94	Madagascar	855

Rank	Country/Entity	College and University Teachers	Rank	Country/Entity	College and University Teachers	Rank	Country/Entity	College and University Teachers
95	Mozambique	833	118	Guyana	492	141	Gambia	155
96	Guinea	805	119	Lesotho	492	142	Suriname	155
97	Cambodia	784	120	Zambia	481	143	Barbados	153
98	Senegal	784	121	Liberia	472	144	Eritrea	144
99	Haiti	777	122	Afghanistan	444	145	New Caledonia	141
100	Paraguay	742	123	Angola	439	146	Central African Republic	139
101	Oman	732	124	Trinidad and Tobago	438	147	Guadeloupe	121
102	Gaza Strip	717	125	Saint Lucia	389	148	Northern Mariana Islands	102
103	Mali	701	126	Brunei	325	149	Martinique	99
104	Ghana	700	127	Niger	315	150	Mauritania	72
105	Macau	663	128	Chad	311	151	French Polynesia	70
106	Congo, Rep. of	656	129	Bahamas	300	152	Grenada	66
107	Bahrain	655	130	Gabon	299	153	Equatorial Guinea	58
108	Cyprus	648	131	Malta	284	154	Bhutan	57
109	Rwanda	646	132	Fiji	277	155	Bermuda	56
110	Qatar	637	133	Virgin Islands (U.S.)	266	156	Netherlands Antilles	51
111	Benin	602	134	Sierra Leone	257	157	Saint Kitts and Nevis	51
112	Burkina Faso	571	135	Réunion	242	158	Dominica	34
113	Burundi	556	136	Malawi	235	159	Faroe Islands	20
114	Mauritius	526	137	Namibia	213	160	Tonga	19
115	United Arab Emirates	510	138	Luxembourg	200	161	Aruba	16
116	Iceland	508	139	Guam	192	162	Djibouti	13
117	Botswana	507	140	Swaziland	190			

Source: UNESCO Statistical Yearbook

20.15 College and University Students

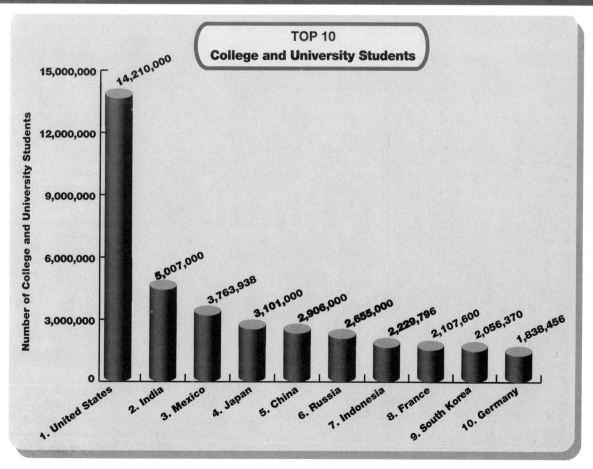

Rank	Country/Entity	College and University Students	Rank	Country/Entity	College and University Students	Rank	Country/Entity	College and University Students
11	Brazil	1,661,034	72	Azerbaijan	89,100	133	Cyprus	7,765
12	Italy	1,601,873	73	Ireland	88,925	134	Bahrain	7,676
13	Philippines	1,582,820	74	Kenya	88,180	135	Oman	7,322
14	Spain	1,398,113	75	Moldova	87,700	136	Malawi	7,308
15	Canada	1,209,386	76	Hong Kong	87,411	137	Mozambique	7,000
16	Turkey	1,161,000	77	Jordan	85,934	138	Mali	6,703
17	Bangladesh	1,032,635	78	Singapore	83,914	139	Angola	6,534
18	Pakistan	953,659	79	Costa Rica	79,959	140	Namibia	6,523
19	Argentina	926,793	80	Lebanon	79,029	141	Guinea	6,245
20	Ukraine	922,800	81	Croatia	77,525	142	Macau	6,145
21	United Kingdom	810,000	82	El Salvador	77,359	143	Zambia	5,270
22	Thailand	809,856	83	Panama	76,839	144	Trinidad and Tobago	5,191
23	Poland	794,600	84	Slovakia	74,322	145	Liberia	5,095
24	Taiwan	751,347	85	Dominican Republic	73,461	146	Botswana	5,062
25	Peru	714,512	86	Libya	72,899	147	Guadeloupe	4,673
26	Egypt	696,988	87	Guatemala	69,532	148	Martinique	4,486
27	South Africa	617,897	88	Uruguay	61,367	149	Tanzania	4,289
28	Australia	604,177	89	Sri Lanka	59,790	150	Burundi	4,256
29	Venezuela	550,783	90	Latvia	55,434	151	Niger	4,060
30	Colombia	510,649	91	Sudan	54,345	152	Lesotho	4,001
31	Iran	478,455	92	Honduras	54,293	153	Malta	3,679
32	Netherlands	408,000	93	Lithuania	54,000	154	Rwanda	3,454
33	North Korea	390,000	94	Côte d'Ivoire	51,215	155	Bahamas	3,201
34	Chile	315,653	95	Kyrgyzstan	49,744	156	Chad	3,049
35	Myanmar (Burma)	309,446	96	Zimbabwe	46,492	157	Gabon	3,000
36	Vietnam	297,900	97	Slovenia	45,951	158	Virgin Islands (U.S.)	2,924
37	Sweden	268,448	98	Madagascar	42,681	159	Central African Republic	2,923
38	Kazakhstan	267,000	99	Paraguay	39,694	160	Mauritania	2,850
39	Romania	255,162	100	Bosnia and Herzegovina	37,541	161	Sierra Leone	2,571
40	Bulgaria	248,571	101	Armenia	36,500	162	Belize	2,469
41	Portugal	236,537	102	Cameroon	33,177	163	Guam	2,385
42	Saudi Arabia	233,710	103	Ethiopia	32,671	164	Mauritius	2,344
43	Algeria	233,019	104	West Bank	30,622	165	Swaziland	2,132
44	Morocco	230,012	105	Albania	30,185	166	Eritrea	2,032
45	Nigeria	228,000	106	Turkmenistan	29,435	167	Somalia	1,692
46	Austria	222,095	107	Uganda	27,586	168	Brunei	1,606
47	Ecuador	206,541	108	Macedonia	27,340	169	Gambia	1,591
48	Iraq	201,984	109	Jamaica	24,200	170	Suriname	1,478
49	Belarus	197,400	110	Estonia	23,169	171	Barbados	1,314
50	Uzbekistan	192,100	111	Nicaragua	22,120	172	New Caledonia	1,207
51	Malaysia	191,290	112	Gaza Strip	20,153	173	Luxembourg	1,100
52	Norway	169,306	113	Kuwait	16,767	174	Northern Mariana Islands	1,097
53	Syria	161,185	114	Senegal	16,733	175	Saint Lucia	870
54	Puerto Rico	156,818	115	United Arab Emirates	13,900	176	Netherlands Antilles	734
55	Denmark	155,661	116	Congo, Rep. of	13,806	177	French Polynesia	701
56	Switzerland	148,024	117	Mongolia	13,800	178	Grenada	651
57	Hungary	141,900	118	Papua New Guinea	13,663	179	Equatorial Guinea	578
58	Czech Republic	139,774	119	Cambodia	11,652	180	Bhutan	519
59	Finland	133,359	120	Haiti	11,546	181	Bermuda	512
60	Yugoslavia	131,689	121	Togo	11,172	182	Palau	509
61	Belgium	123,320	122	Tajikistan	10,000	183	Dominica	484
62	Cuba	122,346	123	Benin	9,964	184	Guinea-Bissau	404
63	Greece	115,284	124	Afghanistan	9,367	185	Comoros	400
64	Bolivia	109,503	125	Ghana	9,274	186	Saint Kitts and Nevis	394
65	New Zealand	105,690	126	Burkina Faso	8,815	187	French Guiana	324
66	Israel	101,700	127	Guyana	8,257	188	Tonga	226
67	Nepal	99,300	128	Réunion	8,058	189	Nauru	200
68	Tunisia	96,101	129	Iceland	7,972	190	Djibouti	130
69	Congo, Dem. Rep. of	93,266	130	Fiji	7,908	191	Vanuatu	124
70	Georgia	93,000	131	Laos	7,800	192	Faroe Islands	91
71	Yemen	90,826	132	Qatar	7,794	193	Aruba	88

Source: UNESCO Statistical Yearbook

Rank	Country/Entity	College and University Student–Teacher Ratio	Rank	Country/Entity	College and University Student–Teacher Ratio	Rank	Country/Entity	College and University Student–Teacher Ratio
1	Madagascar	49.9	52	Norway	16.3	103	Lebanon	11.0
2	Yemen	45.6	53	Sri Lanka	16.2	104	Nicaragua	11.0
3	Martinique	45.3	54	Algeria	16.1	105	Virgin Islands (U.S.)	11.0
4	Paraguay	40.9	55	Ecuador	16.1	106	Zambia	11.0
5	Mauritania	39.6	56	Guatemala	16.0	107	Czech Republic	10.8
6	Guadeloupe	38.6	57	Austria	15.9	108	Liberia	10.8
7	South Korea	33.8	58	Iceland	15.7	109	Northern Mariana Islands	10.8
8	Myanmar (Burma)	33.8	59	Malaysia	15.6	110	Bahamas	10.7
9	Morocco	33.4	60	Burkina Faso	15.4	111	Brazil	10.7
10	Réunion	33.3	61	Angola	14.9	112	Belarus	10.5
11	Cameroon	30.5	62	Cambodia	14.9	113	French Polynesia	10.3
12	Thailand	29.7	63	Haiti	14.9	114	Gambia	10.3
13	Bangladesh	28.7	64	Honduras	14.8	115	Botswana	10.0
14	Fiji	28.5	65	Indonesia	14.8	116	Equatorial Guinea	10.0
15	Pakistan	28.3	66	Peru	14.5	117	Gabon	10.0
16	Gaza Strip	28.1	67	Slovenia	14.5	118	Sierra Leone	10.0
17	Sudan	28.0	68	Canada	14.4	119	Grenada	9.9
18	Italy	27.2	69	Dominican Republic	14.4	120	Moldova	9.9
19	Bolivia	25.7	70	North Korea	14.4	121	New Caledonia	9.9
20	Philippines	23.7	71	Netherlands Antilles	14.4	122	Bulgaria	9.8
21	Turkey	23.2	72	Dominica	14.2	123	Chad	9.8
22	South Africa	22.8	73	Eritrea	14.1	124	Mali	9.6
23	Nepal	22.4	74	Uganda	13.6	125	Suriname	9.5
24	Senegal	21.3	75	Kyrgyzstan	13.5	126	Colombia	9.4
25	Afghanistan	21.1	76	Bosnia and Herzegovina	13.4	127	Macau	9.3
26	Central African Republic	21.0	77	Croatia	13.3	128	Slovakia	9.3
27	Congo, Rep. of	21.0	78	Ghana	13.2	129	Bhutan	9.1
28	Taiwan	20.7	79	Iran	13.2	130	Sweden	9.1
29	Jordan	20.1	80	Vietnam	13.1	131	Bermuda	8.9
30	Denmark	19.5	81	Malta	13.0	132	Barbados	8.6
31	United Arab Emirates	19.2	82	Saudi Arabia	13.0	133	Uruguay	8.6
32	West Bank	19.2	83	Zimbabwe	13.0	134	Kenya	8.1
33	Japan	19.1	84	Niger	12.9	135	Lesotho	8.1
34	Nigeria	18.8	85	Greece	12.6	136	Argentina	7.8
35	Ireland	18.2	86	Venezuela	12.6	137	Guinea	7.8
36	New Zealand	17.7	87	Romania	12.5	138	Mauritius	7.7
37	India	17.5	88	Yugoslavia	12.5	139	Saint Kitts and Nevis	7.7
38	Kuwait	17.5	89	Guam	12.4	140	Burundi	7.6
39	Puerto Rico	17.3	90	Qatar	12.2	141	Hungary	7.3
40	Spain	17.3	91	Singapore	12.2	142	China	7.2
41	United States	17.1	92	Germany	12.1	143	Portugal	6.9
42	Albania	17.0	93	Cyprus	12.0	144	Laos	6.0
43	Iraq	17.0	94	Tonga	11.9	145	Aruba	5.5
44	Tunisia	17.0	95	Trinidad and Tobago	11.9	146	Luxembourg	5.5
45	United Kingdom	17.0	96	Macedonia	11.8	147	Cuba	5.3
46	Ethiopia	16.9	97	Mexico	11.8	148	Rwanda	5.2
47	Guyana	16.8	98	Namibia	11.8	149	Brunei	4.9
48	El Salvador	16.7	99	Bahrain	11.7	150	Faroe Islands	4.6
49	Benin	16.5	100	Malawi	11.4	151	Tanzania	4.4
50	Finland	16.4	101	Swaziland	11.2	152	Saint Lucia	2.4
51	Panama	16.4	102	Poland	11.1			

Source: UNESCO Statistical Yearbook

20.17 College and University Gross Enrollment Ratio

Rank	Country/Entity	College and University Gross Enrollment Ratio	Rank	Country/Entity	College and University Gross Enrollment Ratio	Rank	Country/Entity	College and University Gross Enrollment Ratio
1	Canada	102.9	52	Kuwait	25.4	103	Mauritius	6.3
2	United States	81.1	53	Moldova	25.0	104	Jamaica	6.0
3	Australia	71.7	54	Jordan	24.5	105	China	5.7
4	Finland	66.9	55	Bolivia	22.2	106	Myanmar (Burma)	5.4
5	New Zealand	58.2	56	Hong Kong	21.9	107	Congo, Rep. of	5.3
6	Norway	54.5	57	Malta	21.8	108	Nepal	5.2
7	South Korea	52.0	58	Turkmenistan	21.8	109	Sri Lanka	5.1
8	France	49.6	59	Yugoslavia	21.1	110	Swaziland	5.1
9	Belgium	49.1	60	Czech Republic	20.8	111	Oman	4.7
10	Netherlands	48.9	61	Tajikistan	20.3	112	Bangladesh	4.4
11	United Kingdom	48.3	62	Bahrain	20.2	113	Côte d'Ivoire	4.4
12	Spain	46.1	63	Slovakia	20.2	114	Yemen	4.3
13	Denmark	45.0	64	Thailand	20.1	115	Botswana	4.1
14	Austria	44.8	65	Cyprus	20.0	116	Mauritania	4.1
15	Russia	42.9	66	Ecuador	20.0	117	Nigeria	4.1
16	Germany	42.7	67	Azerbaijan	19.8	118	Vietnam	4.1
17	Belarus	42.6	68	Hungary	19.1	119	Madagascar	3.4
18	Sweden	42.5	69	Romania	18.3	120	Senegal	3.4
19	Armenia	41.8	70	Turkey	18.2	121	Cameroon	3.3
20	Israel	41.1	71	Egypt	18.1	122	Papua New Guinea	3.2
21	Italy	40.6	72	Syria	17.9	123	Togo	3.2
22	Ukraine	40.6	73	El Salvador	17.7	124	Pakistan	3.0
23	Japan	40.3	74	Macedonia	17.5	125	Sudan	3.0
24	Bulgaria	39.4	75	South Africa	17.3	126	Benin	2.6
25	Argentina	38.1	76	Colombia	17.2	127	Zambia	2.5
26	Estonia	38.1	77	Libya	16.4	128	Lesotho	2.4
27	Georgia	38.1	78	Saudi Arabia	15.3	129	Congo, Dem. Rep. of	2.3
28	Greece	38.1	79	Mongolia	15.2	130	Afghanistan	1.8
29	Ireland	37.0	80	Iran	14.8	131	Gambia	1.7
30	Iceland	35.2	81	Mexico	14.3	132	Cambodia	1.6
31	Portugal	34.0	82	Tunisia	12.9	133	Kenya	1.6
32	Singapore	33.7	83	Cuba	12.7	134	Laos	1.5
33	Kazakhstan	32.7	84	Kyrgyzstan	12.2	135	Uganda	1.5
34	Costa Rica	31.9	85	Fiji	11.9	136	Central African Republic	1.4
35	Slovenia	31.9	86	Brazil	11.3	137	French Polynesia	1.4
36	Switzerland	31.8	87	Morocco	11.3	138	Ghana	1.4
37	Uzbekistan	31.7	88	Indonesia	11.1	139	Sierra Leone	1.3
38	Peru	31.1	89	Algeria	10.9	140	Burkina Faso	1.1
39	Chile	30.3	90	Malaysia	10.6	141	Eritrea	1.1
40	Panama	30.0	91	Paraguay	10.3	142	Guinea	1.1
41	Venezuela	28.5	92	Honduras	10.0	143	Burundi	0.9
42	Croatia	28.3	93	Albania	9.6	144	Chad	0.8
43	Lithuania	28.2	94	Nicaragua	9.4	145	Malawi	0.8
44	Barbados	28.1	95	United Arab Emirates	8.8	146	Mali	0.8
45	Philippines	27.4	96	Guyana	8.6	147	Angola	0.7
46	Poland	27.4	97	Guatemala	8.1	148	Ethiopia	0.7
47	Qatar	27.4	98	Namibia	8.1	149	Comoros	0.6
48	Uruguay	27.3	99	Trinidad and Tobago	7.7	150	Rwanda	0.6
49	Lebanon	27.0	100	Zimbabwe	6.9	151	Mozambique	0.5
50	Macau	26.4	101	Brunei	6.6	152	Tanzania	0.5
51	Latvia	25.7	102	India	6.4	153	Djibouti	0.2

Source: UNESCO Statistical Yearbook

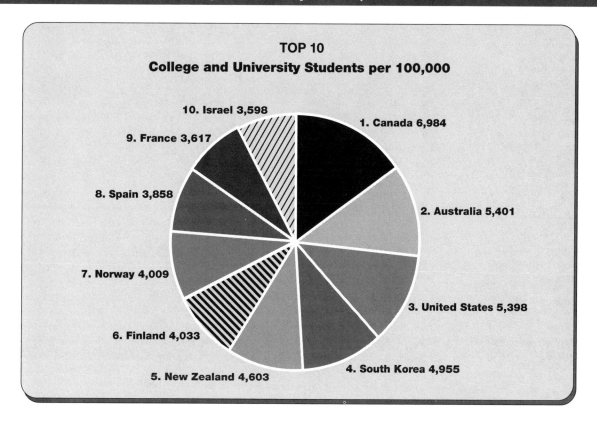

TOP 10
College and University Students per 100,000

- 1. Canada 6,984
- 2. Australia 5,401
- 3. United States 5,398
- 4. South Korea 4,955
- 5. New Zealand 4,603
- 6. Finland 4,033
- 7. Norway 4,009
- 8. Spain 3,858
- 9. France 3,617
- 10. Israel 3,598

Rank	Country/Entity	College and University Students per 100,000	Rank	Country/Entity	College and University Students per 100,000	Rank	Country/Entity	College and University Students per 100,000
11	Netherlands	3,485	37	Estonia	2,670	63	Slovakia	1,715
12	Ireland	3,443	38	Iceland	2,658	64	Egypt	1,674
13	Peru	3,268	39	Germany	2,635	65	Colombia	1,643
14	Denmark	3,261	40	Singapore	2,522	66	Hong Kong	1,635
15	Armenia	3,225	41	Barbados	2,501	67	Azerbaijan	1,619
16	Belgium	3,206	42	Chile	2,412	68	Malta	1,595
17	Japan	3,139	43	Slovenia	2,387	69	Mexico	1,586
18	Italy	3,134	44	Kuwait	2,247	70	Mongolia	1,569
19	United Kingdom	3,126	45	Uruguay	2,179	71	Yugoslavia	1,556
20	Argentina	3,116	46	Bolivia	2,154	72	Iran	1,533
21	Belarus	3,031	47	Jordan	2,136	73	South Africa	1,524
22	Portugal	3,003	48	Thailand	2,096	74	Hungary	1,522
23	Russia	2,998	49	Switzerland	2,085	75	Qatar	1,509
24	Ukraine	2,977	50	Turkmenistan	2,072	76	Romania	1,483
25	Bulgaria	2,942	51	El Salvador	2,031	77	Bahrain	1,445
26	Uzbekistan	2,938	52	Lithuania	2,023	78	Macedonia	1,372
27	Austria	2,933	53	Ecuador	2,012	79	Libya	1,358
28	Panama	2,921	54	Macau	1,995	80	Saudi Arabia	1,316
29	Costa Rica	2,919	55	Moldova	1,976	81	Tunisia	1,253
30	Greece	2,846	56	Turkey	1,960	82	Indonesia	1,167
31	Georgia	2,845	57	Poland	1,946	83	Algeria	1,126
32	Venezuela	2,820	58	Croatia	1,917	84	Suriname	1,124
33	Sweden	2,810	59	Tajikistan	1,890	85	Cuba	1,116
34	Kazakhstan	2,807	60	Syria	1,760	86	Kyrgyzstan	1,115
35	Philippines	2,760	61	Czech Republic	1,741	87	Brazil	1,094
36	Lebanon	2,712	62	Latvia	1,737	88	Morocco	1,075

Rank	Country/Entity	College and University Students per 100,000	Rank	Country/Entity	College and University Students per 100,000	Rank	Country/Entity	College and University Students per 100,000
89	Cyprus	1,069	111	China	461	133	Equatorial Guinea	164
90	Honduras	985	112	Gabon	449	134	Gambia	148
91	Malaysia	971	113	Yemen	407	135	Kenya	143
92	Nicaragua	947	114	Vietnam	404	136	Uganda	142
93	Paraguay	931	115	Botswana	403	137	Laos	134
94	Albania	899	116	Bangladesh	399	138	Central African Republic	131
95	Guyana	846	117	Côte d'Ivoire	396	139	Ghana	127
96	Fiji	757	118	Mauritania	393	140	Cambodia	119
97	Guatemala	755	119	Nigeria	367	141	Sierra Leone	119
98	Namibia	738	120	Oman	334	142	Eritrea	102
99	Trinidad and Tobago	705	121	Papua New Guinea	318	143	Burkina Faso	93
100	Zimbabwe	679	122	Madagascar	316	144	Guinea	93
101	Jamaica	677	123	Senegal	297	145	Malawi	76
102	India	601	124	Pakistan	291	146	Burundi	74
103	Congo, Rep. of	582	125	Cameroon	289	147	Mali	73
104	Mauritius	564	126	Togo	281	148	Angola	71
105	Myanmar (Burma)	564	127	Sudan	272	149	Chad	70
106	Swaziland	543	128	Zambia	241	150	Ethiopia	60
107	United Arab Emirates	521	129	Lesotho	221	151	Niger	55
108	Brunei	518	130	Congo, Dem. Rep. of	212	152	Tanzania	43
109	Nepal	501	131	Benin	208	153	Mozambique	41
110	Sri Lanka	474	132	Afghanistan	165	154	Djibouti	22

Source: UNESCO Statistical Yearbook

20.19 Percentage of Population Over 25 with Postsecondary Education

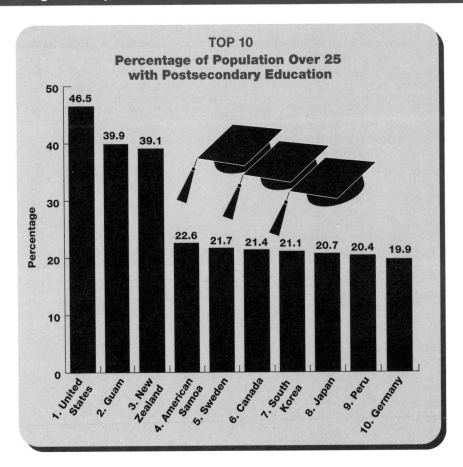

Rank	Country/Entity	Percentage of Population Over 25 with Post-secondary Education	Rank	Country/Entity	Percentage of Population Over 25 with Post-secondary Education	Rank	Country/Entity	Percentage of Population Over 25 with Post-secondary Education
11	Denmark	18.9	35	Luxembourg	10.8	59	Singapore	4.7
12	Philippines	18.7	36	Hong Kong	10.6	60	Egypt	4.6
13	Bermuda	18.4	37	Slovenia	10.4	61	Seychelles	4.6
14	Finland	18.3	38	Bahrain	10.3	62	Fiji	4.5
15	Norway	17.9	39	Hungary	10.1	63	Namibia	4.0
16	Cyprus	17.0	40	Bolivia	9.9	64	Swaziland	3.3
17	Russia	15.1	41	Slovakia	9.5	65	Tonga	2.8
18	Bulgaria	15.0	42	Mexico	9.2	66	Vietnam	2.6
19	Ireland	14.6	43	Netherlands Antilles	8.8	67	Nepal	2.5
20	Estonia	13.7	44	Côte d'Ivoire	8.7	68	Pakistan	2.5
21	Bahamas	13.5	45	Greece	8.7	69	Indonesia	2.3
22	Latvia	13.4	46	Czech Republic	8.5	70	Central African Republic	2.0
23	Qatar	13.3	47	Spain	8.4	71	China	2.0
24	Panama	13.2	48	Uruguay	8.1	72	Mauritius	1.9
25	Ecuador	12.7	49	Poland	7.9	73	South Africa	1.5
26	Kuwait	12.7	50	Portugal	7.7	74	Zambia	1.5
27	Lithuania	12.6	51	New Caledonia	7.5	75	Botswana	1.4
28	Kazakhstan	12.4	52	Aruba	7.0	76	Benin	1.3
29	Chile	12.3	53	Romania	6.9	77	Mauritania	1.3
30	Argentina	12.0	54	Belize	6.6	78	Haiti	0.7
31	Venezuela	11.8	55	Croatia	6.4	79	Burundi	0.6
32	Tajikistan	11.7	56	El Salvador	6.3	80	Uganda	0.5
33	France	11.4	57	Macau	5.9	81	Malawi	0.4
34	Moldova	11.3	58	Zimbabwe	4.9			

Source: UNESCO Statistical Yearbook

20.20 College and University Science Enrollment

Rank	Country/Entity	Science Enrollment as Percentage of Total College and University Enrollment	Rank	Country/Entity	Science Enrollment as Percentage of Total College and University Enrollment	Rank	Country/Entity	Science Enrollment as Percentage of Total College and University Enrollment
1	Dominica	58	27	Myanmar (Burma)	36	53	Jordan	28
2	South Africa	57	28	Belarus	35	54	Kyrgyzstan	28
3	Algeria	52	29	Germany	35	55	Israel	27
4	Romania	51	30	Estonia	34	56	Côte d'Ivoire	26
5	Mozambique	50	31	Latvia	34	57	Honduras	26
6	Russia	49	32	Moldova	34	58	Panama	26
7	Georgia	48	33	Mexico	33	59	Belgium	25
8	Laos	45	34	Switzerland	32	60	Bulgaria	25
9	Seychelles	45	35	Colombia	31	61	El Salvador	25
10	Trinidad and Tobago	45	36	Ireland	31	62	Lesotho	25
11	Guyana	43	37	Philippines	31	63	Paraguay	25
12	Chile	42	38	United Kingdom	31	64	Albania	24
13	Kazakhstan	42	39	Argentina	30	65	Botswana	24
14	Macedonia	41	40	Greece	30	66	Denmark	24
15	Nigeria	41	41	Portugal	30	67	France	24
16	Bahrain	39	42	Sierra Leone	30	68	Mongolia	24
17	South Korea	39	43	Australia	29	69	Tunisia	24
18	Tanzania	39	44	Austria	29	70	Cuba	23
19	Azerbaijan	38	45	Hungary	29	71	Japan	23
20	Croatia	38	46	Morocco	29	72	Kuwait	23
21	China	37	47	Poland	29	73	Madagascar	23
22	Finland	37	48	Solomon Islands	29	74	Tajikistan	23
23	Iran	37	49	Sweden	29	75	Zimbabwe	23
24	Czech Republic	36	50	Syria	29	76	Brazil	22
25	Ethiopia	36	51	Indonesia	28	77	Swaziland	22
26	Hong Kong	36	52	Italy	28	78	Turkey	21

Rank	Country/Entity	Science Enrollment as Percentage of Total College and University Enrollment	Rank	Country/Entity	Science Enrollment as Percentage of Total College and University Enrollment	Rank	Country/Entity	Science Enrollment as Percentage of Total College and University Enrollment
79	Netherlands	20	87	Costa Rica	18	95	Samoa	14
80	New Zealand	20	88	Malawi	18	96	Malta	13
81	Barbados	19	89	Slovenia	18	97	Uganda	13
82	Benin	19	90	Lebanon	17	98	Congo, Dem. Rep. of	11
83	Cyprus	19	91	Nepal	17	99	Mauritania	8
84	Norway	19	92	Togo	16	100	Brunei	6
85	Thailand	19	93	Egypt	15	101	Namibia	5
86	Burkina Faso	18	94	Chad	14			

Source: UNESCO Statistical Yearbook

20.21 Vocational Training Students

While most students go through the main educational stream, a smaller segment chooses vocational education leading directly to employment. Vocational training is looked upon with disfavor by educational policymakers because, while it does provide students with a broad range of know-how and technical skills, it does not give them a grounding in the humanities and social sciences or equip them with university level verbal and language skills. Nevertheless, in many developing countries, a large cohort of children move into the vocational stream, either because general education is too expensive or too time-consuming.

Rank	Country/Entity	Vocational Training Students	Rank	Country/Entity	Vocational Training Students	Rank	Country/Entity	Vocational Training Students
1	China	8,205,000	31	Switzerland	191,696	61	Jordan	30,052
2	Italy	2,661,760	32	Greece	190,443	62	Bangladesh	29,923
3	Germany	2,435,753	33	Denmark	168,417	63	Kenya	29,593
4	Russia	1,923,000	34	Belgium	155,192	64	Georgia	29,300
5	Egypt	1,900,406	35	Puerto Rico	149,191	65	Portugal	28,627
6	Poland	1,729,300	36	Ireland	146,050	66	Moldova	27,943
7	Indonesia	1,405,220	37	Hungary	143,800	67	Estonia	27,806
8	Turkey	1,309,000	38	Israel	142,900	68	Zimbabwe	27,431
9	Japan	1,242,000	39	South Africa	140,531	69	Turkmenistan	26,000
10	Mexico	1,076,700	40	Albania	138,000	70	Myanmar (Burma)	25,374
11	Kazakhstan	984,300	41	Iraq	135,711	71	Congo, Rep. of	25,269
12	South Korea	950,173	42	Belarus	122,400	72	Armenia	25,200
13	Australia	917,801	43	Slovakia	119,853	73	Dominican Republic	22,795
14	Thailand	795,186	44	New Zealand	107,736	74	Angola	19,687
15	Congo, Dem. Rep. of	701,148	45	Libya	94,961	75	Mozambique	19,313
16	Ukraine	618,000	46	Syria	94,204	76	Morocco	17,585
17	United Kingdom	586,000	47	Pakistan	94,000	77	Madagascar	17,419
18	Taiwan	523,412	48	Cameroon	91,779	78	Luxembourg	16,909
19	Netherlands	519,000	49	El Salvador	88,588	79	Cambodia	16,350
20	Nigeria	391,583	50	Azerbaijan	73,000	80	Jamaica	15,898
21	Iran	368,218	51	Uruguay	56,879	81	Tanzania	15,824
22	Romania	345,394	52	Saudi Arabia	49,032	82	Sudan	15,443
23	Peru	270,576	53	Lithuania	49,000	83	Yemen	15,074
24	Cuba	244,253	54	Hong Kong	48,837	84	Réunion	15,055
25	Czech Republic	229,909	55	Malaysia	47,770	85	Ghana	13,232
26	North Korea	220,000	56	Lebanon	45,776	86	Suriname	12,307
27	Bulgaria	213,337	57	Latvia	43,170	87	Côte d'Ivoire	11,037
28	Finland	199,200	58	Uganda	36,063	88	Papua New Guinea	9,941
29	Vietnam	197,500	59	Tajikistan	35,000	89	Singapore	9,476
30	Uzbekistan	194,800	60	Kyrgyzstan	32,005	90	Laos	9,400

Rank	Country/Entity	Vocational Training Students	Rank	Country/Entity	Vocational Training Students	Rank	Country/Entity	Vocational Training Students
91	Guinea	9,278	113	Chad	3,277	135	Mayotte	839
92	Gabon	9,261	114	Swaziland	2,958	136	Guinea-Bissau	825
93	Ethiopia	9,103	115	Croatia	2,660	137	Tonga	824
94	Sri Lanka	8,908	116	Aruba	2,594	138	Saint Lucia	808
95	Burkina Faso	8,808	117	Liechtenstein	2,515	139	Gibraltar	772
96	Mongolia	7,987	118	French Guiana	2,404	140	Qatar	671
97	Zambia	7,982	119	Oman	2,350	141	Monaco	520
98	Sierra Leone	7,756	120	Lesotho	2,326	142	Maldives	452
99	Togo	7,631	121	Cape Verde	2,289	143	Vanuatu	444
100	New Caledonia	7,543	122	Niger	2,110	144	San Marino	428
101	Senegal	7,301	123	Equatorial Guinea	2,105	145	Isle of Man	425
102	Fiji	7,283	124	Faroe Islands	2,090	146	Saint Vincent and the Grenadines	414
103	Bahrain	7,113	125	Mauritius	2,052	147	Kiribati	297
104	Botswana	6,373	126	Brunei	1,966	148	São Tomé and Príncipe	289
105	Netherlands Antilles	5,817	127	Mauritania	1,949	149	Comoros	163
106	Guyana	5,388	128	Bhutan	1,822	150	American Samoa	160
107	Benin	4,873	129	Namibia	1,503	151	Tuvalu	58
108	Somalia	4,809	130	Seychelles	1,338	152	Antigua and Barbuda	46
109	Malta	4,539	131	Eritrea	1,246	153	Nauru	30
110	Cyprus	4,066	132	Western Sahara	1,222			
111	Guam	3,788	133	United Arab Emirates	1,215			
112	Kuwait	3,604	134	Malawi	1,080			

Source: UNESCO Statistical Yearbook

Chapter 21

New Technologies

Internet, Cellular Phones, Faxes, and Computers

The bridge to the twenty-first century is built on four technological developments or machines—the Internet, cellular phones, fax machines, and personal computers. By reducing time and space, advances have helped to bring the world closer together. Although predominantly of Western provenance, it is significant that none of them is associated with any single individual or even corporation. They represent the new era in which great inventions are born out of the work of hundreds of scientists of many nationalities working together and achieving remarkable breakthroughs by concerted effort.

21.1 Internet Hosts

Rank	Country/Entity	Connections per 1,000,000 Persons, 1995	Rank	Country/Entity	Connections per 1,000,000 Persons, 1995	Rank	Country/Entity	Connections per 1,000,000 Persons, 1995
1	Finland	42,229	41	Cyprus	532	81	Kazakhstan	11
2	Iceland	31,007	42	Latvia	525	82	Qatar	11
3	United States	23,012	43	Dominica	521	83	Albania	10
4	Norway	19,289	44	Croatia	515	84	Djibouti	10
5	Australia	17,146	45	Costa Rica	439	85	Egypt	10
6	Sweden	16,405	46	Guam	367	86	Tonga	10
7	New Zealand	14,923	47	Uruguay	346	87	Bolivia	8.9
8	Canada	12,595	48	Comoros	324	88	Tunisia	8.8
9	Switzerland	11,383	49	Bahrain	244	89	Morocco	8.6
10	Netherlands	11,110	50	Malta	231	90	Zimbabwe	8.5
11	Denmark	9,670	51	Argentina	154	91	Barbados	7.7
12	Singapore	7,624	52	United Arab Emirates	154	92	Zambia	7.3
13	United Kingdom	7,513	53	Macau	153	93	Namibia	7.1
14	Austria	6,623	54	Russia	149	94	New Caledonia	5.4
15	Germany	5,794	55	Andorra	147	95	Belize	4.6
16	Israel	5,260	56	Bulgaria	126	96	Jordan	4.4
17	Luxembourg	4,608	57	Brazil	124	97	El Salvador	4.3
18	Ireland	3,747	58	Lithuania	123	98	Iran	4.0
19	Belgium	3,024	59	Turkey	85	99	Uganda	3.1
20	Slovenia	2,948	60	Romania	77	100	Guatemala	2.5
21	Hong Kong	2,858	61	Thailand	68	101	Belarus	2.2
22	Estonia	2,782	62	Fiji	66	102	Azerbaijan	2.1
23	France	2,604	63	Jamaica	65	103	China	1.8
24	Antigua and Barbuda	2,424	64	Colombia	58	104	Saudi Arabia	1.5
25	Japan	2,151	65	Panama	56	105	Uzbekistan	1.5
26	Czech Republic	2,115	66	Venezuela	52	106	Moldova	1.2
27	Hungary	1,546	67	Armenia	46	107	Swaziland	1.1
28	Italy	1,280	68	Ukraine	45	108	India	0.9
29	Taiwan	1,207	69	Ecuador	44	109	Nepal	0.9
30	Portugal	1,187	70	Macedonia	42	110	Senegal	0.7
31	South Africa	1,165	71	Trinidad and Tobago	42	111	Algeria	0.6
32	Spain	1,018	72	Peru	35	112	Kenya	0.6
33	Bahamas	989	73	Nicaragua	34	113	Ghana	0.4
34	Greece	740	74	Philippines	26	114	Guinea	0.3
35	Kuwait	729	75	Solomon Islands	24	115	Sri Lanka	0.3
36	South Korea	653	76	Puerto Rico	23	116	Côte d'Ivoire	0.2
37	Chile	632	77	Lebanon	22	117	Cuba	0.1
38	Poland	598	78	Dominican Republic	18	118	Pakistan	0.1
39	Brunei	549	79	Indonesia	12	119	Ethiopia	0.02
40	Slovakia	543	80	Georgia	11			

Source: World Development Report

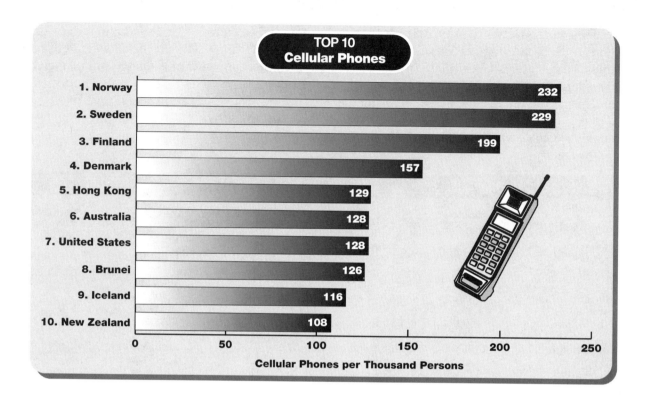

TOP 10 Cellular Phones

Rank	Country	Cellular Phones per Thousand Persons
1.	Norway	232
2.	Sweden	229
3.	Finland	199
4.	Denmark	157
5.	Hong Kong	129
6.	Australia	128
7.	United States	128
8.	Brunei	126
9.	Iceland	116
10.	New Zealand	108

Cellular Phones per Thousand Persons

Rank	Country/Entity	Cellular Phones per 1,000 persons, 1995	Rank	Country/Entity	Cellular Phones per 1,000 persons, 1995	Rank	Country/Entity	Cellular Phones per 1,000 persons, 1995
11	Singapore	98	37	Qatar	33	63	Croatia	7.1
12	United Kingdom	98	38	Martinique	31	64	Turkey	7.1
13	Canada	88	39	Lebanon	30	65	Mexico	7.0
14	Macau	86	40	Malta	29	66	Philippines	6.9
15	Japan	82	41	Greece	26	67	Latvia	6.0
16	Kuwait	70	42	Hungary	26	68	Belize	5.7
17	Italy	67	43	Aruba	25	69	Costa Rica	5.6
18	Switzerland	64	44	Spain	25	70	Czech Republic	4.7
19	Cyprus	61	45	France	24	71	New Caledonia	4.5
20	Netherlands Antilles	59	46	Belgium	23	72	Dominican Republic	4.4
21	Israel	54	47	Estonia	21	73	Grenada	4.4
22	United Arab Emirates	54	48	Barbados	18	74	Trinidad and Tobago	4.4
23	Jersey	51	49	Jamaica	18	75	Ecuador	4.3
24	Austria	48	50	Thailand	18	76	Seychelles	4.3
25	Bahrain	48	51	Venezuela	18	77	Lithuania	4.0
26	Puerto Rico	48	52	West Bank	16	78	Oman	3.7
27	Germany	46	53	Chile	14	79	Paraguay	3.2
28	Taiwan	45	54	Slovenia	14	80	Peru	3.1
29	Ireland	44	55	South Africa	13	81	China	3.0
30	Malaysia	43	56	Uruguay	13	82	Gabon	3.0
31	Andorra	42	57	Mauritius	10	83	Sri Lanka	3.0
32	Guernsey	39	58	Argentina	9.9	84	Fiji	2.8
33	South Korea	37	59	Bahamas	8.6	85	Guatemala	2.8
34	Portugal	34	60	Suriname	8.6	86	Jordan	2.6
35	Guam	33	61	Brazil	8.2	87	Bulgaria	2.5
36	Netherlands	33	62	Colombia	7.1	88	El Salvador	2.5

Rank	Country/Entity	Cellular Phones per 1,000 persons, 1995	Rank	Country/Entity	Cellular Phones per 1,000 persons, 1995	Rank	Country/Entity	Cellular Phones per 1,000 persons, 1995
89	Namibia	2.3	105	Solomon Islands	0.6	121	Egypt	0.2
90	Slovakia	2.3	106	Yemen	0.5	122	Iran	0.2
91	Bangladesh	2.1	107	Ghana	0.4	123	Uzbekistan	0.2
92	Poland	1.9	108	Romania	0.4	124	Zambia	0.2
93	Guyana	1.6	109	Tunisia	0.4	125	Burundi	0.1
94	Cambodia	1.5	110	Kazakhstan	0.3	126	Guinea	0.1
95	Gambia	1.3	111	Laos	0.3	127	India	0.1
96	Tonga	1.2	112	Pakistan	0.3	128	Kenya	0.1
97	Indonesia	1.1	113	Ukraine	0.3	129	Morocco	0.1
98	Nicaragua	1.1	114	Vietnam	0.3	130	Nigeria	0.1
99	Bolivia	1.0	115	Algeria	0.2	131	Tanzania	0.1
100	Saudi Arabia	0.9	116	Angola	0.2	132	Uganda	0.1
101	Azerbaijan	0.8	117	Benin	0.2	133	Georgia	0.04
102	Vanuatu	0.7	118	Cameroon	0.2	134	Malawi	0.04
103	Belarus	0.6	119	Congo, Dem. Rep. of	0.2	135	Myanmar (Burma)	0.04
104	Russia	0.6	120	Cuba	0.2	136	Senegal	0.01

Source: World Development Report

21.3 Fax Machines

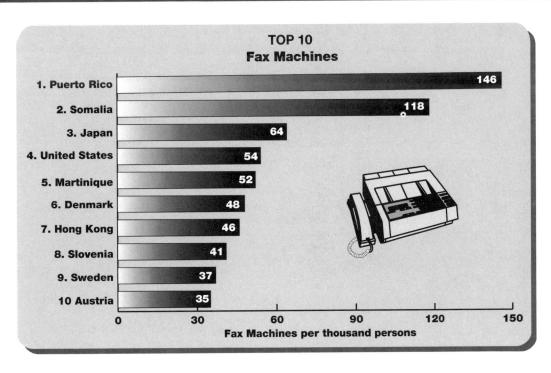

TOP 10
Fax Machines

Rank	Country	Fax Machines per thousand persons
1.	Puerto Rico	146
2.	Somalia	118
3.	Japan	64
4.	United States	54
5.	Martinique	52
6.	Denmark	48
7.	Hong Kong	46
8.	Slovenia	41
9.	Sweden	37
10	Austria	35

Rank	Country/Entity	Fax Machines per 1,000 Persons, 1995	Rank	Country/Entity	Fax Machines per 1,000 Persons, 1995	Rank	Country/Entity	Fax Machines per 1,000 Persons, 1995
11	France	33	18	Australia	26	25	Singapore	19
12	Niger	33	19	Finland	26	26	Canada	18
13	Netherlands	32	20	Israel	25	27	Germany	18
14	Virgin Islands (U.S.)	32	21	Ireland	22	28	Mauritius	18
15	United Kingdom	31	22	Kuwait	21	29	New Zealand	18
16	Norway	30	23	Andorra	20	30	Macau	17
17	Switzerland	28	24	Taiwan	20	31	Belgium	16

Rank	Country/Entity	Fax Machines per 1,000 Persons, 1995	Rank	Country/Entity	Fax Machines per 1,000 Persons, 1995	Rank	Country/Entity	Fax Machines per 1,000 Persons, 1995
32	Qatar	16.0	77	Solomon Islands	2.1	122	Lesotho	0.3
33	Iceland	15.0	78	Tonga	2.0	123	Morocco	0.3
34	Maldives	14.0	79	Bahamas	1.8	124	Syria	0.3
35	New Caledonia	12.0	80	Bulgaria	1.8	125	Algeria	0.2
36	Guernsey	11.0	81	South Africa	1.8	126	China	0.2
37	United Arab Emirates	11.0	82	Trinidad and Tobago	1.6	127	Comoros	0.2
38	Bahrain	9.9	83	Turkey	1.6	128	Djibouti	0.2
39	Cyprus	9.3	84	Greece	1.5	129	Eritrea	0.2
40	Estonia	8.7	85	São Tomé and Príncipe	1.5	130	Kazakhstan	0.2
41	Malta	8.6	86	Argentina	1.4	131	Papua New Guinea	0.2
42	South Korea	8.4	87	Poland	1.4	132	Russia	0.2
43	Slovakia	8.4	88	Yugoslavia	1.4	133	Sierra Leone	0.2
44	Guadeloupe	8.1	89	Brazil	1.3	134	Sudan	0.2
45	Croatia	8.0	90	Cape Verde	1.3	135	Tajikistan	0.2
46	Jersey	8.0	91	Pakistan	1.2	136	Armenia	0.1
47	Seychelles	8.0	92	Chile	1.1	137	Azerbaijan	0.1
48	Jordan	7.3	93	Lithuania	1.0	138	Benin	0.1
49	Czech Republic	7.1	94	Swaziland	1.0	139	Cambodia	0.1
50	Aruba	6.9	95	Thailand	1.0	140	Central African Republic	0.1
51	Barbados	6.8	96	Belarus	0.9	141	Congo, Dem. Rep. of	0.1
52	Brunei	6.8	97	Guatemala	0.9	142	Georgia	0.1
53	Spain	5.2	98	Mongolia	0.9	143	India	0.1
54	Hungary	4.4	99	Romania	0.9	144	Kenya	0.1
55	Saudi Arabia	4.4	100	Zimbabwe	0.9	145	North Korea	0.1
56	French Polynesia	4.1	101	Lebanon	0.8	146	Laos	0.1
57	Dominica	4.0	102	Macedonia	0.8	147	Malawi	0.1
58	Fiji	3.8	103	Venezuela	0.8	148	Mauritania	0.1
59	Vanuatu	3.6	104	Costa Rica	0.7	149	Moldova	0.1
60	Italy	3.5	105	Oman	0.7	150	Rwanda	0.1
61	Uruguay	3.5	106	Suriname	0.7	151	Uzbekistan	0.1
62	Portugal	3.4	107	Gambia	0.6	152	Vietnam	0.1
63	Bangladesh	3.3	108	Peru	0.6	153	Yemen	0.1
64	Grenada	3.1	109	Sri Lanka	0.6	154	Zambia	0.1
65	Malaysia	3.0	110	Guinea-Bissau	0.5	155	Egypt	0.05
66	Micronesia	2.9	111	Iran	0.5	156	Congo, Rep. of	0.04
67	Réunion	2.9	112	Philippines	0.5	157	Cuba	0.04
68	Tunisia	2.8	113	Bhutan	0.4	158	Chad	0.03
69	Colombia	2.6	114	Gabon	0.4	159	Guinea	0.03
70	Ecuador	2.6	115	Indonesia	0.4	160	Myanmar (Burma)	0.03
71	Kiribati	2.5	116	Mozambique	0.4	161	Nepal	0.03
72	Samoa	2.4	117	Paraguay	0.4	162	Ukraine	0.03
73	Togo	2.4	118	Dominican Republic	0.3	163	Burundi	0.02
74	Belize	2.3	119	Equatorial Guinea	0.3	164	Ethiopia	0.02
75	Botswana	2.1	120	Ghana	0.3			
76	Mexico	2.1	121	Latvia	0.3			

Source: World Development Report

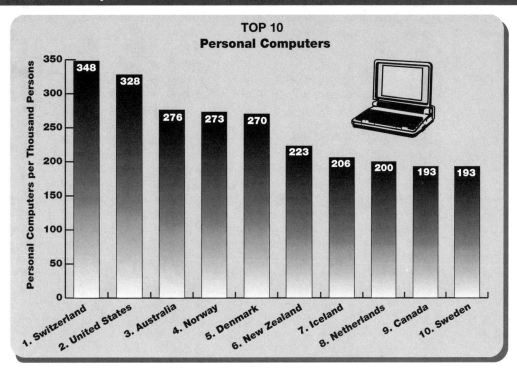

TOP 10
Personal Computers

Rank	Country/Entity	Personal Computers per 1,000 Persons, 1995	Rank	Country/Entity	Personal Computers per 1,000 Persons, 1995	Rank	Country/Entity	Personal Computers per 1,000 Persons, 1995
11	United Kingdom	186	40	Hungary	39	69	Estonia	6.7
12	Finland	182	41	Chile	38	70	Tunisia	6.7
13	Singapore	172	42	Saudi Arabia	35	71	Lithuania	6.5
14	Germany	165	43	Greece	33	72	Peru	5.9
15	Japan	153	44	Mauritius	32	73	Ukraine	5.6
16	Ireland	145	45	Brunei	29	74	Romania	5.3
17	Belgium	138	46	Poland	29	75	Gabon	4.5
18	France	134	47	Belize	28	76	Egypt	4.1
19	Austria	124	48	South Africa	27	77	Nigeria	4.1
20	South Korea	121	49	Mexico	26	78	Ecuador	3.9
21	Hong Kong	116	50	Argentina	25	79	Indonesia	3.7
22	Israel	100	51	Bulgaria	22	80	Algeria	3.0
23	Macau	94	52	Uruguay	22	81	Zimbabwe	3.0
24	Martinique	93	53	Croatia	21	82	Guatemala	2.8
25	Italy	84	54	Trinidad and Tobago	20	83	China	2.1
26	Taiwan	83	55	Russia	18	84	Moldova	2.1
27	Spain	82	56	Venezuela	17	85	Djibouti	1.7
28	Malta	81	57	Colombia	16	86	Morocco	1.7
29	Portugal	61	58	Thailand	15	87	India	1.3
30	Barbados	58	59	Brazil	13	88	Ghana	1.2
31	Kuwait	56	60	Lebanon	13	89	Pakistan	1.2
32	Czech Republic	53	61	Oman	13	90	Sri Lanka	1.1
33	Qatar	52	62	Turkey	13	91	Kenya	0.7
34	Bahrain	50	63	Maldives	12	92	Syria	0.7
35	Slovenia	48	64	Yugoslavia	12	93	Uganda	0.5
36	United Arab Emirates	48	65	Philippines	11	94	Vietnam	0.4
37	Cyprus	41	66	Jordan	8	95	Guinea	0.2
38	Slovakia	41	67	Latvia	7.9			
39	Malaysia	40	68	Senegal	7.2			

Source: World Development Report

There is a direct correlation between a country's technological prowess and the number of its scientists and engineers engaged in research and development. Many of these scientists and engineers are working in industrial and medical research laboratories or are associated with research universities on projects wholly or partly funded by the government. The ranking is slightly misleading because many of the scientists and engineers in Western countries are of foreign origin, even though some of them may be naturalized citizens.

Rank	Country/Entity	Scientists and Engineers in R&D per Million People, 1985–1995	Rank	Country/Entity	Scientists and Engineers in R&D per Million People, 1985–1995	Rank	Country/Entity	Scientists and Engineers in R&D per Million People, 1985–1995
1	Japan	6,309	25	Uzbekistan	1,760	49	Turkey	261
2	United States	3,732	26	Austria	1,631	50	Bolivia	250
3	Sweden	3,714	27	Moldova	1,539	51	Nicaragua	214
4	Norway	3,678	28	Romania	1,382	52	Mexico	213
5	Russia	3,520	29	Italy	1,325	53	Venezuela	208
6	Ukraine	3,173	30	Poland	1,299	54	Benin	177
7	Australia	3,166	31	Spain	1,210	55	Sri Lanka	173
8	Germany	2,843	32	Latvia	1,189	56	Ecuador	169
9	Finland	2,812	33	Portugal	1,185	57	Brazil	168
10	Singapore	2,728	34	Czech Republic	1,159	58	Philippines	157
11	Canada	2,656	35	Hungary	1,033	59	India	149
12	Netherlands	2,656	36	Mongolia	943	60	Thailand	119
13	Denmark	2,647	37	South Africa	938	61	Jordan	106
14	South Korea	2,636	38	Greece	774	62	Guatemala	99
15	France	2,584	39	Tajikistan	709	63	Hong Kong	98
16	Slovenia	2,544	40	Kyrgyzstan	703	64	Malaysia	87
17	United Kingdom	2,417	41	Uruguay	688	65	Central African Republic	55
18	Belarus	2,339	42	Argentina	671	66	Pakistan	54
19	Estonia	2,018	43	Peru	625	67	Burundi	32
20	Croatia	1,978	44	Iran	521	68	Rwanda	24
21	Ireland	1,871	45	Egypt	458	69	El Salvador	19
22	Slovakia	1,821	46	Tunisia	388	70	Nigeria	15
23	Belgium	1,814	47	China	350	71	Madagascar	11
24	New Zealand	1,778	48	Vietnam	308	72	Jamaica	8

Source: World Development Report

Even though most technology originates in developed countries, its production is fairly well dispersed throughout the world for reasons of cheap labor. In many developing nations there are corridors and zones where high-tech industries flourish, mostly in association with U.S. or European firms. The high-tech goods are generally exported to Western countries for hard currency. For many nations, high-technology exports not only bring in much-needed revenues, they also provide employment and promote skills and training.

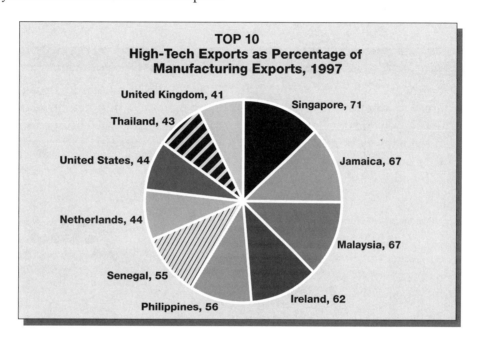

TOP 10
High-Tech Exports as Percentage of Manufacturing Exports, 1997

Singapore, 71
Jamaica, 67
Malaysia, 67
Ireland, 62
Philippines, 56
Senegal, 55
Netherlands, 44
United States, 44
Thailand, 43
United Kingdom, 41

Rank	Country/Entity	High-Tech Exports as Percentage of Manufacturing Exports, 1997	Rank	Country/Entity	High-Tech Exports as Percentage of Manufacturing Exports, 1997	Rank	Country/Entity	High-Tech Exports as Percentage of Manufacturing Exports, 1997
11	Australia	39	32	Norway	24	53	Panama	14
12	Hungary	39	33	Belgium	23	54	Czech Republic	13
13	South Korea	39	34	Dominican Republic	23	55	Guatemala	13
14	Japan	38	35	Algeria	22	56	Ecuador	12
15	Nicaragua	38	36	China	21	57	Greece	12
16	Sweden	34	37	Lithuania	21	58	Poland	12
17	Israel	33	38	Colombia	20	59	India	11
18	Mexico	33	39	Indonesia	20	60	Kenya	11
19	France	31	40	Chile	19	61	New Zealand	11
20	Hong Kong	29	41	Croatia	19	62	Portugal	11
21	Saudi Arabia	29	42	Russia	19	63	Tunisia	11
22	Switzerland	28	43	Brazil	18	64	Peru	10
23	Denmark	27	44	Spain	17	65	Venezuela	10
24	Morocco	27	45	Congo, Rep. of	16	66	Bolivia	9
25	Finland	26	46	El Salvador	16	67	Moldova	9
26	Germany	26	47	Slovenia	16	68	Turkey	9
27	Jordan	26	48	Argentina	15	69	Mozambique	8
28	Canada	25	49	Italy	15	70	Uruguay	8
29	Austria	24	50	Latvia	15	71	Egypt	7
30	Estonia	24	51	Slovakia	15	72	Romania	7
31	Kyrgyzstan	24	52	Costa Rica	14	73	Zimbabwe	6

Rank	Country/Entity	High-Tech Exports as Percentage of Manufacturing Exports, 1997	Rank	Country/Entity	High-Tech Exports as Percentage of Manufacturing Exports, 1997	Rank	Country/Entity	High-Tech Exports as Percentage of Manufacturing Exports, 1997
74	Honduras	4	79	Malawi	3	84	Bangladesh	0
75	Kuwait	4	80	Madagascar	2	85	Central African Republic	0
76	Pakistan	4	81	Mongolia	2	86	Ethiopia	0
77	Paraguay	4	82	Albania	1	87	Nepal	0
78	Cameroon	3	83	Syria	1	88	Yemen	0

Source: World İevelopment Report

21.7 Patent Applications

Patents represent the cutting edge of technological progress and their number provides a clue to the state of research and development in a country, both by individuals working alone out of their homes and those working in groups in research universities and industrial laboratories.

In all countries patents are protected by legislation for a specified number of years, and they also receive international protection from all parties who are signatory to the conventions on industrial and intellectual property.

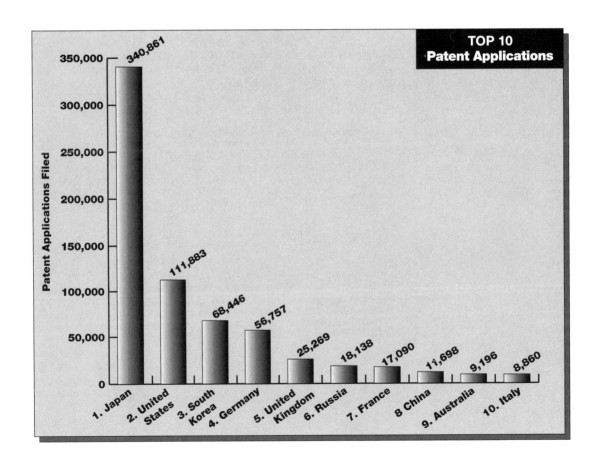

Rank	Country/Entity	Patent Applications Filed, 1996	Rank	Country/Entity	Patent Applications Filed, 1996	Rank	Country/Entity	Patent Applications Filed, 1996
11	Sweden	7,077	38	Bulgaria	318	65	Hong Kong	41
12	Netherlands	4,884	39	Slovenia	301	66	Indonesia	40
13	Ukraine	3,640	40	Moldova	290	67	Vietnam	37
14	Canada	3,316	41	Georgia	289	68	Tajikistan	32
15	Finland	3,262	42	Croatia	259	69	Panama	31
16	Switzerland	2,699	43	Singapore	215	70	Zimbabwe	30
17	Spain	2,689	44	Thailand	203	71	Saudi Arabia	27
18	Brazil	2,655	45	Slovakia	201	72	Uruguay	25
19	Austria	2,506	46	Latvia	197	73	Bolivia	17
20	Denmark	2,452	47	Chile	189	74	Pakistan	16
21	Poland	2,414	48	Venezuela	182	75	Kenya	15
22	Romania	1,831	49	Azerbaijan	165	76	Estonia	12
23	India	1,660	50	Philippines	163	77	Honduras	10
24	Norway	1,550	51	Armenia	162	78	Ecuador	7
25	New Zealand	1,421	52	Kyrgyzstan	126	79	Madagascar	7
26	Israel	1,363	53	Mongolia	114	80	Zambia	6
27	Belgium	1,356	54	Portugal	105	81	Botswana	5
28	Kazakhstan	1,024	55	Lithuania	101	82	El Salvador	3
29	Ireland	925	56	Morocco	90	83	Ethiopia	3
30	Uzbekistan	914	57	Colombia	87	84	Haiti	3
31	Hungary	832	58	Bangladesh	70	85	Malawi	3
32	Belarus	701	59	Turkmenistan	66	86	Congo, Dem. Rep. of	2
33	Czech Republic	623	60	Macedonia	53	87	Guatemala	2
34	Egypt	504	61	Peru	52	88	Lesotho	2
35	Greece	434	62	Sri Lanka	50	89	Albania	1
36	Mexico	389	63	Algeria	48	90	Burundi	1
37	Turkey	367	64	Tunisia	46			

Source: World Development Report

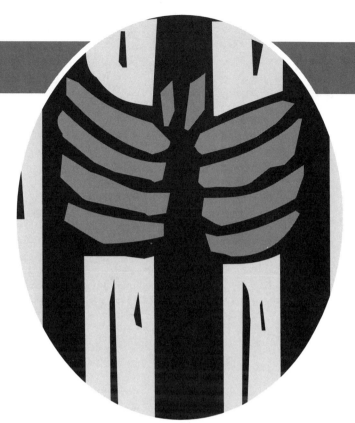

Chapter 22

Crime and Law Enforcement

Crime is essentially local, and, thus, throughout the world, police departments are under the control of local and municipal governments. (The only exceptions are in authoritarian countries where police forces are used as instruments of repression rather than for law enforcement.) The number of people per police officer nationwide is less significant than the number of people per police officer in each city or principality, but it does provide a general idea of the commitment of governments to protect citizens against crime.

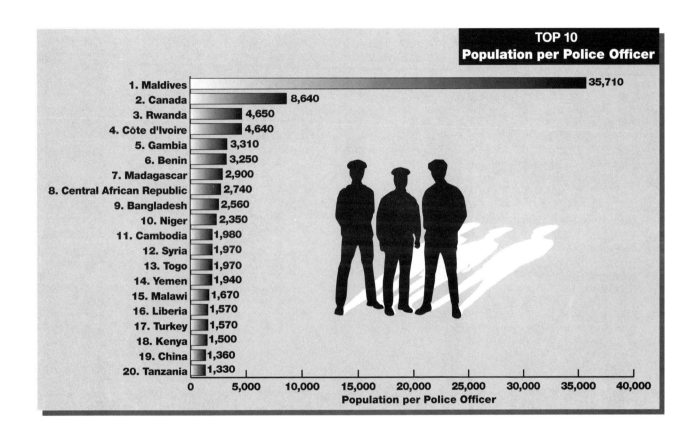

TOP 10 Population per Police Officer

Rank	Country/Entity	Population per Police Officer
1	Maldives	35,710
2	Canada	8,640
3	Rwanda	4,650
4	Côte d'Ivoire	4,640
5	Gambia	3,310
6	Benin	3,250
7	Madagascar	2,900
8	Central African Republic	2,740
9	Bangladesh	2,560
10	Niger	2,350
11	Cambodia	1,980
12	Syria	1,970
13	Togo	1,970
14	Yemen	1,940
15	Malawi	1,670
16	Liberia	1,570
17	Turkey	1,570
18	Kenya	1,500
19	China	1,360
20	Tanzania	1,330

Rank	Country/Entity	Population per Police Officer	Rank	Country/Entity	Population per Police Officer	Rank	Country/Entity	Population per Police Officer
21	Gabon	1,290	34	Chad	990	47	Zimbabwe	750
22	Argentina	1,270	35	Comoros	960	48	Sudan	740
23	Cameroon	1,170	36	Iceland	940	49	Peru	730
24	Philippines	1,160	37	Congo, Dem. Rep. of	910	50	Senegal	730
25	Guinea	1,140	38	Congo, Rep. of	870	51	Pakistan	720
26	Nigeria	1,140	39	South Africa	870	52	Papua New Guinea	720
27	Lesotho	1,130	40	Sri Lanka	860	53	Taiwan	720
28	Indonesia	1,119	41	Algeria	840	54	Hungary	710
29	Ethiopia	1,100	42	Morocco	840	55	Mauritania	710
30	Uganda	1,090	43	Luxembourg	829	56	Italy	680
31	Honduras	1,040	44	India	820	57	Guatemala	670
32	El Salvador	1,000	45	Malaysia	760	58	Liechtenstein	660
33	Nepal	1,000	46	Botswana	750	59	Norway	660

Rank	Country/Entity	Population per Police Officer	Rank	Country/Entity	Population per Police Officer	Rank	Country/Entity	Population per Police Officer
60	Portugal	660	93	Vanuatu	450	126	Saint Vincent and the Grenadines	250
61	Cuba	650	94	Jamaica	430	127	Mauritius	240
62	Myanmar (Burma)	650	95	Oman	430	128	Virgin Islands (U.S.)	240
63	Belgium	640	96	Saint Lucia	430	129	Grenada	230
64	Czech Republic	640	97	Colombia	420	130	Malta	230
65	Finland	640	98	Fiji	407	131	Singapore	230
66	Switzerland	640	99	Haiti	400	132	Hong Kong	221
67	France	630	100	Marshall Islands	400	133	Andorra	220
68	Jordan	630	101	São Tomé and Príncipe	400	134	Réunion	220
69	New Zealand	630	102	Greece	380	135	Israel	210
70	Ghana	620	103	Puerto Rico	380	136	Equatorial Guinea	190
71	Solomon Islands	620	104	Bermuda	370	137	Guyana	190
72	Swaziland	610	105	Poland	370	138	Bahrain	180
73	Denmark	600	106	United Kingdom	350	139	Cyprus	180
74	Sierra Leone	600	107	Greenland	340	140	Panama	180
75	Dominican Republic	580	108	Tunisia	340	141	Gibraltar	170
76	Egypt	580	109	Kiribati	330	142	Uruguay	170
77	Spain	580	110	Netherlands Antilles	330	143	Mali	160
78	Albania	550	111	Sweden	330	144	Iraq	140
79	Afghanistan	540	112	Tonga	330	145	United Arab Emirates	140
80	Somalia	540	113	Venezuela	320	146	Yugoslavia	140
81	Zambia	540	114	United States	318	147	Bahamas	125
82	Lebanon	530	115	Ireland	310	148	Antigua and Barbuda	120
83	Thailand	530	116	Paraguay	310	149	Mongolia	120
84	Netherlands	510	117	Dominica	300	150	Seychelles	120
85	South Korea	506	118	Saint Kitts and Nevis	300	151	Cape Verde	110
86	Costa Rica	480	119	Belize	290	152	Nauru	110
87	Japan	480	120	Tuvalu	290	153	Brunei	100
88	Austria	470	121	Barbados	280	154	Nicaragua	90
89	Chile	470	122	Laos	280	155	Kuwait	80
90	American Samoa	460	123	Saudi Arabia	280	156	Angola	14
91	North Korea	460	124	Trinidad and Tobago	280			
92	Australia	453	125	Ecuador	260			

Source: INTERPOL International Criminal Statistics

Crime

This section presents five rankings on the more serious crimes based on the resources of INTERPOL, or International Criminal Police Organization, the only group currently engaged in the collection of global crime statistics. Because of the limited number of governments cooperating with INTERPOL in its data collection efforts, the rankings are not conclusive and have only limited use for analysis and interpretation. Criminal statistics also suffer from other grave deficiencies built into the reporting system. It is well known that only a certain number of crimes are reported to the police, and of these only a certain percentage are recorded on the police blotter. Only in a few countries is a copy of this record transmitted regularly to the national headquarters, and in even fewer countries are these criminal statistics published. Second, there is no way of verifying whether a greater crime rate is simply the result of better law enforcement or of a better reporting system. Third, many countries deliberately manipulate their crime statistics to maintain a favorable public image.

22.2 Crime Rate

Rank	Country/Entity	Reported Criminal Offenses per 100,000 Persons	Rank	Country/Entity	Reported Criminal Offenses per 100,000 Persons	Rank	Country/Entity	Reported Criminal Offenses per 100,000 Persons
1	Gibraltar	18,316	58	Estonia	2,383	116	Zambia	666
2	Suriname	17,819	59	Maldives	2,353	117	Lebanon	657
3	Saint Kitts and Nevis	15,468	60	Poland	2,351	118	Belarus	650
4	Finland	14,799	61	Spain	2,287	119	Colombia	641
5	Rwanda	14,550	62	Marshall Islands	2,273	120	India	594
6	New Zealand	13,854	63	West Bank	2,226	121	Algeria	584
7	Sweden	12,982	64	Slovenia	2,210	122	São Tomé and Príncipe	558
8	Denmark	10,525	65	Zimbabwe	2,160	123	Guatemala	510
9	Virgin Islands (U.S.)	10,441	66	Tonga	2,100	124	Kenya	484
10	Canada	10,351	67	Réunion	2,097	125	Ecuador	466
11	Netherlands	10,181	68	Dominica	1,956	126	Malaysia	454
12	Guam	10,080	69	Czech Republic	1,911	127	Bosnia and Herzegovina	402
13	United Kingdom	9,880	70	Lesotho	1,885	128	Djibouti	402
14	Greenland	9,360	71	Malta	1,841	129	Panama	380
15	Norway	9,187	72	French Polynesia	1,799	130	Morocco	366
16	French Guiana	8,936	73	Russia	1,779	131	Thailand	351
17	Bermuda	8,871	74	Jamaica	1,723	132	Turkey	339
18	Grenada	8,543	75	Bahrain	1,714	133	Uzbekistan	334
19	Botswana	8,281	76	Latvia	1,597	134	Georgia	325
20	Germany	8,038	77	Sudan	1,565	135	Tajikistan	317
21	Luxembourg	6,933	78	Iceland	1,550	136	Paraguay	313
22	Uruguay	6,806	79	United Arab Emirates	1,496	137	Nigeria	312
23	Bahamas	6,752	80	Macau	1,491	138	Myanmar (Burma)	309
24	France	6,733	81	Japan	1,490	139	Sri Lanka	280
25	Austria	6,314	82	Hong Kong	1,449	140	Ethiopia	263
26	Martinique	6,305	83	Trinidad and Tobago	1,382	141	Kiribati	261
27	Australia	6,279	84	Singapore	1,367	142	Azerbaijan	247
28	Guadeloupe	5,793	85	Croatia	1,334	143	Pakistan	247
29	Belgium	5,769	86	Yugoslavia	1,268	144	Northern Mariana Islands	245
30	Netherlands Antilles	5,574	87	Tanzania	1,250	145	Philippines	230
31	Aruba	5,461	88	Tunisia	1,240	146	Mauritania	225
32	United States	5,374	89	Lithuania	1,199	147	Oman	198
33	Israel	5,191	90	Peru	1,178	148	Iraq	197
34	Antigua and Barbuda	4,977	91	Kuwait	1,171	149	Senegal	190
35	Swaziland	4,853	92	Brunei	1,148	150	Argentina	186
36	Seychelles	4,517	93	Venezuela	1,106	151	Yemen	170
37	Saint Lucia	4,386	94	Ukraine	1,096	152	Mozambique	166
38	Gaza Strip	4,355	95	Chile	1,086	153	Armenia	160
39	Barbados	4,337	96	Nicaragua	1,069	154	Somalia	144
40	Switzerland	4,327	97	Romania	1,039	155	Uganda	140
41	Monaco	4,277	98	South Korea	1,029	156	Central African Republic	135
42	Saint Vincent and the Grenadines	3,977	99	Portugal	988	157	Saudi Arabia	131
			100	Kyrgyzstan	987	158	Guinea-Bissau	129
43	Italy	3,828	101	Libya	951	159	China	128
44	Hungary	3,789	102	Dominican Republic	946	160	Benin	125
45	Egypt	3,693	103	Macedonia	944	161	Brazil	116
46	Guyana	3,682	104	Ghana	942	162	Gabon	114
47	Mauritius	3,430	105	Costa Rica	868	163	Madagascar	112
48	Namibia	3,359	106	Moldova	858	164	Mexico	108
49	Puerto Rico	3,182	107	Malawi	850	165	Gambia	89
50	American Samoa	3,006	108	Mongolia	823	166	Syria	89
51	Greece	2,956	109	Kazakhstan	815	167	Burundi	87
52	Isle of Man	2,867	110	Taiwan	799	168	Iran	77
53	Ireland	2,834	111	Qatar	775	169	Côte d'Ivoire	67
54	Andorra	2,795	112	Papua New Guinea	766	170	Bangladesh	64
55	Slovakia	2,571	113	Jordan	751	171	Indonesia	60
56	Bulgaria	2,522	114	Haiti	701	172	Nepal	44
57	Fiji	2,518	115	Cyprus	689	173	Burkina Faso	41

Rank	Country/Entity	Reported Criminal Offenses per 100,000 Persons	Rank	Country/Entity	Reported Criminal Offenses per 100,000 Persons	Rank	Country/Entity	Reported Criminal Offenses per 100,000 Persons
174	Mali	33	177	Angola	31	180	Togo	11
175	Congo, Rep. of	32	178	Guinea	18			
176	Niger	32	179	Cameroon	11			

Source: INTERPOL International Criminal Statistics

22.3 Burglary Rate

Rank	Country/Entity	Burglaries per 100,000 Persons	Rank	Country/Entity	Burglaries per 100,000 Persons	Rank	Country/Entity	Burglaries per 100,000 Persons
1	Gibraltar	5,250.0	49	Grenada	582.2	97	Uruguay	56.9
2	Netherlands	3,803.0	50	Trinidad and Tobago	567.0	98	Sri Lanka	54.7
3	Netherlands Antilles	3,455.0	51	Spain	555.4	99	Mozambique	45.9
4	Virgin Islands (U.S.)	3,183.7	52	Slovenia	526.4	100	China	45.2
5	United Kingdom	2,404.4	53	Kyrgyzstan	482.4	101	Jordan	43.4
6	New Zealand	2,352.9	54	Fiji	463.7	102	Uzbekistan	40.9
7	Australia	2,131.9	55	Aruba	451.3	103	Qatar	40.8
8	Denmark	2,046.3	56	Zimbabwe	445.3	104	Georgia	40.7
9	Antigua and Barbuda	1,984.4	57	Monaco	407.1	105	Djibouti	40.0
10	Bermuda	1,949.2	58	Latvia	390.4	106	Algeria	39.7
11	Finland	1,934.9	59	Croatia	379.8	107	Kiribati	38.6
12	Germany	1,927.1	60	Venezuela	358.2	108	Maldives	36.1
13	Greenland	1,883.5	61	Greece	330.2	109	Somalia	31.2
14	Sweden	1,615.1	62	Lithuania	325.2	110	Guatemala	27.9
15	Belgium	1,529.5	63	Palau	323.0	111	Indonesia	24.8
16	French Guiana	1,367.3	64	Jamaica	267.7	112	Syria	21.2
17	Bahamas	1,336.5	65	Russia	262.3	113	Côte d'Ivoire	19.5
18	Canada	1,326.2	66	Macau	250.5	114	India	15.6
19	Barbados	1,267.2	67	Guyana	242.6	115	Uganda	15.1
20	Bulgaria	1,174.9	68	French Polynesia	232.7	116	Malawi	13.1
21	Estonia	1,160.7	69	Costa Rica	232.4	117	Rwanda	12.5
22	Austria	1,128.2	70	Hong Kong	222.8	118	United Arab Emirates	10.5
23	Malta	1,079.2	71	Lesotho	221.5	119	Thailand	9.9
24	Dominica	1,078.1	72	Mongolia	204.5	120	Pakistan	9.1
25	Seychelles	1,058.9	73	Cyprus	203.3	121	Azerbaijan	8.4
26	United States	1,041.8	74	Japan	198.1	122	South Korea	6.7
27	Switzerland	973.0	75	Portugal	186.9	123	Ethiopia	6.3
28	Swaziland	941.4	76	Réunion	181.3	124	Gambia	5.6
29	Isle of Man	921.4	77	Dominican Republic	154.0	125	Ghana	5.4
30	Ireland	859.7	78	Zambia	153.5	126	Bangladesh	4.6
31	Luxembourg	855.2	79	Tunisia	143.6	127	Guinea-Bissau	4.0
32	Puerto Rico	853.0	80	Romania	133.2	128	Mali	3.9
33	Belize	833.6	81	Brunei	133.1	129	Benin	3.4
34	Guadeloupe	821.5	82	Nicaragua	110.7	130	Central African Republic	2.7
35	Israel	817.2	83	Malaysia	108.7	131	Mauritania	2.5
36	France	812.6	84	Paraguay	105.1	132	Gabon	2.3
37	Andorra	796.8	85	Nauru	100.0	133	Senegal	2.0
38	Namibia	793.0	86	Tanzania	97.3	134	Botswana	1.9
39	Poland	789.5	87	Norway	95.0	135	Argentina	1.5
40	Saint Lucia	778.0	88	Ecuador	94.4	136	Cameroon	1.2
41	Hungary	767.4	89	Peru	87.0	137	Lebanon	1.2
42	Iceland	704.8	90	Bahrain	86.7	138	Niger	1.0
43	Martinique	641.2	91	Mauritius	85.9	139	Nepal	0.8
44	Guam	634.2	92	Singapore	83.9	140	Guinea	0.7
45	Slovakia	629.8	93	Kenya	76.9	141	Madagascar	0.7
46	Czech Republic	621.5	94	Kuwait	75.9	142	Sudan	0.4
47	Liechtenstein	614.3	95	Northern Mariana Islands	73.7	143	Congo, Rep. of	0.2
48	American Samoa	588.0	96	Papua New Guinea	63.0	144	Myanmar (Burma)	0.1

Source: INTERPOL International Criminal Statistics

22.4 Assault Rate

Rank	Country/Entity	Assaults per 100,000 Persons	Rank	Country/Entity	Assaults per 100,000 Persons	Rank	Country/Entity	Assaults per 100,000 Persons
1	Gibraltar	3,213	57	Czech Republic	89.4	114	Cyprus	17.7
2	Virgin Islands (U.S.)	1,943.2	58	Malawi	82.2	115	Saudi Arabia	17.2
3	Suriname	1,824.4	59	Hungary	79.3	116	Uganda	15.6
4	Saint Lucia	1,193	60	Greece	78.7	117	Japan	14.4
5	Saint Vincent and the Grenadines	986.9	61	Guatemala	77.1	118	Malaysia	14.4
			62	Côte d'Ivoire	73.1	119	Moldova	13.4
6	Greenland	845.0	63	Poland	71.8	120	Ireland	13.3
7	Canada	769.1	64	Macau	67.3	121	Kyrgyzstan	12.6
8	Seychelles	698.7	65	Papua New Guinea	66.7	122	Djibouti	12.4
9	Namibia	657.8	66	Iceland	64.3	123	Isle of Man	12.3
10	Swaziland	589.1	67	Monaco	63.4	124	Madagascar	12.0
11	Australia	560.3	68	Paraguay	62.2	125	Kiribati	11.6
12	Jamaica	552.1	69	Trinidad and Tobago	56.7	126	Mauritius	11.2
13	Bahrain	547.1	70	Kenya	54.1	127	Costa Rica	11.1
14	New Zealand	546.3	71	Switzerland	52.9	128	Sri Lanka	10.8
15	American Samoa	494.0	72	Fiji	51.3	129	Gambia	10.6
16	Antigua and Barbuda	475.0	73	Ethiopia	49.9	130	Zambia	9.5
17	Botswana	431.9	74	Iran	47.7	131	Mozambique	9.2
18	United States	430.2	75	Kuwait	46.5	132	Lithuania	9.1
19	South Korea	410.5	76	Macedonia	46.4	133	Guinea-Bissau	8.7
20	Nauru	400.0	77	Russia	45.8	134	Somalia	8.0
21	Netherlands Antilles	396.0	78	Senegal	44.7	135	Honduras	7.7
22	Ghana	387.4	79	Sweden	42.5	136	Burundi	7.4
23	United Kingdom	362.1	80	Philippines	41.8	137	Belarus	7.0
24	Luxembourg	291.7	81	Qatar	41.7	138	Syria	7.0
25	Belize	275.6	82	Sudan	40.5	139	Morocco	6.7
26	Israel	267.2	83	Guyana	40.2	140	Angola	6.1
27	Bermuda	221.7	84	Finland	40.0	141	Azerbaijan	5.6
28	Guadeloupe	215.2	85	Bulgaria	38.6	142	China	5.2
29	Nicaragua	203.8	86	Mauritania	38.0	143	Indonesia	5.1
30	Zimbabwe	193.6	87	Benin	37.9	144	Libya	4.9
31	Netherlands	191.8	88	Italy	36.8	145	Singapore	4.9
32	Denmark	190.1	89	Andorra	36.5	146	Congo, Rep. of	4.7
33	Martinique	184.9	90	Malta	35.2	147	Romania	4.7
34	Aruba	180.0	91	Iraq	34.7	148	Tajikistan	4.6
35	French Guiana	178.7	92	Belgium	33.0	149	Uzbekistan	4.5
36	Puerto Rico	174.8	93	Ecuador	32.9	150	Burkina Faso	4.1
37	Barbados	170.8	94	Ukraine	32.3	151	Bangladesh	3.6
38	Lesotho	170.6	95	Myanmar (Burma)	31.2	152	Armenia	3.4
39	Uruguay	169.6	96	Dominican Republic	30.8	153	Maldives	3.3
40	Guam	169.3	97	Mexico	30.2	154	Brunei	2.7
41	Slovakia	158.1	98	Estonia	29.3	155	Bosnia and Herzegovina	2.6
42	Venezuela	152.2	99	Lebanon	28.4	156	Austria	2.5
43	Tunisia	134.0	100	Latvia	27.8	157	Niger	2.5
44	Réunion	123.1	101	Thailand	25.4	158	Portugal	1.7
45	Hong Kong	118.8	102	Dominica	25.2	159	United Arab Emirates	1.7
46	Bahamas	115.7	103	Rwanda	25.0	160	Mali	1.1
47	Liechtenstein	114.3	104	Turkey	24.2	161	Nepal	1.1
48	Colombia	110.5	105	Spain	23.5	162	Oman	1.1
49	Germany	108.2	106	Croatia	23.2	163	Egypt	0.7
50	Georgia	107.8	107	Central African Republic	22.8	164	Guinea	0.7
51	Peru	104.3	108	Mongolia	22.8	165	Argentina	0.6
52	French Polynesia	98.9	109	Panama	21.9	166	Tanzania	0.5
53	Grenada	98.9	110	Slovenia	20.9	167	Cameroon	0.1
54	France	98.8	111	Algeria	19.7	168	Pakistan	0.1
55	Chile	96.3	112	Jordan	19.1			
56	Northern Mariana Islands	92.6	113	Gabon	17.9			

Source: INTERPOL International Criminal Statistics

Rank	Country/Entity	Murders per 100,000 Persons	Rank	Country/Entity	Murders per 100,000 Persons	Rank	Country/Entity	Murders per 100,000 Persons
1	Rwanda	12,500.0	57	Iraq	7.1	114	Tajikistan	2.5
2	Swaziland	88.1	58	Lithuania	6.9	115	United Kingdom	2.5
3	Colombia	81.9	59	Barbados	6.8	116	Slovakia	2.4
4	Namibia	72.4	60	Kenya	6.4	117	Switzerland	2.3
5	Lesotho	33.9	61	Pakistan	6.4	118	Ghana	2.1
6	Belize	33.2	62	Tanzania	6.4	119	Israel	2.1
7	Philippines	30.1	63	Bulgaria	5.9	120	Malaysia	2.1
8	Jamaica	27.6	64	Martinique	5.8	121	Tunisia	2.1
9	Guatemala	27.4	65	Uzbekistan	5.5	122	Czech Republic	2.0
10	French Guiana	27.2	66	Armenia	5.4	123	Jordan	2.0
11	Puerto Rico	26.8	67	Costa Rica	5.3	124	Bangladesh	1.9
12	Nicaragua	25.6	68	Canada	5.2	125	Cyprus	1.9
13	Nauru	25.0	69	Bermuda	5.1	126	Maldives	1.9
14	Netherlands	24.9	70	Kiribati	5.1	127	Australia	1.8
15	Estonia	24.3	71	Zimbabwe	5.0	128	Bahrain	1.8
16	Virgin Islands (U.S.)	22.3	72	Denmark	4.9	129	Mauritania	1.8
17	Venezuela	22.1	73	Slovenia	4.9	130	Qatar	1.8
18	Russia	21.8	74	Antigua and Barbuda	4.7	131	Kuwait	1.7
19	Mongolia	19.0	75	France	4.7	132	Singapore	1.7
20	Greenland	18.1	76	Italy	4.7	133	Andorra	1.6
21	Bahamas	17.6	77	Germany	4.6	134	Central African Republic	1.6
22	Saint Lucia	17.0	78	India	4.6	135	Egypt	1.6
23	Ethiopia	16.4	79	Guyana	4.5	136	Hong Kong	1.6
24	Paraguay	15.6	80	Sweden	4.5	137	Brunei	1.5
25	Latvia	14.6	81	Djibouti	4.4	138	Congo, Rep. of	1.5
26	Panama	13.9	82	Hungary	4.3	139	Somalia	1.5
27	Guadeloupe	13.2	83	Lebanon	4.3	140	Gabon	1.4
28	Luxembourg	13.2	84	Dominica	4.2	141	South Korea	1.4
29	Botswana	12.7	85	Mozambique	4.2	142	Morocco	1.4
30	Dominican Republic	11.9	86	Portugal	4.2	143	Senegal	1.4
31	Trinidad and Tobago	11.7	87	Sudan	4.2	144	Syria	1.4
32	Fiji	11.5	88	Myanmar (Burma)	4.1	145	Libya	1.3
33	Chile	11.0	89	San Marino	4.1	146	Aruba	1.2
34	Georgia	10.7	90	Uruguay	4.1	147	Ireland	1.2
35	Ecuador	10.5	91	São Tomé and Príncipe	4.0	148	United Arab Emirates	1.1
36	Kyrgyzstan	10.4	92	Macedonia	3.9	149	Algeria	1.0
37	Saint Vincent and the Grenadines	10.3	93	New Zealand	3.9	150	Japan	1.0
			94	Macau	3.8	151	Norway	1.0
38	Zambia	9.8	95	Northern Mariana Islands	3.8	152	Benin	0.9
39	Uganda	9.5	96	Gibraltar	3.7	153	French Polynesia	0.9
40	Honduras	9.4	97	Turkey	3.6	154	Iceland	0.9
41	Peru	9.3	98	Angola	3.4	155	Saudi Arabia	0.9
42	United States	9.0	99	Burundi	3.3	156	Indonesia	0.8
43	Moldova	8.8	100	Romania	3.3	157	Oman	0.8
44	Ukraine	8.8	101	Mauritius	3.2	158	Isle of Man	0.7
45	Papua New Guinea	8.6	102	Belgium	3.1	159	Finland	0.6
46	Sri Lanka	8.2	103	Malawi	3.1	160	Madagascar	0.6
47	Taiwan	8.2	104	Poland	3.1	161	Guinea	0.5
48	Azerbaijan	8.1	105	Malta	3.0	162	Guinea-Bissau	0.5
49	American Samoa	8.0	106	Belarus	2.9	163	Iran	0.5
50	Guam	7.9	107	Seychelles	2.7	164	Gambia	0.4
51	Grenada	7.8	108	Greece	2.6	165	Argentina	0.3
52	Réunion	7.8	109	Spain	2.6	166	Burkina Faso	0.2
53	Thailand	7.7	110	Austria	2.5	167	China	0.2
54	Suriname	7.6	111	Bosnia and Herzegovina	2.5	168	Niger	0.2
55	Croatia	7.4	112	Côte d'Ivoire	2.5	169	Cameroon	0.1
56	Mexico	7.3	113	Nepal	2.5			

Source: INTERPOL International Criminal Statistics

22.6 Automobile Theft Rate

Rank	Country/Entity	Automobile Theft per 100,000 Persons	Rank	Country/Entity	Murders per 100,000 Persons	Rank	Country/Entity	Murders per 100,000 Persons
1	Switzerland	1,247.4	43	Panama	77.7	85	Côte d'Ivoire	11.9
2	United Kingdom	1,147.3	44	Botswana	73.1	86	Tunisia	11.1
3	Virgin Islands (U.S.)	954.0	45	Swaziland	71.4	87	Qatar	10.5
4	New Zealand	788.6	46	Portugal	65.8	88	Jamaica	9.9
5	Australia	703.0	47	Isle of Man	60.6	89	Kenya	9.7
6	France	667.0	48	Guatemala	58.1	90	Zambia	9.6
7	Denmark	663.3	49	Russia	55.2	91	Romania	9.5
8	Sweden	658.9	50	Finland	53.2	92	Mauritania	9.1
9	United States	591.2	51	Fiji	51.7	93	Zimbabwe	9.1
10	Canada	545.9	52	Hungary	51.1	94	Algeria	8.5
11	Italy	532.8	53	Paraguay	50.3	95	Bahrain	8.2
12	Norway	516.6	54	Ireland	44.3	96	Indonesia	8.0
13	Puerto Rico	482.9	55	Brunei	42.7	97	Gabon	7.5
14	Israel	479.5	56	Ukraine	42.3	98	Singapore	7.2
15	Guadeloupe	453.9	57	Hong Kong	38.9	99	China	6.9
16	Guam	333.6	58	Ecuador	36.5	100	American Samoa	6.0
17	Netherlands	316.8	59	Antigua and Barbuda	35.9	101	Uzbekistan	5.9
18	Belgium	310.7	60	Macedonia	35.1	102	Uganda	5.3
19	Luxembourg	275.5	61	Barbados	34.2	103	Azerbaijan	4.1
20	Germany	260.1	62	Dominica	33.6	104	Pakistan	4.1
21	Spain	253.0	63	Colombia	32.4	105	Sudan	3.4
22	Malta	243.9	64	Guyana	32.2	106	Honduras	3.3
23	Venezuela	239.4	65	Austria	31.8	107	Thailand	3.3
24	Bulgaria	208.0	66	Jordan	28.5	108	Egypt	3.1
25	Aruba	202.5	67	Saudi Arabia	28.5	109	Cyprus	3.0
26	Martinique	192.8	68	Lithuania	28.1	110	Syria	2.9
27	Macau	172.8	69	Japan	27.8	111	Ethiopia	2.3
28	Slovakia	170.6	70	Slovenia	25.1	112	Armenia	2.1
29	Estonia	169.1	71	Dominican Republic	24.8	113	Georgia	1.5
30	Liechtenstein	153.6	72	Costa Rica	23.1	114	Benin	1.3
31	French Guiana	150.6	73	Peru	22.7	115	Philippines	1.2
32	Réunion	137.9	74	Papua New Guinea	22.0	116	Tanzania	0.9
33	Monaco	126.8	75	Croatia	20.9	117	Bangladesh	0.6
34	Taiwan	124.9	76	Northern Mariana Islands	20.8	118	Cameroon	0.2
35	Namibia	115.4	77	Argentina	19.9	119	Congo, Rep. of	0.2
36	Iceland	112.8	78	Kuwait	18.2	120	Guinea-Bissau	0.2
37	Andorra	111.1	79	Turkey	17.0	121	Guinea	0.1
38	Latvia	109.2	80	Djibouti	16.0	122	Madagascar	0.1
39	Poland	109.0	81	Lebanon	13.8	123	Myanmar (Burma)	0.1
40	Greece	100.3	82	Chile	13.1	124	Niger	0.1
41	Czech Republic	95.7	83	Rwanda	12.5			
42	Trinidad and Tobago	86.4	84	Malaysia	12.4			

Source: INTERPOL International Criminal Statistics

Chapter 23

Media

Newspapers

The press, which generally applies to newspapers and magazines, wields an influence on national affairs far beyond its circulation and revenues. In an age where the press's authority and profits have been whittled down by television, radio, and web-based news services, newspapers still act as guardians of the great traditions of freedom of speech and freedom to print. While it cannot compete with the immediacy and visual appeal of television news, it tries to compensate by providing lengthy analyses and in-depth investigative work. After many uncertain decades it has held on to the loyalty of many readers and advertisers. In a few countries, such as the United Kingdom, Germany, and Japan, newspapers still enjoy circulation in the millions, but to attract new readers and keep the old ones, some newspapers have had to resort to sensationalistic journalism. In terms of circulation, the daily press stands more or less where it did twenty years ago, but the contrast among regions is striking. In Africa, nine countries and territories have no newspapers, and in only fifteen of the others does the circulation exceed ten per 1,000 persons; in none does it exceed 100 per 1,000. Circulation rates are high in Europe where it reaches 400 per 1,000. It is more modest in North America where it is 228 per 1,000 in the United States, and 189 per 1,000 in Canada. In Latin America, it drops to 100 per 1,000. Asia presents great contrasts between Japan with 576 per 1,000 and Bangladesh with 6 per 1,000.

23.1 Daily Newspapers

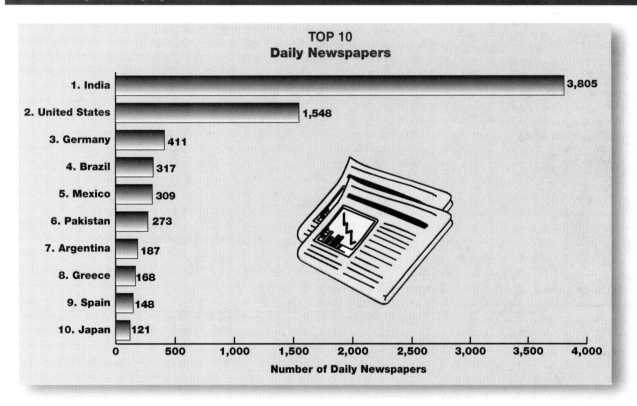

TOP 10
Daily Newspapers

Rank	Country/Entity	Daily Newspapers
1. India		3,805
2. United States		1,548
3. Germany		411
4. Brazil		317
5. Mexico		309
6. Pakistan		273
7. Argentina		187
8. Greece		168
9. Spain		148
10. Japan		121

Number of Daily Newspapers

Rank	Country/Entity	Daily Newspapers	Rank	Country/Entity	Daily Newspapers	Rank	Country/Entity	Daily Newspapers
11	France	118	14	Sweden	94	17	Norway	83
12	Canada	107	15	Ukraine	90	18	Switzerland	80
13	United Kingdom	103	16	Venezuela	89	19	Italy	74

Rank	Country/Entity	Daily Newspapers	Rank	Country/Entity	Daily Newspapers	Rank	Country/Entity	Daily Newspapers
20	Australia	69	74	Liberia	8	128	New Caledonia	3
21	Romania	69	75	Singapore	8	129	Puerto Rico	3
22	Poland	66	76	Syria	8	130	Réunion	3
23	South Korea	62	77	United Arab Emirates	8	131	Senegal	3
24	Turkey	57	78	Armenia	7	132	Suriname	3
25	Finland	56	79	Madagascar	7	133	Swaziland	3
26	Indonesia	56	80	Panama	7	134	Tanzania	3
27	Bangladesh	51	81	Tunisia	7	135	Yemen	3
28	Denmark	51	82	Algeria	6	136	Barbados	2
29	Peru	48	83	Congo, Rep. of	6	137	Bosnia and Herzegovina	2
30	Colombia	46	84	Croatia	6	138	Gambia	2
31	Netherlands	46	85	El Salvador	6	139	Gibraltar	2
32	Malaysia	44	86	Mauritius	6	140	Guyana	2
33	Hong Kong	43	87	Netherlands Antilles	6	141	Lesotho	2
34	Philippines	42	88	Slovenia	6	142	Liechtenstein	2
35	China	38	89	Costa Rica	5	143	Maldives	2
36	Thailand	35	90	Guatemala	5	144	Mali	2
37	Israel	34	91	Honduras	5	145	Mozambique	2
38	Belgium	32	92	Iceland	5	146	Papua New Guinea	2
39	Chile	32	93	Kenya	5	147	Tajikistan	2
40	Uruguay	32	94	Luxembourg	5	148	Uganda	2
41	New Zealand	31	95	Myanmar (Burma)	5	149	Virgin Islands (U.S.)	2
42	Nepal	28	96	Paraguay	5	150	Zimbabwe	2
43	Hungary	27	97	San Marino	5	151	American Samoa	1
44	Nigeria	27	98	Sudan	5	152	Antigua and Barbuda	1
45	Ecuador	24	99	Angola	4	153	Benin	1
46	Austria	23	100	Belize	4	154	Bermuda	1
47	Czech Republic	23	101	Estonia	4	155	Brunei	1
48	Portugal	23	102	Ethiopia	4	156	Burkina Faso	1
49	Latvia	22	103	French Polynesia	4	157	Burundi	1
50	Slovakia	21	104	Ghana	4	158	Côte d'Ivoire	1
51	Saudi Arabia	19	105	Haiti	4	159	Cameroon	1
52	Bulgaria	17	106	Iraq	4	160	Central African Republic	1
53	Cuba	17	107	Jordan	4	161	Chad	1
54	Egypt	17	108	Libya	4	162	Fiji	1
55	Russia	17	109	Moldova	4	163	French Guiana	1
56	South Africa	17	110	Namibia	4	164	Gabon	1
57	Lebanon	16	111	Nicaragua	4	165	Grenada	1
58	Lithuania	16	112	Niger	4	166	Guadeloupe	1
59	Afghanistan	15	113	Oman	4	167	Guam	1
60	Cyprus	15	114	Qatar	4	168	Guinea-Bissau	1
61	Aruba	14	115	Trinidad and Tobago	4	169	Malawi	1
62	Morocco	13	116	Uzbekistan	4	170	Martinique	1
63	Iran	12	117	Vietnam	4	171	Mauritania	1
64	Bolivia	11	118	Albania	3	172	Monaco	1
65	Dominican Republic	11	119	Andorra	3	173	Mongolia	1
66	North Korea	11	120	Azerbaijan	3	174	Rwanda	1
67	Belarus	10	121	Bahamas	3	175	Seychelles	1
68	Congo, Dem. Rep. of	9	122	Bahrain	3	176	Sierra Leone	1
69	Kuwait	9	123	Jamaica	3	177	Somalia	1
70	Macau	9	124	Kyrgyzstan	3	178	Togo	1
71	Sri Lanka	9	125	Laos	3	179	Tonga	1
72	Yugoslavia	9	126	Macedonia	3			
73	Ireland	8	127	Malta	3			

Source: UNESCO Statistical Yearbook

23.2 Daily Newspaper Circulation

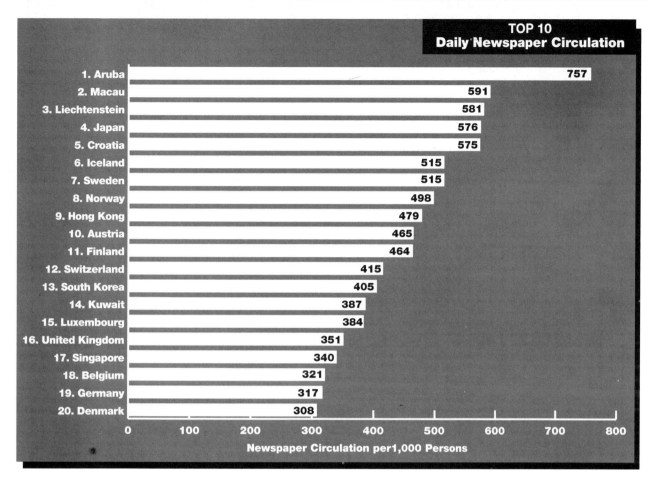

TOP 10
Daily Newspaper Circulation

Rank & Country	Value
1. Aruba	757
2. Macau	591
3. Liechtenstein	581
4. Japan	576
5. Croatia	575
6. Iceland	515
7. Sweden	515
8. Norway	498
9. Hong Kong	479
10. Austria	465
11. Finland	464
12. Switzerland	415
13. South Korea	405
14. Kuwait	387
15. Luxembourg	384
16. United Kingdom	351
17. Singapore	340
18. Belgium	321
19. Germany	317
20. Denmark	308

Newspaper Circulation per 1,000 Persons

Rank	Country/Entity	Newspaper Circulation per 1,000 Persons	Rank	Country/Entity	Newspaper Circulation per 1,000 Persons	Rank	Country/Entity	Newspaper Circulation per 1,000 Persons
21	Netherlands	299	42	Canada	189	63	United Arab Emirates	126
22	New Zealand	297	43	Taiwan	188	64	New Caledonia	123
23	Romania	297	44	Belarus	187	65	Cuba	120
24	Israel	281	45	Puerto Rico	184	66	Ukraine	118
25	Russia	267	46	Slovenia	183	67	Mexico	113
26	Virgin Islands (U.S.)	267	47	Guam	170	68	French Polynesia	112
27	Monaco	263	48	Ireland	170	69	Cyprus	110
28	Netherlands Antilles	260	49	Barbados	159	70	Italy	105
29	Slovakia	256	50	Greece	156	71	Spain	104
30	Australia	255	51	Malta	145	72	Suriname	103
31	Bermuda	254	52	Malaysia	142	73	Costa Rica	102
32	Estonia	242	53	Bulgaria	141	74	Chile	99
33	France	237	54	Poland	141	75	Antigua and Barbuda	94
34	Uruguay	237	55	Argentina	138	76	Namibia	93
35	Hungary	228	56	Qatar	138	77	Yugoslavia	90
36	Latvia	228	57	Lithuania	136	78	Mongolia	88
37	United States	228	58	Lebanon	135	79	Peru	86
38	Czech Republic	219	59	Trinidad and Tobago	135	80	Martinique	84
39	Venezuela	215	60	Bosnia and Herzegovina	131	81	Guadeloupe	83
40	Gibraltar	214	61	Bahrain	128	82	Réunion	83
41	North Korea	213	62	Bahamas	126	83	Tonga	73

Rank	Country/Entity	Newspaper Circulation per 1,000 Persons	Rank	Country/Entity	Newspaper Circulation per 1,000 Persons	Rank	Country/Entity	Newspaper Circulation per 1,000 Persons
84	Ecuador	72	117	Iraq	27	150	Tanzania	8.0
85	Brunei	71	118	Sri Lanka	25	151	Vietnam	8.0
86	Bolivia	69	119	Moldova	24	152	Haiti	7.1
87	Mauritius	68	120	Armenia	23	153	Côte d'Ivoire	7.0
88	Jamaica	66	121	China	23	154	Lesotho	7.0
89	Philippines	65	122	Guatemala	23	155	Uzbekistan	7.0
90	Colombia	64	123	Myanmar (Burma)	23	156	Bangladesh	6.0
91	Egypt	64	124	Sudan	23	157	Guinea-Bissau	6.0
92	Andorra	63	125	Pakistan	22	158	Senegal	6.0
93	Guyana	63	126	Macedonia	21	159	Mozambique	5.0
94	Panama	62	127	Indonesia	20	160	Madagascar	4.5
95	Albania	54	128	Iran	20	161	Mali	4.4
96	Saudi Arabia	54	129	Ghana	18	162	Cameroon	4.0
97	El Salvador	53	130	Nigeria	18	163	Burundi	3.0
98	American Samoa	51	131	Syria	18	164	Congo, Dem. Rep. of	3.0
99	Jordan	48	132	Yemen	17	165	Laos	3.0
100	Thailand	47	133	Zimbabwe	17	166	Malawi	2.6
101	Algeria	46	134	Gabon	16	167	Equatorial Guinea	2.5
102	Tunisia	46	135	Papua New Guinea	15	168	Sierra Leone	2.2
103	Brazil	45	136	Liberia	14	169	Benin	2.0
104	Fiji	45	137	Swaziland	14	170	Gambia	2.0
105	Grenada	45	138	Kenya	13	171	Togo	2.0
106	Honduras	44	139	Libya	13	172	Uganda	2.0
107	Turkey	44	140	Morocco	13	173	Burkina Faso	1.6
108	Paraguay	42	141	Tajikistan	13	174	Niger	1.3
109	Portugal	41	142	Maldives	12	175	Central African Republic	1.0
110	Seychelles	40	143	Afghanistan	11	176	Somalia	1.0
111	Dominican Republic	35	144	Angola	11	177	Belize	0.5
112	South Africa	33	145	French Guiana	11	178	Mauritania	0.5
113	Nicaragua	30	146	Kyrgyzstan	11	179	San Marino	0.5
114	Oman	30	147	Ethiopia	10	180	Chad	0.4
115	Botswana	29	148	Congo, Rep. of	8	181	Rwanda	0.1
116	Azerbaijan	28	149	Nepal	8			

Source: UNESCO Statistical Yearbook

23.3 Magazines and Periodicals

Compared with other forms of media, the world of periodicals is one of great variety. Although magazine publishing remains one of the riskiest enterprises, 600,000 magazines are published worldwide. Many of them die out every year, but enough survive and new ones are added.

Unlike daily newspapers, magazines are published in virtually every country and manage to compete successfully for advertising dollars with newspapers, on the one hand, and the electronic media, on the other.

Rank	Country/Entity	Magazines and Periodicals	Rank	Country/Entity	Magazines and Periodicals	Rank	Country/Entity	Magazines and Periodicals
1	Belgium	13,706	8	Sweden	4,272	15	Philippines	1,570
2	United States	11,593	9	Poland	3,999	16	Thailand	1,522
3	Italy	9,951	10	Turkey	3,554	17	Canada	1,400
4	Germany	9,010	11	Japan	2,926	18	Hungary	1,203
5	Norway	8,017	12	France	2,672	19	Czech Republic	1,168
6	China	6,486	13	Russia	2,592	20	Romania	987
7	Finland	5,711	14	Austria	2,481	21	Portugal	984

Rank	Country/Entity	Magazines and Periodicals	Rank	Country/Entity	Magazines and Periodicals	Rank	Country/Entity	Magazines and Periodicals
22	Iceland	938	42	Cuba	160	62	Zimbabwe	28
23	Slovenia	784	43	Mexico	158	63	Bahrain	26
24	Bulgaria	745	44	Belarus	155	64	Uganda	26
25	Hong Kong	598	45	Albania	143	65	Malaysia	25
26	Luxembourg	508	46	Ghana	121	66	Tajikistan	22
27	Saudi Arabia	471	47	Indonesia	117	67	San Marino	18
28	Estonia	470	48	United Arab Emirates	80	68	Macau	16
29	Slovakia	424	49	Moldova	76	69	Brunei	15
30	Chile	417	50	Macedonia	74	70	Oman	15
31	Yugoslavia	395	51	Uzbekistan	70	71	Rwanda	15
32	Netherlands	367	52	Mauritius	62	72	Botswana	14
33	Malta	359	53	Switzerland	60	73	Qatar	12
34	Croatia	352	54	Madagascar	55	74	South Africa	11
35	Ukraine	321	55	Azerbaijan	49	75	Gambia	10
36	Iran	318	56	Algeria	48	76	Saint Kitts and Nevis	10
37	Lithuania	269	57	Mongolia	45	77	Djibouti	7
38	Egypt	266	58	Armenia	40	78	Congo, Rep. of	3
39	Latvia	213	59	Burkina Faso	37	79	Guinea	3
40	Denmark	205	60	Cyprus	37	80	Monaco	3
41	Ecuador	199	61	Jordan	31			

Source: UNESCO Statistical Yearbook

23.4 Books

In the early 1990s, in the first flush of the information revolution, many felt that print books would soon be extinct. But books continue to thrive and even experience new forms of growth. The number of titles published worldwide has reached one million annually and appear in more than 300 languages. Books in print now number 200 million. The first e-books made their appearance during the turn of the twenty-first century, but the extent of their appeal remains uncertain. Although copyright and intellectual property laws have become more stringent and more extensively enforced, piracy manages to flourish mainly in the developing countries of Asia where legitimately published books have become unaffordable.

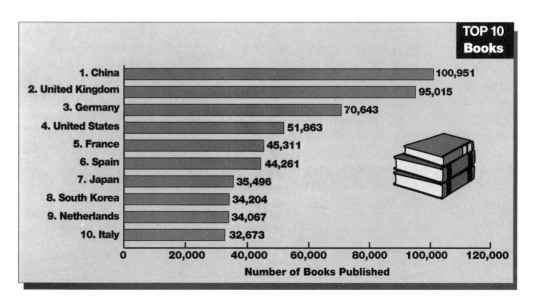

TOP 10 Books

Rank	Country	Number of Books Published
1.	China	100,951
2.	United Kingdom	95,015
3.	Germany	70,643
4.	United States	51,863
5.	France	45,311
6.	Spain	44,261
7.	Japan	35,496
8.	South Korea	34,204
9.	Netherlands	34,067
10.	Italy	32,673

Rank	Country/Entity	Books Published	Rank	Country/Entity	Books Published	Rank	Country/Entity	Books Published
11	Russia	30,390	42	Egypt	3,108	73	Algeria	323
12	Canada	22,208	43	Sri Lanka	2,929	74	Georgia	314
13	Brazil	21,574	44	Slovenia	2,906	75	Uganda	314
14	Switzerland	15,378	45	Lithuania	2,885	76	United Arab Emirates	293
15	Sweden	13,822	46	Yugoslavia	2,799	77	Mongolia	285
16	Finland	12,539	47	Croatia	2,671	78	Malawi	243
17	Denmark	11,973	48	Estonia	2,261	79	Zimbabwe	232
18	India	11,460	49	Peru	1,993	80	Tajikistan	231
19	Poland	10,874	50	Chile	1,820	81	Armenia	224
20	Australia	10,835	51	Latvia	1,677	82	Kuwait	196
21	Iran	10,753	52	Nigeria	1,562	83	Paraguay	152
22	Hungary	10,108	53	Iceland	1,429	84	Pakistan	124
23	Czech Republic	9,309	54	Uzbekistan	1,340	85	Madagascar	114
24	Argentina	9,065	55	Philippines	1,233	86	Eritrea	106
25	Austria	7,987	56	Kazakhstan	1,148	87	Benin	84
26	Thailand	7,626	57	Cyprus	1,040	88	Mauritius	84
27	Norway	6,846	58	Costa Rica	963	89	Belize	70
28	Portugal	6,667	59	Cuba	932	90	Réunion	69
29	Indonesia	6,303	60	Moldova	797	91	Congo, Dem. Rep. of	64
30	Bulgaria	5,925	61	Luxembourg	681	92	Laos	64
31	Vietnam	5,581	62	Macedonia	672	93	Andorra	57
32	Ukraine	5,002	63	Syria	598	94	Brunei	45
33	Israel	4,608	64	Turkmenistan	565	95	Guyana	33
34	South Africa	4,574	65	Tunisia	539	96	Ghana	28
35	Turkey	4,473	66	Jordan	500	97	Trinidad and Tobago	26
36	Romania	4,074	67	Malta	417	98	Oman	24
37	Malaysia	4,050	68	Fiji	401	99	Honduras	22
38	Myanmar (Burma)	3,660	69	Azerbaijan	375	100	Gambia	21
39	Venezuela	3,660	70	Qatar	371	101	Ecuador	11
40	Slovakia	3,481	71	Morocco	354			
41	Belarus	3,346	72	Kyrgyzstan	328			

Source: UNESCO Statistical Yearbook

Radios

Radio is called the hot medium because, unlike television, which is the cool medium, it requires less attention, and listening can be combined with other activities. Most cars are equipped with radios, giving radios a great advantage over television. In many countries radio is the medium closest to total market saturation. Inventions like the Sony Walkman have popularized radio to the extent that it has become truly universal in its ownership. Short wave radio has a global reach and makes it difficult for governments to impose any meaningful form of censorship. The principal drawback of radio is that, like newspapers, its audience is primarily local and is further segmented by interests. However, all-news radio stations, like all-news television networks, are becoming more common.

23.5 Radios

Rank	Country/Entity	Radios (thousands)	Rank	Country/Entity	Radios (thousands)	Rank	Country/Entity	Radios (thousands)
1	United States	520,000	6	United Kingdom	65,400	11	Indonesia	26,000
2	China	215,950	7	Brazil	55,000	12	Canada	22,600
3	Germany	150,000	8	France	50,000	13	Argentina	21,500
4	India	111,000	9	Italy	46,350	14	Australia	21,000
5	Japan	100,000	10	South Korea	42,000	15	Mexico	21,000

Rank	Country/Entity	Radios (thousands)	Rank	Country/Entity	Radios (thousands)	Rank	Country/Entity	Radios (thousands)
16	Ukraine	18,000	70	Portugal	2,220	124	Macedonia	350
17	Nigeria	17,200	71	El Salvador	2,080	125	Bahrain	320
18	Egypt	16,450	72	Honduras	1,910	126	Barbados	300
19	Poland	16,300	73	Jamaica	1,859	127	Burundi	300
20	Iran	13,000	74	Uruguay	1,850	128	Botswana	300
21	Iraq	13,000	75	Tunisia	1,700	129	Papua New Guinea	300
22	Netherlands	12,000	76	Côte d'Ivoire	1,600	130	Somalia	300
23	Spain	12,000	77	Mali	1,600	131	Mongolia	280
24	South Africa	11,200	78	Moldova	1,556	132	Haiti	270
25	Thailand	10,000	79	Cambodia	1,500	133	Suriname	262
26	Uganda	10,000	80	Cameroon	1,500	134	Congo, Dem. Rep. of	240
27	Malaysia	9,500	81	Lithuania	1,420	135	Luxembourg	240
28	Czech Republic	9,100	82	Latvia	1,396	136	Guinea	230
29	Ethiopia	9,000	83	Chad	1,310	137	Namibia	230
30	Turkey	8,800	84	Ghana	1,300	138	Cyprus	210
31	Taiwan	8,620	85	Zambia	1,300	139	Equatorial Guinea	200
32	Philippines	8,300	86	Zimbabwe	1,300	140	Iceland	197
33	Venezuela	8,300	87	Dominican Republic	1,180	141	Central African Republic	180
34	Bangladesh	8,000	88	Croatia	1,100	142	Qatar	180
35	Sweden	7,450	89	Lesotho	1,100	143	Gambia	150
36	Vietnam	7,000	90	Malawi	1,060	144	Gabon	135
37	Hungary	6,250	91	Kuwait	1,000	145	Brunei	125
38	Sweden	5,755	92	Libya	1,000	146	Saint Lucia	100
39	Switzerland	5,600	93	Mauritania	1,000	147	Malta	95
40	Colombia	5,400	94	Sierra Leone	1,000	148	Palau	90
41	Peru	5,300	95	Jordan	980	149	Bahamas	80
42	Denmark	5,200	96	Nicaragua	925	150	Bermuda	80
43	Morocco	5,100	97	Oman	920	151	Micronesia	70
44	Belgium	5,000	98	Turkmenistan	850	152	Dominica	65
45	Finland	4,950	99	Bosnia	840	153	Saint Vincent and the Grenadines	65
46	Austria	4,710	100	Singapore	822			
47	North Korea	4,700	101	Costa Rica	760	154	Comoros	61
48	Romania	4,500	102	Togo	720	155	Cape Verde	57
49	Chile	4,400	103	Paraguay	700	156	Vanuatu	55
50	Bolivia	4,250	104	Yemen	665	157	Antigua and Barbuda	50
51	Greece	4,200	105	Slovakia	630	158	Seychelles	50
52	Bulgaria	3,920	106	Slovenia	630	159	Grenada	45
53	Saudi Arabia	3,800	107	Nepal	625	160	Solomon Islands	45
54	Algeria	3,500	108	Mozambique	620	161	Guinea-Bissau	40
55	Tanzania	3,500	109	Liberia	600	162	Tonga	40
56	Congo, Rep. of	3,480	110	Laos	575	163	Djibouti	35
57	Norway	3,342	111	Guatemala	570	164	São Tomé and Príncipe	31
58	Myanmar (Burma)	3,300	112	Albania	550	165	Belize	30
59	Sri Lanka	3,300	113	Trinidad and Tobago	550	166	Morocco	30
60	Ecuador	3,240	114	Panama	527	167	Maldives	25
61	Belarus	3,200	115	Burkina	513	168	Bhutan	23
62	New Zealand	3,100	116	Swaziland	500	169	San Marino	13
63	Kenya	3,000	117	United Arab Emirates	490	170	Andorra	10
64	Syria	3,000	118	Angola	450	171	Kiribati	6
65	Yugoslavia	2,692	119	Fiji	450	172	Nauru	6
66	Puerto Rico	2,480	120	Niger	440	173	Saint Kitts and Nevis	5
67	Madagascar	2,300	121	Mauritius	410	174	Tuvalu	3
68	Israel	2,250	122	Benin	400			
69	Lebanon	2,247	123	Guyana	380			

Source: UNESCO Statistical Yearbook

23.6 AM Radio Stations

Rank	Country/Entity	AM Radio Stations	Rank	Country/Entity	AM Radio Stations	Rank	Country/Entity	AM Radio Stations
1	United States	4,987	21	Saudi Arabia	43	41	Niger	15
2	Russia	1,050	22	France	41	42	Turkey	15
3	Canada	900	23	Egypt	39	43	Croatia	14
4	Indonesia	618	24	Nigeria	35	44	Israel	14
5	Japan	318	25	Hungary	32	45	South Africa	14
6	China	274	26	Papua New Guinea	31	46	Albania	13
7	Philippines	267	27	Greece	29	47	Lithuania	13
8	Australia	258	28	Mozambique	29	48	Singapore	13
9	United Kingdom	225	29	Malaysia	28	49	Mongolia	12
10	Thailand	200	30	Poland	27	50	Romania	12
11	Spain	190	31	Algeria	26	51	Sri Lanka	12
12	Italy	135	32	Yugoslavia	26	52	Tanzania	12
13	Germany	103	33	Bulgaria	20	53	Cameroon	11
14	India	96	34	Pakistan	19	54	Cyprus	11
15	Nepal	88	35	North Korea	18	55	Sudan	11
16	South Korea	79	36	Angola	17	56	Zambia	11
17	Iran	77	37	Libya	17	57	Congo, Dem. Rep. of	10
18	New Zealand	64	38	Madagascar	17	58	Laos	10
19	Portugal	57	39	Iraq	16	59	Malawi	10
20	Norway	46	40	Kenya	16	60	Uganda	10

Source: UNESCO Statistical Yearbook

23.7 Radios per Capita

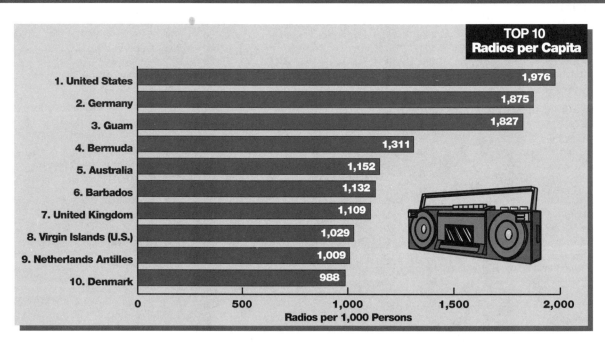

TOP 10 Radios per Capita

	Radios per 1,000 Persons
1. United States	1,976
2. Germany	1,875
3. Guam	1,827
4. Bermuda	1,311
5. Australia	1,152
6. Barbados	1,132
7. United Kingdom	1,109
8. Virgin Islands (U.S.)	1,029
9. Netherlands Antilles	1,009
10. Denmark	988

Radios per 1,000 Persons

Rank	Country/Entity	Radios per 1,000 Persons, 1996	Rank	Country/Entity	Radios per 1,000 Persons, 1996	Rank	Country/Entity	Radios per 1,000 Persons, 1996
11	Monaco	987	15	Dominica	875	19	Canada	803
12	Finland	966	16	New Zealand	866	20	Italy	801
13	South Korea	928	17	France	862	21	Japan	801
14	Czech Republic	884	18	Sweden	844	22	Switzerland	791

Rank	Country/Entity	Radios per 1,000 Persons, 1996	Rank	Country/Entity	Radios per 1,000 Persons, 1996	Rank	Country/Entity	Radios per 1,000 Persons, 1996
23	Antigua and Barbuda	778	79	El Salvador	373	136	Thailand	167
24	Netherlands	775	80	Moldova	358	137	Albania	157
25	Norway	767	81	Honduras	354	138	Dominican Republic	154
26	Jamaica	747	82	Mauritius	353	139	Cambodia	150
27	Iceland	733	83	Ukraine	349	140	Colombia	150
28	Saint Lucia	699	84	Brazil	340	141	Paraguay	144
29	Micronesia	667	85	Vanuatu	327	142	Turkey	141
30	Seychelles	667	86	Slovenia	320	143	Belize	140
31	Puerto Rico	666	87	Tuvalu	319	144	Zambia	139
32	Argentina	637	88	Chile	317	145	Namibia	136
33	Iraq	630	89	Belarus	311	146	Cape Verde	135
34	Suriname	609	90	Qatar	311	147	Indonesia	132
35	Lebanon	601	91	Spain	304	148	Algeria	125
36	Kuwait	591	92	Cyprus	288	149	Gambia	125
37	Macau	591	93	Bahamas	282	150	Tanzania	123
38	Uruguay	591	94	Ecuador	277	151	India	121
39	Hungary	590	95	Liberia	275	152	Laos	121
40	Hong Kong	586	96	Singapore	275	153	Mongolia	121
41	Luxembourg	586	97	South Africa	273	154	Gabon	119
42	Austria	584	98	Egypt	265	155	Slovakia	118
43	Nauru	577	99	Réunion	265	156	Solomon Islands	117
44	Fiji	574	100	Bosnia and Herzegovina	263	157	Philippines	116
45	Gibraltar	573	101	Malta	260	158	Cameroon	115
46	Aruba	571	102	Yugoslavia	256	159	Zimbabwe	113
47	Lesotho	569	103	Chad	240	160	Malawi	112
48	Saint Vincent and the Grenadines	565	104	São Tomé and Príncipe	237	161	Côte d'Ivoire	110
			105	Jordan	234	162	Saint Kitts and Nevis	110
49	Bolivia	553	106	Croatia	230	163	Kenya	103
50	Swaziland	550	107	Mexico	230	164	Maldives	99
51	Latvia	547	108	Peru	225	165	Comoros	97
52	Bahrain	542	109	Costa Rica	224	166	Congo, Rep. of	95
53	Palau	536	110	Portugal	224	167	Vietnam	95
54	San Marino	522	111	Nicaragua	222	168	Congo, Dem. Rep. of	81
55	Uganda	507	112	Sierra Leone	221	169	Kiribati	79
56	Belgium	500	113	Iran	213	170	Ghana	76
57	New Caledonia	495	114	Saudi Arabia	213	171	Pakistan	76
58	Grenada	489	115	Guadeloupe	208	172	Benin	73
59	Equatorial Guinea	488	116	Syria	207	173	Myanmar (Burma)	72
60	French Polynesia	488	117	Botswana	206	174	Papua New Guinea	72
61	French Guiana	486	118	United Arab Emirates	206	175	Bangladesh	67
62	Israel	481	119	Panama	200	176	Djibouti	61
63	Malaysia	476	120	Romania	198	177	Central African Republic	55
64	Guyana	454	121	Morocco	194	178	Guatemala	52
65	Faroe Islands	447	122	Sudan	193	179	Burkina Faso	48
66	Mauritania	444	123	Tunisia	193	180	Niger	48
67	Bulgaria	437	124	Libya	190	181	Yemen	48
68	Trinidad and Tobago	433	125	Northern Mariana Islands	190	182	Burundi	47
69	Mayotte	427	126	Turkmenistan	189	183	Haiti	41
70	Poland	421	127	Martinique	187	184	Somalia	41
71	Brunei	417	128	Sri Lanka	182	185	Angola	39
72	Oman	416	129	Macedonia	179	186	Guinea-Bissau	36
73	Taiwan	402	130	China	178	187	Mozambique	36
74	Greece	400	131	Mali	176	188	Guinea	35
75	Tonga	400	132	Madagascar	173	189	Nepal	29
76	Venezuela	383	133	Nigeria	170	190	Bhutan	28
77	Lithuania	381	134	Togo	170	191	Andorra	6
78	Greenland	374	135	Ethiopia	167	192	North Korea	0.2

Source: UNESCO Statistical Yearbook

Television

Although television is not yet a universal medium like radio, it has become a major influence on modern life in every country. Television is a commanding medium that compels attention. It educates even while it entertains, and it ministers to the eye and the mind through memorable visual images. Because of its potential as a propaganda tool, it is used by the government in many countries as a means of disinformation. In the battle of the media, television always comes in first; radio, second; and newspapers and print media, last. The flip side of television is that its sound bites and flippant analyses often compress and distort reality.

23.8 Television Sets

Rank	Country/Entity	Television Sets (thousands)	Rank	Country/Entity	Television Sets (thousands)	Rank	Country/Entity	Television Sets (thousands)
1	China	300,000	44	Morocco	3,800	87	Jamaica	773
2	United States	204,100	45	Myanmar (Burma)	3,450	88	Costa Rica	750
3	Japan	77,500	46	Bulgaria	3,011	89	Slovenia	745
4	India	57,000	47	Denmark	2,800	90	Jordan	740
5	Russia	56,244	48	Pakistan	2,800	91	Libya	720
6	Brazil	45,000	49	Belarus	2,700	92	Paraguay	710
7	Germany	45,000	50	North Korea	2,700	93	Nicaragua	700
8	United Kingdom	35,800	51.	Finland	2,650	94	Papua New Guinea	700
9	France	33,600	52	Switzerland	2,602	95	Dominican Republic	680
10	Indonesia	28,000	53	Peru	2,350	96	Singapore	650
11	Italy	25,000	54	Norway	2,450	97	Kuwait	630
12	Canada	18,817	55	Sudan	2,300	98	Estonia	610
13	Spain	19,200	56	Cuba	2,200	99	Panama	610
14	Mexico	17,600	57	Algeria	1,945	100	Zambia	600
15	Poland	15,765	58	New Zealand	1,818	101	Angola	550
16	Turkey	15,000	59	Congo, Rep. of	1,800	102	Guinea	500
17	South Korea	14,400	60	Yugoslavia	1,800	103	United Arab Emirates	500
18	Thailand	13,500	61	Ecuador	1,700	104	Uganda	500
19	Argentina	12,000	62	Israel	1,700	105	Kenya	462
20	Ukraine	12,000	63	Azerbaijan	1,600	106	Saudi Arabia	460
21	Vietnam	12,000	64	Bolivia	1,500	107	Honduras	450
22	Australia	11,565	65	Tajikistan	1,500	108	Tanzania	450
23	Iran	9,060	66	Iraq	1,450	109	Trinidad and Tobago	415
24	Philippines	9,000	67	Tunisia	1,400	110	Benin	400
25	Netherlands	7,650	68	Ireland	1,370	111	Bosnia	385
26	Egypt	7,400	69	Lithuania	1,350	112	Macedonia	350
27	Colombia	7,314	70	El Salvador	1,300	113	Madagascar	320
28	Taiwan	7,000	71	Moldova	1,300	114	Albania	300
29	Belgium	4,700	72	Syria	1,300	115	Senegal	290
30	Greece	4,630	73	Latvia	1,213	116	Zimbabwe	290
31	Romania	4,580	74	Georgia	1,200	117	Ghana	265
32	Kazakhstan	4,578	75	Sri Lanka	1,200	118	Bahrain	255
33	Hungary	4,530	76	Puerto Rico	1,160	119	Luxembourg	242
34	Malaysia	4,500	77	Slovakia	1,157	120	Ethiopia	230
35	Sweden	4,202	78	Kyrgyzstan	1,110	121	Mauritius	210
36	Czech Republic	4,200	79	Croatia	1,100	122	Niger	200
37	South Africa	4,200	80	Liberia	1,075	123	Afghanistan	180
38	Nigeria	4,000	81	Uruguay	970	124	Brunei	173
39	Venezuela	4,000	82	Cameroon	960	125	Malta	167
40	Uzbekistan	4,000	83	Armenia	900	126	Mongolia	143
41	Austria	4,000	84	Bangladesh	850	127	Oman	132
42	Chile	4,000	85	Turkmenistan	850	128	Mauritania	132
43	Yemen	3,900	86	Côte d'Ivoire	790	129	Iceland	120

Rank	Country/Entity	Television Sets (thousands)	Rank	Country/Entity	Television Sets (thousands)	Rank	Country/Entity	Television Sets (thousands)
130.	Somalia	118	145	Burkina	46	160	Grenada	15
131	Mali	110	146	Namibia	45	161	Seychelles	14
132	Cyprus	105	147	Congo, Dem. Rep. of	42	162	Lesotho	13
133	Gabon	100	148	Djibouti	42	163	Chad	11
134	Swaziland	90	149	Burundi	40	164	Dominica	10
135	Cambodia	80	150	Equatorial Guinea	37	165	Maldives	10
136	Suriname	80	151	Belize	36	166	Rwanda	10
137	Barbados	75	152	Botswana	35	167	Solomon Islands	6
138	Sierra Leone	73	153	Guyana	35	168	Comoros	2
139	Fiji	70	154	Haiti	35	169	Kiribati	2
140	Bahamas	65	155	Laos	35	170	Micronesia	2
141	Nepal	60	156	Antigua and Barbuda	27	171	Tonga	2
142	Liberia	54	157	Andorra	22	172	Vanuatu	2
143	Mozambique	51	158	Eritrea	22	173	Cape Verde	1
144	Togo	50	159	Central African Republic	17			

Source: UNESCO Statistical Yearbook

23.9 Television Sets per Capita

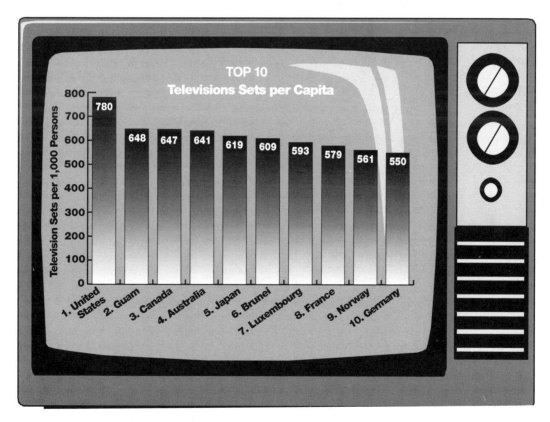

Rank	Country/Entity	Television Sets per 1,000 Persons	Rank	Country/Entity	Television Sets per 1,000 Persons	Rank	Country/Entity	Television Sets per 1,000 Persons
11	Denmark	536	16	Spain	490	21	Malta	448
12	Finland	519	17	Latvia	482	22	Iceland	447
13	New Zealand	506	18	Sweden	476	23	Hungary	444
14	Austria	497	19	Aruba	471	24	Bahrain	442
15	Netherlands	495	20	Belgium	464	25	Greece	442

Rank	Country/Entity	Television Sets per 1,000 Persons	Rank	Country/Entity	Television Sets per 1,000 Persons	Rank	Country/Entity	Television Sets per 1,000 Persons
26	Italy	436	80	Cuba	200	134	Zambia	64
27	Antigua and Barbuda	419	81	Mexico	192	135	India	61
28	Estonia	411	82	Turkmenistan	189	136	Oman	61
29	Poland	408	83	Colombia	188	137	United Kingdom	61
30	Czech Republic	406	84	Mauritius	187	138	Côte d'Ivoire	59
31	Ireland	382	85	Suriname	186	139	Mongolia	59
32	New Caledonia	380	86	Seychelles	184	140	Mauritania	58
33	Russia	380	87	Venezuela	180	141	Angola	51
34	Slovenia	374	88	Macedonia	179	142	Guyana	42
35	Kuwait	373	89	French Polynesia	177	143	Congo, Dem. Rep. of	41
36	Switzerland	370	90	Uzbekistan	176	144	Maldives	40
37	Lithuania	364	91	Jordan	175	145	Nigeria	38
38	Andorra	360	92	French Guiana	170	146	Samoa	38
39	Bulgaria	359	93	Nicaragua	170	147	Senegal	37
40	Hong Kong	359	94	Yugoslavia	170	148	Namibia	29
41	Argentina	347	95	Belize	167	149	Zimbabwe	27
42	Trinidad and Tobago	328	96	Papua New Guinea	163	150	Uganda	26
43	Taiwan	327	97	Vietnam	163	151	United Arab Emirates	26
44	Netherlands Antilles	325	98	Grenada	158	152	Kiribati	25
45	South Korea	321	99	Tunisia	156	153	Liberia	25
46	Puerto Rico	311	100	Ecuador	148	154	Botswana	24
47	Uruguay	310	101	Indonesia	147	155	Madagascar	24
48	Jamaica	306	102	Morocco	145	156	Niger	23
49	Israel	303	103	Paraguay	144	157	Pakistan	22
50	Moldova	300	104	Cyprus	143	158	Micronesia	21
51	Lebanon	291	105	Dominica	141	159	Tonga	20
52	Barbados	284	106	Libya	138	160	Kenya	18
53	Chile	280	107	Martinique	137	161	Congo, Rep. of	17
54	Brazil	278	108	Iran	134	162	Ghana	16
55	Kazakhstan	275	109	Philippines	129	163	Sierra Leone	16
56	Belarus	265	110	Egypt	126	164	Solomon Islands	16
57	Guadeloupe	262	111	Guatemala	122	165	Tanzania	16
58	Tajikistan	258	112	North Korea	115	166	Somalia	13
59	Saudi Arabia	257	113	Macau	113	167	Mali	12
60	China	247	114	Bosnia and Herzegovina	111	168	Togo	12
61	Kyrgyzstan	247	115	South Africa	101	169	Vanuatu	12
62	Yemen	243	116	Peru	100	170	Afghanistan	10
63	Armenia	241	117	Swaziland	96	171	Cambodia	8
64	El Salvador	241	118	Equatorial Guinea	92	172	Bangladesh	7
65	Turkey	240	119	Albania	89	173	Burundi	7
66	Bahamas	233	120	Fiji	89	174	Laos	7
67	Ukraine	233	121	Syria	89	175	Lesotho	7
68	Croatia	230	122	Dominican Republic	87	176	Eritrea	6
69	Panama	229	123	Honduras	80	177	Central African Republic	5
70	Thailand	227	124	Gabon	76	178	Comoros	5
71	Malaysia	226	125	Guinea	76	179	Haiti	5
72	Costa Rica	220	126	Myanmar (Burma)	76	180	Burkina Faso	4
73	Georgia	220	127	Sudan	76	181	Ethiopia	4
74	Singapore	218	128	Cameroon	75	182	Cape Verde	3
75	Slovakia	216	129	Iraq	74	183	Mozambique	3
76	Azerbaijan	212	130	Benin	73	184	Nepal	3
77	Réunion	205	131	Djibouti	73	185	Chad	2
78	Bolivia	202	132	Algeria	71	186	Rwanda	2
79	Romania	201	133	Sri Lanka	66	187	Mayotte	1

Source: UNESCO Statistical Yearbook

23.10 Paper

The production, import, and export of paper are vital indicators of the importance of the print media. It also reveals the linkage of the print media to the environment in general and to trees in particular. Paper production is concentrated in a few countries, such as Canada and Finland, and most other countries are dependent on the few producers for their supplies. Although a decade ago some experts foresaw the advent of a "paperless society," all indications now are that the reverse is true. More paper is used today for printing, packaging, and writing than ever before.

Rank	Country/Entity	Printing and Writing Paper Consumed (metric tons per 1,000 persons)	Rank	Country/Entity	Printing and Writing Paper Consumed (metric tons per 1,000 persons)	Rank	Country/Entity	Printing and Writing Paper Consumed (metric tons per 1,000 persons)
1	Finland	227.4	50	Turkey	10.1	99	Kenya	1.5
2	United States	153.9	51	Colombia	9.1	100	Belize	1.4
3	Denmark	115.7	52	Latvia	8.6	101	Vietnam	1.3
4	Sweden	114.7	53	Jamaica	8.0	102	Bangladesh	1.2
5	Japan	112.9	54	Bahrain	7.6	103	Oman	1.0
6	Switzerland	108.3	55	Saint Lucia	7.5	104	Dominica	0.9
7	United Kingdom	104.1	56	Jordan	7.4	105	Papua New Guinea	0.9
8	Australia	100.5	57	Macedonia	7.1	106	Suriname	0.9
9	Hong Kong	98.4	58	Bahamas	6.9	107	Côte d'Ivoire	0.8
10	Singapore	98.0	59	Kuwait	6.7	108	Grenada	0.8
11	Austria	97.1	60	Paraguay	6.7	109	Comoros	0.7
12	Germany	95.4	61	Tunisia	6.4	110	Nicaragua	0.6
13	Canada	94.0	62	China	5.5	111	Samoa	0.6
14	Belgium	93.6	63	Indonesia	5.5	112	Libya	0.5
15	Netherlands	91.3	64	Russia	5.5	113	Saint Vincent and	0.5
16	Norway	90.6	65	Costa Rica	5.4		the Grenadines	
17	France	76.7	66	Philippines	5.3	114	Tanzania	0.5
18	New Zealand	70.1	67	Ecuador	5.1	115	Togo	0.5
19	Italy	61.2	68	Lithuania	5.0	116	Zambia	0.5
20	Israel	52.2	69	Sri Lanka	4.8	117	Iraq	0.4
21	South Korea	51.3	70	Saudi Arabia	4.6	118	Madagascar	0.4
22	Spain	47.9	71	Romania	4.5	119	Myanmar (Burma)	0.4
23	Iceland	40.4	72	Peru	4.3	120	Cameroon	0.3
24	Ireland	40.1	73	Bulgaria	4.2	121	Cape Verde	0.3
25	United Arab Emirates	38.4	74	El Salvador	4.2	122	Gabon	0.3
26	Malta	37.9	75	Lebanon	4.1	123	Ghana	0.3
27	Portugal	34.2	76	Maldives	4.0	124	Nigeria	0.3
28	Cyprus	34.0	77	Saint Kitts and Nevis	3.9	125	Vanuatu	0.3
29	Malaysia	32.6	78	Albania	3.8	126	Angola	0.2
30	Czech Republic	28.7	79	Guatemala	3.8	127	Haiti	0.2
31	Slovenia	27.6	80	Iran	3.7	128	Mongolia	0.2
32	Hungary	24.0	81	Seychelles	3.5	129	Senegal	0.2
33	Slovakia	23.5	82	Antigua and Barbuda	3.4	130	Uganda	0.2
34	Greece	20.8	83	Egypt	3.2	131	Benin	0.1
35	Estonia	19.9	84	Algeria	2.8	132	Burundi	0.1
36	Argentina	18.4	85	Honduras	2.8	133	Cambodia	0.1
37	Poland	17.0	86	Syria	2.7	134	Central African Republic	0.1
38	South Africa	16.6	87	Morocco	2.5	135	Chad	0.1
39	Chile	16.1	88	Qatar	2.2	136	Congo, Dem. Rep. of	0.1
40	Barbados	14.0	89	Brunei	2.1	137	Ethiopia	0.1
41	Croatia	13.9	90	Dominican Republic	2.1	138	North Korea	0.1
42	Uruguay	13.6	91	Panama	2.1	139	Laos	0.1
43	Thailand	13.1	92	Cuba	2.0	140	Malawi	0.1
44	Brazil	13.0	93	Bolivia	1.9	141	Mauritania	0.1
45	Mexico	12.1	94	India	1.9	142	Nepal	0.1
46	Venezuela	11.3	95	Zimbabwe	1.8	143	Sierra Leone	0.1
47	Mauritius	11.1	96	Pakistan	1.7	144	Sudan	0.1
48	Fiji	10.8	97	Guyana	1.6			
49	Trinidad and Tobago	10.6	98	Moldova	1.6			

Source: UNESCO Statistical Yearbook

Chapter 24

Cities

Cities are virtually mini states. If the ranking of the most populous cities were to be superimposed on the ranking of the most populous countries, Mexico City would rank sixty-fourth, ahead of the majority of the countries of the world. The 1990s was a watershed decade in urban history, marking the first time in human history when more people lived in urban areas than in rural areas. By 2025 more than two-thirds of the world population will be urban dwellers compared with one-third as recently as 1975. Ninety percent of this growth will take place in the Third World. At the turn of the twentieth century, there were only eleven cities worldwide with over one million inhabitants. In 2000 there were 300 and by 2025 there will likely be 570. In the absence of an international organization of cities, similar to the United Nations, data about cities are not collected regularly, and there are some structural dissimilarities between rankings in this section and those in sections on nations. Most available data relate to population, population growth, and area. There are also some scattered data on quality of urban life. The most remarkable fact about cities is density. Urban population densities approach 40,000 per square mile (104,000 per square kilometer) compared to an average of less than 100 per square mile (260 per square kilometer) nationwide. Except in a few cases urban population keeps growing even when the towns and cities have run out of space and there is no room to grow. American cities are much larger geographically than Asian and European cities, which, being older, tend to be more defined. The average size of European cities is about 50 square miles (130 square kilometers). With the advent of cars and mass transit, it became possible for cities to expand beyond their original limits. Thus, cities became nuclei for metropolises and the term "greater" came to be applied to larger cities. Some neighboring cities tend to coalesce, creating twin cities or urban corridors that cover three or more cities, such as Boston–New York–Washington. These in turn breed edge cities or satellite cities, terms that have sometimes displaced the former word "suburb." The areas shown below cover the metropolitan regions.

24.1 Urban Area

Rank	City	Square Miles	Rank	City	Square Miles
1	New York, New York, United States	1,274	19	Washington D.C., United States	357
2	Los Angeles, California, United States	1,110	20	Milan, Italy	344
3	Tokyo, Japan	1,089	21	Seoul, South Korea	342
4	London, United Kingdom	874	22	Sydney, Australia	338
5	Chicago, Illinois, United States	762	23	Melbourne, Australia	327
6	Essen, Germany	704	24	Houston, Texas, United States	310
7	Buenos Aires, Argentina	535	25	Nagoya, Japan	307
8	Mexico City, Mexico	522	26	Boston, Massachusetts, United States	303
9	Osaka-Kobe-Kyoto, Japan	495	27	Berlin, Germany	274
10	Philadelphia, Pennsylvania, United States	471	28	Rio de Janeiro, Brazil	260
11	Detroit, Michigan, United States	468	29	Porto Alegre, Brazil	231
12	Sao Paulo, Brazil	451	30	Birmingham, United Kingdom	223
13	Miami, Florida, United States	448	31	Calcutta, India	209
14	Paris, France	432	32	Karachi, Pakistan	190
15	San Francisco, California, United States	428	33	Manila, Philippines	188
16	Dallas, Texas, United States	419	34	Istanbul, Turkey	165
17	Moscow, Russia	379	35	Montreal, Quebec, Canada	164
18	Manchester, United Kingdom	357	36	Toronto, Ontario, Canada	154

Rank	City	Square Miles	Rank	City	Square Miles
37	Beijing, China	151	62	Madrid, Spain	66
38	St. Petersburg, Russia	139	63	Wuhan, China	65
39	Delhi, India	138	64	Naples, Italy	62
40	Taipei, Taiwan	138	65	Kiev, Ukraine	62
41	Budapest, Hungary	138	66	Lahore, Pakistan	57
42	Santiago, Chile	128	67	Kinshasa, Dem. Rep. of Congo	57
43	Lima, Peru	120	68	Lagos, Nigeria	56
44	Athens, Greece	116	69	Ankara, Turkey	55
45	Chennai, India	115	70	Pusan , South Korea	54
46	Tehran, Iran	112	71	Caracas, Venezuela	54
47	Cairo, Egypt	104	72	Bucharest, Romania	52
48	Bangkok, Thailand	102	73	Bangalore, India	50
49	Baghdad, Iraq	97	74	Tianjin, China	49
50	Mumbai, India	95	75	Yangon, Myanmar (Burma)	47
51	Hyderabad, India	88	76	Surabaya, Indonesia	43
52	Barcelona, Spain	87	77	Shenyang, China	39
53	Bogota, Colombia	79	78	Casablanca, Morocco	35
54	Belo Horizonte, Brazil	79	79	Alexandria, Egypt	35
55	Guangzhou, China	79	80	Dhaka, Bangladesh	32
56	Shanghai, China	78	81	Ahmedabad, India	32
57	Guadalajara, Mexico	78	82	Ho Chi Minh City, Vietnam	31
58	Singapore, Singapore	78	83	Harbin, China	30
59	Monterrey, Mexico	77	84	Chengdu, China	25
60	Jakarta, Indonesia	76	85	Hong Kong, China	23
61	Rome, Italy	69			

Source: 1993 Statistical Abstract of the United States on CD-ROM

24.2 Most Populous Cities

Rank	City	Population	Rank	City	Population	Rank	City	Population
1	Seoul, South Korea	10,229,269	23	Karachi, Pakistan	5,208,132	42	Melbourne, Australia	3,218,100
2	Mumbai, India	9,925,891	24	Santiago, Chile	5,076,808	43	Hyderabad, India	3,145,839
3	Cairo, Egypt	9,900,000	25	Kinshasa, Congo, Dem. Rep. of	4,655,313	44	Singapore, Singapore	3,104,000
4	Mexico City, Mexico	9,815,795				45	Madrid, Spain	3,029,734
5	Sao Paulo, Brazil	9,393,753	26	Shen-Yang, China	4,540,000	46	Buenos Aires, Argentina	2,988,006
6	Jakarta, Indonesia	9,160,500	27	Baghdad, Iraq	4,400,000			
7	Manila, Philippines	8,594,150	28	Calcutta, India	4,399,819	47	Chungking, China	2,980,000
8	Moscow, Russia	8,400,000	29	Ho Chi Minh City, Vietnam	4,322,000	48	Lahore, Pakistan	2,952,689
9	Tokyo, Japan	7,966,195				49	Ahmedabad, India	2,876,716
10	Shanghai, China	7,830,000	30	St. Petersburg, Russia	4,200,000	50	Ankara, Turkey	2,837,937
11	Istanbul, Turkey	7,774,169	31	Yangon, Myanmar (Burma)	4,000,000	51	Harbin, China	2,830,000
12	New York, New York, United States	7,380,906	32	Chennai, India	3,841,396	52	Cheng-tu, China	2,810,000
13	Delhi, India	7,206,704	33	Dhaka, Bangladesh	3,839,000	53	Riyadh, Saudi Arabia	2,800,000
14	London, England	7,007,100	34	Pusan, South Korea	3,813,814	54	Sian, China	2,760,000
15	Beijing, China	7,000,000	35	Sydney, Australia	3,772,700	55	Chicago, Illinois, United States	2,721,547
16	Tehran, Iran	6,750,043	36	Wu-han, China	3,750,000			
17	Hong Kong, China	6,491,000	37	Alexandria, Egypt	3,700,000	56	Surabaya, Indonesia	2,701,300
18	Bogota, Colombia	6,004,782	38	Canton, China	3,580,000	57	Bangalore, India	2,660,088
19	Tientsin, China	5,770,000	39	Los Angeles, California, United States	3,553,638	58	Rome, Italy	2,654,187
20	Lima, Peru	5,706,127				59	Kiev, Ukraine	2,630,000
21	Bangkok, Thailand	5,584,963	40	Berlin, Germany	3,471,418	60	Osaka, Japan	2,602,352
22	Rio de Janeiro, Brazil	5,473,909	41	Yokohama, Japan	3,307,408	61	Taipei, Taiwan	2,595,699
						62	Abidjan, Côte d'Ivoire	2,500,000

Rank	City	Population	Rank	City	Population	Rank	City	Population
63	Nanking, China	2,500,000	117	Kunming, China	1,520,000	171	Tangerang, Indonesia	1,198,300
64	Pyongyang, North Korea	2,500,000	118	Phoenix, United States	1,519,014	172	Lo-yang, China	1,190,000
			119	Lagos, Nigeria	1,518,000	173	Harare, Zimbabwe	1,184,169
65	Tzu-po, China	2,460,000	120	Lan-chou, China	1,510,000	174	San Diego, California, United States	1,171,121
66	Taegu, South Korea	2,449,139	121	Conakry, Guinea	1,508,000			
67	Ta-lien, China	2,400,000	122	An-shan, China	1,500,000	175	Belgrade, Serbia	1,168,454
68	Bandung, Indonesia	2,368,200	123	Dakar, Senegal	1,500,000	176	Guatemala City, Guatemala	1,167,494
69	Chi-nan, China	2,320,000	124	Jiddah, Saudi Arabia	1,500,000			
70	Inchon, South Korea	2,307,618	125	Tang-shan, China	1,500,000	177	Tabriz, Iran	1,166,203
71	Havana, Cuba	2,241,000	126	Surat, India	1,498,817	178	Uu-lu-mu-chi, China	1,160,000
72	Paris, France	2,175,200	127	Brasilia, Brazil	1,492,542	179	Barranguilla, Colombia	1,157,826
73	Algiers, Algeria	2,168,000	128	Quito, Ecuador	1,487,513	180	Almaty, Kazhakstan	1,150,500
74	Hanoi, Vietnam	2,154,900	129	Philadelphia, Pennsylvania United States	1,478,002	181	Dniporpetrovsk, Ukraine	1,147,000
75	Nagoya, Japan	2,152,258						
76	Al-Jizah, Egypt	2,144,000	130	Kyoto, Japan	1,463,601	182	Kuala Lumpur, Malaysia	1,145,342
77	Addis Ababa, Ethiopia	2,112,737	131	Jaipur, India	1,458,183	183	Rosario, Argentina	1,118,984
78	Ch' ang Ch'un, China	2,110,000	132	Kao Hsiung, China	1,434,907	184	Sofia, Bulgaria	1,116,823
79	Tasknet, Uzbekistan	2,107,000	133	Ibadan, Nigeria	1,432,000	185	La Matanza, Argentina	1,111,811
80	Luanda, Angola	2,081,000	134	Kobe, Japan	1,423,380	186	Hantan, China	1,110,000
81	Salvador, Brazil	2,070,296	135	Nizhny Novogorod, Russia	1,400,000	187	Ta-t'ung, China	1,110,000
82	Bucharest, Romania	2,060,551				188	Hiroshima, Japan	1,108,868
83	Ching-tao, China	2,060,000	136	Novosibirsk, Russia	1,400,000	189	Faisalabad, Pakistan	1,104,209
84	Izmir, Turkey	2,017,699	137	Tsitsihar, China	1,380,000	190	Chevabinsk, Russia	1,100,000
85	Nairobi, Kenya	2,000,000	138	Montevideo, Uruguay	1,378,707	191	Kazan, Russia	1,100,000
86	Guayaquil, Ecuador	1,973,880	139	Semarang, Indonesia	1,366,500	192	Ufa, Russia	1,100,000
87	Medellin, Colombia	1,970,691	140	Copenhagen, Denmark	1,362,264	193	Ujung Pandang, Indonesia	1,091,800
88	Mashhad, Iran	1,964,489	141	Dar es Salaam, Tanzania	1,360,850			
89	Tai-yuan, China	1,960,000	142	Palembang, Indonesia	1,352,300	194	Indore, India	1,091,674
90	Medan, Indonesia	1,909,700	143	Fu-shun, China	1,350,000	193	Ning-po, China	1,090,000
91	Beirut, Lebanon	1,900,000	144	Hand-chou, China	1,340,000	194	Donetsk, Ukraine	1,088,000
92	Budapest, Hungary	1,885,000	145	Nan-chang, China	1,350,000	195	Adelaide, Australia	1,081,000
93	Kanpur, India	1,874,409	146	Chang-sha, China	1,330,000	196	Nanning, China	1,070,000
94	Caracas, Venezuela	1,822,465	147	Shih-chia-chuang, China	1,320,000	197	Monterrey, Mexico	1,068,996
95	Accra, Ghana	1,781,100	148	Milan, Italy	1,306,494	198	San Antonio, Texas, United States	1,067,816
96	Hamburg, Germany	1,767,901	149	Yekaterinberg, Russia	1,300,000			
97	Sapporo, Japan	1,756,968	150	Recife, Brazil	1,296,995	199	Adana, Turkey	1,065,544
98	Houston, United States	1,744,058	151	Fukoka, Japan	1,284,741	200	Bhopal, India	1,062,771
99	Baku, Azerbaijan	1,739,900	152	Taejon, South Korea	1,272,143	201	Dallas, Texas, United States	1,053,292
100	Cheng-chou, China	1,710,000	153	Chi-lin, China	1,270,000			
101	Minsk, Ukraine	1,700,000	154	Omdurman, Sudan	1,267,077	202	Antananarivo, Madagascar	1,052,835,
102	Quezon City, Philippines	1,676,644	155	Perth, Australia	1,262,600			
103	Guadalajara, Mexico	1,650,042	156	Kwanggju, South Korea	1,257,504	203	Naples, Italy	1,050,234
104	Warsaw, Poland	1,638,300	157	Nezahualcoyotl, Mexico	1,255,456	204	Odessa, Ukraine	1,046,000
105	Nagpur, India	1,624,752	158	Tbilisi, Georgia	1,253,100	205	Shiraz, Iran	1,042,801
106	Lucknow, India	1,619,115	159	Maracaibo, Venezuela	1,249,670	206	Ludhiana, India	1,042,740
107	Barcelona, Spain	1,614,571	160	Porto Alegre, Brazil	1,237,223	207	Valencia, Spain	1,034,033
108	Chittagong, Bangladesh	1,599,000	161	Munich, Germany	1,236,370	208	Vadodara, India	1,031,346
109	Aleppo, Syria	1,591,400	162	Isfahan, Iran	1,220,595	209	Montreal, Quebec, Canada	1,017,666
110	Pune, India	1,566,651	163	Prague, Czech Republic	1,209,855			
111	Vienna, Austria	1,560,471	164	Cordoba, Spain	1,208,713	210	Birmingham, England	1,017,500
112	Kharkiv, Ukraine	1,556,000	165	Kawassaki, Japan	1,202,511	211	Bursa, Iraq	1,016,760
113	Santo Domingo, Dominican Republic	1,555,656	166	Douala, Cameroon	1,200,000	212	Kalyan, India	1,014,557
			167	Huai-nan, China	1,200,000	213	Pueblo, Mexico	1,007,170
114	Damascus, Syria	1,549,000	168	Omsk, Russia	1,200,000	214	Manaus, Brazil	1,005,634
115	Kuei-yang, China	1,530,000	169	Pao-tai, China	1,200,000	215	Detroit, Michigan, United States	1,000,272
116	Belo Horizonte, Brazil	1,529,566	170	Samara, Russia	1,200,000			

Source: Demographic Yearbook

Urbanization is a universal and irreversible phenomenon. But urban statistics are impaired by serious limitations. The first is that the distinction between urban and rural areas is made in different ways in different countries. Urban status is granted to places with as few as 400 inhabitants in Albania, while in Austria the minimum is 5,000 persons. In Bulgaria urban status is granted to places regardless of size of population, while in Israel it implies predominantly nonagricultural localities. Many other definitions exist: in Sweden, urban areas are defined as regions with less than 200 meters (656 feet) between houses; in Peru, populated centers with 100 or more occupied dwellings; in Iceland, localities with 200 or more inhabitants; in Australia, 250 or more dwellings of which at least 100 are occupied; in Senegal and Yugoslavia, agglomerations of 15,000 or more inhabitants; in South Africa, areas of more than 500 inhabitants; in India,

places having a density of not less than 1,000 persons per square mile where at least three-fourths of the adult population are employed in nonagricultural pursuits; and in Japan, areas (called *shis*) having 50,000 or more inhabitants. Other countries define towns not so much in terms of inhabitants, but in terms of urban characteristics, such as streets, plazas, water supply, sewerage systems, and electric light. In others it is based on administrative status as headquarters of civil divisions. These differences in definition make statistical comparisons difficult, especially on the basis of urban characteristics, such as facilities. Many of the rural areas in the United States are relatively more modernized than the largest towns in Africa. Unrestrained internal migration to the cities also changes the urban percentage of the population more rapidly than the statistics indicate.

24.3 Urban Population

Rank	Country/Entity	Percentage of Urban Population	Rank	Country/Entity	Percentage of Urban Population	Rank	Country/Entity	Percentage of Urban Population
1	Bermuda	100.0	29	Chile	83.5	57	Colombia	70.3
2	Hong Kong	100.0	30	Djibouti	82.8	58	Peru	70.1
3	Monaco	100.0	31	Greenland	81.1	59	Palau	69.4
4	Nauru	100.0	32	South Korea	81.0	60	Switzerland	68.9
5	Singapore	100.0	33	Martinique	80.5	61	Lithuania	68.0
6	Kuwait	97.0	34	Finland	79.7	62	Armenia	67.8
7	Macau	97.0	35	French Guiana	79.4	63	Cyprus	67.7
8	Belgium	96.6	36	Jordan	78.6	64	Bulgaria	67.2
9	Iceland	91.9	37	Japan	78.1	65	Italy	67.1
10	Netherlands	91.0	38	Canada	77.9	66	Ukraine	66.9
11	Western Sahara	90.7	39	Saudi Arabia	77.3	67	Brunei	66.6
12	San Marino	90.1	40	Brazil	75.6	68	Belarus	65.5
13	Uruguay	89.3	41	Spain	75.3	69	Trinidad and Tobago	64.8
14	United Kingdom	89.1	42	Czech Republic	75.2	70	Austria	64.5
15	Argentina	88.4	43	United States	75.2	71	Marshall Islands	64.5
16	Bahrain	88.4	44	Iraq	74.5	72	Bahamas	64.3
17	Qatar	88.0	45	Taiwan	74.5	73	Andorra	62.5
18	Israel	86.9	46	Cuba	74.4	74	Hungary	61.8
19	Luxembourg	85.9	47	France	74.0	75	Iran	61.3
20	Australia	85.3	48	Russia	73.6	76	Poland	61.2
21	Germany	85.3	49	Réunion	73.4	77	Tunisia	61.0
22	Libya	85.3	50	Gabon	73.2	78	South Africa	60.3
23	Malta	85.3	51	Norway	72.0	79	Lebanon	60.1
24	Denmark	85.1	52	Oman	71.7	80	Mayotte	59.7
25	New Zealand	85.0	53	Estonia	71.6	81	New Caledonia	59.4
26	United Arab Emirates	84.0	54	Mexico	71.3	82	Turkey	59.0
27	Venezuela	84.0	55	Puerto Rico	71.2	83	Greece	58.9
28	Sweden	83.9	56	Latvia	71.1	84	North Korea	58.9

Rank	Country/Entity	Percentage of Urban Population	Rank	Country/Entity	Percentage of Urban Population	Rank	Country/Entity	Percentage of Urban Population
85	Macedonia	58.7	127	Uzbekistan	40.7	169	India	25.7
86	Bolivia	57.5	128	Benin	39.6	170	Somalia	25.4
87	Kazakhstan	57.2	129	Bosnia and Herzegovina	39.6	171	Saint Vincent and the Grenadines	24.6
88	Mongolia	57.1	130	Honduras	39.4			
89	Ireland	57.0	131	Mauritius	39.3	172	Myanmar (Burma)	24.0
90	Slovakia	56.8	132	Mauritania	39.1	173	Botswana	23.9
91	Dominican Republic	56.0	133	Côte d'Ivoire	39.0	174	Kenya	23.6
92	Georgia	55.7	134	Liberia	38.8	175	Yemen	23.5
93	Ecuador	55.4	135	Senegal	38.6	176	Swaziland	22.8
94	French Polynesia	55.0	136	Cameroon	38.3	177	Mali	22.0
95	Nicaragua	54.4	137	Guam	38.2	178	Sri Lanka	21.5
96	Romania	54.4	138	Kyrgyzstan	38.2	179	Chad	21.4
97	Croatia	54.3	139	Barbados	37.9	180	Samoa	21.2
98	Azerbaijan	53.8	140	Virgin Islands (U.S.)	37.2	181	Cambodia	21.0
99	Panama	53.7	141	Gambia	36.7	182	Laos	20.7
100	Yugoslavia	53.2	142	Central African Republic	36.5	183	Haiti	20.6
101	Syria	52.2	143	Antigua and Barbuda	36.2	184	Guinea-Bissau	20.3
102	Congo, Rep. of	52.0	144	Albania	35.7	185	Bangladesh	20.2
103	Morocco	51.7	145	Seychelles	35.5	186	Vietnam	20.1
104	Isle of Man	51.1	146	Guyana	35.4	187	Micronesia	19.4
105	Malaysia	50.6	147	Kiribati	35.1	188	Thailand	18.7
106	Paraguay	50.5	148	Guatemala	35.0	189	Tanzania	18.5
107	El Salvador	50.4	149	Nigeria	35.0	190	Vanuatu	17.7
108	Jamaica	50.4	150	Grenada	33.5	191	Lesotho	16.0
109	Algeria	49.7	151	American Samoa	33.4	192	Solomon Islands	15.7
110	Suriname	49.1	152	Namibia	32.8	193	Niger	15.3
111	Slovenia	48.9	153	Tajikistan	32.6	194	Papua New Guinea	15.2
112	Saint Kitts and Nevis	48.9	154	Ghana	32.0	195	Togo	15.2
113	Philippines	48.6	155	Sierra Leone	31.8	196	Afghanistan	15.1
114	Guadeloupe	48.4	156	Sudan	31.3	197	Eritrea	15.1
115	Portugal	48.2	157	Indonesia	30.9	198	Angola	14.2
116	Belize	47.5	158	Tonga	30.7	199	Mozambique	13.2
117	Moldova	46.9	159	Zimbabwe	30.6	200	Burkina Faso	11.7
118	Fiji	46.4	160	Guinea	29.6	201	Uganda	11.3
119	Turkmenistan	46.0	161	Congo, Dem. Rep. of	29.1	202	Malawi	10.7
120	Egypt	44.6	162	Comoros	28.5	203	Ethiopia	9.9
121	Cape Verde	44.1	163	Pakistan	28.3	204	Nepal	9.6
122	São Tomé and Príncipe	44.1	164	Equatorial Guinea	28.2	205	Burundi	6.3
123	Saint Lucia	44.1	165	Northern Mariana Islands	28.0	206	Rwanda	5.4
124	Costa Rica	43.9	166	China	26.4	207	Bhutan	5.3
125	Tuvalu	42.5	167	Madagascar	26.4			
126	Zambia	42.0	168	Maldives	25.9			

Source: World Development Report

24.4 Projected Urban Population Annual Growth Rate

Rank	Country/Entity	Projected Urban Population Annual Growth Rate by Percentage, 1995–2015	Rank	Country/Entity	Projected Urban Population Annual Growth Rate by Percentage, 1995–2015	Rank	Country/Entity	Projected Urban Population Annual Growth Rate by Percentage, 1995–2015
1	Bhutan	6.0	14	Mali	5.0	27	Nigeria	4.5
2	Burundi	6.0	15	Oman	5.0	28	Cambodia	4.4
3	Ethiopia	5.8	16	Tanzania	5.0	29	Equatorial Guinea	4.4
4	Burkina Faso	5.7	17	Angola	4.9	30	Namibia	4.4
5	Solomon Islands	5.7	18	Eritrea	4.9	31	Sudan	4.4
6	Niger	5.6	19	Maldives	4.8	32	Togo	4.4
7	Uganda	5.5	20	Mozambique	4.7	33	Bangladesh	4.3
8	Yemen	5.5	21	Swaziland	4.7	34	Vanuatu	4.3
9	Malawi	5.3	22	Benin	4.6	35	Chad	4.2
10	Nepal	5.3	23	Comoros	4.6	36	Ghana	4.2
11	Laos	5.1	24	Congo, Dem. Rep. of	4.6	37	Sierra Leone	4.2
12	Madagascar	5.1	25	Kenya	4.6	38	Botswana	4.1
13	Lesotho	5.0	26	Guinea	4.5	39	Cameroon	4.1

Rank	Country/Entity	Projected Urban Population Annual Growth Rate by Percentage, 1995–2015	Rank	Country/Entity	Projected Urban Population Annual Growth Rate by Percentage, 1995–2015	Rank	Country/Entity	Projected Urban Population Annual Growth Rate by Percentage, 1995–2015
40	Pakistan	4.1	85	Guyana	2.6	129	Portugal	1.3
41	Papua New Guinea	4.1	86	Morocco	2.6	130	Kazakhstan	1.2
42	Gambia	4.0	87	Saint Vincent and	2.6	131	Australia	1.1
43	Guinea-Bissau	4.0		the Grenadines		132	United States	1.1
44	Gabon	3.9	88	Thailand	2.6	133	Armenia	1.0
45	Mauritania	3.9	89	Vietnam	2.6	134	Canada	1.0
46	Senegal	3.9	90	Egypt	2.5	135	Iceland	1.0
47	Zimbabwe	3.9	91	Turkmenistan	2.5	136	Saint Kitts and Nevis	1.0
48	Cape Verde	3.7	92	Tunisia	2.4	137	Georgia	0.9
49	Congo, Dem. Rep. of	3.7	93	Brunei	2.3	138	Luxembourg	0.9
50	Guatemala	3.7	94	Suriname	2.3	139	Singapore	0.9
51	Haiti	3.7	95	Turkey	2.3	140	Slovakia	0.9
52	Honduras	3.7	96	Dominican Republic	2.2	141	Switzerland	0.9
53	Jordan	3.5	97	Kuwait	2.2	142	Dominica	0.8
54	Paraguay	3.5	98	Panama	2.2	143	Ireland	0.8
55	Saudi Arabia	3.5	99	Albania	2.0	144	Malta	0.8
56	Côte d'Ivoire	3.4	100	Grenada	2.0	145	Cuba	0.7
57	Central African Republic	3.4	101	Peru	2.0	146	Finland	0.7
58	Libya	3.4	102	Saint Lucia	2.0	147	Poland	0.7
59	Zambia	3.4	103	Seychelles	2.0	148	Uruguay	0.7
60	Myanmar (Burma)	3.3	104	Venezuela	2.0	149	Austria	0.6
61	Syria	3.3	105	Bahrain	1.9	150	Croatia	0.6
62	Indonesia	3.2	106	Colombia	1.9	151	Norway	0.6
63	Iran	3.2	107	Jamaica	1.9	152	Romania	0.6
64	Iraq	3.2	108	Kyrgyzstan	1.9	153	France	0.5
65	São Tomé and Príncipe	3.2	109	Mauritius	1.9	154	Greece	0.5
66	Bolivia	3.1	110	United Arab Emirates	1.9	155	Belarus	0.4
67	Algeria	3.0	111	Cyprus	1.8	156	Hong Kong	0.4
68	Nicaragua	3.0	112	North Korea	1.7	157	Slovenia	0.4
69	Sri Lanka	3.0	113	Lebanon	1.7	158	Sweden	0.4
70	Tajikistan	3.0	114	Mexico	1.7	159	Japan	0.3
71	China	2.9	115	Antigua and Barbuda	1.6	160	Lithuania	0.3
72	Philippines	2.9	116	Azerbaijan	1.6	161	Netherlands	0.3
73	Costa Rica	2.8	117	Bahamas	1.6	162	Belgium	0.2
74	India	2.8	118	Brazil	1.6	163	Czech Republic	0.2
75	Uzbekistan	2.8	119	Qatar	1.6	164	Denmark	0.2
76	El Salvador	2.7	120	Barbados	1.5	165	Germany	0.2
77	Malaysia	2.7	121	Israel	1.5	166	Spain	0.2
78	Mongolia	2.7	122	Trinidad and Tobago	1.5	167	Ukraine	0.2
79	Samoa	2.7	123	Moldova	1.4	168	United Kingdom	0.2
80	South Africa	2.7	124	Argentina	1.3	169	Bulgaria	0.1
81	Belize	2.6	125	Chile	1.3	170	Hungary	0.1
82	Djibouti	2.6	126	South Korea	1.3	171	Italy	0.1
83	Ecuador	2.6	127	Macedonia	1.3	172	Estonia	-0.2
84	Fiji	2.6	128	New Zealand	1.3	173	Latvia	-0.3

Source: World Development Report

24.5 Traffic Accidents

Cities, like countries, grow at different rates. Larger cities tend to grow at a slower rate than smaller ones because the former have already reached sizable population levels. Some cities are already showing signs of saturation. They may expand both vertically and horizontally, but only at the expense of the quality of life. Loss of urban quality of life is indicated by overcrowding, noise pollution, air pollution, water shortages, urban travel accidents, greater time spent in traffic jams, and so on. Inner cities continue to decline as jobs and merchants leave for the suburbs. Urbanologists call this process "Calcuttaization," after the Indian city of Calcutta, which is cited as a classic example of urban disintegration stemming from uncontrolled growth.

Rank	Country/Entity	People Injured or Killed per 1,000 Vehicles, 1998	Rank	Country/Entity	People Injured or Killed per 1,000 Vehicles, 1998	Rank	Country/Entity	People Injured or Killed per 1,000 Vehicles, 1998
1	Armenia	347	30	Oman	23	59	Czech Republic	9
2	Central African Republic	138	31	Turkey	23	60	Madagascar	9
3	Uganda	130	32	Portugal	20	61	Slovenia	9
4	Botswana	94	33	Pakistan	18	62	Azerbaijan	8
5	Malawi	89	34	Ecuador	16	63	Belarus	8
6	Senegal	86	35	United States	16	64	Italy	8
7	Benin	74	36	Moldova	15	65	Libya	8
8	Bangladesh	66	37	Yemen	15	66	Lithuania	8
9	India	61	38	Belgium	14	67	Poland	8
10	Jordan	54	39	Iran	14	68	Switzerland	8
11	Zimbabwe	54	40	Japan	14	69	Spain	7
12	Morocco	46	41	Singapore	14	70	France	6
13	Panama	39	42	Austria	13	71	Norway	6
14	Hong Kong	37	43	Canada	13	72	Philippines	6
15	Mauritius	35	44	Malaysia	13	73	Albania	5
16	Chile	33	45	United Kingdom	13	74	Georgia	5
17	South Korea	33	46	Germany	12	75	Iraq	5
18	Peru	32	47	Ireland	12	76	Namibia	5
19	Cambodia	31	48	Macedonia	12	77	Sweden	5
20	Israel	31	49	Ukraine	11	78	Uruguay	5
21	Sierra Leone	30	50	Yugoslavia	11	79	Bulgaria	4
22	Costa Rica	29	51	Greece	10	80	Denmark	4
23	Nicaragua	29	52	Hungary	10	81	Estonia	4
24	Cuba	28	53	Kazakhstan	10	82	Finland	4
25	El Salvador	26	54	Latvia	10	83	Lebanon	3
26	Sri Lanka	26	55	Nigeria	10	84	Netherlands	3
27	Bosnia and Herzegovina	25	56	Russia	10	85	Romania	3
28	Mongolia	25	57	Saudi Arabia	10	86	Venezuela	3
29	Syria	24	58	Slovakia	10	87	Indonesia	1

Source: Economist Intelligence

24.6 Age of Cities

Urban settlements are older than nations; the oldest are believed to date back some 5,600 years. Many of them were essentially riparian settlements, clustered around the great river valleys, such as the Nile, the Indus, the Yangtze, and the Tigris-Euphrates. Most of them were small city-states from which modern nations have grown. Even when a nation became large in terms of size or land area, the city remained the focus of all political and economic activities, serving as the core and magnet of its social life and the showpiece of its culture. To the rest of the world, the city represented the nation, and this tradition survives in the modern usage of a city, such as Washington and New York, Moscow, Beijing, or Paris as a synonym for the respective nations. Some ancient cities have died out, while others have been taken over by conquerors and renamed.

A. EASTERN HEMISPHERE

Rank	City	Age in Years	Rank	City	Age in Years	Rank	City	Age in Years
1	Gaziantep, Turkey	Over 5,600	5	Konya, Turkey	Over 4,600	9	Luxor, Egypt	Over 4,160
2	Jerusalem, Israel	Over 5,000	6	Giza, Egypt	Over 4,568	10	Lisbon, Spain	Over 4,000
3	Kirkuk, Iraq	Over 5,000	7	Sian, Shensi, China	Over 4,200	11	Porto, Portugal	Over 4,000
4	Zurich, Switzerland	Over 5,000	8	Asyut, Egypt	Over 4,160	12	Shaohing, China	Over 4,000

Rank	City	Age in Years
13	Loyong, China	Over 3,900
14	Ankara, Turkey	Over 3,700
15	Changchi, China	Over 3,600
16	Beirut, Lebanon	Over 3,500
17	Liayang, China	Over 3,500
18	Tangier, Morocco	Over 3,500
19	Tel Aviv, Israel	Over 3,470
20	Gaza, Israel	Over 3,450
21	Damascus, Syria	Over 3,400
22	Athens, Greece	Over 3,300
23	La Coruna, Spain	Over 3,200
24	Malaga, Spain	Over 3,200
25	Varanasi, India	Over 3,200
26	Pyongyang, North Korea	Over 3,120
27	Beijing, China	Over 3,100
28	Cadiz, Spain	Over 3,100
29	Hamadan, Iran	Over 3,100
30	Izmir, Turkey	Over 3,100
31	Aleppo, Syria	Over 3,000
32	Changchow, China	Over 3,000
33	Chengchow, China	Over 3,000
34	Foochow, China	Over 3,000
35	Hofei, China	Over 3,000
36	Metz, France	Over 3,000
37	Nanchung, China	Over 3,000
38	Nanking, China	Over 3,000
39	Pisa, Italy	Over 3,000
40	Rome, Italy	Over 3,000
41	Tatung, China	Over 3,000
42	Canton, China	Over 2,900
43	Toulon, France	Over 2,800
44	Syracuse, Italy	Over 2,717
45	Adana, Turkey	Over 2,700
46	Cannes, France	Over 2,700
47	Catania, Italy	Over 2,700
48	Cordova, Spain	Over 2,700
49	Luca, Italy	Over 2,700
50	Messina, Italy	Over 2,700
51	Palermo, Italy	Over 2,700
52	Ravenna, Italy	Over 2,700
53	Reggio de Calabria, Italy	Over 2,700
54	Trebizond, Turkey	Over 2,700
55	Tripoli, Libya	Over 2,700
56	Taranto, Italy	Over 2,690
57	Istanbul, Turkey	Over 2,641
58	Aswan, Egypt	Over 2,600
59	Benghazi, Libya	Over 2,600
60	Constanta, Romania	Over 2,600
61	Hengyang, China	Over 2,600
62	Huelva, Spain	Over 2,600
63	Jerez de la Fronera, Spain	Over 2,600
64	Kaifeng, China	Over 2,600
65	Osaka, Japan	Over 2,600
66	Seville, Spain	Over 2,600
67	Shaoyang, China	Over 2,600
68	Suchow, China	Over 2,600
69	Terni, Italy	Over 2,600
70	Tripoli, Lebanon	Over 2,600
71	Vigo, Spain	Over 2,600
72	Yangchow, China	Over 2,600
73	Yangon, Myanmar (Burma)	Over 2,580
74	Marseilles, France	Over 2,550
75	Besancon, France	Over 2,500
76	Brescia, Italy	Over 2,500
77	Bristol, United Kingdom	Over 2,500
78	Colombo, Sri Lanka	Over 2,500
79	Gaya, India	Over 2,500
80	Kerch, Russia	Over 2,500
81	Kutaisi, Russia	Over 2,500
82	Mathura, India	Over 2,500
83	Monaco	Over 2,500
84	Naples, Italy	Over 2,500
85	Patna, India	Over 2,500
86	Perugia, Italy	Over 2,500
87	Samsun, Turkey	Over 2,500
88	Sialkot, Pakistan	Over 2,500
89	Soochow, China	Over 2,500
90	Stara Zagora, Bulgaria	Over 2,500
91	Tarragona, Spain	Over 2,500
92	Varna, Bulgaria	Over 2,500
93	Cagliari, Italy	Over 2,450
94	Bergamo, Italy	Over 2,400
95	Bologna, Italy	Over 2,400
96	Genoa, Italy	Over 2,400
97	Granada, Spain	Over 2,400
98	Isfahan, Iran	Over 2,400
99	Le Mans, France	Over 2,400
100	Lerida, Spain	Over 2,400
101	Madurai, India	Over 2,400
102	Mainz, Germany	Over 2,400
103	Mantua, Italy	Over 2,400
104	Modena, Italy	Over 2,400
105	Monza, Italy	Over 2,400
106	Neuss, Germany	Over 2,400
107	Nice, France	Over 2,400
108	Omiya, Japan	Over 2,400
109	Patras, Greece	Over 2,400
110	Piraeus, Greece	Over 2,400
111	Regensburg, Germany	Over 2,400
112	Salamanca, Spain	Over 2,400
113	Siena, Italy	Over 2,400
114	Tunis, Tunisia	Over 2,400
115	Alexandria, Egypt	Over 2,315
116	Ancona, Italy	Over 2,300
117	Arezzo, Italy	Over 2,300
118	Constantine, Algeria	Over 2,300
119	Hantan, China	Over 2,300
120	Herat, Afghanistan	Over 2,300
121	Kabul, Afghanistan	Over 2,300
122	Kweilin, China	Over 2,300
123	Milan, Italy	Over 2,300
124	Novara, Italy	Over 2,300
125	Rimini, Italy	Over 2,300
126	Samarkand, Uzbekistan	Over 2,300
127	Trent, Italy	Over 2,300
128	Turin, Italy	Over 2,300
129	Vienna, Austria	Over 2,300
130	Plovdiv, Bulgaria	Over 2,250
131	Consenza, Italy	Over 2,225
132	Antakya, Turkey	Over 2,200
133	Padua, Italy	Over 2,200
134	Salonika, Greece	Over 2,200
135	Sfax, Tunisia	Over 2,200
136	Rheims, France	Over 2,000
137	Toulouse, France	Over 2,000
138	Cairo, Egypt	Over 1,300
139	Annaba, Algeria	Over 1,200
140	Harar, Ethiopia	Over 1,200
141	Fez, Morocco	Over 1,175
142	Mombasa, Kenya	Over 1,100
143	Mogadishu, Somalia	Over 1,075
144	Algiers, Algeria	Over 980
145	Meknes, Morocco	Over 980
146	Oran, Algeria	Over 980
147	Marrakesh, Morocco	Over 900
148	Zaria, Nigeria	Over 900
149	Rabat-Sale, Morocco	Over 800
150	Timbuktu, Mali	Over 800
151	Mansurah, Egypt	Over 750
152	Kano, Nigeria	Over 700
153	Tanta, Egypt	Over 700
154	Funchal, Madeira Islands	Over 550
155	Las Palmas, Canary Islands	Over 505
156	Ouagadougou, Burkina-Faso	Over 500
157	Casablanca, Morocco	Over 468
158	Mputo, Mozambique	Over 440
159	Suez, Egypt	Over 400
160	Luanda, Angola	Over 310
161	Accra, Ghana	Over 300
162	Iwo, Nigeria	Over 300
163	Niamey, Niger	Over 300
164	Porto-Novo, Benin	Over 300
165	Zanzibar, Tanzania	Over 300

B. WESTERN HEMISPHERE

Rank	City	Year of Founding
1	Quito, Ecuador	1000
2	Cuzco, Peru	1100
3	Toluca, Mexico	1120
4	Jalapa, Mexico	1313
5	Mexico City, Mexico	1325
6	Guanajuato, Mexico	1400
7	Arequipa, Peru	1425
8	Queretaro, Mexico	1440
9	Orizaba, Mexico	1457
10	Oaxaca, Mexico	1486
11	Santo Domingo, Dominican Republic	1486

Rank	City	Year of Founding	Rank	City	Year of Founding	Rank	City	Year of Founding
12	Santiago de los Cabelleros, Dominican Republic	1504	50	Potosi, Bolivia	1545	90	Vina del Mar, Chile	1586
13	Santiago de Cuba, Cuba	1514	51	Irapuato, Mexico	1547	91	Corrientes, Argentina	1588
14	Havana, Cuba	1519	52	La Paz, Bolivia	1548	92	San Felix de Guyana, Venezuela	1590
15	Cuernavaca, Mexico	1521	53	Salvador, Brazil	1549	93	Port of Spain, Trinidad and Tobago	1595
16	Managua, Nicaragua	1521	54	Acapulco, Mexico	1550			
17	San Juan, Puerto Rico	1521	55	Concepcion, Chile	1550	94	Santa Cruz, Bolivia	1595
18	Tepic, Mexico	1524	56	Ibague, Colombia	1551	95	Villahermosa, Mexico	1596
19	San Salvador, El Salvador	1525	57	Santo Andre, Brazil	1551	96	Veracruz, Mexico	1599
20	Willemstad, Netherlands Antilles	1527	58	Barquisimeto, Venezuela	1552	97	Moron, Argentina	1600
			59	São Bernardo do Campo, Brazil	1552	98	Quebec, Canada	1608
21	Camaguey, Cuba	1528	60	São Paulo, Brazil	1554	99	Fortaleza, Brazil	1609
22	Merida, Mexico	1528	61	Valencia, Venezuela	1555	100	Santa Fe, New Mexico	1609
23	Taxco, Mexico	1529	62	Guarulhos, Brazil	1560	101	Hampton, Virginia	1610
24	San Miguel, El Salvador	1530	63	Netzahualcoyotl, Mexico	1560	102	Sao Luis, Brazil	1612
25	Lima, Peru	1532	64	Mendoza, Argentina	1561	103	Belem, Brazil	1616
26	Puebla, Mexico	1532	65	San Juan, Argentina	1562	104	Medellin, Colombia	1616
27	Cartagena, Colombia	1533	66	Durango, Mexico	1563	105	Cordoba, Mexico	1617
28	Culiacan, Mexico	1533	67	Niteroi, Brazil	1565	106	Newport News, Virginia	1621
29	Pachuca de Soto, Mexico	1534	68	Rio de Janeiro, Brazil	1565	107	Bucaramanga, Colombia	1622
30	Trujillo, Peru	1534	69	St. Augustine, Florida	1565	108	Albany, New York	1624
31	Olinda, Brazil	1535	70	Caracas, Venezuela	1567	109	New York, New York	1624
32	Recife, Brazil	1535	71	El Valle, Venezuela	1567	110	Georgetown, Guyana	1625
33	Vitoria, Brazil	1535	72	Nova Igacu, Brazil	1567	111	Quincy, Massachusetts	1625
34	Cali, Colombia	1536	73	Celaya, Mexico	1570	112	Salem, Massachusetts	1626
35	San Pedro Sula, Honduras	1536	74	Maracaibo, Venezuela	1571	113	Bridgetown, Barbados	1628
36	Santos, Brazil	1536	75	Cordoba, Argentina	1573	114	Baranquilla, Colombia	1629
37	Uruapan del Progreso, Mexico	1536	76	Santa Fe, Argentina	1573	115	Jersey City, New Jersey	1629
			77	Cochabamba, Bolivia	1574	116	Lynn, Massachusetts	1629
38	Asuncion, Paraguay	1537	78	Aguascalientes, Mexico	1575	117	Boston, Massachusetts	1630
39	Callao, Peru	1537	79	Saltillo, Mexico	1575	118	Cambridge, Massachusetts	1630
40	Guayaquil, Ecuador	1537	80	Leon, Mexico	1576	119	Somerville, Massachusetts	1630
41	Bogota, Colombia	1538	81	San Luis Potosi, Mexico	1576	120	Williamsburg, Virginia	1633
42	Sucre, Colombia	1538	82	Santa Ana, El Salvador	1576	121	Campos, Brazil	1634
43	Tallahassee, Florida	1539	83	Tegucigalpa, Honduras	1578	122	Trois-Rivieres, Quebec	1634
44	Paramaribo, Suriname	1540	84	Monterrey, Mexico	1579	123	Waltham, Massachusetts	1634
45	Mazatlan, Mexico	1541	85	Buenos Aires, Argentina	1580	124	Hartford, Connecticut	1635
46	Morelia, Mexico	1541	86	Coatzacoalcos, Mexico	1580	125	Providence, Rhode Island	1636
47	Santiago, Chile	1541	87	Salta, Argentina	1582	126	Springfield, Massachusetts	1636
48	Guadalajara, Mexico	1542	88	St. John's, Newfoundland	1583	127	Belize, Belize	1638
49	Valparaiso, Chile	1544	89	Joao Pessoa, Brazil	1585			

Source: Library of Congress

Chapter 25

Culture

Culture

Culture defines the intangible quality of national life and a nation's contributions to creative arts, such as literature, music, theater, and art. Culture is the signature of every civilization and it reflects the human quest for excellence. Some cultural characteristics are difficult to quantify and, even when quantified, do not express or reflect the totality of cultural performance or achievement. Wealthier nations are more able to transmit their culture, and about fifteen nations account for 90 percent of the world's cultural achievements. The United States, Germany, France, and the United Kingdom account for 80 percent of all published musical compositions and songs; the United Kingdom produces about one-half of all new theatrical productions; about 80 percent of all books in print are found in American and European libraries; the United States accounts for about 75 percent of all Nobel Prize winners; and the United States and Europe have the finest and largest museums. In sports, as reflected in the Olympic rankings, the United States has a commanding overall lead.

25.1 Olympic Medals (1896–2000)

Rank	Country/Entity	Gold	Silver	Bronze	Rank	Country/Entity	Gold	Silver	Bronze
Summer Games					**Winter Games**				
1	United States	872	659	581	1	Soviet Union/Russia	117	83	77
2	Soviet Union/Russia	517	423	382	2	Germany	108	98	88
3	Germany	374	392	317	3	Norway	93	97	74
4	France	189	195	216	4	United States	65	62	45
5	United Kingdom	188	243	232	5	Austria	42	58	62
6	Italy	179	144	155	6	Finland	40	53	54
7	Hungary	150	134	158	7	Sweden	39	30	26
8	Sweden	138	157	176	8	Switzerland	31	33	35
9	Australia	103	110	139	9	Canada	31	30	33
10	Finland	101	81	114	10	Italy	29	33	25
11	Japan	98	97	103	11	Netherlands	24	27	21
12	China	80	79	64	12	France	20	28	31
13	Romania	74	83	108	13	Japan	13	10	16
14	Netherlands	58	77	64	14	South Korea/Korea	12	4	6
15	Poland	56	72	113	15	United Kingdom	7	4	14
16	Canada	52	80	99	16	Czech Republic	2	2	2
17	Switzerland	50	63	83	17	Bulgaria	2	0	0
18	Bulgaria	48	82	65	18	Poland	1	1	2
19	Denmark	41	63	58	19	China	0	16	6
20	Belgium	37	52	52					

Source: Encyclopedia Britannica

25.2 Nobel Prize Winners (1901–2000)

Rank	Country/Entity	Prizes Won	Rank	Country/Entity	Prizes Won	Rank	Country/Entity	Prizes Won
Peace			**Literature**			**Physics**		
1	United States	16	1	France	13	1	United States	43
2	United Kingdom	11	2	United States	12	2	United Kingdom	19
3	France	10	3	United Kingdom	8	3	Germany	19
4	Sweden	5	4	Germany	7	4	France	8
5	Germany	4	5	Sweden	6	5	Netherlands	7
6	Belgium	3	6	Italy	5	6	Russia	5
7	Norway	3	7	Spain	5	7	Sweden	4
8	South Africa	3	8	Norway	3	8	Switzerland	4
9	Argentina	2	9	Poland	3	9	Austria	3
10	Austria	2	10	Russia	3	10	Italy	3
11	Israel	2	11	Portugal	1	11	Japan	3
12	Russia	2	12	China	1			
13	Switzerland	2						
14	South Korea	1						
Economics			**Medicine and Physiology**			**Chemistry**		
1	United States	23	1	United States	48	1	United States	39
2	United Kingdom	7	2	United Kingdom	18	2	United Kingdom	22
3	Norway	2	3	Germany	14	3	Germany	14
4	Sweden	2	4	France	6	4	France	6
5	France	1	5	Sweden	7	5	Sweden	5
6	Germany	1	6	Switzerland	6	6	Switzerland	5
7	Netherlands	1	7	Austria	5	7	Canada	4
8	Russia	1	8	Denmark	5	8	Japan	2
9	Canada	1	9	Belgium	3	9	Argentina	1
			10	Italy	3	10	Austria	1
						11	Belgium	1
						12	Czech Republic	1
						13	Denmark	1
						14	Finland	1
						15	Italy	1
						16	Netherlands	1
						17	Norway	1
						18	Russia	1

Source: World Almanac

25.3 Libraries

Rank	Country/Entity	Public Libraries	Rank	Country/Entity	Public Libraries	Rank	Country/Entity	Public Libraries
1	Russia	32,200	14	Norway	1,339	27	Philippines	501
2	Germany	20,448	15	France	1,141	28	Finland	461
3	Poland	10,129	16	Japan	1,107	29	Sweden	381
4	United States	9,170	17	Canada	997	30	Thailand	375
5	Czech Republic	8,398	18	Colombia	974	31	Egypt	352
6	Romania	7,181	19	South Africa	720	32	Australia	350
7	Bulgaria	5,591	20	Peru	687	33	Cuba	327
8	Hungary	4,765	21	Sri Lanka	650	34	Israel	320
9	Brazil	3,600	22	Greece	615	35	Tunisia	280
10	China	2,406	23	Netherlands	593	36	Chile	269
11	Belgium	2,351	24	Vietnam	568	37	Taiwan	252
12	Austria	2,081	25	Mexico	557	38	Denmark	250
13	Spain	1,677	26	Iran	507	39	Iceland	234

Rank	Country/Entity	Public Libraries	Rank	Country/Entity	Public Libraries	Rank	Country/Entity	Public Libraries
40	Ecuador	210	52	Afghanistan	55	64	Solomon Islands	8
41	New Zealand	209	53	Saudi Arabia	50	65	Liechtenstein	3
42	Turkey	206	54	Albania	45	66	Ethiopia	4
43	Portugal	178	55	Ireland	31	67	Luxembourg	3
44	South Korea	168	56	Indonesia	30	68	Angola	2
45	United Kingdom	166	57	Venezuela	24	69	Bahamas	2
46	Cyprus	103	58	Benin	18	70	Cape Verde	2
47	Yugoslavia	102	59	Panama	18	71	Malta	2
48	Bolivia	99	60	Syria	14	72	Andorra	1
49	Costa Rica	81	61	Malaysia	13	73	Dominica	1
50	Dominican Republic	68	62	Senegal	10	74	Fiji	1
51	Madagascar	56	63	Ghana	9			

Source: UNESCO Statistical Yearbook

25.4 Film Production

Rank	Country/Entity	Film Production	Rank	Country/Entity	Film Production	Rank	Country/Entity	Film Production
1	India	838	35	Ireland	17	69	Algeria	3
2	China	469	36	Netherlands	16	70	Armenia	3
3	Philippines	456	37	Vietnam	16	71	Colombia	3
4	United States	420	38	Norway	15	72	Croatia	3
5	Japan	238	39	Israel	14	73	Estonia	3
6	Thailand	194	40	Mexico	14	74	Guatemala	3
7	France	141	41	Portugal	13	75	Lithuania	3
8	Italy	96	42	Denmark	12	76	Mali	3
9	Brazil	86	43	Hungary	12	77	Belarus	2
10	Myanmar (Burma)	85	44	Malaysia	12	78	Cameroon	2
11	United Kingdom	78	45	Albania	11	79	Côte d'Ivoire	2
12	Bangladesh	77	46	Bulgaria	11	80	Latvia	2
13	Egypt	72	47	Kazakhstan	10	81	Macedonia	2
14	Pakistan	64	48	Uzbekistan	10	82	Sierra Leone	2
15	Germany	63	49	Romania	9	83	Slovenia	2
16	South Korea	63	50	Belgium	8	84	Syria	2
17	Turkey	63	51	Finland	8	85	Tunisia	2
18	Iran	62	52	Yugoslavia	8	86	Angola	1
19	Spain	59	53	Iceland	7	87	Chile	1
20	Sri Lanka	58	54	Cuba	6	88	Cyprus	1
21	Russia	46	55	Moldova	6	89	Ecuador	1
22	Indonesia	40	56	Ukraine	6	90	Ethiopia	1
23	North Korea	37	57	Burkina	5	91	Ghana	1
24	Switzerland	37	58	Georgia	5	92	Guinea	1
25	Sweden	32	59	Lebanon	5	93	Iraq	1
26	Greece	25	60	Azerbaijan	4	94	Libya	1
27	Singapore	25	61	Bolivia	4	95	Mauritius	1
28	Austria	22	62	Guyana	4	96	Peru	1
29	Canada	22	63	Luxembourg	4	97	Sudan	1
30	Czech Republic	22	64	Morocco	4	98	Tajikistan	1
31	Argentina	21	65	New Zealand	4	99	Tanzania	1
32	Nigeria	20	66	Slovakia	4	100	Uruguay	1
33	Poland	20	67	Venezuela	4			
34	Australia	18	68	Afghanistan	3			

Source: UNESCO Statistical Yearbook

25.5 Annual Movie Attendance

Rank	Country/Entity	Movie Attendance (millions)	Rank	Country/Entity	Film Production	Rank	Country/Entity	Film Production
1	China	14,428.4	29	Poland	17.0	57	Croatia	3.7
2	India	4,300.0	30	Romania	17.0	58	Slovenia	2.9
3	United States	1,200.0	31	Switzerland	16.2	59	Bolivia	2.2
4	Vietnam	345.8	32	Netherlands	16.0	60	Yugoslavia	2.2
5	Russia	140.1	33	Sweden	15.2	61	Azerbaijan	1.9
6	France	130.1	34	Turkey	15.0	62	Tanzania	1.9
7	Japan	127.0	35	New Zealand	14.1	63	Zimbabwe	1.8
8	Germany	124.5	36	Hungary	14.0	64	Costa Rica	1.7
9	United Kingdom	114.6	37	Egypt	12.9	65	Moldova	1.4
10	Lebanon	99.2	38	Belarus	12.5	66	Iceland	1.2
11	Italy	96.7	39	Austria	11.9	67	Estonia	1.0
12	Spain	94.6	40	Norway	11.6	68	Laos	1.0
13	Canada	79.0	41	Ireland	10.4	69	Latvia	1.0
14	Australia	69.0	42	Israel	10.0	70	Cyprus	0.8
15	Portugal	64.0	43	Czech Republic	9.3	71	Kuwait	0.8
16	Mexico	63.0	44	Denmark	8.8	72	Benin	0.7
17	South Korea	47.1	45	Chile	8.0	73	Lithuania	0.7
18	Malaysia	39.4	46	Argentina	7.8	74	Luxembourg	0.7
19	Ukraine	30.8	47	Côte d'Ivoire	7.3	75	Mauritius	0.7
20	Georgia	30.4	48	Ecuador	6.8	76	Kyrgyzstan	0.6
21	Uzbekistan	29.0	49	Greece	6.5	77	Tajikistan	0.4
22	Sri Lanka	27.2	50	Kazakhstan	6.2	78	Madagascar	0.4
23	Iran	26.0	51	Kenya	5.8	79	Malta	0.3
24	Cuba	23.8	52	Slovakia	5.6	80	Rwanda	0.3
25	Venezuela	18.3	53	Finland	5.3	81	Jordan	0.2
26	Singapore	18.1	54	Bulgaria	4.7	82	Macedonia	0.2
27	Morocco	17.3	55	Guinea	3.9	83	Monaco	0.1
28	Belgium	17.2	56	Syria	3.9	84	San Marino	0.1

Source: UNESCO Statistical Yearbook

25.6 Music Sales

Rank	Country/Entity	Millions of Dollars (U.S.)	Rank	Country/Entity	Millions of Dollars (U.S.)	Rank	Country/Entity	Millions of Dollars (U.S.)
1	United States	12,298	9	Netherlands	660	17	Mexico	399
2	Japan	6,762	10	Italy	637	18	Austria	397
3	Germany	3,179	11	Spain	585	19	Denmark	307
4	United Kingdom	2,710	12	South Korea	517	20	India	298
5	France	2,318	13	Belgium	443	21	Argentina	285
6	Brazil	1,394	14	Taiwan	416	22	Indonesia	270
7	Canada	912	15	Sweden	403			
8	Australia	815	16	Switzerland	401			

Rank	Country/Entity	Music Sales per Capita in Dollars (U.S.)	Rank	Country/Entity	Music Sales per Capita in Dollars (U.S.)	Rank	Country/Entity	Music Sales per Capita in Dollars (U.S.)
1	Denmark	58	8	Sweden	44	15	Finland	28
2	Norway	58	9	Belgium	43	16	New Zealand	28
3	Japan	54	10	Netherlands	41	17	Canada	27
4	Switzerland	53	11	United States	40	18	Ireland	23
5	Iceland	50	12	France	39	19	Singapore	20
6	Austria	47	13	Germany	39	20	Cyprus	17
7	United Kingdom	46	14	Australia	31	21	Portugal	16

Source: Economist Intelligence

25.7 Theaters

Rank	Country/Entity	Performing Arts Facilities
1	China	1,756
2	Japan	543
3	Canada	476
4	Netherlands	422
5	United Kingdom	404
6	Brazil	302
7	Spain	301
8	Germany	280
9	Romania	146
10	Poland	144
11	Iraq	132
12	Yugoslavia	123
13	Senegal	105
14	Denmark	100
15	Australia	90
16	Czech Republic	88
17	Greece	88
18	Vietnam	78
19	Bulgaria	67
20	South Africa	51
21	Finland	50
22	Cuba	49
23	Hungary	41
24	Venezuela	41
25	Portugal	37
26	Turkey	31
27	Belgium	30
28	Albania	28
29	Peru	28
30	Sweden	27
31	Mongolia	26
32	Uruguay	25
33	Switzerland	24
34	Nigeria	23
35	Indonesia	22
36	Sri Lanka	22
37	Tunisia	22
38	Chile	20
39	Iran	19
40	United Arab Emirates	18
41	Guinea-Bissau	17
42	Jamaica	16
43	Colombia	14
44	Ireland	14
45	Libya	14
46	Norway	14
47	Bolivia	13
48	Burundi	13
49	Maldives	13
50	Mexico	11
51	Pakistan	11
52	Malaysia	10
53	Costa Rica	9
54	Rwanda	9
55	Ghana	8
56	Algeria	7
57	Suriname	7
58	El Salvador	6
59	Mauritius	6
60	Barbados	5
61	Iceland	5
62	Jordan	5
63	Syria	5
64	Chad	4
65	Cyprus	4
66	Congo, Dem. Rep. of	4
67	Angola	3
68	Bermuda	3
69	Ethiopia	3
70	Fiji	3
71	Guyana	3
72	Dominican Republic	2
73	Luxembourg	2
74	Malawi	2
75	Congo, Rep. of	1
76	Grenada	1
77	Guatemala	1
78	Nicaragua	1
79	Saint Kitts and Nevis	1
80	San Marino	1

Source: UNESCO Statistical Yearbook

25.8 Museums

Rank	Country/Entity	Museums
1	United States	4,440
2	Germany	4,034
3	Australia	1,893
4	United Kingdom	1,868
5	Canada	1,352
6	France	1,300
7	China	967
8	Brazil	778
9	Austria	719
10	Switzerland	699
11	Japan	638
12	Netherlands	625
13	Hungary	571
14	Yugoslavia	565
15	Spain	554
16	Poland	551
17	Greece	478
18	Romania	471
19	India	462
20	Czech Republic	422
21	Norway	401
22	Portugal	314
23	Denmark	285
24	Ukraine	224
25	Bulgaria	223
26	Cuba	216
27	Finland	206
28	Sweden	195
29	Thailand	180
30	Turkey	154
31	South Korea	146
32	Indonesia	131
33	Italy	130
34	New Zealand	98
35	Mexico	93
36	Belarus	86
37	Israel	79
38	Philippines	76
39	Colombia	73
40	Venezuela	54
41	Iceland	53
42	Iran	52
43	Ireland	49
44	Malaysia	43
45	Tunisia	35
46	Egypt	34
47	Syria	33
48	Algeria	28
49	Libya	26
50	Iraq	25
51	Chile	24
52	Puerto Rico	24
53	Bolivia	23
54	Ecuador	23
55	South Africa	22
56	Pakistan	19
57	Cyprus	18
58	Albania	18
59	Guatemala	18
60	Paraguay	18
61	North Korea	17
62	Malta	16
63	Uganda	16
64	Costa Rica	15
65	Bermuda	14
66	Morocco	14
67	Angola	13
68	Bangladesh	13
69	Myanmar (Burma)	12
70	Nigeria	12
71	Peru	12
72	Singapore	12

Rank	Country/Entity	Museums	Rank	Country/Entity	Museums	Rank	Country/Entity	Museums
73	Jordan	11	98	Congo, Dem. Rep. of	5	123	Mali	2
74	Panama	11	99	Guinea	5	124	Papua New Guinea	2
75	Uruguay	11	100	Liechtenstein	5	125	Seychelles	2
76	Zimbabwe	11	101	Madagascar	5	126	Belize	1
77	Taiwan	10	102	Mauritius	5	127	Bhutan	1
78	Namibia	9	103	El Salvador	4	128	Côte d'Ivoire	1
79	Nicaragua	9	104	Ghana	4	129	Equatorial Guinea	1
80	San Marino	9	105	Haiti	4	130	Ethiopia	1
81	Vietnam	9	106	Mongolia	4	131	Fiji	1
82	Afghanistan	8	107	Senegal	4	132	Grenada	1
83	Bahamas	7	108	Antigua and Barbuda	3	133	Guinea-Bissau	1
84	Central African Republic	7	109	Barbados	3	134	Luxembourg	1
85	Kuwait	7	110	Cambodia	3	135	Maldives	1
86	Lebanon	7	111	Malawi	3	136	Saint Kitts and Nevis	1
87	Liberia	7	112	Niger	3	137	Saint Lucia	1
88	Sudan	7	113	Oman	3	138	Saint Vincent and	1
89	Togo	7	114	Suriname	3		the Grenadines	
90	Benin	6	115	United Arab Emirates	3	139	Saudi Arabia	1
91	Burkina Faso	6	116	Andorra	2	140	Sierra Leone	1
92	Dominican Republic	6	117	Bahrain	2	141	Solomon Islands	1
93	Kenya	6	118	Botswana	2	142	Somalia	1
94	Monaco	6	119	Brunei	2	143	Swaziland	1
95	Qatar	6	120	Burundi	2	144	Vanuatu	1
96	Zambia	6	121	Cameroon	2			
97	Chad	5	122	Guyana	2			

Source: UNESCO Statistical Yearbook

Chapter 26

Women

Gender Relations

The Gender-Related Development Index is a composite index devised by the United Nations Development Program (UNDP). It captures the gender inequalities that affect the Human Development Index, or HDI (See Chapter 27). It adjusts HDI by using three variables: life expectancy, in which women have an edge over men, and income and educational attainment (adult literacy and combined primary, secondary, and college enrollment ratios), in which men have an edge. The index disaggregates data to expose areas of gender discrimination and inequality. The index also measures gender-based variations in access to basic national resources and oppor-

tunities. The Gender Empowerment Measure is a composite index also devised by the UNDP. It concentrates on women's participation in the economic, political, and professional spheres. Unlike the Gender-Related Development Index, which is concerned primarily with living standards and basic capabilities, the Gender Empowerment Measure is designed to measure women's access to power. For this purpose, it combines four variables: percentage of seats in national legislatures; percentage of administrative and managerial jobs; percentage of earned income; and percentage of professional and technical workers.

26.1 Gender-Related Development Index

Rank	Country/Entity	Gender-Related Development Index	Rank	Country/Entity	Gender-Related Development Index	Rank	Country/Entity	Gender-Related Development Index
1	Sierra Leone	163	34	Comoros	130	67	Kyrgyzstan	97
2	Niger	162	35	Cambodia	129	68	Algeria	96
3	Burkina Faso	161	36	India	128	69	Guyana	95
4	Mali	160	37	Iraq	127	70	Syria	94
5	Burundi	159	38	Equatorial Guinea	126	71	China	93
6	Ethiopia	158	39	Laos	125	72	Iran	92
7	Guinea	157	40	Cameroon	124	73	Albania	91
8	Mozambique	156	41	Lesotho	123	74	Jordan	90
9	Eritrea	155	42	Kenya	122	75	Paraguay	89
10	Gambia	154	43	Ghana	121	76	Indonesia	88
11	Guinea-Bissau	153	44	Myanmar (Burma)	120	77	Turkmenistan	87
12	Chad	152	45	Papua New Guinea	119	78	Uzbekistan	86
13	Sudan	151	46	Zimbabwe	118	79	Botswana	85
14	Malawi	150	47	Congo, Rep. of	117	80	Mongolia	84
15	Senegal	149	48	Morocco	116	81	Ukraine	83
16	Nepal	148	49	Nicaragua	115	82	Philippines	82
17	Bhutan	147	50	Honduras	114	83	Dominican Republic	81
18	Uganda	146	51	Guatemala	113	84	Peru	80
19	Angola	145	52	Gabon	112	85	Libya	79
20	Haiti	144	53	Egypt	111	86	Ecuador	78
21	Yemen	143	54	Bolivia	110	87	Maldives	77
22	Central African Republic	142	55	Solomon Islands	109	88	Tunisia	76
23	Côte d'Ivoire	141	56	Vietnam	108	89	Armenia	75
24	Bangladesh	140	57	Cape Verde	107	90	South Africa	74
25	Madagascar	139	58	Tajikistan	106	91	Kazakhstan	73
26	Mauritania	138	59	Swaziland	105	92	Belize	72
27	Tanzania	137	60	Oman	104	93	Latvia	71
28	Togo	136	61	El Salvador	103	94	Sri Lanka	70
29	Benin	135	62	Saudi Arabia	102	95	Cuba	69
30	Zambia	134	63	Moldova	101	96	Lebanon	68
31	Nigeria	133	64	Azerbaijan	100	97	Qatar	67
32	Congo, Dem. Rep. of	132	65	Namibia	99	98	United Arab Emirates	66
33	Pakistan	131	66	Georgia	98	99	Jamaica	65

Rank	Country/Entity	Gender-Related Development Index	Rank	Country/Entity	Gender-Related Development Index	Rank	Country/Entity	Gender-Related Development Index
100	Macedonia	64	122	Panama	42	144	Greece	20
101	Suriname	63	123	Colombia	41	145	Spain	19
102	Lithuania	62	124	Thailand	40	146	Switzerland	18
103	Croatia	61	125	Costa Rica	39	147	Germany	17
104	Bahrain	60	126	Trinidad and Tobago	38	148	Barbados	16
105	Estonia	59	127	South Korea	37	149	Austria	15
106	North Korea	58	128	Brunei	36	150	Belgium	14
107	Romania	57	129	Poland	35	151	Japan	13
108	Brazil	56	130	Hungary	34	152	Netherlands	12
109	Turkey	55	131	Hong Kong	33	153	United Kingdom	11
110	Mauritius	54	132	Luxembourg	32	154	Denmark	10
111	Russia	53	133	Uruguay	31	155	Australia	9
112	Fiji	52	134	Cyprus	30	156	New Zealand	8
113	Belarus	51	135	Singapore	29	157	France	7
114	Kuwait	50	136	Portugal	28	158	United States	6
115	Mexico	49	137	Ireland	27	159	Finland	5
116	Argentina	48	138	Slovakia	26	160	Iceland	4
117	Bulgaria	47	139	Czech Republic	25	161	Sweden	3
118	Chile	46	140	Slovenia	24	162	Norway	2
119	Malaysia	45	141	Italy	23	163	Canada	1
120	Malta	44	142	Israel	22			
121	Venezuela	43	143	Bahamas	21			

Source: Human Development Report

26.2 Gender Empowerment Measure

Rank	Country/Entity	Gender Empowerment Measure	Rank	Country/Entity	Gender Empowerment Measure	Rank	Country/Entity	Gender Empowerment Measure
1	Niger	102	30	Georgia	73	59	Panama	44
2	Mauritania	101	31	Mali	72	60	Bulgaria	43
3	Pakistan	100	32	Haiti	71	61	Singapore	42
4	Togo	99	33	Indonesia	70	62	Colombia	41
5	Central African Republic	98	34	Ecuador	69	63	Belize	40
6	Jordan	97	35	Brazil	68	64	Guyana	39
7	Sudan	96	36	Paraguay	67	65	Japan	38
8	India	95	37	Cyprus	66	66	Mexico	37
9	Gambia	94	38	Bolivia	65	67	Slovenia	36
10	Algeria	93	39	Romania	64	68	Guatemala	35
11	United Arab Emirates	92	40	Swaziland	63	69	El Salvador	34
12	Papua New Guinea	91	41	Venezuela	62	70	China	33
13	Equatorial Guinea	90	42	Chile	61	71	Israel	32
14	Malawi	89	43	Thailand	60	72	France	31
15	Egypt	88	44	Uruguay	59	73	Hungary	30
16	Iran	87	45	Dominican Republic	58	74	Poland	29
17	Cameroon	86	46	Cape Verde	57	75	Costa Rica	28
18	Turkey	85	47	Zimbabwe	56	76	Slovakia	27
19	Sri Lanka	84	48	Mozambique	55	77	Italy	26
20	South Korea	83	49	Peru	54	78	Cuba	25
21	Morocco	82	50	Suriname	53	79	Czech Republic	24
22	Zambia	81	51	Latvia	52	80	South Africa	23
23	Bangladesh	80	52	Greece	51	81	Portugal	22
24	Syria	79	53	Lesotho	50	82	Ireland	21
25	Fiji	78	54	Mauritius	49	83	United Kingdom	20
26	Burkina Faso	77	55	Botswana	48	84	Belgium	19
27	Maldives	76	56	Estonia	47	85	Barbados	18
28	Kuwait	75	57	Philippines	46	86	Trinidad and Tobago	17
29	Tunisia	74	58	Malaysia	45	87	Spain	16

Rank	Country/Entity	Gender Empower-ment Measure	Rank	Country/Entity	Gender Empower-ment Measure	Rank	Country/Entity	Gender Empower-ment Measure
88	Bahamas	15	93	Austria	10	98	Finland	5
89	Luxembourg	14	94	Netherlands	9	99	New Zealand	4
90	Switzerland	13	95	Germany	8	100	Denmark	3
91	Australia	12	96	Canada	7	101	Norway	2
92	United States	11	97	Iceland	6	102	Sweden	1

Source: Human Development

Gender Inequalities

Since the World Conference on Women in Beijing in 1995, the body of statistical data illustrating gender inequalities has grown. Until the 1970s, little data were collected on the condition of women at the national or global levels. Data on women were submerged in the general statistics, masking wide disparities in the status of the two sexes. The statistics now available show that in no society do women and men enjoy equal opportunities. The degree of parity varies as well as the speed in closing the traditional gaps. While near equality has been achieved in many Scandinavian countries, women are often treated as second-class citizens in Islamic countries where the rise of fundamentalism has actually made their condition worse. They have little or no access to education, health, or legal and political rights, three key areas of patriarchal hegemony. Women outnumber men two to one among the world's one billion illiterate people. Girls constitute the majority of the 130 million children without access to primary education. Although half the literacy gap between men and women was closed between 1970 and 1990, the number of female illiterates actually increased during the same period. The gender gaps in health are similarly striking. Women's special health needs suffer considerable neglect in poorer countries without proper health facilities. Pregnancy complications are the single largest cause of death among Third World women in their reproductive years. Nearly half a million maternal deaths occur each year in developing countries.

These gaps, although significant, are narrower than those in income and access to employment. Of the estimated 1.3 billion people living in absolute poverty, more than 70 percent are female. The number of rural women living in poverty rose by over 50 percent in the past two decades. Women are getting poor even in rich countries. In the United States women constituted only 40 percent of the poor in 1940 but 64 percent in 1998. Half the female-headed households in the United States are poor. In almost every country, women have a higher rate of unemployment than men. Worldwide, the average wage for women is three-fourths that of men outside agriculture. Further, women are concentrated in low-skill, low-paying jobs and are subject to cultural norms that segregate jobs by gender. Even in developed countries, women have to contend with the glass ceiling. In most cases, women have to combine careers with work at home as a wife and mother. Women face overt legal discrimination in many countries. In Muslim countries governed by the shari'a, women have restricted rights to marry, travel, acquire nationality, manage or inherit property, get credit, and seek employment. They may dress only according to Koranic injunctions (cover their faces and wear only black) and may not go to coeducational institutions or seek medical help from male physicians. Women have little political clout. The political world is essentially male-dominated with women making up less than 6 percent of national legislatures and 6 to 8 percent of cabinets.

26.3 Women's Share of Earned Income

Rank	Country/Entity	Women's Share of Earned Income (percentage)	Rank	Country/Entity	Women's Share of Earned Income (percentage)	Rank	Country/Entity	Women's Share of Earned Income (percentage)
1	Sweden	45	35	Romania	37	69	South Korea	29
2	Latvia	44	36	Thailand	37	70	Luxembourg	29
3	Denmark	42	37	Haiti	36	71	Cyprus	28
4	Estonia	42	38	Sri Lanka	36	72	Morocco	28
5	Finland	42	39	Turkey	36	73	Panama	28
6	Iceland	42	40	Germany	35	74	Bolivia	27
7	Malawi	42	41	Maldives	35	75	Costa Rica	27
8	Mozambique	42	42	Papua New Guinea	35	76	Guyana	27
9	Norway	42	43	Philippines	35	77	Ireland	27
10	Bulgaria	41	44	Austria	34	78	Trinidad and Tobago	27
11	Slovakia	41	45	Belgium	34	79	Venezuela	27
12	Australia	40	46	El Salvador	34	80	Mauritius	26
13	Bahamas	40	47	Japan	34	81	Mexico	26
14	Barbados	40	48	Netherlands	34	82	Suriname	26
15	Burkina Faso	40	49	Portugal	34	83	Egypt	25
16	United States	40	50	Uruguay	34	84	India	25
17	Botswana	39	51	Colombia	33	85	Kuwait	25
18	Central African Republic	39	52	Indonesia	33	86	Tunisia	25
19	Czech Republic	39	53	Israel	33	87	Dominican Republic	24
20	France	39	54	Swaziland	33	88	Peru	24
21	Georgia	39	55	Cape Verde	32	89	Bangladesh	23
22	Hungary	39	56	Greece	32	90	Paraguay	23
23	Mali	39	57	Singapore	32	91	Chile	22
24	New Zealand	39	58	Switzerland	32	92	Fiji	22
25	Poland	39	59	Togo	32	93	Sudan	22
26	Slovenia	39	60	Cuba	31	94	Guatemala	21
27	Zambia	39	61	Italy	31	95	Pakistan	21
28	Canada	38	62	South Africa	31	96	Syria	20
29	China	38	63	Cameroon	30	97	Algeria	19
30	Gambia	38	64	Lesotho	30	98	Ecuador	19
31	United Kingdom	38	65	Malaysia	30	99	Iran	19
32	Zimbabwe	38	66	Spain	30	100	Jordan	19
33	Mauritania	37	67	Brazil	29	101	Belize	18
34	Niger	37	68	Equatorial Guinea	29	102	United Arab Emirates	10

Source: Human Development Report

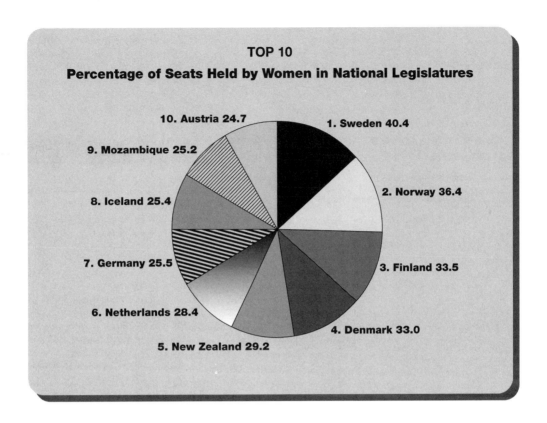

TOP 10

Percentage of Seats Held by Women in National Legislatures

10. Austria 24.7
9. Mozambique 25.2
8. Iceland 25.4
7. Germany 25.5
6. Netherlands 28.4
5. New Zealand 29.2
4. Denmark 33.0
3. Finland 33.5
2. Norway 36.4
1. Sweden 40.4

Rank	Country/Entity	Percentage of Women in National Legislatures	Rank	Country/Entity	Percentage of Women in National Legislatures	Rank	Country/Entity	Percentage of Women in National Legislatures
11	South Africa	23.7	35	Mali	12.2	59	Botswana	8.5
12	Cuba	22.8	36	Philippines	11.6	60	Swaziland	8.5
13	Canada	21.2	37	United Kingdom	11.6	61	Slovenia	7.8
14	China	21.0	38	Hungary	11.4	62	Japan	7.7
15	Australia	20.5	39	Indonesia	11.4	63	Mauritius	7.6
16	Switzerland	20.3	40	Lesotho	11.2	64	Israel	7.5
17	Guyana	20.0	41	United States	11.2	65	India	7.3
18	Luxembourg	20.0	42	Cape Verde	11.1	66	Chile	7.2
19	Spain	19.9	43	Estonia	10.9	67	Georgia	6.9
20	Bahamas	19.6	44	Belize	10.8	68	Uruguay	6.9
21	Trinidad and Tobago	19.4	45	Bulgaria	10.8	69	Brazil	6.7
22	Barbados	18.4	46	Burkina Faso	10.8	70	Tunisia	6.7
23	Belgium	15.8	47	Peru	10.8	71	Thailand	6.6
24	Costa Rica	15.8	48	Malaysia	10.3	72	Bolivia	6.4
25	Suriname	15.7	49	Dominican Republic	10.0	73	Greece	6.3
26	El Salvador	15.5	50	Italy	10.0	74	Maldives	6.3
27	Slovakia	14.7	51	Colombia	9.8	75	Venezuela	6.3
28	Zimbabwe	14.7	52	Panama	9.7	76	Fiji	5.8
29	Mexico	14.2	53	Zambia	9.7	77	Cameroon	5.6
30	Czech Republic	13.9	54	Syria	9.6	78	Malawi	5.6
31	Ireland	13.7	55	Bangladesh	9.1	79	Paraguay	5.6
32	Portugal	13.0	56	France	9.0	80	Romania	5.6
33	Poland	12.7	57	Latvia	9.0	81	Cyprus	5.4
34	Guatemala	12.5	58	Equatorial Guinea	8.8	82	Sri Lanka	5.3

Rank	Country/Entity	Percentage of Women in National Legislatures	Rank	Country/Entity	Percentage of Women in National Legislatures	Rank	Country/Entity	Percentage of Women in National Legislatures
83	Sudan	5.3	90	South Korea	3.0	97	Niger	1.2
84	Iran	4.9	91	Pakistan	2.6	98	Togo	1.2
85	Singapore	4.8	92	Turkey	2.4	99	Mauritania	0.7
86	Ecuador	3.7	93	Egypt	2.0	100	Morocco	0.7
87	Haiti	3.6	94	Gambia	2.0	101	Kuwait	0.0
88	Central African Republic	3.5	95	Papua New Guinea	1.8	102	United Arab Emirates	0.0
89	Algeria	3.2	96	Jordan	1.7			

Source: Human Development Report

26.5 Female College and University Students

Rank	Country/Entity	Female College and University Students per 100,000 Women	Rank	Country/Entity	Female College and University Students per 100,000 Women	Rank	Country/Entity	Female College and University Students per 100,000 Women
1	Canada	7,170	44	Kuwait	2,590	87	United Arab Emirates	1,011
2	United States	5,852	45	Poland	2,462	88	Algeria	1,000
3	Australia	5,405	46	Lithuania	2,285	89	Albania	983
4	New Zealand	5,046	47	Singapore	2,249	90	Fiji	959
5	Armenia	4,820	48	Germany	2,223	91	Honduras	952
6	Norway	4,325	49	Thailand	2,202	92	Morocco	944
7	Finland	4,312	50	Mongolia	2,190	93	Namibia	894
8	Spain	4,127	51	Chile	2,181	94	Malaysia	862
9	France	4,033	52	Moldova	2,103	95	Iraq	861
10	Argentina	3,726	53	Dominican Republic	2,080	96	Indonesia	812
11	Israel	3,703	54	El Salvador	2,013	97	Guyana	804
12	Bulgaria	3,574	55	Turkmenistan	1,960	98	Myanmar (Burma)	715
13	Ireland	3,537	56	Libya	1,930	99	Jamaica	658
14	Portugal	3,530	57	Bahrain	1,922	100	Brunei	640
15	Uzbekistan	3,529	58	Latvia	1,845	101	Trinidad and Tobago	610
16	South Korea	3,507	59	Croatia	1,811	102	Mauritius	537
17	Panama	3,498	60	Hungary	1,796	103	Samoa	509
18	Netherlands	3,456	61	Czech Republic	1,787	104	Swaziland	493
19	United Kingdom	3,409	62	Ecuador	1,705	105	India	445
20	Denmark	3,337	63	Hong Kong	1,701	106	Oman	441
21	Belgium	3,261	64	Malta	1,690	107	Botswana	392
22	Qatar	3,243	65	Slovakia	1,661	108	Sri Lanka	388
23	Italy	3,237	66	Colombia	1,654	109	Zimbabwe	369
24	Philippines	3,223	67	South Africa	1,590	110	Guatemala	358
25	Iceland	3,187	68	Turkey	1,537	111	Sudan	341
26	Sweden	3,184	69	Switzerland	1,525	112	China	318
27	Bahamas	3,136	70	Saudi Arabia	1,508	113	Madagascar	294
28	Ukraine	3,109	71	Macedonia	1,504	114	Gabon	288
29	Russia	3,106	72	Azerbaijan	1,458	115	Congo, Rep. of	271
30	Belarus	3,062	73	Bolivia	1,449	116	Lesotho	255
31	Kazakhstan	3,032	74	Mexico	1,444	117	Vietnam	246
32	Barbados	2,965	75	Suriname	1,418	118	Pakistan	238
33	Georgia	2,862	76	Romania	1,344	119	Nepal	231
34	Austria	2,800	77	Cuba	1,336	120	Côte d'Ivoire	209
35	Greece	2,765	78	Egypt	1,336	121	Papua New Guinea	209
36	Japan	2,765	79	Syria	1,289	122	Nigeria	203
37	Slovenia	2,722	80	Tajikistan	1,240	123	Bangladesh	188
38	Costa Rica	2,677	81	Brazil	1,200	124	Yemen	173
39	Uruguay	2,669	82	Kyrgyzstan	1,145	125	Mauritania	164
40	Estonia	2,651	83	Iran	1,144	126	Senegal	142
41	Venezuela	2,645	84	Tunisia	1,110	127	Zambia	141
42	Lebanon	2,605	85	Paraguay	1,069	128	Belize	133
43	Peru	2,593	86	Nicaragua	1,064	129	Gambia	109

Rank	Country/Entity	Female College and University Students per 100,000 Women	Rank	Country/Entity	Female College and University Students per 100,000 Women	Rank	Country/Entity	Female College and University Students per 100,000 Women
130	Uganda	99	139	Malawi	50	148	Mozambique	21
131	Kenya	90	140	Burkina Faso	43	149	Djibouti	20
132	Togo	89	141	Burundi	41	150	Mali	20
133	Cameroon	88	142	Sierra Leone	41	151	Angola	19
134	Haiti	80	143	Cambodia	35	152	Niger	17
135	Laos	79	144	Central African Republic	35	153	Tanzania	14
136	Benin	75	145	Comoros	33	154	Chad	11
137	Congo, Dem. Rep. of	63	146	Eritrea	27	155	Guinea	10
138	Ghana	54	147	Ethiopia	24			

Source: Human Development Report

26.6 Female College and University Science Enrollment

Rank	Country/Entity	Enrollment as Percentage of Total Female College and University Enrollment	Rank	Country/Entity	Enrollment as Percentage of Total Female College and University Enrollment	Rank	Country/Entity	Enrollment as Percentage of Total Female College and University Enrollment
1	Myanmar (Burma)	61	32	Namibia	31	63	Estonia	25
2	Mongolia	53	33	New Zealand	31	64	Belgium	24
3	Bulgaria	45	34	Poland	31	65	Guyana	24
4	Barbados	44	35	Sierra Leone	31	66	United Kingdom	24
5	Qatar	44	36	Solomon Islands	31	67	Finland	23
6	Kuwait	43	37	France	30	68	Indonesia	23
7	Bahrain	42	38	Syria	30	69	Thailand	23
8	Paraguay	42	39	Chile	29	70	Germany	21
9	Albania	40	40	Slovenia	29	71	Lesotho	21
10	Georgia	40	41	Cyprus	28	72	Malta	21
11	Kyrgyzstan	38	42	Denmark	28	73	Mozambique	21
12	Macedonia	38	43	Dominica	28	74	Iran	20
13	Portugal	38	44	El Salvador	28	75	Hong Kong	19
14	Romania	38	45	Hungary	28	76	Netherlands	17
15	South Africa	38	46	Latvia	28	77	Uganda	17
16	Lebanon	37	47	Morocco	28	78	South Korea	16
17	Argentina	36	48	Tunisia	28	79	Swaziland	16
18	Brunei	36	49	Turkey	28	80	Malawi	15
19	Panama	36	50	Croatia	27	81	Mauritania	15
20	Algeria	35	51	Egypt	27	82	Switzerland	15
21	Cuba	35	52	Greece	27	83	Zimbabwe	14
22	Jordan	35	53	Norway	27	84	Japan	13
23	Brazil	34	54	Philippines	27	85	Tajikistan	13
24	Russia	34	55	Sweden	27	86	Benin	11
25	Trinidad and Tobago	34	56	Austria	26	87	Ethiopia	11
26	Ireland	33	57	Botswana	26	88	Laos	
27	Italy	33	58	Honduras	26	89	Côte d'Ivoire	10
28	Seychelles	33	59	Mexico	26	90	Tanzania	9
29	Colombia	32	60	Samoa	26	91	Burkina Faso	8
30	Israel	32	61	Australia	25	92	Togo	5
31	Madagascar	31	62	Czech Republic	25	93	Chad	3

Source: Human Development Report

26.7 Female Administrators and Managers

Rank	Country/Entity	Female Administrative and Managerial Workers as Percentage of Male
1	Italy	54
2	Honduras	53
3	Australia	43
4	United States	43
5	Canada	42
6	Trinidad and Tobago	40
7	Barbados	39
8	Latvia	39
9	Sweden	39
10	Belize	37
11	Estonia	37
12	Botswana	36
13	Dominica	36
14	Bahamas	35
15	Poland	35
16	Hungary	34
17	New Zealand	34
18	Haiti	33
19	Lesotho	33
20	Philippines	33
21	United Kingdom	33
22	Grenada	32
23	Guatemala	32
24	Norway	32
25	Spain	32
26	Colombia	31
27	Portugal	31
28	Bulgaria	29
29	Seychelles	29
30	Bolivia	28
31	Ecuador	28
32	Iceland	28
33	Panama	28
34	Romania	28
35	Slovenia	28
36	Switzerland	28
37	Uruguay	28
38	Czech Republic	27
39	Slovakia	27
40	El Salvador	26
41	Germany	26
42	Morocco	26
43	Swaziland	26
44	Finland	25
45	Austria	24
46	Peru	24
47	Cape Verde	23
48	Costa Rica	23
49	Ireland	23
50	Mauritius	23
51	Paraguay	23
52	Venezuela	23
53	Greece	22
54	Thailand	22
55	Dominican Republic	21
56	Namibia	21
57	Chile	20
58	Hong Kong	20
59	Israel	20
60	Mali	20
61	Mexico	20
62	Netherlands	20
63	Belgium	19
64	Cuba	19
65	Denmark	19
66	Malaysia	19
67	Georgia	18
68	Brazil	17
69	Eritrea	17
70	South Africa	17
71	Gambia	16
72	Sri Lanka	16
73	Singapore	15
74	Zimbabwe	15
75	Burkina Faso	14
76	Maldives	14
77	Burundi	13
78	Guyana	13
79	Iraq	13
80	Tunisia	13
81	Vanuatu	13
82	China	12
83	Egypt	12
84	Papua New Guinea	12
85	Samoa	12
86	Suriname	12
87	Brunei	11
88	Ethiopia	11
89	Mozambique	11
90	Cameroon	10
91	Cyprus	10
92	Fiji	10
93	Turkey	10
94	Central African Republic	9
95	Congo, Dem. Rep. of	9
96	France	9
97	Ghana	9
98	Japan	9
99	Luxembourg	9
100	Niger	9
101	Mauritania	8
102	Sierra Leone	8
103	Togo	8
104	Indonesia	7
105	Algeria	6
106	Bahrain	6
107	Congo, Rep. of	6
108	Nigeria	6
109	Zambia	6
110	Bangladesh	5
111	Jordan	5
112	Kuwait	5
113	Malawi	5
114	Iran	4
115	South Korea	4
116	Pakistan	4
117	Solomon Islands	3
118	Syria	3
119	Djibouti	2
120	Equatorial Guinea	2
121	India	2
122	Sudan	2
123	United Arab Emirates	2

Source: Human Development Report

26.8 Female Professional and Technical Workers

Rank	Country/Entity	Female Professional and Technical Workers as Percentage of Male	Rank	Country/Entity	Female Professional and Technical Workers as Percentage of Male	Rank	Country/Entity	Female Professional and Technical Workers as Percentage of Male
1	Estonia	68	43	Guyana	48	85	Malawi	35
2	Latvia	67	44	Denmark	47	86	Maldives	35
3	Philippines	64	45	Ecuador	47	87	Vanuatu	35
4	Sweden	64	46	Samoa	47	88	Iran	33
5	Uruguay	64	47	South Africa	47	89	Turkey	33
6	Brazil	63	48	Austria	46	90	South Korea	32
7	Finland	63	49	China	45	91	Sierra Leone	32
8	Poland	63	50	Costa Rica	45	92	Zambia	32
9	Norway	62	51	Fiji	45	93	Morocco	31
10	Suriname	62	52	Guatemala	45	94	Burundi	30
11	Botswana	61	53	Honduras	45	95	Egypt	30
12	Hungary	60	54	Ireland	45	96	Eritrea	30
13	Swaziland	60	55	Mexico	45	97	Papua New Guinea	30
14	Jamaica	59	56	Colombia	44	98	Congo, Rep. of	29
15	Seychelles	58	57	El Salvador	44	99	Jordan	29
16	Slovakia	58	58	Greece	44	100	Sudan	29
17	Bulgaria	57	59	Iraq	44	101	Algeria	28
18	Dominica	57	60	Malaysia	44	102	Equatorial Guinea	27
19	Lesotho	57	61	Netherlands	44	103	Solomon Islands	27
20	Venezuela	57	62	United Kingdom	44	104	Australia	26
21	Canada	56	63	Japan	43	105	Bahrain	26
22	Czech Republic	55	64	Spain	43	106	Burkina Faso	26
23	Romania	55	65	Bolivia	42	107	Nigeria	26
24	Chile	54	66	Georgia	42	108	Switzerland	25
25	Iceland	54	67	Cyprus	41	109	United Arab Emirates	25
26	Israel	54	68	France	41	110	Cameroon	24
27	Paraguay	54	69	Indonesia	41	111	Ethiopia	24
28	Grenada	53	70	Namibia	41	112	Gambia	24
29	Slovenia	53	71	Peru	41	113	India	21
30	United States	53	72	Zimbabwe	40	114	Mauritania	21
31	Portugal	52	73	Belize	39	115	Togo	21
32	Thailand	52	74	Haiti	39	116	Djibouti	20
33	Trinidad and Tobago	52	75	Hong Kong	38	117	Mozambique	20
34	Bahamas	51	76	Luxembourg	38	118	Pakistan	20
35	Barbados	51	77	Mauritius	38	119	Central African Republic	19
36	Belgium	51	78	Kuwait	37	120	Mali	19
37	Dominican Republic	50	79	Singapore	37	121	Sri Lanka	19
38	Germany	49	80	Syria	37	122	Italy	18
39	New Zealand	49	81	Ghana	36	123	Congo, Dem. Rep. of	17
40	Panama	49	82	Tunisia	36	124	Niger	8
41	Cape Verde	48	83	Bangladesh	35			
42	Cuba	48	84	Brunei	35			

Source: Human Development Report

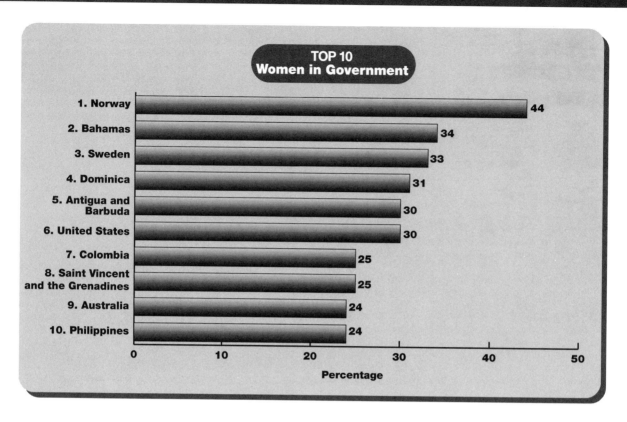

TOP 10 Women in Government

Rank	Country	Percentage
1.	Norway	44
2.	Bahamas	34
3.	Sweden	33
4.	Dominica	31
5.	Antigua and Barbuda	30
6.	United States	30
7.	Colombia	25
8.	Saint Vincent and the Grenadines	25
9.	Australia	24
10.	Philippines	24

Percentage

Rank	Country/Entity	Women in Government as Percentage of Men	Rank	Country/Entity	Women in Government as Percentage of Men	Rank	Country/Entity	Women in Government as Percentage of Men
11	Barbados	23	37	Chile	12	63	Niger	9
12	Costa Rica	21	38	Dominican Republic	12	64	Sri Lanka	9
13	Saint Kitts and Nevis	21	39	Guinea-Bissau	12	65	Tanzania	9
14	Seychelles	21	40	Botswana	11	66	Zambia	9
15	Netherlands	20	41	Ethiopia	11	67	Belgium	8
16	Canada	19	42	Ghana	11	68	Cuba	8
17	Denmark	19	43	Ireland	11	69	Hungary	8
18	Grenada	19	44	Nicaragua	11	70	Iceland	8
19	El Salvador	18	45	Panama	11	71	Japan	8
20	Guatemala	18	46	Zimbabwe	11	72	Kyrgyzstan	8
21	Portugal	18	47	Belize	10	73	Luxembourg	8
22	Honduras	17	48	Benin	10	74	Poland	8
23	New Zealand	17	49	Burkina Faso	10	75	United Kingdom	8
24	Finland	16	50	Ecuador	10	76	Austria	7
25	Guyana	16	51	Estonia	10	77	Gambia	7
26	Latvia	16	52	Fiji	10	78	Germany	7
27	Haiti	14	53	Israel	10	79	Mali	7
28	Lesotho	14	54	Italy	10	80	Mauritius	7
29	Suriname	14	55	Maldives	10	81	Mexico	7
30	Trinidad and Tobago	14	56	Peru	10	82	Namibia	7
31	Brazil	13	57	Spain	10	83	Samoa	7
32	Jamaica	13	58	Uganda	10	84	South Africa	7
33	Mozambique	13	59	Bolivia	9	85	Swaziland	7
34	Slovakia	13	60	Bulgaria	9	86	Switzerland	7
35	Albania	12	61	France	9	87	Angola	6
36	Cape Verde	12	62	Lithuania	9	88	Gabon	6

Rank	Country/Entity	Women in Government as Percentage of Men	Rank	Country/Entity	Women in Government as Percentage of Men	Rank	Country/Entity	Women in Government as Percentage of Men
89	Greece	6	116	Oman	4	143	South Korea	2
90	India	6	117	São Tomé and Príncipe	4	144	Malta	2
91	Kuwait	6	118	Syria	4	145	Pakistan	2
92	Malawi	6	119	Tajikistan	4	146	Papua New Guinea	2
93	Malaysia	6	120	Thailand	4	147	Qatar	2
94	Venezuela	6	121	Turkmenistan	4	148	Russia	2
95	Azerbaijan	5	122	Vietnam	4	149	Senegal	2
96	Bhutan	5	123	Argentina	3	150	Czech Republic	1
97	Cambodia	5	124	Bangladesh	3	151	Djibouti	1
98	Cameroon	5	125	Côte d'Ivoire	3	152	Kazakhstan	1
99	Central African Republic	5	126	Chad	3	153	North Korea	1
100	Cyprus	5	127	Comoros	3	154	Morocco	1
101	Guinea	5	128	Equatorial Guinea	3	155	Sudan	1
102	Kenya	5	129	Georgia	3	156	Ukraine	1
103	Mauritania	5	130	Laos	3	157	Bahrain	0
104	Mongolia	5	131	Paraguay	3	158	Iran	0
105	Saint Lucia	5	132	Romania	3	159	Iraq	0
106	Sierra Leone	5	133	Togo	3	160	Lebanon	0
107	Singapore	5	134	Uruguay	3	161	Libya	0
108	Tunisia	5	135	Uzbekistan	3	162	Madagascar	0
109	Turkey	5	136	Algeria	2	163	Myanmar (Burma)	0
110	Belarus	4	137	Armenia	2	164	Nepal	0
111	Burundi	4	138	Brunei	2	165	Saudi Arabia	0
112	China	4	139	Congo, Dem. Rep. of	2	166	Solomon Islands	0
113	Congo, Rep. of	4	140	Egypt	2	167	United Arab Emirates	0
114	Moldova	4	141	Indonesia	2	168	Vanuatu	0
115	Nigeria	4	142	Jordan	2	169	Yemen	0

Source: Human Development Report

Chapter 27

Global Indexes

The Human Development Index (HDI) is published annually by the United Nations Development Program. The HDI is based on three indicators: (1) longevity, as measured by life expectancy at birth; (2) educational attainment, as measured by a combination of adult literacy (two-thirds weight) and combined primary, secondary, and college enrollment ratios (one-third weight); and (3) standard of living, as measured by real Gross Domestic Product (GDP) per capita in Purchasing Power Parity (PPP). PPP is a concept developed by the United Nations for reducing the distortions introduced in the conversion of various national currencies into U.S. dollars. The PPP conversion factor is the number of units of a country's currency required to buy the same amount of goods and services in the domestic market as a U.S. dollar would buy in the United States. Thus, if a dozen eggs cost $1.00 in the United States, but only 50 cents in Indonesia, then the rupiah's official conversion rate is adjusted upward accordingly. For the construction of the HDI, fixed minimum and maximum values have been established for each of these indicators—life expectancy at birth: 25 years and 85 years; adult literacy: 0 percent and 100 percent; combined enrollment ratio: 0 percent and 100 percent; and real GDP per capita: (PPP$) 100 and 40,000.

Rank	Country/Entity	Human Development Index, 1995	Rank	Country/Entity	Human Development Index, 1995	Rank	Country/Entity	Human Development Index, 1995
1	Canada	0.960	46	Venezuela	0.860	90	Sri Lanka	0.716
2	France	0.946	47	Hungary	0.857	91	Paraguay	0.707
3	Norway	0.943	48	Mexico	0.855	92	Latvia	0.704
4	United States	0.943	49	United Arab Emirates	0.855	93	Kazakhstan	0.695
5	Finland	0.942	50	Saint Kitts and Nevis	0.854	94	Samoa	0.694
6	Iceland	0.942	51	Grenada	0.851	95	Maldives	0.683
7	Netherlands	0.941	52	Poland	0.851	96	Indonesia	0.679
8	Japan	0.940	53	Colombia	0.850	97	Botswana	0.678
9	New Zealand	0.939	54	Kuwait	0.848	98	Philippines	0.677
10	Sweden	0.936	55	Saint Vincent and the Grenadines	0.845	99	Armenia	0.674
11	Spain	0.935				100	Guyana	0.670
12	Austria	0.933	56	Seychelles	0.845	101	Mongolia	0.669
13	Belgium	0.933	57	Qatar	0.840	102	Ukraine	0.665
14	Australia	0.932	58	Saint Lucia	0.839	103	Turkmenistan	0.660
15	United Kingdom	0.932	59	Thailand	0.838	104	Uzbekistan	0.659
16	Ireland	0.930	60	Malaysia	0.834	105	Albania	0.656
17	Switzerland	0.930	61	Mauritius	0.833	106	China	0.650
18	Denmark	0.928	62	Brazil	0.809	107	Namibia	0.644
19	Germany	0.925	63	Belize	0.807	108	Georgia	0.633
20	Greece	0.924	64	Libya	0.806	109	Kyrgyzstan	0.633
21	Italy	0.922	65	Lebanon	0.796	110	Azerbaijan	0.623
22	Cyprus	0.913	66	Suriname	0.796	111	Guatemala	0.615
23	Israel	0.913	67	Bulgaria	0.789	112	Egypt	0.612
24	Barbados	0.909	68	Belarus	0.783	113	Moldova	0.610
25	Hong Kong	0.909	69	Turkey	0.782	114	El Salvador	0.604
26	Luxembourg	0.900	70	Saudi Arabia	0.778	115	Swaziland	0.597
27	Malta	0.899	71	Oman	0.771	116	Bolivia	0.593
28	Singapore	0.896	72	Russia	0.769	117	Cape Verde	0.591
29	Antigua and Barbuda	0.895	73	Ecuador	0.767	118	Tajikistan	0.575
30	South Korea	0.894	74	Romania	0.767	119	Honduras	0.573
31	Bahamas	0.893	75	North Korea	0.766	120	Gabon	0.568
32	Chile	0.893	76	Croatia	0.759	121	São Tomé and Príncipe	0.563
33	Portugal	0.892	77	Estonia	0.758	122	Solomon Islands	0.560
34	Brunei	0.889	78	Iran	0.758	123	Vietnam	0.560
35	Costa Rica	0.889	79	Lithuania	0.750	124	Vanuatu	0.559
36	Argentina	0.888	80	Macedonia	0.749	125	Morocco	0.557
37	Slovenia	0.887	81	Syria	0.749	126	Nicaragua	0.547
38	Uruguay	0.885	82	Algeria	0.746	127	Iraq	0.538
39	Czech Republic	0.884	83	Tunisia	0.744	128	Congo, Rep. of	0.519
40	Trinidad and Tobago	0.880	84	Jamaica	0.735	129	Papua New Guinea	0.507
41	Dominica	0.879	85	Cuba	0.729	130	Zimbabwe	0.507
42	Slovakia	0.875	86	Jordan	0.729	131	Cameroon	0.481
43	Bahrain	0.872	87	Peru	0.729	132	Myanmar (Burma)	0.481
44	Fiji	0.869	88	Dominican Republic	0.720	133	Ghana	0.473
45	Panama	0.868	89	South Africa	0.717	134	Lesotho	0.469

Rank	Country/Entity	Human Development Index, 1995	Rank	Country/Entity	Human Development Index, 1995	Rank	Country/Entity	Human Development Index, 1995
135	Equatorial Guinea	0.465	150	Tanzania	0.358	165	Gambia	0.291
136	Laos	0.465	151	Yemen	0.356	166	Mozambique	0.281
137	Kenya	0.463	152	Nepal	0.351	167	Guinea	0.277
138	Pakistan	0.453	153	Madagascar	0.348	168	Eritea	0.275
139	India	0.451	154	Bhutan	0.347	169	Ethiopia	0.252
140	Cambodia	0.422	155	Central African Republic	0.347	170	Burundi	0.241
141	Comoros	0.411	156	Angola	0.344	171	Mali	0.236
142	Nigeria	0.391	157	Sudan	0.343	172	Burkina Faso	0.219
143	Congo, Dem. Rep. of	0.383	158	Senegal	0.342	173	Niger	0.207
144	Togo	0.380	159	Haiti	0.340	174	Sierra Leone	0.185
145	Benin	0.378	160	Uganda	0.340			
146	Zambia	0.378	161	Malawi	0.334			
147	Bangladesh	0.371	162	Djibouti	0.324			
148	Côte d'Ivoire	0.368	163	Chad	0.318			
149	Mauritania	0.361	164	Guinea-Bissau	0.295			

Source: Human Development Report

27.2 Human Poverty Index

Developed by the United Nations, the Human Poverty Index statistically rates living conditions in both technologically advanced and developing countries. It measures poverty on the basis of six indicators: (1) Gross National Product per capita; (2) daily calorie supply; (3) inflation; (4) infant and maternal health; (5) school enrollment; and (6) life expectancy. It is instructive to compare this ranking with that on Population Below Poverty Line (see Table 7.7) and to remind ourselves that in this most prosperous era for Western nations, the great majority of people worldwide are living in a state of poverty.

Rank	Country/Entity	Human Poverty Index	Rank	Country/Entity	Human Poverty Index	Rank	Country/Entity	Human Poverty Index
1	Niger	62.1	33	Ghana	31.8	65	Ireland	15.2
2	Burkina Faso	58.2	34	Congo, Rep. of	31.5	66	United Kingdom	15.0
3	Sierra Leone	58.2	35	Cameroon	30.9	67	United Arab Emirates	14.5
4	Ethiopia	55.5	36	Iraq	30.1	68	Mongolia	14.0
5	Mali	52.8	37	Namibia	30.0	69	Spain	13.1
6	Burundi	49.5	38	Papua New Guinea	29.8	70	New Zealand	12.6
7	Guinea	49.1	39	Guatemala	29.3	71	Australia	12.5
8	Yemen	48.9	40	Oman	28.9	72	Belgium	12.4
9	Senegal	48.6	41	El Salvador	27.8	73	Mauritius	12.1
10	Mozambique	48.5	42	Myanmar (Burma)	27.5	74	Canada	12.0
11	Madagascar	47.7	43	Algeria	27.1	75	Denmark	12.0
12	Malawi	47.7	44	Kenya	27.1	76	Japan	12.0
13	Bangladesh	46.5	45	Botswana	27.0	77	Thailand	11.9
14	Côte d'Ivoire	46.4	46	Nicaragua	26.2	78	Finland	11.8
15	Pakistan	46.0	47	Vietnam	26.1	79	France	11.8
16	Mauritania	45.9	48	Lesotho	25.7	80	Jamaica	11.8
17	Bhutan	44.9	49	Zimbabwe	25.2	81	Italy	11.6
18	Haiti	44.5	50	Tunisia	23.3	82	Norway	11.3
19	Guinea-Bissau	42.9	51	Peru	23.1	83	Colombia	11.1
20	Sudan	42.5	52	Iran	22.2	84	Panama	11.1
21	Uganda	42.1	53	Honduras	21.8	85	Mexico	10.7
22	Congo, Dem. Rep. of	41.1	54	Bolivia	21.6	86	Germany	10.5
23	Central African Republic	40.7	55	Syria	20.9	87	Jordan	10.0
24	Nigeria	40.5	56	Sri Lanka	20.6	88	Netherlands	8.2
25	Morocco	40.2	57	Indonesia	20.2	89	Sweden	6.8
26	Cambodia	39.9	58	Paraguay	19.1	90	Costa Rica	6.6
27	Tanzania	39.8	59	Philippines	17.7	91	Singapore	6.5
28	Togo	39.8	60	Dominican Republic	17.4	92	Chile	4.1
29	Laos	39.4	61	Libya	17.4	93	Uruguay	4.1
30	Zambia	36.9	62	China	17.1	94	Trinidad and Tobago	3.3
31	India	35.9	63	United States	16.5			
32	Egypt	34.0	64	Ecuador	15.3			

Source: Human Development Report

Appendix

Sources of Global Statistics

TITLE OF PUBLICATION	NAME OF ORGANIZATION
Accident/Incident Reporting (ADREP) Annual Statistics	International Civil Aviation Organization
ACP Basic Statistics	European Community
African Socio-economic Indicators 1990–91	United Nations
African Statistical Yearbook 1988–89 Vol. I, Part 1 North Africa	United Nations
African Statistical Yearbook 1988–89 Vol. I, Part 2 West Africa	United Nations
African Statistical Yearbook 1988–89 Vol. II, Part 3 East and Southern Africa	United Nations
African Statistical Yearbook 1988–89 Vol. II, Part 4 Central Africa, Others in Africa	United Nations
Agricultural Income	European Community
Agricultural Markets: Prices	European Community
Agricultural Prices: Price Indices and Absolute Prices	European Community
Agriculture Statistical Yearbook	European Community
Agrifacts: A Handbook of UK and EEC Agricultural and Food Statistics	Wyre College
Animal Production Quarterly Statistics	European Community
Annual Bulletin of Coal Statistics for Europe	United Nations
Annual Bulletin of Electric Energy Statistics for Europe	United Nations
Annual Bulletin of Gas Statistics for Europe	United Nations
Annual Bulletin of General Energy Statistics for Europe	United Nations
Annual Bulletin of Housing and Building Statistics for Europe	United Nations
Annual Bulletin of Statistics	International Tea Committee
Annual Bulletin of Steel Statistics for Europe	United Nations
Annual Bulletin of Trade in Chemical Products	United Nations
Annual Bulletin of Transport Statistics for Europe	United Nations
Annual Oil Market Report	International Energy Agency
Annual Report of the International Iron and Steel Institute	International Iron and Steel Institute
Annual Review and Assessment of the World Tropical Timber Situation	International Tropical Timber Organization
Annual Summary of Merchant Ships Completed	Lloyds Register of Shipping
Areas Under Vines, Results of the Annual Surveys	European Community
ASEAN Selected Statistics	Association of South-East Asian Nations Secretariat
Association of European Airlines Yearbook	Association of European Airlines
Balance of Payments Statistical Yearbook, Part I	International Monetary Fund
Balance of Payments Statistical Yearbook, Part II	International Monetary Fund
Balance of Payments: Geographical Breakdown	European Community
Balances of Payments of OECD Countries	Organization for Economic Cooperation and Development
Bank Profitability: Statistical Supplement—Financial Statements of Banks	Organization for Economic Cooperation and Development
Basic International Chemical Industry Statistics	Chemical Industries Association
Basic Science and Technology	Organization for Economic Cooperation and Development
Basic Statistical Data on Selected Countries	Commonwealth Secretariat
Basic Statistics of the Community	European Community
The Best 'N' Most in DFS	Generation Publications
BP Review of World Gas	British Petroleum Company Pic
BP Statistical Review of World Energy	British Petroleum Company Pic

TITLE OF PUBLICATION	NAME OF ORGANIZATION
Bulletin-Consumption Statistics for Milk and Milk Products	International Dairy Federation
Bulletin de IOIV	Bulletin de IOIV
Bulletin of Labour Statistics	International Labour Organization
Bulletin of Regional Health Information	World Health Organization
Bulletin of Statistics on World Trade in Engineering Products	United Nations
Bulletin of the Lead and Zinc Study Group: Lead and Zinc Statistics	International Lead and Zinc Study Group
Cancer Incidence in Five Continents	International Agency for Research on Cancer
Caricom's Trade	Caribbean Community Secretariat
Carriage of Goods—Inland Waterways	European Community
Carriage of Goods—Railways	European Community
Carriage of Goods—Road	European Community
Casualty Return	Lloyds Register of Shipping
Censuses of Population in the Community Countries 1981–82	European Community
Civil Aviation Statistics of the World, Doc. 9180	International Civil Aviation Organization
Climatological Normals (CLINO) for CLIMAT and CLIMAT Ship Stations	World Meteorological Organization
Coal Information	International Energy Agency
Cocoa Market Report	E D & F Main Cocoa Limited
Comacon Data	Vienna Institute for Comparative Economic Studies
Commodity Trade Statistics	United Nations
Community Survey of Orchard Fruit Trees	European Community
Comparative Information on Productivity Levels and Changes in APO Member Countries	Asian Productivity Organization
Compendium of Social Statistics and Indicators	United Nations
Compendium of Statistics and Indicators of the Situation of Women	United Nations
Compendium of Tourism Statistics	World Tourism Organization
Construction Statistics Yearbook	United Nations
Consumer Price Index	European Community
Consumer Prices in the EEC	European Community
Cotton: Review of the World Situation	International Cotton Advisory Committee
Cotton: World Statistics, Bulletin of the International Cotton Advisory Committee	International Cotton Advisory Committee
Country Reports, Central and Eastern Europe	European Community
Country Statements	International Textile Manufacturers Federation
Crop Production, Quarterly Statistics	European Community
Demographic Statistics	European Community
Demographic Trends in OECD Member Countries	Organization for Economic Co-operation and Development
Demographic Yearbook	United Nations
Digest of Statistics No. 379, Series T—No. 50, Traffic—Commercial Air Carriers	International Civil Aviation Organization
Digest of Statistics No. 381, Series OFOD—No. 44, On Flight Origin and Destination	International Civil Aviation Organization
Digest of Statistics No. 382, Series R—No. 30, Civil Aircraft on Register	International Civil Aviation Organization
Digest of Statistics No. 383, Series AT—No. 31, Airport Traffic	International Civil Aviation Organization
Digest of Statistics No. 385, Series FP—No. 44, Fleet—Personnel, Commercial Air Carriers	International Civil Aviation Organization
Digest of Statistics No. 397, Series F—No. 45, Financial Data, Commercial Air Carriers	International Civil Aviation Organization
Digest of Statistics No. 398, Series TF—No. 10, Traffic by Flight Stage	International Civil Aviation Organization
Digest of Statistics No. 399, Series AF—No. 9, Airport and Route Facilities, Financial Data and Summary Traffic Data	International Civil Aviation Organization
Digest of Statistics on Social Protection in Europe, Vol. 1, Old Age	European Community
Digest of Statistics on Social Protection in Europe, Vol. 2, Invalidity/Disability	European Community
A Digest of Trade Statistics	Caribbean Community Secretariat

TITLE OF PUBLICATION	NAME OF ORGANIZATION
External Trade and Balance of Payments	European Community
External Trade Statistical Yearbook	European Community
External Trade, System of Generalized Tariff Preferences, Imports 1988, Vol. I	European Community
External Trade, System of Generalized Tariff Preferences, Imports: 1988, Vol. II	European Community
Facts and Figures	European Patent Office
Family Budgets: Comparative Tables, Vols. I and II	European Community
Family Planning and Child Survival Programs as Assessed in 1991	The Population Council
FAO Production Yearbook	Food and Agriculture Organization
FAO Trade Yearbook	Food and Agriculture Organization
FAO Yearbook of Fishery Statistics: Catches and Landings	Food and Agriculture Organization
FAO Yearbook of Fishery Statistics: Commodities	Food and Agriculture Organization
Farm Structure 1985 Survey: Main Results	European Community
Farm Structure: 1985 Survey Analysis of Results: Economic Size and Other Gainful Activities	European Community
Farm Structure: 1985 Survey Analysis of Results: Regional Structure of Agricultural Production	European Community
Fatal Accident Statistics for Passenger Air Transport Services CAA Paper 83014	Civil Aviation Authority
Fearnley's Review	Fearnleys Review
Fertilizer Yearbook	Food and Agriculture Organization
Financial Market Trends	Organization for Economic Cooperation and Development
Fisheries, Yearly Statistics	European Community
Flows and Stocks and Fixed Capital: 1964–89	Organization for Economic Cooperation and Development
The Food Aid Monitor: World Food Aid Flows, Transport and Logistics	World Food Programme
Food Aid Shipments	International Wheat Council
Food Consumption Statistics	Organization for Economic Cooperation and Development
Foreign Trade by Commodities, Vols. I to V, Series C	Organization for Economic Cooperation and Development
Foreign Trade Statistics for Africa, Direction of Trade Series A	United Nations
Foreign Trade Statistics of Asia and the Pacific	United Nations
Forestry Statistics	European Community
Gas Prices	European Community
General Government Accounts and Statistics	European Community
Geographical Distribution of Financial Flows to Developing Countries, Disbursements, Commitments, Economic Indicators: 1986–89	Organization for Economic Cooperation and Development
Government Finance Statistics Yearbook	International Monetary Fund
Government Financing of Research and Development	European Community
Grain Market Report	International Wheat Council
Handbook of Industrial Statistics	United Nations Industrial Development Organization
Handbook of International Trade and Development Statistics	United Nations Conference on Trade and Development
Human Development Report	United Nations
Human Settlements Basic Statistics	United Nations
IBA Quarterly Review	International Bauxite Association
Indicators of Industrial Activity	Organization for Economic Cooperation and Development
Industrial Production Quarterly Statistics	European Community
Industrial Property Statistics, Part I, Patents	World Intellectual Property Organization
Industrial Property Statistics, Part II, Trademarks and Service Marks, Utility Models, Industrial Designs, Varieties of Plants, Micro-organisms	World Intellectual Property Organization

TITLE OF PUBLICATION	NAME OF ORGANIZATION
Industrial Property Statistics, Publication A (Supplement to Industrial Property) No. 11	World Intellectual Property Organization
Industrial Statistics Yearbook, Vol. I General Industrial Statistics	United Nations
Industrial Statistics Yearbook, Vol. II Commodity Production Statistics	United Nations
Industrial Structure Statistics	Organization for Economic Cooperation and Development
Industrial Trends Monthly Statistics	European Community
Industry Statistical Yearbook	European Community
Information on Man-made Fibres	Comite International de la Rayonne et des Fibres Synthetiques
International Cocoa Organization Annual Report	International Cocoa Council Organization
International Comparisons of Energy Data	European Community
International Cotton Industry Statistics	International Textile Manufacturers Federation
International Direct Investment Statistics Yearbook	Organization for Economic Cooperation and Development
International Financial Statistics	International Monetary Fund
International Financial Statistics Yearbook	International Monetary Fund
International Historical Statistics, Africa and Asia	Macmillan Press Limited
International Historical Statistics, The Americas and Australia	Macmillan Press Limited
International Historical Statistics, Europe 1750–1988	Macmillan Press Limited
The International Markets for Meat	General Agreement on Tariffs and Trade
The International Markets for Meat, Arrangement Regarding Bovine Meat 12th Annual Report	General Agreement on Tariffs and Trade
International Molasses and Alcohol Report	F O Licht
International Narcotics Control Board—Narcotic Drugs, Estimated World Requirement Statistics for 1990	United Nations
International North Pacific Fisheries Commission Statistical Yearbook	International North Pacific Fisheries Commission
International Narcotics Control Board—Psychotropic Substances, Statistics for 1990	United Nations
International Pacific Halibut Commission, Annual Report	International Pacific Halibut Commission
International Sea-borne Trade Statistics: Yearbook 1984–85	United Nations
International Railway Statistics, Statistics of Individual Railways	International Union of Railways
International Steel Statistics Summary Tables	Iron and Steel Statistics Bureau
International Sugar and Sweetener Report	F O Licht
International Textile Machinery Shipment Statistics	International Textile Manufacturers Federation
International Trade Statistics Vol. I	General Agreement on Tariffs and Trade
International Trade Statistics Vol. II	General Agreement on Tariffs and Trade
International Trade Statistics Yearbook, Vol. I Trade by Country	United Nations
International Trade Statistics Yearbook, Vol. II Trade by Commodity	United Nations
International Whaling Statistics	International Whaling Commission
Intra-European Country to Country Traffic	Association of European Airlines
Iron and Manganese Ore Databook	Metal Bulletin Books Limited
The Iron and Steel Industry	Organization for Economic Cooperation and Development
Iron and Steel, Yearly Statistics	European Community
Joint Production of Lead and Zinc	International Lead and Zinc Study Group
Know More About Oil, World Statistics	Institute of Petroleum
Labour Force Survey, Results 1991	European Community
Labour Force Statistics	Organization for Economic Cooperation and Development

TITLE OF PUBLICATION	NAME OF ORGANIZATION
OECD Financial Statistics Part 1 Section 1 International Markets	Organization for Economic Cooperation and Development
OECD Financial Statistics Part 1 Section 2 Domestic Markets Interest Rates	Organization for Economic Cooperation and Development
OECD Financial Statistics Part 2 Financial Accounts of OECD Countries	Organization for Economic Cooperation and Development
OECD Financial Statistics Part 3 Non-Financial Enterprises Financial Statements	Organization for Economic Cooperation and Development
Oil and Energy Trends	Basil Blackwell Limited
Oil and Energy Trends, Annual Statistical Review	Basil Blackwell Limited
Oil World	International Energy Agency
Oil World	Ista Mieik Gmbh
Oil World Annual	Ista Mieik Gmbh
Oil, Chemical and Combined Carriers	E A Gibson Shipbrokers Limited
OPEC Annual Statistical Bulletin	Organization of Petroleum Exporting Countries
OPEC Bulletin	Organization of Petroleum Exporting Countries
Operating Experience with Nuclear Power Stations in Member States in 1990	International Atomic Energy Agency
Operation of Nuclear Power Stations	European Community
Platinum	Johnson Mathey
Pocket Profiles	Inter-American Development Bank
Population and Vital Statistics Report	United Nations
Portrait of the Regions: Vol. I Germany, Beneiux, Denmark; Vol. II France, United Kingdom, Ireland; Vol. III Portugal, Spain, Italy	European Community
Price Structure of the Community Countries in 1985	European Community
Price of Agricultural Products and Selected Inputs in Europe and North America	United Nations
The Pulp and Paper Industry	Organization for Economic Cooperation and Development
Pulp and Paper International Annual Review	Pulp and Paper International
The Purchasing Power of Working Time: An International Comparison	International Metalworkers' Federation
Purchasing Power Parties and Real Expenditures	Organization for Economic Cooperation and Development
Quarterly Bulletin of Cocoa Statistics	International Cocoa Council Organization
Quarterly Bulletin of Statistics	Food and Agriculture Organization
Quarterly Labour Force Statistics	Organization for Economic Cooperation and Development
Quarterly Market Review	International Sugar Organization
Quarterly National Accounts	Organization for Economic Cooperation and Development
Quarterly National Accounts ESA	European Community
Quarterly Oil Statistics and Energy Balances	International Energy Agency
Raw Material EC Supply	European Community
Recent Demographic Developments in Europe	Council of Europe
Reference Tables	British Paper and Board Industry Federation
Regions Statistical Yearbook	European Community
Register of Liquified Gas Carriers	E A Gibson Shipbrokers Limited
Report of the UN High Commissioner for Refugees, General Assembly Official Records: 46th Session, Supplement No. 12	United Nations
Report for the Crop Year	International Wheat Council
Results of the Business Survey Carried Out Among Managements in the Community	European Community
Retail Price Indices, Statistical Bulletin of the South Pacific	South Pacific Commission
Retailing in the European Single Market 1993	European Community

TITLE OF PUBLICATION	NAME OF ORGANIZATION
Revenue Statistics of OECD Member Countries	Organization for Economic Cooperation and Development
Review of Fisheries in OECD Member Countries	Organization for Economic Cooperation and Development
Review of Maritime Transport	United Nations Conference on Trade and Development
Rubber Statistical Bulletin	International Rubber Study Group
Services: Statistics on International Transactions	Organization for Economic Cooperation and Development
Shipping Statistics	Institute of Shipping Economics and Logistics
Shipping Statistics and Economics	Drewry Shipping Consultants Limited
Shipping Statistics Yearbook	Institute of Shipping Economics and Logistics
Shipping Trade, Trends and Statistics	Drewry Shipping Consultants Limited
Short-term Review of International Pulp and Paper Markets	Jaakko Poyry
Silicon Carbide	Elsevier Advanced Technology
Situation de la Production Latiere et du Controle Laitier dans les Organismes Pays Members	Federation Nationale des de Controle Laitier
Social Indicators of Development	The World Bank
A Social Portrait of Europe	European Community
Social Protection Expenditure and Receipts	European Community
South Pacific Economies	South Pacific Commission
Standardized Input-Output Tables of ECE Countries for Years Around 1975	United Nations
The State of the World's Children	United Nations Children's Fund
Statistical Appendices to AEA Yearbook	Association of European Airlines
Statistical Brief	Chamber of Shipping
Statistical Bulletin	International Commission for the Conservation of Atlantic Tunas
Statistical Bulletin	International Sugar Organization
Statistical Bulletin Fishery Statistics for 1988	North West Atlantic Fisheries Organization
Statistical Indicators for Asia and the Pacific	United Nations
Statistical Report on Road Accidents	European Conference of Ministers of Transport
Statistical Trends in Transport	European Conference of Ministers of Transport
Statistical Yearbook for Asia and the Pacific	United Nations
Statistical Yearbook for Latin America and the Caribbean	United Nations
Statistics and Indicators on Women in Africa	United Nations
Statistics of Road Traffic Accidents in Europe	United Nations
Statistics of World Trade in Steel	United Nations
Statistics on Children in UNICEF Assisted Countries	United Nations Children's Fund
Statistics on Housing in the European Community	Ministry of Housing, Physical Planning and the Environment (Netherlands)
Steel Consumption by User Branch	European Community
The Steel Market in 1991	United Nations
Steel Market in 1991 and the Outlook for 1992	Organization for Economic Cooperation and Development
Steel Statistics of Developing Countries	International Iron and Steel Institute
Steel Statistical Yearbook	International Iron and Steel Institute
Structure and Activity of Industry: Annual Enquiry Main Results	European Community
Structure and Activity of Industry: Data by Regions	European Community

TITLE OF PUBLICATION	NAME OF ORGANIZATION
Structure and Activity of Industry: Data by Size of Enterprises	European Community
Sugar Yearbook	International Sugar Organization
Tanker Charter Record	Basil Blackwell Limited
Telecommunications: Profile of the Worldwide Telecommunications Industry	Elsevier Advanced Technology
Tourism Annual Statistics	European Community
Tourism in Europe, Trends	European Community
Tourism Policy and International Tourism in OECD Member Countries	Organization for Economic Cooperation and Development
Transport and Communications Annual Statistics	European Community
Travel and Tourism Barometer	World Tourism Organization
Trends in Developing Economies	The World Bank
Trends in the Hotel Industry	Pannell Kerr Forster
Trends in the Transport Sector	European Conference of Ministers of Transport
Tungsten Statistics	United Nations Conference on Trade and Development
UN Statistical Yearbook	United Nations
UNCTAD Commodity Yearbook	United Nations Conference on Trade and Development
UNCTAD Statistical Pocket Book	United Nations Conference on Trade and Development
Unemployment	European Community
UNHCR Activities Financed by Voluntary Funds. Report for 1990–91 and Proposed Programmes and Budget for 1992	United Nations
Part 1: Africa	
Part 2: Asia and Oceania	
Part 3: Europe and North America	
Part 4: Latin America	
Part 5: South West Asia, North Africa and the Middle East	
Part 6: Overall Allocations	
Uranium—Resources, Production and Demand	Organization for Economic Cooperation and Development
Urea Statistics	International Fertilizer Industry Association
Western European Living Costs	Confederation of British Industry
Women and Political Power Survey (carried out among the National Parliaments existing as from 3.10.96)	Inter-Parliamentary Union
Wool Facts 1991–92	International Wool Secretariat
World Air Transport Statistics	International Air Transport Association
World Bulk Fleet	Fearnleys
World Bulk Trades	Fearnleys
The World Cocoa Market: An Analysis of Recent Trends and of Prospects to the Year 2000	International Cocoa Council Organization
World Crop and Livestock Statistics	Food and Agriculture Organization
World Debt Tables, Vol. 1, Analysis and Summary Tables	The World Bank
World Debt Tables, Vol. 2, External Finance for Developing Countries, Country Tables	The World Bank
World Energy Statistics and Balances	International Energy Agency
World Fleet Statistics	Lloyds Register of Shipping
World Footwear Markets	Satra Footwear Technology Centre
World Health Statistics Annual	World Health Organization
World Investment Directory Vol. I Asia and the Pacific	United Nations
World Investment Directory Vol. II Central and Eastern Europe	United Nations
The World Market for Dairy Products	General Agreement on Tariffs and Trade

TITLE OF PUBLICATION	NAME OF ORGANIZATION
World Metal Statistics	World Bureau of Metal Statistics
World Metal Statistics Quarterly Summary	World Bureau of Metal Statistics
World Metal Statistics Yearbook	World Bureau of Metal Statistics
World Mineral Statistics Vol. 1 Metals and Energy	British Geological Survey
World Mineral Statistics Vol. 2 Industrial Minerals	British Geological Survey
World Oil Trade Review of International Oil Movements	Basil Blackwell Limited
World Population Projections	The World Bank
World Population Prospects	United Nations
World Rice Statistics, 1987	International Rice Research Institute
World Road Statistics, 1986–90	World Road Federation
Worldwide Rubber Statistics	International Institute of Synthetic Rubber Products
World Rubber Statistics Handbook	International Rubber Study Group
World Stainless Steel Statistics	World Bureau of Metal Statistics
World Statistics in Brief, United Nations Statistical Pocketbook	United Nations
World Steel in Figures	International Iron and Steel Institute
World Sugar and Sweetener Yearbook	F O Licht
World Tables	The World Book
World Trade Stainless, High Speed and Other Alloy Steel	Iron and Steel Statistics Bureau
World Trade Steel	Iron and Steel Statistics Bureau
World Transport Data	International Road Transport Union
Worldwide Hotel Industry	Horwath International
Yearbook of Common Carrier Telecommunications Statistics	International Telecommunication Union
Yearbook of Forest Products	Food and Agriculture Organization
Yearbook of International Horticultural Statistics	International Association of Horticultural Statistics
Yearbook of Labour Statistics	International Labour Organization
Yearbook of Nordic Statistics	Nordic Council of Ministers and the Nordic Statistical Secretariat
Yearbook of Tourism Statistics, Vol. 1	World Tourism Organization
Yearbook of Tourism Statistics, Vol. 2	World Tourism Organization

Index